Washington Real Estate Law

Alan Tonnon, J.D.

Rockwell Publishing Company

Copyright © 2005
By Rockwell Publishing, Inc.
13218 N.E. 20th
Bellevue, WA 98005
(425)747-7272 / 1-800-221-9347

Fourth Edition

ISBN: 1-887051-19-8

PRINTED IN THE UNITED STATES OF AMERICA

Cover design: Alisa Oh

Table of Contents

1 An Introduction to Law and the Legal System

Outline

D. Limitations on adjudication
   1. case or controversy
   2. statute of limitations
   3. res judicata
VII. A Civil Lawsuit
  A. The dispute
  B. Starting a lawsuit
  C. Pretrial discovery
  D. Settlement negotiations
  E. Jury or judge
  F. The trial
  G. Appeal
  H. Collecting a judgment

Key Terms

- substantive/procedural
- affirm/modify/reverse/remand
- criminal/civil
- prejudicial error
- plaintiff/defendant
- subject matter jurisdiction
- damages
- federal question
- tort
- diversity jurisdiction
- unconstitutional
- case or controversy requirement
- due process
- declaratory relief
- equal protection
- statute of limitations
- discovery rule
- state action
- res judicata
- statute/ordinance
- summons/complaint/answer
- bill
- garnishment
- veto/override
- personal jurisdiction
- codification
- service of process
- case law
- pretrial discovery
- stare decisis
- deposition/interrogatories
- precedent
- settlement
- equitable/common law remedies
- opinion
- injunction
- judicial review
- fact witness/expert witness
- statutory construction
- direct/cross examination
- trial record
- jury instructions
- exhibit
- burden of proof
- question of fact/of law
- standard of proof
- trier of fact
- appellant/appellee

Chapter Overview

This chapter is a broad survey of the legal system in the United States, with a particular focus on Washington's legal system. It begins with a discussion of the nature and purposes of the law, and explains some fundamental legal categories and concepts. It goes on to discuss the sources of law: constitutions, legislatures, courts, and administrative agencies. It also examines the judicial system in detail, and describes a typical lawsuit from its outset through enforcement of the judgment.

You should come away from this chapter with a better understanding of how laws are made, how legal rights are enforced, and how legal disputes are resolved. This information serves as a foundation for the material covered in the rest of the book.

Law and the Real Estate Profession

The law has a tremendous impact on the work of a real estate agent. Hundreds of federal, state, and local laws control the use and transfer of real property. These laws affect property values as well as the structure of various real estate transactions. In addition, the real estate profession itself is strictly regulated. Laws prescribe the agent's qualifications and his or her duties to clients, customers, and employees.

The law's impact on the real estate profession is steadily expanding. In some areas of law (environmental law, for example), regulations have multiplied dramatically. In other areas, legal standards of conduct are being raised by judges: a landlord or a broker might now be held liable for an oversight that would not have been the basis for a lawsuit 15 years ago.

Avoiding liability is one of the most compelling reasons to learn about the law. Even if you would never consider doing anything dishonest, an honest mistake could leave you threatened with a lawsuit. A firm grasp of your duties toward the buyer and seller minimizes the risk of a lawsuit.

Sometimes a well-informed agent can also prevent litigation between the buyer and seller. By recognizing issues that are common causes of lawsuits, you can help the buyer and seller clarify their agreement and avoid misunderstandings.

Learning about the law is not just a matter of memorizing rules. It's important to understand where the rules come from and what backs them up. It's one thing to memorize the phrase "A real estate agent must disclose all material facts to his or her client." But who made that rule? What happens if that rule is ignored? How is it enforced? Can the rule be challenged or changed? Knowing how the legal system works gives the rule substance. In learning how laws are developed, you'll see that it is sometimes possible to influence the process to advance the interests of your clients or yourself.

Of course, learning about the law won't enable you to give clients legal advice, or to act without legal advice yourself. But it will give you a clearer sense of when legal advice is needed. And when it is needed, you'll be much better equipped to assist a client's lawyer or your own lawyer in analyzing the situation and preparing the case.

The Nature and Role of the Law

The law is a system of rights and duties established and enforced by a government. It takes the form of general rules that citizens and everyone else in the government's domain must obey.

Example: The law sets forth rights and duties connected with land ownership. As a landowner, Brown has a legal right to the exclusive possession of his property. This creates a corresponding legal duty for others to avoid entering the property without permission. If someone violates this rule, the government will enforce Brown's rights by ejecting the trespasser.

On the other hand, Brown has a legal duty to maintain the property so that a person entering it at his request will be reasonably safe. If Brown fails to live up to this duty and someone is injured as a result, the government will enforce Brown's duty by requiring him to pay compensation to the injured person.

Functions of the Law

The law serves a number of related functions. It:

- establishes order,
- resolves disputes,
- enforces promises,
- prevents exploitation, and
- promotes equality.

First and foremost, law establishes order. Without law, might makes right: the strong and ruthless use violence and the threat of violence to dominate anyone who is weaker. But a legal system establishes rules of conduct based on considerations other than brute force. A court or similar tribunal provides a forum for resolving disputes without violence. Thus, the law makes it easier for people to live together peacefully.

An important function of the law in any complex society is the enforcement of promises. Commerce depends on promises: a builder who agrees to construct a house must be able to rely on the owner's promise to pay for the house. Otherwise, the builder would have to demand payment in advance; but in that case, the owner would have to rely on the builder's promise to go through with the work. By enforcing certain promises called **contracts**, the law makes it possible to plan ahead and to deal with strangers.

In the United States today, the law reflects widely accepted ideas of fairness and equality. We have laws intended to protect people not merely from physical force, but also from many forms of exploitation. For example, a real estate agent is not allowed to take unfair advantage of a buyer by misrepresenting or concealing facts about a property. We also have laws that promote equal treatment: a real estate agent may not refuse to show a couple a house because of their race or religion.

Morality and Efficiency

The passage of laws preventing exploitation and promoting equality is an example of **sociological jurisprudence**: using the law as a tool for reforming society. But law has also been used as a tool for oppression. For example, in the 1850s and 1860s, many white Californians felt their jobs were threatened by a flood of Chinese immigrants who were willing to work for low wages. The state and city governments responded to this situation by issuing tax and licensing laws designed to create social and economic hardships for the Chinese.

It's clear that a society's laws are closely connected to its ideas of justice and morality. But although the law reflects and often changes with public morality, they are by no means the same thing. There are many moral issues that the law does not address, leaving them up to the individual's conscience, to the family, to churches and other organizations, and to public opinion.

Morality is not the only force that shapes the law. Efficiency, rather than justice, is the goal of many rules. When there are two ways of doing something, both may be equally effective. Yet a law (a building code, for example) may arbitrarily choose one method and require everyone to use it, because uniform procedures help society run more smoothly.

Historical Background

When English settlers colonized the New World, they brought English law with them. After gaining its independence, the United States retained many aspects of English law and legal institutions. These are still the foundation of the U.S. legal system.

For example, judges in the U.S. have played almost as great a role in establishing rules of law as our legislatures have (see the discussion of sources of law, below). This is based on the English model, and it contrasts with the European tradition. In France, Germany, Spain, and Italy, lawmaking has been more strictly reserved to the legislatures, and judicial decisions have not carried nearly as much weight.

In addition, many of our basic legal concepts and rules were inherited directly from England. This history accounts for much of the strange legal terminology that is especially common in real property law: "escheat," "emblements," and "appurtenance" were all part of English law centuries ago. Early English law based on court decisions was known as the **common law** of England. As a result, long-established rules based on English law are sometimes referred to as "common law rules."

Legal Categories and Concepts

In today's complicated society, the law covers a vast territory. Mapping out some fundamental categories and concepts will make it easier to explore.

Substantive Law and Procedural Law

One of the most basic divisions in the law is the distinction between substantive law and procedural law. **Substantive law** establishes and defines rights and duties. **Procedural law** sets forth the methods of enforcing substantive rights.

> **Example:** The rule that a landowner has the exclusive right to possess his or her own land is substantive law: it gives a landowner a legal right. If the landowner is prevented from exclusive possession because another person has trespassed and refuses to leave, the landowner can start a lawsuit. There are rules prescribing how to sue someone: file a complaint with the court, send a summons to the other party within a certain number of days, and so forth. These rules setting forth the procedure for enforcing the right to possess the land one owns are procedural law.

Criminal Law and Civil Law

Another fundamental distinction is the one between criminal law and civil law. A person who fails to live up to a legal duty, or fails to respect another's legal right, may cause harm to another person or to property. The failure may be accidental or deliberate. The injury may be slight or serious; it may be physical, emotional, or financial.

Someone who has been injured as a result of another's act generally has the right to sue that other person for compensation. The government offers a forum (the courts) for resolving the dispute. One individual suing another is called a **civil suit**, a civil action, or civil litigation.

- **Plaintiff**—The person who starts the lawsuit.
- **Defendant**—The person being sued.
- **Litigant**—Both plaintiff and defendant may be called litigants.

Certain harmful or potentially harmful acts are classified as **crimes**. In general, crimes are those acts that are particularly dangerous to society.

> **Example:** Accidentally rear-ending another car causes harm, but it isn't a crime. Drunk driving is a crime (even if the driver has not caused an accident) because it has the potential to cause a great deal of harm.

Because crimes are so disruptive, the government takes a greater interest in them than it does in other harmful acts. Instead of simply offering the injured person an opportunity to sue, the government itself (represented by the public prosecutor) sues the person accused of a crime. The government may start a criminal action without the victim's cooperation, or even if there was no victim. A civil suit, on the other hand, will take place only if the injured person decides to start one.

Civil suits and criminal suits have different purposes, so they offer different remedies. The goal of a civil suit is simply to compensate the injured person for the harm that was done. The remedy granted is usually a monetary award (called damages), paid by the person who caused the harm to the person who was harmed. A damages award is usually limited to the financial losses that the injured person incurred. These might include lost profits or wages, or money spent on repairs or hospital bills.

A criminal suit has broader goals: to punish the wrongdoer and prevent him or her from committing more crimes, and to deter others from committing similar crimes. The penalties are not based on paying for the damage done. A person convicted of a crime might have to pay a heavy fine to the government, even if the criminal act (such as drunk driving) did not result in any actual damage. He or she might also have to serve a jail sentence.

It's important to note that the same harmful act might lead to both a criminal action and a civil action.

> **Example:** A drunk driver causes an accident, injuring several people. The government brings a criminal action against the driver, resulting in a fine and a jail sentence. However, the criminal action does not compensate the victims. They will have to sue in civil court to force the driver to pay for their medical expenses, lost wages, and car repairs.

Real estate lawsuits are nearly always civil, not criminal. The exceptions to this rule are cases involving fraud, conversion of funds, or a violation of a specific law. For example, the victim of a fraud can bring a civil suit for compensation. But if the fraud was serious enough, the government will also impose criminal penalties.

Since most real estate disputes do not involve crimes, the focus of this chapter (and of the book as a whole) will be on civil law.

Basic Civil Law Concepts

As our laws have grown more and more complex, it has become necessary for most lawyers to specialize in a particular area of law. Their specialties correspond to all the different areas in which disputes arise: real estate law, corporate law, family law, personal injury law, and so on. But there are three fundamental categories underlying all of these specialties:

- contracts,
- torts, and
- property.

Each of these categories represents a group of basic legal concepts, relationships, and principles.

Contracts. A **contract** is a legally binding promise. When two people enter into a contractual relationship, they voluntarily take on legal duties toward one another.

> **Example:** If Chin contracts to sell his bike to Martinez in exchange for $100, Chin has a legal duty to give Martinez the bike, and Martinez has a legal duty to pay Chin $100. Without the contract, Chin had no duty to give Martinez the bike, and Martinez had no duty to pay Chin $100. By entering into the contract, they voluntarily assumed these duties.

A whole body of rules governs the legal relationships created by contracts. These rules apply to real estate contracts, employment contracts, and sales contracts—and apply whether the contract concerns tomatoes, a condominium, or commercial shipping. In Chapter 7, we'll discuss contract law in detail, as it applies to contracts concerning real property.

Torts. Other legal duties are not voluntarily assumed but are instead imposed by law. The law imposes the duty on everyone to take reasonable care to avoid injuring another person or damaging someone else's property. A failure to behave as a reasonable person would behave is a breach of this imposed duty and is called a **tort**. Torts are sometimes referred to as "civil wrongs," to distinguish them from criminal wrongs, or crimes.

> **Example:** Running desperately through the depot to catch a train, Garner accidentally knocks Harrison down. Harrison's arm is broken in the fall. Garner has breached the legal duty to use reasonable care in passing through a public place. In other words, Garner has committed a tort against Harrison.

Tort law is the body of rules concerning legally imposed duties and standards of reasonable conduct. There are rules for intentional and unintentional acts; public places and private homes; family members, business associates, and total strangers.

Property. The third fundamental category, **property law**, concerns ownership of or an interest in real or personal property. It includes rules for acquiring and losing property ownership, and rules about the rights and duties associated with property ownership.

> **Example:** Greenstreet deeds a property called Blackacre to Hall. The law grants Hall, as the owner, the right to use, encumber, will, sell, or ignore Blackacre. The law (in the form of a zoning ordinance) also places some restrictions on Hall's use of the property: Hall may build a house on Blackacre, but not a shopping mall. And the law imposes a duty on Hall to pay taxes on the property. These rights and duties are automatic consequences of ownership.

- **Contract**—A legally binding promise.
- **Tort**—A civil wrong.
- **Property Law**—Law concerning ownership of (or an interest in) real or personal property.

Nearly every specialized area of law involves contract, tort, and property issues to some degree. For example, a lawyer specializing in maritime law might have to deal with the legal problems arising from a contract to ship goods to Japan, an accident at sea in which crew members were injured, and the transfer of ownership of a vessel.

Contract, tort, and property issues can also be tangled up together in a single legal problem.

> **Example:** Jones and Bailey are neighbors. Jones has an easement over Bailey's property for a driveway leading to his own property. Jones and Bailey disagree about where the boundary between their lots is located.
> Jones leased his house to Collins. Jones believes the lease expired at the end of the summer, but Collins won't give up possession, claiming the lease was supposed to last until the end of the year. One day Collins slips in the driveway and breaks her collarbone.

It's not clear whether she was on Jones's property or Bailey's property when she slipped, because of the boundary dispute.

In order to determine whether either Jones or Bailey must compensate Collins for her injury, the lawyers will have to sort out contract issues (Had the lease expired? What evidence can be introduced to prove the contents of the agreement between Jones and Collins?); property issues (Who owned that part of the driveway? Did Jones have a responsibility to maintain the easement? Did Collins have a right to use the easement, or was she trespassing?); and tort issues (Did Collins slip because someone failed to make the driveway reasonably safe? Or was it because of her own carelessness?).

Sources of Law

Who makes the laws? The simple answer is that the government does. But in the United States, "the government" has numerous elements that play a role in lawmaking. Governmental power is divided between the federal government and the 50 independent state governments, and in each state there are regional and local governmental bodies. To complicate matters even more, there are different sources of law within the federal government and each of the state governments.

A single legal problem can involve both state and federal laws, and may be the subject of constitutional provisions, statutes, court decisions, and administrative regulations, all at the same time.

Fig. 1.1 Sources of law

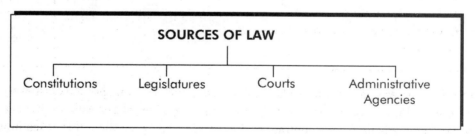

Constitutions

A constitution is a grant of power to a government. It sets forth the government's basic structure and defines the limits of the government's power.

A constitution is, in effect, the fundamental law with which all other laws must comply. In issuing a new law, a government sometimes exceeds its constitutional power. Then the new law is **unconstitutional**: it is an illegal law, and cannot be enforced. Even a constitutional law can be applied by a government official in a way that oversteps the limits of the government's power. In that case, the law still stands, but the official's action is unconstitutional and illegal.

Constitutions are intended to be long-lasting documents that provide government stability. They can be changed (**amended**), but the procedure for amending a constitution is more difficult than the procedure for changing an ordinary law.

In the United States, there is a federal Constitution that applies to the whole country, and each of the states has its own constitution as well.

The Federal Constitution

The United States Constitution was drawn up at the Constitutional Convention in 1787, approved by the states, and adopted in 1789. The Constitution declares itself to be the "supreme law of the land" (Article VI, Section 2).

Power of Federal and State Governments. The U.S. Constitution defines the relationship between the federal government and the state governments. Only the federal government may make laws concerning certain matters; these include interstate commerce, wars and the military, immigration, bankruptcy, copyrights and patents, and currency (Article I, Section 8).

In many other areas, both the federal government and the state governments can and do make laws. Discrimination and environmental protection are examples.

Certain matters are left up to the state governments, such as the ownership and transfer of real property. As a result, most of the laws affecting a parcel of land are the laws of whichever state the land is located in.

If there's a conflict between a federal law and a state law, the stricter rule prevails. If a federal air pollution law is tougher than a Washington air pollution law, a factory in Washington must comply with the federal standard. But if the federal law is looser than the Washington law, the factory must comply with the Washington standard.

Protection of Individual Rights. The first ten amendments to the U.S. Constitution are known as the **Bill of Rights**. They were adopted in 1791. The Thirteenth, Fourteenth, and Fifteenth Amendments were added soon after the Civil War. Together, these amendments protect the rights of individuals by limiting government power. The protections range from freedom of religion to the right to a jury trial.

Some of these amendments have a particular impact on property and the real estate profession. These include the following guarantees:

- due process,
- equal protection,
- just compensation, and
- no unreasonable searches or seizures.

Due process. According to the Fifth and Fourteenth Amendments, no one shall be "deprived of life, liberty, or property without due process of law." This is known as the due process requirement. Due process includes a fair hearing by an impartial judge.

> **Example:** A real estate agent is accused of grossly misrepresenting the condition of a home. The Washington State Department of Licensing has the power to revoke an agent's license for this misconduct. But a real estate license is considered "property" for the purposes of the due process requirement. As a result, the Department of Licensing cannot deprive the agent of his license without first holding a hearing that gives the agent an opportunity to tell his side of the story.

Equal protection. The Fourteenth Amendment also provides that the government may not deny an individual the "equal protection of the laws." The equal protection requirement prohibits governments from adopting laws that unfairly discriminate between different groups of people.

Most laws involve some sort of discrimination. For example, a law that says a person must have a real estate license to negotiate the sale of land can be said to discriminate against people who don't have licenses. But that discrimination is not considered unfair, since people with licenses are usually better qualified to negotiate land sales than people without licenses. However, discrimination on the basis of race, ethnic background, or gender is considered unfair. That kind of discrimination violates the equal protection requirement.

Just compensation. Another provision of the Fifth Amendment prevents the government from taking private property for public use "without just compensation." The government has the power to turn your land into a public garden or parking lot, but the Constitution requires the government to pay you for it. (See the discussion of eminent domain and condemnation in Chapter 8.)

Unreasonable searches and seizures. The Fourth Amendment prevents the government from making "unreasonable searches and seizures" of an individual's person or property. A search warrant issued by a judge is required, and a warrant may be issued only if there is "probable cause" for a search.

The Fourth Amendment is primarily applied in criminal cases. In that context, probable cause means that the government must have reasonable grounds for believing that a search will uncover items used in the commission of a crime. But the Fourth Amendment also applies to "administrative searches," such as a routine inspection by the fire department or health department. A search warrant is required to inspect a residence or business, unless there is an emergency or the owner or occupant consents to the inspection.

It is not necessary to show that there is probable cause to believe the administrative search will uncover a code violation in a particular building. A legitimate government interest in conducting inspections in that neighborhood is a sufficient basis for the issuance of a search warrant. (*Camara v. Municipal Court*, 387 U.S. 523 (1967) and *See v. City of Seattle*, 387 U.S. 541 (1967).)

State action. To claim the rights guaranteed by the Constitution, there must be state action involved, which is action by a government or a government official. The federal

Constitution's protection of individual rights is primarily protection against abuses by the government. It generally does not protect a person against actions taken by private individuals or entities.

> **Example:** The First Amendment protects freedom of speech. A city cannot pass a law or take action to prevent groups of protesters from gathering on city sidewalks or in city parks for political rallies. That interference with their freedom of speech would violate the First Amendment.
>
> On the other hand, as far as the federal Constitution is concerned, the owner of a shopping center may prevent the same groups from gathering in the center's mall or parking lot. Because the shopping center is private property, this policy does not involve state action, so it is not considered a violation of the First Amendment. (*Hudgens v. NLRB*, 424 U.S. 507 (1976).)
>
> However, a city or state may pass a law requiring shopping center owners to allow peaceful protests on their property. Such a law would make it illegal for a shopping center owner to interfere with an orderly protest, even though preventing the orderly protest would not be a violation of the federal Constitution. (*PruneYard Shopping Center v. Robins*, 447 U.S. 74 (1980).)

- **Due Process**—The right to a fair hearing by an impartial judge.
- **Equal Protection**—Everyone has the right to equal protection of the laws. The government may not adopt laws that unfairly discriminate between different groups of people.
- **Just Compensation**—If the government takes private land, it must pay fair compensation.
- **Unreasonable Search and Seizure**—The government may not seize or search private property without probable cause. A search warrant is usually required.
- **State Action**—Action by a government or a government official.

Washington's State Constitution

The Washington state constitution was adopted in 1889. It begins with a Declaration of Rights. Among many other guarantees, it provides that everyone has a right to acquire, possess, and protect property.

Many of the state constitutional rights overlap those rights protected by the U.S. Constitution, such as freedom of speech and due process of law. But in some cases, the Washington constitution may offer greater protection than the U.S. Constitution.

Legislatures: Statutory Law

Legislative bodies are the dominant source of new laws in the United States. Representatives elected to the U.S. Congress, the 50 state legislatures, and county and city councils across the country make hundreds of new laws every year. The laws adopted by Congress and the state legislatures are called **statutes**. The laws adopted by county and city councils are generally called ordinances.

The Legislative Process

The members of a legislative body write and adopt laws through a process of argument and compromise. Each legislative body has its own procedures. As an example, here is a brief outline of the procedures used in Congress.

Congress is divided into two houses, the Senate and the House of Representatives. A proposed law (called a bill) is introduced in each house, often at the suggestion of a government agency (such as the Department of Housing and Urban Development) or a lobbying group (such as the National Association of Realtors®).

In each house, a legislative committee (such as the Banking Committee or the Ways and Means Committee) analyzes and redrafts the bill. A Senate committee and a House committee often make different changes in the bill, so that two different versions develop.

Next, the whole Senate and the whole House each consider and vote on their versions of the bill. If a majority in either house votes against the bill, it dies. If a majority in each house votes in favor of the bill, the two versions must be reconciled. A conference committee made up of members from both houses works out a compromise version of the bill. If a majority in each house votes for this version, the bill is passed.

The final stage of the legislative process involves the president. The president can express approval of the bill by signing it, or can take no action on it. Either way, the bill becomes law. But if the president vetoes the bill, it will not become law unless Congress votes to override the veto. To override a presidential veto, a two-thirds majority in each house must vote in favor of the bill. If the bill can't muster the required support in Congress, it dies. If the veto is overridden, however, the bill becomes law in spite of the president's disapproval.

The Washington legislature follows a similar procedure. It also is divided into two houses, the state senate and the state house of representatives. The state governor has the power to veto legislation.

A citizen can influence the legislative process. First, of course, you can vote for representatives who seem likely to promote your interests. You can also join or organize a lobbying group that will propose new legislation or revisions to the representatives. And when the Congress, the legislature, or a local council is considering a proposal that you support or oppose, you can urge your representatives to vote for or against it.

Codification

Once a new statute or ordinance has been formally adopted, it is published. It is the legislative body's pronouncement of what the law on a given issue will be, from the effective date forward.

Some statutory laws are simple and clear; many are long and confusing. Some address a very narrow issue; others cover a large area. As we'll discuss later in this chapter, many statutory laws are interpreted or supplemented by court decisions. At times a legislative body will gather up all the laws on a particular subject (court decisions as well as statutory laws), reconcile them and clarify them, then set them out systematically in a comprehensive statute called a code. This process is called **codification**.

Revised Code of Washington (RCW)

The **Revised Code of Washington**, referred to as the **RCW**, is the compilation of state laws currently in effect. The RCW can be located online at the Washington State Legislature's website: www.leg.wa.gov/rcw/. You can view the statutes organized by title, or search the text of the RCWs for a particular keyword or phrase.

The Courts: Case Law

Although legislative bodies are the main source of new law, the courts are also an important source. However, judges do not issue general rules in the same way that legislative bodies do. A legislative body can make laws on any subject it chooses (as long as it doesn't violate the federal or state constitution). But a judge can only address a point of law if it is at issue in a lawsuit. Because the rules of law developed by judges are extracted from decisions reached in court cases, they are referred to as **case law.**

Lawmaking and Dispute Resolution

A judge's primary task is resolving disputes. One person accuses another of breaching a contract; the other denies it. They can't work out their disagreement, so there is a lawsuit. The judge acts as a referee and settles the argument by applying the law to the facts of the particular dispute.

But in the course of resolving a dispute, a judge will often have to engage in a form of lawmaking. Applying the law to the facts is not a mechanical process. Nearly every case presents a new combination of circumstances, and many raise issues that have not been settled by existing law. A judge will often have to extend and reshape established rules of law, and sometimes will have to forge new ones.

> **Example:** Adams sells his house to Baker. The floors in the house are covered with wall-to-wall carpeting, and Baker assumes that the carpeting will stay with the house. However, when Adams moves out, he removes all of the carpeting and takes it with him. Adams never told Baker that he intended to take the carpeting with him when he left.
>
> A lawsuit arises concerning whether or not the carpeting was included as part of the sale. The judge rules that wall-to-wall carpeting is a fixture that remains with the house and is considered part of the sale unless specifically excluded by the seller. Adams is required to pay damages to Baker for the removal of the carpeting.

The way the judge decides this issue will, of course, directly affect Adams and Baker, the parties involved in the lawsuit. But under certain circumstances, the judge's conclusion will affect not only Adams and Baker, but everyone who is in a similar situation. In other words, the judge's decision will become a rule of law.

Stare Decisis and Precedent

A judge's decision in a specific case can become a rule of law applied to all cases because of the **doctrine of stare decisis**. The doctrine holds that once a judge has decided a particular point of law, other judges faced with the same issue must decide it the same way. ("Stare decisis" is a Latin phrase that means, roughly, "to abide by the decision.")

Since the judge in the example above ruled that wall-to-wall carpeting is a fixture that is included as part of the sale, the doctrine of stare decisis would require another judge in a later case involving a similar issue to also rule that wall-to-wall carpeting is a fixture. The first judge's decision is called a **precedent**, and under certain circumstances it is considered binding on other judges.

- **Stare Decisis**—A doctrine requiring judges to abide by previous judicial decisions.
- **Precedent**—A previously decided case that serves as an example for a similar case arising later.
- **Jurisdiction**—An area under the authority of a particular court.

Stare decisis is not a law, but a policy that judges have followed for centuries (we inherited it from the English common law). It tries to ensure that two people who do the same thing will be treated the same way by the law. That fits with our sense of fairness; it also makes the law more predictable. If a binding precedent holds that wall-to-wall carpeting is a fixture, sellers are given warning that they cannot take the carpeting with them unless they specifically exclude it from the sale.

Not every court decision is a binding precedent for all other judges, however. It depends, for the most part, on three factors:

- jurisdiction,
- position in the court hierarchy, and
- a written opinion.

For a judge to be bound by the decision of another court, the other court must be in the same jurisdiction. A **jurisdiction** is the area under the authority of a particular court. For example, the jurisdiction of the Washington Supreme Court is the state of Washington. A decision of the Washington Supreme Court is not binding on a Nevada state court.

Within each jurisdiction, courts are arranged in a hierarchy, with numerous courts on the lowest level and a smaller number of courts on each higher level. There may be just one judge or several judges on a given court, depending on its function and the population of the area it serves. A judge is required to follow the precedents decided by a higher court in the same jurisdiction.

For example, suppose Intermediate Court A hears a case involving wall-to-wall carpeting and rules that wall-to-wall carpeting is a fixture that is part of the sale. All the judges on Lower Courts A1, A2, and A3 must follow that precedent if a similar case is brought before them.

Fig. 1.2 An imaginary, simplified court system

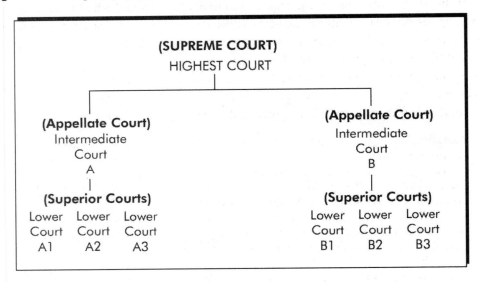

But when a judge on Lower Court B2 decides a similar case, he or she is free to hold that wall-to-wall carpeting is not a fixture and can be removed by the seller. That's because Lower Court B2 is not in the same jurisdiction as Intermediate Court A.

Intermediate Court B is also not bound by the precedents of Intermediate Court A, since Court A is not higher than Court B. Both intermediate courts are bound by the decisions of the Highest Court, however.

A judge is expected to follow the earlier decisions of his or her own court, but he or she has the power to depart from these precedents. Conditions may have changed significantly since the earlier case was decided, or the earlier decision may simply seem wrong. If so, the judge may modify the rule or overrule the precedent altogether.

Example: Two years later, Intermediate Court A hears another wall-to-wall carpeting case. The judges on Intermediate Court A would ordinarily follow their own court's precedent, but this time they reconsider the earlier decision and decide to overrule it. They hold that wall-to-wall carpeting is not a fixture unless it has been completely glued to the floor in such a manner that it is unremovable. (Note that if the earlier case had been decided by the Highest Court, rather than by Intermediate Court A, the precedent could not be overruled by Intermediate Court A. Judges can't overrule precedents decided by a higher court.)

No decision can be a binding precedent unless a written **opinion** is published. In addition to stating the court's decision, an opinion describes the facts of the case and the court's reasoning: why it concluded that wall-to-wall carpeting is a fixture. Some courts publish an opinion for every case decided; others publish opinions only for their most important cases.

By reading the higher court's opinion, a lower court judge can determine how similar the facts of the earlier case were to the case he or she is deciding, and whether the same reasoning applies. When the facts are significantly different, the current case is **distinguished** from the earlier case. If the current case can be distinguished, the lower court judge can reach a different result than was reached in the earlier case.

Even though judges are not bound by lower court decisions or decisions from other jurisdictions, they often take those decisions into consideration. A well-reasoned opinion from another jurisdiction can have a great deal of persuasive influence.

> **Example:** A judge in Washington is deciding a case involving a very unusual type of easement. Although no other court in Washington has ever dealt with such an easement, courts in other states have. The Washington judge reads opinions from courts in New York, Florida, and Alabama. The Florida court decided the easement was valid, but the New York and Alabama courts decided it was invalid.
>
> The Florida court's reasoning makes much more sense to the Washington judge than the other courts' reasoning. He decides to rule that the easement in his case is valid, and writes an opinion that is based on the Florida court's arguments.

The process of deciding cases and the relationship of different courts are more complicated than this initial discussion might suggest. They will be examined in greater detail later in this chapter.

Administrative Agencies

Over the past few decades, another source of law has become increasingly important in the United States: federal, state, and local administrative agencies. Executives (the president, governors, and mayors) and legislative bodies do not have the time or the expertise to take care of all the details of a complex area of law, so they create administrative agencies to handle specific areas.

There are agencies concerned with nearly every aspect of society. Federal agencies range from the Department of Housing and Urban Development and the Environmental Protection Agency to the Internal Revenue Service. Washington state agencies include the Department

Fig. 1.3 How cases are cited

Case Law Citations

Judicial opinions are published in books called **case reporters**. Case citations—references to particular cases in the reporters—are given in a standardized form.

Example: *Rodgers v. Rainier Nat'l Bank*, 111 Wn.2d 232, 757 P.2d 976 (1988)

The citation includes the name of the case, followed by the volume (111) of the case reporter (Wn.2d) where the opinion can be found. Then it states the page number (232) the opinion begins on. Washington cases can also be found in the Pacific Reporter. The second cite tells you that this opinion is also found in volume 757 of the Pacific 2nd Reporter (P.2d) beginning on page 976. The citation ends with the year that the case was decided, in parentheses (1988).

There are separate case reporters for most state appellate courts in the country, as well as federal case reporters. In addition, there are regional reporters that compile important cases from state courts in a given region (the Pacific Reporter and the Northeastern Reporter, for example). Each reporter's title has its own abbreviation for purposes of citation. Following are the abbreviations that someone in Washington State is most likely to encounter.

State Court Decisions
Decisions of the Washington Supreme Court:
    Washington Reports   Wash. or Wn.2d

Decisions of the Washington Court of Appeals:
    Washington Appellate Reports   Wn. App.

Decisions from superior courts in Washington and 14 other western states:
    Pacific Reporter   P. or P.2d

Federal Court Decisions
Decisions of the United States Supreme Court:
    United States Reports   U.S.
    Supreme Court Reporter   S.Ct.

Decisions of the United States Courts of Appeals (including the Ninth Circuit):
    Federal Reporter   F., F.2d, or F.3d

Decisions of the United States District Courts:
    Federal Supplement   F. Supp. or F. Supp. 2d

A citation to a case from a federal Court of Appeals includes the circuit number in parentheses, along with the year the case was decided. A Ninth Circuit decision would be cited like this: *Trident Center v. Connecticut General Life Ins. Co.*, 847 F.2d 564 (9th Cir. 1988).

A citation to a case from a federal district court includes the name of the district in the parentheses. A decision from the Eastern District of Washington would be cited like this: *Barron v. Safeway Stores, Inc.*, 704 F. Supp. 1555 (E.D. Wash. 1988).

of Licensing and the Department of Labor and Industries. Every county and city also has a zoning authority, a building department, a planning commission, and so forth.

Rulemaking

An administrative agency is usually given broad powers within its area of authority. This includes the power to issue regulations that have the force of law. For example, the Director of the Department of Licensing has issued regulations prohibiting the discriminatory sales practices called blockbusting and steering (see Chapter 12). A real estate agent who violates these regulations may have his or her license revoked. The Director also has the power to fine agents for violations.

Before issuing a new regulation, an agency is generally required to publish a notice of its intention to do so. This gives interested parties (such as real estate agents or home-owners) the opportunity to express their ideas and concerns. The regulation must, of course, be constitutional. Furthermore, it also must not exceed the authority granted to the agency by the legislative body or executive that created it. In Washington, a public hearing is required to be held on the proposed new rule. In some cases the agency may ask for additional written comments.

Adjudication and Enforcement

Detailed regulations give rise to many disagreements: licenses, permits, and benefits may be denied or revoked; rules may be violated. These disputes would overwhelm the court system, so most of them are decided by the agencies themselves.

Many of these disputes are handled through an informal negotiation process. But when a significant liberty or property interest (such as a real estate license) is at stake, the agency usually must hold a formal administrative hearing in order to comply with the Constitution's due process requirement. These cases are decided by administrative law judges.

An administrative law judge is part of the agency, and is an expert in the agency's area of authority. But he or she is supposed to consider disputes impartially, rather than taking the agency's point of view. If you're unhappy with an administrative law judge's decision, you can appeal to the superior court. However, a court is not very likely to overturn the agency's decision. If the agency's record of the case contains substantial evidence to support the decision, the court will simply consider whether the agency has exceeded its grant of power or incorrectly followed a required administrative procedure. If not, the court will affirm the agency's ruling.

How Laws Interact

Constitutional provisions, statutes, case law, and administrative regulations are not isolated from one another. They are often complementary, and a judge may apply all of them in resolving a lawsuit. There is also interaction between the different kinds of laws: a statute or a regulation can be held unconstitutional by a court; new case law can be developed to interpret a statute; a new statute can replace case law.

Judicial Review

Earlier in the chapter, the concept of unconstitutionality was introduced. If a law exceeds the limits of government power as outlined in the U.S. Constitution (or the state constitution), it is unconstitutional.

Judges determine whether statutes, ordinances, or regulations are unconstitutional. The Constitution did not expressly assign that role to them, but in an early case the U.S. Supreme Court declared that the judiciary had that power. (*Marbury v. Madison*, 5 U.S. (1 Cranch) 137 (1803).) **Judicial review** of legislation and regulations is established and accepted today.

Judges do not routinely review all of the statutes adopted by a legislative body or all of an administrative agency's regulations. Someone who believes he or she has been harmed by an unconstitutional statute or regulation must file a lawsuit challenging the law's constitutionality before a court will review it.

Once a court decides that a law is unconstitutional, it cannot be enforced. At that point, the legislative body or administrative agency may try to revise the statute or regulation to bring it within constitutional limits.

Fig. 1.4 How laws interact

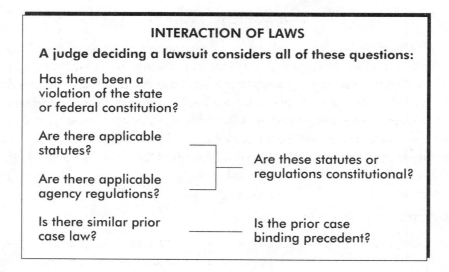

Statutory Construction

The most common kind of interaction between different types of laws occurs when a judge applies a statute in a lawsuit. This is a straightforward task when the facts of the case clearly fall inside or outside of the statute's rule. But it often isn't clear whether the statute covers a particular situation or not, so the judge must decide. This process of interpretation is called **statutory construction**. Judges have to interpret administrative regulations in the same way.

In interpreting a statute or regulation, the judge's goal is to carry out the intention of the legislature or the administrative agency. When judges interpret a statute or a regulation, case law is grafted onto the statutory or regulatory law. A whole series of cases may develop the meaning of a single statutory phrase such as "discrimination." One case says you cannot discriminate against disabled people; another case says that while you cannot discriminate against disabled people, those infected with HIV are not disabled.

The legislature may disagree with some of the case law that develops throughout this process of interpretation. It can then rewrite the statute to make it clear that those infected with HIV are indeed considered to be disabled persons and cannot be discriminated against. The revised statute will cancel out any case law that conflicts with it. An administrative agency can revise its regulations in the same way.

But the process of judicial interpretation will begin all over again with the revised statute or regulation. There's no such thing as a perfectly clear rule that covers all possible cases and requires no interpretation. This interaction between statutes, regulations, and court decisions is a necessary part of the law.

The Judicial System

As you've seen, judges resolve disputes by interpreting and applying existing laws, and developing new ones if necessary. This section focuses on the structure of the judicial system. It explains the different functions of trial and appellate courts, and outlines the state and federal court systems. It also describes some rules that limit access to the courts.

Both the federal and state systems are overcrowded; there are too many cases and not enough judges to hear them, which often causes long delays. So procedures and limitations have been developed to help reserve the courts' resources for the cases where adjudication is most necessary and most likely to be effective.

Trial Courts and Appellate Courts

The fundamental court proceeding in a lawsuit is the **trial**. The general outlines of a trial are no doubt familiar to you: lawyers present arguments and evidence, witnesses testify and are cross-examined, and a jury or a judge decides the case. Trials take place in a jurisdiction's lower courts, so those are often referred to as **trial courts**.

If you're dissatisfied with the outcome of a trial, you generally have the opportunity to appeal at least once. On appeal, you are asking a higher court in the same jurisdiction to reconsider the trial court's decision. A court that has the power to review the decisions of lower courts is called an **appellate court**, and is said to have **appellate jurisdiction**. (Trial courts are said to have **original jurisdiction** because they hear cases for the first time.)

Many people expect an appeal to be just like another trial, but it is a very different proceeding. To try every appealed case all over again would be extremely expensive, both for the parties and for the court system. So the evidence is not presented again, the witnesses do not testify again, and there is no jury.

Instead, the appellate court reviews the **trial record**, which includes a word-for-word transcript of everything that the lawyers, witnesses, and trial judge said in the courtroom. The record also includes any exhibits that were introduced at the trial. An **exhibit** is documentary or physical evidence: a listing agreement, a deed, fingerprints, or an old tire.

In reviewing the record, the appellate court is looking for errors committed by the trial judge. Most appellate courts will only change a trial court's decision if:

- the judge committed an error,
- the error concerned a question of law, and
- the error was prejudicial.

Questions of Fact and Questions of Law. All the issues in a trial can be classified as either questions of fact or questions of law. A **question of fact** is any question about what actually took place: Did Abernathy tell Barlow she could lease the apartment for nine months or for a year and a half? A **question of law**, on the other hand, is any question about what the law is on a particular point: Is a lease for a year and a half valid if it isn't in writing?

Questions of fact are decided by the trier of fact. In a jury trial, the trier of fact is the jury. In a non-jury trial, the trier of fact is the judge. Questions of law are always decided by the judge, regardless of whether there is a jury.

An appellate court generally accepts the trier of fact's conclusions on questions of fact. The trier of fact had a better opportunity to assess the evidence than the appellate court. The trier of fact heard the testimony firsthand and could observe the witnesses as they were testifying, whereas the appellate judges only read a transcript of the testimony. So if the trier of fact concluded that Abernathy told Barlow she could lease the apartment for a year and a half, the appellate court will assume that conclusion is correct. An exception is made only if the trier of fact's findings are completely unsupported by the evidence.

An appellate court's main focus is on the questions of law, reviewing the record to see if the trial judge decided any of those incorrectly. The trial judge may have made a mistake about an established point of law (substantive or procedural). Or the trial judge may have ruled on an issue that had never been decided before, and the appellate court might disagree with the ruling. In either case, the trial court is said to have committed an error.

Prejudicial Error and Harmless Error. If the appellate court finds that the trial judge committed an error, it considers whether the error was prejudicial or harmless. A **preju-dicial** error is one that adversely affects a substantial right of one of the litigants. This is generally interpreted to mean an error that may make a difference in the outcome of the trial. If the trier of fact would almost certainly have reached the same final decision if the error had not been made, the error is considered **harmless**.

The Appellate Decision. If the appellate court does not find any error in the record, or decides that the error was harmless, it will **affirm** the trial court's decision. If it decides that there was prejudicial error, it will **modify** or **reverse** the decision.

When a trial court's decision is reversed, the appellate court may substitute its own ruling for the trial court's judgment, or it may **remand** the case back to the lower courts. If the case is remanded, the appellate court may order the original trial judge to conduct additional proceedings, or it may order a new trial.

Whereas a trial is presided over by a single judge, an appeal is usually heard by a panel of three or more judges. Sometimes not all of the judges on an appellate panel agree on how a case should be decided. Then the decision will be reached by majority vote.

Second Appeal. A litigant dissatisfied with the result of an appeal may appeal again, to an even higher court. But while a first appeal is generally an **appeal by right**, a second appeal is often **discretionary**. The litigant petitions the high court to hear the case, but the high court may refuse. In fact, because the courts are so crowded, the great majority of discretionary appeals are turned down.

State Courts and Federal Courts

Just as there is a federal legislature (Congress) and 50 state legislatures, there is a federal court system and 50 state court systems. But the federal court system isn't centralized in Washington, D.C.; there are federal courts in every state, along with the state courts. The jurisdictions of federal courts and state courts overlap.

Taking a closer look at the concept of jurisdiction will make it easier to understand the two systems and their relationship to one another. You have already seen how a court's jurisdiction can be limited to a particular geographical area: the Washington state courts don't have authority over what takes place in Nevada. But jurisdiction can be limited in other ways as well.

A court's jurisdiction may be limited to a certain type of lawsuit, such as tax cases or patent cases. The types of cases that a court has authority to hear are called its **subject matter jurisdiction**. A court that is not limited to a specific subject is called a court of **general jurisdiction**.

Fig. 1.5 The Washington state court system

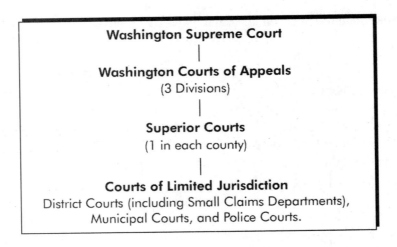

There may also be monetary limits on a court's jurisdiction. For example, some courts can only hear a case if the amount of money involved in the dispute (called the **amount in controversy**) is more than $10,000. Other courts can only hear a case if the amount in controversy is less than $4,000.

Limitations like these define the jurisdiction of the various state and federal courts. We'll look at the Washington state court system, then at the federal system, and then at the relationship between the two.

District and Municipal Courts

The trial courts at the lowest level of the hierarchy are the district, municipal, and police courts. District courts share jurisdiction with the higher level superior courts over criminal matters such as misdemeanors, gross misdemeanors, and criminal traffic cases (such as driving under the influence, hit-and-run, and driving with a suspended license), as well as civil cases involving damages for personal or property injury, or contract disputes, in amounts up to $50,000. With certain exceptions, such as convictions for driving while intoxicated and some game violations, those convicted of criminal offenses in district court may only be sentenced up to $5,000 in fines, a year in jail, or both.

District courts have exclusive jurisdiction over traffic infractions (such as speeding tickets) and small claims disputes.

Small Claims Departments. Each district court has a small claims department for resolving minor civil disputes quickly and inexpensively. The amount in controversy must be $4,000 or less.

To save time and expense, the small claims process is simplified in several respects. There is no jury. Neither the plaintiff nor the defendant can be represented by a lawyer in the courtroom (although they are allowed to consult a lawyer about the case). The plaintiff gives up the right to an appeal. The defendant still has the right to an appeal, since he or she was not the one who chose the small claims court.

Municipal and Police Courts. Violations of municipal or city ordinances are handled in municipal and police courts. Some cities contract with district courts to handle such cases. As in district courts, a judge may impose fines of up to $5,000, a year in jail, or both.

Judges. District court judges are elected to a four-year term. Municipal and police court judges are either elected or appointed, depending on the particular statutory provisions under which the courts were established. It is not a requirement that a district or municipal court judge be an attorney.

Superior Courts

Superior courts have concurrent jurisdiction over the matters that can be filed in district courts (except for traffic infractions and small claims disputes). In addition, superior courts are the trial courts for all cases that exceed the limits of district and municipal court jurisdiction. Thus, superior courts try serious criminal cases (felonies). They also try civil cases. There is no minimum amount in controversy requirement to bring a case in superior court. However, since a case cannot be brought in district court if the amount in controversy exceeds $50,000, most superior court cases are for over $50,000. Most civil cases in which the plaintiff is seeking a non-monetary remedy (such as an injunction) are also brought in superior court. In addition, superior courts can hear appeals in cases that were decided in the district or municipal court.

There is one superior court in each county, and the number of judges on the court depends on the county's population. There are 29 judicial districts in the state and nearly 174 superior court judges. Counties with large populations usually comprise one district, while in less populated areas there are several counties in one district. In very rural counties, judges rotate among the counties as needed.

Although not required to, a superior court judge will usually try to follow precedents decided by other judges on the same court. A King County superior court judge will follow another King County judge's lead. A judge on another superior court (the superior court in Spokane County, for example) may disregard the King County precedent altogether.

Juvenile Court. Juvenile court is a division of the superior court that deals with youths under the age of 18. It handles cases involving youths who commit offenses or who are abused or neglected.

Judges. Like district court judges, superior court judges are elected to four-year terms. Vacancies between elections are filled by the governor. Superior court judges must be attorneys admitted to practice in the state of Washington.

Some courts employ court commissioners to ease the judges' caseloads. Most commissioners are attorneys licensed to practice in Washington. Working under the direction of the presiding judge, the commissioner assumes many of the same powers as a superior court judge. However, a commissioner does not preside over criminal cases or jury trials.

Washington Courts of Appeals

A litigant who is unhappy with a superior court's decision has a right to a review by one of the state courts of appeals. These courts have appellate jurisdiction in all matters except criminal cases involving the death penalty. (Death penalty cases are appealed directly from superior court to the state supreme court.)

An opinion by a state court of appeals is published only if it involves a new and important issue, or changes an established rule. The state is divided into three appellate divisions. A published decision from one of the three appellate divisions is binding precedent within that division. However, the three divisions are semi-independent. A court of appeals in one division is not bound to follow precedents decided by another division.

The decisions of any of the courts of appeals are binding precedents for all the trial courts in the state (district, municipal, and superior courts). This is true even when the trial court is not in the same appellate district as the court of appeals that established the precedent.

> **Example:** A Spokane County superior court judge is hearing a case involving breach of contract. In resolving the questions of law that the case presents, the judge looks first for precedents decided by Division Three of the Court of Appeals, because Spokane is in Division Three. But the judge finds that the main point of law in the case has never been addressed by Division Three. That doesn't mean the judge gets to make up her own mind about the issue. She must do further research to determine whether the courts of appeals in either of the other two divisions have decided the question yet. It turns out that Division One has established a precedent on the issue. The Spokane superior court judge must follow the Division One precedent, even though Spokane is not in that division.

What if the judge had found two conflicting precedents, one from Division One and one from Division Two? She could choose between the two. That kind of conflict would eventually be cleared up by the highest court in the state system, the Washington Supreme Court.

Judges. The judges on the courts of appeals serve six-year staggered terms. This ensures that not all judges will be up for re-election at the same time. The only requirement for office is that the prospective judges be attorneys admitted to practice law in the state of Washington.

Washington Supreme Court

The Washington Supreme Court is the state's highest court. It consists of a chief justice and eight associate justices. A criminal defendant who has been sentenced to death has the right to appeal to the state supreme court directly from superior court. Most other cases must go from superior court to a court of appeals before they can be appealed to the supreme court.

An appeal to the Washington Supreme Court from a court of appeals decision is discretionary. The supreme court will generally hear an appeal only if the case presents a particularly important legal question, or if the courts of appeals have developed conflicting precedents. The supreme court can resolve these conflicts because its decisions are binding on all other Washington state courts. One of the supreme court's most important functions is making the law uniform throughout the state. All supreme court opinions are published; they are the final word on Washington law.

Judges. Just like the court of appeals judges, the supreme court justices are elected to staggered six-year terms. The only requirement for office is that the prospective justice be an attorney admitted to practice law in the state of Washington. Any midterm vacancies are filled by the governor.

United States District Courts

The U.S. District Courts are the main trial courts of the federal system. There are dozens of district courts across the country, with at least one in each state. Washington has two district courts, a Western District Court (located in Seattle and Tacoma) and an Eastern District Court (located in Spokane). A federal district court judge's decision is binding on other federal judges in the same district, but not on federal judges in other districts. So a judge in the Eastern District of Washington must follow Eastern District precedents, but doesn't have to follow Western District precedents. The U.S. District Courts can hear cases that fall into one of three categories:

1. The United States government is a party.
2. A federal question is presented.
3. There is diversity of citizenship, and the amount in controversy is more than $75,000.

Cases in which the United States is a party include suits involving federal crimes: interstate car theft, racketeering, drug smuggling, and so forth. The U.S. can also be a party in a civil suit. For example, a defense contractor might sue the U.S. Army over a contract dispute. That case could be tried in a federal district court, since the army is a branch of the U.S. government.

The district courts also have jurisdiction over civil cases in which a **federal question** is presented. A federal question is any issue regarding the application or interpretation of the U.S. Constitution, a federal statute, or a U.S. treaty. If a group of political protesters sues a city for interfering with their First Amendment right to freedom of speech, the case could be heard in a federal district court.

The third category of federal district court jurisdiction covers civil cases in which there is **diversity of citizenship** and the amount in controversy is more than $75,000. Diversity of citizenship exists when the plaintiff and the defendant are not citizens of the same state. If a citizen of Alabama sues a citizen of Washington, or if a citizen of Washington sues a citizen of Brazil, the case can be heard in federal district court if more than $75,000 is at stake. This is called **diversity jurisdiction**.

Judges. All federal judges are appointed by the president and confirmed by the Senate. The Constitution provides that they will hold office "during good behavior," which generally means for life or until they retire.

United States Courts of Appeals

The result of a trial in a U.S. district court can be appealed (by right) to one of the U.S. Courts of Appeals. There is a federal court of appeals for each of eleven circuits. Each circuit covers several states (see Figure 1.6). There is an additional court of appeals in Washington, D.C., which is called the D.C. Circuit. Washington is in the Ninth Circuit, along with Oregon, California, Montana, Idaho, Nevada, Arizona, Alaska, Hawaii, and Guam. The decision of a U.S. district court sitting in any of those states (for instance, the District Court for the Eastern District of Washington, or the Idaho District Court), could be appealed to the Ninth Circuit Court of Appeals.

There are 39 judges on the Ninth Circuit, which is the largest federal appeals court. Most appeals are heard by panels made up of three of the circuit's judges. A Ninth Circuit decision is a binding precedent for all the U.S. district courts within the circuit.

> **Example:** A judge on the U.S. District Court for the Western District of Washington rules that a broker's hiring policies violated federal employment discrimination statutes. If a case involving similar hiring policies comes before the U.S. District Court for the Eastern District of California, the judge does not have to follow the Western District

Fig. 1.6 The federal court system

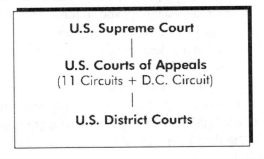

Fig. 1.7 The federal judicial circuits

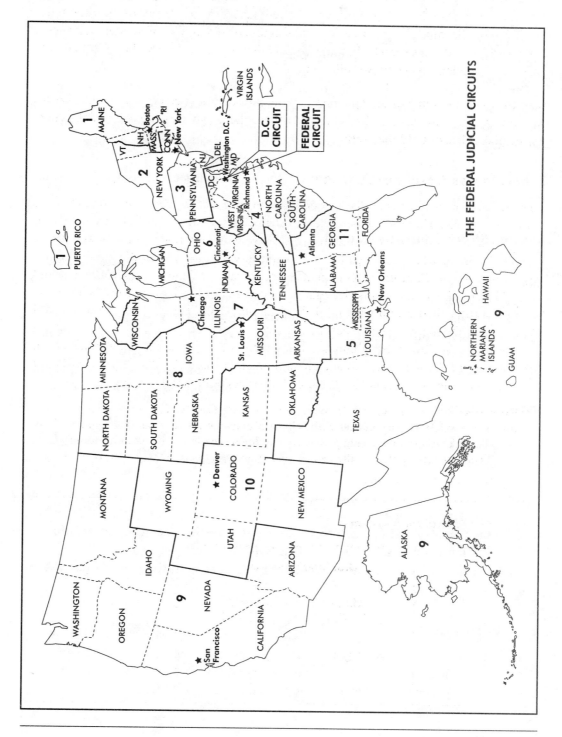

THE FEDERAL JUDICIAL CIRCUITS

of Washington's decision. He or she may decide that the hiring policy did not violate the federal statute.

However, it's a different matter if the Washington broker appeals to the Ninth Circuit, and a three-judge panel affirms the Washington district court's decision. Now a district court in California (or Hawaii, Arizona, or any Ninth Circuit state) is required to follow the precedent and hold that the hiring policy violated the statute.

Other circuit courts of appeals do not have to follow the Ninth Circuit's precedent. And district courts in other circuits—the District Court for the Western District of Kentucky, or for the Southern District of New York—are also free to ignore the Ninth Circuit's decision. But a decision by one of the U.S. Courts of Appeals usually has significant persuasive value for other courts.

Not every opinion of the U.S. Courts of Appeals is published, but all the opinions that decide new issues or change old rules are.

United States Supreme Court

The U.S. Supreme Court is made up of a chief justice and eight associate justices. Although it is the highest and most influential court in the country, its jurisdiction is limited just as the jurisdiction of the lower federal courts is limited.

The Supreme Court has original jurisdiction in a few special types of cases: for example, a lawsuit involving officials of a foreign government, or a lawsuit filed by a state against a citizen of a different state. However, even though the Court is empowered to conduct the trials in these cases, they will usually take place in a U.S. district court instead. The only trials that must take place in the Supreme Court are those for cases in which one state is suing another state.

The Supreme Court has appellate jurisdiction in all cases decided by the U.S. Courts of Appeals. Its decisions in these cases are binding precedents for all other courts. This gives the Supreme Court power to resolve conflicts between the decisions of U.S. Courts of Appeals in different circuits.

All appeals to the Supreme Court are discretionary. A litigant files a petition requesting a hearing, and the Supreme Court decides whether or not to grant the request. Petitions are filed for thousands of cases each year, but the Court hears less than five percent of them. Although "I'll take my case all the way to the Supreme Court!" is a standard threat, it can rarely be carried out. The U.S. Court of Appeals is the end of the line for the overwhelming majority of federal cases.

Specialized Courts

There are a few specialized federal courts with narrow subject matter jurisdiction. The U.S. Tax Court hears only cases involving the federal tax laws, the Federal Circuit Court hears only cases concerning patents or foreign trade, and the U.S. Bankruptcy Court hears nothing but bankruptcy cases.

Fig. 1.8 Specialized federal courts

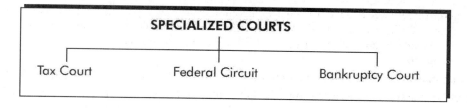

Federal and State Court Jurisdiction

Because federal jurisdiction and state jurisdiction overlap, the relationship between the two court systems is complicated. We'll start with the simpler cases—those that must be heard in federal court and those that must be heard in state court—before moving on to the cases that can be heard in either one.

Exclusive Jurisdiction

Federal Court. In some federal statutes, Congress has included a requirement that lawsuits based on the statute can be brought only in federal court. For example, cases involving the Voting Rights Act of 1965 cannot be heard in state court. The same is true for suits regarding patents, copyrights, immigration, admiralty, and a number of other subjects that are controlled by federal statutes. Very few cases involving real property are in this category.

State Court. Any case that does not fall within the jurisdiction of the federal courts must be brought in state court. In other words, a case has to be heard in state court if:

- the U.S. government is not a party,
- no federal question is presented, and
- there is no diversity of citizenship (or there is diversity but the amount in controversy is $75,000 or less).

For example, most real estate cases must be brought in state court rather than federal court. In a typical real estate lawsuit, the plaintiff and the defendant are citizens of the same state, only questions of state law are involved, and the U.S. government is not a party.

Concurrent Jurisdiction

Either State or Federal Court. The reason state and federal jurisdiction overlap is that the cases that may be brought in federal court do not have to be. A state court can hear a diversity of citizenship case, even if the amount in controversy is over $75,000. A state court can also hear a federal question case, except if it concerns those subjects (like patents) that Congress has expressly reserved for the federal courts.

When a state trial court decides a federal question case, the decision can be appealed only in the state system. In other words, the case must be taken to one of the Washington courts of appeals, rather than to the Ninth Circuit Court of Appeals. On a second appeal, it would go to the Washington Supreme Court.

From that point, there is the possibility of a third appeal, to the U.S. Supreme Court. The U.S. Supreme Court will review the decision of a state supreme court if (and only if) the case presents an important federal question. It will not interfere in cases that involve only questions of state law.

Choosing Between Federal and State Court. When a case could be filed in either state or federal court, why does the plaintiff choose one over the other? The reasons aren't clear-cut. Sometimes federal court is chosen just because the plaintiff's lawyer is accustomed to federal court and is more familiar with federal court procedures. Some lawyers believe that federal court judges tend to be better qualified or more sophisticated, since they are appointed rather than elected.

At times, the federal or state courts gain a reputation for favoring plaintiffs or defendants in a particular type of case. Civil rights cases are the most prominent example. In the 1960s (and later), state courts in southern states were seen as more likely to support racial segregation than the federal courts in those states. As a result, a southern plaintiff claiming that his or her civil rights had been violated would almost invariably choose to bring the case in federal court.

Limitations on Adjudication

Our judicial system has several rules that bar lawsuits in specific situations. It's important to understand these limitations, as they can prevent an aggrieved plaintiff from being able to sue.

Case or Controversy

As a general rule, a lawsuit must involve an active conflict, not just a theoretical or potential conflict. Based on Article III of the U.S. Constitution, this is known as the **case or controversy requirement**.

> **Example:** The landlord of a large new apartment building wonders if it is necessary to go to the expense of installing various security devices. If he doesn't install them, would he be liable if one of the apartments were burglarized? Could a tenant have them installed and then deduct the cost from the rent?

The landlord can consult a lawyer about these issues. The lawyer will give his or her opinion about what a court would probably decide if these cases arose. But a court would refuse to consider these hypothetical questions.

A judge won't issue a binding decision on what this landlord's duty is unless one of the apartments is actually burglarized and the tenant sues the landlord, or unless a tenant actually deducts the installation costs and the landlord sues for the deducted portion of the rent.

In some situations, however, a court has discretion to grant **declaratory relief**. This means that instead of requiring a problem to reach a crisis, the court will let the parties know in advance what their duties under a contract are, or what their property rights are. A **quiet title action** is an example of declaratory relief. If there is a possible claim against a property holder's title (a boundary dispute, for example), he or she can ask a court to decide whether or not the claim is valid. The title holder does not have to wait for the potential claimant to sue. Without a quiet title action, the title holder might be reluctant to develop the property, since it could turn out to belong to someone else.

Statute of Limitations

A statute of limitations precludes a court from hearing a case if too much time has passed since the conflict arose. The reason for these time limits is that it becomes more and more difficult to prove or disprove a claim as years go by. Evidence is often lost, and witnesses' memories fade.

The time limits vary depending on the type of case. In Washington, most contract suits must be filed within six years after the breach occurred if the contract was in writing, or within three years if the contract was oral. A suit to recover possession of real property must be filed within ten years.

It's important to note that in certain types of cases, the statute of limitations doesn't start running until the injury or loss is discovered, even if the wrongful act occurred much earlier. This is called the **discovery rule.**

> **Example:** Six months after she purchases a house, a buyer learns that the seller acted fraudulently in the transaction. The time limit for the buyer to bring an action against the seller doesn't begin until the buyer discovers the fraud.

The statute of limitations may offer special protection to a minor or incompetent person. In many cases, the statute of limitations does not begin to run until the minor reaches the age of majority, or the incompetent person regains competence.

Anyone thinking about starting a lawsuit should find out the limitations period for that type of action, and keep it in mind. Once the statutory period has run out, you've lost your legal remedy for good.

Res Judicata

"Res judicata" is a Latin phrase meaning "the thing has been decided." The doctrine of **res judicata** holds that once a dispute between two parties has been tried and appealed and a final judgment has been issued, the same dispute cannot be tried again. The dissatisfied party can't start a new lawsuit on the same question, hoping to find a more sympathetic judge or a more persuasive lawyer. The purpose of the doctrine is simple: finality. It puts the case to rest, at least as far as the court system is concerned. Without res judicata, some parties would go on suing each other over the same matter forever. That would make the courts even more crowded than they already are.

A Civil Lawsuit

Now we'll take a closer look at the litigation process. This section follows a simple civil lawsuit from its filing to the enforcement of the final judgment. The entire process would probably take at least several months; in many cases, it takes years.

The Dispute

Henry Palermo has lived near the Little Spokane River for many years. The lot to the west of his property had always been vacant, until Claire Mulligan bought it six months ago. Mulligan has had the lot cleared and regraded in preparation for the construction of a house.

Recently, very heavy rains occurred and Palermo's house was flooded. The water caused considerable damage to the house and yard and many of Palermo's belongings were ruined, including expensive stereo and recording equipment and a large record collection. Palermo had let his homeowner's insurance lapse two months earlier.

Since his house was never flooded before, Palermo believes Mulligan's clearing and regrading next door changed the pattern of runoff and caused the flooding. He explains this to Mulligan, and says she should help pay for the damage. Mulligan is furious. She tells Palermo his property flooded simply because it rained so hard, and that the changes she made in her property had nothing to do with it. In the course of a ten-minute conversation, the neighbors become enemies.

So Palermo consults a lawyer. The lawyer evaluates Palermo's claim by researching the law (looking up statutes and case law) about drainage onto adjoining property. He decides Palermo has a fairly strong case. Washington law holds that a landowner who disturbs the natural flow of surface waters may be liable for resulting damage to adjacent property.

Mulligan also hires a lawyer to look into the matter. Her lawyer concludes that it would be difficult for Palermo to prove that Mulligan's clearing caused his property to flood. Unless Palermo can prove that in court, Mulligan will not be held liable for the damage.

The two lawyers discuss their clients' positions. Palermo's lawyer says that unless Mulligan pays Palermo $60,000, Palermo will sue her. Mulligan's lawyer says that Mulligan won't pay Palermo a nickel, because the damage was not her fault.

Starting a Lawsuit

Palermo and his lawyer decide to proceed with a lawsuit. Palermo's lawyer starts the suit (*Palermo v. Mulligan*) by filing a **complaint** in the superior court of the county where Mulligan and Palermo live. The complaint outlines the dispute, explains how the plaintiff (Palermo) believes his legal rights have been violated by the defendant (Mulligan), and asks the court to grant judgment in the plaintiff's favor. Palermo asks the court to order Mulligan to prevent any future flooding and pay him $60,000.

Choosing a Court. What kind of court a lawsuit takes place in depends on the jurisdictional issues we discussed earlier. The case must come within the court's jurisdictional limits—geographical, subject matter, and monetary limits. This case had to be brought in state court, because Mulligan and Palermo are both citizens of Washington, and the case does not involve any federal laws (the laws concerning drainage and flooding are state laws). And since the amount in controversy is $60,000, the case had to be filed in superior court rather than in district or municipal court.

Fig. 1.9 Starting a lawsuit

STARTING A LAWSUIT

1. Plaintiff files a complaint.
2. Defendant is served with summons and copy of complaint.
3. Defendant files a notice of appearance and answer.
4. Pretrial discovery takes place.
5. Settlement negotiations may take place.
6. The trial takes place.

Personal Jurisdiction. Even when a case is within a particular court's jurisdictional limits (geographical, subject matter, and monetary limits), that court can hear the case only if it has authority over the defendant. That authority is referred to as **personal jurisdiction.**

A court ordinarily acquires personal jurisdiction over a defendant by service of process. **Service of process** means delivery of a **summons** and a copy of the complaint to the defendant. The summons is simply a notice informing the defendant that the complaint has been filed, and that he or she must file a response with the court.

Service of process usually must take place in the state where the court sits. In most cases, the plaintiff has a process server take the summons and complaint to the defendant's home or business and hand it directly to the defendant. If the defendant tries to evade the process server, service can be accomplished by publication, or through an agent of the defendant.

Jurisdiction Over Property. A court must also have jurisdiction over any property at issue in a lawsuit. Washington courts have jurisdiction over all real and personal property within the state's boundaries.

The Defendant's Answer. A summons and complaint was served on Mulligan at her home. Now her lawyer has 20 days to prepare a **notice of appearance and answer** and file it with the court.

In the answer, a defendant may challenge the court's jurisdiction. The defendant may also deny the plaintiff's allegations, discuss facts that the plaintiff left out of the complaint, or make a **counterclaim** against the plaintiff. Mulligan's answer simply denies that the clearing and regrading on her property were the cause of Palermo's flood damage.

If a defendant fails to respond to the complaint, in some cases the plaintiff can win the case by default. A **default judgment** would then be entered against the defendant.

The complaint, the answer, and other additional documents filed with the court are called **pleadings**.

Pretrial Discovery

Once a lawsuit has been started, both the plaintiff and the defendant are given an opportunity to find out more about the disputed facts through the **discovery process**. The rules of discovery require each side to provide the other with information upon request. They also enable a litigant to obtain information from reluctant witnesses.

One method of acquiring information during discovery is a deposition. In a **deposition**, one party's lawyer questions the other party or a witness about the case. The **deponent** (the person responding to the lawyer's questions) is under oath, just as if he or she were testifying in court. A word-for-word transcript of the deposition can be used as evidence in the trial.

Interrogatories are another important discovery tool. They are like a deposition conducted by mail instead of in person. One party's lawyer sends a series of questions to the other party; the other party must send back answers. Interrogatories are also answered under oath.

Palermo's lawyer sends Mulligan interrogatories asking about the clearing and grading process, and about what measures were taken regarding runoff. Mulligan's lawyer sends Palermo interrogatories asking about the extent of the water damage, and about flooding in previous years. In addition, each side deposes the other party about the facts of the dispute. If Mulligan and Palermo fail to show up for their depositions or fail to answer the interrogatories, they may be fined for contempt of court.

Settlement Negotiations

Litigation is almost always expensive, time-consuming, and unpleasant. Both parties must weigh those costs against what they stand to gain, and how likely they are to win, if the case goes to trial.

Throughout the litigation process, Palermo's and Mulligan's lawyers negotiate to **settle** the case. In a settlement, the defendant pays the plaintiff a sum of money (or agrees to do or to refrain from doing something) so that the plaintiff will call off the lawsuit.

Soon after the action is filed, on the advice of her lawyer, Mulligan offers to pay Palermo $2,000 and install culverts to rechannel runoff, if he will drop the suit. On the advice of his lawyer, Palermo refuses this offer; he will take the case to trial unless Mulligan pays him $30,000 and rechannels the runoff. As each lawyer learns more about the facts of the case through the discovery process, he re-evaluates his client's claim. Palermo's lawyer may realize that it will be much more difficult than he first thought to prove that it was Mulligan's clearing and grading that caused Palermo's property to be flooded. Or Mulligan's lawyer may realize that it may be much easier to prove that than he thought.

On the basis of these re-evaluations, the gap between the parties' settlement offers narrows. As the trial date approaches, Palermo is asking only $21,000 to settle, and Mulligan is offering $10,000. It is extremely likely that Palermo and Mulligan will come to an agreement. Over 95% of civil cases settle or are decided by arbitration rather than going through a trial. (The percentage may be even higher in some counties, especially where there is a backlog of cases and it might be quite some time before the case would ever get to trial.)

In some cases, however, the parties are unable to settle. It may be that the facts of the case are unclear, or that the laws governing the case are ambiguous. Or it may be that the litigants are unusually stubborn, or extremely angry with one another. We'll assume that for some combination of these reasons, Palermo and Mulligan do not settle, and the case proceeds to trial.

Jury or Judge

The U.S. Constitution and the Washington Constitution guarantee litigants the right to trial by jury. That right applies in most civil cases, but some cases (and certain issues within some cases) cannot be tried by a jury. It depends on the remedies requested by the plaintiff.

Common Law and Equitable Remedies. The remedies awarded in civil cases are classified either as common law remedies or as equitable remedies. A **common law remedy** is generally an award of money (damages). An **equitable remedy**, on the other hand, usually involves an **injunction**: an order to do something, or to refrain from doing something.

> **Example:** If the court ordered Mulligan to install culverts and plant protective vegetation, that would be an equitable remedy. If Mulligan were ordered to pay Palermo $25,000, that would be a common law remedy.

Equitable remedies can be awarded only when money would not adequately correct the problem. Specific performance, contract reformation, foreclosure, and quiet title are all equitable remedies.

For historical reasons, a jury is not allowed to decide equitable issues. If a plaintiff is asking only for an equitable remedy (such as foreclosure), the case cannot be heard by a jury. If a plaintiff is asking for both types of remedies (such as damages and an injunction), a jury may hear the case. The jury will decide on the common law remedy, but the judge will decide on the equitable remedy.

Choosing a Jury. Even when a lawsuit does not involve any equitable issues, a jury isn't automatically assigned to the case. One or both of the parties must request a jury. If neither party does, the judge will decide the questions of fact as well as the questions of law.

When should a litigant request a jury? It's an intuitive choice rather than a scientific one. Juries are supposed to be more sympathetic than judges in some cases. A jury hearing a personal injury suit may be more likely to feel compassion for the plaintiff than a judge, who might have heard dozens of similar cases. A jury may tend to side with the underdog, and favor an individual against a large corporation.

On the other hand, if a litigant's case is based on a complicated legal argument or on detailed technical or scientific evidence, a jury might have a hard time understanding it. And jury trials take longer and are more expensive than non-jury trials.

Although Palermo's lawyer thinks that a jury would feel sorry for his client because of the property damage, he decides not to request a jury. Palermo's case depends too much on technical proof that Mulligan's changes caused the flooding. Mulligan's lawyer decides to request a jury. He hopes the jury will feel that Mulligan did nothing unreasonable, and that it is unfair to hold her responsible for Palermo's misfortune.

Jurors are taken from a pool of citizens chosen at random. Both lawyers have an opportunity to question the potential jurors, to learn about their backgrounds and discover their personal prejudices. Those who seem biased against or in favor of one of the parties may be eliminated from the jury. A jury in district court consists of up to six people. A jury in superior court consists of six or twelve people.

The Trial

Presentation of the Evidence. The plaintiff's case is presented first. The plaintiff's lawyer makes an **opening statement**, telling his or her client's version of the events that gave rise to the lawsuit. This explanation helps the judge and jurors understand the point of the evidence and testimony the lawyer is about to present. The defendant's lawyer can also make an opening statement at this point, or wait until after the plaintiff's case has been fully presented.

The plaintiff's lawyer examines witnesses whose testimony supports his or her client's version of the facts. There are two types of witnesses, fact witnesses and expert witnesses.

A **fact witness** is someone who had an opportunity to observe events connected with the dispute. For example, Palermo's lawyer has some of his client's neighbors testify that there were even heavier rains three years earlier, yet Palermo's property did not flood. A fact witness is only supposed to describe events he or she personally observed, and is not allowed to offer opinions about the facts.

An **expert witness** is someone who has expert knowledge of a subject, either through experience or education. Litigants hire expert witnesses to evaluate their claims. If the expert's opinion supports the litigant's case, the expert is paid to testify at the trial. Palermo's lawyer calls two engineering consultants to testify about the effect of Mulligan's clearing and grading on her property's drainage. The lawyer also examines an appraiser, who testifies about how much it will cost to repair or replace the water-damaged property.

Fig. 1.10 The trial

THE TRIAL

1. Opening statements
2. Presentation of evidence
   (plaintiff goes first)
   - fact witnesses
   - expert witnesses
   - physical or documentary evidence
3. Closing arguments
4. Jury instructions

The initial questioning of witnesses by the lawyer who called them to testify is the **direct examination**. Immediately after the direct examination of a witness, the opposing lawyer has a chance to **cross-examine** that witness. In the cross-examination, the opposing lawyer tries to cast doubt on the witness's testimony and bring out any facts that are unfavorable to the other side. Then the first lawyer has a chance to repair any damage done on cross-examination by **redirect examination** of the witness. Sometimes the opposing lawyer will cross-examine the witness a second time.

Court rules provide that some testimony (or documentary or physical evidence) cannot be used in court because it is considered unreliable or unfair. Such testimony or evidence is inadmissible.

> **Example:** Testimony must be relevant to the issues involved in the dispute. If a neighbor testifying on behalf of Palermo says, "Mrs. Mulligan struck me as a troublemaker," Mulligan's lawyer can object. The witness's impression of Mulligan has no bearing on whether or not her activities caused Palermo's property to flood. The witness's comment is irrelevant and therefore inadmissible.

A lawyer can object to a witness's testimony, or to the other lawyer's questioning, on a variety of grounds: a fact witness is giving an opinion; a minister is being asked to divulge confidential information; the other lawyer is leading the witness (asking yes or no questions, instead of asking witness to describe the events in his or her own words).

If the judge agrees with the objecting lawyer that the questioning is improper, the judge will tell the witness not to answer. If the judge agrees that testimony already given is inadmissible, he or she will tell the jury to disregard the witness's remarks, and may have them stricken from the trial record.

When the plaintiff's lawyer has finished presenting evidence, it is the defense lawyer's turn. The same procedure is repeated: direct and cross-examination of the defendant's witnesses, with objections from the lawyers and rulings on admissibility by the judge. The plaintiff's lawyer then has a chance to present additional evidence to rebut the defendant's case. Finally, each lawyer makes a **closing argument,** explaining how all the evidence fits together.

Jury Instructions. After all the evidence has been presented, the judge gives the jury instructions about the law that applies to the case.

> **Example:** The judge explains that Washington law does not hold a landowner responsible for damage caused by the natural flow of surface water from his or her property onto adjoining property. However, if the landowner changes the natural pattern of drainage, he or she is liable for the resulting damage. The judge points out that this liability does not depend on whether the defendant intended to cause damage, nor on whether the defendant was careless.

The jury instructions include an explanation of the **burden of proof**. Here, as in most cases, the plaintiff has the burden of proof. That is, it is up to Palermo to prove that Mulligan's clearing and regrading were the cause of the damage. Mulligan is not required to prove that her changes did not cause the damage.

The judge will also explain that the plaintiff must prove his claim by a **preponderance of the evidence.** In other words, the jury doesn't have to be absolutely certain that Mulligan's changes caused the damage. It is enough if Palermo convinced the jury that it is more likely than not that Mulligan's changes were the cause. This is the **standard of proof** used in nearly all civil cases. (In criminal cases, where the defendant has so much at stake, a stricter standard of proof is applied: the prosecution must prove its case **beyond a reasonable doubt**.)

The Decision. In a civil case in Washington, 5 out of 6 or 10 out of 12 jurors must agree on the decision; a unanimous verdict is not necessary. However, in a criminal trial, the decision must be unanimous (all of the jurors must agree). If there is a **hung jury**—that is, the jury cannot agree on a verdict after deliberating for a long time—the case must be tried all over again before a new jury.

The jury in *Palermo v. Mulligan* votes 10 to 2 in favor of the plaintiff. Most of the jurors found Palermo's expert witnesses more convincing than Mulligan's expert witnesses. The jurors concluded that the flooding would not have occurred if Mulligan had not cleared and regraded her lot.

The jury awards Palermo $26,000 to repair and replace his water-damaged property. This is significantly less than the $60,000 he requested. The jury wasn't willing to believe that Palermo's stereo equipment and record collection were worth as much as the appraiser testified. The lower award may also reflect some sympathy for Mulligan.

In addition to the jury's damages award, the judge issues an injunction ordering Mulligan to install culverts that will rechannel runoff. Based on the experts' testimony, the judge specifies changes that will prevent future flooding of Palermo's property, without damaging Mulligan's property.

In hindsight, Mulligan and her lawyer appear to have miscalculated. Mulligan would have been better off accepting Palermo's $21,000 settlement offer, instead of going through with the trial in the hope of avoiding liability altogether.

Appeal

Both Mulligan and Palermo have the right to appeal the superior court decision to the Washington Court of Appeals. After the lower court's judgment has been entered, there is a limited period (usually 60 days) for filing a **notice of appeal**.

If Mulligan were to appeal, she would be the **appellant**, and Palermo would be the **appellee**. If Palermo were to appeal, he would be the appellant, and Mulligan would be the appellee. Both of them decide not to appeal, however. Since the jury's fact conclusions cannot be challenged on appeal, neither Palermo nor Mulligan could expect to gain much, and they are both very tired of the whole thing.

Collecting a Judgment

Just because the jury has awarded Palermo $26,000 doesn't mean that Mulligan will take out her checkbook and pay him on the spot. It can take a long time to collect a judgment; some are never collected.

Judgment Liens. Mulligan (the **judgment debtor**) doesn't pay the judgment immediately, so Palermo (the **judgment creditor**) secures his interest by claiming a lien against Mulligan's real property. If Mulligan still fails to pay the judgment, Palermo can **foreclose** on the lien, hoping to collect his $26,000 from the proceeds of a forced sale of the property. (Liens on real property are discussed in more detail in Chapter 3.)

Judgment liens can also attach to some personal property, such as business equipment and inventory. However, many types of personal property are exempt from judgment liens, including the debtor's household furnishings and clothing.

Garnishment. When a judgment debtor is a wage earner, the judgment creditor can use wage garnishment to collect the judgment in installments. An **earnings withholding order** is served on the debtor's employer, who must set aside the debtor's earnings for the creditor. The amount of money required to support the debtor and his or her family is exempt from garnishment.

A judgment debtor's bank account may also be garnished. For instance, money in a savings account could be garnished and collected to pay the judgment.

These collection devices are cumbersome, and they aren't always successful. Some defendants turn out to be "judgment-proof:" they have no wages and no assets, or assets that are either exempt from judgment liens or already heavily encumbered with other liens. Inability to collect a judgment may be a real hardship for a judgment creditor who owes his or her own lawyer a substantial fee. That can make winning a lawsuit a hollow victory.

Conclusion

Lawsuits can be extremely time-consuming, frustrating, and expensive. However, you can reduce the risk of litigation if you are familiar with real estate law and understand your duties and obligations toward your clients and other parties.

Chapter Summary

- The law is a system of rights and duties established and enforced by a government. It maintains order, resolves disputes, enforces promises, and prevents exploitation. The law reflects a society's ideas of justice, but also serves other goals, such as efficiency.

- Substantive law defines rights and duties, while procedural law sets forth the methods for enforcing substantive rights.

- The government brings a criminal action to punish a wrongdoer and protect society. In a civil action, on the other hand, an injured party sues for compensation. Some wrongful acts can lead to both criminal and civil penalties.

- Contracts, torts, and property are the fundamental concepts of civil law. Contract law concerns voluntarily assumed duties; tort law concerns the duties of reasonable conduct imposed by law; property law concerns the duties inherent in ownership.

- Federal and state constitutions, legislative bodies, courts, and administrative agencies are the sources of law in the United States. Constitutions protect individual rights by limiting government power. Within those constitutional limits, legislative and administrative bodies issue general rules in the form of statutes, ordinances, and regulations.

- Courts apply those rules to resolve lawsuits. In the process of interpreting the rules, judges develop case law. The doctrine of stare decisis requires judges to follow established precedents, so that the law will be evenhanded and predictable.

- A court system is a hierarchy of trial courts and appellate courts. An appeal is not a second trial. The appellate court reviews the trial record for prejudicial errors, focusing primarily on questions of law rather than fact.

- The federal and state court systems are independent, with overlapping jurisdictions. Federal jurisdiction is limited to cases involving federal questions, diversity of citizenship, or the U.S. government. State courts can hear any cases except those that Congress has expressly reserved for the federal courts.

- The case or controversy requirement, statutes of limitation, and the doctrine of res judicata limit access to the courts. But the court systems are severely overcrowded in spite of these rules.

- A civil suit begins when the plaintiff files a complaint with the court and has a summons served on the defendant. The pretrial discovery process gives each side access to information the other might prefer to conceal. The parties' lawyers try to negotiate a settlement, to save the expense and trouble of a trial.

- Litigants have a right to trial by jury on any issue that does not involve an equitable remedy. In the trial, each side presents testimony and other evidence favorable to its case. Evidence is only admissible if it meets established standards of reliability and fairness.

- If the plaintiff wins, he or she may have to resort to garnishment or a lien to collect the judgment.

Chapter Quiz

1. The main historical influence on law in the United States was:
   a. Spanish law
   b. feudal law
   c. European law
   d. English law

2. When one individual sues another, the lawsuit is called:
   a. a civil action
   b. an equity suit
   c. declaratory relief
   d. criminal litigation

3. The primary purpose of most civil lawsuits is to:
   a. punish a wrongdoer
   b. compensate a person who has been harmed
   c. protect society
   d. deter crime

4. A person who commits a tort:
   a. will be prosecuted by the government
   b. will be held liable for breach of contract
   c. has violated the standards of reasonable conduct imposed by law
   d. must pay a fine or serve a jail term

5. An unconstitutional law:
   a. exceeds the powers granted to the government
   b. can only be enforced retroactively
   c. may be used to modify a Supreme Court decision
   d. violates the case or controversy requirement

6. The constitutional provision that guarantees a fair hearing by an impartial judge is known as the:
   a. equal protection clause
   b. stare decisis rule
   c. administrative law doctrine
   d. due process requirement

7. Which of the following would be most likely to issue an ordinance?
   a. The Bellevue City Council
   b. The Department of Licensing
   c. The Washington House of Representatives
   d. The King County Superior Court

8. Codification refers to:
   a. reviewing statutes or regulations to determine whether they are constitutional
   b. enforcing substantive rights
   c. combining scattered, piecemeal laws into a comprehensive statute
   d. interpretation of a contract by an appellate court

9. The main purpose of the doctrine of stare decisis is to:
   a. limit access to the courts
   b. prevent courts from exceeding their subject matter jurisdiction
   c. clarify ambiguous statutes
   d. make court decisions more consistent and predictable

10. A binding precedent can be overruled:
   a. by a lower court within the same jurisdiction
   b. by the same court that established it
   c. only by a court with original jurisdiction
   d. only by a court higher than the court that established it

11. A current case is distinguished from a precedent when:

    a. it was decided in a different jurisdiction
    b. it violates the doctrine of res judicata
    c. its facts are significantly different
    d. it overrules the precedent

12. When a precedent is not binding on a particular court:

    a. the judge may still consider it and follow it if it is persuasive
    b. it cannot be admitted into evidence during the trial
    c. the judge may not refer to it in his or her opinion
    d. the judge is not allowed to follow it

13. An administrative law judge:

    a. works in the small claims division of a municipal court
    b. is concerned only with procedural law
    c. resolves disputes involving an administrative agency's regulations
    d. All of the above

14. Which of these usually takes place during an appeal?

    a. Expert witnesses testify
    b. The trial transcript is reviewed
    c. New documentary evidence is introduced
    d. A new jury is chosen

15. Which of these is a question of law?

    a. Was the broker required to put the earnest money in a trust account?
    b. Did the tenant inform the landlord that the railing was broken?
    c. Did the real estate agent inspect the attic?
    d. Was the buyer told that the agent was representing the seller?

16. A prejudicial error is one that:

    a. involves racial discrimination
    b. is committed during the discovery process
    c. involves administrative regulations
    d. may have affected the outcome of the trial

17. When an appellate court can choose whether or not to review a lower court's decision, the appeal is called a/an:

    a. appeal by favor
    b. appeal by right
    c. discretionary appeal
    d. grant review

18. Which of these can limit a court's jurisdiction?

    a. Geographical boundaries
    b. Subject matter of the case
    c. Amount of money at issue in a case
    d. All of the above

19. What's the difference between district and municipal courts?

    a. Municipal courts hear criminal cases and district courts don't
    b. Municipal courts handle violations of city ordinances
    c. Municipal courts have small claims divisions and district courts don't
    d. All of the above

20. Able is going to sue Beckett for breach of contract, claiming $75,000 in damages. Which kind of state court can Able file suit in?

    a. Municipal court
    b. District court of appeals
    c. Circuit court of appeals
    d. Superior court

21. To start a lawsuit, the plaintiff files a/an:

    a. deposition
    b. summons and complaint
    c. answer
    d. interrogatory

22. A jury is not allowed to:

    a. grant an equitable remedy
    b. grant a damages award
    c. decide a criminal case
    d. decide a superior court case

23. Unlike an expert witness, a fact witness:

    a. testifies during the appeal
    b. should not state his or her opinions while testifying
    c. may not be cross-examined
    d. All of the above

24. In most civil lawsuits, the case must be proven by a preponderance of the evidence. This is known as the:

    a. burden of proof
    b. reasonable doubt rule
    c. standard of proof
    d. standard of doubt

25. If a judgment debtor refuses to pay a judgment:

    a. there is nothing the judgment creditor can do except wait and hope that he or she will eventually be paid
    b. the judgment creditor may have the debtor's wages and bank account garnished
    c. the judgment creditor can claim a lien against the debtor's property
    d. Both b) and c)

2 The Nature of Real Property

Outline

I. Land Description
   A. Misrepresenting boundaries
      1. seller's liability
      2. broker's liability
      3. broker's duty
II. Methods of Description
   A. Metes and bounds descriptions
      1. point of beginning
      2. compass bearings
      3. conflicting elements
   B. Government survey descriptions
      1. meridians and base lines
      2. townships and sections
      3. government lots
   C. Lot and block descriptions (recorded plat)
   D. Air lots
   E. Description problems
      1. correcting the description (reformation)
      2. possession
      3. acquiescence or agreement
      4. boundary line agreement
      5. common grantor
      6. court decision
III. Attachments
   A. Natural attachments
      1. naturally occurring vs. cultivated
      2. doctrine of emblements
   B. Fixtures
      1. method of attachment
      2. intention of the annexor
      3. adaptation to the realty
      4. relationship of the parties
      5. written agreement
      6. mobile homes
      7. secured financing and fixtures
IV. Appurtenances
   A. Air rights
      1. use of airspace
      2. sale of airspace
   B. Water rights
      1. riparian rights

      2. appropriative rights
      3. disappearance of riparian rights
      4. navigable waters
      5. non-navigable waters
    C. Mineral rights
      1. mineral deed
      2. mineral reservation
      3. mineral lease
      4. mineral rights option
    D. Support rights
      1. lateral support
      2. subjacent support
    E. Oil and gas rights
      1. rule of capture

Key Terms

- metes and bounds
- monument
- course
- point of beginning
- compass bearing
- natural monument
- government survey
- meridian
- base line
- range line
- township
- section

- government lot
- lot and block
- air lot
- datum
- bench mark
- reformation
- adverse possession
- attachment
- boundary line agreement
- recognition and acquiescence
- doctrine of emblements

- fixture
- constructive annexation
- annexor
- trade fixture
- appurtenance
- riparian rights
- appropriative rights
- navigable waters
- lateral support
- subjacent support
- rule of capture

Chapter Overview

This chapter will provide you with basic information about real property. You will learn how real property is described, what is included as part of the real property, and what rights accompany real property ownership. This information will help you understand the obligations of property sellers and real estate agents involved in real estate transactions.

Case Example:

In 1983, the Connall family put their property up for sale. They told the broker that the property had been surveyed before they bought it, and that the property was 5 acres. They pointed out the boundaries to the broker. The broker later pointed out these same boundaries to potential buyers, the Hoffmans. Part of the property contained a corral, cattle chute, barn, and shed. These were important to the Hoffmans because they owned a horse and wanted to get involved with 4-H activities.

Shortly after the Hoffmans purchased the property, a neighbor told them that a recent survey showed that part of the corral, cattle run, and horse shed were actually 18 to 21 feet on his property. The Hoffmans brought a lawsuit against the Connalls and the broker for misrepresenting the property's boundaries. *Hoffman v. Connall*, 108 Wn.2d 69, 736 P.2d 242 (1987).

Are the corral, cattle chute, barn, and shed part of the real property? Would the Connalls be liable for misrepresenting the boundaries? Should the broker be held liable? Was the broker negligent in not verifying the seller's statements concerning the boundaries? How could the broker have discovered where the real boundaries were located?

After reading this chapter, you will be able to answer these and other questions concerning the nature of real property. The actual outcome of the case of *Hoffman v. Connall* is given below.

Land Description

Knowing where the boundaries to a piece of property lie is important to the seller, the buyer, and the real estate agent. Boundary problems are one of the most common causes of real estate lawsuits. When people buy property, they want to know exactly what they are buying and how much property is included.

Misrepresenting Boundaries

In the case of *Hoffman v. Connall*, the seller and the broker were sued for misrepresenting the location of the property's boundaries. The Connalls were found liable, but the broker was not. The court found that the broker had made an innocent misrepresentation.

Seller's Liability. Although a specific case's outcome might vary depending on its facts, in Washington owners are typically found liable for misrepresenting the boundaries of their property. This is true even if the misrepresentation was innocent. Owners are presumed to know the character and attributes of the property they are conveying. If they are mistaken about the boundaries, they can be held liable for that mistake.

Broker's Liability. In Washington, brokers are not usually held liable for making innocent misrepresentations, unless they knew something that indicated the seller's statements were false.

Broker's Duty. It is the broker's duty to avoid making any false representations to a buyer. A broker cannot simply take the word of the seller, but instead must be alert to potential misrepresentations, and should employ reasonable efforts to confirm or refute statements made by the seller.

In *Hoffman v. Connall*, the court decided that there was no evidence to indicate that anything was wrong with the boundaries pointed out by the Connalls, and the broker had no reason to investigate further. Therefore, the broker was not held liable. However, if the broker had reason to suspect that the boundaries were not accurate, and still did not investigate, he would have been held liable.

Although there was nothing to make the broker believe the boundaries might have been wrong, it would have been a good idea to check the original survey mentioned by the Connalls. If the Connalls, the Hoffmans, or the broker had checked the land description and confirmed the boundaries before the sale, the misrepresentation and resulting lawsuit could have been avoided.

Methods of Description

As you can see, it is extremely important to know a property's true boundaries. Documents such as deeds, mortgages, and purchase agreements must contain complete and accurate descriptions. Ambiguous or uncertain descriptions are not legally adequate and will cause the instrument to be invalid.

There are many methods for describing property, but the three most commonly used systems of land description are:

- metes and bounds,
- government survey, and
- lot and block.

Metes and Bounds Descriptions

The metes (measurements) and bounds (boundaries) system is the oldest of the three methods of describing land. It was used by the original colonists as they settled in this country. This method is still frequently used in rural areas and is especially common in many eastern states.

The **metes and bounds** method of description identifies a parcel of land by describing its outline or boundaries. The boundaries are fixed by reference to three things:

1. **monuments**, which may be natural objects such as rivers or trees, or man-made objects such as roads or survey markers;
2. **courses** or directions, in the form of compass readings; and
3. **distances**, measured in any convenient unit of length.

A **metes and bounds** description gives a starting point and then proceeds around the boundary by describing a series of **courses** (compass readings) and distances. The description continues until the boundary has been described all the way around to the point of beginning.

Point of Beginning. A metes and bounds description always starts at some convenient and well-defined point that can be easily identified (such as the old oak tree in Figure 2.1).

Fig. 2.1 A metes and bounds description

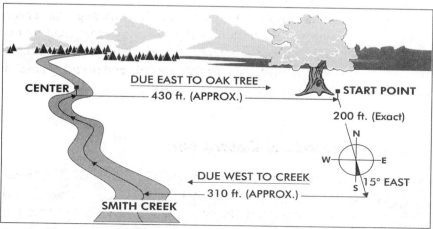

A tract of land located in Spokane County, described as follows: "Beginning at the oak tree, thence south 15° east, 200 feet, thence north 90° west, 310 feet more or less to the centerline of Smith Creek, thence northwesterly along the centerline of Smith Creek to a point directly west of the oak tree, thence north 90° east, 430 feet more or less to the point of beginning."

The starting point is referred to as the **point of beginning** or **POB**. The point of beginning is always described by reference to a monument.

    Examples: "The SW corner of the intersection of 1st Street and 2nd Avenue," or "200 feet north of the old oak tree."

Note that the point of beginning does not have to be a monument itself, it must simply refer to a monument. In the second example above, the old oak tree is a monument, and the POB is 200 feet north of the tree.

Although older metes and bounds descriptions often refer to natural monuments such as "the old oak tree," present-day descriptions generally refer to government survey lines as monuments. This helps avoid problems that may occur if the original monument is moved or destroyed.

Compass Bearings. In a metes and bounds description, a direction is described by reference to a compass point. The compass directions are described in terms of the degree of deviation from north or south. Thus, northwest or 315° is written as north 45° west, since it is a deviation of 45° to the west of north. Similarly, south southeast or 157½° is written as south 22½° east, since it is a deviation of 22½° to the east of south. East and west are both written relative to north: north 90° east and north 90° west, respectively.

Fig. 2.2 Compass bearings

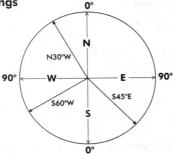

Compass bearings are given by reference to north or south.

Conflicting Elements. In a metes and bounds description, discrepancies sometimes occur between the various elements of the description. This is usually because the original surveyor made a mistake. For instance, if the description calls for a course of "320 feet in a northerly direction to the corner of the Smith farmhouse" and the Smith farmhouse is really in a northwesterly direction, there is a discrepancy that must be resolved. To help surveyors resolve problems like these, an order of priority for the various elements has been set up:

1. natural monuments (e.g., "Sander's Creek"),
2. then man-made monuments (e.g., "Avondale Road"),
3. then courses (e.g., "south 8° east"),
4. then distances (e.g., "310 feet"),
5. then names (e.g., "the Holden Ranch"), and
6. then the area or quantity of acreage (e.g., "80 acres").

> **Example:** A land description reads "east 380 feet to the midpoint of Sander's Creek." It is actually 390 feet to the midpoint of Sander's Creek. The reference to Sander's Creek takes precedence over the distance. The property will extend clear to the middle of the creek, not just 380 feet.

Government Survey Descriptions

A second method of land description is the **government survey** method. This method emerged after the American Revolution, when the federal government owned huge amounts of undeveloped land. Land speculators and settlers were moving into the territories, and Congress was anxious to sell some of the land in order to increase revenues and diminish the national debt. Since using the metes and bounds method of description for all of this property was not feasible, a new system called the government survey method was developed. This method of description is used mainly in states west of the Mississippi.

This system of land description is also called the rectangular survey method because it divides the land into a series of rectangles or grids. Each grid is composed of two sets of lines, one set running north/south and the other east/west.

Meridians and Base Lines. The original north/south line in each grid is called the principal meridian. Each principal meridian is given its own name, such as the Willamette Meridian, which runs through the western part of Oregon and Washington. The original east/west line in each grid is called a **base line.** There are 35 principal meridians and 32 base lines across the country. (See Figure 2.4.)

Additional east/west lines, called **correction lines**, run parallel to the base lines at intervals of 24 miles. Additional north/south lines—called **guide meridians**—are also established at 24-mile intervals. Because of the curvature of the earth, all true north/south lines converge as they approach the North Pole. Therefore, each guide meridian only runs as far as the next correction line. Then a new interval of 24 miles is measured and a new guide meridian is run. This is done to correct for the curvature of the earth, so that the lines remain approximately the same distance apart and do not converge. (See Figure 2.5.)

The large squares created by the intersection of guide meridians and correction lines are further divided into smaller tracts of land by additional north/south lines running at six-mile intervals, called **range lines**. These range lines divide the land into columns called **ranges**. Additional east/west lines run at six-mile intervals from the correction lines and are called **township lines**. The east/west lines divide the land into rows or tiers called **township tiers**.

Townships and Sections. The square of land located at the intersection of a range and a township tier is called a **township**. It is identified by its position relative to the principal meridian and base line. (See Figure 2.6.)

> **Example:** The township located in the fourth tier north of the base line and the third range east of the principal meridian is called "township 4 north, range 3 east" or "T4N, R3E."

Each township measures 36 square miles. A township is divided into 36 sections which are one square mile each. The sections are always numbered 1 through 36 in a specified

Fig. 2.3 Government survey lines

North/South lines	East/West lines
principal meridian	base line
guide meridians	correction lines
range lines	township lines
ranges	township tiers

sequence. (See Figure 2.7.) Parcels of land smaller than sections can be identified by reference to sections and partial sections. (See Figure 2.8.)

> **Example:** "The northwest quarter of the southwest quarter of section 12, township 4 north, range 3 east," or "the NW ¼ of the SW ¼ of section 12, T4N, R3E."

Grid systems are identical across the country, so it is necessary to include in the description the name of the principal meridian that is being used as a reference. (Since each principal meridian has its own base line, it is not necessary to specify the base line.) The county and state where the land is situated should also be included, to avoid any possible confusion. Thus, a complete description of a township would be T4N, R3E of the Willamette Meridian, Yakima County, State of Washington.

Government Lots. Because of the curvature of the earth, the convergence of range lines, and human surveying errors, it is impossible to keep all sections exactly one mile square. Government regulations provide for any deficiency or surplus to be placed in the north and west sections of a township. These irregular sections are called **government lots** and are referred to by a lot number. Government lots can also result when a body of water or other obstacle prevents an accurate square-mile section from being surveyed. (See Figure 2.9.)

Lot and Block Descriptions (Recorded Plat)

In terms of surface area, more land in the United States is described by the government survey method than by any other land description system. However, in terms of number of properties, the lot and block or recorded plat system is the most important land description method. It is the method used most frequently in metropolitan areas.

Under this system, land is described by reference to lots and blocks (groups of lots surrounded by streets) that are mapped out by a surveyor on a subdivision **plat** (map) that is subsequently recorded in the county where the land is located. After the map is recorded, any reference to one of the numbered lots on the specified plat will be a sufficient legal description of the lot. (See Figure 2.10.)

> **Example:** A lot and block description might read as follows: Lot 2, Block 4 of Tract number 45, in the city of Everett, county of Snohomish, state of Washington, as per map recorded in Book 22, page 36, of maps, in the office of the recorder of said county.

Since a detailed description of the lot is already on file in the recorder's office, that description may be incorporated into any legal document simply by reference. However, that is not usually done in Washington. Typically, a complete legal description is included in each document.

Plat maps frequently contain a wealth of information above and beyond the detailed description of property boundaries. Other information that may be listed includes:

- measurements of area,
- locations of various easements,

Fig. 2.4 The principal meridians and base lines in the United States

Fig. 2.5 The basic composition of the government survey system

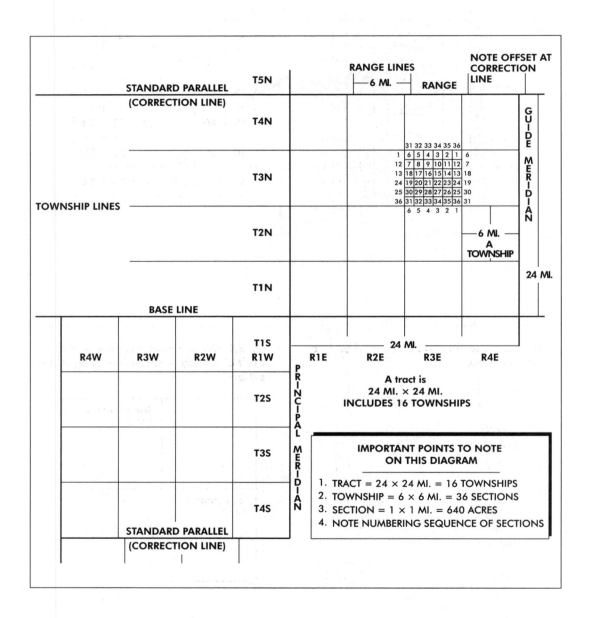

Fig. 2.6 Township 4 North, Range 3 East

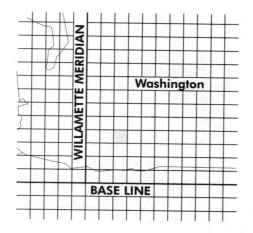

Fig. 2.7 A township contains 36 sections, numbered in this sequence

6	5	4	3	2	1
7	8	9	10	11	12
18	17	16	15	14	13
19	20	21	22	23	24
30	29	28	27	26	25
31	32	33	34	35	36

Fig. 2.8 A section can be divided up into smaller parcels

NW ¼ 160 ACRES	NE ¼ 160 ACRES
SW ¼ 160 ACRES	NE ¼ of SE ¼ 40 ACRES

10 ACRES — SE ¼ of SE ¼ of SE ¼

Fig. 2.9 Government lots may be the result of a body of water intruding into a section

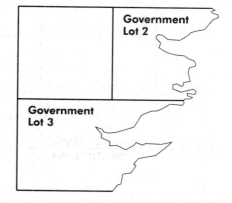

Government Lot 2

Government Lot 3

- right-of-way dimensions,
- location of survey markers,
- proposed streets, blocks, and lots of the subdivision,
- records of conditions and restrictions applying to the land,
- topographical details such as elevation, and
- school sites and recreational areas.

However, examination of a plat map is not a substitute for a thorough title search and should not be treated as such.

Air Lots

Not all real property can be described simply by reference to a position on the face of the earth. Some forms of real property, such as condominiums, also require description in terms of elevation above the ground. When describing the location of a condominium or other air-space, you can't simply measure the height from the ground, because the ground is not a stable and exact legal marker.

The United States Geodetic Survey and most large cities have established datums and bench marks as legal reference points for measuring elevation. A **datum** is an artificial horizontal plane, such as sea level. A **bench mark** is a point whose elevation has been officially measured relative to a datum. For example, a bench mark may be a metal or concrete marker, often placed in a sidewalk or other stable position.

> **Example:** A metal disk located in the sidewalk at the corner of Oak and Elm streets has the following words engraved on it: "Bench Mark No. 96, seventeen feet above River City Datum."

Surveyors use the datum or a bench mark as a reference point in describing air lots.

> **Example:** A surveyor plotting a condominium unit on the 16th floor of a new building being built on Elm Street calculates that the floor of the unit will be 230 feet above the sidewalk. He therefore shows in his survey that the floor of the unit is located 247 feet

---

Fig. 2.10 A plat map

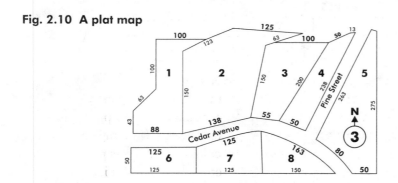

above the River City Datum as established by Bench Mark 96, because Bench Mark 96 is 17 feet above the datum.

Description Problems

A discussion of land description would not be complete without reviewing some of the problems that arise with land descriptions and their possible solutions. Some typical problems that might occur are:

- incorrect descriptions,
- indefinite or ambiguous descriptions,
- omission of part of the description,
- adjoining owners disagreeing over boundary lines, and
- modern surveys that don't match the original survey lines.

These problems can often be cured by:

- correcting the description,
- possession,
- agreement or acquiescence,
- the common grantor theory, or
- litigation and a court decision.

Correcting the Description. When an error occurs in a land description, the problem can often be solved simply by having the party who transferred the property give a new deed with the correct description. When this is not possible, a court order can be obtained to correct the description. This is called a **reformation**.

Possession. Sometimes a description problem or boundary dispute can be resolved by possession.

> **Example:** John Thompson owns property in Lincoln County and Spokane County, and both pieces of property are referred to as the "Thompson Ranch." Thompson conveys property to Maria Alberti. The deed identifies the property as the "Thompson Ranch," but does not specify which county the land is located in.
> Such a description is legally insufficient. However, if Alberti occupies the ranch in Lincoln County, the deed could be held valid, since her possession of the Lincoln County ranch makes it obvious which ranch was referred to in the deed.

A boundary dispute may also be resolved by adverse possession. Under the doctrine of **adverse possession**, the claimants must show that they treated the property as if they owned it, in a way that could not escape the true owner's notice. Their possession of the property must be exclusive, actual, open, notorious, hostile, and uninterrupted for a period of ten years. If the adverse possessor is acting under color of title or has paid all taxes on the property, the time limit is only seven years. (Adverse possession is discussed in more detail in Chapter 8.)

Acquiescence or Agreement. Another method of solving a boundary dispute is called **recognition and acquiescence**. A claimant must show that the boundary is well-defined and has been acquiesced to for ten years. This method is similar to adverse possession, except that possession is with the acquiescence of the true owner instead of being hostile.

Boundary Line Agreement. Parties may also simply agree on a boundary. For example, neighbors may agree to build a fence and have the fence serve as the boundary line. A boundary line agreement will become binding on the parties and all subsequent owners if it is put in writing and signed and acknowledged in the same manner as a deed. The boundary line agreement must use legal descriptions and include a survey map that has been filed in the county where the land is located.

Common Grantor. If a common grantor has clearly designated a boundary, that boundary will be binding on all subsequent owners of the property, even if it was not the true or original boundary.

Case Example:

In 1957, the Corletts purchased a piece of property. In 1958, they bought the neighboring piece of property and built a fence on what they thought was the boundary line between the two properties. In 1970, the Corletts sold the west parcel to the Youngs, and in 1977, the Youngs sold it to the Rosses. Then, in 1978, the Corletts sold the east parcel to the Winanses.

The Winanses had a survey done that showed the fence was not the true property line. The Winanses brought a quiet title action to establish the fence as the property line. The Rosses wanted the original boundary line to be upheld.

The court found that the new boundary (the fence) was established by a common grantor. (Remember the Corletts originally owned both pieces of property and they put up the fence.) When the Corletts sold the west lot to the Youngs, it was with the understanding that the fence was the boundary. Thus, the court found that the Corletts and the Youngs had agreed on a new boundary. Visual inspection of the property showed

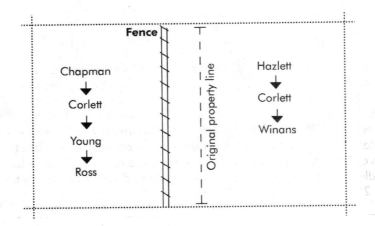

a fence that was clearly meant to be the dividing line. Therefore, the new boundary designated by the common grantor became the true boundary for all subsequent purchasers. *Winans v. Ross*, 35 Wn. App. 238, 666 P.2d 908 (1983).

Court Decision. Problems often arise in connection with the government survey method of land description. When much of the West was originally surveyed, the surveyors worked under harsh conditions, with inadequate tools and equipment by today's standards. Errors were frequently made. When these errors are discovered, the court normally attempts to maintain the line as intended by the original surveyors.

Case Example:

Two parcels of land were designated government lot numbers 5 and 6. They were established as government lots because of the presence of Crescent Lake. The Wicks owned lot 5, and the Ericksons owned lot 6. The original official government plat was produced in 1857 and showed that the lake crossed the north/south line between the lots, as shown in diagram number 1.

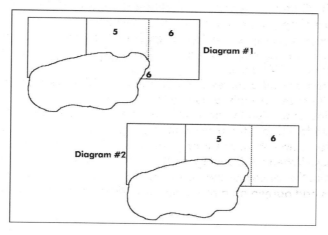

A more modern survey showed that the lake was actually 51 feet from the north/south line, as shown in diagram number 2. In a lawsuit concerning ownership of the chunk of property below the rim of the lake, the Wicks attempted to establish that their lot failed to close at the lake and actually continued on past the rim of the lake. They argued that the piece below the rim was actually part of their property.

The court stated the intent of a new survey should be to ascertain where the original surveyors placed the boundaries, not where modern surveyors would place them. Therefore, the Wicks' lot should close at a point as near as possible to the one shown on the original government survey. The Wicks did not own property beyond that point, regardless of how a modern survey team would divide the property today. *Erickson v. Wick*, 22 Wn. App. 433, 591 P.2d 804 (1979).

Attachments

You are involved in a real estate transaction. Because you checked on the land description, you now have a clear idea exactly how much property is being conveyed. But the land description does not mention the house and garage built on the property, nor the lovely rose garden and collection of gardening tools. Are these included in the sale?

Anytime there is a sale or transfer of land, it is important to be able to distinguish between real property (what is included in the sale) and personal property (what can be removed by the seller). Buyers and sellers, landlords and tenants, owners and creditors often disagree about whether an item is personal property or part of the realty. These disagreements can lead to lawsuits.

> **Example:** A buyer sues a seller because the seller took the built-in washer and dryer with him and the buyer assumed they were included in the purchase price.

When there is a conflict like this, the real estate agent may end up paying for the disputed item out of his or her own pocket to keep the peace. Thus, it is important for all of the parties (seller, buyer, and agent) to know what things are included in the sale of the real property.

Most people automatically think of the land itself when they hear the term "real property." But real property is more than just rocks and dirt. Things attached to the land, like buildings and fences, and things growing on the land, like trees and shrubs, are called **attachments**, and they are considered part of the real property.

There are two main categories of attachments:

- natural attachments (such as trees and crops), and
- man-made attachments (fixtures).

Natural Attachments

Natural attachments are things growing on the property. There are two types of natural attachments:

- naturally occurring trees and plants; and
- plants grown and cultivated by people.

Naturally Occurring vs. Cultivated. Both types of natural attachments are generally considered part of the real property. However, the crops produced by cultivated plants are treated as personal property.

> **Example:** The cultivated trees in an apple orchard would be considered part of the real estate, but the apples produced would be personal property.

Naturally occurring trees and plants, once severed from the land, may also be considered personal property.

Example: Standing timber growing on the land is considered part of the real property. However, once cut (severed from the land), it becomes personal property.

Personal property is governed by a different set of rules than real property. Washington has adopted a statute called the **Uniform Commercial Code (UCC)** to deal with the sale of goods. The UCC defines crops as goods and governs their sale. The UCC has eliminated some of the old legal distinctions between the two types of natural attachments.

Under the UCC, crops that are specifically identified in a contract may be considered personal property even before they are actually severed from the land.

Example: Farmer Beardsley sells the timber on his east 40 acres to a lumber company. The contract provides that the trees are to be cut. The lumber company owns the trees from the date of the contract and they are considered personal property, even while they are still attached to the land.

Doctrine of Emblements. A special rule called the **doctrine of emblements** applies to crops planted by tenant farmers. If the tenancy is for an indefinite period of time, and the tenancy is terminated (through no fault of the tenant) before the crop is ready for harvest, the tenant has the right to re-enter the land and harvest the crop.

Example: For several years, a farmer has been renting a large field from his neighbor. They have a year-to-year lease; it is automatically renewed each June until one of the parties gives the other notice of termination.

In April, the neighbor tells the farmer the lease will end in June because she's planning to sell her land. The farmer has the right to enter the property in the autumn to harvest the crops he planted, even though the lease has ended.

To fall within this rule, the crop must be produced annually, by the labor and industry of the farmer. For example, if the crop is wild mushrooms, which were not planted or cultivated by the farmer, the rule does not apply. If the crops are an annual product of perennial plants, such as apples or strawberries, the right to re-enter and harvest applies only to the first crop that matures after the tenancy has ended.

Fixtures

Fixtures are man-made attachments. They are items that were once personal property, but are now attached to the real estate in such a way that they are considered part of the real property. For instance, a pile of lumber and a batch of nails are considered personal property. But are they still personal property if they are used to build a barn?

Whether a particular item is a fixture or personal property is a question that real estate agents deal with constantly. Earlier, we referred to a dispute over a built-in washer and dryer. Are these items fixtures? What about a tool shed? A freestanding swimming pool? A swing set?

To avoid controversy over this issue, the real estate agent should discuss these kinds of items with the parties, making sure that each person knows what is and is not included in the sale. Of course, to be able to do this, the agent must know what is normally considered a fixture and what is considered personal property.

The courts have come up with a series of tests to determine when an item is a fixture.

Method of Attachment. When an item is permanently attached to the land, it becomes part of the real estate. An attachment is considered to be permanently attached when it is:

- permanently resting on the land (like houses and barns and other buildings),
- affixed to the land by roots (as with trees and shrubs),
- embedded in the earth (like sewer lines or septic tanks), or
- attached by any enduring method (such as by cement, plaster, nails, bolts, or screws).

Genuine physical attachment (called **actual annexation**) is not absolutely necessary for an item to be considered a fixture. Mere attachment by the force of gravity may be sufficient.

> **Example:** An outbuilding on the Parkers' property is simply resting on the ground, without any foundation. Even so, it is considered to be a fixture, part of the real property.

An item may also be considered a fixture if it is enclosed within a room or building in such a manner that it cannot be removed without dismantling it or tearing down part of the building.

Constructive annexation. Some completely movable items are regarded as so strongly connected with the property that they are considered fixtures, even though they are not actually attached to the realty. This is called the **doctrine of constructive annexation**.

> **Example:** A firm that manufactures widgets sells its main processing plant. The widget-making machine weighs four tons and is bolted to the floor. It is clearly a fixture. The key to turn on the widget-maker and the specialized tools used to repair the machine, though easily moved, are also considered fixtures.

The doctrine of constructive annexation also applies to items that have been temporarily removed for servicing or repair, such as built-in appliances.

> **Example:** Mr. Adams sells his house to Mr. Brown. At the time of the sale, the built-in dishwasher is at a repair shop. The dishwasher is still considered part of the sale, and its ownership transfers to Mr. Brown at the time of the sale.

Intention of the Annexor. The method of attachment test can be rigid and may lead to inconsistent results. Therefore, the courts have decided that the intention of the annexor is the more important test. (The **annexor** is the person who placed the item on the property.) This test asks this question: "Did the annexor intend the item to become part of the realty or to remain personal property?" If the annexor intended the item to become part of the realty, then the item will generally be considered real property. Conversely, if the annexor

Fig. 2.11 Fixture tests

```
                    FIXTURE TESTS
              • Method of attachment
              • Intention of the annexor
              • Adaptation to the realty
              • Relationship of the parties
              • Evidence of written agreement
```

didn't intend the item to become part of the real property, the item will be considered personal property.

There must be objective evidence of the owner's intent; the secret intent of the owner does not control. Each of the other tests (including the method of attachment) is viewed as objective evidence of the owner's intent.

> **Example:** A property owner installed a birdbath by embedding it in concrete. This permanent method of attachment is evidence that she intended the birdbath to become part of the realty. She cannot claim that she secretly intended to take it with her when she moved, and that it should therefore be considered personal property.

Adaptation to the Realty. When an item is essential to the use and operation of the property, or was designed specifically for use in a particular location, such as pews in a church, it is probably a fixture.

> **Example:** Computers placed in a general purpose office building are normally considered personal property. However, components of a computer system housed in a specially built computer facility have been held to be fixtures.

Relationship of the Parties. When attempting to determine intent, a court considers the relationship of the parties, such as landlord-tenant, seller-buyer, or owner-creditor.

> **Example:** If a tenant screws a lamp fixture into the wall, it is generally assumed that she intends to take the lamp with her when she moves. Items installed by a tenant are usually personal property; both the landlord and the tenant would expect the tenant to remove the item.
>
> However, if an owner installs a similar lamp fixture, it is generally assumed that he is attempting to improve the property, without thought of removing the lamp later. A lamp installed by an owner would probably be considered a fixture, and a buyer could assume that it would stay with the property.

Trade fixtures. A tenant who installs items for the purpose of carrying on a trade or business usually intends to remove the items at the end of the lease. Such items are called

trade fixtures. The general rule is that trade fixtures may be removed unless there is a contrary provision in the lease or the trade fixtures have become an integral part of the property.

Case Example:

Hahn ran an auto painting business in a building leased from the Whitneys. When Hahn left, he removed and took a furnace that the Whitneys claimed was a fixture. Hahn had installed the furnace to help dry paint and keep the employees warm. The court determined that this was a trade fixture that could be removed by the tenant. *Whitney v. Hahn,* 18 Wn.2d 198 (1946).

If the trade fixture has become an integral part of the property, but the tenant wants to remove it anyway, the tenant has the duty to restore the property to its original condition or compensate the owner for any damage caused by removing the fixture.

> **Example:** A tenant installed refrigeration units in a grocery store. Removing the units created a hole in the roof, ceiling, and wall. The tenant was required to repair the damage to the leased premises.

Allowing tenants to remove trade fixtures encourages efficiency in business. Tenants are more likely to install new equipment if they know they can take the equipment with them when they leave. Trade fixtures that are not removed when the tenant leaves automatically become the owner's property.

A rule similar to the trade fixtures rule applies to items installed by agricultural tenants for the purpose of farming the land. Certain farming equipment and items such as small tool sheds or prefabricated henhouses are called **agricultural fixtures** and may be removed by the tenant farmers when they leave the property.

Written Agreement. Regardless of any of the previously discussed considerations, if there is a written agreement between the parties stipulating how a particular item is to be treated, a court will respect and enforce the written agreement.

> **Example:** A seller planned to take certain shrubs from the property when she left. She informed the buyer of her intention and included a statement in the sales agreement specifying which shrubs she intended to remove. The written agreement allows her to remove the shrubs even though they would normally be considered part of the realty.

Case Example:

Frank Montgomery leased some property from a realty company. The 15-year lease provided that upon its expiration, Montgomery could remove all the structures he had placed on the premises. Montgomery placed a cabin on the property. Although a cabin would normally be a fixture, in this case the cabin was considered Montgomery's personal property because of the specific agreement in the lease. Although this is a New Mexico case, Washington law also recognizes that a written agreement supersedes all other considerations. *Garrison General Tire Service, Inc. v. Montgomery*, 75 N.M. 321, 404 P.2d 143 (1965).

Mobile Homes. A mobile home is classified as personal property until it is permanently attached to the realty by removing the wheels and mounting the unit on a foundation. (As personal property, mobile homes may be sold without a real estate license, and the sales are subject to sales tax laws.)

Secured Financing and Fixtures. A special problem with fixtures may arise when secured financing is involved, as occurs when a borrower and a lender agree that personal property or fixtures will secure a loan or credit line. Article 9 of the Uniform Commercial Code (UCC) governs secured transactions.

When a loan is made or credit extended, a security agreement specifies the terms of the transaction and a financing statement is filed. A **financing statement** gives constructive notice that a security interest exists in the item. Any later purchasers of the real estate are put on notice by this filing. If a default occurs, the articles can be repossessed by the holder of the security interest.

> **Example:** Dave Roberts owns an office building that is mortgaged to State Bank. He purchases a central air conditioning unit and has it installed on a concrete slab in back of the office. He buys the air conditioner on credit, and the seller files a financing statement to give notice of its interest.
>
> Dave defaults on his payments to the bank and to the air conditioning company. Normally, a central air conditioner would be considered a fixture, and upon default ownership of the air conditioner would pass to the bank along with the office building. However, since a financing statement has been filed, the air conditioning company can repossess the air conditioner.

Anyone involved in a real estate transaction should check with the county recorder's office, the office of the Secretary of State, and the U.C.C. Division of the Department of Licensing to be sure there are no financing statements giving notice of an interest in any of the fixtures on the property.

Appurtenances

Once you know the boundaries of the real property, and what items are included in the sale, you also need to become familiar with the property rights that transfer with the property ownership.

One of the best ways to understand real property and its accompanying rights is to imagine it as an **inverted pyramid** with its tip at the center of the earth and its base extending out into the sky. A property owner has rights to the surface of the land within the boundaries of the property, plus everything under or over the surface that falls within the pyramid. This includes rights to oil and minerals beneath the surface, plus certain air and water rights.

An **appurtenance** is a right, privilege, or improvement that is associated with a piece of real property. Examples of appurtenances are the rights to use air, water, and minerals in or on the land. When real property is sold or transferred, these rights are normally transferred along with the property, but they may be sold separately or limited by past transactions. When you are involved in a real estate transaction it is important to be aware of these rights and how they can be limited.

Air Rights

According to the inverted pyramid idea, a property owner's rights would theoretically extend to the upper limits of the sky. However, through the Air Commerce Act of 1926 and the Civil Aeronautics Act of 1938, Congress declared that the United States government has complete control over U.S. airspace.

Use of Airspace. Although the government has restricted air rights, property owners still have the exclusive right to use the lower reaches of airspace over their property, so long as they do nothing to impede or interfere with normal air traffic. Property owners also have the right not to be harmed or damaged by use of the airspace above their property.

> **Example:** The classic example is an airport built near a chicken farm. The noise of the airplanes flying over the chicken farm causes the chickens to stop laying eggs. If the farmer can prove that he has suffered actual harm, he may be able to recover damages.

Sale of Airspace. A property owner may sell rights to the airspace above the property separately from the surface land. As population increases and real estate prices rise, the sale of airspace has become more common, especially in large metropolitan areas.

> **Example:** The New York Central and New Haven railroads had tracks running across real estate in a prime location. They sold rights to the airspace above the tracks for an enormous sum. The purchasers acquired the airspace plus a surface easement necessary for the construction and support of buildings. The Park Avenue Development (a large development of commercial buildings) was subsequently built above the tracks.

Water Rights

Water is a vital resource all across the country. Because of its importance, water has been the source of much legislation and litigation, particularly in the arid West. Questions arise as to ownership of the water, the right to use the water, and ownership of a lake or stream bed.

Fig. 2.12 The inverted pyramid

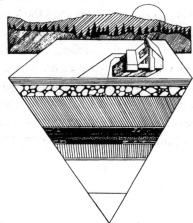

The two main types of water rights are riparian rights and appropriative rights.

Riparian Rights. Riparian rights arise on lands that are bordered or crossed by water, or contain a body of water within their boundaries. Under the riparian rights system, every landowner who has land touching the water has an equal right to use the water.

All riparian owners have the right to take water for domestic uses such as drinking, bathing, and watering a personal garden. Riparian landowners who are situated upstream may not diminish the water flow in quantity, quality, or velocity. All riparian owners may use the water for swimming, boating, or other recreational purposes. However, no landowner can divert water for use on non-riparian land (land that does not adjoin the water).

> **Example:** Davis and Carelton both owned property along Blueberry Creek. Davis, the upstream owner, decided to turn a field across the road into a rice paddy. He diverted so much water from the stream that there wasn't enough for Carelton to water his garden. A court could prohibit Davis from using the water in this way, because it was used on non-riparian land, was not a domestic use, diminished the flow of water, and interfered with Carelton's right to use the water.

The common law of England recognized riparian rights. This law was originally used in the Washington Territory (before Washington became a state), and is still used in some states. However, as water rights and water law became a more significant issue, many western states moved away from riparian rights to a system of appropriative rights.

Appropriative Rights. Under the system of appropriative rights, the right to use water in a way that diminishes the normal quantity is established by obtaining a water permit from the state government. Once a permit is obtained, water may be used on any land for the purpose specified in the permit application.

Under the **prior appropriation system**, if two parties both have appropriation permits for the same body of water, first in time is first in right. This means that the party who obtained a permit first can use the full amount of water specified in the permit, even if this leaves too little water for those who obtain permits later.

> **Example:** Consider the previous example. Now suppose that instead of relying on riparian rights, Davis obtained a permit to use the amount of water necessary to turn one of his fields into a rice paddy. The permit was granted because an experiment to determine the feasibility of growing rice was considered a beneficial use of the water. Davis will be allowed to divert the amount of water specified in his permit, even if it diminishes the normal flow of the creek.

Washington's Water Code (RCW 90.03.010) establishes prior appropriation as the dominant water law of the state, and explains the procedure for obtaining an appropriation permit. In Washington, the prior appropriation system applies to underground water as well as surface water.

Disappearance of Riparian Rights. When the Water Code was first passed in 1917, it provided that any existing riparian rights that were not put to a beneficial use would be lost. Later case law established 1932 (15 years after the enactment of the water law) as the date by which unused riparian rights must be put to use or be forfeited. Landowners who were exercising their riparian rights and putting the water to a beneficial use retained those rights.

> **Example:** In 1915, Shoemaker and Bertoldo each purchased a piece of property that bordered on Houseman Lake. When they acquired the property, they automatically acquired riparian rights to the lake water. Shoemaker and Bertoldo each used the lake for fishing and swimming, and Bertoldo also used water from the lake to water his garden.
>
> It is now 1938. Bertoldo can still use water from the lake to water his garden, but if Shoemaker wants to start a garden and use lake water, he will have to apply for a permit. Shoemaker has lost his riparian rights because he was not using them. Now he cannot use any of the lake water in a way that would diminish the quantity unless he obtains a permit. (Note that he can still use the water for recreation.)

In 1967, a new provision in the Water Act required that all claims to water rights not already certified by the state must be recorded by July of 1974. This meant that any riparian rights (any water rights that were not granted under the permit system) had to be recorded. Property owners did not have to get permits; they simply had to claim and record their rights. Any water rights not claimed were deemed relinquished.

> **Example:** Consider the example of Bertoldo above. If he (or his heirs) wanted to continue using water from the lake, he had to record his claim by 1974. If he failed to record, he would lose his right to use the lake water. If he failed to record his claim but he still wanted to use the water after 1974, he would have to apply for a permit.

The effect of this new provision was that after 1974, unless a water right has been recorded or a permit has been granted, the only rights a property owner has to water bordering his property are those rights that do not diminish the quantity. Those rights include boating, swimming, and other recreational or aesthetic uses. Additional water rights may only be acquired through compliance with the permit system.

Navigable Waters. The question of whether or not a body of water is **navigable** is significant because it affects ownership of lake beds, riverbeds, and beaches. The Washington Supreme Court has stated that for a particular body of water to be navigable, it must be "capable of being used practically for the carriage of commerce."

It is obvious that some large bodies of water, like Lake Washington, Lake Chelan, and the Columbia River, would be considered navigable. However, on many smaller lakes and rivers, it is a more difficult question. The answer can sometimes be found only when there is a lawsuit concerning the issue and a decision is rendered by the state supreme court.

All navigable waterways in the United States are owned and controlled by the federal or state government. When land borders on an ocean, sea, or navigable lake or river, the property owner owns only the land above the mean high water mark. Land below the high water mark and all lake or river beds of navigable waters are owned by the government.

There is a public easement for right-of-way on all navigable waters, which means that the public has the right to use the waterways for transportation. The public also has the right to make reasonable use of the surface of the water (for swimming and boating, for example) unless specifically prohibited. A landowner who owns property bordering navigable waters may also apply for a permit that would allow him or her to use a certain specified amount of water for a designated beneficial purpose.

Non-navigable Waters. If a small lake is completely within the boundaries of one landowner's property, the landowner owns the lake bed. If a non-navigable lake or stream is bordered by several different landowners, ownership of the lake or stream bed is generally divided by tracing lines from each property boundary to the center of the lake or stream. Each owner has title to the parcel of the lake bed or stream bed adjoining his or her land. (See Figure 2.13.) Each also has the riparian right to the reasonable use of the entire surface of the lake or stream for purposes such as swimming and boating.

Case Example:

A developer attempted to erect an apartment building over a portion of Bitter Lake. Even though there was no question that the developer was building only on the portion of the lake bed it owned, the court required the building to be removed because it interfered with the rights of the other landowners around Bitter Lake to make reasonable use of the surface of the lake. *Bach v. Sarich*, 74 Wn.2d 575, 445 P.2d 648 (1968).

Fig. 2.13 Small non-navigable lake

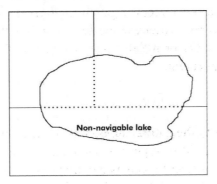

Non-navigable lake

Mineral Rights

A landowner generally owns all minerals located in or under his or her property. Minerals are considered real property until they are extracted, at which point they become personal property. A landowner may sell mineral rights separately from the actual land. This type of sale is sometimes called a **horizontal division**. The right to own and use the surface property is divided from ownership of or rights to the subsurface minerals. The four main methods of dividing mineral rights are:

1. **Mineral deed**—A mineral deed transfers all rights to the minerals, and also grants the rights necessary to conduct mining operations to obtain the minerals. This usually includes the rights of access, development, processing, and transportation.
2. **Mineral reservation**—A mineral reservation is similar to a mineral deed, except that the owner sells or transfers the surface property and retains the mineral rights for him or herself.

Case Example:

Burlington Northern Railroad sold property to the Weyerhaeuser Company but retained the mineral rights for itself. The deed specifically reserved to the railroad "all minerals of any nature whatsoever, including coal, iron, natural gas and oil, upon or in said land. . ." Weyerhaeuser purchased the land and all of its accompanying rights, except the mineral rights, which were kept by the railroad. *Weyerhaeuser Co. v. Burlington Northern, Inc.*, 15 Wn.App. 314, 549 P.2d 54 (1976).

3. **Mineral lease**—Under a mineral lease, the lessee is given the right to mine and has title to the minerals obtained, but the lessor retains a future right in

the minerals. The property owner is usually compensated by royalty payments based on a percentage of the value of the extracted minerals.

4. **Mineral rights option**—A mineral rights option grants the right to explore for the presence of minerals. After exercising this option, the mining company would then decide whether or not to lease or purchase the mineral rights as stated in the option agreement.

Support Rights

A landowner has the right to the natural support of the land provided by surrounding land. **Lateral support** is the right to support from adjacent land. This right applies not only to land, but also to improvements such as buildings, so long as the added weight of the improvements is not the cause of the problem. The slipping and sliding of the soil must occur because of the soil's own weight and not because of the superimposed weight of improvements.

> **Example:** Smith and Jones own property next to each other. Smith builds a house on his property. There is no problem with soil slippage. A few years later, Jones decides to level his property before building. He brings in bulldozers and removes several feet of soil near Smith's property line.
> The soil on Smith's property begins to slide. This destroys expensive landscaping, and several cracks develop in the foundation of Smith's house. Jones may be liable for the damage to Smith's property, since his bulldozing removed vital lateral support.

Subjacent support is the right to support from the underlying earth. This right is significant when the property is divided horizontally and rights to underlying minerals or oil and gas are transferred to someone else. The underlying owner may be liable for damage to the surface property caused by excavations in the supporting earth.

Oil and Gas Rights

Washington does not produce large quantities of oil or natural gas. However, when the issue arises, Washington follows the non-ownership theory, which holds that underground oil and gas are not subject to ownership, because of their migratory nature. Under this theory, a property owner cannot actually own the oil or gas until it is pumped to the surface, where it becomes personal property.

Oil and gas in their natural state lie trapped under great pressure beneath the surface of the earth. However, once an oil or gas reservoir has been tapped, the oil and gas begin to flow toward the point where the reservoir was pierced by the well, since this is the area of lowest pressure. By drilling a well, a property owner could theoretically drain an oil or gas reservoir that lay beneath his or her own property and beneath several neighbors' property as well.

Rule of Capture. Once oil or gas is pumped to the surface, it is governed by the rule of capture. This rule specifies that if a property owner drills on his or her own land, he or she owns all of the oil or gas produced, even though it may have migrated from under a neighbor's land.

This rule stimulates oil and gas production. If the neighbors want to protect their interests in the oil or gas that lies beneath their property, they must drill offset wells, in order to keep all of the oil or gas from migrating to one well. The outcome is that more oil or gas is produced in a shorter amount of time because more wells are drilled.

Since landowners usually do not have the necessary skill, experience, or equipment to drill for oil or gas themselves, they often enter into lease agreements with oil or gas companies who drill the wells and extract the oil or gas. There is no standard lease form, but oil and gas leases generally include an initial cash amount paid for granting the lease, a specified lease term, a method by which the lease term may be extended if necessary, and the amount of royalties to be paid to the landowner based on the amount of oil or gas actually extracted.

Conclusion

As you can see, a sale or transfer of real property includes much more than just the land. You need to know where the property boundaries lie and what attachments or fixtures are included. Knowing how property is described and what rights go along with the property will help you avoid many of the problems that commonly arise in real estate transactions.

Case Problem

The following is a hypothetical case problem. Most of the facts are taken from a real case. Based on what you have learned from this chapter, make a decision on the issues presented, and then check to see if your answer matches the decision reached by the court.

The Facts

Henry Timm rented a house from his brother from 1948 through 1972. During that time he made many improvements to the home. Upon his brother's death, the house was put up for sale and advertised as "remodeled." Timm participated in the arrangements for the sale and knew that it was being advertised as remodeled.

When the house was sold, Timm moved out, taking with him:

1. a kitchen sink and cabinet combination installed to modernize the kitchen,
2. an exhaust fan constructed in a wall to replace a window,
3. two baseboard heaters, and
4. carpeting attached to the floor by nailing strips and staples.

A dispute developed over whether or not these items were fixtures that should have remained with the house. At the trial, Timm said that he considered these items his personal property and always intended to take them with him. However, he had never previously expressed this intention.

The Question

Which of the items listed above, if any, would be considered fixtures?

The Answer

In the case of *Kane v. Timm*, 11 Wn. App. 910, 527 P.2d 480 (1974), the court found that all of the items were fixtures except for the baseboard heaters.

Consider all of the tests used to determine whether an item is a fixture. The intention of the annexor is the most significant test. Although Timm said that he always intended to take these items with him, he had not previously expressed this intent. A secret intent cannot govern; there must be objective evidence of intent.

The kitchen sink and cabinet unit were installed to modernize the kitchen. This implies an intent for the items to remain in the kitchen. Remember also that Timm knew that the house was advertised as "remodeled." If the updated items were removed, it could hardly be considered remodeled.

The exhaust fan was built into the wall to replace a window. So constructed, it was specifically adapted to this particular realty.

The carpet was attached by nailing strips and staples, fairly permanent methods of attachment. The baseboard heaters were probably resting on the floor, with no actual attachment to the property.

As to the relationship of the parties, although Timm was renting the property from his brother, he lived on the premises for 24 years—longer than many people live in homes they own. It is likely that when Timm improved the property, he intended the improvements to remain with the property.

None of the items were trade fixtures, and there was no written agreement concerning them.

Chapter Summary

- Knowing the correct boundaries of real property is important to the buyer, the seller, and the real estate agent. A seller may be held liable for innocently misrepresenting property boundaries. A broker will not usually be held liable for an innocent misrepresentation, but should use reasonable efforts to determine if a seller's statements are accurate.

- The three main methods of land description are metes and bounds, government survey, and lot and block. The lot and block method is the system used most frequently in metropolitan areas.

- The two types of attachments to real property are natural attachments and man-made attachments (fixtures). The tests to determine whether an item is a fixture include: method of attachment, intention of the annexor, adaptation to the realty, relationship of the parties, and written agreement.

- An appurtenance is a right, privilege, or improvement associated with real property, such as air, water, oil and gas, and mineral rights. These rights are normally transferred along with the property, but they may be severed and sold separately.

- The use of water is regulated by one of two systems: the riparian rights system or the appropriative rights system. Prior appropriation is the dominant water law in the state of Washington. To acquire an appropriative right, you must obtain a permit from the government.

Checklist of Problem Areas

Real Estate Licensee's Checklist

❑ Any sale of property raises questions as to which items are fixtures. A real estate agent should be aware of which items the seller plans to remove and which will remain with the real property. The following are some items that often cause disputes:

- carpeting (in general, unattached rugs are personal property, but wall-to-wall carpeting specially cut to fit the room and tacked to the floor is a fixture),
- drapes and venetian blinds,
- mirrors and chandeliers,
- appliances such as refrigerators, stoves, microwave ovens, and air conditioners (the method of attachment is important here—a freestanding refrigerator or a microwave oven that can be removed by merely disconnecting an electric plug is generally personal property, but a built-in unit may be considered a fixture),
- special landscaping such as expensive trees or shrubs,
- play equipment such as swing sets and slides, and
- birdbaths, sundials, or statues in the garden or yard.

❑ Most listing agreements and purchase and sale agreements contain a clause that lists included items. Sometimes the listed items are different, depending on which form is used. An agent should make sure that both the listing agreement and the earnest money agreement list the same items, so that problems don't arise later.

❑ If an agent has any reason to doubt a seller's statement regarding the size of the property, or if a seller is not sure of the exact boundaries of the property, the agent should check the land description to find out where the boundaries are and exactly how much property there is. If there are questions or problems concerning the true boundaries of the property, the agent should recommend that the property be surveyed.

❑ An agent should check to see if all appurtenant rights (oil, mineral, etc.) pass with the property, or if any rights have already been transferred or sold to another party, or if the seller plans to retain any appurtenant rights. The preliminary title report will indicate whether any rights have been transferred to another party, if the seller isn't sure.

Seller's Checklist

❑ A seller should be very sure of the boundaries of the property before describing these boundaries to an agent or buyer. Remember, a seller can be held liable for making an innocent misrepresentation. If the seller is unsure, the land description should be checked or a new survey performed.

❑ If a seller wants to remove items that might be considered fixtures, a written list of excluded items should be incorporated into the purchase and sale agreement. It may be advisable to simply remove certain items before showing the property. This way there can be no questions later about whether or not the item was meant to be included.

❑ If a seller wants to retain any rights (such as mineral rights), there must be a clear provision in the earnest money agreement and in the deed that severs these rights from the surface property.

Buyer's Checklist

❑ A buyer should ask where the boundaries of the property lie. If the agent or seller is uncertain, the buyer should request a copy of the land description or request a new survey.

❑ A buyer should ask specific questions concerning whether or not certain items are fixtures that will transfer with the property.

❑ A buyer should ask whether a financing statement has been filed on any of the fixtures.

❑ Before purchasing property, a buyer should check to see if the air, mineral, oil, and gas rights are still appurtenant to the property, or if they have been separated from the land and already sold to another.

Chapter Quiz

1. A portion of a metes and bounds description states "thence south 275 feet to the edge of the old gravel pit." A recent survey shows that it is actually 280 feet to the old gravel pit. The property:

   a. will end at 275 feet because distances take precedence over monuments
   b. will end at the edge of the gravel pit because monuments take precedence over distances
   c. will have to be resurveyed and a new description provided
   d. None of the above

2. Under the government survey method of land description, a township is divided up into how many sections?

   a. 12
   b. 20
   c. 36
   d. 42

3. New guide meridians are established at each correction line:

   a. because of the curvature of the earth, so that the lines don't converge
   b. because of the curvature of the earth, so that the lines don't convect
   c. because when the surveying was first begun, 24 miles was the largest interval they could survey
   d. Both a) and c)

4. A government lot:

   a. is a lot owned by the government
   b. is a parcel of land of irregular shape or size
   c. must be described using the lot and block system
   d. None of the above

5. The method of land description used most often in large metropolitan areas is:

   a. rectangular survey
   b. lot and block
   c. metes and bounds
   d. government survey

6. If the tenancy is terminated before a crop is ready to harvest, a tenant farmer has the right to re-enter the land and harvest the crop. This rule is known as the doctrine of:

   a. fructus industriales
   b. constructive annexation
   c. emblements
   d. appurtenance

7. Kirk Horten is in the process of selling his house to Susan Bianucci. At the time of closing, the dishwasher is at the repair shop. Under the doctrine of constructive annexation, the dishwasher:

   a. will not be considered part of the sale
   b. is a fixture that will be considered part of the sale
   c. will have to be conveyed under a separate contract since it was not actually present at the time of the sale
   d. None of the above

8. In determining whether or not an item is a fixture, the most important test is the:

   a. relationship of the parties
   b. adaptation to the realty
   c. intention of the annexor
   d. character of the item

9. Trade fixtures:

   a. are considered real property and cannot be removed by the tenant
   b. must be specified in the lease to be removable
   c. are generally removable
   d. None of the above

10. A candy maker has a two-year lease. The lease specifies that any improvements the tenant makes to the property will remain with the property and pass to the owner upon termination of the lease. The candy maker installs a marble counter to roll the candy on. When the lease is up:

    a. the candy maker may remove the marble counter because it is a trade fixture
    b. the candy maker may remove the counter because it is not a fixture
    c. the candy maker may not remove the counter because of the written agreement
    d. the candy maker may not remove the counter because he did not ask the owner if he could install it

11. Western Pacific Railroad has tracks that run through downtown Metropolis. Western Pacific owns the strip of land that the tracks are located on. Megacorp wants to purchase the airspace above the tracks to build a shopping complex. Which of the following is true?

    a. Megacorp must purchase the air rights from the federal government, since it has control over airspace
    b. Megacorp can purchase the air rights from Western Pacific Railroad
    c. Megacorp cannot purchase the air rights; unlike other appurtenant rights, they can't be sold separately from the land
    d. None of the above

12. Abe Carelton owns two sections of property. One borders along Red Rock Creek, and the other section is across the road and does not adjoin the creek. Abe uses water from the creek to irrigate his crops on both sections of property. This use of the water:

    a. is illegal
    b. is legal since he has a riparian right to the use of the water
    c. is legal if he has obtained a permit giving him an appropriative right to the water
    d. None of the above

13. Allison Simmons owns property along a navigable river.

    a. Allison owns the section of the river bed adjoining her property and running to the middle of the river
    b. The government owns and controls the riverbed
    c. Allison is not entitled to any use of the water since it is owned by the government
    d. Both b) and c)

14. Greg Majeski has horizontally divided his property and sold all the mineral rights to a mining corporation along with the necessary rights to obtain the minerals. This type of a mineral sale is called a:

    a. mineral deed
    b. mineral reservation
    c. mineral lease
    d. mineral option

15. In dealing with oil and gas rights, the rule of capture provides that:

    a. a property owner can only own the oil and gas captured from beneath his or her own land. Oil or gas that migrates from beneath a neighbor's land is owned by the neighbor

    b. a property owner who drills on his or her own land owns all of the oil or gas produced even though some of the oil or gas may have migrated from under a neighbor's land

    c. oil and gas remain real property even after being captured

    d. None of the above

3 Interests in Real Property

Outline

I. Estates
  A. Freehold estates
    1. fee simple estates
      a. fee simple absolute
      b. fee simple defeasible
        i. fee simple determinable
        ii. fee simple subject to condition subsequent
    2. life estates
      a. future possessory interests
      b. trusts
  B. Leasehold estates
    1. estate for years
    2. periodic tenancy
    3. tenancy at will
    4. tenancy at sufferance
    5. wrongful possession
II. Encumbrances
III. Easements (Nonfinancial Encumbrances)
  A. Appurtenant easements
  B. Easements in gross
  C. Creation of easements
    1. express easement
      a. grant
      b. reservation
      c. plat map
    2. implied easement
      a. prior use
      b. by necessity
    3. estoppel
    4. prescription
  D. Maintenance and repair of easements
  E. Termination of easements
    1. express termination
    2. implied termination
    3. estoppel
    4. prescription
  F. Easements vs. licenses
  G. Encroachments
  H. Private restrictions

IV. Liens (Financial Encumbrances)
  A. mortgages and deeds of trust
  B. construction liens
  C. judgment liens
  D. tax liens
  E. lien priority
  F. protecting the debtor

Key Terms

- freehold estate
- fee simple estate
- fee simple absolute
- fee simple defeasible
- life estate
- life tenant
- pur autre vie
- estate in remainder
- remainderman
- estate in reversion
- waste
- leasehold
- estate for years

- periodic tenancy
- tenancy at will
- tenancy at sufferance
- wrongful possession
- encumbrances
- easement
- appurtenant
- in gross
- runs with the land
- dominant tenement
- servient tenement
- estoppel
- prescription

- hostile
- merger
- license
- encroachment
- specific lien
- general lien
- redemption
- construction lien
- foreclosure
- priority
- judgment lien
- special assessment
- homestead exemption

Chapter Overview

Interests in real property refer to the rights or claims people have in property. Do they actually "own" the property or are they simply leasing it? Do they have an immediate interest or a future interest? Do they have the right to possess the property, or is their interest an easement or lien?

The answers to these questions are significant to the seller, the buyer, and the real estate agent, since a person can only sell or transfer the interest that he or she owns. For example, if you are renting a house, you may assign your lease to someone else, but you can't sell the house because you don't actually own it.

Before purchasing property, a buyer must be sure the seller owns the type of interest that the buyer wants to purchase. It is also important to find out if other people have any interests in the property, such as mortgages, easements, or judgment liens.

This chapter describes the various interests in property, including how they are created and terminated and how they affect the property.

Estates

An **estate** is an interest in land that is—or may become—possessory. In other words, the person who holds the interest currently has, or may have in the future, the right to possess the property. The various types of estates can be distinguished by their duration and when they may be possessed. A present interest gives a person the right to immediate possession of the property. A future interest gives a person the right to possess the property only at some future date.

Freehold Estates

Under the English feudal system, all land was owned by the king. The king parceled out land to his followers in return for certain services. These men often created subtenancies by renting out portions of their properties. The modern American system that allows several different people to possess interests or estates in the same piece of property grew out of that feudal system. Many of the legal terms still used in discussing real estate came out of that system.

The term "freehold" originally referred to the holdings of a freeman under the English system. A freeman was allowed to sell his rights in the property, as long as the new owner agreed to give the same services to the lord or king, who held a higher interest in the property.

In modern usage, a freehold estate may still be sold, and unless specifically stated otherwise, the new owner acquires the same type of ownership held by the previous owner.

A **freehold estate** is a possessory interest in real property that is of uncertain duration, which means that the length of time of ownership is unspecified and indefinite. There are two main categories of freehold estates:

- the fee simple estate, and
- the life estate.

Fee Simple Estates

Normally, when a person is referred to as the "owner" of property, it is assumed that he or she holds a fee simple estate. A **fee simple estate** is the highest and best interest that can exist in land. A fee simple is always:

1. inheritable,
2. transferable, and
3. perpetual.

That an estate is **inheritable** means quite simply that it can be inherited—left to someone in a will, or automatically passed to heirs upon death if there is no will. A fee simple estate is also freely **transferable**, which means that it can be sold, divided, or even given away with no restrictions. Finally, a fee simple is **perpetual**, meaning that a person who holds a fee simple estate has the right to possess the property for an indefinite period of time. Since there is no specified termination date, a fee simple estate can theoretically be held forever (in perpetuity) by the titleholder or heirs.

The fee simple estate is divided into two subcategories:

1. fee simple absolute, and
2. fee simple defeasible.

Fee Simple Absolute. A **fee simple absolute** is essentially the same type of fee simple estate described above: inheritable, transferable, and perpetual. In a typical sale of property, the real estate agent and the buyer assume that the seller holds a fee simple absolute title and that this same interest will pass to the new buyer. However, it is important to recognize that not every estate is a fee simple absolute. The grantor of property can qualify the estate being transferred and specify that it is not a pure fee simple absolute. Such qualifications create what are called fee simple defeasible estates.

Fee Simple Defeasible. When transferring property, the grantor may want to include certain conditions concerning the use of the property. As long as these conditions are met or a specified future event does not occur, the **fee simple defeasible** is also for an indefinite period of time, just like the fee simple absolute. However, a defeasible estate can be defeated, or undone, upon the happening of the future event specified by the grantor.

There are two types of defeasible fees:

• fee simple determinable (sometimes called a qualified fee), and
• fee simple subject to condition subsequent (sometimes called a conditional fee).

A **fee simple determinable** estate will automatically revert back to the grantor, or the grantor's heirs, if certain qualifications are not met. This type of estate is usually created by using the words "so long as," "which," "while," "during," or "until."

> **Example:** Wilmington Elementary School was located next to property owned by Mrs. Martin. In 1988, Mrs. Martin transferred her property as a gift to the Mountain View School District. The deed specified "so long as it is used for school purposes." For many years the property was used at recess as a playground by the children at Wilmington Elementary.
>
> In 2005, due to population changes and the failure of school levies, the Mountain View School District closed down Wilmington Elementary. After that point, none of the property was used for school purposes. Mrs. Martin's property automatically reverts back to her, or to her heirs.

A **fee simple subject to condition subsequent** is an estate that may revert back to the grantor if certain conditions are not met. The conditions are usually expressed with the words "if," "provided that," or "on the condition that." When the conditions are not met, the grantor or heirs have the right, at their option, to terminate the estate and reacquire the property. This estate is similar to a fee simple determinable, except that the termination is not automatic. The grantor or heirs must take legal steps to terminate the estate; they are said to have the **power of termination**.

> **Example:** Consider the example used above. Suppose the deed said "provided that it is used for school purposes." When the property was no longer used for school purposes, it would not automatically revert to Mrs. Martin. She would have to take legal steps to terminate the estate.

The fee simple determinable estate can produce harsh outcomes, because if a condition is not met, the property automatically reverts back to the grantor. To avoid this inflexible result, courts generally try to construe the terms of a grant of a defeasible fee as conditional rather than determinable. Automatic reversion is thus avoided; action by the grantor is required to terminate the estate.

Life Estates

A **life estate** is an estate that is based on someone's lifetime. For example, Harrison dies, leaving his farm to a charity, but grants a life estate to his wife. Harrison's wife may possess and live on the property for the remainder of her life, but upon her death, the farm will automatically pass to the charity.

Life estates are often used to simplify the division of property in a will or to avoid the expense of probate. A life estate is usually measured by the life of the holder of the life estate.

> **Example:** To avoid the expense of probating his will after death, Bob deeds his property to his son Stan, but reserves a life estate for himself. Bob has the right to use and possess the property for the rest of his lifetime, but upon his death, the property automatically passes to Stan.

The above example describes an **express reservation** of a life estate to the original owner of the property. A life estate may also be created by **express grant** to someone other than the original owner.

A life estate may also be based on the life of someone other than the holder of the life estate. This is called a life estate **pur autre vie** (for another's life). This type of estate is sometimes used to create security for ailing parents or disabled children who are unable to provide for themselves.

> **Example:** Bob's mother is afflicted with Alzheimer's disease and is unable to take care of herself. His sister Charlotte has been taking care of their mother. Bob deeds his property to Charlotte so long as their mother is still alive. Upon their mother's death, the property is to pass to Bob's son Stan.
>
> Charlotte has a life estate based on their mother's life. Charlotte has the right to use and possess the property only so long as their mother is alive. When their mother dies, the property automatically passes to Stan.

Their mother is the **measuring life**. The life estate lasts only as long as her lifetime. Charlotte is the holder of the life estate. She has the right to possess the property, and is called the **life tenant**.

The life tenant has an ownership interest in the land that can be sold, leased, or mortgaged. Remember, however, that a person can only sell, lease, or mortgage the interest he or she owns. In the example above, if Charlotte, the life tenant, sells her interest in the property, the new buyers have only purchased a life estate. The buyers' interest ends with the death of the mother, the measuring life.

Future Possessory Interests. When a life estate is given, an interest also passes to the person who will receive the property when the life estate ends. This is a **future possessory interest**, since he or she does not have the right to possess the property until sometime in the future (at the death of the measuring life). There are two types of future possessory interests:

- estates in remainder, and
- estates in reversion.

Case Example:

In his will, George left his second wife, Wilma, a life estate in the family home, with the remainder interest to his six adult children from a previous marriage.

After George's death, Wilma had the right to use and possess the property for the rest of her lifetime. Upon her death, the property was to pass automatically to the children. *In re Estate of Campell*, 87 Wn. App. 506 (1997).

In the above example, George's children hold an **estate in remainder**. Although they do not have the right to possess the property right now, they have a current interest in the remainder of the estate (the estate that will begin when the life estate terminates). George's children are called the **remaindermen**.

When the property is designated to return to the original grantor at the end of the life estate, the grantor has an **estate in reversion**.

A life tenant has certain duties towards the property. A life tenant may not use or abuse the property in any way that would permanently damage the property or reduce its market value. Such abuse is called **waste**. This term implies neglect or misconduct, and does not include ordinary depreciation of property due to age and normal use.

A life tenant must allow for reasonable inspection of the property by the holder of the future possessory interest. He or she is permitted to check for possible waste. If waste is discovered, the holder of the future possessory interest may bring a legal action for damages. An action for waste may be brought at any time, against either the life tenant, or if the life tenant has died, against the life tenant's estate.

Trusts. In modern practice, life estates are seldom used because trusts provide the same benefits, with the additional safety factor of a trustee who looks out for the interests of the specified party.

When a trust is created, a trustee is given legal title to property that he or she holds for the life of the beneficiary. Upon the death of the beneficiary, the property is disposed of as provided for by the creator of the trust.

Leasehold Estates

A **leasehold estate** is a more limited interest in property than a freehold estate. The holder of a leasehold estate—the **tenant**—does not own the property but merely leases or rents the property. This gives the tenant the right to exclusive possession of the property for a time.

Although most real estate agents deal with the sale of property, some are involved in renting or leasing property. Even for an agent who deals only with sales, a knowledge of the different types of leasehold estates is important. If a sale involves rental property, the potential buyer may want to know what kind of leases the current tenants hold, and if or when their leases could be terminated.

In Washington, three different kinds of leasehold estates are recognized:

- tenancy for a specific term (also called estate for years or term tenancy),
- periodic tenancy, and
- tenancy at will.

We'll also discuss the tenancy at sufferance, which is similar to the above tenancies but isn't actually an estate.

Estate for Years

The **estate for years** lasts for a specific time period. Despite its name, this type of estate is not required to have a term of one year or a period of years. It may be for three months, six months and five days, two years, or any period with a specific beginning and ending date.

> **Example:** Ramon is a college student renting an apartment for one semester. The lease gives him the right to possess the apartment from August 20 until December 31. Ramon's tenancy is an estate for years because it is for a specific time period.

With an estate for years, neither party is required to give notice to terminate the lease agreement. The lease terminates automatically at the end of the specified rental period. If the parties want to terminate the lease before the specified end of the lease period, they may do so by mutual consent. The termination of an estate for years by mutual consent is called **surrender**.

Fig. 3.1 Types of estates

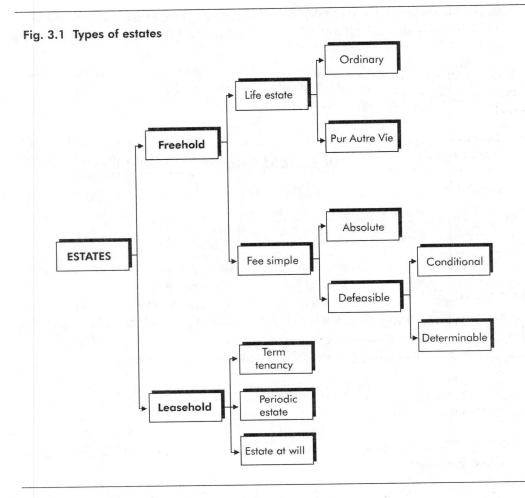

Unless specifically prohibited by the lease, an estate for years is assignable by the tenant. This means that a tenant may sublease or assign the interest in the lease to another party. The lease agreement is not terminated, but is merely taken over by someone else.

Periodic Tenancy

A **periodic tenancy** continues from period to period until terminated by proper notice from one of the parties. The length of the period is usually one month, but may be any specified time period. A periodic tenancy automatically renews itself from period to period, and thus continues for an indefinite length of time. No specific or automatic termination date exists; the tenancy ends only when one of the parties gives proper notice of termination. In Washington, a periodic tenancy may be terminated by written notice from either party (landlord or tenant) 30 days or more before the end of the rental period.

Example: Carl Schmidt is leasing office space on a month-to-month basis. His landlord gives Carl written notice of termination on March 10. Since it is less than 30 days until the end of March, Carl has the right to continue to occupy the space through March and April. The March 10 notice is more than 30 days before the end of the April rental period, so Carl has to vacate the space by the end of April.

If the tenancy is covered by the Residential Landlord-Tenant Act (RLTA), it may be terminated by written notice from either party 20 days or more before the end of the rental period.

Example: Now suppose that Carl Schmidt is renting an apartment on a month-to-month basis. His landlord gives Carl written notice of termination on March 10. Since it is more than 20 days until the end of the month, Carl will have to vacate the apartment by April 1.

Many residential apartment leases begin as estates for years, with a specified time period such as one year or six months. After the specified time period is up, the tenancies often continue as periodic tenancies, usually from month to month.

Tenancy at Will

Under a **tenancy at will**, the tenant is in possession of the property by permission or at the will of the owner. A tenancy at will has no specified termination date and no periodic time limits. Usually no rent is paid, or else rent is given in some form that has no reference to periods of time.

In Washington, a landlord may terminate a tenancy at will at any time, and must simply give the tenant a "reasonable time" in which to vacate.

Case Example:

Paul Najewitz occupied a house on some property in return for keeping the property in repair. This was considered a tenancy at will because it was for an indefinite term and no periodic rent was required.

The tenancy was terminated when demand for possession was made by the owner. The only right Najewitz had after that was a reasonable time in which to vacate. *Najewitz v. Seattle*, 21 Wash. 2d 656, 152 P.2d 722 (1944).

Note that unlike the estate for years or the periodic tenancy, a tenancy at will cannot be assigned. Also, the tenancy at will automatically expires upon the death of either the landlord or the tenant.

Tenancy at Sufferance

A **tenancy at sufferance** is created when a tenant comes into possession of a property lawfully and under a valid lease, but then holds over after the lease has expired. The tenant continues in possession of the property, but without the consent of the landlord.

Example: Joe has a one-year lease with Landlord Sam. At the end of the term, Joe refuses to move out. Joe initially obtained possession of the property legally (under a valid lease), but is remaining on the property without Sam's consent.

The tenancy at sufferance technically isn't an estate at all. The tenant (referred to as a **holdover tenant**) has no possessory interest in the property and the landlord isn't required to give the tenant a notice of termination. However, the landlord must follow proper legal procedures to evict the tenant.

Wrongful Possession

A tenant is in **wrongful possession** of the property if he or she no longer has the legal right to remain. A landlord may bring an action for unlawful detainer against tenants in wrongful possession. **Unlawful detainer** is the legal action taken to evict a tenant. Evictions will be discussed in more detail in Chapter 13. Some examples of tenants in wrongful possession are:

- tenants who hold over after the expiration of a specific lease term (tenants at sufferance);
- tenants who continue in possession after being given proper notice of termination; and
- tenants who fail to pay the rent and continue in possession after being given notice requiring payment of rent or surrender of the premises.

Encumbrances

A freehold estate is a possessory interest in real property with ownership rights; a leasehold estate is a possessory interest without ownership rights. The third type of interest in real property is a nonpossessory interest. Someone who holds a nonpossessory interest in property has a claim or right concerning the property, but does not have the right to possess the property. Nonpossessory interests are called **encumbrances** because they encumber or burden the title.

Encumbrances may be financial or nonfinancial in nature. Nonfinancial encumbrances, such as easements, affect the use or physical condition of the property. Financial encumbrances, referred to as liens, affect only the title.

Easements (Nonfinancial Encumbrances)

An **easement** is a right owned by one party to use the land of another for a particular purpose. Easements affect the value and use of property, so real estate agents and prospective buyers should find out whether a property is subject to any easements. A standard title insurance report will list the recorded easements, but usually won't list unrecorded easements. Agents and buyers should ask the seller about easements, and should also keep an eye out for any indication that the property is used by someone other than the seller (a neighbor, for instance).

An easement may be either positive or negative. A **positive easement** authorizes a party to do something on another person's land or to take something from the land. The most common example of a positive easement is the right to cross another's land, often called a right-of-way easement or access easement.

> **Example:** Johnson has an easement to cut across the corner of Eldridge's property to reach her mailbox, instead of having to go the long way around by the road. This is a positive easement because it grants Johnson the right to do something on another person's land.

Instead of granting a right, a **negative easement** prohibits a landowner from doing something on his or her own land.

> **Example:** A planned unit development contains areas that are to be maintained as "greenbelts" (in their natural condition). The property owners in the development are restricted from placing any buildings or cutting down any trees or plants in the greenbelt areas.

The greenbelt rule is a negative easement, because it prevents the owners from doing something on their own property that they would otherwise be permitted to do. "Negative easement" is really just another name for a restrictive covenant. Restrictive covenants are explained in Chapter 11. This chapter focuses on positive easements.

Positive easements are classified as either:

- appurtenant easements, or
- easements in gross.

Appurtenant Easements

An **appurtenant easement** benefits a particular piece of land. The land that receives the benefit is called the **dominant tenement**. The piece of land over which the easement runs is called the **servient tenement**. "Tenement" is a real estate term that refers to the land and all of the rights that go along with the land.

Probably the most common example of an appurtenant easement is a right-of-way easement providing access across one parcel of land to another.

> **Example:** Albright owns a landlocked piece of property with no access to the road. Albright has a right-of-way easement to travel over Schindler's neighboring property to reach the road.
>
> This is a positive easement because it grants Albright the right to do something. The Schindler property is the servient tenement because the easement runs across it. The Albright property is the dominant tenement because it is the property that benefits from the easement.

An appurtenant easement **runs with the land**, which means that if the land is transferred (sold, inherited, or given away), the easement is also transferred, even if the easement is not mentioned in the deed. An appurtenant easement cannot be sold separately from the property. Whoever owns the dominant property also owns the easement.

> **Example:** Using the example above, if Albright sold her property to Crowther, then Crowther would also acquire the right-of-way easement across the Schindler property.

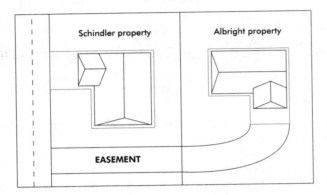

Easements in Gross

An **easement in gross** belongs to an individual or a commercial entity. There is no dominant tenement involved with an easement in gross. There is only a servient tenement across which the easement runs.

> **Example:** Andy lives down the road from Carter. Carter grants Andy a personal easement to cross Carter's property and fish in Carter's lake.

This is a personal easement in gross that will not pass with the land. If Andy sells his property, the new owner does not receive the easement. If Andy dies, the easement will be extinguished. A personal easement in gross such as the one in the example cannot be sold or assigned.

Most easements in gross are commercial rather than personal. Unlike personal easements in gross, commercial easements in gross are freely assignable and transferable.

> **Example:** The Greentown Electric Company has an easement in gross to enter property to install and service its power lines. When Mega-Electric buys Greentown Electric, it also purchases the easement.

Note, however, that a commercial easement for a specific purpose cannot normally be sold for another purpose. For example, the electric company could not sell its easement for power lines to the local sewer district to run sewer lines through the easement.

When showing property to prospective buyers, a real estate agent should be able to explain all utility easements affecting the property. An average residence may be subject to easements for the water company, the electric company, the gas company, a cable T.V. company, and the telephone company, just to name a few. All of these easements can have an impact on the value of the property.

> **Example:** If the electric company has an easement running through your backyard and installs unsightly power lines, this easement may seriously decrease the value of the property.

Creation of Easements

An easement (whether appurtenant or in gross) may be created in any of the following ways:

- express grant or reservation,
- plat maps,
- implied from prior use or necessity,
- estoppel, or
- prescription.

Express Easement. An **express easement** is generally written in a deed or other legal document that sets forth the boundaries and specifications of the easement.

The most effective way to create an easement is to describe the easement in a deed. The easement may be described in the deed passing title to the property, or there may be a separate deed describing only the easement.

A deed or other document may create an easement by express grant or express reservation.

When an easement is created by **express grant**, the property owner expressly grants a specific right to use the property (the easement) to another.

> **Example:** David sells the west half of his property to Martha. In the deed, he expressly grants Martha the right to use the private road located on his half of the property.

An **express reservation** is similar to an express grant, except that instead of giving away the easement, the landowner reserves it for himself or a third party.

> **Example:** David sells the east half of his property to Martha. In the deed, he expressly reserves to himself the right to use the private road now located on Martha's half of the property.

Plat maps. Another way of creating an express easement is by recording a **plat map**. If a landowner subdivides and sells land according to a recorded plat, the purchasers acquire easements to use the roads, alleys, and all common areas shown on the plat. These areas are considered dedicated for public use.

Case Example:

In 1956, Haven Lake Development Company recorded the Haven Lake plat map. Approximately one year later, a map entitled "Access Easement-Lots 251 thru 256" was also recorded, showing an easement access road that originated on lot 255 and crossed lot 254.

Forty years later, the current owner of lot 255 attempted to access his lot via an easement across lot 254. The owners of lot 254 sued to quiet title.

The original plat map did not reflect any easement, and the mere filing of the subsequent document was insufficient to amend the original plat. Therefore, the no grant of easement existed.

Implied Easement. An **implied easement** is presumed to exist because of certain facts that tend to show that the parties meant to create an easement. This type of easement arises only when the tract of land was originally under common ownership (owned by the same individual) and then was severed or divided into two or more parcels.

There are two situations in which an easement by implication may develop. An easement may be implied from prior use, or may be implied because of obvious necessity.

For an easement to be **implied from prior use**, the use giving rise to the easement must have been going on for a long time, and must be apparent from a visual inspection of the property at the time of sale. The use must also be reasonably necessary for the enjoyment of the dominant tenement.

Example: John owns two adjacent, heavily forested mountain properties. Parcel A is accessible only by two roads. One road is often impassable due to weather conditions; the other road is located on Parcel B.

John sells Parcel A to Tina, but objects when Tina wants to reach her property using the road located on Parcel B, which John still owns. If a court determines Tina's use of the road is reasonably necessary, she will have an easement by implication.

Fig. 3.2 Methods of creating easements

CREATION OF EASEMENTS			
Express	**Implied**	**Estoppel**	**Prescription**
1. Express grant	1. Implied from prior use		
2. Express reservation	2. Implied by necessity		
3. Plat maps			

If the easement is essential to a parcel of property, the court may find an **easement by necessity** even if there is no apparent prior use.

> **Example:** If a lot is completely landlocked with no access to roads, and no express easement has been given, an easement by necessity may be found to provide access to the road.

Estoppel. The legal doctrine of **estoppel** prevents a person from asserting rights or facts that are contrary to previous acts or conduct.

> **Example:** Bianca has a house on several acres. It is too far out in the country to be connected to the city sewer system, so the house is connected to a large septic system capable of handling several houses. Bianca divides her property and sells half to Carl. No mention is made of the septic system. Carl builds a house on his property. Bianca watches and says nothing as Carl hooks up his plumbing to the septic system on her property.
>
> An easement has been created by estoppel. Because of her failure to object, Bianca cannot now claim that Carl had no right to hook up to the septic system.

Prescription. An **easement by prescription** is created when someone makes long and continuous use of another's property without the permission of the owner. To acquire an easement by prescription, use of the easement must be **open and notorious**. This means that the use must be obvious and visible to any landowner who keeps reasonably well informed about the property.

The use must also be **hostile** or **adverse**, meaning without the permission or consent of the owner, or against the owner's interests. An owner may acquiesce to the use, but not give permission. In other words, if the owner is aware of the use and does not object—but also does not give permission—the use is hostile. But if the owner gives consent or permission, a license has been granted, and an easement by prescription cannot develop.

In Washington, the use must be **continuous and uninterrupted** for ten years. Continuous does not mean constant use, but only a continuous use that is normal for that property.

> **Example:** Mr. Rose and Mr. Green both own summer cottages on a hill above the beach. There are steps to the beach cut into the rocky hillside on Mr. Rose's property. Every summer for the last 12 years, Mr. Green has used these steps to get to the beach. This is a continuous use even though Mr. Green never uses the steps in winter.

Note also that a continuous and uninterrupted use does not necessarily mean use by only one person.

> **Example:** Michael and Patrick own adjoining property. For two years, Michael drives across a corner of Patrick's property without Patrick's permission. Then Michael sells his property to Donovan. For another four years, Donovan drives across the same corner. Then Donovan sells to Maureen. Maureen drives across Patrick's property for another five years.

Maureen may be able to claim a prescriptive easement. The time periods in which Michael, Donovan, and Maureen drove across the property can be added together to make up the required ten years. This adding of time periods is called **tacking**.

Note that there can be no prescriptive easements against government property.

Maintenance and Repair of Easements

Neither party has a duty to maintain or repair an easement unless this duty is specifically spelled out in the easement grant. However, if an easement is allowed to fall into such a state of disrepair that it is totally unusable, the easement may be lost.

> **Example:** Consider our previous example of the right-of-way easement. Albright has the right to drive across the Schindler property. Unless spelled out in a written agreement, if the Schindlers do not use this driveway, they have no duty to maintain it. They cannot block or obstruct the drive, but they are not responsible for any repairs or upkeep.
>
> The easement holder also has no duty to repair or maintain the driveway. Albright can let it fall into disrepair if she likes. Although Albright has no duty to repair, she has the right to take all steps necessary to make the easement usable. If she chooses, she can repair or maintain it as much as needed.

Where a private road or driveway is used by the landowner and an easement gives another party the right to use the same road or driveway, both parties must divide the cost of repairs in proportion to their use of the road.

Termination of Easements

There are several methods by which easements may be terminated or cease to exist. These correspond roughly to the ways easements are created.

Express Termination. Just as easements may be expressly created, they may be expressly terminated.

Written agreement. The parties may agree on an express termination date that is specified when the easement is granted, or there may be a later written agreement, called a **release**.

Automatic termination. Most easements do not expire automatically. However, if the grant of the easement specifies a time period, the easement expires or automatically terminates at the end of the time period. An easement may be granted for life. This type of easement automatically terminates upon the death of the person who was the measuring life.

Condemnation. An easement may be terminated through **condemnation**, which occurs when the state takes private property for a public use. If the state condemns either the dominant or the servient property, the easement may be lost. However, the owner of the easement (the owner of the dominant property) is entitled to compensation for the value of the easement.

Fig. 3.3 **Methods of terminating easements**

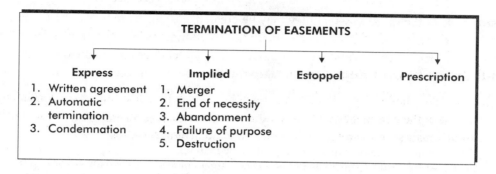

Fig. 3.3 Methods of terminating easements

Example: Adams has an easement to maintain a billboard on Barton's property. The state condemns Barton's property because they are going to build a new highway across it. The state compensates Barton for the value of his property, and must also compensate Adams for loss of the value of her easement.

Implied Termination. An easement may be terminated without any express agreement, by the actions of the parties or by circumstances beyond the control of the parties.

Merger. When the owner of the easement (the dominant property) also becomes the owner of the property subject to the easement (the servient property), the easement is extinguished by **merger**. The need for an easement no longer exists. You cannot have an easement in your own property, since an easement is defined as an interest in another's land.

Necessity ends. If an easement is created by necessity, the easement automatically terminates once the necessity disappears.

Abandonment. An easement may cease to exist if the owner **abandons** it. Although non-use alone is not enough to terminate an easement, it may be evidence of an intent to abandon. Abandonment is usually proven by a clear act or expression of the owner's intent to abandon.

> **Example:** Abernathy has an easement to cross Simpson's property to reach the lake. Abernathy has not used the easement for nine years and has planted a rose garden across the area where the path to Simpson's property used to be.

Failure of purpose. If an easement has been created for a particular purpose, it terminates when the purpose ceases or has been fulfilled.

> **Example:** B&D Railroad had an easement for railroad tracks across a corner of Farmer Brown's property. B&D discontinued using this track, removed the rails, and subsequently went bankrupt. The easement terminated because the purpose of the easement ceased.

Destruction of servient tenement. When an easement exists in a building rather than in the land, the involuntary destruction of the building will terminate the easement.

Estoppel. In the same way that they may be created, easements may also be terminated by estoppel. If the conduct of the easement holder (dominant property owner) leads the servient property owner to assume that the easement holder does not intend to use the easement, and the servient property owner takes some action in reliance on this, the easement holder may be prevented from later trying to enforce the easement.

> **Example:** Max sold half of his property to Sylvia but reserved to himself an easement to walk across the corner of Sylvia's property to get to his mailbox. After several years, Max put up a fence blocking off the path to the mailbox.
>
> Sylvia naturally assumed that Max was no longer going to use the path, so she set up her garden shed in the corner over the path. Two years later Max took down the fence and told Sylvia she would have to move the shed so that he could use the easement to get to his mailbox.
>
> By building the fence, Max led Sylvia to believe that he did not intend to use the easement. Sylvia reasonably relied on his conduct when she built the shed. Max could be estopped (prevented) from now claiming the right to use the easement.

Prescription. Actions by the owner of the servient property that interfere with the easement could extinguish the easement by prescription. There must be an open, continuous, and uninterrupted interference with the easement for ten years.

> **Example:** Consider the example just above. Now suppose Sylvia (the owner of the servient property) built the fence across the easement. The fence has been in place blocking off the easement for 14 years. Max's easement is probably terminated by prescription.

Easements vs. Licenses

Like an easement, a **license** grants permission to enter another's property for a specific purpose. But a license does not create an interest in the property.

There are several differences between easements and licenses. Easements are often for an indefinite period of time, but licenses are usually more temporary. While an easement cannot be revoked, a license may be revoked by the grantor at any time. If revoked, money damages may have to be paid, but a court could not force the grantor to reinstate the license.

Easements are usually created by written agreement or through action of law, while licenses are often created by simple verbal agreement. A license is a purely personal right that cannot be sold or transferred and becomes invalid if the licensee dies.

> **Example:** Carl is having his driveway repaved, so he makes arrangements with his neighbor Karen to park his car in her driveway for two weeks. After only one week, Carl dies. The license automatically terminates. Carl's son does not have the right to park the car in Karen's driveway for the remaining week unless he makes a new arrangement with Karen.

Note that since a license is revocable by the landowner, it is not actually considered an encumbrance or an interest in the property.

Also, because a license is created through permission of the landowner, the use is not hostile. Therefore, no claim of adverse possession can be brought by the licensee.

Encroachments

An **encroachment** is a structure or object, such as a fence or garage, that extends over the property line and intrudes onto an adjacent neighbor's land. Most encroachments are un-intentional, resulting from a mistake concerning the exact location of the property line.

A court can order an encroachment to be removed through an ejectment action. Alternatively, if the cost of removal would be too high, the court may order the encroacher to pay damages to the neighbor.

Technically, an encroachment is not an encumbrance because it is not a right or interest held by the encroacher. However, if an encroachment is ignored, it could ripen into a prescriptive easement or even title by adverse possession.

Private Restrictions

Private restrictions (also known as deed restrictions) are restrictions on the use of a property that were imposed by a previous owner. Like easements, private restrictions are encumbrances that limit a property owner's use of his or her land. Private restrictions are discussed in Chapter 11.

Liens (Financial Encumbrances)

A **lien** is a financial interest in property that gives a creditor the right to have a debt paid out of the debtor's property if the debtor fails to pay. The lienholder does not own or have a right to possess the property, but could cause the property to be sold to satisfy the lien.

Both buyers and sellers will be concerned about liens against property because liens decrease the property's value. Existing liens against a property will not prevent its transfer or sale, but the transfer does not eliminate the liens. The new owner takes the property subject to those liens. Thus, it is extremely important for a buyer to know what liens are attached to a property before purchasing it.

A real estate agent should always find out if there are any outstanding liens on the property. Liens are generally filed in the office of the county recorder in the county where the property is located.

Voluntary liens are liens the owner places against his or her own property. These liens are usually placed in order to secure repayment of a debt.

> **Example:** Mortgages and deeds of trust are voluntary liens. A property owner borrows money and provides a lien on specific property as security for the debt.

Involuntary liens (sometimes called statutory liens) arise through operation of law without the property owner's consent. Involuntary liens are created to protect those who have valid financial claims against the owner of the real property.

> **Example:** When taxes are assessed, a tax lien arises against the property. If the taxes are not paid, the property can be sold to satisfy the lien.

Liens are also classified as either general or specific. A **general lien** attaches to all of the debtor's property. A **specific lien** attaches only to a particular piece of property. A deed of trust is an example of a specific lien. It attaches only to the particular property offered as security for the loan.

Some of the most common types of liens against real estate are:

- mortgages and deeds of trust,
- construction liens,
- judgment liens, and
- tax liens.

Mortgages and Deeds of Trust

Mortgages and deeds of trust are voluntary, specific liens created by a contract between a borrower and a lender. The borrower's property is used as security for the loan. If the borrower fails to repay the loan as agreed, the lender can sell the property and use the proceeds to repay the loan.

When property transfers to a new buyer, it remains subject to any existing mortgages or deeds of trust. So whether the seller will pay off an existing mortgage or deed of trust—or whether it is assumable by the buyer—are questions that must be answered before close of the sale. Both mortgages and deeds of trust will be discussed in more detail in Chapter 10.

Construction Liens

A person who supplies materials or performs work on property may be entitled to claim a **construction lien** against the property to secure payment for the labor or materials. For example, if a general contractor is building a house on a piece of property and is not paid for his services, he can obtain a lien against the property for the amount owed. The lien allows the property to be sold to satisfy the debt. A construction lien is created by filing a notice of the claim at the office of the recorder in the county where the property is located.

In addition to or instead of filing the lien, a laborer or supplier could sue the property owner for the amount due. However, litigation is time-consuming and expensive, and even if you win, it is sometimes difficult to collect the judgment.

The right to file a construction lien can be waived. When a construction contract is drawn up, it may include a provision that states that liens may not be filed on the property. This type of provision is called a **waiver**. Such a waiver must be stated clearly and unambiguously in the contract.

Every state now has some type of construction lien law. It's important to be aware of the time limits contained in Washington's construction lien law.

Time Limits. Initially, to establish and preserve the right to a construction lien, laborers and suppliers must give the general contractor and property owner a written **pre-claim notice** of the right to claim a lien. This pre-claim notice must be served personally or by certified or registered mail. For new construction of a single-family residence, notice must be given within ten days of first supplying services or materials. For remodels, repairs, or commercial projects, notice must be given within 60 days of beginning work. Pre-claim notices are not required, however, from claimants who have contracted directly with the owner.

A **lien claim** must be filed within 90 days after last performing work or furnishing materials for the project. A lien filed more than 90 days after labor or materials were last furnished is invalid. The 90-day time period starts to run when the particular claimant stops providing labor or supplies, not when the entire project is completed.

Thirty days after work or delivery of materials ends, the property owner may choose to record a **notice of cessation**. This notice can only be recorded within ten days after the 30-day period expires. The purpose of a notice of cessation is to limit the lien claim period by establishing the date that work ended. A laborer or supplier can still assert that his or her work ended on a later date, but the lien claim must be filed within 60 days after the notice of cessation was recorded.

Foreclosure. Construction liens must be foreclosed judicially. (Foreclosure is discussed in Chapter 10). A legal action to foreclose this type of lien must be brought within eight months after the lien was recorded, in the county where the real estate is located.

> **Example:** New plumbing is being put into the Montgomery Building. Karl is the one who supplied the new pipes. The last load of pipes was delivered on May 15, 2004. When Karl still had not been paid by July 1, 2004, he filed a construction lien against the property.

Fig. 3.4 Construction lien priority

CONSTRUCTION LIEN PRIORITY

1. First, to people who performed labor;
2. Next, any contributions owed to employee benefit plans;
3. Then to people who furnished materials or equipment;
4. Then to the subcontractors; and
5. Finally, to the original or general contractor.

On April 15, 2005, Karl attempts to file a legal action to foreclose. However, Karl will not be successful because it has been over eight months since the lien was recorded.

Priority. Often, there is more than one construction lien against the same piece of property. If the property is sold to satisfy these liens, the proceeds from the sale will be applied according to the order of priority.

Termination of Construction Liens. A construction lien is terminated by the payment of the debt upon which the lien is based. In Washington, an owner may also release an existing lien by giving a bond or paying the amount owed into court to cover any potentially valid claims (the funds are controlled by the court). This system benefits the property owner since the property is not tied up by a lien. It also benefits the lienholder since the money is available to pay any valid claims, and cannot be removed by the property owner.

If a lien foreclosure action is filed, but is not prosecuted to judgment within two years, the court has discretion to dismiss the action for want of prosecution. This dismissal cancels the lien. The purpose of this rule is to prevent property from being encumbered by a lien for an unreasonable amount of time.

> **Example:** A contractor filed a construction lien and subsequently filed a legal action for foreclosure on February 4, 2003. However, the foreclosure action still had not been prosecuted by February 5, 2005. Since it has been over two years, the court can dismiss the action.

Judgment Liens

Judgment liens arise from a court's determination that one party owes money to another. The court enters a judgment, and the winner (the judgment creditor) can obtain a **judgment lien** against property owned by the loser (the judgment debtor). This type of lien is involuntary and general. It arises by operation of law and automatically attaches to all of the debtor's property in the county where the judgment was entered, except for the debtor's homestead (principal residence). The judgment will attach to homestead property only if the judgment creditor records an **abstract of judgment** with the county recorder.

If the debtor owns property in other counties, the judgment creditor may file an abstract of judgment in other counties and attach those additional properties. The judgment lien also attaches to any property acquired by the debtor during the lien period.

> **Example:** Glen owns two acres of land in Snohomish County. A lawsuit was filed against him. Glen lost the case and a judgment was entered against him. The winner obtained a lien against Glen's property for the judgment amount. Two months later, Glen's father died, leaving Glen ten acres of property, also in Snohomish County. The judgment lien also attaches to this property.

Once a judgment lien has attached, the debtor must pay the judgment to free the property from the lien. If it is not paid, the property can be sold to satisfy the judgment.

Termination of Judgment Liens. Like any lien, a judgment lien is terminated by payment of the amount owed. Judgment liens also terminate according to statutory limitations.

In Washington, a judgment lien is generally only valid for ten years after the date of entry of the judgment. However, within 90 days before a judgment lien expires, the lienholder can apply for an order extending the period for an additional ten years. The lienholder must apply to the court that issued the judgment and pay a filing fee.

Also, note that a judgment lien for child support lasts for ten years after the child's 18th birthday.

Tax Liens

Property Taxes. Real property is assessed (appraised) and then taxed according to its value. Property taxes are involuntary and specific liens. In Washington, property taxes become a lien on the first day of January in the year in which the taxes are levied. The levy of property taxes takes place in October.

Therefore, taxes levied in October of 2004 are actually considered to have become a lien against the property on January 1, 2004, even though the taxes are not payable until the next year.

Tax bills are typically mailed about the middle of February. One-half of the property tax is due and payable by April 30, and the second half must be paid by October 31. Delinquent taxes are subject to interest and penalties.

A buyer usually pays all of the real estate taxes that become due in the year following the purchase, even though the lien for these taxes arose prior to the time of purchase.

Taxpayers in Washington are given a three-year grace period before property is foreclosed because of property tax liens. The owner must be given notice of the impending foreclosure sale. In other words, three years after the taxes became delinquent, the owner is given notice of application for a judgment foreclosing the lien.

The taxpayer has the right to redeem the property at any time up to the date of the foreclosure sale by paying the delinquent amount plus any interest and costs or penalties. Once the foreclosed property has been sold, the purchaser takes title immediately. The former owner has no further redemption rights at that point.

Special Assessments. Municipalities may levy taxes called **special assessments** to pay for local improvements such as road paving or sewer lines. Special assessments are levied only against those properties that actually benefit from the improvements. (The properties that benefit must pay their share of the cost of the improvements.) If a special assessment is not paid, it becomes an involuntary, specific lien against the property.

After a special assessment becomes delinquent by two installment payments, or if the final installment is over one year late, the local taxing authority can begin foreclosure proceedings. These proceedings must commence within ten years after the last installment becomes delinquent.

Fig. 3.5 Types of liens

LIENS				
	Voluntary	Involuntary	General	Specific
Mortgages	X			X
Deeds of trust	X			X
Construction Liens		X		X
Property assessments		X		X
Judgment liens		X	X	
IRS liens		X	X	

Income Tax Liens. If federal income taxes are not paid, another type of tax lien will arise. Income tax liens are involuntary and general. They apply to all property owned by the taxpayer, both personal and real.

Other Tax Liens. Counties, cities, and nonpolitical units with taxing powers (such as school and irrigation districts) are also authorized to use liens as security devices when taxes are not paid.

Lien Priority

It is not unusual for one piece of property to have several types of liens placed against it. One property may be subject to a mortgage, a construction lien, and a tax lien. Often the total amount of the liens is more than the property will bring at a forced sale, and all the liens cannot be paid in full. Since liens are not paid on a pro rata basis, it must be determined which liens should be paid first.

As a general rule, the priority of liens depends on the order in which they were created. **Lien priority** is established by date of recording. In other words, the lien recorded first gets first priority for payment.

However, there are some exceptions to this rule. Property tax liens and special assessment liens are superior to all other liens against the property. They have first priority, even if another lien was created first. (The lien for general property taxes is superior to a lien for a special assessment, even if the special assessment lien was created first.) Also, the date used to determine the priority of construction liens is the date work first started on the project, rather than the date the lien was recorded.

Example: Margaret Smith's property has the following liens against it:

- a mortgage recorded March 9, 1999;
- property tax liens that attached January 1, 2003 and January 1, 2004;
- a lien for a judgment entered June 2, 2004;
- a special assessment lien that attached July 6, 2004;
- a construction lien recorded August 16, 2004 (but work on the project started May 19, 2004).

When the property is sold at a foreclosure sale, the liens would be paid out of the proceeds of the sale in the following order:

1. property tax liens
2. special assessment lien
3. mortgage
4. construction lien
5. judgment lien

Protecting the Debtor

When a creditor forecloses a lien, the amount of money obtained from the foreclosure sale is not always enough to cover the amount owed on the debt. To recover any remaining balance, the creditor may get a **deficiency judgment**, which is a personal judgment against the debtor ordering the debtor to pay the creditor the remaining amount owed.

Example: The Osgoods borrowed money from the bank to buy some property. When the Osgoods defaulted on the loan, the lender foreclosed on the mortgage. The loan amount was $225,000, but the property sold for only $215,000. The lender may obtain a deficiency judgment against the Osgoods for the $10,000 shortfall.

There are, however, some limitations on the right to obtain a deficiency judgment. For example, no deficiency judgment is available after a trustee's sale under a deed of trust. (See Chapter 10.)

Homestead Laws. Another way of protecting debtors is through homestead laws. While homestead laws do not protect family residences from all types of liens, they can sometimes protect families from the forced sale of their home. Homestead laws reflect a belief by the legislature that a person's obligation to support dependents is as important as the payment of debts.

Washington law provides for an automatic **homestead exemption** for certain property used as a principal residence. Under the law, a **homestead** (a family dwelling, along with the land and any outbuildings) is exempt from the foreclosure of judgment liens for up to the total net value of the property, or $40,000, whichever is less. The exemption begins as soon as the owner begins residing on the property.

Case Example:

In 1995, RMC, a construction company, attempted to foreclose on a judgment lien against a home owned by the Hyppas. At that time, the homestead exemption amount was $30,000. The property, valued at $145,000, was encumbered by liens totaling more than $130,000.

The total of the $30,000 homestead exemption and the $130,000 in liens exceeded the home's market value. The court thus held that there was no net value on which RMC could execute. *Miller Constr. Co. v. Coltran*, 87 Wn. App. 112 (1997).

An owner can obtain homestead protection in advance, for property he or she is planning to reside on, by recording a **declaration of homestead** for that property. The declaration of homestead must contain a legal description of the property and an estimate of its cash value. A person can have only one homestead at a time, so if the owner already has a homestead, he or she must record a declaration of abandonment of homestead on the other property.

Use of the homestead exemption is rare, mainly because the exemption does not protect the debtor against all claims. The homestead exemption does not offer protection against:

- mortgages or deeds of trust,
- construction liens,
- tax liens,
- liens for child support or spousal maintenance obligations, or
- liens imposed by a condominium or homeowners association.

Conclusion

As you can see, many different people may have various interests in the same piece of property. The interests others may have in your property affect your right and ability to use, possess, or sell the property. Encumbrances and conditions on your title affect your right to use your property. And liens affect the value of your property and your ability to sell it quickly and easily.

Case Problem

The following is a hypothetical case problem. Most of the facts are taken from a real case. Using what you've learned from this chapter, make a decision on the issues presented, and then check to see if your answer matches the real decision by the court.

The Facts

Doris Smith and Eugene Breen owned adjoining land. A dirt road leading to the back of both their properties ran astride the boundary line. The road had existed since at least the 1930s and had been used jointly and amicably by the various owners of both pieces of property for over 30 years.

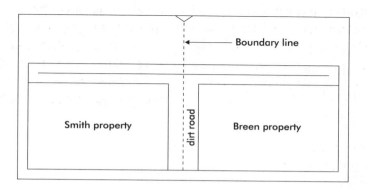

In 1966, Smith and Breen both tried to assert ownership of the entire road. Breen began parking his truck on the road, blocking Smith's passage. Smith's attorney wrote Breen a letter requesting that he not block the road. The letter apparently had no effect, so Smith brought a lawsuit to enjoin Breen from blocking the road, and claiming sole ownership of the road (Smith claimed that she alone maintained the road). Breen counterclaimed, asserting that he had acquired title to the entire roadway by blocking Smith's access.

The Questions

Who was the rightful owner of the road? Had Breen obtained ownership by blocking Smith's use of the road? Could Smith claim sole ownership because she had been the only one to maintain the road? If an easement existed, what type was it and how was it established?

The Answer

Neither party had sole ownership of the road, and both had the right to use it equally. If Breen had successfully blocked the road from use by Smith for over ten years, he might have been able to terminate Smith's easement by prescription. However, Smith objected to the blocking, and the time period was not nearly long enough.

Nor did Smith have a valid claim simply because she maintained the road. There is no specific requirement that the owner of an easement make repairs or perform maintenance.

A prescriptive easement may be acquired by clear proof that the land was used in an open, notorious, continuous, and uninterrupted manner for ten years, that the use was adverse to the owner, and that the owner had knowledge of the use.

In this case, both parties' predecessors had been using the entire width of the roadway as if it belonged to them. For more than 30 years neither asked the other for permission to use the road, and there was no challenge to the use of the road.

In the case of *Smith v. Breen*, 26 Wn. App. 802, 614 P.2d 671 (1980), the court found that the use of Smith's property by Breen and his predecessors, and the use of Breen's property by Smith and her predecessors, had ripened into mutual easements by prescription. Both Smith and Breen had an equal right to use the roadway because both had acquired a prescriptive easement.

Chapter Summary

- An estate is an ownership interest in property that is or may become possessory. The highest and best interest is the fee simple. There are two types of fee simple estates: the fee simple absolute and the fee simple defeasible.

- The defeasible fee may end if certain events occur or conditions are not met. A defeasible fee may be determinable or conditional.

- The term of a life estate is measured by someone's lifetime. A life estate based on someone else's life is called a life estate "pur autre vie." The person who will receive the property when the life estate ends has an estate in remainder or an estate in reversion. Today, trusts are used more frequently than life estates.

- A leasehold estate is a non-ownership, possessory interest in property. There are three types of leasehold estates: the estate for years, the periodic tenancy, and the tenancy at will. The tenancy at sufferance is not a true leasehold estate.

- An encumbrance is a nonpossessory interest in real property. Encumbrances may be nonfinancial or financial in nature.

- Easements may be appurtenant or in gross. Creation of an easement may be express, implied, by estoppel, or by prescription.

- A license is similar to an easement but is not considered an interest in property. A license is usually more temporary than an easement. An encroachment is a structure or object that extends over the property line onto an adjacent property.

- A lien is a financial interest in property that gives a creditor the right to have the property sold upon default and the debt paid out of the sale proceeds. A lien may be specific or general, and either voluntary or involuntary. Some examples of liens are mortgages, deeds of trust, construction liens, judgment liens, and tax liens.

Checklist of Problem Areas

Real Estate Licensee's Checklist

❑ Find out the type of estate the seller owns when taking a listing. For example, ask the seller whether there are conditions or restrictions on the property, or whether the seller owns a fee simple absolute or only a life estate.

❑ Are there liens against the property?

❑ Look for obvious visible easements and ask the owner and check the files for recorded easements. If there are easements, how do they affect the property?

Seller or Lessor's Checklist

❑ What liens will you be expected to pay off out of the sale proceeds?

❑ If you are a seller and own an easement, will you retain the easement or will it pass with the sale of the property?

❑ If the property has been leased, does the lease provide a specific termination date? If no termination date is provided, how much notice must the landlord give the tenant? Does the lease fall under the Residential Landlord-Tenant Act (RLTA)? If so, the notice period may be different.

Buyer or Tenant's Checklist

❑ If you are a buyer, verify what kind of estate is being sold. Is it a fee simple absolute or is it a conditional fee or life estate?

❑ If you are a buyer, find out if any easements burden the property. How do these easements affect the property financially and aesthetically?

❑ A buyer takes property subject to a valid lease. If there is currently a tenant on the property, the new owner must recognize and follow the terms of the tenant's lease. A new owner can terminate the lease only through proper notification.

❑ A tenant must be aware of how much notice is required before termination. Is the tenancy covered by the RLTA?

❑ The tenant should also remember that notice of termination must be in writing—verbal notice is not sufficient. If the tenant does not give sufficient notice, he or she may be liable for an additional rent payment, even if the tenant has already vacated the premises.

Chapter Quiz

1. The highest and best interest that can exist in land is called a:

   a. leasehold estate
   b. fee simple estate
   c. conditional fee
   d. life estate

2. The type of estate called a fee simple subject to condition subsequent is based on certain express conditions. If these conditions are not met:

   a. the property will automatically revert back to the grantor
   b. the grantor has the "power of termination" but must take legal steps to terminate
   c. the property automatically reverts to the state
   d. None of the above

3. Jean grants Mary a life estate in some property. Upon Mary's death, the property is to pass to David. David is called:

   a. the reverter
   b. a pur autre vie
   c. the remainderman
   d. the primary holder

4. When discussing life estates, waste is defined as:

   a. the years until the life tenant dies
   b. lost revenue while the property cannot be sold
   c. permanent damage or abuse to property which reduces its market value
   d. None of the above

5. Roger rents a house in Yakima. The lease gives him the right to possess the house from September 1, 2004 through May 31, 2005. This type of tenancy is called a:

   a. periodic or month-to-month tenancy
   b. tenancy for a specific term
   c. tenancy at will
   d. tenancy at sufferance

6. Alice is renting an apartment on a month-to-month basis. The tenancy is covered by the Residential Landlord-Tenant Act. If Alice wants to move, she must give her landlord:

   a. 10 days' written notice
   b. 20 days' written notice
   c. 30 days' written notice
   d. No notice is required

7. Lori owns a landlocked piece of property, but she has a right-of-way easement to drive across her neighbor's property. This is a(n):

   a. appurtenant easement
   b. negative easement
   c. easement in gross
   d. None of the above

8. The Riverside Power Company has a commercial easement in gross to run a power line through your backyard. The power company is purchased by Mega-Corp Power. The easement:

   a. is automatically extinguished
   b. may not be sold since it is an appurtenant commercial easement
   c. may be sold since it is a commercial easement in gross
   d. may be sold since it is a negative easement

9. In order to acquire an easement by pre-scription in Washington, the use must be continuous and uninterrupted for:

   a. 5 years
   b. 10 years
   c. 15 years
   d. 20 years

10. Jones owns an easement to walk across Farley's property to reach his mailbox. Then Farley sells his property to Jones. The easement no longer exists because it has terminated through:

    a. merger
    b. abandonment
    c. failure of purpose
    d. destruction of the dominant tenement

11. A mortgage is a(n):

    a. involuntary, specific lien
    b. involuntary, general lien
    c. voluntary, specific lien
    d. voluntary, general lien

12. A construction lien must be filed within how many days after cessation of work on the project?

    a. 30 days
    b. 45 days
    c. 60 days
    d. 90 days

13. In Washington, one-half of the assessed property tax is due and payable before:

    a. January 1
    b. March 15
    c. April 30
    d. June 1

14. In paying liens:

    a. mortgages always have first priority
    b. lien priority is established by date of recording
    c. property tax liens are superior to other liens
    d. Both b) and c)

15. In Washington, the homestead exemption is:

    a. $20,000
    b. $30,000
    c. $40,000
    d. $50,000

4 Co-Ownership of Real Property

Outline

I. Forms of Co-ownership
   A. Community property
      1. when community property rules apply
         a. meretricious relationships
      2. classifying the property
      3. legal consequences
   B. Tenancy in common
      1. rights and duties of tenants in common
         a. contribution
         b. waste
      2. transfer and encumbrance
      3. terminating a tenancy in common
   C. Joint tenancy
      1. creating a joint tenancy
         a. the four unities
      2. rights and duties of joint tenants
         a. right of survivorship
         b. making the title marketable
         c. simultaneous death
      3. terminating a joint tenancy
      4. advantages and disadvantages of joint tenancy
      5. husband and wife choosing co-ownership
II. Ownership by Associations
   A. Corporations
      1. creation
      2. management
      3. liability
      4. nonprofit corporations
   B. General partnerships
   C. Limited partnerships
   D. Limited liability companies
   E. Joint ventures
   F. Syndicates

Key Terms

- concurrently
- severalty
- community property
- separate property
- meretricious relationship
- commingling
- joinder
- tenancy in common
- contribution
- waste
- partition

- joint tenancy
- right of survivorship
- unity of possession
- unity of interest
- unity of time
- unity of title
- marketable title
- severance
- corporation (domestic or foreign)
- shareholders

- nonprofit corporation
- articles of incorporation
- partnership (general or limited)
- partnership property
- limited liability company (member-managed or manager-managed)
- joint venture
- syndicate

Chapter Overview

Ownership of real property is frequently shared by more than one person. Two, ten, or two hundred people can own the same piece of property at the same time (**concurrently**). This chapter explains the forms that concurrent ownership can take.

The first section of the chapter focuses on the various ways in which co-owners can hold title, such as community property or tenancy in common. The second part of the chapter describes ownership by associations of two or more persons, such as partnerships.

Forms of Co-ownership

When property is owned by one individual, he or she holds title **in severalty**. In Washington, when property is owned by more than one individual, they can hold title in one of three ways:

- community property,
- tenancy in common, or
- joint tenancy.

Many prospective co-owners are unaware of these various forms of co-ownership, and wind up with one or another by default. However, the way in which title is held is very important, as it determines who controls the property. It can also have dramatic consequences when co-ownership ends, whether voluntarily or through dissolution or death. Co-owners need to understand these effects and deliberately choose the type of ownership they want.

Real estate agents should make sure that buyers realize the importance of the form of co-ownership. However, when an agent raises the subject, the buyers often ask for help in choosing how to take title. This is beyond the licensee's area of expertise; at that point, he or she must advise the buyers to consult a lawyer. Even a well-intentioned licensee who gives buyers friendly advice may end up charged with the unauthorized practice of law.

Fig. 4.1 Forms of co-ownership

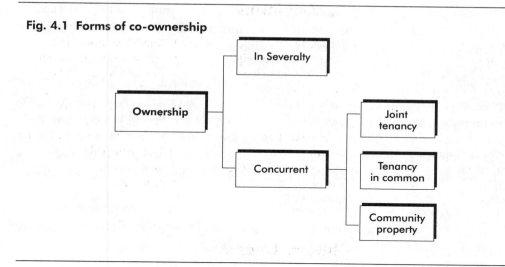

In addition, if the buyers make the wrong choice based on the agent's advice, the agent could be liable for damages.

Even though a real estate licensee should avoid advising buyers about forms of co-ownership, the licensee nevertheless needs at least a general understanding of the subject. Whenever a legal document is executed, the agent needs to know whether only one co-owner's signature is sufficient, or whether all the co-owners need to sign. For the parties, this can mean the difference between an effective sale and a void transaction. For the agent, it can mean the difference between a commission and a lawsuit.

Community Property

Community property is one of the most common forms of co-ownership in this state. Outside of Washington, only Arizona, California, Idaho, Louisiana, Nevada, New Mexico, Texas, and Wisconsin have community property systems. In most other states, married couples co-own property as **tenants by the entirety**. Tenancy by the entirety is similar to joint tenancy (discussed below).

The concept of community property is based on Spanish law. Early Washington settlers had little contact with Spain or the Spanish culture. However, they did pattern many of their early laws on California's legal system, and California has a history that is rich with Spanish influence.

When Community Property Rules Apply

Under community property rules, all property owned by a married couple is classified either as the **separate property** of one spouse, or as the **community property** of both spouses. These classifications determine a couple's rights and duties in regard to the property.

Community property rules apply only to property acquired during a marriage. If a couple is not legally married, they cannot acquire community property, no matter how long they have lived together or how much their relationship resembles a marriage.

In some states, a couple that has lived together for a certain number of years in a marriage-like relationship is considered legally married, even though there has been no marriage ceremony, and no marriage license has been obtained or signed. This kind of marriage is called a **common law marriage**. Washington law does not provide for common law marriages. However, if a couple has met the common law marriage requirements of another state before moving to Washington, they will be considered legally married when they move to Washington, and the property they acquire while living in Washington will be considered community property.

Note that although property acquired by an unmarried couple is not community property, both parties may have a common interest in that property. The property rights of each party depend on the type of relationship that exists between them.

Meretricious Relationships. In the past, a distinction was made between an "innocent relationship" and a "meretricious relationship." A relationship was considered innocent if one or both of the parties believed in good faith that a valid marriage existed, even when it did not. A **meretricious relationship** existed when both parties lived together with full knowledge that a lawful marriage did not exist. If the couple's relationship was innocent, the court would protect the rights of the innocent party (or parties, if both believed a valid marriage existed). The property accumulated during such a relationship would usually be divided fairly and equitably.

However, if the relationship were meretricious (both parties knew that they were not validly married), property was simply presumed to belong to the party named in the legal title. This often produced inequitable results.

> **Example:** Tim and Sarah lived together for 20 years without ever marrying. During this time, they bought a house. Title to the house was in Tim's name alone. When Tim and Sarah separated, Tim retained sole ownership of the house because title was in his name. Any money or effort Sarah put into the house was lost, simply because title was not in her name.

But over the last few decades, the distinction between an innocent and a meretricious relationship has been blurred, if not eliminated. Courts now simply examine the nature and extent of the relationship and the property accumulations, and try to make a just and equitable disposition of the property.

> **Example:** If Tim and Sarah from the previous example were separating today, the courts might very well divide the property accumulated during their relationship evenly between them, regardless of whose name was on the title. This is especially true if they had children and purported to live as a married couple for those 20 years.

The nature and duration of the relationship between an unmarried couple affects the division of their property. The Washington Supreme Court has mentioned several factors that should be considered when determining how property should be divided. These factors include:

- continuous cohabitation,
- duration of the relationship,
- purpose of the relationship,
- pooling of resources,
- pooling of services for joint projects,
- who acquired the property,
- monetary and labor contributions,
- whether or not there are children,
- who is to care for the children, and
- the general condition in which each of the parties will be left.

Based on these factors, a court may divide property evenly between the partners, award it to the person who has title to it, or award it in some other fair and equitable manner.

Classifying the Property

While problems can arise when dividing property between an unmarried couple, the question of an equitable division of property occurs most frequently when a validly married couple divorces. Who receives what portion of the property depends on whether the property is classified as community property or separate property.

The idea behind the community property system is that a marriage is a partnership. The husband and wife each work for the good of the partnership. Any money or property acquired through the skill or labor of either spouse during the marriage belongs to the marital community, not just to the individual who earned it. This means that the salaries of both husband and wife are community property. And even if only one spouse works outside the home for wages (for example, while the other spouse works inside the home raising children), those wages are community property, and belong to both spouses.

In addition, anything purchased with community funds or with community credit (for example, an item purchased with a credit card issued to both spouses) is community property.

The principle behind community property is favored so strongly that it is presumed that any property purchased during marriage belongs to the community, even if title is held in the name of only one spouse, unless it can be proven otherwise.

Example: Suppose Tim and Sarah were married for nine years. During their marriage, they bought a house. Title to the house is in Tim's name alone. When they divorce, the house is presumed to be community property even though title is in Tim's name.

On the other hand, everything acquired before marriage remains separate property after marriage. This includes money accumulated before marriage, and items purchased with money accumulated before marriage.

Example: Sarah earns her living as a bus driver. While she was single, she accumulated $15,000 in savings. Even after her marriage to Tim, that $15,000 remained Sarah's separate property. Anything purchased with separate property funds is also separate property. So if Sarah uses her $15,000 to buy a car during her marriage, the car is also her separate property.

Gifts. Property or money acquired by gift, will, or inheritance is also separate property, even if it is received during the marriage. For example, if Veronica's father leaves her $25,000 in his will, that $25,000 is Veronica's separate property, even if she acquired it during her marriage to Phil.

The rationale behind this rule is that a gift, a legacy, or an inheritance is not earned by the skill or labor of a spouse. But if a gift is actually given in exchange for services rendered, either in the past or in the future, it is considered community property rather than separate property.

Example: Phil's elderly mother gives him her sailboat. It is understood between them that the sailboat is Phil's compensation for helping his mother with housekeeping and other chores. The sailboat is not a true gift. Because Phil "earned" it, the sailboat is community property rather than separate property.

Note that a gift purchased with community funds by one spouse for the other spouse is the recipient spouse's separate property.

Example: Veronica buys Phil a Rolex watch with money she has saved from her salary. Even though the watch was purchased with community funds, the watch becomes Phil's separate property.

Rents and Profits. Ordinarily, any appreciation in separate property and any rents or profits generated by separate property are also separate property. However, if the appreciation or profits are the result of a spouse's effort, skill, or labor, they are community property instead.

Example: Phil owns an apartment building as his separate property. If he hires a property management company and is not actively involved in managing the building himself, the rents it generates will be his separate property. But if he spends time and energy on maintaining the building and leasing the apartments, the rents will be at least partly community property.

Community Property Agreements. Some couples choose to sign **community property agreements**, which makes all property owned by either of them community property, no matter when or how it was acquired. Most community property agreements provide that:

1. all property owned by either spouse is converted to community property;
2. all property later acquired will be community property; and
3. upon the death of one spouse, all community property will immediately vest in the survivor.

Note that a community property agreement avoids the necessity for probate when one spouse dies. All of the deceased spouse's property has been converted to community property by the agreement, and all community property automatically vests in the surviving spouse. An attorney should be consulted prior to preparing a community property agreement, because the agreement could disrupt more sophisticated estate planning.

Commingling. Even without a community property agreement, separate property will sometimes become community property. This occurs when separate funds are mixed, or **commingled**, with community funds so that they are impossible to distinguish.

> **Example:** Returning to the previous example, suppose that when Sarah got married she put her $15,000 into a joint checking account. Both she and Tim contributed to the account and used funds from the account. It is no longer clear whether the money remaining in the account is Sarah's $15,000 or community funds.
>
> Under these circumstances, the $15,000 might well be considered a gift to the community and will no longer be considered Sarah's separate property.

Separation. The rules change when a married couple is living separately or if a decree of separation has been issued. Then the income earned and property acquired by each spouse is considered his or her separate property. This rule applies only to a "defunct marriage," and does not apply when the spouses are separated for other reasons.

Fig. 4.2 Community vs. separate property

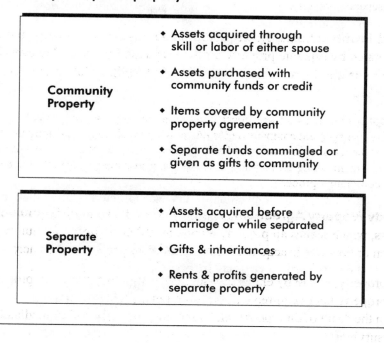

Case Example:

A husband and wife experience a long separation due to the wife's confinement in a mental institution outside of Washington. Acquisitions by the husband during the separation were considered community property, not his separate property. *Rustad v. Rustad*, 61 Wn.2d 1176, 377 P.2d 414 (1963).

When a married person wins a personal injury suit, the damages award is community property if it is received while the couple is living together. If the couple is living apart, the damages award is usually the separate property of the injured spouse. However, if the injury occurred while the couple was still living together, a portion of the award may be community property.

Case Example:

Ronna and William Brown were married in 1967. In 1979, Ronna was injured in a car accident. Approximately six months later, Ronna instituted a dissolution action. At trial, Ronna had not yet recovered any damages for the accident. The trial court said any recovery should be divided as follows:

- lost earnings and diminished earning capacity from the date of the accident until the date of the separation is community property and should be awarded one-half each to Ronna and William;
- lost earnings and diminished earning capacity after the date of separation is Ronna's separate property;
- out-of-pocket expenses prior to trial had already been reimbursed in full (otherwise, expenses paid by community funds would probably have been reimbursed);
- expenses occurring after trial should be awarded to the party incurring the expense; and
- recovery for all other damages (probably referring to "pain and suffering") is Ronna's separate property.

In re Marriage of Brown, 100 Wn.2d 729, 675 P.2d 1207 (1984).

A different rule applies if the personal injury was inflicted by the other spouse, rather than a third party. Then the damages award is the injured spouse's separate property, regardless of whether the couple is living together.

Separate and Community Property Interests. Sometimes there are both separate and community interests in a single property. This commonly occurs in two situations: when the property is paid for over time, and when the property is improved during the marriage.

When property is paid for over time (as with a deed of trust or an installment contract), some payments may be made with separate funds and some with community funds. This is especially likely to occur with a major purchase, such as a home.

Example: Doreen and Dimitri purchased a residence for $200,000. They used Doreen's separate funds to make the $40,000 downpayment. However, their $160,000 loan was a community obligation (both Doreen and Dimitri signed the loan documents). They proceed to use community funds to make the monthly payments on the loan.

The house is community property, but Doreen has a separate property interest in the home in the same proportion that the downpayment had to the purchase price (20%). If ten years later the property is worth $350,000, Doreen's separate interest has increased to $70,000 (20% of $350,000).

Another common example would be one spouse purchasing a home before the marriage, and then making the mortgage payments on the home after the marriage with community funds. The home would be the purchasing spouse's separate property, but the community would have an interest in it in proportion to the amount of principal payments made with community funds.

Community property—either community funds, or the time, skill, and labor of one of the spouses—is often used to improve separate property. That gives the marital community an interest in the property.

Example: Terri inherits a house from her mother. This is her separate property. Since Terri and Sam already have a home, Terri decides to lease the inherited house. In preparing the house for rental, Terri spends $10,000 in community funds on repairs and improvements. The house is still Terri's separate property, but Terri and Sam's marital community now has an interest in it.

This interest is proportionate to the community's contribution (the $10,000 plus Terri's time and efforts). Although most of the rent generated by the property will be Terri's separate property, a portion will be Terri and Sam's community property.

The same process works in reverse. Let's say Terri's mother left her $10,000, which she used to improve the home she and Sam own as community property. Then Terri would have a separate interest in the home along with the community's interest.

Legal Consequences

The way in which property is classified has a significant bearing on each spouse's rights and interests in that property: each spouse owns his or her separate property in severalty; each has an undivided ½ interest in all community property.

Management and Control. Equal control of community property is the general rule. Equal control means that either spouse can act unilaterally, without the other's consent.

Example: Lowell and Gina own a car as community property. One day a passerby offers Lowell $5,000 for the car. That strikes Lowell as a very good price, so he accepts the offer without consulting Gina.

When Lowell tells Gina he sold the car, she's very annoyed. But it's too late to do anything about it; Lowell's unilateral action was legally binding.

One exception to this rule is that when one spouse operates a business, the other spouse has no right to interfere in its management, even though the business is community property.

Joinder Requirements. There are several important limitations on a spouse's right to unilateral management and control of community property. Some transactions require both a husband and a wife to act jointly; this is called a **joinder requirement**.

One spouse can't give away community property without the other's consent. If Lowell had given away the car, Gina could have demanded it back. Also, one spouse can't sell, lease, or encumber the couple's household furnishings without the other's consent. And one spouse can't purchase, transfer, or encumber community real property without the other spouse's consent.

It is crucial for real estate agents to remember this joinder requirement, and to obtain the signature of both spouses on any contract involving community property. Otherwise, the contract is voidable.

> **Example:** Instead of selling their car, Lowell decides to sell their home. He finds a buyer and signs a purchase and sale agreement. Since Lowell cannot transfer community real property without Gina's consent (and signature), the purchase and sale agreement is not a valid contract.

There are very few exceptions to this joinder requirement. One of the exceptions is that joinder is not required in an estoppel situation. If a neighbor builds a garage over the property line because Lowell said it was okay, Gina is estopped from objecting to the encroachment, even though she didn't give her approval.

Remedies for Unauthorized Acts. When only one spouse enters into a transaction regarding community real property, the transaction is not binding on the other spouse. If the nonacting spouse wants to, he or she may void the transaction, even when the other party acted in good faith. Any payment received from the other party (for example, an earnest money deposit) must be refunded.

For real estate agents, buyers, and lienholders, the rule is simple: always determine whether a property owner is married. If the owner is married, the safest course is to have his or her spouse:

- sign a quitclaim deed transferring any interest he or she might have in the property to the acting spouse, or
- co-sign all the documents involved in the transaction (the listing agreement, purchase and sale agreement, and deed).

These steps are not necessary if the property is the acting spouse's separate property. However, if it turns out that the community has an interest in the property, the buyer could lose the property, and the broker could lose the commission.

Case Example:

Roy and Billee Haueter owned an apartment building they wanted to sell. On October 3, 1982, Roy signed an exclusive listing contract with Larry Klaas. Billee testified that she did not know about this listing agreement.

On November 29, 1982, the Haueters sold the apartment house through Dennis Weybright. Weybright received a 6% commission on the sale.

Klaas brought a lawsuit for breach of his exclusive listing agreement. The court entered a judgment against Roy Haueter individually. No judgment was entered against the community because the court found that Billee Haueter had not authorized the listing with Mr. Klaas and did not ratify the contract. *Klaas v. Haueter*, 49 Wn. App. 697, 745 P.2d 870 (1987).

In this case example, the sale itself was valid. The problem arose because an unwary broker did not have both husband and wife sign an exclusive listing agreement. The fact that Klaas won a judgment against Roy Haueter individually means that he is entitled to the full amount from Roy. However, since no judgment was entered against Billee, Klaas may have a harder time actually collecting the money.

Liability for Debts. A creditor's rights against a married person's property are determined by its classification as separate or community property. One spouse's separate property is shielded from liability for the other spouse's premarital debts.

> **Example:** When Lois and Joe got married, Lois already owned a home, and Joe owed a large judgment in connection with an automobile accident. Since the home is Lois's separate property, the judgment against Joe cannot become a lien against the home.

Separate property is also protected from debts the other spouse incurs during the marriage, unless the debts were incurred for necessities such as food and clothing. Thus, if Joe's automobile accident occurred during the marriage, Lois's separate property still could not be reached by the judgment creditor.

Fig. 4.3 Liability for debts

	Other Spouse's Premarital Debt	Other Spouse's Debt Incurred During Marriage
Separate Property	SAFE	SAFE*
Community Property	NOT SAFE**	NOT SAFE

* unless debt is for necessities
** except earnings kept in separate account

Community property, on the other hand, can be reached by the premarital creditors of either spouse. The nondebtor spouse can protect his or her earnings by keeping them apart from all other community funds, in an account that the debtor spouse has no access to. However, this won't shield the earnings from debts the other spouse contracts for during the marriage.

And, finally, all community property is liable for the debts either spouse incurs during the marriage. Referring back to the example above, if the home were community property and Joe's accident occurred during the marriage, the judgment lien against Joe would attach to the home, even though Lois had nothing to do with the automobile accident.

Division of the Property on Dissolution. When a marriage is dissolved, the court presiding over the dissolution can divide and award the couple's community property.

As a very general rule, community property is divided between the spouses equally. However, courts often distribute it differently in order to produce more equitable results. Separate property is excluded from this process; the court cannot award one spouse's separate property to the other spouse.

In determining whether property is separate or community property, the court relies on two legal presumptions that strongly favor community property:

1. all property acquired during the marriage is presumed to be community property, unless it was a gift or inheritance, and
2. after several years of marriage, everything the couple owns is presumed to have been acquired during the marriage.

These presumptions apply even if the title to the property states that it is separate property.

Either spouse may rebut these presumptions with evidence that the property is actually separate property.

> **Example:** When Todd married Nancy, he owned a car and had $20,000 in savings. The car and the money were his separate property. During the marriage, Todd used his $20,000 to buy some land. The deed to the property says, "Todd Smith, a married man, as his sole and separate property."
>
> In the couple's dissolution proceedings, the court presumes that both the car and the land are community property. It is up to Todd to rebut this presumption by showing that they are his separate property. He must present evidence that he owned the car before the marriage, and that he purchased the land with funds he possessed before the marriage.

It can be especially difficult to prove that property is separate when it has changed form during the marriage (from a grand piano to cash to a motorcycle), or when separate funds have been commingled with community funds. It may be necessary to go through a complicated process of tracing the couple's expenditures. Community expenses are presumed to have been paid out of community funds, and separate expenses are presumed to have been paid out of separate funds.

When there are both separate and community interests in the same piece of property, the court will likely order some form of reimbursement. Typically, a spouse must reimburse the community for contributions to his or her separate property, and the community must reimburse a spouse for separate contributions to community property.

Disposition of Property at Death. When a married person dies, the probate court determines what part of the estate is separate property and what part is community property. The property is then distributed according to the will, or if there is no will, according to the rules of intestate succession. (See Chapter 8 for more information about wills and intestate succession.)

A married person is free to will his or her separate property to anyone. In addition, both spouses have the right to will their undivided ½ interest in all community property to someone other than his or her spouse.

> **Example:** Jules and Maria own a home as community property. Maria wills her ½ interest in the property to her friend, Josephine. When Maria dies, Jules and Josephine each own an undivided ½ interest in the property as tenants in common.

If a married person dies without having made a valid will, all the community property vests in the surviving spouse.

> **Example:** Bud and Rena had four children. Bud never got around to writing a will. When he dies, Rena receives full title to their home, car, furniture, and other community property. She now owns all of this in severalty, and the children have no rights in it.

The separate property of the intestate spouse (the spouse who died without leaving a will), is divided between the surviving spouse and the deceased's children. The spouse receives an undivided ½ interest in the separate property and the children share the remaining ½ interest. All of these interests are held as tenants in common.

> **Example:** Bud also owned some land as his separate property. When Bud dies, Rena receives an undivided ½ interest in the land. Each of their four children receives an undivided ⅛ interest in the land (a ½ interest divided among four children).

If both husband and wife die at the same time (in an accident, for example), each spouse's ½ interest in the community property is distributed as if that spouse survived the other spouse.

Tenancy in Common

Tenancy in common is the most basic form of concurrent ownership. It is the residual category: co-ownership that doesn't fit into any of the other categories is a tenancy in common by default. If a deed transferring land to two unmarried individuals doesn't specify how they are taking title, they take title as **tenants in common**.

Co-owners who choose tenancy in common should make that clear in the deed, by adding "as tenants in common" after their names. If they own unequal shares in the property, that should be stated in the deed as well.

> **Example:** When Zowalskie and Martinez bought Baker's tract of land, they decided to take title as tenants in common. Zowalskie came up with ⅔ of the purchase price, and Martinez contributed ⅓. Their deed reads, "Zowalskie, a single woman, with an undivided ⅔ interest, and Martinez, a single woman, with an undivided ⅓ interest, as tenants in common."

When a deed does not state each co-tenant's fractional interest, the law presumes that the interests are equal. In a lawsuit, a tenant in common can overcome that legal presumption by submitting evidence that the contributions to the purchase price were unequal.

> **Example:** Zowalskie paid ⅔ of the purchase price, and Martinez paid ⅓. However, their deed simply states, "Zowalskie, a single woman, and Martinez, a single woman, as tenants in common."
>
> Zowalskie and Martinez subsequently have a serious disagreement, and they take each other to court over the property. Because the deed doesn't state what fractional interest each of them owns, the judge presumes that each has a ½ interest.
>
> But Zowalskie presents evidence (a canceled check) showing that she paid ⅔ of the purchase price. This establishes that Zowalskie has a ⅔ interest in the property, and Martinez has only a ⅓ interest.

Rights and Duties of Tenants in Common

In principle, there's no limit to how many tenants in common can share a property. There are also no restrictions on how they divide up the ownership. One tenant in common might own a ½ interest, and 50 others might each own a $1/100$ interest.

The interests owned by tenants in common are always **undivided**: each tenant has a right to possess and occupy the whole property, no matter how small his or her share of ownership is. Similarly, no co-tenant can exclude another co-tenant from any portion of the property. This rule is referred to as **unity of possession**. This concept is best illustrated by contrasting tenancy in common with ownership in severalty.

> **Example:** Abernathy owns a large tract of land. She deeds the east ⅔ of it to Bernstein, and the west ⅓ to Corman.
>
> Bernstein and Corman each own their portion of the tract in severalty. They are not co-owners; they are sole owners of two separate properties. Each holds the entire bundle of rights to his portion, and has the right to exclude all others from his portion. Bernstein can exclude Corman from the east ⅔ and Corman can exclude Bernstein from the west ⅓.
>
> On the other hand, suppose Abernathy deeds her entire tract to Bernstein and Corman as tenants in common, with Bernstein taking an undivided ⅔ interest and Corman taking an undivided ⅓ interest. Now they are co-owners of a single property, sharing a single bundle of rights. Both have the right to possess and occupy the whole tract; neither can exclude the other from any part of it. Even though Bernstein's interest in

the property is twice as great as Corman's, Bernstein can't fence off ⅔ of the property and tell Corman to keep out.

One tenant in common does not have a right to charge another co-tenant rent. If Bernstein chooses to live on the property while Corman chooses not to, Corman is not entitled to collect rent from Bernstein. But Corman may be allowed to offset the rental value of the property against his share of the property's expenses.

As an extension of the unity of possession rule, each co-tenant has a right to an equal share of any products or income generated by the property. Diamonds from a mine or apples from an orchard belong to all the tenants in common. If they lease out the property to someone else, the co-tenants share the collected rent equally.

Contribution. All tenants in common are required to share the property's expenses: maintenance, insurance, taxes, mortgage payments, and so forth. Unless otherwise agreed, each tenant's share of expenses is proportionate to his or her ownership interest. Thus, Bernstein is liable for ⅔ of the expenses, and Corman is liable for ⅓ of the expenses.

A co-tenant who pays more than his or her share of the expenses can demand reimbursement from the other tenants in common. This is called the **right to contribution**.

The right to contribution also applies to property improvements, but only when the other tenants in common have agreed to the improvement.

> **Example:** Armstrong, Bennett, and Crane own a house as tenants in common. Armstrong and Bennett want to add a deck, but Crane is opposed to the project. Armstrong pays a carpenter to build the deck. Armstrong is entitled to reimbursement from Bennett, but not from Crane.

As you might guess, this rule often leads to disputes over whether a particular project (a new cedar roof, for example) was an improvement or necessary maintenance.

Waste. A tenant in common is liable to the other tenants for any waste he or she commits on the property (just as a life tenant is liable to a remainderman for waste). For instance, if Armstrong drives a car through the garage wall, she will have to compensate Bennett and Crane for the damage.

Transfer and Encumbrance

A tenant in common is free to sell, will, or encumber his or her undivided interest without the consent of the other tenant(s). A tenant in common's interest can also be transferred involuntarily, by foreclosure or bankruptcy.

> **Example:** Drew, Giles, and Magraw are tenants in common. Drew mortgages her undivided ⅓ interest, but that mortgage doesn't encumber Giles's or Magraw's interest.
> Drew dies, leaving all her property to her friend, Lohr. Now Giles, Magraw, and Lohr are tenants in common, and Lohr's undivided ⅓ interest is encumbered by the mortgage.

Lohr can't make the mortgage payments, so eventually the bank forecloses. Warner purchases Lohr's ⅓ interest at the foreclosure sale. Now Giles, Magraw, and Warner are tenants in common.

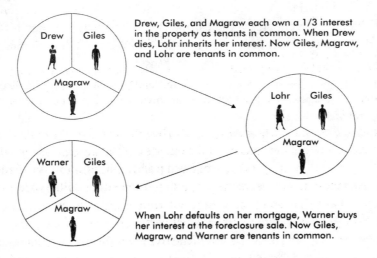

To transfer or encumber the whole property, all the tenants in common must sign the deed, deed of trust, or other instrument.

> **Example:** Williams, McNeil, Pohto, and Starbuck are tenants in common. Investments, Inc. offers them a great deal of money for their land. Williams, McNeil, and Pohto leap at the offer. But Starbuck (who holds an undivided $1/16$ interest) turns it down, because of his sentimental attachment to the property.
> Williams, McNeil, and Pohto can sell their combined undivided $15/16$ interest in the property without Starbuck's consent, but they can't sell the whole property. Investments, Inc. insists on all or nothing. The others plead with Starbuck, but he won't budge. Investments, Inc. withdraws its offer.

What if Williams, McNeil, and Pohto all signed a deed that purported to convey the whole property to Investments, Inc.? The deed would effectively convey their undivided $15/16$ interest, but not the whole property. Investments, Inc. could withdraw from the transaction or sue for damages.

The real estate agent who represented Investments, Inc. in the sale might be in trouble. She probably relied on the title insurance company to figure out who owned the property and who needed to sign the deed. The title officer slipped up—it happens, though not often. By failing to double check, the real estate agent exposed herself to liability for negligence. She might even be accused of participating in a fraud, if she knew about Starbuck's interest.

Terminating a Tenancy in Common

Agreement. A tenancy in common can be terminated by agreement. The co-tenants can agree to change their tenancy in common to one of the other forms of concurrent ownership (joint tenancy or community property, if they are married). Or they can agree to divide their property, so that each owns a portion of the property in severalty. This division by agreement is called **voluntary partition**.

> **Example:** Ames wills 20 acres of vacant land to Bakke and Church as tenants in common. Bakke and Church agree that they'd each rather have half the property instead of sharing the whole property.
>
> They have the land surveyed and divided into two ten-acre parcels. Bakke deeds her undivided ½ interest in the east ten acres to Church, and Church deeds his undivided ½ interest in the west ten acres to Bakke. Now each owns a ten-acre tract in severalty.

Judicial Partition. A tenancy in common can also be terminated by the unilateral action of one of the co-tenants, without the consent of the other(s). If Bakke wants to end the tenancy in common, but Church does not, Bakke can file a **partition action** in superior court.

Everyone with a recorded interest in the property (co-tenants and lienholders) is brought into the partition suit as a defendant. The judge determines the status and priority of all the liens against the property, and what interest each party holds. Then the judge terminates the tenancy in common by partitioning the property. Each former co-tenant is granted a share proportionate to his or her ownership interest.

Whenever possible, the judge will order the property to be physically divided. But physical division often won't work. For example, if the property Bakke and Church owned as tenants in common included a house, it would not be practical to divide it in half.

When physical partition is impractical or inequitable, the judge can order the property sold. The sale proceeds are then divided among the former co-tenants according to their ownership interests. Or, in some cases, a judge may order part of the property sold and part of it physically divided.

A tenant in common may oppose a physical division of the property. He or she can present evidence to show that the divided property would be worth substantially less than the proceeds from a sale of the whole property. In this case, the judge should order the property sold instead of physically divided.

Joint Tenancy

Joint tenants have a relationship similar to that of tenants in common: each joint tenant has an undivided interest in, and shares possession of, the whole property.

But the distinguishing feature of joint tenancy—the **right of survivorship**—comes into play if one of the joint tenants dies. When a joint tenant dies, his or her interest in the property passes automatically to the surviving joint tenant(s).

> **Example:** Craft, Kaskell, and Rusnak buy a vacation home together. Sometime later, Craft dies. If Craft, Kaskell, and Rusnak were tenants in common, Craft's undivided interest would pass to his heirs. Kaskell, Rusnak, and Craft's heirs would then own the property as tenants in common.

But if Craft, Kaskell, and Rusnak were joint tenants, from the moment of Craft's death, Kaskell and Rusnak own the whole property. Because of the right of survivorship, Craft cannot will her interest to her heirs.

Creating a Joint Tenancy

Since joint tenancy has such a radical effect on the disposition of property, it isn't something co-owners can slip into by default. Specific rules exist for creating and maintaining a joint tenancy. If these rules are not followed when the property is acquired, or if they are broken during the period of ownership, the joint tenancy fails and the right of survivorship is lost. Instead of a joint tenancy, the co-owners will either have a tenancy in common or, if they're a married couple, community property.

The Four Unities. To create a joint tenancy, the **four unities of title** must exist:

1. unity of possession,
2. unity of interest,
3. unity of time, and
4. unity of title.

Unity of possession means that all co-tenants have the right to occupy the whole property. A tenancy in common also requires the unity of possession.

Unity of interest means that all the joint tenants must have an equal interest in the property. If there are two joint tenants, each must have a ½ interest; if there are three joint tenants, each must have a ⅓ interest; and so on. If Scovel has a ¼ interest and Dimarco has a ¾ interest, they aren't joint tenants.

Unity of time means that all of the joint tenants must acquire their interests in the property at the same moment.

Unity of title means that the joint tenants all must take title through the same deed or will.

> **Example:** Connelly deeds an undivided ½ interest in his property to Dreyer. Two months later, Connelly deeds an undivided ½ interest in the same property to Cree. Dreyer and Cree cannot be joint tenants, because they acquired title at two different times, through two different deeds. Although there is unity of interest and unity of possession, there is no unity of time and no unity of title. As a result, there is no joint tenancy.

However, it is possible for a property owner to create a joint tenancy by deeding the property to him or herself and others.

> **Example:** Karen has owned some land for many years. When her children, Bill and Clarisse, reach adulthood, Karen deeds the property "to Karen, Bill, and Clarisse, as joint tenants."
> This new deed satisfies the unity of time and the unity of title requirements, even though Karen originally acquired the property long before and through a different deed than Bill and Clarisse.

Note that joint tenants may agree among themselves to give one joint tenant exclusive possession of the property. Such an agreement does not destroy the joint tenancy. The agreement can even be entered into at the same time that the co-owners acquire the property, without preventing the creation of a joint tenancy.

Other Requirements. A joint tenancy can only be created in writing. The deed or will must expressly state the intention to create a joint tenancy. It's best to have the deed or will state that title is held either "as joint tenants" or "in joint tenancy."

Courts have disagreed over whether any other language is sufficient evidence of an intent to create a joint tenancy. However, it is clear that the phrase "with the right of survivorship" will not create a joint tenancy by itself. And even the words "as joint tenants" or "in joint tenancy" only establishes a presumption that there was an intent to create a joint tenancy. A court will consider evidence presented to rebut the presumption: for example, evidence showing that the grantor, the testator, or the new co-owners had confused joint tenancy with tenancy in common.

Rights and Duties of Joint Tenants

Once co-owners manage to establish a joint tenancy, they have similar rights and duties as tenants in common: the right to contribution, the right to the products and rents from the property, and the duty to avoid waste. A joint tenant can also encumber his or her own interest without the others' consent. But in addition, joint tenants have a right that tenants in common don't have: the right of survivorship.

Right of Survivorship. As explained earlier, when a joint tenant dies, his or her interest in the joint tenancy property passes directly to the surviving joint tenants.

> **Example:** Kunz, Dodd, and King are joint tenants. Because of the unity of interest rule, each has an undivided ⅓ interest in the joint tenancy property.
> When King dies, Dodd and Kunz still own the property as joint tenants, but now each has an undivided ½ interest, since they automatically acquired King's interest.

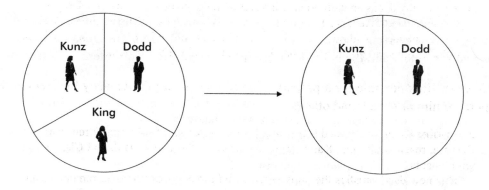

A joint tenancy interest cannot be willed or inherited, because it no longer belongs to the joint tenant at the moment of his or her death. As a result, joint tenancy property does not need to go through the probate process. This can spare the surviving joint tenants considerable expense and delay. However, joint tenancy property doesn't escape federal estate taxes. The deceased joint tenant's interest is treated as part of his or her estate for federal estate tax purposes.

The surviving joint tenants take the interest free and clear of any liens. The deceased joint tenant's deed of trust, judgment lien, or other debts are extinguished on his or her death. (In contrast, when a tenant in common dies, his or her heir takes the property interest subject to any existing liens and debts.)

Because a lien against one joint tenant's interest is so easily lost, few creditors are willing to accept such an interest as security. But a lien against the entire property—a deed of trust signed by all the joint tenants, for example—is not lost if one or more of the joint tenants dies.

Making the Title Marketable. Although surviving joint tenants acquire the deceased joint tenant's interest automatically at the moment of death, they must take steps to clear their title.

This can be accomplished by recording proof of the death, such as a court decree or a certified copy of the death certificate. The survivors should also record a sworn statement (an affidavit) that identifies the deceased as one of the property's joint tenants and identifies themselves as the surviving joint tenants. In addition, they should record a certificate of inheritance tax release.

Until these steps have been taken, the surviving joint tenants' title is not **marketable**. That means the public record presents some question about the validity of their title.

A title company will refuse to insure a title unless it is marketable. Here again, however, a real estate agent can't rely absolutely on the title company. The agent needs to know the rules and double check to make sure they've been followed. When surviving joint tenants sell property, the buyer should not go through with the transaction until the proof of death, affidavit, and tax release have all been recorded.

Simultaneous Death. If all the joint tenants die at once, each tenant's interest in the joint tenancy property passes according to his or her will. Each joint tenant's interest is probated separately and the heirs of each joint tenant receive their interests as tenants in common.

> **Example:** Debra and Tim own property as joint tenants. They are killed at virtually the same moment when an earthquake hits their house.
> Debra's undivided ½ interest in the property passes to her heirs, Samuel and Zeke, by intestate succession. Tim had written a will leaving all his property to his friend Cliff, so Cliff takes Tim's undivided ½ interest in the joint tenant property.
> After the probate process is completed, Samuel, Zeke, and Cliff are tenants in common. Samuel and Zeke each have an undivided ¼ interest, and Cliff has an undivided ½ interest.

Terminating a Joint Tenancy

Partition. Just like tenants in common, joint tenants can agree to partition their property, or one joint tenant can bring suit for judicial partition. Either way, by breaking the unity of possession, partition eliminates the right of survivorship and ends the co-ownership.

Merely filing a partition action does not terminate the joint tenancy; it ends only when the court's partition judgment is entered. Thus, if one of the joint tenants dies during the trial, the right of survivorship is still effective.

Severance. A joint tenancy is also terminated when it is **severed**, which can occur in a number of different ways, including transfer, declaration, and agreement. Severance ends the joint tenancy and eliminates the right of survivorship, but unlike partition, it does not terminate the co-ownership. Instead, severance changes a joint tenancy into a tenancy in common or community property.

Each joint tenant has the power to sever the joint tenancy by transferring his or her interest. A transfer severs a joint tenancy by breaking the unities of time and title.

> **Example:** Adams and Buzzell own some land as joint tenants. Buzzell sells her undivided ½ interest in the property to Wall. Now Adams and Wall each own an undivided ½ interest, but they are tenants in common, not joint tenants.

An involuntary transfer of a joint tenant's interest also severs the joint tenancy. This includes transfers due to bankruptcy or foreclosure.

A transfer (either voluntary or involuntary) severs the joint tenancy only in regard to the transferred interest. When there are just two joint tenants, that ends the joint tenancy altogether. When there are more than two joint tenants, however, the co-owners who did not transfer their interests remain joint tenants in relation to one another.

> **Example:** Kennedy, Jordan, and Chin are joint tenants. Kennedy deeds her interest to her friend, Peabody. That severs the joint tenancy as far as Kennedy's undivided ⅓ interest is concerned, so Peabody is not a joint tenant. Peabody is a tenant in common in relation to Jordan and Chin. But Jordan and Chin are still joint tenants in relation to one another.
>
> If Peabody were to die, her interest would pass to her heirs, since the right of survivorship does not apply to her.
>
> But if Jordan dies, Chin (rather than Jordan's heirs) acquires Jordan's interest, because the right of survivorship was still effective between Jordan and Chin. On Jordan's death, Chin has an undivided ⅔ interest, and Peabody still has an undivided ⅓ interest. Chin and Peabody are tenants in common.

Historically, the law did not allow a person to deed property to him or herself. So the severing joint tenant had to deed his or her interest to an intermediate called a **strawman**. Like any other transfer, this severed the joint tenancy. The strawman would then deed the property back to the former joint tenant, who would take title as a tenant in common.

In Washington (and most other states), this straw transaction is no longer necessary. A joint tenant may sever the joint tenancy simply by deeding his or her interest in the property to him or herself.

Case Example:

Mr. and Mrs. Riddle owned some real property as joint tenants. Mrs. Riddle retained an attorney to plan her estate. The attorney explained to her that the joint tenancy property would go to her husband upon her death.

Mrs. Riddle wanted to terminate the joint tenancy so she could dispose of the property by will. The attorney prepared a deed by which Mrs. Riddle granted her ½ interest in the property to herself. He also helped Mrs. Riddle write a will leaving her ½ interest to someone other than her husband. Mrs. Riddle died a few weeks after executing these documents.

When he discovered what his wife had done, Mr. Riddle sued Mrs. Riddle's estate. Following an established precedent, the trial court held that Mrs. Riddle's deed to herself had not severed the joint tenancy. By right of survivorship, Mr. Riddle now owned the entire property in severalty.

But this decision was reversed on appeal. Overruling the precedent, the appellate court held that the deed had severed the joint tenancy. Mrs. Riddle's ½ interest passed according to her will, not by the right of survivorship. *Riddle v. Harmon*, 102 Cal. App. 3d 524 (1980).

Transferring the property is not the only way to sever a joint tenancy. One of the co-owners can simply declare in writing that the joint tenancy is severed. And executing any written instrument that shows an intention to sever the joint tenancy also may be held to sever it.

Example: Kunz and Lambert own a house as joint tenants. They enter a written agreement stating that Lambert is to have the right to will his interest in the property to his heirs.

This agreement suggests an intention to sever the joint tenancy, since the right of survivorship is a basic characteristic of a joint tenancy. For that reason, a court would probably hold that the agreement caused a severance.

In this example, it is the written document that caused the severance, because it was evidence of an intention to sever. Note that a joint tenant's unilateral attempt to will the joint tenancy property will not automatically cause a severance (although it may be used as evidence of an intent to sever).

Recording requirement. Unless all the joint tenants have agreed to the severance, a deed, declaration, or other document severing the joint tenancy must be recorded to be effective. If the severance document has not yet been recorded and the severing joint tenant dies, the property will still pass to the surviving joint tenants as required by the right of survivorship.

Mutual consent agreement. Joint tenants may agree among themselves that their joint tenancy can only be severed by mutual consent, and not by the unilateral action of one tenant. If one joint tenant later deeds his or her interest to someone else, the transfer will not be effective, and the joint tenancy won't be severed.

> **Example:** Ramsey and Pomerenke agree that their joint tenancy can be severed only by mutual consent. Later Ramsey deeds his undivided ½ interest to Thorne. Because of the mutual consent agreement, the deed to Thorne is invalid, and the joint tenancy is not severed.

There are two important exceptions to this rule. First, if Thorne was a good faith purchaser, received the interest in exchange for value, and was not aware of the mutual consent agreement, the deed is valid and the joint tenancy is broken.

Second, if one joint tenant murders another joint tenant, the joint tenancy is severed. This prevents the murderer from gaining the victim's interest in the property through the right of survivorship. The rule applies to voluntary manslaughter (killing under extreme provocation) as well as to premeditated murder.

Advantages and Disadvantages of Joint Tenancy

Co-owners who take title as joint tenants usually choose to do so to avoid probate, and to enable the surviving tenant to take the property free of the other's liens and debts. These are substantial advantages, if in fact one of the parties dies during the period of co-ownership.

But the right of survivorship is very easily lost through severance. Although a severance document must be recorded to be effective, a co-owner who has no reason to suspect that the joint tenancy has been severed is not likely to check the public record. He or she may be in for a shock if the other co-owner dies and the deceased's interest in the property becomes part of the deceased's estate.

As mentioned above, co-owners can prevent this kind of surprise by agreeing that their joint tenancy cannot be severed except by mutual consent. But that arrangement can create the opposite problem, making it difficult to get out of the joint tenancy. If one of the joint tenants is unwilling to consent to a severance, the others must file a partition action. Like any lawsuit, a partition action can be expensive, time-consuming, and stressful.

Husband and Wife Choosing Co-ownership

A husband and wife may share title to property as joint tenants or as tenants in common, rather than holding it as community property. For example, a married couple may choose to own their home in joint tenancy: that way, if one spouse dies, his or her interest is automatically transferred to the other spouse, without having to wait for probate to be completed.

However, in Washington, there is a very strong presumption in favor of community property. There must be conclusive evidence showing that a couple understood the various forms

Fig. 4.4 Characteristics of co-ownership

	Joint Tenancy	Tenancy in Common	Community Property
Creation presumed	No	Yes	Yes
Equal right to possession	Yes	Yes	Yes
Equal interests	Yes	No	Yes
Right of survivorship	Yes	No	No
Each co-owner can convey undivided interest	Yes	Yes	No
Each co-owner can will undivided interest	No	Yes	Yes

of ownership and specifically wanted a form other than community property. Otherwise, the court will presume that the property is community property.

Statutory law provides that property co-owned by a husband and wife is presumed to be community property, even if the title to the property states that it is owned in joint tenancy. If a husband and wife want to own property as joint tenants, they must take other steps (such as stating in the deed that the property is not intended to be community property) to be sure that the presumption of community property can be refuted.

In dissolution proceedings, real estate held in joint tenancy is presumed to be community property, regardless of what the deed says. The spouse who objects to this classification must present evidence to rebut the presumption, showing that the couple truly intended a joint tenancy and not community property.

A joint tenancy between husband and wife is not severed by dissolution of the marriage, and the court does not have the power to award joint tenancy property in the property settlement.

When a spouse dies, his or her interest in property held in joint tenancy with the other spouse vests automatically in the survivor. But the heirs and devisees of the deceased spouse may try to establish that it really was community property, rather than a joint tenancy.

Example: The deed to Rick and Samantha's home says, "Rick and Samantha, in joint tenancy." Rick dies, and his will provides that his undivided ½ interest in the home goes to Deborah, his daughter by a previous marriage.

If the home was truly owned in joint tenancy, Rick's interest in it could not be willed. The right of survivorship would automatically vest Rick's interest in Samantha. Rick's attempt to will his interest to Deborah would not sever the joint tenancy.

But Deborah wants to establish that the home was really held as community property, not in joint tenancy. In the probate court, she may argue that Rick and Samantha didn't really understand what a joint tenancy was, and didn't intend to create one. Deborah can use her father's attempt to will his interest to her as evidence that there wasn't a joint tenancy, as well as the absence of language in the deed stating that the property should not be considered community property.

If Deborah succeeds in proving that the home was community property, the court will award her Rick's undivided ½ interest, in accordance with his will. Deborah and Samantha would then own the home as tenants in common. (And then, because of hard feelings generated by the lawsuit, either Deborah or Samantha would probably bring a partition action to end the co-ownership.)

Ownership by Associations

The second aspect of real property co-ownership is ownership by associations—businesses, nonprofit groups, and other organizations—rather than individuals. Depending on its form, an association may be a legal entity separate from its individual members or owners.

Title to property can be held in an association's name. Ownership by associations overlaps with the different forms of co-ownership discussed in the first part of the chapter. For example, a business organization may hold property in severalty, or it may be a tenant in common with other organizations or individuals.

A business organization generally can't be a joint tenant, however, since the right of survivorship is the key trait of a joint tenancy. Artificial entities such as corporations potentially have perpetual existence, which would prevent a joint tenant from acquiring any genuine survivorship right.

A real estate agent should understand when and how an association can hold title to real property. Most importantly, he or she needs to know who can sign (and who must sign) on behalf of an association to enter into contracts and transfer property.

Corporations

The most sophisticated form of association is the **corporation**. The ownership interests in a corporation are divided into **shares**. The corporation is owned by **stockholders** or **shareholders**, individuals who purchase shares in the company as an investment. The money invested provides the corporation with operating capital.

A corporation may have only a few shareholders, or it may have hundreds. But the corporation is legally a separate entity from its shareholders. The law treats it as an artificial individual: it can enter into contracts, own property, incur debts, sue and be sued. Because of this special legal status, corporations are closely regulated by state and federal laws.

Creation. To start a corporation in Washington, its organizers (the **incorporators**) file **articles of incorporation** with the secretary of state's office. The articles establish the corporation's name, list the name and address of each incorporator, explain the share structure, and include a general statement of purpose.

A **domestic corporation** is one organized in compliance with Washington law. A **foreign corporation** is one organized under the laws of another state, or in another country. A foreign corporation involved in Washington real estate transactions must be registered by the secretary of state to do business in Washington.

Management. A corporation's shareholders may have very little direct involvement in its management. They receive an annual report and may inspect the corporate records. They may also attend an annual meeting and vote on some major issues.

The real power behind a corporation is its **board of directors**. The directors govern the corporation's affairs in accordance with its bylaws. They appoint corporate **officers**—the president or chief executive officer (CEO), vice president, treasurer, and corporate secretary—who run the business on a day-to-day basis.

The officers are not automatically authorized to convey or encumber the corporation's real property. These actions must be expressly authorized by a resolution of the board. A title company will usually require proof of the authorization before insuring a transaction.

Liability. The primary advantage of the corporate form of organization is that shareholders are protected from liability for the corporation's debts.

> **Example:** A few years ago, Mendez spent $3,000 on stock in the ABC Corporation. His shares are now worth $3,600.
>
> The ABC Corporation is found liable for an injury caused by a defective product it manufactured, and a $250,000 judgment is entered against the corporation. The judgment creditor can file a lien against the corporation's assets if the judgment is not paid.
>
> However, the creditor cannot proceed against Mendez to collect the judgment. His home, bank accounts, and other property are protected from liability, because the corporation is a separate legal entity. Mendez may lose his $3,600 investment if the corporation goes out of business because of the judgment, but that is the extent of his liability.

In theory, all stockholders have this protection from liability. But in fact, creditors often require the personal guaranties of the major stockholders before they will make large loans to or enter into a lease with a corporation.

Nonprofit Corporations. Until now, our discussion of corporations has been limited to for-profit corporations—businesses organized for the purpose of generating a profit that is distributed to its shareholders. Now let's take a moment to discuss **nonprofit corporations,** which are subject to some different rules.

Nonprofit corporations may be organized for charitable, political, social, religious, or professional purposes. Examples of nonprofit corporations include homeowners associations, social clubs, charities, and service organizations. Note that labor unions and cooperative organizations are excluded from nonprofit corporation status, as are organizations subject to state banking or insurance laws.

In contrast to a for-profit corporation, a nonprofit corporation must be structured so that it shares neither ownership nor revenues with individuals or other corporations. So a nonprofit corporation cannot issue stock or distribute income to its members, directors, or officers. It is also prohibited from lending money or credit to directors or officers.

However, nonprofit corporations are permitted to earn revenues, and may pay reasonable compensation to or confer benefits on members, directors, or officers for services rendered. And a nonprofit corporation may also make distributions to its members upon final liquidation of the corporation and its assets.

General Partnerships

A **general partnership** is simply an association of two or more individuals as co-owners of a business run for profit. It doesn't have the formal structure of a corporation or other business organization. Although a partnership can own property, for most other purposes the law does not recognize a general partnership as an entity independent from its members.

Creation. General partnerships are usually created by express agreement (either oral or written). In Washington, they can also be created by implied agreement, based on the actions of the parties. However, having a common interest in a business transaction doesn't automatically create a partnership. The parties must intend to carry on a definite, ongoing business as co-owners, sharing the management and profits. When that is their intention, they have a partnership, whether they call it that or not.

In Washington, general partners are not required to file any paperwork to form a partnership. However, an affidavit of partnership may be filed in the county recorder's office. Although this is not a legal requirement, some lenders or title insurance companies may require such a filing before participating in any transactions with the partnership.

Management and Profits. A general partnership agreement can provide for almost any allocation of rights and duties between the partners. If the agreement doesn't address an issue (or if it is an implied agreement), then the allocation will be according to statute. The rules outlined here are the statutory rules; most of them can be altered in a partnership agreement.

All general partners have an equal voice in the management and control of the business. The partnership is legally bound by the actions of one partner, as long as the partner is acting within the scope of his or her authority. (Each partner is an agent and a fiduciary of the partnership, so the agency rules explained in Chapters 5 apply.)

Unless otherwise agreed, the partners all share in the profits equally, even if their contributions to the business are unequal. In fact, some partners may only contribute skill or labor, without making any capital contributions at all. Partners usually divide losses in the same way they share profits.

Fig. 4.5 Partnership liability

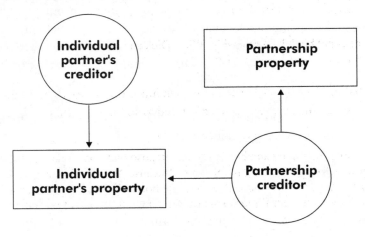

Liability. General partners have unlimited liability for the acts of the partnership. Each partner can be made to pay the full amount of any partnership debts out of his or her own pocket.

> **Example:** Power, Quen, and Roberts own the PQR Company, a general partnership. Both the PQR Company and the individual partners are sued for breach of a construction contract, and a judgment is entered against them for $95,000. Neither the individual partners nor the PQR Company pay the judgment, so the judgment creditor claims a lien against Power's home. Power ends up paying the entire $95,000 to protect his home from foreclosure.

Power can then demand reimbursement from Quen and Roberts for their share of the judgment, and can sue them if they don't pay. This personal liability is the main disadvantage of a general partnership. It contrasts sharply with the protection enjoyed by a corporate shareholder.

Partnership Property. All property that general partners bring into the business at the outset, and all that they later acquire for the business, is **partnership property**. Anything purchased with partnership funds is presumed to be partnership property.

Real estate may be acquired in the partnership name. If title is acquired in the partnership name, it can be conveyed only in the partnership name. Note that partnership property can be encumbered or conveyed in the name of the partnership with the signature of any authorized partner. When there are several partners and they live in different cities, this can save a lot of time and expense.

Every partner is an agent of the partnership, and thus the acts of any partner will bind the partnership. However, a partner cannot bind the partnership by acts that exceed his or her authority if the third party knows that the partner is acting beyond his or her authority.

Example: Tom, Dick, and Harry own TDH Enterprises, a general partnership. The partnership owns some land, but the title to the land is in Tom's name. Tom sells the land to his brother. Tom and his brother are trying to cheat the partnership out of the property. They both know that the land is actually partnership property and that Dick and Harry would not approve of the sale.

The sale does not bind the partnership. When Dick and Harry find out about the sale, they can recover the land from Tom's brother.

On the other hand, if a partner conveys partnership property to a good faith purchaser who doesn't realize that the partner is not authorized to sell it, the partnership can't recover the property.

Example: Using the same example as above, suppose that Tom sells the land to Arthur, who is an innocent, good faith purchaser. Because Arthur believes that Tom has authority to sell the land, the partnership will be bound by the sale. Dick and Harry can sue Tom for violating his duties to the partnership, but they can't get the land back from Arthur.

Unless otherwise agreed, each partner has a right to possess all partnership property for partnership purposes. A partner has no right to possess partnership property for any other purpose, except with the consent of the other partners.

A partner can't transfer his or her interest in partnership property to someone outside the partnership, except when all of the partners assign the whole property. But (unless otherwise agreed) one partner may assign his or her interest in the partnership itself to an outsider. That gives the assignee a right to share in the partnership's profits. It does not make the assignee a partner, however, or give him or her the right to interfere in the management of the business.

Also, if a judgment is entered against a partner personally, his or her interest in the partnership property cannot be used to enforce the judgment.

Example: Abernathy and Bowen own A&B Company, a general partnership. They also own a building as partnership property.

Bowen is involved in an automobile accident, and a judgment is entered against her. The judgment creditor cannot claim a lien against A&B Company's building. (The creditor could claim a lien if the judgment were against the partnership rather than Bowen.) But Bowen's interest in the partnership itself can be reached by her judgment creditor: the creditor can garnish Bowen's share of the profits.

When a partner dies, his or her interest in partnership property vests in the surviving partners. The deceased partner's estate has a right to an accounting and a share of the partnership profits, but it does not have an interest in the partnership property.

Limited Partnerships

A **limited partnership**, like a general partnership, is an association of two or more persons as co-owners of a business. A limited partnership has one or more general partners, plus one or more limited partners. The rights and duties of general partners in a limited partnership are the same as in a general partnership. The limited partners, however, have limited liability and a limited role in management.

Think of a limited partnership as a compromise between a general partnership and a corporation. Limited partners cannot participate in the management of the business to the extent that general partners do, although they may have a greater role than corporate shareholders. Like corporate shareholders, limited partners are protected from the business's debts. As a result, limited partnerships are more strictly regulated than general partnerships.

A limited partnership must file a certificate of limited partnership at the office of the secretary of state. This form includes the name and address of all general partners. It must also include an address where the names and addresses of all limited partners may be found. The names and addresses of the limited partners do not have to be filed with the secretary of state, but they must be available for inspection at the address listed in the form. If the certificate of limited partnership is not filed, or the names and addresses are not available as required, all of the partners may be considered general partners.

A limited partner has no control over partnership property, which is controlled solely by the general partners.

Limited Liability Companies

The **limited liability company (LLC)** is a relatively new type of business entity that has quickly gained popularity across the country. Owners and investors, especially real estate owners and investors, choose the limited liability company form of business because of its many advantages. First, there is great flexibility in structuring the management of a limited liability company. Second, members of an LLC are subject only to limited liability for the company's obligations. And last, an LLC can be set up so that it is taxed as a partnership. Limited liability companies in Washington are governed by the state Limited Liability Company Act.

Creation. An LLC is created when an LLC agreement is drawn up and a certificate of formation is filed with the state. In the LLC agreement, members can choose virtually any manner of allocating income, losses, or appreciation among themselves. Once the LLC is created, initial and annual reports must be filed with the state and an annual fee must be paid.

Management. LLCs have the flexibility of a general partnership when it comes to managing the business. Management of the LLC is placed in the hands of its members, unless the certificate of formation assigns management to one or more managers.

In a **member-managed** limited liability company, every member has agency authority; that is, all managing members can bind the LLC with their actions. Unless the LLC agreement provides otherwise, all decisions are made by the majority of LLC members. However, the LLC agreement may create a structure in which certain persons or classes of members have different management powers, duties, and voting rights.

In a **manager-managed** limited liability company, ordinary members do not act as agents of the LLC. Unless the LLC agreement provides otherwise, designated managers may be appointed or removed by a majority of the members and do not need to be members of the LLC.

Liability. An attractive aspect of the LLC form is that its members enjoy limited liability like that of corporation shareholders or limited partners. However, members and managers will be liable for any acts or omissions except those constituting gross negligence, intentional misconduct, or a knowing violation of the law.

Taxation. A major disadvantage to the corporate form of ownership is the double taxation imposed on corporations and their stockholders. Income is first taxable at the corporate level, and is then taxable at the stockholder level when it is distributed as dividends. Income earned by an LLC, on the other hand, is taxed at only one level—the member level. LLC income is taxed as the personal income of each member, in the same manner as partnership income.

As you can see, LLCs offer a unique combination of advantages. By using this form of business entity, an owner can take advantage of the best attributes of both a corporation and a partnership.

Joint Ventures

A **joint venture** is similar to a partnership, but is formed for a single transaction or a related series of transactions, not as an ongoing business. There are no formal requirements for the creation of a joint venture. The parties simply agree to work together on a project and to share the profits or losses.

A joint venture is not an entity separate from its individual members; however, title to property can be held in the joint venture's name.

Syndicates

A **syndicate** is not a recognized legal entity. Like "company," the term "syndicate" can be used to refer to virtually any business organization. The XYZ Syndicate might be a corporation, general partnership, limited partnership, or trust, and it would hold title accordingly.

Conclusion

Ownership of real property by married persons is subject to community property laws in Washington. There is a very strong presumption in favor of community property. Property is presumed to belong to the marital community unless specific evidence shows otherwise. Certain transactions concerning community property require the consent and signature of both spouses. This requirement is especially significant to a real estate agent, since neither spouse can transfer or encumber community real property without the other spouse joining in the transaction.

Co-ownership of property also includes tenancy in common and joint tenancy. The biggest difference between tenancy in common and joint tenancy is the right of survivorship enjoyed by joint tenants.

Many legal presumptions exist in the area of co-ownership. If you want a form of ownership that differs from the applicable presumptions, you must clearly and specifically set out your wishes in writing.

Real estate agents also need to be familiar with property ownerships by associations such as corporations, partnerships, and limited liability companies. Each has different characteristics in terms of organizational structure, personal liability, and taxation.

Case Problem

The following is a hypothetical case problem. Most of the facts are taken from a real case. Make a decision on the issues presented and then check to see if your answer matches the decision reached by the court.

The Facts

Edward and Margaret were married and had signed a community property agreement. This agreement provided that:

1. all separate property owned by either spouse was converted to community property;
2. all property acquired later would be community property; and
3. upon the death of one spouse, all community property would vest in the survivor.

Edward's father transferred some property to Edward and his brother Richard as a gift. The deed expressly provided that the brothers took title as joint tenants.

Upon Edward's death, a dispute arose between Richard and Margaret. Richard claimed that the property was a gift in joint tenancy, and that upon Edward's death the property would belong to Richard by the right of survivorship.

Margaret claimed that because of the community property agreement, half of the property belonged to her.

The Questions

How will the court decide who gets the property? Was it separate property or community property? Which takes precedence, the joint tenancy right of survivorship, or the community property agreement? If it is community property, how much of the property would Margaret get?

The Answer

The court held that because of the community property agreement, the joint tenancy interest conveyed to Edward became community property at the time of the conveyance. It was never Edward's separate property because the community property agreement provided that all property then owned or later acquired would be community property. The joint tenancy was actually created not between Richard and Edward individually, but between Richard and the community of Edward and Margaret.

The court also stated that it is the policy of the law to favor community property and disfavor joint tenancies, so the community property agreement controlled.

Under the community property agreement, upon Edward's death, Margaret acquired all the community property. Therefore Richard retained his half of the joint tenancy property and Margaret became sole owner of the other half.

The conversion of Margaret's share of the community property into her separate property acted to sever the joint tenancy. Richard and Margaret now hold as tenants in common, each holding an undivided one-half interest in the whole. *Lyon v. Lyon*, 100 Wn.2d 409, 670 P.2d 272 (1983).

Summary

- All property owned by a married couple in Washington is either the separate property of one spouse or the community property of both. Husband and wife have equal control over the community property. The joinder requirement prevents the transfer or encumbrance of community real property without the signature of both spouses. An unauthorized transfer is voidable by the nonconsenting spouse. Community property is not subject to partition.

- A tenancy in common is the most basic form of co-ownership. Tenants in common may have unequal interests, their interests are undivided, and they share possession of the whole property. A tenant in common's interest can be freely transferred or willed. A tenancy in common may be terminated by partition, either voluntarily or by court order.

- A joint tenancy requires the four unities (time, title, interest, and possession). The key characteristic of joint tenancy is the right of survivorship. It prevents a joint tenant from willing his or her interest, but makes probate of the property unnecessary. The transfer of a joint tenant's interest severs the joint tenancy by breaking the unities of time and title. Severance does not terminate the co-ownership, but changes it to tenancy in common or community property.

- Title to real property can be held by associations of individuals: corporations, general partnerships, limited partnerships, or limited liability companies. Each form of organization has advantages and disadvantages in terms of management, taxation, regulation, and liability.

- General partners have equal rights of possession and control of partnership property. One partner cannot transfer or encumber his or her undivided interest in the property separately from the other partners' interests.

- The limited liability company has become a popular form of business entity because it combines the tax benefits of a partnership with the limited personal liability of a corporation.

Checklist of Problem Areas

Real Estate Licensee's Checklist

❑ Have both husband and wife signed the listing agreement and the purchase and sale agreement?

❑ What kind of interest does the seller have in the property? Is it owned in severalty, or is the seller a tenant in common or joint tenant?

❑ If the seller is a tenant in common or a joint tenant, are the other owners aware of the sale? Will the buyer be an owner in severalty or will he or she be a co-owner? Is the buyer aware of his or her status?

Seller's Checklist

❑ Are you selling separate or community property? If it is community property, has your spouse agreed to the sale and signed the listing and purchase and sale agreement?

❑ If you are a tenant in common or a joint tenant, you may sell your interest in the property without your co-tenants' consent. However, you may sell only your portion, not the entire property.

❑ If you hold property as a joint tenant, selling your interest alone will sever the joint tenancy. Severing changes a joint tenancy into a tenancy in common. Does the buyer realize that he or she is purchasing only an undivided interest in the property?

❑ If you hold property as a joint tenant, have you signed any kind of agreement specifying that the property may only be severed by mutual consent?

Buyer's Checklist

❑ Are you purchasing property as your separate property or as community property? If the property will be community property, has your spouse signed the purchase and sale agreement? If the property will be separate property, is this clearly specified and is the property purchased with your separate funds?

❑ Will you hold ownership in severalty or as a tenant in common or joint tenant? If you're attempting to create a joint tenancy, has the four unities requirement been met?

Chapter Quiz

1. Anderson and Baker own a house in Seattle. Anderson has an undivided ¾ interest in the property and Baker has an undivided ¼ interest. They hold the property as:

   a. tenants in common
   b. joint tenants
   c. tenants by the entirety
   d. community property

2. In Washington, a married person cannot hold title to real property:

   a. as his or her separate property
   b. in a partnership
   c. as a tenant by the entirety
   d. as a joint tenant

3. When title to property is held in severalty:

   a. the property cannot be transferred or encumbered without the consent of a majority of the co-owners
   b. the property is owned by one individual
   c. none of the owners can be a corporation
   d. the property cannot be willed

4. The only one of the four unities required for a tenancy in common is the unity of:

   a. time
   b. title
   c. interest
   d. possession

5. When Schultz and White took title to the house as joint tenants, they agreed that only White would live there. What effect did this agreement have on the joint tenancy?

   a. It severed the joint tenancy; unity of possession is essential
   b. It did not sever the joint tenancy if Schultz and White stated that they did not intend to sever it
   c. It did not sever the joint tenancy as long as Schultz is charging White rent
   d. It severed the joint tenancy by partitioning the property

6. Adams, Kester, and Calhoun own some land as tenants in common. Adams and Kester each have an undivided ¼ interest, and Calhoun has an undivided ½ interest. Calhoun wills all his property to Davis. When Calhoun dies, who owns the land?

   a. Adams and Kester each have an undivided ½ interest
   b. Adams and Kester each have an undivided ¾ interest
   c. Adams and Kester each have an undivided ¼ interest, and Davis has an undivided ½ interest
   d. Adams, Kester, and Davis each have an undivided ⅓ interest

7. Ayers, Burns, and Cervas own some land as joint tenants. When Cervas dies, Ayers and Burns each have a ½ undivided interest, because of:

   a. the right of survivorship
   b. unity of possession
   c. the rules of intestate succession
   d. the doctrine of severalty

8. Alton, Barrit, and Carter own a house as joint tenants. Barrit mortgages her interest in the property. Which of the following is true?

    a. If Barrit defaults on her mortgage, the lender can foreclose on the entire property
    b. The mortgage is void
    c. The mortgage severs the joint tenancy
    d. If Barrit dies, the lender loses its lien against the property

9. Ames, Barry, and Carlson own some land as joint tenants. Carlson sells his interest in the property to Delaney. Which of the following is true?

    a. Ames and Barry each hold an undivided ⅓ interest as joint tenants, and Delaney holds an undivided ⅓ interest as a tenant in common
    b. Ames and Barry each hold an undivided ¼ interest as joint tenants, and Delaney holds an undivided ½ interest as a tenant in common
    c. Ames, Barry, and Delaney each hold an undivided ⅓ interest as joint tenants
    d. Ames, Barry, and Delaney each hold a ⅓ interest in severalty

10. A married couple might choose to hold real property in joint tenancy rather than as community property in order to:

    a. avoid paying property taxes
    b. avoid the probate process
    c. prevent one spouse from conveying his or her interest in the property without the other's consent
    d. prevent a mortgage foreclosure

11. Harry and Wilma are a married couple; they own some land as community property. Harry wills all his property to Annette. When Harry dies, who owns the land?

    a. Wilma owns the land in severalty
    b. Wilma has an undivided ⅔ interest and Annette has an undivided ⅓ interest
    c. Wilma and Annette each have an undivided ½ interest
    d. Wilma, Annette, and Harry's minor child each have an undivided ⅓ interest

12. Which of these is a spouse's separate property?

    a. A house he or she bought before the marriage
    b. A house purchased during the marriage using his or her own earnings as a downpayment
    c. A house he or she received during the marriage in exchange for services rendered to a family member
    d. None of the above; all real property owned by a married person is community property

13. Fong did not consent to any of these transactions involving community property. He can void the transfer or encumbrance in each case except one. Which one?

    a. His wife sold the couple's boat to a neighbor
    b. His wife gave the couple's boat to a neighbor
    c. His wife sold the couple's vacant lot to her cousin
    d. His wife mortgaged the couple's residence

14. The ZAP Corporation owns some land in severalty. In order to sell the land, who must sign the sale documents?

    a. The CEO and at least one member of the board of directors
    b. A majority of the directors
    c. A majority of the stockholders
    d. Corporate officers authorized to sell it by a resolution of the board of directors

15. The LMNOP company is a general partnership. Partnership funds were used to purchase a building for the company's offices. The building is partnership property:

    a. only if the deed lists all the partners and expressly states that they are tenants in partnership
    b. even though the title is in one partner's name alone
    c. only if the title is in the partnership's name
    d. as long as none of the partners is a married person

5 Introduction to Agency

Outline

I. Basic Agency Definitions
II. Agency Authority
   A. Types of agents
   B. Types of authority
   C. Agency liability issues
III. Creating an Agency Relationship
   A. Express agreement
   B. Ratification
   C. Estoppel
   D. Implication
   E. Creating a real estate agency
IV. Terminating the Agency Relationship
   A. Termination by operation of law
   B. Termination by action of the parties
   C. Terminating a real estate agency
V. Real Estate Agency Relationships
   A. Agency relationships: historical background
   B. Types of real estate agency relationships
      1. seller agency
      2. buyer agency
      3. dual agency
      4. non-agency
   C. Employee vs. independent contractor
      1. relationship between broker and principal
      2. relationship between salesperson and broker

Key Terms

- agent
- principal
- subagent
- universal agent
- general agent
- special agent
- actual authority

- express authority
- implied authority
- apparent authority
- ostensible agency
- vicarious liability
- imputed knowledge
- ratification

- agency by estoppel
- renunciation
- revocation
- implication
- independent contractor
- retainer
- in-house transaction

Chapter Overview

The term "real estate agent" is commonly used, but few people stop to think about what the "agent" part really means. This chapter explains what an agent is, discusses how an agency relationship is created and terminated, and describes the specific agency relationships that exist in the real estate business.

Rules defining and governing agency relationships are found in general agency law, a body of law that applies to agency relationships in nearly any context, such as between lawyer and client, or between trustee and beneficiary. Since 1997, real estate agency relationships have also been subject to Washington's real estate agency statute: the Real Estate Brokerage Relationships Act. This statute is based on general agency law, but contains important changes that address agency issues that are specific to the real estate field.

Basic Agency Definitions

An **agent** is someone who is authorized to represent or act for someone else—the **principal**—in dealings with other parties. In the real estate business, the agent is the real estate broker and the principal may be either the property seller or the buyer. Persons outside the agency relationship who deal with the principal through the agent are called **third parties**.

A **subagent** is an agent (or representative) of the agent. For example, real estate brokers often hire salespeople to perform functions such as acquiring listings and marketing properties. A salesperson who takes a listing would be an agent of the broker and a subagent of the principal (the seller).

Agency Authority

In an agency relationship, the agent receives authority from the principal to perform certain actions, and the agent also takes on certain duties and responsibilities. The amount and type of authority determines what type of agency relationship is created, and what liability the agency assumes. Note that an agent may be liable for any harm caused by actions that exceed the authority granted by the principal.

Types of Agents

A **universal agent** is authorized by the principal to do everything that can be done by a lawfully designated representative. This type of agent has the highest degree of authority.

> **Example:** A guardian charged with the care of someone who is mentally incompetent to manage his own affairs is a universal agent.

A **general agent** has authority to handle all matters for the principal in certain specified areas.

> **Example:** A property manager is a general agent if she has the authority to market and maintain the property, hire and fire maintenance personnel, enter lease agreements on the owner's behalf, and take full responsibility for managing property on behalf of the owner.

A **special agent** has limited authority to do a specific thing or conduct a specific transaction. Most real estate agents are special agents. Their authority is usually limited by the principal to a single function or transaction.

> **Example:** A seller hires a broker to find a buyer for a particular piece of property. The broker is authorized to negotiate with third parties—but not to sign a contract on the seller's behalf.

Types of Authority

There are two types of authority: actual and apparent.

Actual Authority. Authority specifically given by the principal is called **actual authority**. Actual authority may be either express or implied.

Express authority is specifically communicated by the principal to the agent, either orally or in writing. **Implied authority** is the authority necessary to carry out the duties expressly authorized by the principal. Implied authority does not have to be expressed, because it is required by the agent to fulfill his or her responsibilities.

> **Example:** A listing agreement gives a real estate agent express authority to find a ready, willing, and able buyer for a property. The agent is generally assumed to have the implied authority to do what is necessary to find that buyer. This includes activities

Fig 5.1 Types of Agency Authority

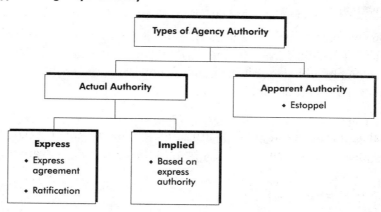

such as advertising, placing "for sale" signs on the property, showing the property, and negotiating and transmitting offers.

Apparent Authority. In contrast to actual authority, an agent may have only **apparent authority** to do something. This situation may occur when a person has no actual authority to act, but the principal's words or conduct lead a third party to believe that this person's actions are authorized. In other words, the principal negligently or deliberately allows it to appear that the person (the **apparent agent** or **ostensible agent**) has authority to act on behalf of the principal.

A principal will be bound by acts performed within the scope of an ostensible agent's apparent authority, as long as the principal was aware of the acts and made no effort to deny that they are authorized.

Agency Liability Issues

As we stated earlier, agency authority carries with it certain duties and responsibilities. If an agent fails to live up to those duties and responsibilities, he can be held liable for any harm he causes. Washington's real estate agency law significantly changed an agent's level of liability in two significant ways: regarding vicarious liability and regarding imputed knowledge.

Vicarious Liability. A **tort** is a negligent or intentional wrongful act that causes injury or financial harm to another person. Someone who commits a tort may be sued by the injured party and required to compensate her.

In some states a principal may be held liable for his agent's torts, under the legal theory of **vicarious liability**. But Washington's real estate agency statute eliminated most vicarious liability between a real estate agent and his principal. This means that a seller or buyer is generally not liable for an act, error, or omission by his broker, a salesperson working for another broker, or another subagent.

Exceptions. Two exceptions do exist to this exclusion from liability. A principal may be liable for her real estate agent's actions if:

1. the principal participated in or authorized the act, error or omission; or
2. the principal benefited from the act, error, or omission, and a court determines that it is highly probable that the injured party would be unable to enforce a judgment against the agent or subagent.

Likewise, an agent will not be held vicariously liable for the act, error, or omission of a subagent, unless the agent participated in or authorized the act, error, or omission. Note, however, that a broker may still be held liable for the actions of his affiliated licensees.

Imputed Knowledge. Previously, under general agency law, a principal was considered to have notice of any information that his agent had—even if the agent never actually told the principal. In other words, the agent's knowledge was automatically **imputed** to the principal. As a result, the principal could be held liable for failing to disclose a problem to a third party, even if the agent never informed the principal of the problem.

However, the real estate agency law eliminated the imputed knowledge rule. A principal in a real estate transaction is no longer automatically held to have notice of facts known by his real estate agent.

Creating an Agency Relationship

It is important for both the principal and the agent to understand how and when an agency relationship is created. Under general agency law, an agency relationship may originate in several different ways: express agreement, ratification, estoppel, and implication.

Express Agreement

Most agencies are created by **express agreement**: the principal appoints someone to act as her agent and the agent accepts. An express agency agreement may be written or oral.

Although agency relationships are usually created in writing, a written agreement is not required. An oral agreement will create an agency just as effectively. The agent will be held to the same degree of responsibility and must perform all the agency duties owed to the principal. If the agent is negligent or does not carry out the required duties, the principal may sue the agent for damages.

Ratification

Even without a specific understanding or agreement, an agency relationship may still be created. An agency is created by **ratification** when the principal gives approval after the fact to acts performed by:

- a person who is without authority to act for the principal, or
- an agent whose actions exceed the authority granted by the principal.

The principal may ratify unauthorized acts expressly. Alternatively, if the principal is aware of the acts, does nothing to stop them, and accepts the benefit of these acts, an agency relationship is created by ratification.

Estoppel

Estoppel is a legal doctrine under which a person is prevented from asserting rights that are inconsistent with previous representations or actions. A situation may occur where the principal has not authorized an agency, but the principal's acts or behavior mislead someone into believing that an agency existed. The principal's previous acts (conduct, words, or even silence in not disavowing the agency) prohibit him or her from denying the existence of an agency relationship. This is called an **agency by estoppel**.

Agency by estoppel protects innocent third parties who have reasonably assumed that a person acting like an agent was an agent. The principal is held responsible because he or she allowed such a belief, or failed to advise the third party that the agent was acting without authority.

It's important to note that the estoppel doctrine will not be used against a principal who has no knowledge of someone claiming agency. Note also that a third party has a duty to make a reasonable effort to discover the scope of the agent's authority. A principal won't be estopped from denying an agency relationship when a reasonable effort by the third party would have shown that the degree of agency claimed did not exist.

Implication

An agency may be created by **implication** when one person behaves toward another in a way that suggests or implies that he or she is acting as that other person's agent. If the other person reasonably believes an agency relationship exists, and the supposed agent fails to correct that impression, he or she may owe the other person agency duties.

Agency by implication resembles agency by estoppel, but a significant difference exists. An agency by estoppel requires the principal to acknowledge that an agency relationship exists, to protect the interests of a third party. An agency by implication requires the agent to acknowledge that an agency relationship exists, to protect the principal's interests.

Creating a Real Estate Agency

In Washington, the Real Estate Brokerage Relationships Act imposed new rules concerning how agency relationships are created in real estate transactions. Under this statute, an agency relationship between a real estate licensee and a client begins when the licensee undertakes to provide real estate services for the client. The agency relationship begins regardless of whether or not any fee has been paid to the agent.

An agency relationship with a seller typically begins with the execution of a written listing agreement. On the other hand, an agency relationship with a buyer begins automatically when a licensee performs real estate brokerage services for the buyer.

> **Example:** A prospective buyer visits a real estate brokerage and tells a salesperson that he's interested in buying a home. The salesperson asks the buyer about his price range and the type of house he's interested in. The buyer and salesperson then go look at some homes listed for sale that may fit the buyer's needs.
>
> Under the real estate agency statute, the salesperson and her broker have automatically become agents for the buyer, since the salesperson is performing brokerage services for the buyer.

There is an important exception to this rule concerning buyer agency. A licensee working with a buyer does not automatically become the buyer's agent if a written agreement exists to the contrary, such as a listing agreement with the seller, a written dual agency agreement with both parties, a written subagency agreement with the seller, or a written non-agency agreement.

Example: Returning to the previous scenario, suppose the salesperson shows the buyer one of her own listings. Because the brokerage already has a written agreement with the seller, the salesperson and broker won't be representing the buyer if she decides to buy this house. They will represent the seller.

Terminating the Agency Relationship

Now that you are familiar with how an agency is created, it is important to understand how and when an agency relationship will end. Once the agency is terminated, the agent is no longer authorized to represent the principal.

Under general agency law, an agency may be terminated either by operation of law or by the acts of the parties.

Termination by Operation of Law

An agency relationship may be terminated by operation of law. This means the agency will automatically end upon the occurrence of certain specified events. An agency is terminated by operation of law in the following situations:

- expiration of the agency term,
- fulfillment of the agency's purpose,
- death, incapacity, or bankruptcy of either party, and
- extinction of the subject matter.

Expiration of the Agency Term. If no specific termination date is included in the listing agreement, the listing is considered terminated after a "reasonable time." If a dispute arises over when the listing agreement expired, the court will determine what is considered reasonable under the circumstances of the particular case.

Fulfillment of Agency's Purpose. Perhaps the most common reason for termination is that the purpose of the agency has been accomplished.

> **Example:** A property owner hires a real estate broker to sell some property. Once the property is sold and all of the details addressed, the agency relationship terminates.

Death, Incapacity, or Bankruptcy. An agency will be terminated by the death or bankruptcy of either the agent or the principal. In addition, most states provide that the agency terminates if either party becomes mentally incompetent. Generally, the agent has no authority to act after either the death or incompetence of the principal, even if the agent is unaware of the principal's death or incompetence.

Extinction of Subject Matter. If the subject matter of an agency is extinguished, the agency automatically terminates. The subject matter of a real estate agency is the property in question—if it is extinguished (e.g., sold, condemned, or destroyed), the agency is terminated.

Termination by Action of the Parties

An agency may also be terminated through action of the parties, by:

- mutual agreement,
- renunciation by the agent, or
- revocation by the principal.

Mutual Agreement. An agency is a consensual relationship, which means that it is entered into by the consent of both parties. If both parties agree, the agency may be terminated by mutual agreement, with no liability or obligation to either party.

Renunciation. Because of the consensual nature of agency, each party in an agency relationship has the power to terminate the agency. The agent may **renounce** his or her agency at any time. However, if a contract exists and the agent renounces it, the agent may be liable to the principal for damages resulting from breach of the contract.

When a real estate agent signs a contract with a principal, he or she agrees to provide personal, professional skills. Since this is a personal services contract, the principal cannot demand specific performance as a remedy (see Chapter 7). A court cannot force a person to perform personal services, because that would violate the constitutional prohibition against involuntary servitude. Therefore, only monetary damages are awarded.

Revocation. A principal may **revoke** the grant of agency powers at any time by firing the agent. However, if revoking the agency breaches a contractual agreement, the principal may be liable for any damages suffered by the agent because of the breach.

> **Example:** Alan Bertoldo is planning to sell his house. He signs an exclusive listing agreement with broker Susan Yamamoto. In the meantime, he starts dating a real estate agent who convinces him to switch the listing to her brokerage company. Alan revokes his grant of agency to Susan and tells her that he is changing brokers.

Alan has the right to revoke the agency, but he is also liable for the consequences. He will probably be required to pay damages to Susan. He could end up having to pay the full commission amount to Susan because he breached the exclusive listing agreement. Alan's new agent may also be in trouble because of her actions. She interfered with another agent's exclusive listing, and convinced Alan to breach his agreement. (This type of problem is discussed in Chapter 7.)

An exception to the usual rules about revocation occurs when an agent has an interest in the property. When agency is coupled with an interest, the principal does not have the right to revoke the agency. Also, the death, incompetence, or bankruptcy of the principal does not terminate the agency.

Example: A broker loans funds to a contractor to complete the building of a home. In addition to agreeing to repay the loan, the contractor agrees to give the broker an exclusive right to sell the property when the home is completed. Before the home is sold, the contractor dies. The agency is not automatically terminated by the contractor's death, because the broker has an interest in the property.

Terminating a Real Estate Agency

Under Washington's Real Estate Brokerage Relationships Act, a real estate agency relationship ends when one of the following occurs:

1. Completion of performance by the licensee (the terms of the agency agreement are fulfilled).
2. Expiration of the agency term as agreed by the parties. (Note that an exclusive listing agreement should always specify a termination date. That is a legal requirement in some states, although it is not required in Washington.)
3. Termination of the relationship by mutual consent.
4. Notification from one party to the other that the agency is terminated.

Once an agency relationship has terminated, the agent can no longer represent the principal. However, under the agency statute, the agent still owes two duties to the principal even after the relationship has ended:

1. The agent must account for all money and property received during the relationship.
2. The agent must not disclose confidential information about the principal that was learned during the agency relationship.

Real Estate Agency Relationships

Washington's Real Estate Brokerage Relationships Act fundamentally changed how real estate agency relationships work. To better understand these relationships under the current law, we'll first take a look at how they worked under the old rules.

Agency Relationships: Historical Background

Previously, under general agency law, buyers and sellers in a transaction were often confused about which party each of the various real estate agents represented. In particular, buyers often believed that the agent they were working with was representing them, when in fact the agent was almost always representing the seller.

Unilateral Offer of Subagency. This confusion stemmed from a standard provision found in most listing agreements, called a "unilateral offer of subagency." This provision stated that any member of the multiple listing service who found a buyer for a listed property automatically represented the seller. In other words, the selling agent became a subagent of the seller.

This provision made it difficult to create a buyer agency. In order to represent a buyer in a particular sale, a licensee had to reject the offer of subagency and enter into a separate written agreement with the buyer. Thus, nearly all licensees represented the seller.

Inadvertent Dual Agency. Under the circumstances, it was easy for a buyer to assume—incorrectly—that the selling agent represented the buyer. After all, the selling agent often worked with the buyer on a continuous and friendly basis, encouraging the buyer's loyalty by going out of his or her way to meet the buyer's needs. As a result, the buyer often told the selling agent confidential information.

But the selling agent represented the seller and had a duty to pass that confidential information along to the seller—which came as an unpleasant surprise to the buyer. And often the selling agent would let his or her natural desire to help the buyer interfere with the fiduciary duties owed to the seller. This confusion caused trouble for everyone, and sometimes resulted in the creation of an inadvertent dual agency.

> **Example:** Mattucci, a salesperson, worked for Fairfield Realty. Over the course of several weeks, he showed the Kaplans many homes. He liked the Kaplans and worked hard to find them the right house. He gave them tips on buying and discussed their finances with them at length. Understandably, the Kaplans believed that Mattucci was their agent. But Mattucci did not have an agency agreement with the Kaplans, and so (under the traditional presumption) he was acting in the capacity of a seller's agent.
>
> The Kaplans decided to make an offer on a house listed by Broker Eisner. They told Mattucci they were willing to pay the full listing price, but wanted to make an initial offer of $5,000 less.
>
> If Mattucci failed to disclose to the seller that the Kaplans were willing to pay full price, he would be breaching his duty of loyalty to the seller. However, his conduct had caused the Kaplans to believe that he was representing them. Thus, if Mattucci did disclose this information to the seller, the Kaplans could claim that he had breached his duty of loyalty to them. And because he was inadvertently acting as agent for both parties, both could claim that he acted as a dual agent without their consent.

Offer of Cooperation. In the 1990s, as buyers became more interested in having their own agents to represent them, many multiple listing services replaced the unilateral offer of subagency in their listing agreements with an "offer of cooperation." Under this provision, other members of the MLS acted only as cooperating agents, not as subagents. A cooperating agent was simply any member of the MLS who attempted to find a buyer. Each individual cooperating agent could decide whether he or she would represent the seller or the buyer in a given transaction.

Despite this change, many cooperating agents continued to act as the seller's agent. They did not offer to represent the buyer or enter into an agency agreement with the buyer, so the traditional presumption that they were representing the seller continued.

Real Estate Agency Statute. To help eliminate confusion over agency representation, many states (including Washington) passed agency disclosure laws. These laws require real estate agents to disclose to both the buyer and the seller, in writing, the identity of the party they represent. In addition, the Washington State Legislature also passed the Real Estate Brokerage Relationships Act, which became effective in 1997.

Under the current law, a real estate licensee who works with a buyer is presumed to be the buyer's agent, unless a written agreement exists to the contrary. This rule has two important benefits. First, it turns the buyer's natural assumption—that the licensee working with the buyer is acting as the buyer's agent—into reality. Second, it significantly reduces the danger of inadvertent, undisclosed dual agency. Because a licensee represents the buyer he or she is working with, there is no conflict between the licensee's desire to help the buyer and the licensee's agency duties.

Types of Real Estate Agency Relationships

Under the Real Estate Brokerage Relationships Act, four types of real estate agency relationships exist:

- seller agency,
- buyer agency,
- dual agency, and
- non-agency.

It's important to note that these agency relationships are created independent of any fees being paid from the principal to the real estate agent.

Seller Agency. Although traditionally real estate agents nearly always represented the seller, under the real estate agency statute the only licensees representing the seller are the listing broker and listing salesperson. The listing agreement creates a seller agency relationship.

Under the terms of the listing agreement, the primary task of a seller's agent is to find a buyer for the seller's property at a price that is acceptable to the seller. To accomplish this, the seller's agent advises the seller about preparing the property for sale, helps the seller decide on the listing price, markets the property to advantage, and negotiates on the seller's behalf with selling agents and buyers.

Seller's agents and buyers. Throughout a transaction, a seller's agent must use his or her best efforts to promote the interests of the seller. Yet the seller's agent may also provide some services to a prospective buyer.

> **Example:** Susie is the seller's agent. A prospective buyer, Bart, doesn't have his own agent but wants to make an offer on the house. Susie helps Bart fill out a purchase offer form and apply for financing.

These services are considered to be in the best interests of the seller, and thus do not violate Susie's duties to the seller. Of course, Susie must disclose to Bart that she is acting as the seller's agent, not his agent.

A seller's agent must be very careful to treat the buyer fairly, but must not act as if he or she is representing the buyer. In other words, the agent must fully disclose all known material facts and answer the buyer's questions honestly—but should not give the buyer advice, such as how much to offer for the listed property.

> **Example:** Sanjay, a salesperson, lists Giselle's house for sale. The listing price is $299,000 but Sanjay believes Giselle will be willing to accept an offer of $290,000. Sanjay shows the house to a prospective buyer who asks him, "How low do you think the seller will go?"
>
> Sanjay must make it clear that he represents Giselle and cannot divulge confidential information to any prospective buyer. If he were to divulge such information, Giselle could sue for breach of agency duties.

In some cases, the seller's agent has had a previous relationship with the buyer. In this situation it may be difficult for the agent to represent the seller's interests without feeling some loyalty to the buyer as well.

> **Example:** Returning to the previous example, suppose Giselle is pleased with how Sanjay handled the sale of her home and subsequently asks Sanjay to help her find a new home. Sanjay shows Giselle one of his own listings.
>
> Under the circumstances, Giselle may believe that Sanjay is acting as her agent. However, because of the listing agreement, Sanjay is the seller's agent and he must make that fact clear to Giselle. Furthermore, he needs to remind Giselle that he is obligated to disclose to the seller any material information Giselle tells him and that in all negotiations, he will be representing the seller's best interests.
>
> Remember that a real estate agent cannot disclose confidential information about a principal even after an agency terminates. So Sanjay cannot disclose to the seller anything confidential about Giselle that he learned during his agency relationship with her.

In transactions like this, where the listing salesperson is also the selling salesperson, a seller's agent may still come up against the problem of inadvertent dual agency. But aside from that situation, a seller's agent will rarely face that problem under current law.

Buyer Agency. Under Washington's real estate agency law, a buyer is automatically represented by the agent he or she is working with (unless there is a written agreement to the contrary). Although this relationship is created automatically, a buyer and broker may decide to enter into a written **buyer representation agreement**, which typically includes the following:

- the duration of the agency;
- the general characteristics of the property the buyer wants;
- the price range;
- the conditions under which a fee will be earned;

- who will pay the fee; and
- a description of the broker's duties.

The advantages of buyer agency include confidentiality and loyalty, objective advice, help with negotiations, and access to more homes.

Confidentiality and loyalty. A buyer's agent owes agency duties to the buyer, including the duties of confidentiality and loyalty.

> **Example:** Malia, a salesperson, has shown Tony two homes he likes. The first is large fixer-upper listed for $260,000. The other is a small, newer house priced at $249,000. If Tony bought the larger house, Malia would receive a larger commission. But the smaller house better suits Tony's needs, and since Malia must put Tony's interests before her own, she advises him to purchase the smaller house.
>
> Malid suggests Tony start with an offer of $239,000. Tony agrees, but tells Malia he is willing to pay full price. Because Malia is Tony's agent, she cannot tell the seller that Tony is willing to pay full price. Had she been the seller's agent, however, she would have been required to disclose that fact to the seller.

Objective advice. A seller's agent will present the property in the most positive light and may use expert sales techniques to convince the buyer to sign on the dotted line. But a buyer's agent can be relied upon to give the buyer objective advice about the pros and cons of a particular home. For example, the buyer's agent will point out various issues important to the buyer, such as energy costs, the need for future repairs, and property value trends.

Help with negotiating. Buyers often feel uncomfortable negotiating for a property, especially one they really want to buy. They may be afraid to make a mistake through ignorance, or they may feel pressured to make a high offer quickly before someone else snaps up the property. A buyer's agent can use his or her negotiating skills and knowledge of the real estate market to help the buyer get the property on the best possible terms.

Access to more properties. A buyer may arrange to compensate her agent if the buyer purchases any home, even one not listed with a broker. This frees the buyer's agent to pursue less traditional means of searching for properties, and to show the buyer properties that are for sale by owner, properties with open listings, and properties in foreclosure or probate proceedings.

Buyer's agent's compensation. A buyer's agent may be compensated in a variety of ways. The three most common are:

- a retainer,
- a seller-paid fee, and/or
- a buyer-paid fee.

A **retainer** is a fee paid up front before services are provided. Some buyer's agents collect a retainer when a buyer agency relationship begins, to ensure that their services won't go entirely uncompensated. The retainer is usually nonrefundable but will be credited against any fee or commission the agent earns.

In many cases, a buyer's agent is paid by the seller through a commission split. In a **commission split**, a cooperating broker who procures a buyer is entitled to the selling broker's portion of the commission, regardless of which party the cooperating broker represents. Note that accepting a seller-paid fee does not create any agency duties toward the seller.

> **Example:** Shelley lists her property with Broker Sato and agrees to pay him 6% of the sales price. The listing agreement includes a clause that entitles any cooperating broker who procures a buyer to the selling broker's portion of the commission.
>
> Broker Ross has a buyer agency agreement with prospective buyer Graham, who offers $250,000 for Shelley's house. Shelley accepts the offer. When the transaction closes, Shelley pays a $15,000 commission; $7,500 goes to Broker Sato and $7,500 goes to Broker Ross.

Most buyer representation agreements also provide for compensation by means of a commission split when the buyer purchases a home listed through an MLS. However, a buyer representation agreement may provide for a **buyer-paid fee** instead. The buyer-paid fee might be based on an hourly rate, essentially making the agent a consultant. Alternatively, a buyer's agent may charge a percentage fee, so that the commission is a percentage of the purchase price. A third possibility is a flat fee—a specified sum that is payable if the buyer purchases a property found by the agent.

Some buyer agency agreements provide that the buyer's agent will accept a commission split if one is available; otherwise the buyer pays the fee (for example, if the property was for sale by owner).

Dual Agency. A **dual agency** relationship exists wherever a licensee represents both the seller and the buyer in the same transaction. Because the interests of the buyer and seller usually conflict, it's hard to represent them both without being disloyal to one or both.

> **Example:** Buyer Brant and Seller Amy are both represented by Broker Tyler. Amy tells Tyler that she's in a hurry to sell and will accept any reasonable offer. Brant tells Tyler that he's very interested in the house and is willing to pay the full asking price.
>
> Should Tyler tell Brant how eager Amy is to sell? And should Tyler tell Amy that Brant is willing to pay full price?

Clearly, it's impossible for a dual agent to fully represent both parties. Thus, instead of the duty of loyalty, Washington law imposes on a dual agent the duty to refrain from acting to the detriment of either party. The dual agent must do his or her best to act impartially and treat both clients equally.

The dual agent must inform both parties that neither will receive full representation. Certain facts must necessarily be withheld from each party; the dual agent cannot divulge confidential information about one party to another party.

> **Example:** Returning to the previous scenario, Broker Tyler must not tell Brant that Amy will accept any reasonable price. Similarly, Tyler must not tell Amy how much Brant is willing to pay.

Both parties must give their informed written consent to the dual agency. A licensee who acts as a dual agent without full disclosure and written consent has violated the real estate license law and is subject to disciplinary action.

In-house transactions. Dual agencies now occur most often in in-house transactions. An **in-house transaction** occurs when both the listing salesperson and the selling salesperson work for the same broker. In this situation, the listing salesperson represents only the seller, the selling salesperson represents only the buyer, and the broker is a dual agent, representing both parties.

> **Example:** Salesperson Paul works for Broker Tina. Paul has shown Buyer Wanda several houses over the course of a few weeks. Finally, Paul shows Wanda a house listed by Salesperson Philip, who also works for Broker Tina. Wanda decides to make an offer on this house.
>
> In this transaction, Paul, the selling salesperson, is the buyer's agent. Philip, the listing salesperson, is the seller's agent. And Tina, the broker, is a dual agent.

Non-Agency. In some transactions, a real estate licensee might choose to act only as a facilitator and refuse to assume any agency duties at all. This arrangement is called non-agency and is legal under Washington's real estate agency law.

A non-agent will still owe general statutory duties to any party he or she works with. (These duties are discussed fully in Chapter 6.) There is no way for a licensee to opt out of the duties of disclosure, reasonable skill and care, honesty and good faith, and so on.

Employee vs. Independent Contractor

One final aspect of real estate agency relationships to consider is whether or not a licensee acting as an agent is an employee of the principal.

Relationship between Broker and Principal. When a broker becomes an agent for the principal, he or she is working for the principal, but is not considered the principal's employee. A broker is usually an independent contractor in relation to the principal. The factors used to determine whether someone is an independent contractor or an employee include:

- the principal's degree of supervision and control,
- whether the work schedule is set by the principal,
- who decides how the job will be carried out, and
- whether the principal withholds taxes and social security contributions.

An **independent contractor** is generally hired to perform a particular job and to use his or her own judgment as to how the work will be done. In contrast, an **employee** is hired to perform whatever jobs the employer requires and is given guidelines and instructions as to how to perform each task.

Real estate brokers generally decide what hours they will work and use their own judgment as to the best methods for selling a particular piece of property. They are not controlled by the seller, and the seller does not withhold any income taxes or make contributions to social security for the broker. Therefore, the broker is generally held to be an independent contractor.

Relationship between Salesperson and Broker. Although some real estate salespersons are employees of a broker or brokerage firm, most are independent contractors. The Internal Revenue Service considers a real estate salesperson to be an independent contractor if:

1. the individual is a licensed real estate agent;
2. compensation is directly related to sales rather than to hours worked; and
3. the services are performed pursuant to a written contract that states the individual will not be treated as an employee for federal tax purposes.

In Washington, there is usually a written contract between the broker and the salesperson (although that is not a legal requirement). This contract should specify whether the salesperson is working as an employee or as an independent contractor.

Brokers cannot exercise the same degree of control over an independent contractor as they do over an employee. However, a broker is still liable for his or her salesperson's actions, since the salesperson is the broker's agent (a subagent). Washington license law requires brokers to adequately supervise their sales agents or risk disciplinary action. (Note that this supervision requirement does not turn a salesperson into an employee.)

State laws differ in regard to the treatment of independent contractors in the area of unemployment and worker's compensation. In Washington, independent contractors licensed to sell real estate are not eligible to receive unemployment compensation. However, they are eligible to receive worker's compensation.

Fig. 5.2 Distinction between employee and independent contractor

Employee
- Broker withholds taxes, social security
- Broker controls activities
- May receive employee benefits

Independent Contractor
- Pays own taxes, social security
- Controls own activities
- May not receive employee benefits

Conclusion

Real estate brokers and salespeople work as agents. The broker is the agent of the principal, and the salesperson is the agent of the broker or subagent of the principal. To understand their duties and responsibilities, agents should be aware of how their agency relationships were created, how much authority has been given, and when the relationships will terminate. Agents need to be familiar both with general agency law and Washington's real estate agency statute.

Case Problem

The following is a hypothetical case problem. Most of the facts are taken from a real case. Make a decision on the issues presented and then check to see if your answer matches the decision reached by the court.

The Facts

In August 1983, Holst listed her property for sale with Fear, a salesperson with Fireside Realty.

Rader was interested in the property. He contacted Fireside Realty and spoke with Bourgeois, another agent. Bourgeois showed Rader the property and answered questions about its condition.

Rader told Bourgeois he would offer $250,000 for the property. Bourgeois said Holst would probably not accept that price, and asked what Rader's highest offer would be. Rader responded $300,000 and Bourgeois wrote up an offer for that amount.

On October 19, Holst accepted the $300,000 offer and the parties signed a purchase and sale agreement. The agreement stated that the "Listing Agent" was "Charles Fear of Fireside Realty" and the "Selling Agent" was "Art Bourgeois of Fireside Realty."

The agreement was subject to the property being staked by a surveyor, to an inspection of the buildings, and to marketable title. At Rader's request, Bourgeois obtained survey bids as well as bids for removing timber from the property. He also took Rader through the buildings for inspection and discussed the issue of marketable title with Rader and the closing agent. Bourgeois did not tell Holst about the timber bids.

After the sale closed, Holst brought a lawsuit against Fireside Realty, Fear, and Bourgeois. The suit alleged that Bourgeois had acted as Rader's agent and that Fireside Realty had acted as a dual agent without informing Holst or obtaining her consent. Fireside denied that Bourgeois had agreed to represent Rader, and that even if it had acted as a dual agent, it had adequately disclosed the dual agency in the purchase and sale agreement.

The Questions

Did Fireside Realty act as a dual agent in the transaction? And if so, did it adequately disclose its dual agency to the parties involved?

What if the current real estate agency law is applied (as opposed to common law agency rules, which were in effect at the time the events in this case took place)?

The Answer

The court held that when a brokerage lists a property for sale, it owes a duty to the seller not to act as the buyer's agent without the seller's consent. The court found that it was reasonable to infer that Bourgeois had acted as Rader's agent. It also found that it was reasonable to infer that Fireside had breached its duty to Holst by not adequately disclosing the existence of a dual agency. *Holst v. Fireside Realty*, 89 Wn. App. 245 (1997).

Under the current real estate agency statute, it's clear that Bourgeois became Rader's agent as soon as he began providing brokerage services to Rader, such as showing Rader the property and answering questions about it. Fireside Realty would have been acting as a dual agent. Fear and Bourgeois would have been required to disclose this fact and obtain the parties' written consent to the dual agency.

Chapter Summary

- An agent may be universal, general, or special. Most real estate agents are special agents.

- An agent may have actual or apparent authority. Actual authority may be express or implied.

- An agency relationship may created by express agreement, ratification, estoppel, or implication. Under the real estate agency statute, an agency relationship between a licensee and client generally begins when the licensee begins providing real estate services for the client.

- An agency relationship may be terminated by expiration of the term, operation of law, mutual agreement, renunciation, or revocation.

- The real estate agency statute defines four types of real estate agency relationships: seller agency, buyer agency, dual agency, and non-agency.

- Previously, buyer agency was rare under general agency law. Under the current real estate agency statute, however, a buyer agency is usually created as soon as a licensee begins working with a buyer.

- A real estate broker is an independent contractor in relation to the principal. Most real estate salespersons work as independent contractors rather than as employees of the broker.

Checklist of Problem Areas

Real Estate Licensee's Checklist

❑   How much authority has been given by the principal?

❑   What type of agent are you?

❑   Have you signed a written listing agreement or buyer representation agreement? Remember that you can become a buyer's agent without a written agreement.

❑   Do you know when the agency will terminate, or what consequences you may suffer if you renounce the agency agreement?

Seller's Checklist

❑   How much authority have you given to the agent?

❑   Have any of your actions created an agency relationship by ratification or estoppel, even if there is no express agency agreement?

❑   Do you know when the agency will terminate, or what consequences you may suffer if you revoke the agency agreement?

Buyer's Checklist

❑   Do you know how your agent will be compensated?

Chapter Quiz

1. Most real estate agents are considered:
   a. general agents
   b. universal agents
   c. special agents
   d. total agents

2. An apparent agent is one who:
   a. has actual authority from the principal
   b. appears to be the agent of another but does not have actual authority
   c. is an agent working for the buyer instead of the seller
   d. None of the above

3. A real estate agency agreement:
   a. is usually in writing
   b. may be oral
   c. may be created by estoppel
   d. All of the above

4. A real estate salesperson who decides what hours she will work, is compensated solely by commission, and pays her own social security contributions would be considered:
   a. an ostensible broker
   b. an independent contractor
   c. an employee
   d. None of the above

5. Once an agency relationship has been created, the agency may terminate when:
   a. both parties agree
   b. the agent renounces
   c. the principal revokes
   d. Any of the above

6. An example of something that will cause the agency relationship to terminate by operation of law is the:
   a. death of the principal
   b. bankruptcy of the broker
   c. loss of the agent's license
   d. All of the above

7. After an agency relationship terminates, the agent still owes the principal the duty of:
   a. disclosure of material facts
   b. confidentiality
   c. reasonable care and skill
   d. loyalty

8. An agency relationship can be created in any of the following ways, except:
   a. ratification
   b. verification
   c. estoppel
   d. oral agreement

9. Dual agency is:
   a. legal as long as the agent consents to the arrangement in writing
   b. legal as long as both principals give their informed consent to the arrangement in writing
   c. legal as long as the agent receives equal compensation from both principals
   d. illegal in Washington state

10. In Washington, a real estate agency relationship is created when a licensee:

    a. obtains an acceptance to a valid offer
    b. makes an appointment to meet with a seller
    c. first undertakes to provide brokerage services
    d. places an advertisement for buyers or sellers in the newspaper

11. To create an agency relationship, all of the following are necessary, EXCEPT:

    a. in writing
    b. lawful objective
    c. competent parties
    d. mutual agreement

12. In a typical broker/salesperson relationship, which of the following is true?

    a. The salesperson is licensed to represent members of the public directly
    b. The salesperson is classified as an independent contractor, responsible for paying her own taxes
    c. The broker is required to withhold unemployment and industrial accident insurance premiums from the salesperson's paychecks
    d. The broker is required by law to withhold income and social security taxes from the salesperson's paychecks

13. Under Washington law, a seller is not vicariously liable for the actions of his broker unless:

    a. the broker has a bad reputation in the community and the seller should have known the broker would do something illegal
    b. the seller is bankrupt
    c. the seller knew that the broker had a grudge against the buyer and might do something to harm her
    d. the seller benefitted from the act and the broker is bankrupt

14. Which of the following would not result in the termination of a listing?

    a. Owner revokes agent's authority
    b. Broker dies before property is sold
    c. Listing salesperson dies before property is sold
    d. Property owner is declared incompetent before property is sold

15. Renunciation of an agency occurs:

    a. automatically, when the agency term expires
    b. after a reasonable time
    c. when the agent unilaterally terminates the agency
    d. when the agency contract is breached before the term expires

6 Agent's Duties and Responsibilities

Outline

Key Terms

- fiduciary
- secret profit
- confidential information
- reasonable care and skill
- actual fraud
- constructive fraud
- misrepresentation
- puffing
- material fact
- latent defect
- agency disclosure
- Director of Department of Licensing
- core curriculum
- commingling
- unprofessional conduct
- cease and desist order

Chapter Overview

In Chapter 5 you learned what an agent is and how an agency relationship is created and terminated. In this chapter, you will learn about the duties involved in an agency relationship. Under Washington's real estate agency statute, an agent owes certain duties to all parties he or she works with, such as prospective buyers. An agent also owes specific duties to his or her principal.

We'll also take a look at the duties and responsibilities imposed on salespersons and brokers by Washington's real estate license law.

Agent's Duties to the Principal

As we discussed in the previous chapter, agency relationships in Washington used to be governed solely by general agency law. A real estate agent owed certain duties to his or her principal, called **fiduciary duties**. A **fiduciary** is someone who occupies a position of special trust in relation to another person. The fiduciary duties owed to the principal included loyalty, reasonable care and skill, obedience and good faith, and disclosure of material facts.

In 1997, Washington's Real Estate Brokerage Relationships Act went into effect, replacing fiduciary duties with **statutory duties**. Specifically, an agent in a real estate transaction now owes his or her principal the following duties:

- loyalty,
- disclosing conflicts of interest,
- confidentiality,
- advising the principal to seek expert advice, and
- good faith and continuous effort.

Loyalty

A real estate agent owes the principal a duty of **loyalty**, which means that the principal's interests must be put above the interests of the agent or any other party. For example, an agent cannot make a **secret profit**, which is any profit or financial benefit from a transaction that is obtained by the agent without the knowledge or authorization of the principal. So if an agent accepts a kickback for referring the principal's business, he will have breached his duty of loyalty.

> **Example:** Amy is helping Saul find a home. She shows him a home that he likes, but it needs some repairs. Saul asks Amy to recommend a contractor for the repairs and she gives him the name of Braeburn Construction. She doesn't tell Saul that she is friends with the owner.
>
> When Saul hires Braeburn to do the repairs, the owner gives Amy a small percentage of the contract price. Amy has breached her duty of loyalty to Saul.

Conflicts of Interest

An agent also has a duty to disclose to the principal any **conflicts of interest** that may exist, such as a relationship between the agent and a prospective buyer. So if the buyer is a friend, relative, or business associate of the agent, or a company in which the agent has an interest, the agent must disclose this fact to the principal. The disclosure must take place before the principal decides whether to accept the buyer's offer.

> **Example:** Kroeger signs a 30-day exclusive listing agreement with Cascadia Realty. Stoddard, a salesperson with Cascadia, shows the property to his mother, who makes an offer on the house. Stoddard is in a hurry when he presents the offer, and neglects to tell Kroeger of the relationship between himself and the potential buyer. Kroeger accepts.
>
> Even if Kroeger suffers no injury from the relationship and neither Stoddard nor his mother gains any advantage, the duty to disclose conflicts of interest has been breached.

Confidentiality

The duty of **confidentiality** prohibits an agent from disclosing any confidential information about the principal, even after the agency has ended. Washington's real estate agency law defines **confidential information** as information from or concerning a principal that:

1. was acquired by the licensee during the course of an agency relationship with the principal;
2. the principal reasonably expects to be kept confidential;
3. the principal has not disclosed or authorized to be disclosed to third parties;
4. would, if disclosed, operate to the detriment of the principal; and
5. the principal personally would not be obligated to disclose to the other party.

For example, if the agent represents the seller, the agent must not reveal (or make any personal use of) the fact that the seller is willing to accept less than the listing price, unless the seller has authorized such a disclosure.

Expert Advice

Real estate agents must be careful not to perform any acts beyond their skill and ability. An agent has a duty to advise the principal to **seek expert advice** on any matters relating to the transaction that are beyond the agent's expertise.

Agents should never claim to have expertise in areas in which they have no special training or skills. For example, if questions arise as to a home's structural soundness, the agent should advise the principal to contact a home inspector.

> **Example:** Pat lists his house for sale with Celina. An interested buyer approaches Pat and proposes a seller-financed transaction. Pat asks his agent, Celina, for advice in

structuring the financing. Although Celina is familiar with seller-financed transactions, she must advise Pat to seek the advice of an attorney.

Good Faith and Continuous Effort

A real estate agent has a duty to make a **good faith and continuous effort** to fulfill the terms of the agency agreement. A seller's agent must make a good faith and continuous effort to find a buyer for the property; a buyer's agent must make a good faith and continuous effort to find a suitable property to purchase.

Note that once a seller has entered into a purchase and sale agreement, the seller's agent is not required to seek out additional buyers. And once a buyer has entered into a purchase and sale agreement, the buyer's agent need not search for additional properties to show the buyer.

Agent's Duties to All Parties

Although a real estate agent's main responsibility is to his or her principal, the agent also owes certain duties to any party he or she works with. Previously, under general agency law the agent only owed the duty of honesty and fair dealing to third parties. But Washington's real estate agency law replaced that general duty with a statutory list of duties that are owed to any party the agent renders services to, regardless of which party the agent represents. In fact, the agent owes these duties even if she is not representing any of the parties.

An agent owes the following duties to any party involved in a transaction (including the principal):

- reasonable care and skill,
- honesty and good faith,
- presenting all written communications,
- disclosure of material facts,
- accounting,
- providing a pamphlet on agency law, and
- disclosing any existing agency relationship.

Under the real estate agency statute, a breach of any of these statutory duties is grounds for disciplinary action under Washington's real estate license law.

Reasonable Care and Skill

In performing their duties, real estate agents must use the degree of care and skill ordinarily employed by others competently engaged in the same business. This means that an

Fig. 6.1 Types of Fraud

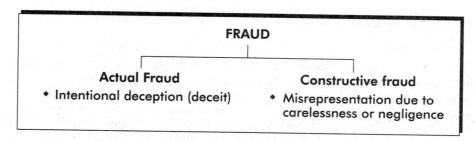

agent's actions will be compared to what is expected of other competent real estate agents. Failing to act competently, reasonably, or carefully may be considered negligence.

Honesty and Good Faith

A real estate agent has the duty to act with honesty and good faith toward any party. Making inaccurate statements or misrepresentations to prospective buyers or sellers is a breach of this duty and may be considered fraud. Most fraud cases arise because of spoken or written statements that are untrue. However, fraud can also arise through conduct.

> **Example:** The downstairs bathtub in a house was never correctly plumbed, causing dry rot beneath the tub. One day when the owner steps into the tub, his foot goes through the bottom of the tub clear to the ground, leaving a gaping hole in the tub. Instead of telling the buyer about the hole, or leaving it in plain view for the buyer to see, the seller places a decorative non-skid mat in the tub, completely hiding the hole.

Fraud can be classified as either actual or constructive. **Actual fraud** (often called deceit) exists when an intentional deception takes place. This is usually accomplished by deliberately misrepresenting or concealing a material fact.

> **Example:** A house is located in an area with flooding problems caused by heavy run-off every spring. The basement of the house has flooded seven times in the last ten years. There are water marks on the basement walls showing how high the water rises. The seller paints the basement walls just before selling, in order to conceal the water marks.

On the other hand, **constructive fraud** does not arise because of a deliberate statement or act, but out of a misrepresentation made through carelessness or negligence.

A party to whom inaccurate statements or misrepresentations have been made has the right to rescind the transaction and/or sue the agent for damages. And if an agent knows that statements made by the seller are false, but passes them on to the buyer anyway, the agent may be liable for misrepresentation.

Case Example:

The Farrells listed their laundromat for sale with Score, a real estate broker. Score located a potential buyer named Robinson.

Score told the Farrells that Robinson had a good job with Standard Oil, which he would retain after the purchase while his wife managed the laundromat. He also said that Robinson had sufficient stock in Standard Oil to buy out the Farrells, but he did not want to cash in the investment at that time. Based on these representations, the Farrells accepted Robinson's offer and executed a promissory note to Score for his commission.

Robinson took possession of the laundromat and made payments for seven months. He was unable to make any further payments. After negotiating with the Farrells, the contract was rescinded and Robinson returned the laundromat business to the Farrells.

The Farrells sued Score to cancel the promissory note for his commission. The court found that Score had known Robinson could raise the downpayment funds only by resigning from Standard Oil and thereby receiving an annuity benefit. Score also knew that Robinson possessed only a small amount of stock worth approximately $320.

The court held that a principal is entitled to rely on representations made by a broker concerning the financial ability of the intended purchaser. Intentional misrepresentation of the potential buyer's financial condition constitutes fraud. Since the Farrells' acceptance of Robinson as a purchaser was induced through the broker's misrepresentation as to his financial condition, they were entitled to cancellation of the note. *Farrell v. Score,* 67 Wn.2nd 957, 411 P.2d 146 (1966).

Similarly, if an agent knows the seller is intentionally concealing a material fact but says nothing to the buyer, the agent may be liable.

Case Example:

When taking a listing, the broker asked the sellers if the property had any problems. The sellers said no. However, the broker had sold this same home to the sellers and knew that it had chronic sewage and drainage problems. He did not inform the buyers of the problem, and in fact told them there were "no problems."

In the words of the court, three days after closing, "the toilets in the house erupted with raw sewage." The broker was held liable for his failure to disclose the material defects to the buyers, even though the sellers had informed him that no defects existed. *McRae v. Bolstad,* 101 Wn.2d 161, 676 P.2d 496 (1984).

Puffing, Predictions, and Opinions. Misrepresentations that can give rise to legal action should not be confused with mere opinions, predictions, or puffing.

- Opinion—"I think this is the best buy on the market."
- Prediction—"This house could double in value over the next ten years."
- Puffing—"This is the finest house in the neighborhood; it has a fantastic view."

In order to prove fraud based on a misrepresentation, it is necessary to show that a person relied on the misrepresentation. Statements that are mere opinions, predictions, and puffing are not considered the types of statements that a reasonable person would rely on in making a decision to buy property, because of their nonfactual or exaggerated nature.

> **Example:** The broker tells a buyer, "This is a great little house; you'll be very happy here." After purchasing the house, the buyer is not happy. He discovers several problems and decides it is not a great house at all.
>
> Even if it isn't a great house, the broker is not liable for his statement because it was mere puffing—a statement of opinion made to induce the purchaser to buy, but not relating to any specific material fact.

In general, recovery is not available for fraud or misrepresentation based on statements of opinion. However, an agent should be very cautious in voicing unsubstantiated opinions or predictions. If it is considered a professional or expert opinion, it could lead to liability for negligence.

Present Written Communications

Any type of written communication, including all written offers, to or from either party must be presented to the other party in a timely manner. Even if an offer seems totally unacceptable, the agent must inform the principal of the offer, because the principal—not the agent—decides which offer is acceptable. The agent must relay an offer to the principal even if its acceptance means a smaller commission, because the agent's first loyalty is to the principal.

> **Example:** A broker is aware of two potential purchasers for a property. The first party offers $200,000 and the second party offers $225,000. Instead of telling the seller of the $225,000 offer, the broker arranged two sales: a sale from the seller to the first buyer for $200,000 and a second sale from that buyer to the second buyer from $225,000. In this way, the broker earned two sales commissions.
>
> The original seller sues the broker, accusing him of failing to let the seller know there was a higher offer for the property. The court awards the seller the amount of the second commission plus compensatory damages.

Disclosure of Material Facts

A real estate agent has the duty to disclose a **material fact** to a party if the agent is aware of the fact, and it is not apparent or readily ascertainable by the party.

Previously, no clear definition of the term "material fact" existed, making it difficult for agents to determine whether a particular fact required disclosure. However, Washington's real estate agency law now defines a "material fact" as information that:

1. has a substantial negative impact on the property's value or on a party's ability to perform, or
2. defeats the purpose of the transaction.

For example, the property's true value is a material fact that the agent must disclose to the principal. Misleading the principal as to the value of the property or withholding information that affects its value would be a breach of the licensee's duty to disclose material facts. A licensee should also inform the principal of any information or recent events that may affect the value of the property, such as zoning changes or plans to build a new school in the neighborhood.

For a seller's agent, the buyer's financial position may be material information that must be disclosed. Financial information regarding the buyer is considered material if the seller would have refused to enter into the agreement if the information were known at the time the contract was made. If the agent misrepresented or failed to disclose detrimental financial information concerning the buyer, the broker may lose the right to a commission. Essentially, the broker failed to produce a buyer who was financially able to complete the sale.

> **Example:** A buyer made an offer on a property that complied with all the terms desired by the seller. However, the broker failed to disclose to the seller that the buyer did not make enough money to keep up with the monthly payments. At the last minute, the seller began to have doubts about the transaction and refused to sign the purchase and sale agreement.
>
> The broker was not entitled to the commission. Even though the buyer's offer met the terms required by the seller, the buyer was not a "ready, willing, and able" buyer.

Latent Defects. A common example of a material fact that must be disclosed is a latent defect. A **latent defect** is one that would not be discovered through ordinary inspection. A licensee must disclose any known latent defect to the parties.

> **Example:** When taking a listing from a seller, the agent notices a crack in the home's foundation that is almost entirely hidden from view. This is a latent defect and must be disclosed to the seller as well as to any potential buyers.

What is Not Material. The real estate agency law excludes certain types of information from the material fact disclosure requirement. Specifically, it isn't considered material if the property may have been the site of any crime, suicide, or other death, gang-related activity, political or religious activity, or other occurrence that doesn't adversely affect the physical condition of or title to the property.

> **Example:** An agent is showing a buyer a home in which a brutal homicide occurred three years ago. This information is not considered a material fact and need not be disclosed to the buyer.

Note, however, that if the buyer asked the agent whether any crimes had occurred on the property, the agent would have to answer honestly. Regardless of whether or not the information requested is a material fact, the agent is obligated to answer questions honestly and in good faith.

Criminal activity will be considered a material fact if it affects the property's physical condition.

> **Example:** A house for sale previously contained an illegal drug lab. It's possible that the house may be contaminated by dangerous chemical residues left behind that substantially affect the condition of the property. This is a material fact and must be disclosed to prospective buyers.
>
> On the other hand, if the property has been thoroughly cleaned, inspected by qualified personnel, and declared to pose no health hazard, there is nothing affecting the property's physical condition. The existence of the drug lab probably does not need to be disclosed.

The Washington State Human Rights Commission has stated that questions about Acquired Immune Deficiency Syndrome (AIDS) or any of its related conditions are improper questions by any prospective landlord, tenant, home buyer, or seller.

The guidelines specifically prohibit an agent from engaging in discussion about or disclosing whether a tenant, owner, or resident had AIDS. AIDS is considered a disability under the Washington State Law Against Discrimination. It is an unfair practice for an appraiser to lower the value of real property because a person with AIDS resides in the property or is a neighbor to the property. The presence of AIDS is not a factor that should be discussed or disclosed during a real estate transaction.

Seller Disclosure Statement. Washington requires all sellers of residential property (defined as a residential dwelling of one to four units) to give the buyer a disclosure statement. The purpose of the statement is to disclose the seller's knowledge regarding the condition of the property, including the condition of the buildings and utilities, the existence of any easements and encumbrances, and other material information. (See the Seller Disclosure Statement, Figure 6.2.) The disclosure statement is for disclosure purposes only, and is not to be considered a part of the sales agreement.

The seller must give the buyer the disclosure statement within five days of the signing of a purchase and sale agreement, unless the buyer and seller agree to a different timeframe. The buyer can waive the right to receive the statement. Within three business days of receiving the statement, the buyer can either "approve and accept" the disclosure statement or rescind the sales agreement. The choice to accept or rescind is at the complete discretion of the buyer. If the buyer decides to rescind the agreement, he or she must notify the seller in writing within the three-day period and will then be entitled to a full refund of the earnest money deposit.

If the seller refuses to give the buyer a disclosure statement within the statutory time period (or by a later deadline the buyer has agreed to), the buyer has the right to rescind the purchase and sale agreement at any time until closing.

Fig. 6.2 Seller Disclosure Statement

NWMLS Form No. 17
W.A.R. Form No. D-5
Rev. 7/03
Page 1 of 5 Pages

© Copyright 2003
Northwest Multiple Listing Service
ALL RIGHTS RESERVED

SELLER DISCLOSURE STATEMENT †

SELLER: _____

† To be used in transfers of residential real property, including multi-family dwellings up to four units; new construction; condominiums not subject to a public offering statement, certain timeshares, and manufactured and mobile homes. See RCW Chapter 64.06 and Section 43.22.432 for further explanations.

INSTRUCTIONS TO THE SELLER
Please complete the following form. Do not leave any spaces blank. If the question clearly does not apply to the property write "NA." If the answer is "yes" to any asterisked (*) item(s), please explain on attached sheets. Please refer to the line number(s) of the question(s) when you provide your explanation(s). For your protection you must date and initial each page of this disclosure statement and each attachment. Delivery of the disclosure statement must occur not later than five (5) business days, unless otherwise agreed, after mutual acceptance of a written purchase and sale agreement between Buyer and Seller.

NOTICE TO THE BUYER
THE FOLLOWING DISCLOSURES ARE MADE BY THE SELLER ABOUT THE CONDITION OF THE PROPERTY LOCATED AT

_____,

CITY _____, COUNTY _____ ("THE PROPERTY") OR AS LEGALLY DESCRIBED ON THE ATTACHED EXHIBIT A. SELLER MAKES THE FOLLOWING DISCLOSURES OF EXISTING MATERIAL FACTS OR MATERIAL DEFECTS TO BUYER BASED ON SELLER'S ACTUAL KNOWLEDGE OF THE PROPERTY AT THE TIME SELLER COMPLETES THIS DISCLOSURE STATEMENT. UNLESS YOU AND SELLER OTHERWISE AGREE IN WRITING, YOU HAVE THREE (3) BUSINESS DAYS FROM THE DAY SELLER OR SELLER'S AGENT DELIVERS THIS DISCLOSURE STATEMENT TO YOU TO RESCIND THE AGREEMENT BY DELIVERING A SEPARATELY SIGNED WRITTEN STATEMENT OF RESCISSION TO SELLER OR SELLER'S AGENT. IF THE SELLER DOES NOT GIVE YOU A COMPLETED DISCLOSURE STATEMENT, THEN YOU MAY WAIVE THE RIGHT TO RESCIND PRIOR TO OR AFTER THE TIME YOU ENTER INTO A PURCHASE AND SALE AGREEMENT.

THE FOLLOWING ARE DISCLOSURES MADE BY SELLER AND ARE NOT THE REPRESENTATIONS OF ANY REAL ESTATE LICENSEE OR OTHER PARTY. THIS INFORMATION IS FOR DISCLOSURE ONLY AND IS NOT INTENDED TO BE A PART OF ANY WRITTEN AGREEMENT BETWEEN BUYER AND SELLER.

FOR A MORE COMPREHENSIVE EXAMINATION OF THE SPECIFIC CONDITION OF THIS PROPERTY YOU ARE ADVISED TO OBTAIN AND PAY FOR THE SERVICES OF QUALIFIED EXPERTS TO INSPECT THE PROPERTY, WHICH MAY INCLUDE, WITHOUT LIMITATION, ARCHITECTS, ENGINEERS, LAND SURVEYORS, PLUMBERS, ELECTRICIANS, ROOFERS, BUILDING INSPECTORS, ON-SITE WASTEWATER TREATMENT INSPECTORS, OR STRUCTURAL PEST INSPECTORS. THE PROSPECTIVE BUYER AND SELLER MAY WISH TO OBTAIN PROFESSIONAL ADVICE OR INSPECTIONS OF THE PROPERTY OR TO PROVIDE APPROPRIATE PROVISIONS IN A CONTRACT BETWEEN THEM WITH RESPECT TO ANY ADVICE, INSPECTION, DEFECTS OR WARRANTIES.

Seller ☐ is/ ☐ is not occupying the property.

I. SELLER'S DISCLOSURES:
* If you answer "Yes" to a question with an asterisk (*), please explain your answer and attach documents, if available and not otherwise publicly recorded. If necessary, use an attached sheet.

	YES	NO	DON'T KNOW
1. TITLE			
A. Do you have legal authority to sell the property? If not, please explain.	☐	☐	☐
*B. Is title to the property subject to any of the following?	☐	☐	☐
(1) First right of refusal	☐	☐	☐
(2) Option	☐	☐	☐
(3) Lease or rental agreement	☐	☐	☐
(4) Life estate	☐	☐	☐
*C. Are there any encroachments, boundary agreements, or boundary disputes?	☐	☐	☐
*D. Are there any rights of way, easements, or access limitations that may affect Buyer's use of the property?	☐	☐	☐
*E. Are there any written agreements for joint maintenance of an easement or right of way?	☐	☐	☐
*F. Is there any study, survey project, or notice that would adversely affect the property?	☐	☐	☐
*G. Are there any pending or existing assessments against the property?	☐	☐	☐
*H. Are there any zoning violations, nonconforming uses, or any unusual restrictions on the property that would affect future construction or remodeling?	☐	☐	☐
*I. Is there a boundary survey for the property?	☐	☐	☐
*J. Are there any covenants, conditions, or restrictions which affect the property?	☐	☐	☐

PLEASE NOTE: Covenants, conditions, and restrictions which purport to forbid or restrict the conveyance, encumbrance, occupancy, or lease of real property to individuals based on race, creed, color, sex, national origin, familial status, or disability are void, unenforceable, and illegal. RCW 49.60.224.

SELLER'S INITIAL: _____ DATE: _____   SELLER'S INITIAL: _____ DATE: _____

1

1
2
3
4
5
6
7
8
9
10
11
12
13
14
15
16
17
18
19
20
21
22
23
24
25
26
27
28
29
30
31
32
33
34
35
36
37
38
39
40
41
42
43
44
45
46
47
48
49
50
51
52
53
54
55
56

NWMLS Form No. 17
W.A.R. Form No. D-5
Rev. 7/03
Page 2 of 5 Pages

SELLER DISCLOSURE STATEMENT

	YES	NO	DON'T KNOW	
2. WATER				57
				58
A. Household Water				59
(1) The source of water for the property is: ☐ Private or publicly owned water system				60
☐ Private well serving only the subject property * ☐ Other water system				61
*If shared, are there any written agreements?	☐	☐	☐	62
*(2) Is there an easement (recorded or unrecorded) for access to and/or maintenance of the water source?	☐	☐	☐	63 / 64
*(3) Are there any known problems or repairs needed?	☐	☐	☐	65
(4) During your ownership, has the source provided an adequate year round supply of potable water?	☐	☐	☐	66 / 67
If no, please explain: _____				68
*(5) Are there any water treatment systems for the property?	☐	☐	☐	69
If yes, are they: ☐ Leased ☐ Owned				70
B. Irrigation				71
(1) Are there any water rights for the property, such as a water right, permit, certificate, or claim?	☐	☐	☐	72 / 73
*(a) If yes, have the water rights been used during the last five-years?	☐	☐	☐	74
*(b) If so, is the certificate available?	☐	☐	☐	75
C. Outdoor Sprinkler System				76
(1) Is there an outdoor sprinkler system for the property?	☐	☐	☐	77
*(2) If yes, are there any defects in the system?	☐	☐	☐	78
*(3) If yes, is the sprinkler system connected to irrigation water?	☐	☐	☐	79
3. SEWER/ON-SITE SEWAGE SYSTEM				80
A. The property is served by:				81
☐ Public sewer system ☐ On-site sewage system (including pipes, tanks, drainfields, and all other component parts)				82
☐ Other disposal system				83
Please describe: _____				84
B. If public sewer system service is available to the property, is the house connected to the sewer main?	☐	☐	☐	85
If no, please explain: _____				86 / 87
C. Is the property subject to any sewage system fees or charges in addition to those covered in your regularly billed sewer or on-site sewage system maintenance service?	☐	☐	☐	88 / 89
D. If the property is connected to an on-site sewage system:				90
*(1) Was a permit issued for its construction, and was it approved by the local health department or district following its construction?	☐	☐	☐	91 / 92
(2) When was it last pumped? _____	☐	☐	☐	93
*(3) Are there any defects in the operation of the on-site sewage system?	☐	☐	☐	94
(4) When was it last inspected? _____			☐	95
By whom: _____				96
(5) For how many bedrooms was the on-site sewage system approved? _____ bedrooms			☐	97
E. Are all plumbing fixtures, including laundry drain, connected to the sewer/on-site sewage system?	☐	☐	☐	98 / 99
If no, please explain: _____				100
*F. Have there been any changes or repairs to the on-site sewage system?	☐	☐	☐	101
G. Is the on-site sewage system, including the drainfield, located entirely within the boundaries of the property?	☐	☐	☐	102 / 103
If no, please explain: _____				104
H. Does the on-site sewage system require monitoring and maintenance services more frequently than once a year?	☐	☐	☐	105 / 106
If yes, please explain: _____				107

SELLER'S INITIAL: _____ DATE: _____   SELLER'S INITIAL: _____ DATE: _____   108

2

NWMLS Form No. 17
W.A.R. Form No. D-5
Rev. 7/03
Page 3 of 5 Pages

SELLER DISCLOSURE STATEMENT

NOTICE: IF THIS SELLER DISCLOSURE STATEMENT IS BEING COMPLETED FOR NEW CONSTRUCTION WHICH 109
HAS NEVER BEEN OCCUPIED, SELLER IS NOT REQUIRED TO COMPLETE THE QUESTIONS LISTED IN ITEM 4 110
(STRUCTURAL) OR ITEM 5 (SYSTEMS AND FIXTURES). 111

	YES	NO	DON'T KNOW	
4. STRUCTURAL				113
*A. Has the roof leaked?	☐	☐	☐	114
*B. Has the basement flooded or leaked?	☐	☐	☐	115
*C. Have there been any conversions, additions or remodeling?	☐	☐	☐	116
*(1) If yes, were all building permits obtained?	☐	☐	☐	117
*(2) If yes, were all final inspections obtained?	☐	☐	☐	118
*D. Do you know the age of the house?	☐	☐	☐	119
If yes, year of original construction: _____				120
*E. Has there been any settling, slippage, or sliding of the property or its improvements?	☐	☐	☐	121
*F. Are there any defects with the following: (If yes, please check applicable items and explain.)	☐	☐	☐	122

☐ Foundations	☐ Decks	☐ Exterior Walls	123
☐ Chimneys	☐ Interior Walls	☐ Fire Alarms	124
☐ Doors	☐ Windows	☐ Patios	125
☐ Ceilings	☐ Slab Floors	☐ Driveways	126
☐ Pools	☐ Hot Tub	☐ Sauna	127
☐ Sidewalks	☐ Outbuildings	☐ Fireplaces	128
☐ Garage Floors	☐ Walkways	☐ Wood Stoves	129
☐ Siding	☐ Other _____		130

	YES	NO	DON'T KNOW	
*G. Was a structural pest or "whole house" inspection done?	☐	☐	☐	131
If yes, when and by whom was the inspection completed?				132
_____				133
*H. During your ownership, has the property had any wood destroying organisms or pest infestations?	☐	☐	☐	134
I. Is the attic insulated?	☐	☐	☐	135
J. Is the basement insulated?	☐	☐	☐	136
5. SYSTEMS AND FIXTURES				137
*A. If any of the following systems or fixtures are included with the transfer, are there any defects?				138
If yes, please explain: _____				139
Electrical system, including wiring, switches, outlets, and service	☐	☐	☐	140
Plumbing system, including pipes, faucets, fixtures, and toilets	☐	☐	☐	141
Hot water tank	☐	☐	☐	142
Garbage disposal	☐	☐	☐	143
Appliances	☐	☐	☐	144
Sump pump	☐	☐	☐	145
Heating and cooling systems	☐	☐	☐	146
Security system ☐ Leased ☐ Owned	☐	☐	☐	147
Other _____	☐	☐		148
*B. If any of the following fixtures or property is included with the transfer, are they leased?				149
(If yes, please attach copy of lease.)				150
Security System	☐	☐	☐	151
Tanks (type): _____	☐	☐	☐	152
Satellite dish	☐	☐	☐	153
Other: _____	☐	☐	☐	154

SELLER'S INITIAL: _____ DATE: _____   SELLER'S INITIAL: _____ DATE: _____   155

3

NWMLS Form No. 17
W.A.R. Form No. D-5
Rev. 7/03
Page 4 of 5 Pages

SELLER DISCLOSURE STATEMENT

	YES	NO	DON'T KNOW	

6. COMMON INTERESTS — 156, 157

A. Is there a Home Owners' Association? ☐ ☐ ☐ — 158

Name of Association _____ — 159

B. Are there regular periodic assessments? ☐ ☐ ☐ — 160

_____ per ☐ month ☐ years — 161

☐ Other _____ — 162

*C. Are there any pending special assessments? ☐ ☐ ☐ — 163

*D. Are there any shared "common areas" or any joint maintenance agreements (facilities such as walls, fences, landscaping, pools, tennis courts, walkways, or other areas co-owned in undivided interest with others)? ☐ ☐ ☐ — 164, 165, 166

7. GENERAL — 167

*A. Have there been any drainage problems on the property? ☐ ☐ ☐ — 168

*B. Does the property contain fill material? ☐ ☐ ☐ — 169

*C. Is there any material damage to the property from fire, wind, floods, beach movements, earthquake, expansive soils, or landslides? ☐ ☐ ☐ — 170, 171

D. Is the property in a designated flood plain? ☐ ☐ ☐ — 172

E. Has the local (city or county) planning agency designated your property as a "frequently flooded area"? ☐ ☐ ☐ — 173, 174

*F. Are there any substances, materials, or products on the property that may be environmental concerns, such as asbestos, formaldehyde, radon gas, lead-based paint, fuel or chemical storage tanks, or contaminated soil or water? ☐ ☐ ☐ — 175, 176, 177

*G. Are there any tanks or underground storage tanks (e.g., chemical, fuel, etc.) on the property? ☐ ☐ ☐ — 178

*H. Has the property ever been used as an illegal drug manufacturing site? ☐ ☐ ☐ — 179

*I. Are there any radio towers in the area that may cause interference with telephone reception? ☐ ☐ ☐ — 180

8. LEAD BASED PAINT (Applicable if the house was built before 1978.) — 181

A. Presence of lead-based paint and/or lead-based paint hazards (check one below): — 182

☐ Known lead-based paint and/or lead-based paint hazards are present in the housing (explain). _____ — 183, 184

☐ Seller has no knowledge of lead-based paint and/or lead-based paint hazards in the housing. — 185

B. Records and reports available to the Seller (check one below): — 186

☐ Seller has provided the purchaser with all available records and reports pertaining to lead-based paint and/or lead-based paint hazards in the housing (list documents below). — 187, 188

_____ — 189

☐ Seller has no reports or records pertaining to lead-based paint and/or lead-based paint hazards in the housing. — 190

9. MANUFACTURED AND MOBILE HOMES — 191

If the property includes a manufactured or mobile home, — 192

*A. Did you make any alterations to the home? ☐ ☐ ☐ — 193

If yes, please describe the alterations: _____ — 194

*B. Did any previous owner make any alterations to the home? ☐ ☐ ☐ — 195

If yes, please describe the alterations: _____ — 196

*C. If alterations were made, were permits or variances for these alterations obtained? ☐ ☐ ☐ — 197

10. FULL DISCLOSURE BY SELLERS — 198

A. Other conditions or defects: — 199

*Are there any other existing material defects affecting the property that a prospective buyer should know about? ☐ ☐ ☐ — 200, 201

SELLER'S INITIAL: _____ DATE: _____   SELLER'S INITIAL: _____ DATE: _____ — 202

4

NWMLS Form No. 17
W.A.R. Form No. D-5
Rev. 7/03
Page 5 of 5 Pages

SELLER DISCLOSURE STATEMENT

B. Verification 203

The foregoing answers and attached explanations (if any) are complete and correct to the best of Seller's knowledge and Seller has 204
received a copy hereof. Seller agrees to defend, indemnify and hold real estate licensees harmless from and against any and all claims 205
that the above information is inaccurate. Seller authorizes real estate licensees, if any, to deliver a copy of this disclosure statement to 206
other real estate licensees and all prospective buyers of the Property. 207

Date: _____ Date: _____ 208

Seller _____ Seller _____ 209

II. BUYER'S ACKNOWLEDGEMENT 210

Buyer hereby acknowledges that: 211

A. Buyer has a duty to pay diligent attention to any material defects that are known to Buyer or can be known to Buyer by utilizing diligent 212
attention and observation. 213

B. The disclosures set forth in this statement and in any amendments to this statement are made only by the Seller and not by any real 214
estate licensee or other party. 215

C. Buyer acknowledges that, pursuant to RCW 64.06.050 (2), real estate licensees are not liable for inaccurate information provided by 216
Seller, except to the extent that real estate licensees know of such inaccurate information. 217

D. This information is for disclosure only and is not intended to be a part of the written agreement between Buyer and Seller. 218

E. Buyer (which term includes all persons signing the "Buyer's acceptance" portion of this disclosure statement below) has received a copy 219
of this Disclosure Statement (including attachments, if any) bearing Seller's signature(s). 220

F. If the house was built prior to 1978, Buyer acknowledges receipt of the pamphlet *Protect Your Family From Lead in Your Home*. 221

DISCLOSURES CONTAINED IN THIS DISCLOSURE STATEMENT ARE PROVIDED BY SELLER BASED ON SELLER'S ACTUAL 222
KNOWLEDGE OF THE PROPERTY AT THE TIME SELLER COMPLETES THIS DISCLOSURE. UNLESS BUYER AND SELLER 223
OTHERWISE AGREE IN WRITING, BUYER SHALL HAVE THREE (3) BUSINESS DAYS FROM THE DAY SELLER OR SELLER'S 224
AGENT DELIVERS THIS DISCLOSURE STATEMENT TO RESCIND THE AGREEMENT BY DELIVERING A SEPARATELY 225
SIGNED WRITTEN STATEMENT OF RESCISSION TO SELLER OR SELLER'S AGENT. IF SELLER DOES NOT GIVE YOU A 226
COMPLETED DISCLOSURE STATEMENT, THEN YOU MAY WAIVE THE RIGHT TO RESCIND PRIOR TO OR AFTER THE TIME 227
YOU ENTER INTO A SALE AGREEMENT. 228

BUYER HEREBY ACKNOWLEDGES RECEIPT OF A COPY OF THIS DISCLOSURE STATEMENT AND ACKNOWLEDGES THAT 229
THE DISCLOSURES MADE HEREIN ARE THOSE OF THE SELLER ONLY, AND NOT OF ANY REAL ESTATE LICENSEE OR 230
OTHER PARTY. 231

DATE: _____ DATE: _____ 232

BUYER: _____ BUYER: _____ 233

BUYER'S WAIVER OF RIGHT TO REVOKE OFFER 234

Buyer has read and reviewed the Seller's responses to this Seller Disclosure Statement. Buyer approves this statement and waives Buyer's right 235
to revoke Buyer's offer based on this disclosure. 236

DATE: _____ DATE: _____ 237

BUYER: _____ BUYER: _____ 238

BUYER'S WAIVER OF RIGHT TO RECEIVE COMPLETED SELLER DISCLOSURE STATEMENT 239

Buyer has been advised of Buyer's right to receive a completed Seller Disclosure Statement. Buyer waives that right. 240

DATE: _____ DATE: _____ 241

BUYER: _____ BUYER: _____ 242

If the answer is "Yes" to any asterisked (*) items, please explain below (use additional sheets if necessary). Please refer to the line number(s) of 243
the question(s). 244

_____ 245
_____ 246
_____ 247
_____ 248
_____ 249
_____ 250

SELLER'S INITIAL: _____ DATE: _____   SELLER'S INITIAL: _____ DATE: _____ 251

5

It's important to note that under Washington's disclosure law, the information in the disclosure statement is based on the seller's actual knowledge of the property. The information in the statement may not be considered to be representations made by the real estate agent. Furthermore, the statement is not a warranty from either the seller or the real estate agent. Neither the seller nor the agent will be liable for any inaccuracies in the statement unless they had personal knowledge of the inaccuracies.

No Duty to Investigate. Some states require licensees to inspect the property and report their findings to the buyer. In Washington, however, the real estate agency law provides that an agent has no duty to investigate anything unless he or she specifically agrees to do so. The agent is not required to inspect the property, investigate either party's financial position, or independently verify statements made by either party or any reasonable source.

> **Example:** A seller tells his broker that the house has never had any problems with termites. The agent has no duty to verify the seller's statement. When a potential buyer then asks the broker if the house has ever had termite problems, the broker says no. If it turns out that the house does in fact have termite problems, the agent is not liable for passing the seller's statement on to the buyer.

Accounting

A real estate broker must be able to account for any trust funds she accepts in a transaction. Trust funds are funds and other valuables that the broker receives on behalf of a client. Trust funds must not be mixed, or commingled, with the broker's own funds. In addition, the broker must report to the client on the status of the trust funds on a regular basis.

Real Estate Agency Law Pamphlet

A real estate agent must give each party he renders services to a pamphlet containing the provisions of Washington's real estate agency law—the Real Estate Brokerage Relationships Act. This pamphlet must be given to each party before the party signs an agency agreement, consents to a dual agency, or waives any agency rights.

Agency Disclosure

Before a party signs an offer in a real estate transaction that is being handled by a real estate agent, the agent must disclose whether the agent represents the buyer, seller, both parties, or neither. This disclosure must be made to the party in writing.

License Law

Of course, before a real estate broker or salesperson can act as an agent, he or she must be duly licensed. The requirements for obtaining a real estate license are set forth in Washington's real estate license law. The license law also contains the grounds for disciplinary action against a licensee and lists the procedures that must be followed in disciplinary proceedings. The license law is administered by the Real Estate Division of the Washington State Department of Licensing.

Administration of the License Law

The license law and its accompanying rules and regulations are enforced by the Director of the Department of Licensing. The Director, who is appointed by the Governor, has the authority to issue and deny licenses and to take disciplinary action in response to license law violations. With the advice and approval of the Real Estate Commission, the Director also issues the rules and regulations that govern the activities of real estate licensees.

The Director and six commissioners make up the Real Estate Commission, which oversees the license examinations. The commissioners, who are also appointed by the Governor, advise the Director on real estate industry issues. Each commissioner must have at least five years of experience in the real estate profession.

In legal proceedings involving the Real Estate Division of the Department of Licensing, the Director is represented by the Washington State Attorney General. The Attorney General also advises the Director on license law issues.

Obtaining a License

A real estate broker or salesperson license is acquired by meeting the applicable age and education requirements, successfully completing the required clock hours of educational instruction in real estate, paying all fees, and passing the appropriate license examination. For information about the exact requirements for licensure, you should contact the Department of Licensing.

Renewing a License. Real estate licenses are renewed every two years. For a licensee who is a natural person, the renewal date is his or her birthday. If the licensee is a corporation, partnership, or other business entity, the renewal date is the date on which the license was issued. A licensee must submit proof that he or she has completed any required continuing education, and must pay the renewal fee. If the renewal application is late, the licensee must pay a late penalty in addition to the renewal fee.

Continuing education requirement. For each license renewal, a broker or salesperson must complete 30 clock hours of approved continuing education courses. Courses used to fulfill this continuing education requirement must have been started after the initial license was issued. If a licensee completes more than 30 clock hours in a two-year period, up to 15 hours may be carried forward for credit into the following renewal period.

Any course used to fulfill pre-license requirements cannot be used to fulfill a continuing education requirement.

Beginning June 1, 2004, licensees must complete a three-hour **core curriculum** requirement as part of their 30 hours. The core curriculum hours cover contemporary real estate issues and may be presented as an independent course or as part of a longer course.

Other License Regulations

A broker licensed in Washington must maintain an office in Washington. The licenses of the broker and any affiliated licensees must be prominently displayed in the office. Failure to meet this requirement may result in disciplinary action.

> **Example:** A Bellevue broker's license was suspended for six months for failing to maintain an accessible office with a properly displayed license.

If a broker shares an office with another business, the other business must be compatible with real estate brokerage activity. The two businesses must operate independently and maintain separate records. If two different brokerages share an office, they must be physically separated within the building, and must display separate identifying signs.

To open and maintain a branch office, a broker must pay a branch license fee. A duplicate of the broker's license showing the branch office address is issued and must be displayed in the branch office.

If a licensee changes locations, he or she must notify the Director of the Department of Licensing and surrender the license showing the old address. A new license with the new address will then be issued upon payment of a small fee.

If an affiliated licensee leaves a broker's employ, the broker must immediately surrender the person's license to the Director. The license ceases to be effective at the moment of termination, regardless of whether the licensee quit or was fired. The license is inactive until the licensee begins working for a new broker and a new license is issued. Note that if the salesperson or associate broker was terminated due to conduct that would be grounds for disciplinary action under the license law, the broker must submit a written statement to the Director, describing the reason for termination.

Retention of Records

The license law requires every broker to keep adequate records of all real estate transactions (even transactions that do not close), and to retain those records for at least three years. However, it's good business practice to keep records for longer than three years, as a broker's liability extends for a number of years after the transaction date.

At a minimum, a broker must keep the following real estate records:

1. Trust account records:
   a. duplicate receipt books or cash receipt journal recording all receipts;
   b. pre-numbered checks with check register, cash disbursement journal, or check stubs;
   c. validated duplicate bank deposit slips;

    d. client's accounting ledger summarizing all funds received and all funds disbursed for each real estate or business opportunity transaction or each property management account, contract, or mortgage collection account;

    e. separate ledger sheets for each tenant, lessee, vendee, or mortgagor; and

    f. reconciled bank statements and canceled checks.

2. A transaction folder containing all agreements, contracts, documents, leases, closing statements, and correspondence for each real estate or business opportunity transaction, rental, lease, contract, or mortgage collection account.

All records should be accurate, posted, up-to-date, and kept at an address where the real estate broker is licensed to maintain a real estate office.

Trust Funds

The handling of trust account money and records is an area where many real estate brokers run into problems. Current Washington guidelines require that all money collected for any reason related to the sale, rental, lease, or option of real estate or business opportunities or contract or mortgage collections must be placed in a trust account no later than the first banking day following its receipt.

There are only two exceptions to this rule: 1) if the purchase and sale agreement specifically states that the deposit check is to be held for a period of time, or 2) if the money collected was in connection with real estate, contracts, deeds of trust, or a business owned by the broker.

Funds belonging to the broker must never be deposited in the trust account. Commingling of trust fund money with the broker's personal funds or other general funds is grounds for license revocation.

Aside from being required by law, it is to the broker's advantage to place all client funds in special accounts. If client funds are commingled with the broker's own funds, the broker would be personally liable for any loss.

> **Example:** A broker places a client's earnest money deposit in his office safe. He intends to take it to the bank sometime next week. Over the weekend, his office is robbed and the money is stolen. The broker is personally liable for this money, no matter how unforeseeable the loss.

The broker may not disburse any trust funds before closing (or before a condition in the purchase agreement has been fulfilled) without a written release signed by both the buyer and the seller. However, if the parties have designated an escrow agent in writing, the broker may transfer funds to the escrow agent ahead of time, to allow the checks to clear by the closing date. And when a purchase agreement terminates according to its own terms before closing, the broker may disburse funds as provided in the agreement with a written rescission agreement.

Trust Accounts. In Washington, real estate trust accounts must be interest-bearing, demand deposit accounts in a banking institution within the state.

Example: An associate broker in Belfair was fined $200 for failing to place money received into proper real estate trust accounts.

A broker must maintain a pooled interest-bearing account called a "Housing Trust Fund Account" for deposits of $10,000 or less. The interest that accrues on this account is to be paid to the Department of Licensing at least quarterly. Twenty-five percent of the money goes to the Real Estate Education Account and 75% goes to the State Housing Trust Fund. The Housing Trust Fund is used for low-income housing grants and loans.

For deposits over $10,000, the broker must disclose in writing to the client or customer that he or she has an option as to how the funds will be handled. The money can go into the broker's pooled Housing Trust Fund Account, with the interest paid to the state. Alternatively, a separate interest-bearing account can be established and the interest paid to the client or customer.

The broker must keep records of the accrued interest, disposition of the interest, and payment of service fees for all trust accounts. Bank service charges can be paid out of a trust account only if the interest is sufficient to cover them. Otherwise, the charges must be paid out of the broker's own funds.

Disciplinary Action

A real estate licensee or license applicant may be subject to disciplinary action under the license law for either:

- engaging in unprofessional conduct, or
- engaging in an activity that is listed in the license law as being grounds for disciplinary action.

The license law defines **unprofessional conduct** as including any of the following:

1. the commission of any act involving moral turpitude, dishonesty, or corruption relating to real estate activities, regardless of whether the act constitutes a crime;
2. misrepresentation or concealment of a material fact in obtaining or reinstating a license;
3. false, deceptive, or misleading advertising;
4. incompetence, negligence, or malpractice that harms or may harm a consumer;
5. having any business or professional license suspended, revoked, or restricted by any government entity;
6. failure to cooperate with the Director of the Department of Licensing in the course of an investigation, audit, or inspection;
7. failure to comply with an order issued by the Director;
8. violating any lawful rule made by the Director;

9. aiding or abetting an unlicensed person to perform real estate activities that require a license;
10. practice or operation of a business or profession beyond the scope of practice or operation as defined by law;
11. any type of misrepresentation in the conduct of real estate activities;
12. failure to adequately supervise or oversee staff, whether employees or independent contractors, to the extent that consumers may be harmed or damaged;
13. being convicted of any gross misdemeanor or felony relating to real estate activities; or
14. interference with an investigation or disciplinary action by willfully misrepresenting facts, or by threatening, harassing, or bribing customers or witnesses to prevent them from providing evidence.

The license law further provides that a licensee is subject to disciplinary action for:

- being convicted of forgery, embezzlement, extortion, fraud, or similar offenses;
- making or authorizing statements that he or she knew (or could have known by the exercise of reasonable care) were false;
- converting trust funds to his or her own use;
- failing to disclose information or to produce records for inspection upon request by the Director;
- selling real estate according to a plan that endangers the public interest, after the Director has objected in writing;
- accepting money from more than one party in a transaction without first disclosing this to all interested parties in writing;
- accepting a profit on expenditures made for a principal without disclosing it to the principal;
- accepting compensation for an appraisal contingent on reporting a predetermined value;
- issuing an appraisal for property in which he or she has an interest without disclosing that interest in the appraisal report;
- falsely claiming to be a member of a state or national real estate association;
- directing a client or customer to a lending institution or escrow company in expectation of a kickback, without disclosing that expectation to the party he or she is representing;
- buying, selling, or leasing property (directly or through a third party) without disclosing that he or she holds a real estate license;
- any conduct in a real estate transaction which demonstrates bad faith, dishonesty, untrustworthiness, or incompetency.

In addition, violating any provision of the license law or its accompanying regulations is grounds for disciplinary action. This means that if a licensee fails to comply with any of the license law requirements discussed earlier (such as maintaining records or displaying a license), the licensee will be subject to disciplinary action.

Disciplinary Procedures

If the Director investigated a licensee's actions and finds evidence of a license law violation, the Director serves the licensee with a statement of charges. The licensee must be given notice of his or her right to file a request for a hearing within 20 days of receiving the statement of charges. If the licensee doesn't request a hearing, he or she is considered in default. At that point, the Director may enter a decision based on whatever facts are available.

If the licensee requests a hearing, the Director must set a hearing date as soon as is convenient but not less than 30 days after the statement of charges was served. Note that the hearing may be held sooner only if the Director has issued an immediate license suspension.

The hearing is typically conducted by an administrative law judge and each side may present arguments and evidence and cross-examine hostile witnesses. Both the licensee and the Department of Licensing may be represented by lawyers.

If the Department proves the accusation by a preponderance of the evidence, the Director may impose any of the sanctions permitted under the license law. An order imposing sanctions is mailed to the licensee and the sanctions become effective as soon as the order is received. But if the accusation is not proved, the case is dismissed and no further action is taken.

A licensee is entitled to appeal the results of the hearing to the superior court within 30 days of the decision. Any sanctions imposed in the Director's order remain in effect during the appeal process. However, the Director may choose to stay the sanctions during the appeal if it is appropriate to do so.

Sanctions for License Law Violations

The license law permits the following sanctions against a licensee or license applicant who is found to have violated the license law:

- revocation of the license;
- suspension of the license for a fixed or indefinite term;
- restriction or limitation of real estate activities;
- satisfactory completion of a specific program of remedial education or treatment;
- monitoring of real estate activities according to the Director's order;
- censure or reprimand;
- compliance with conditions of probation for a designated period of time;
- payment of a fine for each violation found by the Director of up to $5,000 per violation;
- denial of an initial or renewal license application; or
- other corrective action.

Fines collected by the Department are placed into the Real Estate Education Account and used for licensee education.

Following a disciplinary hearing, the Director may issue a **cease and desist order** to prevent a licensee or unlicensed person from continuing to violate the law. If the Director determines that a delay would cause irreparable harm to the public, a temporary cease and desist order may be issued even before any hearing takes place. The licensee must be informed of his or her right to a hearing to determine whether the temporary order should be canceled, modified, or made permanent. If the licensee requests the hearing, it must take place within 30 days, unless the licensee asks for a later date.

Alternatively, the Director can ask a court for an injunction ordering a licensee or unlicensed person to stop violating the law. The court may appoint a receiver to take over or close a real estate office operating in violation of the law, until a hearing can be held.

A violation of the license law is a gross misdemeanor, and in certain cases the Director may recommend criminal charges be filed against the violator. The case is handled by the prosecuting attorney in the county where the violation occurred. If the prosecuting attorney fails to act, the Director may ask the state Attorney General to take action instead.

Conclusion

Most real estate brokers and agents are honest and hardworking, and very few intentionally commit fraud. But only the very lucky get through a lengthy real estate career without some problems arising. Most get into trouble because of carelessness or mistakes.

The real estate agency statute spells out a licensee's duties to his or her principal and to third parties. Make sure you are informed of these duties, and keep up-to-date on current laws and requirements.

The license law contains additional requirements for salespersons and brokers, including licensing requirements and grounds for disciplinary action. Obviously, you need to be very familiar with these regulations as well.

Case Problem

The following is a hypothetical case problem. Most of the facts are taken from a real case. Based on what you have learned from this chapter, make a decision on the issues presented, and then check to see if your answer matches the court's decision.

The Facts

Marjorie Belote and a co-owner owned over 1,000 acres of wheat land in Whitman County. On May 19, 1970, a written 90-day listing on the property was given to broker Owen F. Koller at a listing price of approximately $500,000.

Koller telephoned the owners to see if they would be interested in trading the farm for a building in Lewiston, Idaho, owned by Gerald Anderson. For purposes of a trade, this building and the adjacent parking lot were worth approximately $400,000. The owners said they were not interested in a trade, but wanted an outright sale.

In June, Koller contacted the owners several times about the exchange and sent them a brochure on the building. After much insistence by Koller, the owners finally flew to Lewiston to inspect the building and arranged to have the building appraised.

Without the owners' approval, Koller obtained a copy of their appraisal of Anderson's building and gave it to Anderson. The owners were very upset when they learned that Anderson had a copy of the appraisal, because they had paid $300 for it and considered it privileged information. Some negotiation concerning the trade occurred, but the trade never took place. The listing agreement expired and the owners had no further contact with Koller.

In October, Anderson began to negotiate with the owners for the direct purchase of the property without a trade. Anderson eventually purchased the property in January.

The owners later learned that their broker, Koller, had been a friend of Anderson for several years and had made a number of sales on his behalf. They discovered that Koller and Anderson had agreed that if a trade of the building for the property were made, Koller would receive a commission from Anderson of approximately $24,000.

Koller never disclosed to the owners that this agreement existed. It further appeared that Anderson was willing to make a direct sale at any time if a trade could not be arranged. It was clearly always the owners' preference to make a direct sale, but Koller never disclosed this possibility to the owners.

On the brochures of the building that Koller sent to the owners, the following information appeared:

"FARM & BUSINESS REALTY INC."
Suite 209 Davenport Hotel, Spokane, Wash. 99201
MA4-2121
Owen F. Koller—Broker

Koller brought a lawsuit against the owners claiming that he was entitled to a commission, since they sold the property to a purchaser whom he introduced to the property during the term of the exclusive listing agreement.

The Questions

Is Koller entitled to the commission? Did Koller breach any duty? Was the information printed on the brochure enough to inform the owners that Koller was also an agent for Anderson, and their subsequent negotiation proof that they approved of the dual agency?

The Answer

In the case of *Koller v. Belote*, 12 Wn. App. 194, 528 P.2d 1000 (1974), the court held that Koller was not entitled to a commission. The court also awarded $1,071 to the owners for transportation costs and expenses in visiting Lewiston at Koller's insistence.

The court found that Koller had failed to disclose the existence of a dual agency relationship and obtain the parties' consent. The mere transmittal of a brochure upon which the broker's name was listed was not enough to satisfy this duty of disclosure.

In addition, Koller failed to disclose a potential conflict of interest: his long-standing friendship with the prospective buyer. Furthermore, he placed his own interests above those of the principals by pushing the trade over a direct sale, which was clearly contrary to the express desires of the owners.

The court also found that Koller had breached his duty to the sellers by transmitting confidential information (the appraisal) to Anderson.

Note that this case was decided prior to the enactment of Washingon's Real Estate Brokerage Relationships Act. Under the current law, Koller would also have been required to give a real estate agency law pamphlet to each of the parties and make a written agency disclosure to each party before the sales contract was signed.

Chapter Summary

- Real estate agency relationships in Washington are governed by general agency law and the real estate agency statute.

- A real estate agent must put her principal's interests above her own, cannot make any secret profits, and must disclose any conflicts of interest. She cannot disclose any confidential information about her principal, even after the agency ends. She must advise the principal to seek expert advice when necessary. She must also make a good faith and continuous effort to fulfill the agency agreement's terms.

- A secret profit is any financial benefit obtained by the agent as a result of the agency that was not authorized by the principal.

- When dealing with any party in a transaction (including the principal), a real estate agent must use reasonable care and skill and act with honesty and good faith. He must present all written communications and disclose all material facts in a timely manner. He must be able to account for all funds received in a transaction. He must give a real estate agency law pamphlet to every party to whom he provides services. Before a party signs an offer, he must make a written agency disclosure to each party in the transaction.

- Inaccurate statements or misrepresentations may be considered fraud. Fraud may be actual or constructive.

- An agent is not responsible for innocently passing on a seller's inaccurate statements.

- Puffing, predictions, and opinions are generally not actionable. A licensee has no duty to inspect the property or independently investigate or verify statements made by either party or a reasonable source.

- A material fact is one with a substantial negative impact on the property's value or a party's ability to perform, or that would defeat the purpose of the transaction.

- A latent defect is one that would not be discovered through an ordinary inspection. Any known latent defects must be disclosed to the parties.

- The license law sets forth the requirements for obtaining and renewing a license. Licensees must complete continuing education courses to renew a license.

- Grounds for disciplinary action and disciplinary procedures are contained in the license law.

- If a licensee is found to have violated the license law, his or her license may be suspended or revoked. A licensee is entitled to notice and hearing before such sanctions are imposed.

Checklist of Problem Areas

Real Estate Licensee's Checklist

❏ Have you made the required agency disclosure statement and included written confirmation in the purchase and sale agreement?

❏ Have you provided the real estate agency law pamphlet to all appropriate parties?

❏ Have all of your statements to the seller and to the buyer been truthful and accurate?

❏ Have you fully disclosed all material facts to the seller and to the buyer, as required and allowed by your agency relationship?

❏ Have you disclosed a dual agency relationship or any personal, financial, or business relationship between yourself or your selling agents and potential buyers?

❏ Is the potential purchaser the agent, or a friend, relative, or business associate of yours, or someone in your brokerage?

Principal/Seller's Checklist

❏ Do you understand the terms of the contract (listing agreement) signed with the broker, and are you aware of the consequences if you breach this agreement?

❏ Have you been truthful with the agent and with potential buyers concerning all material facts about the property?

❏ Have you made clear to your agent what terms of sale are acceptable to you? Does your agent know what personal information he may disclose to potential purchasers?

❏ Have you asked the agent to provide you with relevant financial information about the buyer?

❏ Is the commission agreement perfectly clear? Do you and the broker both understand and agree on how much the commission will be and when it will become payable?

Buyer's Checklist

❏ Make sure you know who the agent is working for—even though the agent is showing you property and answering your questions, he or she may be the seller's agent.

❑ Remember that you can't rely on puffing, opinions, or predictions. Such statements, even if untrue, are generally not actionable.

❑ Ask questions—the agent or seller may simply forget to tell you certain things if you don't ask. But also note that the rule of "caveat emptor" no longer applies. The agent and seller must disclose all material facts even if you don't ask.

❑ Do you know your rights under Washington's disclosure law? Have you examined the seller's disclosure statement carefully?

Chapter Quiz

1. A listing broker should disclose all of the following to a purchaser, EXCEPT:

   a. the listed property has a latent defect

   b. the broker is aware of some problems with the septic tank

   c. the property owner has expressed a willingness to accept less than the asking price

   d. the property is currently classified as a nonconforming use

2. Without the seller's permission, a broker tells a potential buyer that her client is experiencing financial difficulties and needs to sell immediately at any cost. The broker:

   a. was obligated to disclose this information to the buyer

   b. has breached the duty of good faith and loyalty to the principal by disclosing this information to the buyer

   c. should have disclosed this information if it helped to close a sale

   d. was right to disclose this information only if the buyer had already made an offer

3. A property is listed for $208,950. The broker finds an interested buyer who wants to offer $183,000, which is well below what the broker knows the seller will accept. What should the broker do?

   a. Write the offer and submit it to the seller as is

   b. Write the offer but don't submit it to the seller

   c. Refuse to write the offer because, as agent for the seller, the broker is authorized to reject unacceptable offers

   d. Refuse to write the offer and notify the seller in writing of that refusal

4. It is 28° in January in Spokane. The furnace in a seller's house is broken. He has been heating the house by using the fireplace and several portable heaters. Before a buyer comes to look at the house, he puts out the fire and hides the heaters. He tells the buyer that the furnace works great. The seller is guilty of:

   a. constructive fraud

   b. actual fraud

   c. puffing

   d. negligence

5. A real estate agent tells potential buyers, "This is a great old house. They just don't build them like they used to." This statement would be considered:

   a. a misrepresentation

   b. constructive fraud

   c. self-dealing

   d. puffing

6. A buyer tells the listing agent in confidence that there are going to be some zoning changes that will have a favorable effect on the property. The listing agent passes this information on to the seller. The agent:

   a. has fulfilled his fiduciary duty to the seller

   b. has violated the license law

   c. may owe damages to the buyer

   d. has committed a crime

7. Harold wants to list his house with Angela. He asks her what the property is worth. Angela says she is no expert, but the house is probably worth $275,000 and he should consider listing it at $278,500. However, she warns him that if he wants an accurate, professional assessment of the home's value, he should ask an appraiser. Harold relies on Angela's estimate and lists the house at $278,000. He turns down three offers for $262,000, thinking the price is too low. He later discovers his house is really worth $260,000. Before Harold can relist it at the lower price, the stock market crashes, interest rates go sky-high, and Harold's property value decreases by $20,000. Harold sues Angela for breach of her fiduciary duty, asking for $20,000 in damages.

   a. Angela will be held liable because she misrepresented Harold's property value
   b. Angela will probably not be liable because she did not hold herself out as an expert and recommended that Harold ask an appraiser
   c. Angela will not be held liable because it is not her fault that the economy suffered such a severe setback
   d. Angela will be held liable because she was not able to find a ready, willing, and able buyer at her suggested listing price

8. Cheryl Burgess hired broker Tom Osling to sell her property. Tom is a limited partner in a local land development company that purchased the property. Tom did not tell Cheryl that he had any interest in the company that purchased the property.

   a. Tom did not need to disclose this information, since he was only a limited partner and not a full, general partner
   b. Tom breached his duty to Cheryl by not disclosing this information, and may be considered a dual agent
   c. Tom did not need to disclose this information since it was only a business relationship
   d. Tom could not be charged with dual agency, since he received no commission from the development company

9. Broker Bob has a listing to sell Sam's house for $319,000. Bob's sister is interested in purchasing the house. Bob tells Sam that the purchaser is his sister and that her offer is $317,000. Sam says he doesn't care who the buyer is, but he won't go below $318,000. They close the deal at $318,000.

   a. The sale is invalid because a broker can't sell to a member of his family
   b. Bob adequately fulfilled his duty by disclosing who the buyer was to Sam
   c. The sale is valid, but Bob cannot earn any commission on the transaction
   d. Bob should have told his sister that she would have to work through another broker

10. Real estate trust accounts must be:

    a. interest-bearing
    b. demand deposit accounts
    c. opened in a Washington depository institution
    d. All of the above

11. Once an agent has obtained a real estate license, it must be renewed:

    a. every two years
    b. every three years
    c. every four years
    d. only if revoked or suspended

12. Which of the following is an example of commingling?

    a. Paying trust account service charges from the interest generated by the account
    b. Depositing an employee's paycheck in a client's trust account
    c. Placing the buyer's deposit in a trust account
    d. Depositing rent from a commercial rental account in a trust account

13. The law requires brokers to keep adequate records of real estate transactions and to retain these records:

    a. until the transaction has completely closed
    b. for one year
    c. for three years
    d. for six years

14. After a disciplinary hearing against a licensee, the Director of the Department of Licensing has the power to:

    a. sentence the licensee to jail time of up to 90 days
    b. file criminal charges against the licensee
    c. require the licensee to pay restitution to the injured party
    d. temporarily suspend the license

15. When a licensee appeals a disciplinary action to the superior court:

    a. the results of the Director's disciplinary hearing are set aside
    b. the sanctions imposed by the Director remain in effect throughout the appeals process
    c. the sanctions imposed by the Director are stayed until the appeals process is complete
    d. the licensee has no right of appeal

7 Contract Law

Outline

I. Contract Classifications
   A. Express vs. implied
   B. Unilateral vs. bilateral
   C. Executory vs. executed
   D. Valid, void, voidable, or unenforceable
II. Contract Formation
   A. Capacity
   B. Mutual consent
      1. offer
      2. termination
      3. acceptance
      4. consent freely given
         a. fraud
         b. undue influence
         c. duress
         d. mistake
   C. Consideration
   D. Lawful purpose
   E. The statute of frauds
   F. Promissory estoppel
III. Modification of a Contract
   A. Assignment or novation
   B. Accord and satisfaction
   C. Release
IV. Breach of Contract
   A. Substantial performance vs. material breach
   B Conditions
   C. Tendering performance
V. Remedies for Breach
   A. Arbitration
   B. Lawsuit
   C. Damages
      1. certainty requirement
      2. mitigation requirement
      3. liquidated damages
   D. Equitable remedies
      1. injunction
      2. rescission
      3. specific performance
   E. Interference with contract

VI. Real Estate Contracts
    A. Employment agreements
    B. Listing agreements
       1. types of listing agreements
       2. basic elements
    C. Purchase and sale agreements
    D. Options
       1. consideration for an option
       2. relation back
       3. assignment
       4. termination
       5. right of first refusal

Key Terms

- express/implied contract
- unilateral/bilateral contract
- executory/executed contract
- valid contract
- void
- voidable
- unenforceable
- disaffirm
- capacity
- emancipated minor
- offer
- acceptance
- objective intent
- revocation
- mailbox rule
- counteroffer
- fraud

- undue influence
- duress
- business compulsion
- unilateral mistake
- consideration
- severable
- statute of frauds
- promissory estoppel
- detrimental reliance
- assignment
- novation
- accord and satisfaction
- material breach
- substantial performance
- time is of the essence
- contingency clause
- tender offer
- anticipatory repudiation

- mandatory arbitration
- contractual arbitration
- statute of limitations
- parol evidence rule
- damages
- mitigate
- liquidated damages
- equitable remedies
- injunction
- rescission
- cancellation
- specific performance
- integration clause
- extender clause
- bump clause
- option
- relation back
- right of first refusal

Chapter Overview

A **contract** is an agreement to do (or not do) a certain thing. It doesn't have to be a legal document; a spoken promise, a bus pass, and a movie ticket are all examples of contracts. To be enforced by a court, a contract must be made according to the rules of contract law. These rules are designed to protect the parties against misunderstandings and false claims.

A typical real estate sales transaction involves a number of contracts: an employment agreement between a broker and a salesperson; a listing agreement; a purchase and sale agreement; a title insurance policy; an escrow agreement; and a security instrument, such as a deed of trust. Because contracts are such an integral part of real estate transactions, it's essential for real estate agents to understand basic contract law.

This chapter discusses forming and modifying a contract, the remedies available when a contract is breached, and several specific types of contracts used in real estate transactions.

Contract Classifications

There are four fundamental ways of classifying all contracts. Every contract is:

- either express or implied,
- either unilateral or bilateral,
- either executory or executed, and
- either valid, voidable, void, or unenforceable.

Express vs. Implied. An **express** contract is an agreement that has been expressed in words, either spoken or written. If Miller asks Simpson, "Will you cut my hair for $10?" and Simpson says, "OK," they have an express contract. An **implied** contract, on the other hand, hasn't been put into words. Instead, the agreement is implied by the actions of the parties.

> **Example:** Ferris offers to mow George's lawn for $5. George accepts and is pleased with the work. Without being asked, Ferris begins coming on the first Saturday of every month to mow George's lawn. George pays Ferris in cash after each job is finished.
>
> One Saturday Ferris shows up to mow the lawn and is greeted by a housesitter who says George is on vacation for a few days. Ferris goes ahead and mows the lawn anyway. Under their implied contract, George is obligated to pay for the mowing job.

Some contracts are partly express and partly implied. When you order a meal in a restaurant, it's understood that you agree to pay the price on the menu, although you don't actually say that to the waiter.

Unilateral vs. Bilateral. A contract is **unilateral** when only one party makes a legally binding promise to the other party. A contract is **bilateral** when each party makes a binding promise to the other.

> **Example:** Krouse tells Jackson, "I'll pay you $100 if you paint my fence this week." Jackson says, "Sure, I'll do it tomorrow morning." They have a bilateral contract, because Jackson has promised to paint the fence, and Krouse has promised to pay.
>
> Now suppose that Krouse says, "Paint my fence this week and I'll pay you $100," but Jackson doesn't commit herself. This is a unilateral contract, since only Krouse has made a promise. If Jackson paints the fence, Krouse is bound to pay her $100. But Krouse can't require Jackson to paint the fence, because she didn't promise to do it.

Executed vs. Executory. An **executed** contract is one that has been fully performed—both parties have done what they promised to do. An **executory** contract has not yet been fully performed. One or both of the parties have not begun to carry out their promises, or are in the process of carrying them out. Contracts start out executory and end up executed.

Valid, Void, Voidable, or Unenforceable. A **valid** contract is an agreement that meets all the legal requirements for contract formation outlined in the next section of this chapter. If one of the parties doesn't fulfill his or her side of the bargain (he or she **breaches** the contract), the other can sue to have the contract enforced.

But many agreements don't meet one or more of the requirements for contract formation. These agreements are usually considered legally void. In the eyes of the law, a **void** contract is actually not a contract at all; it can't be enforced in court. If both parties fulfill their promises, fine. But if one breaches and the other sues, the judge will rule that no contract was formed, and will refuse to enforce the agreement.

In certain situations, an agreement that is missing a legal requirement is not void, but rather **voidable** by one party. This generally occurs when one party has taken advantage of the other in some way. For example, if someone has signed a contract as a result of undue influence exerted by the other party, the injured party can choose whether or not to go through with the contract. The injured party can **disaffirm** the contract—that is, ask a court to terminate it. If the injured party chooses not to disaffirm, the agreement will be enforceable. In the next section, we'll cover the various situations in which a contract is voidable rather than void.

Finally, some contracts are **unenforceable** even when they are not void or voidable. For example, a valid contract becomes unenforceable when the statute of limitations runs

Fig. 7.1 Contracts

Type of contract	Legal Effect	Example
Void	No contract at all	An agreement for which there is no consideration
Voidable	Valid until rescinded by one party	A contract with a minor
Unenforceable	Party may not sue for performance	A contract where the limitations period has expired
Valid	Binding and enforceable	An agreement with all the requirements for a valid contract

out. Or maybe all the requirements for contract formation were met, but there isn't proper evidence to prove that in court. (This problem often occurs with oral contracts.) A contract is also likely to be unenforceable if it is vaguely worded.

Contract Formation

A valid contract must have these four elements:

- capacity to contract,
- mutual consent,
- consideration, and
- a lawful purpose.

These requirements apply to all contracts. In addition, certain contracts (especially real estate contracts) must be in writing and signed to be enforceable.

Capacity

To enter into a valid contract, a person must be at least **18 years old** and must also be legally **competent**. This requirement protects minors and the mentally disabled, who otherwise might enter into contracts without fully understanding the consequences.

Minority. If a minor enters into a contract, the contract is voidable, but only by the minor. The minor can decide whether he wants to go through with the transaction. If not, the minor can go to court to disaffirm the contract. But if the minor does want to go through with it, the other party is bound.

> **Example:** Martinson, who is only 17, signs a contract to buy some property from Stuart. A week later, Stuart decides it wasn't a very good deal. However, only Martinson can disaffirm the contract. Stuart must fulfill the terms of the contract if Martinson chooses to go through with it.

A minor must disaffirm a voidable contract before he turns 18, or within a reasonable time after turning 18.

Note, however, that a contract with an emancipated minor is valid. An **emancipated minor** is a person under 18 who:

- is or has been married,
- is on active duty in the armed forces, or
- has a declaration of emancipation from a court.

Incompetence. A person who is entirely without understanding cannot make a contract. After a person has been declared incompetent by a court (because of mental disability, retardation, or senility), any contract he or she enters into is void. If the person made a contract before the declaration of incompetence but while of unsound mind, the court-appointed guardian can ask the court to have that contract set aside.

In a few cases, if a person was under the influence of alcohol or other drugs at the time of entering into a contract, it will be voidable. But to disaffirm the contract, the person will usually have to prove that he or she was involuntarily intoxicated.

Necessities Exception. An exception to these capacity rules applies to a minor or an incompetent person who contracts to buy necessities (such as food, clothing, shelter or medicine). In this situation, the contract is not voidable and he or she must pay the reasonable value of those items.

Note that this exception applies only to necessities and not to items such as a new car, video game system, or sports equipment.

> **Example:** Jenelle, who is 16, goes on a spending spree at the mall. She buys a $900 new stereo system, paying $100 cash and signing a contract agreeing to pay the balance over the next 6 months. When she goes home, her parents take one look at the stereo and tell her to take it back. Because Jenelle is a minor, she can return the stereo, disaffirm the contract, and get her money back.

Mutual Consent

For a contract to be a binding obligation, all the parties must consent to its terms. This mutual consent is sometimes referred to as a "meeting of the minds." It is achieved through **offer and acceptance**.

Offer. The process of forming a contract begins when one person (the **offeror**) makes an offer to another (the **offeree**). To be the basis for a contract, an offer must:

- express an intent to contract, and
- have definite terms.

The intent to contract must be **objective intent** (what the offeror says and does) rather than **subjective intent** (what the offeror is actually thinking). If you say or do something that a reasonable person could interpret as a serious expression of the intention to make a contract ("I'll sell you a dozen roses for $15"), that may be a legally binding offer even if you don't have any roses and never really intended to come up with them.

Case Example:

Warren Treece, vice president of Vend-A-Win (a corporation that distributed punchboards), spoke before the Washington State Gambling Commission in support of punchboards. During his speech, Treece offered to pay $100,000 to anyone who could find a crooked punchboard. His statement brought laughter from the audience.

Vernon Barnes heard a news report of Treece's statement. Several years earlier, Barnes had purchased two fraudulent punchboards. Barnes telephoned Treece, told him that he had two crooked punchboards and asked if Treece's offer was serious. Treece told Barnes the offer was serious, that the money was being held in escrow, and asked Barnes to bring in the punchboards for inspection.

The punchboards were inspected and found to be rigged and dishonest. However, Treece refused to pay Barnes the $100,000. Barnes brought a breach of contract action against Treece.

In his defense, Treece argued that his statement was made in jest, and could not be construed as an offer that could be accepted to form a contract.

The court found that although the original statement drew laughter from the audience, Treece's subsequent statements and conduct showed a serious intent.

The court found that there was a binding unilateral contract: Treece had promised to pay $100,000 to anyone who found a crooked board, and Barnes had found two crooked boards. The court awarded judgment for Barnes in the amount of $100,000. *Barnes v. Treece*, 15 Wn. App. 437, 549 P.2d 1152 (1976).

On the other hand, a casual remark or a joke is not a binding offer. Because of the nature of the remark, the tone of voice, or the situation, a reasonable person should not interpret the statement as a serious offer.

Example: Rico paid $65,000 for a sports car. After it breaks down for the second time in a week, Rico tells Paulson, "I'm so tired of this piece of junk I'd sell it for ten bucks." Paulson pulls out her wallet and hands Rico a ten dollar bill.

Rico is not required to sell Paulson the car for ten dollars, because his statement was not a binding offer. A reasonable person would not have interpreted his remark as a serious expression of an intent to contract.

An offer must have **definite terms**—it won't be binding if it is too vague. It should state at least such basic terms as the subject matter, the time for performance, and the price. In some cases, a court will fill in the blanks with a reasonable time or a reasonable price.

Example: A waiter describes the day's "Seafood Special" without stating the dish's price. A restaurant diner orders and eats the dish without knowing its price. Unless the restaurant charges an unreasonably high price for the dish, a contract has been formed and the diner is obligated to pay for his meal.

However, if too many terms are left unspecified (for example, during preliminary negotiations for a contract), no contract has been formed.

If an offer to purchase involves financing, terms such as the interest rate or length of the loan term must be included in the offer.

Case Example:

The Setterlunds signed a purchase and sale agreement to purchase commercial real estate from the Firestones. The agreement provided that the sellers were to accept a promissory note and deed of trust as security for the $205,000 balance of the purchase price. However, a note and deed of trust were never attached to the agreement.

The Firestones did not go through with the sale and the Setterlunds sued for specific performance of the purchase contract.

The Firestones argued that the purchase and sale agreement was too indefinite to permit specific performance because the note and deed of trust were not attached. Thus, essential terms and conditions were missing. Since no note was attached, the parties had never agreed on an interest rate (a very important point with a balance of $205,000).

Preliminary agreements (such as purchase and sale agreements) must be definite enough to allow the court to enforce the agreement without having to supply important missing terms. In this case, the court would have needed to supply the missing interest rate.

The court found that the purchase and sale agreement was not definite enough to be enforced by specific performance. The Firestones could not be forced to go through with the sale. *Setterlund v. Firestone*, 104 Wn.2d 24, 700 P.2d 745 (1985).

Using pre-printed forms for real estate contracts such as listing agreements and purchase and sale agreements helps eliminate the possibility of vagueness. The pre-printed forms have spaces to fill in the contract's essential terms, making it less likely that a term will be overlooked.

Termination. An offer is not legally binding until it is accepted by the offeree. It can be accepted at any time before it terminates. An offer can be terminated by one of four events:

- lapse of time,
- death or incapacity of one of the parties,
- revocation by the offeror, or
- rejection by the offeree.

Lapse of time. Many offers state that they will expire at a certain time, such as "after five days" or "on March 30." When an offer doesn't specify an expiration date, a court will generally rule that it expired after a reasonable time. But even when an offer includes an expiration date, it may end sooner, through one of the other methods of termination.

Death or incapacity. An offer is terminated if either of the parties dies or becomes incompetent before it is accepted.

Revocation. If an offeror revokes the offer before the offeree accepts it, it is terminated—the offeree has lost the chance to accept it. This is true even if the offer stated that it was irrevocable, or that it would not expire until a particular date.

Case Example:

In July 1975, Seattle First National Bank foreclosed against the Knights' property. On December 16, 1976, the Knights learned that the bank was negotiating with Johnston to buy the property. At a meeting with the bank's attorney, Mrs. Knight was told that the bank would sell the property back to the Knights for the amount then owing (approximately $22,000). Mrs. Knight claimed that the bank told her it would not conclude the sale with Johnston for two or three weeks.

On December 22, with Johnston's approval, the bank entered into an agreement to sell the property to Patrick.

The Knights brought a lawsuit against the bank and argued that the offer by the bank to sell to them was an oral agreement to extend the time for redemption and that it was a binding agreement.

The court held that the bank's offer to Mrs. Knight was an offer that could be revoked or withdrawn any time before acceptance. The bank withdrew its offer when it sold to Patrick. *Knight v. Seattle First National Bank*, 22 Wn. App. 493, 589 P.2d 1279 (1979).

Note that the result would have been different if the Knights had paid the bank to keep the offer open for a few weeks. When an offeree pays or gives something to the offeror in exchange for holding an offer open, the offer cannot be revoked during the specified period. (See the discussion of options at the end of this chapter.) But without such a payment, an offer can be revoked at any time before it is accepted.

A revocation is effective as soon as it is communicated to the offeree. When it is not communicated directly (in person or over the telephone), the revocation is effective at the time it is received by the offeree. So if a notice of revocation is mailed to the offeree, the offer is not revoked until the revocation is delivered.

Rejection. An offer is also terminated when it is rejected by the offeree. If I reject your offer on Monday, I can't change my mind and call back on Tuesday to accept it. If you're still interested in the deal, we can start the process of offer and acceptance over again. But your original offer was terminated by my rejection, and if you've lost interest, I can no longer hold you to your offer.

Acceptance. When an offer is accepted, a contract is formed. At that point, the parties are legally bound. Neither party can back out unless the other is willing to call off the contract.

There are four basic requirements for acceptance:

- an offer can only be accepted by the offeree;
- an acceptance must be communicated to the offeror;
- an acceptance must be made in the manner specified; and
- an acceptance must not vary the terms of the offer.

Fig. 7.2 Offer and acceptance

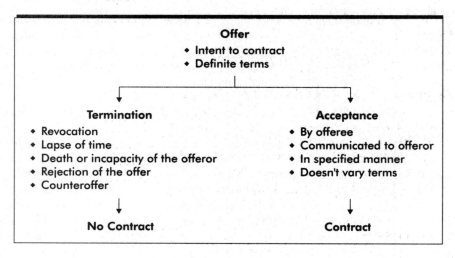

Offer
- Intent to contract
- Definite terms

Termination
- Revocation
- Lapse of time
- Death or incapacity of the offeror
- Rejection of the offer
- Counteroffer

↓

No Contract

Acceptance
- By offeree
- Communicated to offeror
- In specified manner
- Doesn't vary terms

↓

Contract

Accepted by the offeree. The first of these requirements—that an offer can be accepted only by the offeree—may sound obvious. But it means that if Jeremy makes an offer to Arthur and Arthur decides not to accept it, Amy can't accept the offer and force Jeremy to deal with her. Of course, Jeremy may be willing to work with Amy, but in legal terms any contract between Jeremy and Amy is based on a new offer, not on the offer Jeremy made to Arthur.

Communicated to the offeror. An acceptance must be communicated to the offeror. You may already have decided to accept my offer, but until you let me know that you've accepted it, I can still revoke it.

> **Example:** Seller is selling waterfront property. Seller's agent tells Buyer that the frontage is about 800 feet. Buyer signs a purchase and sale agreement offering to buy the property and the agent delivers it to Seller. In the meantime, Buyer discovers that the frontage is only 700 feet. Buyer notifies Seller that he will not go through with the purchase.
>
> Seller sues. Seller claims that he signed the purchase and sale agreement the day he received it. But since he hadn't sent it back to Buyer yet, the acceptance was not communicated and Buyer still had the right to revoke.

Mailbox rule. When an acceptance is not communicated directly (in person or over the telephone), it is effective as soon as the message is sent, even though the offeror may not receive it immediately. This is called the **mailbox rule**: the acceptance creates a binding contract when the offeree drops it in the mailbox. In recent years, the widespread use of fascimiles and email raises the issue of whether the mailbox rule also applies to these methods of communicating offers and acceptances.

Manner of acceptance. As mentioned earlier, certain types of contracts (including most contracts concerning real property) are required by law to be in writing and signed. For those contracts, only a written, signed acceptance will bind the offeree.

> **Example:** Adams writes Bing a letter offering to sell him her house for $250,000. It's an excellent offer, so Bing calls Adams on the phone and says he's accepting it.
>
> Two hours later, Bing changes his mind. He can call Adams back and withdraw his acceptance, because it wasn't in writing.

However, other types of contracts do not necessarily require a written acceptance. Any reasonable method of acceptance will usually be effective, unless the offer specifies how it is to be accepted. If the offer specifies a particular method (such as "in writing," "by registered mail," or "by delivering a cashier's check"), the acceptance will not bind the offeror unless those instructions are followed.

> **Example:** Wallace offers to sell his antique car to Savala. The offer states it is to be accepted by registered mail. Savala drops by Wallace's office and tells him that she's accepting the offer. Wallace can still revoke the offer, because Savala did not accept the offer in the manner specified.

Of course, an offeror can waive this requirement. If Wallace chooses to treat Savala's spoken acceptance as effective, a contract is formed.

Note that generally, silence cannot be the specified manner of acceptance.

> **Example:** Xavier writes Zigler a letter offering to buy her sailboat for $2,000. The letter says, "If you have not rejected this offer by Saturday, I will consider it accepted." Zigler receives the letter but never replies.
>
> Xavier goes to Zigler's house with $2,000 and demands the boat. Zigler is not required to let him have it. Her silence in response to Xavier's letter was not an acceptance, and no contract was formed.

But if the offeree accepts the benefits of the offer, silence may be construed as acceptance. If Xavier had enclosed a $2,000 check with his letter and Zigler cashed it, she would be deemed to have accepted his offer and would be required to let him have the boat.

Acceptance must not vary the offer's terms. To create a contract, the offeree must accept the terms exactly as offered. The offeree can't modify the terms of the offer or add any new terms.

Case Example:

The Flerchingers listed their ranch for sale with a brokerage and the listing expired without a sale. Koller, a salesperson at the brokerage, later went into business for himself and continued to seek a buyer for the Flerchinger property without the owners' knowledge.

Koller contacted Watson, who offered $150,000 for the property. Koller then attempted to get the Flerchingers to sign a purchase and sale agreement under which Koller would receive a $7,000 commission upon closing.

The Flerchingers signed the purchase and sale agreement, but only after the price was raised to $155,000 and a provision was added giving them the buildings and pasture for their cattle until October and possession of the current hay crop. After the Flerchingers signed the agreement, Koller edited out the new clause.

Koller never obtained Watson's signature to this agreement and after May 26, all parties treated the agreement as terminated.

The next month, Watson approached the Flerchingers directly and they reached a new agreement. Upon learning of the sale, Koller sued for a commission and lost. Although the Flerchingers eventually sold to Watson, it was not an acceptance of the original offer. Each change constituted a new offer or counteroffer. *Koller v. Flerchinger*, 73 Wn.2d 857, 441 P.2d 126 (1968).

Because the Flerchingers added terms (the additional $5,000 and retention of hay and pasture until October), they technically did not accept Watson's offer. Instead, they made a counteroffer. A **counteroffer** is essentially a new offer—now the Flerchingers are the offerors, and Watson is the offeree. To create a binding contract, Watson would have had to accept the Flerchingers' counteroffer (which he didn't do). Further negotiations took place before an agreement was finally reached.

A counteroffer terminates the original offer, just as a rejection would. If your counteroffer is rejected, it's too late to go back and accept the original offer. You can start again with a new offer identical to the original offer. But if the original offeror has had a change of heart, you can no longer hold him or her to the original offer. It's important to keep this in mind, since a real estate transaction often involves a series of offers and counteroffers. Each counteroffer terminates the previous offer.

Consent Freely Given. Offer and acceptance are the expression of mutual consent to the terms of an offer. But to create a binding contract, consent must be freely given. It is not freely given when it is the result of one of these negative influences:

- fraud,
- undue influence,
- duress, or
- mistake.

Any of these makes a contract voidable by the party who was harmed. The injured party may choose to go ahead with the contract or disaffirm it. To disaffirm, the victim must be able to show that the negative influence was the key to his or her consent.

Fraud. A victim of fraud must prove that he or she would not have entered into the contract if the other party had not misrepresented the effect of the agreement or made false promises. Recall from our discussion of fraud in Chapter 6 that fraud may be actual or constructive. For example, a seller who intentionally hides cracks in the basement and assures the buyer the foundation is sound is committing actual fraud. A seller who innocently points out incorrect lot boundaries may be committing constructive fraud.

It's also important to distinguish between fraud in the inducement and fraud in the execution of the contract. When **fraud in the inducement** occurs, a party understands what he is signing, but his signature is induced by fraud. The contract is voidable by the defrauded party.

> **Example:** A real estate salesperson convinces an owner to sign a listing agreement by falsely claiming the house is worth $100,000 more than its true value. This is fraud in the inducement.

When **fraud in the execution** is committed, the defrauded party does not know what he is signing and did not intend to enter into such a contract at all.

> **Example:** Two days before a sale closes, the listing agent hands his client a stack of papers, telling him that his signature is needed on each document for closing purposes. The client signs the documents, without realizing that one of the documents is actually a deed granting his property to the salesperson. This is fraud in the execution.

Undue influence. Taking unfair advantage of another person by using your influence over them is considered **undue influence**. A contract is voidable if you persuade someone to sign it by taking advantage of his or her trust in you, his or her weakness of mind (due to senility or exhaustion, for example), or his or her necessities or distress (drug addiction, for example). Undue influence often involves telling the victim that documents must be signed immediately, and that there's no time to consult a lawyer.

Case Example:

In 1972, John F. Jeanes was a Christian Science practitioner who met Nancy Ferguson when she was considering making a full commitment to Christian Science. They fell in love and began considering marriage. During their relationship, Nancy received treatment from John several times a week. At trial, she testified that she exalted practitioners in her mind and that she trusted John because of her affection for him and because of his role as a practitioner.

When Nancy decided to purchase an apartment building, John helped her locate some suitable property and began to encourage Nancy to take him on as a partner in the purchase. When Nancy declined, John became angry, telling her she was ungrateful and that her refusal violated the tenets of Christian Science. He also told her she was financially, intellectually, and emotionally incapable of buying and operating the property alone.

Nancy finally agreed to accept John as an equal partner. Nancy advanced nearly $13,000, while John provided less than $3,000, saying he had other immediate obligations and would pay more later. John later paid another $500 but never made any more payments. Whenever Nancy brought up the subject, he would assure her that he would pay later, and frequently became angry with her for bringing it up. Because of their close relationship, Nancy tolerated the delay and was confident that John would ultimately pay.

The relationship between Nancy and John ended in 1975. John subsequently refused to help pay an upcoming balloon payment on the apartment building's mortgage. Nancy also unsuccessfully attempted to secure a quitclaim deed from John. Nancy attempted to buy John out, but he refused to respond.

In 1978, Nancy filed an action to quiet title. The court found that John's performance as a practitioner had an immense influence upon Nancy, causing her to have an extraordinary amount of trust and confidence in him. It further found that John's emotional and spiritual influence over Nancy made her particularly susceptible to his influence. Where one party is under the domination of another, a transaction induced by unfair persuasion is the result of undue influence and is voidable.

The court found that the partnership agreement in the apartment house between Nancy and John was subject to rescission for undue influence. John was awarded the amount of his contribution plus interest, and title to the apartment house was quieted in Nancy's name alone. *Ferguson v. Jeanes*, 27 Wn. App. 558, 619 P.2d 369 (1980).

Duress. Illegal imprisonment or confinement, threats of bodily harm, threats of injury to a person's reputation, or the use of other means to coerce a person into doing what he or she otherwise would not do are all examples of **duress**. Any contract that is signed under duress is voidable by the injured party. This is true even if the actions or threats are taken against a third party, such as the person's spouse, child, or parent.

Washington courts have extended the concept of duress to include business compulsion. **Business compulsion** is a form of duress in which a person is threatened with a serious business loss. Entering into a disadvantageous contract because of financial necessity does not constitute business compulsion. For the doctrine to apply, the victim must prove that the offending party caused or contributed to the problem and exerted the pressure that brought about the decision to enter into the agreement.

For example, it is a form of business compulsion to coerce someone into signing a contract by threatening to take some action that will be financially disastrous for the victim, such as withholding a payment owed to the victim, or starting a groundless lawsuit in bad faith. However, the acts or threats of one party cannot amount to duress if there is a legal right to do the threatened act. For instance, threatening to bring a valid lawsuit is not duress.

Mistake. Unlike the other negative factors that can make a contract voidable, mistake does not usually involve any bad faith or villainy. If both parties are mistaken about some fact or law that is important to their contract, either of them may disaffirm the contract. This is known as **mutual mistake**.

Case Example:

Simonson and Teeter formed Northwest Furnace & Equipment Company. Teeter supplied the business expertise and Simonson supplied the capital. Fendell was hired as the general manager.

Simonson became disenchanted with the business and offered to sell his interest to Teeter and Fendell. Fendell wanted proof of the business's financial condition before negotiating to buy out Simonson. The parties conducted a complete inventory and the company accountant prepared a financial statement. The statement indicated the business was solvent and operating at a profit; all three believed this to be accurate.

The parties signed a contract in which Fendell and Teeter agreed to buy Simonson's interest for $75,000 by December 30, 1978.

In mid-December Fendell and Teeter discovered that $48,000 in accounts payable had been mistakenly omitted from the financial statement. The business was not making a profit and was actually insolvent.

Simonson brought a lawsuit seeking enforcement of the contract. Fendell and Teeter argued for rescission of the contract due to mutual mistake.

The court found that all parties believed the business was solvent and operating at a profit when the contract was signed. Since the contract would not have been formed but for the mutual mistake, Fendell and Teeter were entitled to rescission and the contract was not enforceable. *Simonson v. Fendell*, 101 Wn.2d 88, 675 P.2d 1218 (1984).

When only one of the parties to a contract is mistaken (**unilateral mistake**), the contract is not voidable unless the other party knew about the mistake and did nothing to correct it.

Consideration

Even after an offer has been accepted, there is no valid contract unless it is supported by consideration. **Consideration** is something of value exchanged by the parties. A contract can't be a one-way street: each party must give something to the other. The exchange of consideration is what distinguishes a contractual promise from the promise of a gift.

> **Example:** If Alan promises Barry his sweater in exchange for Barry's wheelbarrow, they have a contract. Each has given the other some consideration: Alan gave Barry a promise, and Barry gave Alan a promise.
>
> But if Alan promises Barry his sweater and Barry promises Alan nothing in return, there is no contract. The sweater is a gift.
>
> The distinction becomes important if, after making the promise, Alan fails to give Barry the sweater. In the first case, where Alan received consideration for his promise (Barry's promise to give him the wheelbarrow) Barry can sue Alan to enforce the promise.
>
> But in the second case, Barry can't sue Alan. The courts will not enforce a promise that is not supported by consideration. It wasn't nice of Alan to break his promise, but since the sweater was a gift instead of a contractual obligation, the law won't get involved.

Consideration can be anything of value—a sweater, $10, or a split-level ranch house. The consideration for most contracts is a promise to give something of value, as in the example above. For this reason, the parties to a contract are sometimes referred to as the **promisor** (the party making a promise) and the **promisee** (the party who is to receive the benefit of a promise).

In a typical real estate contract, the buyer promises to pay the seller money, and the seller promises to transfer title to the buyer. By exchanging promises they create an executory contract; when they fulfill their promises (when the buyer actually pays the seller and the seller actually gives the buyer the deed) the contract is executed.

To provide consideration for a contract, a promisor must either do something that benefits the promisee, or give something up. Promising to not do something can be consideration—for example, promising to stop smoking. Or if you don't smoke, promising never to start can be consideration.

But an empty promise is not consideration for a contract: if you've never smoked, promising to quit can't be consideration. And something that you've already done can't be consideration.

> **Example:** Andrew quit smoking, and Aunt Bernice is very pleased. Aunt Bernice says to Andrew, "Because you quit smoking, I'm going to buy you a yacht." This is not a contract; since Andrew had already quit smoking, he didn't really give Aunt Bernice anything (or give up anything) in exchange for Aunt Bernice's promise.

Also, promising to do something that you're already legally obligated to do (or promising to refrain from doing something that you're obligated to refrain from doing) is not consideration.

> **Example:** Williams agrees to build a house for Kessner for $200,000. When the house is over halfway done, Williams says, "You're going to have to pay me another $30,000 if you want me to finish this project." Kessner meekly agrees. This is not an enforceable contract; Williams can't sue Kessner for the additional $30,000, because Williams was already obligated to finish the house for $200,000.

Adequacy. It's important to understand that the value of the consideration one party gives doesn't have to equal the value of what the other gives. In other words, even though one party struck a bad bargain, the contract is still enforceable.

> **Example:** Peterson's house was appraised at $300,000. He's anxious to sell it very quickly, because he thinks he may have to leave the country in a hurry. When Marshall offers $215,000 for the house, Peterson accepts, and they execute a written contract.
>
> As it turns out, Peterson won't have to leave the country. He wants to back out of the sale, but Marshall wants to go through with it. Although Peterson's consideration is worth much more than what Marshall is giving, their contract is binding.

Of course, when the consideration is grossly unequal, that may be a sign that there was fraud, undue influence, duress, or mistake involved in the contract negotiations. But unless one of those negative factors is proven, the contract is enforceable.

Lawful Purpose

The purpose of a contract (sometimes called the "object" of the contract) must be lawful at the time the contract is made. If one person promises to pay another for committing

Fig. 7.3. Elements of a valid real estate contract

A Valid Real Estate Contract
◆ Capacity
◆ Mutual consent
◆ Lawful objective
◆ Consideration
◆ In writing

an illegal act, their contract is void and cannot be enforced by a court. This may seem obvious; a hit man is unlikely to take his employer to court to collect his fee, and the employer is unlikely to sue him for failing to carry out the murder. But the requirement has a considerably broader application. Even when a contract's purpose does not violate an express provision of the law, a court may refuse to enforce it if it is contrary to public policy or accepted morals.

> **Example:** Lara asks Kerr, a contractor, to remodel her basement. Lara wants the job completed as soon as possible and Kerr offers to do the work without obtaining the required construction permits. Lara agrees and they sign a contract. This contract is void for lack of a lawful purpose.

Many contracts have more than one purpose, and they are often **severable**—one part can be enforced without the other. When part of a contract is legal and part is illegal, a court may set aside the illegal part and enforce the rest. But when a contract has a single purpose, if any of the consideration is unlawful, the entire contract is void.

The Statute of Frauds

The law that requires certain contracts to be in writing and signed is commonly known as the **statute of frauds**. As the name suggests, the writing requirement is intended to prevent fraudulent claims. The parties to an unwritten contract are likely to disagree later about what each agreed to do or whether they agreed to do anything. Putting a contract in writing helps eliminate that kind of dispute, because the document is solid evidence of the existence of an agreement and its essential terms.

Application. The statute of frauds applies to any agreement that, by its terms, will not be performed within one year from the time it is made. It also applies to a promise to pay another's debt, or guarantee payment of another's debt.

Most importantly for licensees, the statute of frauds applies to any agreement authorizing or employing an agent or broker to sell or purchase real estate for compensation or a commission, and to any agreement for the purchase and sale of real estate. To be enforceable, these contracts must be in writing and signed.

The statute of frauds does not apply to a commission-splitting agreement between two brokers. If a listing broker orally agrees to share a commission with another broker, they have a valid contract. The cooperating broker can sue the listing broker to collect his or her share.

The writing required by the statute of frauds doesn't have to be a formal legal document. A note or memorandum is enough, if it indicates there is an agreement between the parties and it is signed.

Case Example:

Seck, a real estate broker, had known Foulks for a long time. Foulks asked Seck to help him sell his ranch in Sacramento County, and Seck agreed.

However, Foulks refused to give Seck a formal listing agreement. "You know dog-gone well, you know me, I'm not going to cheat you out of a commission," Foulks said. But Seck took out one of his business cards and jotted down the basic terms of the listing on the back of the card. It looked like this:

310 M/L
2000 per acre
½ down
bal. 5 years
5% int
quarterly with int
keep taxes up to date
½ mineral rights
6% comm
10/1/65

Seck then asked Foulks to initial and date the card. Foulks wrote, "3/24/65 GWF."

Seck found a buyer for the ranch, but Foulks refused to pay Seck a commission. When Seck sued, Foulks argued that the notes on the business card weren't enough to comply with the statute of frauds. But the court disagreed. The court said that all Seck needed was a written, signed memorandum indicating the fact of employment. This requirement was fulfilled by "6% comm" and Foulks's initials on the business card. *Seck v. Foulks*, 25 Cal. App. 3d 556, 102 Cal. Rptr. 170 (1972).

This case clearly shows that in order to satisfy the statute of frauds, the writing doesn't have to be very formal. Although this is a California case, Washington also follows the rule that a writing is sufficient to satisfy the statute of frauds if it clearly indicates the agreement between the parties and is signed.

To comply with the statute of frauds, a contract only needs to be signed by "the party to be charged"—that is, the one who's being sued. For example, it didn't matter that Seck hadn't signed the business card, as long as Foulks had. A full signature is unnecessary; initials are enough. In fact, anything that the signer intends as a signature will do. But it may be difficult to prove that a wavy line or an "X" was someone's signature if that person later denies it.

Once you've signed a contract, you're bound by its terms, even if you claim you never read it. An illiterate person should ask someone trustworthy to explain all the terms of a written agreement before signing it. The same is true for a person signing a document written in a foreign language. Of course, if someone convinces another person to sign a document by misrepresenting its contents, fraud has occurred and the contract is voidable.

Promissory Estoppel

Often, people are not aware that the four elements we just discussed (capacity, mutual consent, consideration, and lawful purpose) are required for a valid contract, and as a result are surprised to discover that a promise someone made to them is unenforceable. The outcomes of some contract lawsuits can seem very unfair.

To prevent unfairness in at least some cases, the courts have developed the doctrine of **promissory estoppel** (also called the doctrine of **detrimental reliance**). Under this doctrine, a court may enforce a promise that is lacking consideration, a signed writing, or some other contract requirement.

A party attempting to enforce a promise under the theory of promissory estoppel must show the court that the following type of situation exists:

1. Able made a promise to Brown;
2. Able should have expected that his promise would cause Brown to take some action;
3. Brown did take action, in reasonable reliance on Able's promise; and
4. as a result, Brown will be harmed if Able's promise is not enforced.

In such a case, a court may decide to enforce the promise, even though no valid contract exists.

> **Example:** Martha, Stan's mother, bought a large tract of land and promised to give it to Stan. Stan cleared and fenced the land, built a house on it, and moved in with his wife.
>
> Two years later, Martha and Stan have a fight. Martha tells Stan and his wife to get off her property, but they refuse to leave. Martha sues to regain possession of her land.

Martha's promise to Stan was not originally enforceable, since Stan did not give Martha any consideration in exchange for her promise, and there was no signed writing. But the court uses the doctrine of promissory estoppel to rule in Stan's favor. Martha should have realized that her promise would induce action by Stan, and she was in fact aware of all his work on the property. Stan's reliance on Martha's promise was reasonable, so the court rules that Stan and his wife are entitled to possession of the property.

Note that the doctrine of promissory estoppel will be applied only when the promisee's reliance on the promise was reasonable. For example, a real estate broker without a written listing cannot use promissory estoppel to collect a commission. A broker is supposed to know that a written agreement is necessary—it is not reasonable for a broker to rely on a client's oral promise.

Modification of a Contract

When both parties agree that their written contract contains an error or omission, they can simply correct it. But to make a more substantial change in the contract, they usually must exchange additional consideration. In effect, the modification is a separate contract; like any other contract, it must be supported by consideration or it is unenforceable.

Assignment or Novation

When one party transfers his or her rights and duties under a contract to another person, it is either an **assignment** or a **novation**.

As a general rule, either party to a contract may **assign** their contractual rights to another party. But this right may be limited by the contract itself: a contract often provides that one party can't assign it without the other party's consent.

> **Example:** Lightfoot and Tanner sign a two-year residential lease. It provides that Tanner, the tenant, cannot assign her rights under the lease (the right to live on the property) to anyone else without Lightfoot's permission.
>
> However, the contract doesn't prevent Lightfoot from assigning his rights to someone else without Tanner's permission. Lightfoot assigns the lease to Clarke; Lightfoot is the assignor and Clarke is the assignee. Now Tanner is required to pay rent to Clarke.

Even without a provision prohibiting assignment, a contract for personal services, such as a listing agreement, cannot be assigned without consent. If I contract to have you play the piano at a party, you can't send your sister over instead of showing up yourself. A contract also can't be assigned without consent if the assignment would significantly change the other party's duties or increase his or her risks.

It's important to keep in mind that an assignor isn't relieved of all liability under the contract. Suppose the assignee doesn't carry out his or her contractual duties. The other party sues, but the assignee turns out to be judgment-proof (has no money or assets). The assignor is **secondarily liable**, and can be required to pay the other party if the assignee doesn't.

To avoid secondary liability, a party who wants to withdraw from a contract should request a novation instead of an assignment. In a **novation**, a new person takes the place of one of the parties, and the withdrawing party is completely relieved of liability connected with the contract.

But a novation can be arranged only with the other original party's consent. A novation is essentially a new contract, so it must comply with all the rules for contract formation, including the mutual consent requirement.

Note that the term "novation" doesn't necessarily refer to the substitution of a new party. It can also refer to the substitution of a new obligation in place of the original one. If the original parties tear up a two-year lease and execute a five-year lease, a novation has occurred.

Accord and Satisfaction

Sometimes a promisee agrees to accept something different or less than what the original contract required the promisor to provide. This kind of agreement is called an **accord**; it does not have to be supported by separate consideration. To extinguish the promisor's original obligation, the promisee executes a **satisfaction**—a document expressly stating that the promisor's performance has been accepted in satisfaction of the obligation.

Release

A contractual obligation can be eliminated altogether if the promisee grants the promisor a release. An oral release is valid if the promisee receives some new consideration; a written release doesn't have to be supported by new consideration. If the contract had to be in writing because of the statute of frauds, the release should also be in writing.

Breach of Contract

Now that you are familiar with how contracts are created and modified, let's take a look at what happens when a contract is breached.

If one party to a contract performs his or her side of the bargain, the other party is required to perform, too. But if one party fails to perform (**breaches** the contract), the other is not required to perform. If I agree to build you a house for $250,000 and I don't build the house, you don't owe me $250,000.

Substantial Performance vs. Material Breach

In most cases, each party carries out the promised performance to the other's satisfaction. And in certain cases, one party clearly fails to do what he or she promised. But sometimes it's not so clear-cut.

> **Example:** One party to a contract, Abernathy, does everything he promised, but the other party, Bono, feels that the quality of Abernathy's work was substandard. Or Abernathy does nearly everything promised, but some details are overlooked Or Abernathy does everything promised, but takes longer to do it than agreed. In these cases, there is room for argument about whether or not the contract was breached. Is Bono required to perform his side of the bargain?

The answer to that question depends on whether there has been substantial performance or a material breach. If Abernathy hasn't fulfilled every detail of the contract but has carried out its main objectives, that may be treated as **substantial performance**. Although Bono may be able to sue for damages because of the unfulfilled details, they don't excuse Bono from performing his side of the bargain.

If Abernathy fails to perform some important part of the contract, or performs very badly, that will be treated as a **material breach**. If Abernathy commits a material breach, Bono is excused from fulfilling his promises. If Bono doesn't perform, he won't be liable to Abernathy for breach of their contract, because Abernathy already breached it. (If Bono has already fully performed, Abernathy will be required to pay him damages for breach of contract.)

What provisions of a contract are so important that failure to fulfill them amounts to a material breach? That depends on all the circumstances of each case. If the promisee emphasized to the promisor that a particular detail of the contract was especially important, failure to comply with that detail may be a material breach. On the other hand, if the promisee acted as though a detail was unimportant, failure to comply with it isn't a material breach.

> **Example:** Grace hires Jorgen to build her a house based on her design. According to the plans, the hallways are to be a standard three feet wide. After construction is completed, Grace inspects the house and determines that the hallways are a half inch too wide. She is angry and withholds her final payment to Jorgen, who in turn sues for payment on their contract. A court would likely find that Jorgen has substantially performed and no material breach has occurred.

Time is of the Essence. Many standard contract forms state that "time is of the essence." The purpose of including that phrase is to emphasize that timely performance is crucial. That makes failure to meet a deadline a material breach. Otherwise, a delay isn't a material breach, as long as performance is completed within a reasonable time after the deadline. However, note that the phrase often doesn't have any real effect. Unless the parties actually insist on timely performance, a court is likely to hold that the "time is of the essence" clause has been waived. So if you want to treat delay as a material breach, you must let the other party know.

Conditions

Contracts often include one or more **conditions** (sometimes called **contingency clauses**). A **condition** makes the promisor's obligation depend on the occurrence of a particular event. If the event does not occur, the promisor can withdraw without liability for breach of contract. For example, many purchase and sale agreements are contingent on the buyers qualifying for financing, or on the results of an appraisal, termite inspection, or soil test.

When a contract is conditional, the promisor must make a good faith effort to fulfill the condition. He or she can't deliberately prevent its fulfillment in order to get out of the contract.

Case Example:

The Egberts agreed to buy a 98-acre field from Mrs. Way. The offer to purchase was conditional on Mrs. Way clearing flaws in the title within one year. Encumbrances on the title included state inheritance tax and federal estate tax liens.

Within the next year, Mrs. Way failed to file tax returns necessary to release the encumbrances on the property. The Egberts filed suit for specific performance.

The court found that Mrs. Way had an obligation to make a good faith effort to clear the tax liens on the property. By her own admission, she had done nothing to pay these taxes. The court ordered Mrs. Way to perform her part of the contract. *Egbert v. Way*, 15 Wn. App. 76, 546 P.2d 1246 (1976).

A condition can be waived by the party it was intended to benefit or protect.

Example: A purchase and sale agreement is contingent on a satisfactory termite inspection. If the results of the inspection are unsatisfactory, the buyer can withdraw from the purchase unless the seller corrects the problems revealed.

The inspection shows that the house is infested with termites. The seller informs the buyer that she is not going to correct the problem, but the buyer decides to go ahead with the purchase. The buyer has a right to waive the condition, because it was included in the contract for his protection.

When a condition is included for the benefit of both parties, however, neither one can waive it without the other's consent.

Tendering Performance

In many cases, Party A has reason to believe that Party B is not going to fulfill the contract. The time for performance has arrived, and Party B hasn't taken any steps toward carrying out her side of the bargain. Before Party A can sue Party B for breach of contract, Party A must offer to perform his side of the bargain. This offer of performance is called a **tender offer** or simply a **tender**.

Example: Lin contracted to buy Maxwell's house, but Maxwell suspects Lin doesn't plan to go through with the purchase. Maxwell must offer to deliver the deed to Lin as promised in their contract. If Lin refuses to pay Maxwell and accept the deed, Lin is in default, and Maxwell may sue.

A tender must be made in good faith. In other words, the tendering party must be willing and able to perform everything he or she promised, fully and immediately. The tender must be unconditional, unless the contract contained a condition that the other party hasn't fulfilled yet.

It is not necessary to tender performance when there has been an **anticipatory repudiation**. If Lin repudiates the contract by notifying Maxwell that she won't perform, Maxwell can file suit for breach without making a tender. The tender would be a waste of time. But an anticipatory repudiation must be a clear, unequivocal statement. Maxwell can't infer repudiation from Lin's behavior or from a vague remark.

Remedies for Breach

When a promisor has performed badly, or has refused to perform at all (either by anticipatory repudiation or by rejecting the tender offer), he or she has breached the contract. Then the promisee can turn to the legal system for help in enforcing the contract.

Arbitration

As we discussed in Chapter 1, the courts are overflowing with litigation, and it can take years for a case to get to trial. Because of these long delays, more and more contracts include an arbitration provision.

Arbitration is an alternative to the court system. An arbitrator performs the functions of a judge, reviewing the evidence and resolving the dispute. Arbitration is usually much more informal than a trial; the discovery process is limited and the rules of evidence are relaxed. Thus, arbitration is typically both faster and less expensive than a trial.

Arbitration may be required by law if the amount of damages is less than a certain amount (currently $35,000) and the only relief sought is money damages. This is called **mandatory arbitration** and is designed to ease court congestion. In other cases, parties to a dispute can agree to submit to arbitration instead of going to court. Parties to a contract may include an arbitration provision in the contract, agreeing in advance to arbitrate if a dispute arises. This is called **contractual arbitration** and is intended to save the parties time and money.

Unless otherwise agreed, the arbitrator's decision will be legally binding on the parties—the loser can't just shrug it off. The results of mandatory arbitration may be appealed in superior court. But parties agreeing to contractual arbitration typically give up the appeal right, in the effort to save time and money.

As you can see, an arbitration provision in a contract has a significant effect on the parties' rights in the event of a breach. An arbitration clause should be clearly explained to any party signing a contract. Otherwise, parties to a real estate transaction might sign a contract containing an arbitration provision without truly understanding the legal consequences.

Lawsuit

A breach of contract often is the first step towards a lawsuit. A lawsuit must be brought within a certain specified time period. The laws that set forth the time period requirements are known as **statutes of limitations**. In Washington, a lawsuit based on a written contract must be filed within six years after the breach occurred. An action based on an oral contract must be brought within three years.

The parties to a contract can agree to a shorter limitation period than the one prescribed by statute, but the period must not be unreasonably short.

These limitation periods apply even when the suing party was not aware of the breach at the time it occurred. But there's an exception for cases involving fraud or mistake: time doesn't start to run until the injured party discovers the fraud or mistake.

Interpretation of the Contract. In order to decide whether a contract has been breached (and if it has, what the plaintiff's remedy should be), the court must interpret the parties' agreement. In doing so, the court tries to determine (and enforce) what the parties intended at the time they entered the contract.

When the contract is in writing, the court is supposed to determine the parties' intention from the written document alone. If the language in the document is clear and unambiguous, the court will not hear evidence about the contract negotiations or any oral agreements that contradict the terms of the written agreement.

> **Example:** Tiokasin is going to lease a townhouse from Lane for nine months. The written lease form clearly states that rent is due on the first of each month. Before signing the lease, Tiokasin asks Lane if she can pay the rent on the fifteenth of each month instead, and Lane agrees. However, they don't change the lease form to reflect this agreement.
>
> Later Tiokasin and Lane wind up in court. Tiokasin wants to testify that Lane agreed to accept the rent on the fifteenth of each month. But this testimony will not be allowed, because it contradicts the written agreement between the parties.

This is known as the **parol evidence rule**. ("Parol" is a legal term that means "spoken.") This rule, like the statute of frauds, is intended to cut down on false claims and prevent people from weaseling out of what they agreed to do.

If the written contract is ambiguous, the judge will let the parties testify about their contract negotiations to shed light on the meaning of the document. Often the evidence presented doesn't clear up the ambiguity. In that case, the court will interpret the contract against the party that was responsible for the ambiguity—usually the one that drafted the document. If neither party is to blame, the court will interpret the provision in favor of the promisor: at the time the contract was made, what did the person making the promise believe that the other person understood?

Damages

Once the court has concluded that a breach of contract has occurred, it must decide on a remedy. The most common remedy for breach of contract is a **damages** award: the breaching party is ordered to pay a sum of money to the nonbreaching party. How much? The award is supposed to be the amount that will put the nonbreaching party in the position he or she would have been in if the other party had fulfilled the contract.

> **Example:** Perkins contracted to clear Hanawalt's property for $10,000, but he quit the project soon after starting. So Hanawalt hired Lopez to carry out the job. Lopez charged her $12,000.
>
> Hanawalt sues Perkins for breach of contract, and Perkins is ordered to pay her $2,000. If Perkins had not breached the contract, it would have cost Hanawalt only $10,000 (rather than $12,000) to have her property cleared. The $2,000 judgment against Perkins represents the difference between what the job actually cost Hanawalt and what it would have cost her if Perkins hadn't breached: $12,000 – $10,000 = $2,000.

However, if Lopez had charged Hanawalt only $9,000 to clear the property, Hanawalt would actually have been better off as a result of Perkins's breach. The job would have cost her $1,000 less than it would have if Perkins had fulfilled their contract. In that case, Hanawalt would not be entitled to a judgment against Perkins, because she wasn't damaged by his breach. The purpose of a contract lawsuit is to compensate the promisee for actual damages, not to punish the promisor for breaching.

Certainty Requirement. To be the basis for a damages award, a loss resulting from breach of contract must be proven with certainty. Occasionally a damages award includes lost profits: "If Harrison hadn't breached the contract, I could have opened my store a month earlier, and I would have made at least $1,000 of profit during that month." But in most cases, lost profits are considered too uncertain to be included in the judgment. Who knows whether the store would have turned a profit if it had been open that month? It might even have lost money. Unless the evidence proves that there would have been a profit, and that it would have been at least a certain amount, lost profits are not awarded.

Mitigation Requirement. The nonbreaching party in a contract dispute is required to **mitigate** damages. That means the nonbreaching party must do what he or she can to reduce losses resulting from the other party's breach.

> **Example:** Hernandez leases an apartment to Tyler for one year; Tyler has agreed to pay $1,000 a month. Two months later, Tyler decides she doesn't like the place, so she moves out and doesn't make any further rent payments. That's clearly a breach of contract.
>
> But Hernandez can't simply sue Tyler and expect a judgment for $10,000 (the additional amount she would have received if Tyler had honored the lease). Hernandez is required to mitigate her damages by trying to rent the apartment again.
>
> If Hernandez immediately finds a new tenant for $1,000 a month, Tyler will not be liable for any of her unpaid rent. However, Tyler might be required to reimburse

Hernandez for expenses incurred in renting the apartment again, such as any leasing fee and the cost of cleaning, painting, advertising, etc.

Suppose no one will rent the apartment for $1,000 a month, but someone rents it for $900 a month. Then Tyler will be liable to Hernandez for the difference between what Hernandez actually collects and what she would have collected if Tyler hadn't breached: $100 per month, for 10 months. The damages award would be $1,000 ($100 × 10 = $1,000), plus any expenses Hernandez incurred in renting the apartment.

Liquidated Damages. To lessen the possibility of expensive litigation, some contracts include a **liquidated damages** provision. The parties agree in advance that if there is a breach, the damages will be set at a specified sum or calculated according to a specified formula. The nonbreaching party will accept the liquidated damages instead of suing for actual damages.

As a general rule, a court will enforce a liquidated damages provision if the amount is reasonable and does not constitute a penalty, and the type of harm is such that it is difficult to ascertain or estimate the actual damages accurately.

There are restrictions on liquidated damages for certain types of contracts. In the case of a residential lease, a liquidated damages clause is void unless it would be extremely difficult to calculate the actual damages after a breach. The same rule applies to a consumer loan for the purchase of personal property. That standard is hard to meet, so a liquidated damages provision in a residential lease or a consumer loan contract is rarely enforceable.

In a contract to purchase residential real property, the buyer's deposit may be treated as liquidated damages, as long as certain statutory requirements are met:

1. The total deposit to be forfeited may not exceed 5% of the purchase price.
2. The contract must include a clause that provides substantially as follows: "In the event the purchaser fails, without legal excuse, to complete the purchase of the property, the earnest money deposit made by the purchaser shall be forfeited to the seller as the sole and exclusive remedy available to the seller for such failure."
3. If the real estate is being purchased for personal, family, or household purposes, the provision described above must be in a typeface that is at least as large as the text of the rest of the agreement, and it must be separately initialed or signed by the parties.

If these requirements are not met, the liquidated damages provision will not be enforced, and the seller will have to sue the buyer for breach of contract in order to obtain damages.

In a contract to purchase commercial property, a liquidated damages provision will be held valid if the amount specified in the agreement was a reasonable estimate of just compensation for the anticipated breach at the time the agreement was entered into.

Equitable Remedies

A damages award—a sum of money intended to compensate the nonbreaching party—is the standard remedy in a contract dispute. But money doesn't always do the trick. In some cases, alternative remedies are available.

Injunctions. An **injunction** is a court order directing a person to do something or refrain from doing something (see Chapter 1). Sometimes one party to a contract can obtain an injunction to prevent the other party from breaching.

To get an injunction, it's usually necessary to convince the court that the other party is about to breach the contract, and that the breach will cause **irreparable harm**. That doesn't actually mean it has to cause harm that could never be fixed; it simply must be harm that can't be adequately redressed by a damages award.

> **Example:** A restrictive covenant in Nelson's deed protects the enormous oak tree that has stood for 150 years on the boundary between her property and Locke's property. Locke learns that Nelson is planning to chop down the tree in spite of the restrictive covenant. He obtains an injunction to prevent Nelson from breaching the covenant.
>
> An injunction is an appropriate remedy because a damages award would not compensate Locke for the loss of a tree that took 150 years to grow.

Rescission. Sometimes one party to a contract doesn't want to enforce the other party's promise. Instead, he or she just wants to undo the contract completely, as if it never happened. In that case, he or she may ask a court to **rescind** the contract. When a contract is rescinded, each party returns any consideration the other has given. All of their contractual obligations are terminated.

Rescission is available under a variety of circumstances. Whenever a voidable contract is disaffirmed—because of lack of capacity, fraud, undue influence, duress, or mistake—the court will rescind it. A contract can also be rescinded without going to court, if both parties agree. One party can request court-ordered rescission if the other party failed to provide

Fig. 7.4 Breach of contract

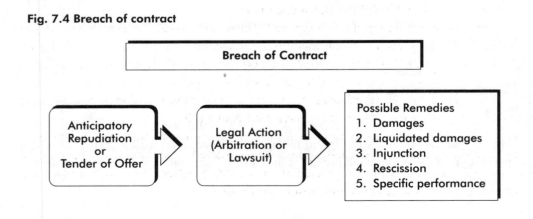

the promised consideration, or if that consideration turned out to be void. A court will also rescind an unlawful contract (unless the unlawfulness was clear from the contract's terms and the parties were equally at fault—then a court will refuse to become involved in any way).

In some situations, the parties may prefer to **cancel** their contract instead of rescinding it. When a contract is canceled, all further obligations are terminated, but the parties aren't required to return what they've already received under the contract.

Specific Performance. Sometimes the nonbreaching party to a contract doesn't want to be compensated for the harm that resulted from the other's breach. Instead, the nonbreaching party wants to make the other party do what he or she promised to do. This is called **specific performance**: the court orders the breaching party to carry out the performance he or she promised in the contract.

Specific performance is generally not granted when a damages award will be just as effective. For example, a car dealer won't be ordered to sell you a particular car when you could get an identical one from another dealer. (If you have to pay more at the second dealer, the first dealer will be ordered to pay you the difference as a damages award.) But if the subject of a contract is unique, then specific performance is an appropriate remedy. A damages award won't enable you to buy an identical item, because there isn't another just like it.

Specific performance is most often used in enforcing real estate contracts, because a piece of real property is generally unique. A damages award may not be sufficient compensation for breach of an agreement to transfer real property.

A preference in favor of specific performance exists where the agreement is in writing, is certain in its terms, is fair and just, is for valuable consideration, and is capable of being enforced without hardship to either party.

In many circumstances, a court cannot grant specific performance. For example, it can never be a remedy for breach of a personal services contract, because no one can be forced to work for someone or to employ someone. Specific performance also can't be ordered for an agreement to procure the act or consent of another person, such as when a husband has agreed to persuade his wife to sign a document.

You can't be ordered to perform a contract if it wasn't just and reasonable, or if you didn't receive legally adequate consideration. For example, if you agreed to sell your $250,000 house for $175,000, the contract is enforceable even though the consideration is inadequate. But although you may be required to pay damages to the buyer, you can't be forced to complete the sale. Furthermore, a buyer can't be ordered to complete a purchase of real property when the seller doesn't have marketable title.

You also can't be ordered to perform if the other party hasn't fulfilled all the conditions he or she agreed to. And finally, you can't be ordered to perform if your consent to the contract was obtained by misrepresentation or unfair practices, or if your consent was given because of mistake, misapprehension, or surprise.

In spite of all these restrictions, specific performance is a common remedy when a seller breaches a purchase and sale agreement.

Interference with Contract

Sometimes one of the parties to a contract is persuaded to breach it by a third party that is outside the contractual relationship. For example, another real estate agent might convince your client to breach the listing agreement he has with you. Or a real estate agent might persuade a seller to breach a binding sales contract and accept a better offer.

These acts may constitute a tort called **interference with contractual relations**. The nonbreaching party can file a tort lawsuit against the third party, in addition to filing a contract lawsuit against the breaching party. To win the tort suit, the plaintiff must show that the defendant (the third party):

1. was aware of the contract,
2. intentionally interfered with the contract,
3. causing a breach of the contract,
4. that resulted in damages.

A tort called **interference with prospective economic advantage** is similar to interference with contractual relations, but the plaintiff doesn't need to show that he or she had a binding contract with another person. It's only necessary to prove that they had an economic relationship and the defendant was aware of that relationship. For example, a seller's broker without a written listing agreement could sue a buyer and another broker for interference with prospective economic advantage.

Real Estate Contracts

A real estate agent is expected to be familiar with several different types of contracts. Each of these real estate contracts is simply a particular application of the basic rules of contract law outlined in the first part of this chapter.

As you've seen, the statute of frauds requires most of the contracts used in a real estate transaction to be in writing. Even when a signed written document isn't required by law, it's always wise to have one. The parties to a contract can draft a document for themselves, but it's much safer to use standard forms or to have lawyers do the drafting. A real estate agent preparing a contract must use approved forms, with minimal additions and changes, or risk liability for the unauthorized practice of law.

Whenever a document is executed in the course of a real estate transaction, the agent must see to it that each party receives a copy at the time of signing. That includes copies of any modifications of the agreements, too. Under the real estate license law, a broker must keep copies of all documents pertaining to a transaction for at least three years.

Some of the contracts commonly used in real estate transactions will be discussed in later chapters: title insurance policies (Chapter 8); escrow instructions (Chapter 9); mortgages, deeds of trust, and installment land contracts (Chapter 10); and leases (Chapter 13).

This section examines broker/salesperson employment contracts, listing agreements, purchase and sale agreements, and options. Forms for each of these types of contracts are published by a number of different companies. Although the forms are standardized in a general sense, their details vary. Keep in mind that the provisions discussed here are not necessarily required by law, and are not necessarily included in every form. Also remember that the parties may choose to alter some of the pre-printed provisions in a form.

Employment Agreements

It's a good business practice for a broker to have a written **employment agreement** with each affiliated licensee who works for him or her. The agreement should be signed by both parties and should state the main terms of the employment relationship, such as duties, supervision, compensation, and termination.

Most standard contract forms include a paragraph stating that the document represents the entire agreement between the parties. This is called an **integration clause**. When a contract contains an integration clause, neither party can rely on any oral promises or side agreements that the other makes. Any terms that are not included in the written document are unenforceable.

> **Example:** Zimmerman is a new salesperson. Before signing the employment contract, Zimmerman says he's concerned because a provision in the contract states that his share of a commission won't be payable unless the commission is collected. The broker says, "Oh, don't worry about that. I always act fast to collect from any client who doesn't pay right away. You'll always get your money."
>
> But as it turns out, the broker doesn't always take the trouble to collect from difficult clients. On one occasion, Zimmerman ended up with nothing to show for a lot of work.
>
> Zimmerman's employment contract contains an integration clause, which makes the written document the complete agreement between Zimmerman and the broker. Therefore, the broker's statement is not an enforceable promise. If their employment agreement had not contained an integration clause, Zimmerman could have treated the broker's statement as a contractual promise and sued the broker for damages resulting from the breach of contract.

Listing Agreements

A **listing agreement** is also a type of employment contract, but it is between a seller and a broker. As we have seen, a broker cannot sue for a commission unless the listing is in writing and signed by the client. The listing agreement need not be a formal legal document, but it must indicate the fact of employment—either expressly, with a statement indicating that the signer is employing the broker, or by implication, through a reference to the broker's compensation.

Fig. 7.5 Broker/Salesperson Employment Contract

NWMLS Form No. 127A
Rev. 2/04
Page 1 of 2

BROKER/ASSOCIATE AGREEMENT
(Independent Contractor Agreement)

© Copyright 2004
Northwest Multiple Listing Service
ALL RIGHTS RESERVED

IT IS AGREED by and between _____ (herein referred to as the "Broker")

and _____ (herein referred to as the "Associate"), as follows:

1. **LICENSES:** Each of the parties hold appropriate real estate licenses issued by the State of Washington.

2. **OFFICE ASSOCIATION:** Associate agrees to exert his/her best efforts to promote Broker's, Broker's office's and Associate's reputation and business.

3. **INDEPENDENT CONTRACTOR STATUS:** The parties agree that Associate is an independent contractor for federal tax and all other purposes and is not an employee of, or partner with, the Broker. Under federal law, remuneration paid Associate must be directly related to sales or other out put rather than to salary or the number of hours worked, or the independent contractor status will be lost for federal income tax purposes. Notwithstanding the foregoing, Washington State License law requires the broker to supervise associate's real estate activities. Associate agrees to comply with broker's directions and procedures in this regard.

4. **BROKER TO PROVIDE OFFICE AND OFFICE PROCEDURES:** Broker shall, in common with other Associates of the office, make available office space, office equipment, local telephone service, receptionist, business secretarial assistance, office signs, office advertising, membership in listing and/or referral services selected by Broker, and use of maps and other sales materials. To allow Associate an equal opportunity in the matter of customers, sales and listings, and to promote the image of the parties and the office, Broker agrees to maintain rules regarding use of the office: days it will be open; office procedures; floor time; inquiries; leads; and other sales opportunities.

5. **ASSOCIATE RESPONSIBILITY - BUSINESS EXPENSES:** Associate shall be responsible to pay for his/her own license and business fees; automobile and other transportation; long distance phone charges; entertainment; insurance; and other business expenses.

   From time-to-time, unusual expenses involved in listing and/or sale, such as out-of-town travel, extended long distance charges, and brochures, may, by advance agreement of the parties, be deducted from a commission prior to division between Broker and Associate.

6. **ASSOCIATE'S ADVERTISING:** Associate is responsible to pay for his/her own advertising, over and above general office advertising by the Broker. Notwithstanding this, it is understood that the State Real Estate Code imposes certain restrictions on advertising and signs. Associate agrees not to utilize any advertising, signs, brochures or other solicitation materials without Broker's advance approval thereof.

7. **ASSOCIATE'S AUTO INSURANCE:** Associate agrees to at all times maintain, at Associate's expense, automobile liability and property damage insurance covering Associate's own car and any other car that may be used in conduct of Associate's business. The limits on said policy shall be as approved by Broker. In the absence of such approval the policy limit shall be at least $1,000,000 single limit. Broker shall be named co-insured and a copy of the policy shall be given to Broker.

8. **ASSOCIATE'S TAXES:** Associate shall be responsible to file and pay quarterly estimated, and annual federal income tax returns; and any other taxes required of an independent contractor. Broker will file any required notices or returns (such as IRS Form 1099) on all monies received by Associate through Broker.

   Broker shall pay any applicable State, County and/or City Business & Occupation Taxes on the entire commission, and the amount of such tax shall be deducted from the commission prior to division between Broker and Associate.

   At Broker's request, Associate will pay one-half of the medical aid and supplemental retirement portions of any industrial insurance premiums which Washington law requires the Broker to pay on independent contractors.

9. **BROKER OWNS RECORDS:** All maps, manuals, log books, printed materials, and supplies; client, customer, and transaction records, electronic or printed; and any other records, related to or received through the Broker's office (the "Broker's Property") are the exclusive property of and remain owned by Broker. Any amount paid by Associate for the Broker's Property shall be for use of the Broker's Property and shall create no ownership interest therein.

10. **ASSOCIATE TO RETURN BROKER'S PROPERTY:** Associate agrees to return all of Broker's Property described in paragraph 9, above, to Broker prior to separating from Broker's office (including transfer to another real estate office).

11. **MULTIPLE LISTING SERVICE:** Associate shall be responsible for paying all membership fees and costs for joining the multiple listing service (the "MLS") (or other real estate associations). Associate acknowledges that all proprietary information, passwords, keys, keyboxes, forms, and other services and information provided by the MLS are furnished for the use of Associate only and may not be disclosed, loaned, or distributed to anyone except in accordance with MLS Rules and agreements.

    Associate agrees to indemnify and hold Broker harmless from any liability, including MLS fines and damage suits, resulting from misuse of MLS property and disclosure or distribution of passwords and other proprietary information in violation of MLS rules and agreements to third persons, including without limitation moving companies, insurance companies, oil companies, clients, customers, employees, assistants, licensees, or anyone else.

12. **COMPLIANCE WITH BYLAWS & RULES:** Both the Broker and Associate agree to comply with all rules and regulations and agreements of the MLS, Board of Realtors or other real estate associations to which either or both of the parties may belong. Each party hereby agrees to save the other harmless from violation of any such Rules or Regulations or breach of any agreements each of them may enter with the MLS, Board, or association.

13. **MANDATORY MEMBERSHIP:** If Broker (now or in the future) belongs to any MLS, Board of Realtors, or association which requires that (as a condition of Broker's membership) all of those associated with Broker must belong, then Associate agrees to immediately apply for and maintain membership and pay (when due) all dues or other charges levied by such Board. In the event of Associate's failure to do so, Broker may terminate this Agreement and/or deduct required dues or charges from the next commission or other monies due Associate.

INITIALS: BROKER _____ DATE _____ ASSOCIATE _____ DATE _____

Reprinted with permission, Northwest Multiple Listing Service. No endorsement implied.

NWMLS Form No. 127A
Rev. 2/04
Page 2 of 2

BROKER/ASSOCIATE AGREEMENT
(Independent Contractor Agreement)
(continued)

14. **PROPERTY INVESTMENT:** Associate may acquire, for personal investment or residence, property listed with Broker's office or through a Multiple Listing Service, provided that the Broker and any other Associate's portion of the commission provided in the listing is paid at closing. Broker or other office Associate(s) may likewise acquire property listed by Associate, provided that the Associate's portion of the commission provided in the listing is paid at closing.

15. **OWNERSHIP - LISTINGS:** It is understood that all listings, sales and other agreements obtained or negotiated by Associate shall, in accordance with state law, be in the name of and be the property of Broker, subject to Associate's share of any commission.

Earnest money, lease deposits and other money; Purchase and Sale Agreements; Listing Agreements; Leases; and any other wholly or partially executed instruments or documents shall be immediately delivered to the Broker's possession in accordance with state law. Associate shall be entitled to copies thereof for his/her own records.

Associate has no authority, express or implied, to represent anything to a purchaser, seller or anyone else unless it is contained in the Listing Agreement and there are no reasonable grounds for Associate to suspect that it is otherwise; or unless Associate is specifically authorized by the Broker, in the instance, to make the representation.

16. **TERMINATION:** This Agreement may be terminated, at any time, without cause, by either party giving notice to the other.

If Associate contemplates termination of this Agreement, Associate will make every effort to close any pending sales in which Associate is interested. In the event that any such sale does not close prior to termination of this Agreement and in the Broker's opinion is necessary or appropriate for the Broker or others in the office to attend to any matters concerning the sale (including changes in financing; securing of occupancy agreements; removal of contingencies; and any other usual or unusual matters required to close the sale) then the Broker shall be authorized to deduct up to 50% of the Associate's share of the commission and pay the same to himself/herself or other Associates according to their participation in the matters necessary to close the sale.

Associate agrees not to, in any way, induce or encourage an owner to terminate a listing (or sale) following termination of this Agreement.

17. **ARBITRATION:** Any and all disputes between Associate and Broker, or between Associate and other Associates in Broker's office, arising from matters occurring, all or in part , prior to termination of this Agreement, shall be resolved by arbitration, rather than suit. Each of the parties shall, within five days of being requested to do so by the other, name one arbitrator. The two arbitrators shall within five days of their appointment, appoint a third arbitrator. The dispute shall be heard within thirty days thereafter, in accordance with state statutes governing arbitration, and the decision of the arbitrators shall be final and binding upon the parties subject only to statutory review by the Superior Court. Alternatively, the parties may agree to submit the dispute to a Board of Realtors or Multiple Listing Service which offers such arbitration services.

18. **COMMISSIONS:** The parties shall share commissions in accordance with the Addendum attached hereto.

DATED this_____ day of _____ , _____ .

_____   _____
BROKER SIGNATURE   **ASSOCIATE SIGNATURE**

COMMISSION AGREEMENT
ADDENDUM TO BROKER/ASSOCIATE
AGREEMENT BETWEEN

_____ , BROKER

AND _____ , ASSOCIATE

DATED _____

A. Associate shall not be entitled to any salary, draws or compensation of any nature other than the listing fees and commission shares set forth hereinafter.

B. Associate shall have no claim to a listing fee or commission share except from money actually received by Broker.

C. All commissions and other monies must be paid to Broker alone. State law prohibits Associate from receiving commissions other than from the Broker holding his/her license.

D. Multiple listing dues, listing fees owed Associate or others (including other Brokers), Business and Occupation Taxes, Industrial Insurance, and other expenses agreed to in the Broker/Salesman Agreement, shall be deducted from the commission prior to determining Broker's and Associate's shares. In addition, Broker shall be entitled to deduct, from Associate's commission share, unpaid amounts owed Broker or multiple listing services or Board of Realtors for dues or any other reason. The net amount is the "commission" below.

E. Commissions shall be divided_____ % to the Associate and _____ % to the Broker.

F. Associate shall be entitled to the following listing fee (both before and after termination of this Agreement) for each exclusive listing obtained by Associate for Broker and sold by Associate or by others:

DATED this_____ day of _____ , _____ .

_____   _____
BROKER SIGNATURE   **ASSOCIATE SIGNATURE**

Remember that even without an enforceable listing agreement, a real estate licensee may owe agency duties to the client. Those duties are based on agency law, not on contract law. And these agency duties are in addition to—and independent of—the contractual duties the broker takes on in a listing agreement.

Because a listing agreement is a personal services contract, it can be assigned to another broker only with the client's consent. The assignment, like the original contract, must be in writing. It should be signed by the assignor and the assignee, as well as the client.

Types of Listing Agreements. A broker's right to a commission also depends on the type of listing agreement used. Under an **exclusive right to sell listing**, the owner agrees to list the property with only one broker. That broker is entitled to a commission if the property sells during the listing term, regardless of who sells it (even if the one who sells it is the owner). Most brokers prefer this type of listing.

In an **exclusive agency listing**, the owner agrees to list with only one broker but retains the right to sell the property him or herself without being obligated to pay the broker a commission. The broker is entitled to a commission if he or she or any other licensee sells the property, but not if the owner sells it.

Whenever an agent takes an exclusive agency or exclusive right to sell listing, the beginning and ending dates for the listing period must be stated in the employment agreement.

Under an **open listing** agreement, the owner is only obligated to pay a commission to the agent who sold the property or was the procuring cause of the sale. To be the **procuring cause,** the broker must be primarily responsible for the parties' agreement. Since an open listing is a non-exclusive agreement, the seller is free to give listings to other agents as well. The sale of the property terminates all open listings.

If two brokers contribute to a particular sale, a dispute may arise over which broker was the procuring cause. Whether a broker was the procuring cause is a question of fact that is determined by examining all of the circumstances surrounding the particular transaction.

> **Example:** The principal gave open listings to five different brokers, Aimes, Baker, Kimoto, Dahl, and Edwards. Aimes and Baker both showed the property to the same buyer. Aimes brought the buyer to the property for the first time, but it was Baker who successfully negotiated the offer that the principal accepted.
>
> Aimes claims that she should receive at least part of the commission. But the agent who effectuated the sale is considered the procuring cause, so Baker is the one entitled to the commission.

Basic Elements. A listing agreement must identify the property to be sold or leased. The street address is generally useful, but is not enough to identify the property with certainty. That usually isn't an issue, but it can become one if the client decides not to sell and tries to avoid paying a commission. It's a good practice to attach a legal description of the property to the contract as an exhibit. Any pages attached to a contract should be dated and initialed by the parties, to show that the attachments were intended to be part of the agreement.

Fig. 7.6 Listing Agreement

NWMLS Form No. 1A
W.A.R. Form No. L-102-R
Exclusive Sale
Rev. 12/96
Page 1 of 3 pages

EXCLUSIVE SALE AND LISTING AGREEMENT

© Copyright 1996
Washington Information Network
ALL RIGHTS RESERVED

The undersigned Seller ("Seller") hereby grants to _____ , ("Broker") 1

from date hereof until midnight of _____ , the sole and exclusive right to submit offers to purchase, and to receipt 2

for deposits in connection therewith, the real property ("the Property") commonly known as _____ 3

in the City of _____ , County of _____ , State of Washington, Zip _____ ; and legally 4

described as: LOT _____ , BLOCK _____ , DIVISION _____ 5

_____ VOL _____ , PAGE _____ _____. 6

_____ 7

1. **DEFINITIONS.** For purposes of this Agreement: (a) "MLS" means the Northwest Multiple Listing Service; and (b) "sell" includes a contract to sell; an exchange or 8
contract to exchange; an option to purchase; and/or a lease with option to purchase. 9

2. **AGENCY/DUAL AGENCY.** Seller authorizes Broker to appoint _____ to act as Seller's Listing Agent(s). It is understood and 10
agreed that this Agreement creates an agency relationship with Listing Agent(s) and Broker only, not with any other sales persons of Broker; provided, Seller 11
authorizes Broker to appoint other salespersons affiliated with Broker as subagents to act on Seller's behalf as and when needed, at Broker's discretion. Any 12
broker or salesperson, other than Broker or Listing Agent, who procures a prospective buyer for the Property will not be representing Seller and may represent the 13
Buyer. Accordingly, for the purposes of this Agreement, the term "Broker" means Listing Agent(s) including any subagents and Listing Agent's Broker, Designated 14
Broker or Branch Manager, unless expressly stated otherwise. 15

Seller agrees that if the Property is sold to a buyer represented by one of Broker's salespersons other than Listing Agent(s), then Seller consents to Broker acting 16
as a dual agent. Seller further agrees that if the Property is sold to a buyer who Listing Agent also represents, then Seller consents to Listing Agent(s) and Broker 17
acting as dual agents. Seller agrees that different sales persons affiliated with Broker may represent different sellers in competing transactions involving the 18
same buyer and that this shall not be considered action by Broker that is adverse or detrimental to the interests of either seller, nor shall it be considered a 19
conflict of interest on the part of Broker. Seller acknowledges receipt of the pamphlet entitled "The Law of Real Estate Agency." 20

If Broker acts as a dual agent, then Broker shall be entitled to the entire commission payable under this Agreement plus any additional compensation Broker 21
may have negotiated with the Buyer. 22

3. **COMMISSION.** If (a) Broker procures a Buyer on the terms in this Agreement, or on other terms acceptable to Seller; or (b) Seller directly or indirectly or through 23
any person or entity other than Broker, during the term hereof, sells the Property; then Seller will pay Broker a commission of (fill in one and strike the other) 24
_____ % of the sales price, or _____ . Further, if Seller shall, within six months after the expira- 25
tion of this Agreement, sell the Property to any person to whose attention it was brought through the signs, advertising or other action of Broker, or on information 26
secured directly or indirectly from or through Broker, during the term of this Agreement, then Seller will pay Broker the above commission. Provided, that if a 27
commission is paid to a member of MLS or a cooperating MLS in conjunction with a sale, the amount of commission payable to Broker shall be limited to the 28
amount of commission which would have been payable pursuant to this Agreement less any commission so paid to another member of MLS. Provided further, 29
that if Seller cancels this Agreement without legal cause, Seller may be liable for damages incurred by Broker as a result of cancellation, regardless of whether 30
Seller pays a commission to another MLS member. 31

4. **KEYBOX.** Broker is authorized to install a keybox on the Property. Such keybox may be opened by a master key held by all members of MLS and their sales- 32
people. A master key also may be held by affiliated third parties such as inspectors and appraisers who cannot have access to the Property without Broker's 33
prior approval which will not be given without Broker first making reasonable efforts to obtain Seller's approval. 34

5. **SELLER'S WARRANTIES AND REPRESENTATIONS.** Seller warrants that he/she has the right to sell the Property on the terms herein and that the Property 35
information on the additional pages to this Agreement is correct. Further, Seller represents that to the best of Seller's knowledge, there are no structures or 36
boundary indicators that either encroach on adjacent property or on this Property. Seller understands that Broker and other members of MLS will make 37
representations to prospective buyers based on the Property information on the additional pages to this Agreement. Seller agrees to indemnify and hold Broker 38
and other members of MLS harmless in the event the foregoing warranties and representations are incorrect. 39

6. **CLOSING COSTS.** Seller agrees to furnish and pay for a buyer's policy of title insurance showing marketable title to the Property. Seller agrees to pay real estate 40
excise tax and one-half of any escrow fees or such portion of escrow fees and any other fees or charges as provided by law in the case of FHA or VA financed sale. 41
Rent, taxes, interest, reserves, assumed encumbrances, homeowner fees and insurance are to be prorated between Seller and Buyer as of the date of closing. 42

7. **MULTIPLE LISTING.** Broker shall cause this listing to be published by MLS. Broker may refer this listing to any other cooperating multiple listing service at Bro- 43
ker's discretion. Broker shall cooperate with all other members of MLS, or of a multiple listing service to which this listing is referred, in working toward the sale of 44
the Property. Regardless of whether a cooperating MLS member is the agent of the Buyer, the Seller, neither or both, the member shall be entitled to receive the 45
selling office's share of the commission. SELLER UNDERSTANDS AND AGREES THAT THE PROPERTY INFORMATION ON THE ADDITIONAL PAGES OF 46
THIS AGREEMENT WILL BE GIVEN TO PROSPECTIVE BUYERS AND TO OTHER COOPERATING MEMBERS OF MLS WHO DO NOT REPRESENT THE SELLER 47
AND, IN SOME INSTANCES, MAY REPRESENT THE BUYER. IT IS UNDERSTOOD THAT MLS IS NOT A PARTY TO THIS AGREEMENT AND ITS SOLE 48
FUNCTION IS TO FURNISH THE DESCRIPTIVE INFORMATION ON THE ADDITIONAL PAGES OF THIS LISTING TO ITS MEMBERS, WITHOUT VERIFICATION 49
AND WITHOUT ASSUMING ANY RESPONSIBILITY FOR SUCH INFORMATION OR IN RESPECT TO THIS AGREEMENT. 50

8. **DISCLAIMER/SELLER'S INSURANCE.** Neither Broker, MLS, nor any members of MLS or of any multiple listing service to which this listing is referred shall be res- 51
ponsible for loss, theft, or damage of any nature or kind whatsoever to the Property and/or to any personal property therein, including entry by the master key to 52
keybox and/or at open houses. Seller is advised to notify Seller's insurance company that the Property is listed for sale and ascertain that the Seller has 53
adequate insurance coverage. If the Property is to be vacant during all or part of the term of this listing, Seller should request that a "vacancy clause" be 54
added to Seller's insurance policy. 55

9. **BROKER'S RIGHT TO MARKET THE PROPERTY** Seller shall not commit any act which materially impairs Broker's ability to market and sell the Property under the 56
terms of this Agreement. In the event of breach of the foregoing, Seller agrees to pay Broker a commission in the above amount, or at the above rate applied to 57
the listing price herein, whichever is applicable. Broker shall be entitled to show the Property at all reasonable times. Broker need not submit to Seller any offers 58
to lease, rent, execute an option to purchase, or enter into any agreement other than for immediate sale of the Property. 59

10. **REAL PROPERTY TRANSFER DISCLOSURE STATEMENT.** Unless Seller is exempt under RCW 64.06, Seller shall provide to Broker as soon as reasonably prac- 60
ticable a completed and signed "Real Property Transfer Disclosure Statement" (W.A.R. Form D-5 or NWMLS Form 17). Seller agrees to indemnify, defend and 61
hold Broker harmless from and against any and all claims that the information Seller provides on W.A.R. Form D-5 or NWMLS Form 17 is inaccurate. 62

11. **DAMAGES IN THE EVENT OF BUYER'S BREACH** In the event Seller retains earnest money as liquidated damages on Buyer's breach, any costs advanced or com- 63
mitted by Broker on Seller's behalf shall be paid therefrom and the balance divided equally between Seller and Broker. 64

12. **ATTORNEYS' FEES.** In the event either party employs an attorney to enforce any terms of this Agreement and is successful, the other party agrees to pay reason- 65
able attorneys' fees. In the event of trial, the successful party shall be entitled to an award of attorneys' fees and expenses; the amount of the attorneys' fees and 66
expenses shall be fixed by the court. The venue of any suit shall be the county in which the property is located. 67

DATED THIS _____ DAY OF _____ , _____ .   Are the undersigned the sole owner(s)? ☐ YES ☐ NO 68

BROKER (COMPANY) _____   SELLER _____ 69

BY _____   SELLER _____ 70

Reprinted with permission, Northwest Multiple Listing Service. No endorsement implied.

NWMLS Form 1 Rev. 7/02
Copyright 2002
Northwest Multiple Listing Service
All Rights Reserved

RESIDENTIAL Exclusive Listing Agreement (page 2 of 3)
LISTING INPUT SHEET

• Indicates Required information   ( ) Indicates Maximum Choice

PROPERTY TYPE 1

LISTING #

• COUNTY

• TAX ID#

• Listing Office ID#   (Listing Office Name & Phone No. including area code)

• LAG-Listing Agent ID#   (Listing AgentName & Phone No. including area code)

Co Listing Office ID#   **Co Agent - ID #**

• AREA   **• Community/District**

• Street # (HSN)   **Modifier**

❑ E ❑ NW ❑ SW
❑ N ❑ S ❑ W
❑ NE ❑ SE
Direction

• Street Name

❑ Av Ct ❑ Cir ❑ Dr ❑ Lp ❑ St ❑ Terr
❑ Av Pl ❑ Cr St ❑ Dr Ct ❑ Pkwy ❑ St Ct ❑ Wy
❑ Ave ❑ Ct ❑ Hwy ❑ Place ❑ St Dr
❑ Blvd ❑ Ct Av ❑ Lane ❑ Rd ❑ St Pl
Suffix

❑ E ❑ NE ❑ SW
❑ N ❑ NW ❑ W
❑ KPN ❑ S
❑ KPS ❑ SE
Post Direction

Unit #

• CITY

• ZIP Code   + 4

❑ Thomas ❑ RR-Mason ❑ Totem
❑ RR-Kitsap ❑ RR-Thurston ❑ Yellow
❑ RR-Jeff ❑ RR-Lewis ❑ Unknown
• MAP BOOK

• Map Page **• Top Map Coord.**

Show Map Link (Y/N)   ❑ (by default 'Yes')   **• Side Map Coord.**

• Listing Price

• Internet Advertising (Y/N)   ❑   (by default 'Yes')

Show Address to Public (Y/N)   ❑   (by default 'Yes')

• Primary Photo By (1) ❑ Agent/Office ❑ No Photo ❑ NWMLS Photographer

Photographer Instructions

• SOC (Selling Office Com.)   **Selling Office Commission Comments**

• Number of Bedrooms   **• Total Bathrooms**

❑ Square Feet ❑ Acres
ASF - Total   **Lot Size**

• Year Built   **• Listing Date**   **• Expiration Date**

• School District   (see Code List)

• Occupant Type Owner/Presale/Tenant/Vacant   ❑   (O/P/T/V)

• Owner's Name   **• Owner's Phone**

• Occupant's Name   **• Phone to Show**

• Owner's City and State

Marketing Remarks. CAUTION! The comments you make in the following lines are limited to descriptions of the land and improvements only. These remarks will appear in the client handouts and websites. (500)

Confidential Agent-Only Remarks. Comments in this category are for agent's use only. (250)

Legal Description. (100)

Driving Directions to Property (125)

LOCATION

Lot Number

Block

Plat/Subdivision/Building Name

❑
• Preliminary Title Ordered (Y/N)

LISTING INFORMATION
• Possession (3)
❑ Closing   ❑ Closing + 3 Days
❑ Negotiable   ❑ Subject to Tenant's Rights
❑ See Remarks

• Showing Information (No Limit)
❑ Appointment   ❑ Call Listing Office
❑ Day Sleeper   ❑ Gate Code Needed
❑ MLS Keybox   ❑ Other Keybox
❑ Owner-Call First ❑ Pet in House
❑ Power Off   ❑ Renter - Call First
❑ Security System ❑ Vacant
❑ See Remarks

• Form 17 (1)   ❑ Not Provided
❑ Provided   ❑ Exempt

• Tax Year

• Annual Taxes $

• Senior Exemption   ❑ (Y/N)

Monthly Homeowner Dues $

Monthly Rent - if rented $

• Potential Terms (10)
❑ Assumable   ❑ Cash Out
❑ Conventional   ❑ Farm Home Loan
❑ FHA   ❑ Lease/Purchase
❑ Owner Financing ❑ Rehab Loan
❑ State Bond   ❑ VA
❑ Variable Price Listing ❑ See Remarks

NWMLS Form 1 Rev. 7/02
Copyright 2002
Northwest Multiple Listing Service
All Rights Reserved

RESIDENTIAL Exclusive Listing Agreement (page 3 of 3)
LISTING INPUT SHEET

Listing Address:

PROPERTY
TYPE 1

LAG #

SITE INFORMATION

Lot Dimensions

Waterfront Footage

Lot Topog./Veg. (4)
- ❑ Brush
- ❑ Equestrian
- ❑ Garden Space
- ❑ Partial Slope
- ❑ Rolling
- ❑ Steep Slope
- ❑ Wooded
- ❑ Dune
- ❑ Fruit Trees
- ❑ Level
- ❑ Pasture
- ❑ Sloped
- ❑ Terraces

View (4)
- ❑ Bay
- ❑ City
- ❑ Jetty
- ❑ Mountain
- ❑ Partial
- ❑ Sound
- ❑ See Remarks
- ❑ Canal
- ❑ Golf Course
- ❑ Lake
- ❑ Ocean
- ❑ River
- ❑ Territorial

Lot Details (4)
- ❑ Alley
- ❑ Cul-de-sac
- ❑ Dead End Street
- ❑ High Voltage Line
- ❑ Private
- ❑ Corner Lot
- ❑ Curbs
- ❑ Open Space
- ❑ Paved Street
- ❑ Sidewalk

Waterfront (4)
- ❑ Bank-High
- ❑ Bank-Medium
- ❑ Bulkhead
- ❑ Beach Rights
- ❑ Creek
- ❑ Lake
- ❑ River
- ❑ Bank-Low
- ❑ No Bank
- ❑ Bay
- ❑ Canal
- ❑ Jetty
- ❑ Ocean
- ❑ Sound

Site Features (10)
- ❑ Arena-Indoor
- ❑ Athletic Court
- ❑ Boat House
- ❑ Cable TV
- ❑ Disabled Access
- ❑ Dog Run
- ❑ Fenced-Partially
- ❑ Gated Entry
- ❑ Hot Tub/Spa
- ❑ Patio
- ❑ RV Parking
- ❑ Sprinkler System
- ❑ Arena-Outdoor
- ❑ Barn
- ❑ Cabana/Gazebo
- ❑ Deck
- ❑ Dock
- ❑ Fenced-Fully
- ❑ Gas Available
- ❑ Green House
- ❑ Outbuildings
- ❑ Propane
- ❑ Shop
- ❑ Stable

Pool (1)
- ❑ Above Ground
- ❑ Community
- ❑ Indoor
- ❑ In-Ground

BUILDING INFORMATION

• Sewer (2)
- ❑ Sewer Connected
- ❑ Septic
- ❑ Sewer Available

Basement (2)
- ❑ Daylight
- ❑ Partially Finished
- ❑ Unfinished
- ❑ Fully Finished
- ❑ Roughed In
- ❑ None

• Parking Type (4)
- ❑ Carport-Attached
- ❑ Garage-Attached
- ❑ None
- ❑ Carport-Detached
- ❑ Garage-Detached

• Total Covered Parking

Approved for # of Bedrooms (septic)

Builder

New Constructions U=Under Construction, P=Presale, C=Completed

• STYLE Code

• Building Information
- ❑ Additional Dwelling
- ❑ PUD
- ❑ Stick Built On Lot
- ❑ Manufactured Home
- ❑ Stick Built Off Site
- ❑ Zero Lot Line

Manufactured Home Serial No.

Manufactured Home Manufacturer

Manufactured Home Model Name

Foundation (2)
- ❑ Concrete Block
- ❑ Post & Block
- ❑ Poured Concrete
- ❑ Tie Down
- ❑ Concrete Ribbon
- ❑ Post & Pillar
- ❑ Slab
- ❑ See Remarks

Building Condition (1)
- ❑ Average
- ❑ Fair
- ❑ Fixer
- ❑ Good
- ❑ Remodeled
- ❑ Restored
- ❑ Under Construction
- ❑ Very Good

• Roof (2)
- ❑ Built-up
- ❑ Composition
- ❑ Metal
- ❑ Torch Down
- ❑ Cedar Shake
- ❑ Flat
- ❑ Tile
- ❑ See Remarks

• Exterior (2)
- ❑ Brick
- ❑ Log
- ❑ Stone
- ❑ Wood
- ❑ See Remarks
- ❑ Cement/Concrete
- ❑ Metal/Vinyl
- ❑ Stucco
- ❑ Wood Products

Architecture (1)
- ❑ Cabin
- ❑ Cape Cod
- ❑ Colonial
- ❑ Contemporary
- ❑ Craftsman
- ❑ Spanish/SW
- ❑ Tudor
- ❑ Victorian
- ❑ See Remarks

INTERIOR FEATURES
(Approximate Square Footage Excluding Garage)

Finished   **Unfinished**

Square Footage Source

Leased Equipment

Water Heater (Type/Location)

• Energy Source (4)
- ❑ Electric
- ❑ Oil
- ❑ Propane
- ❑ See Remarks
- ❑ Natural Gas
- ❑ Pellet
- ❑ Wood

• Heating/Cooling (4)
- ❑ Baseboard
- ❑ Heat Pump
- ❑ Radiant
- ❑ Stove/Free Stdg
- ❑ Forced Air
- ❑ Insert
- ❑ Radiator
- ❑ Wall

Floor Covering (4)
- ❑ Ceramic Tile
- ❑ Fir/Softwood
- ❑ Slate
- ❑ Wall to Wall Carpet
- ❑ Concrete
- ❑ Hardwood
- ❑ Vinyl
- ❑ See Remarks

Interior Features (10)
- ❑ Bath Off Master
- ❑ Ceiling Fan(s)
- ❑ Disabled Access
- ❑ Fireplace in Master BR
- ❑ Hot Tub/Spa
- ❑ Jetted Tub
- ❑ Sauna
- ❑ Skylights
- ❑ Vaulted Ceilings
- ❑ Wet Bar
- ❑ 2nd Kitchen
- ❑ Built-in Vacuum
- ❑ Dining Room
- ❑ Dble Pane/Strm Wind
- ❑ High Tech Cabling
- ❑ Intercom
- ❑ Pantry
- ❑ Security System
- ❑ Solarium/Atrium
- ❑ Walk-in Closet
- ❑ Wired for Generator

Appliances That Stay (10)
- ❑ Dishwasher
- ❑ Dryer
- ❑ Microwave
- ❑ Refrigerator
- ❑ Washer
- ❑ Double Oven
- ❑ Garbage Disposal
- ❑ Range/Oven
- ❑ Trash Compactor
- ❑ See Remarks

Total Number of Fireplaces

No. of Full Bathrooms (1.0)

No. of ³/₄ Bathrooms (.75)

No. of ¹/₂ Bathrooms (.5)

ROOM LOCATION

Level (1) U for Upper M for Main L for Lower
S for Split G for Garage

Entry	[U]	[M]	[L]	[S]
Living Room	[U]	[M]	[L]	
Dining Room	[U]	[M]	[L]	
Kitchen w/Eating Space	[U]	[M]	[L]	
Kitchen	[U]	[M]	[L]	
Master Bedroom	[U]	[M]	[L]	
Bonus Room	[U]	[M]	[L]	
Den/Office	[U]	[M]	[L]	
Family Room	[U]	[M]	[L]	
Rec Room	[U]	[M]	[L]	
Extra Fin. Room	[U]	[M]	[L]	[G]

No. of Bedrooms U___ M___ L___
No. of Full Baths U___ M___ L___ G___
No. of ³/₄ Baths U___ M___ L___ G___
No. of ¹/₂ Baths U___ M___ L___ G___
No. of Fireplaces U___ M___ L___
Utility Rooms U___ M___ L___ G___
Approved Accessory Dwelling Unit U___ M___ L___

UTILITY / SCHOOL

• Water Source (2)
- ❑ Community
- ❑ Private
- ❑ Shared Well
- ❑ See Remarks
- ❑ Individual Well
- ❑ Public
- ❑ Shares

Water Company

Power Company

Sewer Company

Elementary School

Junior High/Middle School

Senior High School

Bus Line Nearby Y/N ___

INITIALS: _____   _____   _____
   Seller   Date   Seller   Date   Agent   Date

A provision stating the amount (or rate) of the broker's commission is another key part of every listing agreement. Remember that because the amount or rate is always negotiable as a matter of law, it must not be pre-printed on the listing agreement form. The figure has to be filled in for each transaction.

Provisions affecting the commission. A listing agreement should state the sales price and terms that the client is willing to accept. The client can refuse any offer that doesn't meet these terms without being liable for a commission. Of course, if the broker presents an offer that doesn't meet the listing terms and the client accepts it anyway, he is liable for the commission.

Generally, a broker is hired to find a **ready, willing, and able** buyer who meets the specific requirements established by the seller. A buyer is considered ready and willing if the buyer makes an offer that meets the terms stipulated by the seller. A buyer is considered able if he or she has the financial ability to complete the purchase. This means that the buyer must have one of the following:

1. enough cash to complete the sale;
2. a strong enough credit rating and enough personal assets to ensure that he or she can complete the sale; or
3. a binding commitment for a loan to finance the purchase.

Under the terms of most listing agreement forms, the broker is entitled to a commission even if the transaction never closes, as long as the client and a ready, willing, and able buyer have agreed on the essential terms of a sale. It doesn't have to work that way, however. The seller can add a condition to the listing agreement, making liability for the commission depend on the sale actually closing, or on some other event.

Even under a standard listing agreement, if the contract between the buyer and seller is conditional (contingent on the results of an inspection, for example) the seller isn't liable for a commission unless the condition is either fulfilled or waived by the parties.

Most exclusive listing forms make the client liable for a commission if she withdraws the property from sale or does anything to make it unmarketable.

Extender clauses. Exclusive listing forms usually include an extender clause (also called a safety clause or carryover clause). An **extender clause** makes the client liable for a commission during a specified period after the listing expires, if the property is sold to someone the broker dealt with during the listing term. This makes it difficult for a buyer and seller to conspire to deprive the broker of a commission by waiting until the listing expires before signing a purchase and sale agreement.

In some forms, the extender clause requires the client to pay the commission if the broker merely introduced the buyer to the property during the listing term. In other forms, the extender clause has a stricter requirement, so that the client has to pay the commission only if the broker was the procuring cause of the sale.

An extender clause often includes some safeguards for the seller. It may require the broker to provide a list of the people he or she negotiated with, so the seller won't become liable for a commission without realizing it. It may also state that if the seller signs a listing agreement with another broker during the carryover period, the seller will not be liable for a commission to the first broker. Without that provision, the seller could become liable for two commissions on the same sale, one to the first broker and one to the second broker. Some forms do not include these safeguards, so a seller should beware.

Purchase and Sale Agreements

The general term for a contract between a buyer and a seller of real property is **purchase and sale agreement**, or something similar. In Washington, purchase and sale agreements, particularly those prepared by real estate agents for their clients and customers, are sometimes called **earnest money agreements**.

In most transactions, the buyer puts up an earnest money deposit at the same time he or she makes an offer to purchase. The written offer also serves as the buyer's receipt for the deposit. If the seller decides to accept the offer, he or she signs the form, and it becomes the parties' contract.

In Washington, there is no single standard purchase and sale agreement form. A number of different forms are prepared and distributed by organizations such as the Washington Association of Realtors, various multiple listing associations, and some individual brokerage companies. A sample form from the Northwest Multiple Listing Service is included for illustrative purposes. No recommendation or criticism of any particular form is intended.

The basic elements of a purchase and sale agreement are fairly simple. The agreement must:

- identify the parties and the property,
- state the price and the method of payment, and
- state the time for delivery of title and possession.

Most purchase and sale agreements are quite detailed. It's very important for the contract to state all the terms of the parties' agreement clearly and accurately. The closing of the transaction will follow the terms set forth in the agreement. Who is required to do what and when depends on the purchase and sale agreement. Anything that isn't clear can lead to a dispute.

The Parties. When a purchase and sale agreement is being signed, ask two key questions regarding the parties:

- Does everyone who is signing have the capacity to contract?
- Is everyone with an ownership interest signing?

If any of the parties is underage or incompetent, the contract will be voidable or void.

Property Description. A full legal description of the property should be attached as an exhibit to the contract. Include a reference to the attachment in the space provided for the description (for example, "see Exhibit A"). The parties must initial and date each page of the attachment to incorporate it into their agreement.

Terms of Sale. The purchase and sale agreement should state all the terms of the sale as clearly as possible: what is and isn't included in the sale, the total price, and the method of payment.

Any personal property that will be included in the sale should also be listed. Some forms have a paragraph entitled "Included Items," which lists personal property included in the sale. This list should be reviewed and items deleted or added as necessary. When adding included items, be specific; write in "washer, dryer, refrigerator" rather than "all major appliances."

The seller doesn't warrant the condition of the personal property, but he or she does promise that it is free of liens. If the seller wants to exclude any fixtures from the sale, they must also be listed.

An addendum should be added which specifies the financing arrangements: the type of loan, principal amount, interest rate (and whether it is fixed or variable), amortization period, loan term, and monthly payments. In addition, the total sales price should be clearly stated.

Contingencies. Most agreements between buyers and sellers are conditional. Any conditions or contingencies must be spelled out in the purchase and sale agreement or in an attached addendum. This section should state exactly what must occur in order to fulfill each condition. It should explain how one party is to notify the other when a condition has been fulfilled or waived. It should also state a time limit; if the condition is not fulfilled by that date, the contract will be void. Finally, it should explain the parties' rights in the event that the condition is not met or waived.

If a real estate agent believes that a contingency clause in a purchase and sale agreement may affect the date of closing or the date that possession will transfer, the agent should explain this to the parties.

Financing. Nearly all residential transactions are contingent on the buyer's ability to obtain financing. The buyer is required to make a diligent, good faith effort to obtain financing on the terms stated in the purchase and sale agreement, but if no lenders are willing to make a loan on those terms, the buyer can terminate the agreement without forfeiting the deposit. That's why it's particularly important to describe the financing arrangements in detail. If the buyer must obtain financing within a specific time period, he or she must notify the seller in a timely manner of the failure to obtain the financing or risk losing the deposit.

If seller financing is going to be used for part of the purchase price, it is imperative to refer to and attach the appropriate finance documents to the purchase and sale agreement. If the real estate contract or note and deed of trust are not referred to and attached to the agreement, the agreement will not be enforceable.

Fig. 7.7 Purchase and Sale Agreement

NWMLS Form 21
Residential Purchase & Sale Agreement
Revised 03/03
Page 1 of 4

©Copyright 2003
Northwest Multiple Listing Service
ALL RIGHTS RESERVED

RESIDENTIAL REAL ESTATE PURCHASE AND SALE AGREEMENT
SPECIFIC TERMS

1. **Date:** _____ , _____   **MLS No.:** _____

2. **Buyer:** _____

3. **Seller:** _____

4. **Property:** Tax Parcel Nos.: _____ (_____ County)
   Street Address: _____
   _____ Washington _____
   Included Items: ☐ stove/range ☐ refrigerator ☐ washer ☐ dryer ☐ dishwasher ☐ hot tub ☐ fireplace insert
   ☐ wood stove ☐ satellite dish ☐ security system ☐ other _____
   Legal Description:

5. **Purchase Price:** _____

6. **Earnest Money:** (To be held by ☐ Selling Broker ☐ Closing Agent)
   Personal Check: _____
   Note: _____
   Other (_____): _____

7. **Default:** (check only one) ☐ Forfeiture of Earnest Money ☐ Seller's Election of Remedies

8. **Title Insurance Company:** _____

9. **Closing Agent:** ☐ a qualified closing agent of Buyer's choice ☐ _____

10. **Closing Date:** _____

11. **Possession Date:** ☐ on Closing ☐ _____ calendar days after Closing ☐ _____

12. **Offer Expiration Date:** _____

13. **Counteroffer Expiration Date:** _____

14. **Addenda:** _____
    _____

    Inspection Addendum: ☐ NWMLS 35A ☐ NWMLS 35B ☐ Other ☐ None

15. **Agency Disclosure:** Selling Licensee represents ☐ Buyer ☐ Seller ☐ both parties ☐ neither party
    Listing Agent represents ☐ Seller ☐ both parties

16. **Services of Closing Agent for Payment of Utilities:** ☐ Requested (Attach NWMLS Form 22K) ☐ Waived

Buyer's Signature	Date	Seller's Signature	Date
Buyer's Signature	Date	Seller's Signature	Date
Buyer's Address		Seller's Address	
City, State, Zip		City, State, Zip	
Phone	Fax	Phone	Fax
Buyer's E-mail Address		Seller's E-mail Address	
Selling Broker	MLS Office No.	Listing Broker	MLS Office No.
Selling Licensee (Print)		Listing Agent (Print)	
Phone	Fax	Phone	Fax

NWMLS Form 21
Residential Purchase & Sale Agreement
Revised 03/03
Page 2 of 4

©Copyright 2003
Northwest Multiple Listing Service
ALL RIGHTS RESERVED

RESIDENTIAL REAL ESTATE PURCHASE AND SALE AGREEMENT
GENERAL TERMS
(continued)

a. **Purchase Price.** Buyer agrees to pay to Seller the Purchase Price, including the Earnest Money, in cash at Closing, unless otherwise specified in this Agreement. Buyer represents that Buyer has sufficient funds to close this sale in accordance with this Agreement and is not relying on any contingent source of funds or gifts, except to the extent otherwise specified in this Agreement.

b. **Earnest Money.** Buyer agrees to deliver the Earnest Money within 2 days after mutual acceptance of this Agreement to Selling Licensee who will deposit any check to be held by Selling Broker, or deliver any Earnest Money to be held by Closing Agent, within 3 days of receipt or mutual acceptance, whichever occurs later. If the Earnest Money is held by Selling Broker and is over $10,000.00 it shall be deposited into an interest bearing trust account in Selling Broker's name provided that Buyer completes an IRS Form W-9. Interest, if any, after deduction of bank charges and fees, will be paid to Buyer. Buyer agrees to reimburse Selling Broker for bank charges and fees in excess of the interest earned, if any. If the Earnest Money held by Selling Broker is over $10,000.00 Buyer has the option to require Selling Broker to deposit the Earnest Money into the Housing Trust Fund Account, with the interest paid to the State Treasurer, if both Seller and Buyer so agree in writing. If the Buyer does not complete an IRS Form W-9 before Selling Broker must deposit the Earnest Money or the Earnest Money is $10,000.00 or less, the Earnest Money shall be deposited into the Housing Trust Fund Account. Selling Broker may transfer the Earnest Money to Closing Agent at Closing. If all or part of the Earnest Money is to be refunded to Buyer and any such costs remain unpaid, the Selling Broker or Closing Agent may deduct and pay them therefrom. The parties instruct Closing Agent to: (1) provide written verification of receipt of the Earnest Money and notice of dishonor of any check to the parties and licensees at the addresses and/or fax numbers provided herein; and (2) commence an interpleader action in the Superior Court for the county in which the Property is located within 30 days of a party's demand for the Earnest Money (and deduct up to $250.00 of the costs thereof) unless the parties agree otherwise in writing.

c. **Included Items.** Any of the following items located in or on the Property are included in the sale: built-in appliances; wall-to-wall carpeting; curtains, drapes and all other window treatments; window and door screens; awnings; storm doors and windows; installed television antennas; ventilating, air conditioning and heating fixtures; trash compactor; fireplace doors, gas logs and gas log lighters; irrigation fixtures; electric garage door openers; water heaters; installed electrical fixtures; lighting fixtures; shrubs, plants and trees planted in the ground; and all bathroom and other fixtures. However, items identified in Specific Term No. 4 are included only if the corresponding box is checked. If any of the above Included Items are leased or encumbered, Seller agrees to acquire and clear title at or before Closing.

d. **Condition of Title.** Buyer and Seller authorize Selling Licensee, Listing Agent or Closing Agent to insert, attach or correct the Legal Description of the Property. Unless otherwise specified in this Agreement, title to the Property shall be marketable at Closing. The following shall not cause the title to be unmarketable: rights, reservations, covenants, conditions and restrictions, presently of record and general to the area; easements and encroachments, not materially affecting the value of or unduly interfering with Buyer's reasonable use of the Property; and reserved oil and/or mining rights. Monetary encumbrances not assumed by Buyer shall be paid by Seller on or before Closing. Title shall be conveyed by a Statutory Warranty Deed. If this Agreement is for conveyance of a buyer's interest in a Real Estate Contract, the Statutory Warranty Deed shall include a buyer's assignment of the contract sufficient to convey after acquired title.

e. **Title Insurance.** Seller authorizes Buyer's lender or Closing Agent, at Seller's expense, to apply for a standard form owner's policy of title insurance, with homeowner's additional protection and inflation protection endorsements if available at no additional cost, from the Title Insurance Company. The Title Insurance Company is to send a copy of the preliminary commitment to both Listing Agent and Selling Licensee. The preliminary commitment, and the title policy to be issued, shall contain no exceptions other than the General Exclusions and Exceptions in said standard form and Special Exceptions consistent with the Condition of Title herein provided. If title cannot be made so insurable prior to the Closing Date, then as Buyer's sole and exclusive remedy, the Earnest Money shall, unless Buyer elects to waive such defects or encumbrances, be refunded to the Buyer, less any unpaid costs described in this Agreement, and this Agreement shall thereupon be terminated. Buyer shall have no right to specific performance or damages as a consequence of Seller's inability to provide insurable title.

f. **Closing.** This sale shall be closed by the Closing Agent on the Closing Date. If the Closing Date falls on a Saturday, Sunday, or legal holiday as defined in RCW 1.16.050, the Closing Agent shall close the transaction on the next day that is not a Saturday, Sunday, or legal holiday. "Closing" means the date on which all documents are recorded and the sale proceeds are available to Seller. Seller shall deliver keys to Buyer on the Closing Date or on the Possession Date, whichever occurs first.

Initials: BUYER: _____ DATE: _____ SELLER: _____ DATE: _____

BUYER: _____ DATE: _____ SELLER: _____ DATE: _____

RESIDENTIAL REAL ESTATE PURCHASE AND SALE AGREEMENT
GENERAL TERMS
(continued)

g. Possession. Buyer shall be entitled to possession at 9:00 p.m. on the Possession Date. Seller agrees to maintain the Property in its present condition, normal wear and tear excepted, until the Buyer is entitled to possession. 55 56

h. Closing Costs and Prorations. Seller and Buyer shall each pay one-half of the escrow fee unless this sale is FHA or VA financed, in which case it shall be paid according to FHA or VA regulations. Taxes for the current year, rent, interest, and lienable homeowner's association dues shall be prorated as of Closing. Buyer agrees to pay Buyer's loan costs, including credit report, appraisal charge and lender's title insurance, unless provided otherwise in this Agreement. If any payments are delinquent on encumbrances which will remain after Closing, Closing Agent is instructed to pay them at Closing from money due, or to be paid by, Seller. Buyer agrees to pay for remaining fuel in the fuel tank if, prior to Closing, Seller obtains a written statement as to the quantity and current price from the supplier. Seller agrees to pay all utility charges, including unbilled charges. Unless waived in Specific Term No. 16, Seller and Buyer request the services of Closing Agent in disbursing funds necessary to satisfy unpaid utility charges in accordance with RCW 60.80 and Seller agrees to provide the names and addresses of all utilities providing service to the Property and having lien rights (attach NWMLS Form 22K Identification of Utilities or equivalent). 57–67

i. Sale Information. The Listing Agent or Selling Licensee is authorized to report this Agreement (including price and all terms) to the Multiple Listing Service that published it and to its members, financing institutions, appraisers, and anyone else related to this sale. Buyer and Seller expressly authorize all lenders, financial institutions, Closing Agents, appraisers, title insurance companies, and others related to this Sale, to furnish the Listing Agent and/or Selling Licensee, on request, any and all information and copies of documents concerning the status, progress and final disposition of financing, appraisal, Closing, title condition, and any other matter concerning this sale, including buyer's credit report. In addition, Buyer shall provide any additional consent or authorization necessary to permit Buyer's lender or financing institution to provide information concerning the status, progress and final disposition of financing to the Listing Agent and/or Selling Licensee. 68–76

j. FIRPTA - Tax Withholding at Closing. The Closing Agent is instructed to prepare a certification (NWMLS Form 22E or equivalent) that Seller is not a "foreign person" within the meaning of the Foreign Investment In Real Property Tax Act. Seller agrees to sign this certification. If Seller is a foreign person, and this transaction is not otherwise exempt from FIRPTA, Closing Agent is instructed to withhold and pay the required amount to the Internal Revenue Service. 77–80

k. Notices. Unless otherwise specified in this Agreement, any notice required or permitted in, or related to, this Agreement (including revocations of offers or counteroffers) must be in writing. Notices to Seller must be signed by at least one Buyer and shall be deemed given only when the notice is received by Seller, by Listing Agent or at the licensed office of Listing Agent. Notices to Buyer must be signed by at least one Seller and shall be deemed given only when the notice is received by Buyer, by Selling Licensee or at the licensed office of Selling Licensee. Receipt by Selling Licensee of a Real Property Transfer Disclosure Statement, Disclosure of Information on Lead-Based Paint and Lead-Based Paint Hazards, Public Offering Statement and/or Resale Certificate shall be deemed receipt by Buyer. Selling Licensee and Listing Agent have no responsibility to advise of receipt of a notice beyond either phoning the party or causing a copy of the notice to be delivered to the party's address shown on this Agreement. Buyer and Seller must keep Selling Licensee and Listing Agent advised of their whereabouts in order to receive prompt notification of receipt of a notice. 81–91

l. Computation of Time. Unless otherwise specified in this Agreement, any period of time stated in this Agreement shall start on the day following the event commencing the period and shall expire at 9:00 p.m. of the last calendar day of the specified period of time. Except for the Possession Date, if the last day is a Saturday, Sunday or legal holiday as defined in RCW 1.16.050, the specified period of time shall expire on the next day that is not a Saturday, Sunday or legal holiday. Any specified period of 5 days or less shall not include Saturdays, Sundays or legal holidays. Time is of the essence of this Agreement. 92–97

m.Facsimile and E-mail Transmission. Facsimile transmission of any signed original document, and retransmission of any signed facsimile transmission, shall be the same as delivery of an original. At the request of either party, or the Closing Agent, the parties will confirm facsimile transmitted signatures by signing an original document. E-mail transmission of any document or notice shall not be effective unless the parties to this Agreement otherwise agree in writing. 98–101

n. Integration. This Agreement constitutes the entire understanding between the parties and supersedes all prior or contemporaneous understandings and representations. No modification of this Agreement shall be effective unless agreed in writing and signed by Buyer and Seller. 102–104

Initials: BUYER: _____ DATE: _____ SELLER: _____ DATE:_____ 105
BUYER: _____ DATE: _____ SELLER: _____ DATE:_____ 106

NWMLS Form 21
Residential Purchase & Sale Agreement
Revised 03/03
Page 4 of 4

RESIDENTIAL REAL ESTATE PURCHASE AND SALE AGREEMENT
GENERAL TERMS
(continued)

o. **Assignment.** Buyer may not assign this Agreement, or Buyer's rights hereunder, without Seller's prior written consent, unless provided otherwise herein. 107 108

p. **Default.** In the event Buyer fails, without legal excuse, to complete the purchase of the Property, then the following provision, as identified in Specific Term No. 7, shall apply: 109 110

   i. **Forfeiture of Earnest Money.** That portion of the Earnest Money that does not exceed five percent (5%) of the Purchase Price shall be forfeited to the Seller as the sole and exclusive remedy available to Seller for such failure. 111 112

   ii. **Seller's Election of Remedies.** Seller may, at Seller's option, (a) keep the Earnest Money as liquidated damages as the sole and exclusive remedy available to Seller for such failure, (b) bring suit against Buyer for Seller's actual damages, (c) bring suit to specifically enforce this Agreement and recover any incidental damages, or (d) pursue any other rights or remedies available at law or equity. 113 114 115 116

q. **Attorneys' Fees.** If Buyer or Seller institutes suit against the other concerning this Agreement, the prevailing party is entitled to reasonable attorneys' fees and expenses. 117 118

r. **Offer.** Buyer agrees to purchase the Property under the terms and conditions of this Agreement. Seller shall have until 9:00 p.m. on the Offer Expiration Date to accept this offer, unless sooner withdrawn. Acceptance shall not be effective until a signed copy is actually received by Buyer, by Selling Licensee or at the licensed office of Selling Licensee. If this offer is not so accepted, it shall lapse and any Earnest Money shall be refunded to Buyer. 119 120 121 122

s. **Counteroffer.** Seller agrees to sell the Property under the terms and conditions of this Agreement. If Seller makes a counteroffer, Buyer shall have until 9:00 p.m. on the Counteroffer Expiration Date to accept the counteroffer, unless sooner withdrawn. Acceptance shall not be effective until a signed copy is actually received by Seller, by Listing Agent or at the licensed office of Listing Agent. If the counteroffer is not so accepted, it shall lapse and any Earnest Money shall be refunded to Buyer. If no expiration date is specified for a future counteroffer, the counteroffer shall expire at 9:00 p.m. on the second day after the counteroffer is signed by the last party making the counteroffer, unless sooner withdrawn. 123 124 125 126 127 128 129

t. **Agency Disclosure.** Selling Broker represents the same party that Selling Licensee represents. Listing Broker represents the same party that the Listing Agent represents. If Selling Licensee and Listing Agent are different salespersons affiliated with the same Broker, then both Buyer and Seller confirm their consent to that Broker representing both parties as a dual agent. If Selling Licensee and Listing Agent are the same salesperson representing both parties then both Buyer and Seller confirm their consent to that salesperson and his/her Broker representing both parties as dual agents. All parties acknowledge receipt of the pamphlet entitled "The Law of Real Estate Agency." 130 131 132 133 134 135 136

u. **Commission.** Seller and Buyer agree to pay a commission in accordance with any listing or commission agreement to which they are a party. The Listing Broker's commission shall be apportioned between Listing Broker and Selling Broker as specified in the listing. Seller and Buyer hereby consent to Listing Broker or Selling Broker receiving compensation from more than one party. Seller and Buyer hereby assign to Listing Broker and Selling Broker, as applicable, a portion of their funds in escrow equal to such commission(s) and irrevocably instruct the Closing Agent to disburse the commission(s) directly to the Broker(s). In any action by Listing or Selling Broker to enforce this paragraph, the prevailing party is entitled to court costs and reasonable attorneys' fees. 137 138 139 140 141 142 143

v. **Cancellation Rights/Lead-Based Paint.** If a residential dwelling was built on the Property prior to 1978, and Buyer receives a Disclosure of Information on Lead-Based Paint and Lead-Based Paint Hazards (NWMLS Form 22J) after mutual acceptance, Buyer may rescind this Agreement at any time up to 3 days thereafter. 144 145 146

w. **Property Condition Disclaimer.** Real estate brokers and salespersons do not guarantee the value, quality or condition of the Property. Some properties may contain building materials, including siding, roofing, ceiling, insulation, electrical, and plumbing materials, that have been the subject of lawsuits and/or governmental inquiry because of possible defects or health hazards. In addition, some properties may have other defects arising after construction, such as drainage, leakage, pest, rot and mold problems. Real estate licensees do not have the expertise to identify or assess defective products, materials, or conditions. Buyer is urged to retain inspectors qualified to identify the presence of defective materials and evaluate the condition of the Property. 147 148 149 150 151 152 153

Initials: BUYER: _____ DATE: _____ SELLER: _____ DATE: _____ 154

      BUYER: _____ DATE: _____ SELLER: _____ DATE: _____ 155

Sale of buyer's home. Many purchases are contingent on the buyer's ability to sell his or her current home. In fact, even when that isn't an express condition, it may be a hidden condition. Often a buyer won't have enough money for a downpayment unless the current home is sold. As a result, he or she can't qualify for the loan described in the financing contingency without selling the current home.

If the buyer will not be able to obtain financing unless his or her current home is sold, it's best to make the sale of the current home an express condition in the purchase and sale agreement. Otherwise, the seller may be misled into believing that the buyer has a much better chance of obtaining the necessary loan than he or she actually has. The contingency clause should state whether it will be fulfilled once the buyer accepts an offer, or whether the sale of the current home must actually close.

Inspections. The transaction will likely be made dependent on one or more satisfactory property inspections, such as a physical inspection, a geological inspection, or a pest control inspection. If an appraisal notes that pests might be a problem, a pest control inspection may be required by the lender before it will fund the loan.

Bump clause. Including a **bump clause** enables the seller to keep the property on the market pending the fulfillment of a condition. While bump clauses are used when there's a good chance that any condition won't be fulfilled on time, they are most often used when a transaction depends on the sale of the buyer's home. If the seller receives another offer before the buyer's home is sold, the seller can demand that the buyer waive the condition or cancel their contract.

Release of contract. When one transaction fails because a condition is not met, the seller may want to enter into another agreement with a second buyer. In this situation, it's advisable for the seller to include an express condition in the second purchase and sale agreement, making it contingent on the failure of the first agreement and on the first buyer's release of all claims. The seller should not proceed with the second transaction without first clearly establishing that the first agreement is terminated and the first buyer has no right to enforce it. The best way to accomplish this is by asking the first buyer to execute a release of contract form in which the parties agree to rescind the contract.

Encumbrances and Condition of Title.
A seller must note the condition of title, and specify any encumbrances or defects. The seller usually agrees to obtain a standard title insurance policy for the buyer.

Closing and Date of Possession.
The purchase and sale agreement should provide a specific date for closing. Possession of the property is usually transferred to the buyer on the closing date, but the parties can make other arrangements. The seller may want a few extra days for vacating the property. Or the buyer may want to take possession before closing. In either case, the parties should execute a separate rental agreement in addition to the purchase and sale agreement.

A clause is often included which states that "**time is of the essence:**" performance on or before the exact date set out in the purchase and sale agreement is one of the essential

Fig. 7.8 Types of real estate contracts

Real Estate Contracts
◆ Employment agreements
◆ Listing agreements
◆ Earnest money agreements
◆ Options

elements of the contract. Remember, though, that a court may hold that a "time is of the essence" clause has been waived unless the parties actually insist on timely performance.

Escrow and Closing. It's a good idea for a purchase and sale agreement to include arrangements for the escrow. When the parties set the closing date, they should take into account the time needed for fulfilling any conditions. If the closing date is approaching and an inspection report is not yet available, or it looks like some other contingency won't be met on time, the parties may want to move the closing date by executing a written extension agreement.

Deposit. The buyer's deposit is an expression of good faith—it is evidence of a serious intention to buy the property. The funds may be immediately deposited in an escrow account or the broker may hold the deposit check uncashed until the seller has accepted the buyer's offer. Then if the seller rejects the offer, the check can easily be returned to the buyer. The conditions for handling the deposit must be specified in the offer.

The purchase and sale agreement should not only acknowledge receipt of the deposit, it should explain the circumstances under which the deposit will be refunded or forfeited. The parties have the option of treating the deposit as liquidated damages. If the buyer defaults, the seller will keep the deposit as liquidated damages instead of suing for actual damages.

Funds deposited in escrow are not released automatically if there is a dispute. If the seller wants to retain the deposit as liquidated damages, the escrow agent will usually not release that money to the seller without the buyer's consent. It may be necessary to sue or submit the matter to arbitration in order to establish that the buyer is in default and the seller is entitled to liquidated damages.

Agency Disclosure. An agency disclosure clause must be included. The listing agent states which party (or parties) he or she is representing in the transaction. When there is a selling agent in addition to the listing agent, the selling agent must also indicate which party he or she represents. By signing the purchase and sale agreement, the seller and buyer accept these characterizations of the agency relationships. (See Chapter 6.)

Other Provisions. Additional provisions may be included, such as what utilities the property is connected to, whether there are any leased fixtures, the condition of a well or septic tank, and type of insulation.

Acceptance. The seller accepts the buyer's offer as set forth in the document. The seller also agrees to compensate the broker.

In most cases, the seller's agreement to pay the broker is merely a reaffirmation of the commission agreement in an earlier written listing. But if the broker has taken the risk of operating under an oral or implied listing agreement, this written provision will satisfy the statute of frauds.

Under the compensation provision of the purchase and sale agreement, if the buyer defaults, the broker is usually entitled to half of the damages the seller receives. In practice, this generally means that the broker will take half of the forfeited deposit. However, the broker is not allowed to receive more in damages than he or she would have received as a commission if the transaction had closed.

Counteroffers. Often a seller is unwilling to accept the buyer's offer as written, but would accept slightly different terms. Remember that when an offeree varies any terms in an offer, it becomes a counteroffer instead of an acceptance. The original offeror (the buyer) is not bound unless he or she chooses to accept the seller's counteroffer.

When a seller wants to make a counteroffer, some agents simply cross out the appropriate terms on the buyer's purchase and sale agreement and replace them with the seller's new terms. The seller signs the agreement and initials and dates the changes. Then if the buyer is willing to accept the counteroffer, he or she also initials and dates the changes. This approach may work if the changes are minor and there is enough space to indicate them clearly. But the agreement may become difficult to read. Sometimes an agent fails to get every change initialed, so that it isn't clear whether the parties ever reached an agreement on all of the terms.

It's clearer and more professional to write any counteroffer on another form or a separate attachment. There are many forms specifically designed for this purpose.

Options

An **option** is a contract that gives one party the right to do something, but not the obligation to do it. In real estate, the most common type of option is an option to purchase. An option to purchase gives one party (the **optionee**) the right to buy the property of the other (the **optionor**) at a designated price within a specific time period. Within that period, the optionee may choose to exercise the option—that is, enter into a contract to buy the property. But the optionee is under no obligation to exercise the option.

Example: Sullivan is interested in buying Hubbard's house, but hasn't quite made up his mind. He asks Hubbard to grant him an option to purchase the house for $250,000. Hubbard agrees and writes up an option agreement in which Sullivan agrees to pay $250 to keep the option open for two weeks.

A week later, while Sullivan is still making up his mind, he hears that Pirandello is planning to offer Hubbard $275,000 for the house. Sullivan decides he does want to buy the house, so he exercises his option. Hubbard is bound to sell her house to Sullivan for $250,000, instead of selling it to Pirandello for $275,000.

Note that an option to purchase real property must be in writing and signed. The written option agreement should be as specific as possible, identifying the parties and the property, and stating all the terms of the potential sale. The option must also be exercised in writing.

Consideration for an Option. Consideration paid for an option contract is not refundable. If the optionee decides not to exercise the option, he or she can't demand that the optionor return the consideration. In the previous example, if Sullivan had decided not to buy the house, he would have lost the $250. If consideration is paid for an option, then the option cannot be revoked. Sullivan paid consideration of $250, so Hubbard could not revoke the option.

To make an option irrevocable, very little consideration is necessary. But if the consideration is not legally adequate, the optionee will not be able to sue for specific performance.

Example: Hubbard granted Sullivan an option to purchase her house for $250,000. Sullivan gave Hubbard $15 to keep the option open for two weeks. During that period, Pirandello offers Hubbard $275,000 for the house. Hubbard can't revoke Sullivan's option because he gave her consideration.

However, Hubbard decides to breach the option contract and sell the house to Pirandello. When Sullivan sues Hubbard for breach of contract, the court rules that $15 was not adequate consideration for a two-week option on a $250,000 house. Sullivan is entitled to damages for breach of contract, but not specific performance. The court cannot order Hubbard to sell the house to Sullivan for $250,000.

Relation Back. When an option is exercised, the interest the optionee acquires in the property **relates back** to the time the option was granted. In the eyes of the law, it's as though the optionee purchased the property when the option was granted, rather than when the option was exercised.

Example: Entwhistle gave an exclusive listing on her house to B&D Realty. This listing was to expire on July 15. On May 20, Entwhistle gave Sumner an option to purchase her house for $340,000. Both parties agreed that the option would not be exercised until after B&D's listing expired.

Sumner exercised his option and purchased the house on August 20. B&D Realty sued for its commission. Entwhistle would be required to pay the commission.

Even though the option was not exercised until August, it was entered into in May. When Sumner exercised the option, his interest in the property related back to the time the option was granted. In effect, he is held to have purchased the property in May rather than in August. Since the listing agreement was still in effect in May, B&D is entitled to the commission.

This rule makes it particularly important for a real estate purchaser to check the public record for any options recorded against the property he or she intends to buy. When an option is exercised, any rights acquired since the option was granted are cut off, if the person who acquired the rights had actual or constructive knowledge of the option.

> **Example:** Dunn buys Schauer's property in March. Dunn doesn't know that Nguyen has an option to purchase the property that won't expire until June. But since Nguyen recorded her option in February, Dunn is charged with constructive knowledge of the option. Without realizing it, Dunn has taken the property subject to Nguyen's option.
>
> In May, Nguyen decides to exercise the option. She can require Dunn to convey the property to her, just as if it were still owned by Schauer.

However, keep in mind that until an option is exercised, it is only a contract right, not an interest in the property. So an option can't be used as security for a mortgage, and it isn't a lien.

Assignment. An option agreement can generally be assigned, unless the contract states that assignment is prohibited. An option to purchase may be included in a lease. If the lease is assigned, the option is assigned too, even when the assignment doesn't specifically mention the option.

Termination. When an optionee has given consideration for the option, the death of the optionor does not terminate the option. The option contract is binding on the optionor's heirs, and the optionee can still exercise it.

An option terminates automatically if it is not exercised before its expiration date. But if the option agreement was recorded, it can still be a cloud on the title after it has expired. A title insurance company will not simply ignore a recorded option after its expiration date—they can't be sure that the optionor didn't grant an extension. So when a recorded option is no longer effective, a document canceling the option should be recorded. To make absolutely sure that the optionee doesn't have any claim on the property, title insurers often require a quitclaim deed from the optionee to the optionor.

Right of First Refusal. A right of first refusal (sometimes called a **right of preemption**) is not the same thing as an option. Someone who holds a **right of first refusal** has the right to buy the property only when and if the owner decides to sell it. The owner can't be required to sell the property against his or her will, unlike an optionor.

Rights of first refusal are sometimes included in leases for office space. If adjacent space on the same floor becomes vacant, the lessor must offer the lessee the chance to expand into that space before it can be offered to a new tenant. Co-owners of property sometimes grant each other the right of first refusal; if one co-owner decides to sell his or her share, the other has the right to buy it instead of letting it go to a stranger.

Homeowners associations occasionally use rights of first refusal to maintain some control over who moves into the area. When a homeowner decides to sell, the association can buy the property to prevent its sale to someone the members consider undesirable. In this way, preemption rights have sometimes been used as a tool for racial discrimination. That practice is illegal (see Chapter 12).

Conclusion

Anyone participating in real estate transactions should have a general knowledge of how contracts are formed, and what is required for them to be valid and enforceable. It's also important to know what kinds of things cause a contract to be void, and what actions or problems would be considered a breach of contract.

If you participate in many transactions, you're likely to encounter situations where one party does not fulfill the terms of a contract. It then becomes important to know what the possible solutions are. A contract may be rescinded or canceled. The contract may provide for liquidated damages, or a court may order one party to pay the other a certain amount of damages. In some instances, the court may even order specific performance.

Virtually all real estate transactions involve at least one contract of one type or another. An understanding of contract law can help you deal more competently and securely with all of the contracts used in the industry.

Case Problem

The following is a hypothetical case problem. Most of the facts are taken from a real case. Based on what you have learned from this chapter, make a decision on the issues presented and then check to see if your answer matches the court's decision.

The Facts

Kreger entered into a purchase and sale agreement with Hall for the purchase of 15 acres of land, making a $1,000 initial deposit. The agreement provided that upon Hall furnishing title clear of encumbrances, Kreger would pay $11,500 in cash at closing on February 1, 1965. The agreement specified that Hall could use the cash received at closing to pay off encumbrances. The balance of the purchase price was to be paid in annual installments.

The property was encumbered by a $10,000 mortgage. Hall told Kreger he intended to pay off the mortgage with funds he expected to receive in a fire insurance claim settlement.

On January 28, 1965, Hall wrote to Kreger demanding that Kreger deposit the $11,500 downpayment for closing of the sale by February 1. Otherwise, Hall stated that all rights of the purchaser would be terminated.

Kreger responded that he was ready, willing, and able to make the downpayment, upon the furnishing of title clear of encumbrances, and that if the mortgage was not yet satisfied, it should be paid out of the downpayment. In the alternative, Kreger offered to assume the mortgage and remit to Hall any balance remaining over the amount of the encumbrance.

Hall did not want to use the downpayment for this purpose, and intended to satisfy the mortgage from the fire insurance payments. However, payment of the insurance settlement was taking longer than expected.

On January 29, 1965, Hall entered into a purchase and sale agreement for the sale of the property to Parker, upon the same terms as the agreement with Kreger, except that the Parker agreement did not require that the encumbrance be satisfied out of the downpayment.

Upon discovering that Hall had entered into an agreement with someone else, Kreger filed a lawsuit for specific performance of his purchase and sale agreement. Kreger claimed that he was ready, willing, and able to make the downpayment, but that the seller failed to deliver a report showing clear title.

Hall alleged that the contract with Kreger was forfeited, since Kreger failed to pay the sum required on February 1, 1965.

The Questions

Was the purchase and sale agreement forfeited? Was Kreger entitled to specific performance of the agreement? What happens to Parker (the second purchaser)?

The Answer

The trial court found that there was no forfeiture of the agreement by Kreger. The agreement provided for payment on February 1. Kreger was ready, willing, and able to pay on this date, but Hall had not provided clear title. Even though Kreger knew that Hall intended to pay off the mortgage with the fire insurance money, this did not change the terms of the agreement. The contract provided that title was to be free of encumbrances, and Kreger was not required to pay until presented with clear title. Kreger had not forfeited the agreement because he was at all times ready to perform.

Kreger was entitled to specific performance of the agreement. The court directed Kreger to deposit into court the sum of $10,500 ($11,500 minus Kreger's earnest money deposit of $1,000). Payment from this amount was used to satisfy the encumbrance. Hall was then required to execute a contract for the balance of the sales price as provided for in the purchase and sale agreement.

The alleged sale to Parker was junior to the prior rights of Kreger. Hall had no right to sell the property to Parker while there was still an enforceable agreement with Kreger. If Parker was damaged, he might have a cause of action against Hall. *Kreger v. Hall*, 70 Wn.2d 1002, 425 P.2d 638 (1967).

Chapter Summary

- An express contract has been put into words, either spoken or written. An implied contract is not put into words, but rather is implied by the actions of the parties.

- A contract is unilateral when only one party makes a promise. In a bilateral contract, each party makes a binding promise to the other.

- A valid contract meets all legal requirements. If the contract does not meet one or more of the legal requirements, it is void. A contract is voidable if one party could enforce the contract, or could choose not to go through with it. Sometimes a contract is simply unenforceable due to lack of evidence, vague or ambiguous wording, or because the statute of limitations has run out.

- The four essential elements for a valid contract are capacity to contract, mutual consent (an offer and acceptance), consideration, and lawful purpose.

- Acceptance must not vary the offer's terms. If it does, it is a counteroffer rather than acceptance.

- In order to create a binding contract, consent must be given freely. A contract may be voidable if consent was obtained by fraud, undue influence, duress, or mistake.

- The statute of frauds provides that certain contracts must be in writing, such as contracts for the sale of real estate, contracts which cannot be performed within a year, or agreements to pay another's debt.

- There are many remedies for breach of contract. The dispute may be resolved through arbitration or a civil lawsuit. Damages may be ordered, or the breaching party may be required to pay the amount specified in a liquidated damages provision. There are also equitable remedies that might be granted, such as injunctions, rescission, or specific performance.

- Listing agreements, purchase and sale agreements, and option agreements are types of real estate contracts.

Checklist of Problem Areas

Real Estate Licensee's Checklist

❑ Does the listing agreement or purchase and sale agreement meet all of the requirements for a valid contract?

❑ If the buyer has made an offer, did the seller accept the offer—or make changes in the acceptance so that it is actually a counteroffer? You are only entitled to a commission if you find a buyer who meets the seller's terms, or whose offer is accepted by the seller.

❑ Is the contract, including all of its terms, clear to both parties? Remember that a contract is voidable for mutual mistake.

Seller's Checklist

❑ Is the listing agreement, option, or purchase and sale agreement you signed a valid contract?

❑ If you breach the contract, what kind of damages could you be liable for? Is there a provision for liquidated damages? Could specific performance be required?

Buyer's Checklist

❑ Has there been actual acceptance of your offer, or merely a counteroffer made?

❑ Does the seller have the capacity to contract? In other words, is he or she 18 or older and mentally competent?

❑ If the seller breached the contract, what kind of damages would you be entitled to?

❑ If you breach the contract (refuse to buy after signing a purchase and sale agreement), what kind of damages could you be liable for?

Chapter Quiz

1. Sam tells his teenage neighbor, "I'll pay you $10 if you mow my lawn on Saturday." The teenager says, "I'm not sure if I can. I'll let you know later." What type of promise is this?

    a. Bilateral
    b. Unilateral
    c. Executed
    d. Implied

2. On May 15, Sharon offers to sell her property to Bill. The offer provides for acceptance by mail. On May 18, Bill mails a letter to Sharon accepting the offer. On May 19, before receiving Bill's letter, Sharon calls Bill on the phone to tell him that she is revoking the offer. Which of the following is true?

    a. Sharon can still revoke because she notified Bill before she received the acceptance
    b. Sharon can still revoke because Bill should have accepted by telephone
    c. Sharon cannot revoke because acceptance is held to be communicated as soon as it is sent, even though not yet received
    d. Sharon cannot revoke because it has been more than three days since she made the offer

3. Art offers to buy Kevin's house for $235,000. Kevin says "I'll accept your offer, but at $238,000." This is known as:

    a. a partial acceptance
    b. a unilateral acceptance
    c. an implied offer
    d. a counteroffer

4. White owns some beautiful beachfront property. He is a reputable businessman with a wife and children. Many years ago, White was involved in a scandal involving drugs and sex. The whole thing was hushed up at the time and White has since mended his ways.

    Johnson was White's roommate in college. He is now a struggling real estate broker. He visits White and tells him he wants an exclusive listing on the beachfront property or he will tell everyone about White's past. This is an example of:

    a. duress
    b. business compulsion
    c. mutual mistake
    d. unlawful purpose

5. Smith agrees to sell his property to Carlucci. The property is worth approximately $500,000. Smith says he will give it to Carlucci for $250,000 and some cocaine. This contract:

    a. is enforceable
    b. is not entirely void; just the illegal part is void
    c. lacks adequate consideration
    d. is void

6. The statute of frauds requires:

    a. that all contracts be in writing
    b. that certain contracts be in writing
    c. that a contract is not enforceable if it is fraudulent
    d. None of the above

7. Tom and Val have been neighbors for 20 years. Both have five acres of property on which they grow apples and peaches. For the last few years, Val has been severely crippled with arthritis. She promised Tom that if he would work her property and harvest the fruit along with his own for five years, she would sell the property to him for half its market value. Tom works as promised and starts to make arrangements to purchase the property. But Val changes her mind and refuses to sell the property to Tom unless he pays full market value.

a. Tom has no recourse because there was no written contract
b. This is still a valid contract even though it is not in writing
c. Even though no written contract exists, Tom may still have an action against Val based on promissory estoppel
d. Even though no written contract exists, Tom may still have an action against Val based on accord and satisfaction

8. The purchase and sale agreement contains a clause providing that it will not be binding unless the buyers qualify for financing. This type of clause is known as a:

a. repudiation clause
b. contingency clause
c. declaratory clause
d. None of the above

9. When comparing arbitration to an action that goes to trial:

a. arbitration is usually cheaper but takes longer
b. arbitration is usually faster, but costs much more
c. arbitration is usually both faster and cheaper
d. arbitration is usually slower and more expensive

10. In Washington, a lawsuit based on breach of a written contract generally must be filed within how many years after the breach occurred?

a. Two years
b. Four years
c. Six years
d. Eight years

11. A contract contains a provision stating how much each party will have to pay in the event of a breach. This is called:

a. a liquidated damages provision
b. an equitable remedy
c. a personal injunction
d. None of the above

12. Krebs breaches a contract to sell his property to Barkley. Barkley decides that he doesn't want to try to enforce the contract. He just wants to undo the contract and get his earnest money deposit back. This is called:

a. an injunction
b. rescission
c. specific performance
d. mitigation

13. Woods agrees to sell his $200,000 house to Yatz for only $90,000. When the time comes, Woods suddenly refuses to perform. Yatz brings a lawsuit against Woods asking for specific performance.

a. Specific performance will probably be granted because property is unique
b. Specific performance will probably not be granted because the consideration is inadequate
c. Specific performance will probably be granted because the amount of consideration is irrelevant
d. Specific performance will probably not be granted because it is hardly ever granted in cases involving real estate

14. Which of the following is not a contract?
    a. A listing agreement
    b. A purchase and sale agreement
    c. An option
    d. None of the above

15. An option:
    a. must be supported by consideration
    b. obligates the optionee to exercise the option
    c. is an implied contract if supported by consideration
    d. is revocable by the optionor

8 Title to Real Property

Outline

Key Terms

- alienation
- deed
- grantor
- grantee
- conveyance
- granting clause
- power of attorney
- attorney in fact
- acknowledgment
- donative intent
- acceptance
- general warranty deed
- covenant of seisin
- covenant of right to convey
- covenant against encumbrances
- covenant for quiet enjoyment
- covenant of warranty
- special warranty deed

- quitclaim deed
- cloud on title
- after-acquired title
- will
- testament
- testator (testatrix)
- bequeath
- codicil
- legatee
- devise
- devisee
- executor (executrix)
- probate
- nuncupative will
- testamentary capacity
- holographic will
- involuntary alienation
- intestate succession
- escheat
- foreclosure

- suit for partition
- quiet title action
- adverse possession
- tacking
- color of title
- condemnation
- eminent domain
- dedication
- title insurance
- standard coverage policy
- extended coverage policy
- abstract of title
- recording
- grantor-grantee index
- book of plats
- actual notice
- constructive notice
- race-notice statute
- bona fide purchaser
- Torrens system

Chapter Overview

The process of transferring ownership of real property from one person to another is called **alienation**. A property owner may voluntarily transfer property by a number of different methods, such as selling it to an arm's length buyer or leaving it to friends in a will. Property may also be transferred involuntarily (against the owner's wishes), as in a foreclosure sale or when the property is condemned. This chapter describes the various types of transfers. It also explains title insurance and the recording system.

Voluntary Alienation

Deeds

The most common method of voluntary alienation is by deed. A **deed** is a document used by an owner of real property (the **grantor**) to transfer all or part of an interest in the property to another party (the **grantee**). This process of transferring (alienating) real property by deed is called **conveyancing**.

In order to be valid, a deed must meet specific requirements and contain certain elements. It must:

1. be in writing,
2. contain words of conveyance and a description of the property,

3. identify the grantee,
4. be signed and acknowledged by a competent grantor, and
5. be delivered to and accepted by the grantee.

Written. The statute of frauds requires any transfer of an interest in real property to be in writing. A transfer of real property cannot be accomplished orally.

Words of Conveyance. The core of a deed is the granting clause. This is the portion of the deed that actually sets forth words that convey the property to the new owner. The **granting clause** must express the intention to transfer ownership of the property or an interest in the property.

The requirement for words of conveyance is easily satisfied. Usually one word, such as "convey," is sufficient. However, deeds often contain several words of conveyance. (Attorneys sometimes like to use five or six words when one would do.) A typical granting clause might state:

"Grantors . . . do hereby give, grant, bargain, sell, and convey unto the said grantees forever . . ."

Description of Property. The property being conveyed must be adequately described in the deed. A legal description should always be included.

Identifiable Grantee. For a deed to transfer title, it must name an existing and identifiable grantee.

Example: A deed to "Tom Jones and his wife" is adequate to transfer the property to Tom and his wife. Even though the wife was not actually named in the deed, she was identifiable as Tom's wife.

Note that the grantee does not have to be competent. Property can be transferred to someone who is a minor or mentally incompetent. Essentially, the only requirement is that the grantee be alive and identifiable.

Example: John executes a deed to transfer his property to Mary. Unknown to John, Mary had recently passed away. Mary's heirs argue that they are entitled to the property. However, they have no legal right to the property because it never transferred to Mary. A deed cannot transfer property to a dead grantee. The deed is void and the property remains John's. If he wishes it to go to Mary's heirs, he must deed it to them.

The grantee may be a corporation or other legal entity (such as a partnership or trust), rather than a human being. Normally, these entities are adequate grantees so long as they legally exist. In other words, they must meet the requirements for incorporation, or be licensed, or have the proper certificates on file, so that they can be recognized as an existing legal entity.

Competent Grantor. Every deed must name an identifiable grantor. The grantor is the person who conveys or transfers the property or an interest in the property. If a mistake is made in the spelling of the grantor's name or it is spelled differently in different parts of the deed, it will not invalidate the deed, as long as it is clear who the grantor is meant to be.

> **Example:** In the body of the deed the name of the grantor is spelled "Reily," but the signature at the bottom of the deed is spelled "Reilly." A deed names the grantor as "Jane Elizabeth Hawthorne," but the signature is written as "Jane E. Hawthorne." Both of these deeds would probably be valid.

In addition to being clearly identifiable, the grantor must also be competent (of legal age and sound mind). If the grantor is mentally incompetent or under legal age, the deed is void or voidable by the grantor.

Marital status. Marital status can affect the grantor's right to convey the property, since Washington is a community property state. So it's a good idea to state clearly in the deed whether the grantor is married or single, although that is not a legal requirement.

Corporate grantor. Under the law, a corporation is considered a person for certain purposes. A corporation has the right to transfer real property. There are specific rules governing the transfer of real property by a corporation. Normally, a resolution of the board of directors is required before a corporate officer can execute a deed.

Signature of Grantor. To be valid, a deed must be signed by the grantor. (The grantee's signature is not required.) Although the grantor's signature is not required to be in any certain place, it is important to make it clear that the signature applies to the entire document. Usually the signature is found at the end of the document.

In certain situations, the deed may be signed by a mark. A mark may be used if the grantor is illiterate or physically disabled and cannot write his or her own name. If the grantor signs by a mark, his or her name should be written or typed near the mark, and the act of making the mark should be witnessed.

Power of attorney. A deed may be signed by the grantor's **attorney in fact**: someone the grantor has authorized to act on his or her behalf. The grantor gives the attorney in fact (not necessarily a lawyer) this authority to act in a written document called a **power of attorney**. The power of attorney must be recorded in the county where the property is located. A power of attorney may be revoked by the grantor at any time.

When the attorney in fact is signing a deed or other document for the grantor, he or she usually signs the grantor's name and then places his or her name beneath it.

> **Example:** *Andrew C. Thompson*
> by *Margaret L. Pierson*, his Attorney in Fact

For a signature by power of attorney to be effective, the grantor must be alive and competent when the deed is delivered. The death of the grantor or the attorney in fact automatically revokes the power of attorney. Therefore, the grantee should make sure that the power of attorney is still in effect, and that the grantor is alive and competent.

Fig. 8.1 Requirements of a valid deed

```
                        A VALID DEED

I hereby grant ....................... words of conveyance
Greenacres Farm ................... adequate description of property
To Harry Carter ...................... identifiable, living grantee
(signed) Sam Smith ................. signature of competent grantor
```

Acknowledged. Washington requires all deeds to be acknowledged. **Acknowledgment** is a formal declaration made by the grantor that the document has been signed voluntarily. Acknowledgment usually occurs when the grantor signs the deed in front of a notary public and states that it is a free and voluntary act. Acknowledgment may also be taken by several other officers or public officials specified in state statutes (such as a judge, court clerk, or county auditor).

The person who takes the acknowledgment fills in a **certificate of acknowledgment**, which states that the grantor appeared and acknowledged that he or she executed the instrument as a free and voluntary act.

Someone who has an interest in the property may not take the acknowledgment. For instance, if you are deeding property to your nephew (who is a notary public), he may not acknowledge the deed, because he is the grantee and therefore has an interest in the property.

The document must be read to a blind grantor before the acknowledgment is taken. Similarly, if the grantor does not speak or understand English, the acknowledgment should not be taken until it is clear that the document has been translated into a language that the grantor understands.

Delivery, Donative Intent, and Acceptance. Even if a deed contains all of the required elements, it will not not transfer title until it is delivered by the grantor, with the intent to pass title, and is accepted by the grantee. Actual physical delivery of the deed is usually necessary, although the grantee may accept delivery of the deed through an agent. Valid delivery cannot occur without **donative intent**: the grantor must intend to pass title and surrender control. It is the intent of the grantor that governs.

Case Example:

Proctor was a married real estate broker. In 1964, he hired Zee Forsythe as a saleswoman. From 1964 to 1966, Proctor acquired certain property in Forsythe's name. In 1967, Forsythe signed a contract for the purchase of a lot. Proctor supplied the downpayment. They planned to construct a home, and Forsythe signed a $10,000 mortgage.

Proctor asked Forsythe to marry him, told her he loved her, gave her several gifts, and purchased a plaque to be installed in the home which read, "From Norman to Zee with love."

During this time, there were several dealings by Proctor on Forsythe's behalf that required her to sign numerous papers, some of them in blank.

Sometime later, a dispute arose concerning ownership of the property. Proctor claimed ownership based on two quitclaim deeds and a mortgage bearing Forsythe's signature, which showed the property to be transferred from her to Proctor. Forsythe claimed that these documents were not intentionally or knowingly signed by her, and requested that they be set aside.

One of the deeds that Forsythe claims was signed in blank showed that two typewriters were used at separate times to complete the instrument.

The court found an express intent by Proctor to make a gift to Forsythe. It further found a lack of intent by Forsythe to convey title back to Proctor, because the documents were not knowingly or intentionally signed. This rendered the deed and mortgage in Proctor's name void, and the property was awarded to Forsythe. *Proctor v. Forsythe*, 4 Wn. App. 238, 480 P.2d 511 (1971).

Case Example:

Susan Fenich quitclaimed 80 acres to her granddaughter, Helene Bull. The purpose of this deed was to transfer the property to Helene if Helene's mother (Mary) predeceased the grandmother (Susan).

This deed was given to an attorney. Susan died in 1949, while Mary was still living. Susan's will left almost all of her property to Mary. A lawsuit arose regarding the 80 acres. One of the issues was whether the deed from Susan to Helene was valid.

The court found there was no intent to make a present transfer, and therefore there was no delivery. The deed was delivered to an attorney, not to Helene, and was not to be effective unless Mary predeceased Susan. Therefore the deed from Susan to Helene was not effective and did not transfer title. *Bull v. Fenich*, 34 Wn. App. 435, 661 P.2d 1012 (1983)

Although it is rare, constructive or implied delivery may be found valid if the intention of the grantor can be adequately shown. A deed may also sometimes be given to a third person to give to the grantee.

Example: Appleby signs a deed to Bertinelli as grantee and hands the deed to Bertinelli's lawyer, with the intention of transferring ownership to Bertinelli here and now. This is delivery to an agent of the grantee, and it is effective to transfer title.

Delivery must take place during the grantor's lifetime. Just as a deed cannot be given to a dead grantee, it cannot be delivered by a dead grantor.

Example: Upon Mr. Grant's death, a deed is found in his safety deposit box. The deed is from Mr. Grant to his niece. The deed is void for want of delivery, since Mr. Grant was dead before the niece ever received the deed.

Not only is it necessary that the grantor intend to transfer ownership or an interest in property, it is also necessary that the grantee accept that transfer. If there is a dispute concerning acceptance, the courts generally try to find in favor of acceptance. But in some circumstances, the grantee may not want to accept, either for personal reasons, or because it would not be in his or her best interest.

Example: Moynihan owns property worth $10,000 that he wants to deed to his son. However, the property has a tax lien on it for $12,000. The son does not want to accept the property because of the tax liability.

Putting a deed in escrow is also a form of delivery. For escrow to be valid, complete and irrevocable delivery must occur. When a deed is placed in escrow, the depositor must give up all possession or control over the deed.

Other Elements. Many deeds contain other elements that seem to be standard, but actually are not required. For instance, almost all deeds are dated, but it is not a legal requirement that the deed contain the date of conveyance.

Another item sometimes included is the grantee's signature. Although a deed must contain the grantor's signature, the grantee does not need to sign.

The deed also does not have to contain a recital of the specific consideration for which the property is being transferred. However, it is helpful to include a recital of consideration to show that a transaction was a purchase rather than a gift, since the grantee of a gift deed may be vulnerable to claims by the grantor's creditors. The recital of consideration generally does not contain the actual purchase price, but may simply state: ". . . for $10.00 and other valuable consideration." Consideration can take forms other than money, such as love and affection, waiver of a right, or performance of a service.

Types of Deeds

There are three main types of deeds used in Washington: the general warranty deed, the special warranty deed, and the quitclaim deed.

Warranty Deed. A **general warranty deed** contains certain assurances or guarantees by the grantor:

1. The grantor has good title to the land conveyed: at the time of executing and delivering the deed, the grantor actually owned the land. This is called the **covenant of seisin**.

2. The grantor has the right to the convey the land: the grantor either has title to the land or is an agent of the owner with the authority to transfer the interest. This is called the **covenant of right to convey**.

3. The property is free from undisclosed encumbrances. This is called the **covenant against encumbrances**.

4. The grantor promises quiet and peaceable possession of the premises: the grantee's possession will not be threatened by any lawful claim made by a third party. This is called the **covenant of quiet enjoyment**.

5. The grantor is required to defend the title against anyone who may lawfully have a claim to it. This is called the **covenant of warranty**.

If the grantee suffers damages or loses the property because the title was not as promised, or covenanted, he or she may sue the grantor for damages. For instance, if there was an encumbrance such as a tax lien, and the grantee had to pay this lien, the grantee could sue the grantor for the amount of his or her damages.

The general warranty deed is the most comprehensive and most commonly used of all the deeds, and it gives the grantee the most protection.

Special Warranty Deed. The next type of deed is the **special warranty deed** (also called a **bargain and sale deed**). In this type of deed, the grantor only guarantees his or her own actions. Essentially, the grantor conveys the same interest in property and quality of title as acquired from the last owner. The grantor promises:

1. Nothing the grantor has done has encumbered the property. However, the grantor does not guarantee against any encumbrances that he or she may not be aware of.

2. The grantor also promises the grantee quiet enjoyment against the grantor and his or her heirs and assigns. This assures the grantee that he or she will not be evicted or disturbed by the grantor claiming a right to the property. However, it does not protect the grantee against other claims.

Under a special warranty deed, the grantor is liable if the grantee is disturbed by some claim arising through an act of the grantor. However, if an outstanding title is asserted by an outside third party, the grantor is not liable.

> **Example:** Roberts purchased property from Fenniman. Roberts then sold the property to Yamagato. Roberts gave Yamagato a special warranty deed.
> Unknown to Roberts, Fenniman was a clever crook who had sold the same property to several people. One of these other people appeared and claimed title to the property. Roberts cannot be held liable.

Quitclaim Deed. A **quitclaim deed** simply conveys whatever interest the grantor has. It contains no warranties of any sort. A quitclaim deed will convey nothing at all if the grantor had no interest in the property when the deed was executed.

Example: Able and Baker are neighbors and good friends. They don't know where the boundary line is between their property. A fence runs between the properties 30 yards from Baker's house. Baker thinks his true property line is actually 32 yards from the house. Able and Baker both want to sell their property, but don't want to hire a surveyor. Baker gives Able a quitclaim deed for the two yards of property on the other side of the fence.

Years later, when a survey is done, it is found that the fence is right on the true boundary line. Baker's quitclaim deed didn't actually transfer any interest, since Baker didn't really own the two yards on the other side of the fence.

A common reason for using a quitclaim deed is to cure **clouds on the title**. These could be defects or technical flaws in an earlier conveyance, such as a misspelling of one of the parties' names, or an error in the description of the estate.

A quitclaim deed is also used when the grantor is unsure of the validity of his or her title and wants to avoid any warranties.

Example: A grantor holds title to the property by virtue of an inheritance that is being challenged in probate court. If the grantor wants to transfer the property, he or she will probably use a quitclaim deed.

After-acquired Title. Sometimes a grantor may acquire good title after previously attempting to convey good title to a grantee. When the grantor obtains good title, it will automatically pass to the grantee by operation of law, if the transfer was by a general warranty deed or special warranty deed. This is referred to as **after-acquired title**.

Example: Seller conveyed her property to Buyer on June 1, by a general warranty deed. However, Seller did not have valid title to the property on June 1, because she held title under a forged deed. On August 12, Seller received good title to the property under a properly executed deed. Buyer automatically acquired good title to the property on August 12.

After-acquired title normally does not pass to a grantee under a quitclaim deed. A quitclaim deed transfers only the grantor's current interest. If the grantor did not have valid title at the time of the quitclaim deed, the grantee could not receive title then, and would not receive any after-acquired title. (However, title would pass if the quitclaim deed included a clause specifically expressing an intent to pass after-acquired title.)

Wills

A **will** (or testament) is a common form of voluntary alienation. Before discussing wills, it is helpful to know the general terminology. The person making out the will is called the **testator** (sometimes a female testator is referred to as the **testatrix**). A testator **bequeaths** personal property (known as a **bequest**) to a **legatee** and **devises** real property to a **devisee**. An amendment to a will is called a **codicil**. The **executor** is named in the will and is the person who carries out the directions in the will, under the supervision of the probate court. **Probate** is the process by which a will is proved valid and its directions are carried out.

Requirements for a Valid Will. In Washington, any person of sound mind who is at least 18 years old may make a will leaving personal and real property to others. To be valid, a will generally must be:

1. in writing,
2. signed by a competent testator, and
3. attested to by two or more competent witnesses.

In writing. Generally, a will must be in writing to be valid. Under limited circumstances, Washington will recognize a **nuncupative** (oral) will used to dispose of personal property. However, real estate can never be devised by a nuncupative will.

Signature. Except for nuncupative wills, a will must be signed by the testator in order to be valid. However, as with deeds, a will may be signed by a mark or by someone acting for the testator. In Washington, if the will is signed by someone other than the testator, it must be signed under the direction of or at the request of the testator and in the testator's presence. The person who signs for the testator must also sign his or her own name and state that the testator's name was subscribed at the testator's request.

Just as the grantor of a deed must be competent, so must a person making out a will. The test for **testamentary capacity** is whether the party has sufficient mind and memory to understand the transaction, comprehend the nature and extent of the estate property, and recollect the "objects of his or her bounty."

The law presumes the validity of a will. However, if the person making the will was incompetent when the will was executed, the will is invalid. To invalidate a will, the evidence of incompetency must be clear, cogent, and convincing.

Fig. 8.2 Will terminology

WILL TERMINOLOGY

Testator/Testatrix: one who makes a will
Bequeath: to transfer personal property by will
Devise: to transfer real property by will
Codicil: an amendment to a will
Executor/Executrix: carries out directions in the will
Probate: procedure to prove a will's validity

Case Example:

Ernest and Elva Eubank had an estate worth approximately $500,000. They had no children. In 1977, they executed wills that left $20,000 to Kermit Lighter (Elva's brother), along with other smaller bequests. The residuary estate was bequeathed half to J.E. Marvin (Ernest's cousin) and the remaining half to Marvin's six children.

On September 8, 1984, Ernest and Elva executed a new will that made Kermit Lighter residuary legatee, and gave only $40,000 to Marvin and $10,000 to each of the Marvin children.

The Marvins petitioned to invalidate the 1984 will, claiming lack of capacity and also undue influence by Kermit Lighter.

Dr. Ebert had treated both Ernest and Elva since 1955. He testified that he had diagnosed Elva in 1981 as suffering from senile dementia or an Alzheimer's-like syndrome. He testified that by June 1984, he felt she was unable to care for herself and was not oriented as to time, place, or self. In his opinion, she was not competent to understand a legal document or to comprehend the nature and extent of her holdings, and he was not confident that Elva could know the objects of her bounty.

Dr. Ebert and Dr. Murphy, a neurologist, also testified that Ernest was not competent.

James Simonton, the Eubanks' trust officer at the bank, visited the Eubanks in September of 1984. Although he had seen them approximately every two months, neither Ernest nor Elva recognized him. Simonton, who is an attorney, testified that in his opinion, neither of the Eubanks had sufficient mind or memory to understand a complicated legal document, to know the extent of their property, or to know the objects of their bounty.

The trial court found testamentary incapacity to execute the 1984 wills. *Matter of Estate of Eubank*, 50 Wn. App. 611, 749 P.2d 691 (1988).

Witnesses. Washington requires two or more competent witnesses to sign their names to the will in the presence of the testator. To validate the will, the witnesses must be able to testify that the testator signed the will or acknowledged the signature in their presence.

Any competent adult may normally act as a witness. However, someone who is a beneficiary under the will should not act as a witness. A beneficiary may serve as a witness to validate the will; however, he may not then take under the will. If a beneficiary acts as a witness, all devises, legacies, and gifts made to him will be void, unless there are two other competent witnesses.

Example: Ethel Crabtree signs her will and has it witnessed by her nephew and her next-door neighbor. Ethel bequeaths $10,000 to her nephew in the will and leaves the remainder of her estate to a charitable organization. The will is valid because it was attested to by two witnesses. The nephew can testify as a valid witness to the will. However, the bequest to the nephew may be void, because he is a beneficiary acting as a witness and there is only one other witness.

Example: Elinor Martindale signs her will and has it witnessed by her chauffeur, the cook, and the gardener. In the will, Elinor bequeaths $1,000 to the chauffeur. This bequest is valid, because there are two other witnesses besides the beneficiary.

Foreign wills. If a will is made by someone in another state in a manner that meets the laws of that state, Washington will recognize the will as valid, even if it does not meet all of Washington's requirements.

> **Example:** Some states recognize holographic wills, even though they are not witnessed. A **holographic will** is a will written entirely in the testator's handwriting. Washington, however, does not recognize holographic wills. Taylor lives in a state where holographic wills are valid, and he writes a holographic will. He later moves to Washington and does not make a new will. When he dies, Washington will recognize the holographic will, since it was valid in the state where it was executed.

Revocation of a Will. A will may be revoked by a subsequent written will, or by being burnt, torn, canceled, obliterated, or destroyed with the intent and for the purpose of revoking the will. This destruction may be done directly by the testator, or by another person in the testator's presence and at the testator's direction.

If a will is lost or destroyed inadvertently or as a result of fraud, the court may still take proof of the will and establish it. A will must be proved by at least two witnesses.

Family Rights under a Will. In Washington, when a married person dies, one-half of any community property goes to the surviving spouse. The other one-half of the community property and any separate property may be disposed of by will. Children do not have an absolute right to inherit and may be specifically disinherited in a will.

Involuntary Alienation

Involuntary alienation is any transfer of ownership or an interest in property that occurs without any action by the owner or against the owner's wishes. In several instances involuntary alienation occurs automatically, such as when a person dies without leaving a will, or dies without leaving any heirs. Property ownership may also be transferred due to adverse possession, a court decision, or government action. And finally, ownership may change due to environmental or geological changes in the land itself.

Intestate Succession

Someone who dies without leaving a valid will is said to have died **intestate**. Intestate succession is the method of distributing the property of a person who dies without leaving a will (or whose will is invalid). The people who take property by intestate succession are called **heirs**. Intestate succession is strictly governed by statute and is supervised by the probate court. The probate court normally appoints an administrator to carry out the statutory distribution of the property.

Escheat

When a person dies intestate and without leaving any heirs, his or her property **escheats** to the state. The state acquires title to all of the deceased person's property.

Fig. 8.3 Transfer of a deceased person's property

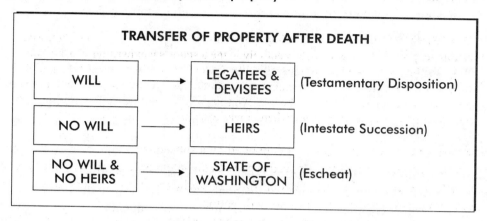

TRANSFER OF PROPERTY AFTER DEATH

WILL	→	LEGATEES & DEVISEES	(Testamentary Disposition)
NO WILL	→	HEIRS	(Intestate Succession)
NO WILL & NO HEIRS	→	STATE OF WASHINGTON	(Escheat)

Case Example:

John Adomaitis died intestate and without leaving any heirs. John died a resident of Illinois, but he left approximately $7,500 on deposit at the Seattle First National Bank.

A dispute arose concerning whether Illinois or Washington was entitled to this money. The court found that when a person dies without surviving heirs, leaving personal property located in the state of Washington, that property escheats to the state of Washington. *O'Keefe v. State Department of Revenue*, 79 Wn.2d 633, 488 P.2d 754 (1971).

In order for a person to die without leaving any heirs, there must be no living **issue** (issue includes children, grandchildren, great-grandchildren, etc.), and no parents, issue of the parents, grandparents, or issue of the grandparents. Obviously, this doesn't happen often.

If no heirs have appeared within four months after the decedent's death, the court may order payment of claims and expenses out of the estate. After ten months, if no heirs have appeared, personal property may be sold under order of the court. Real property cannot be sold to satisfy any debts until all of the proceeds of the personal property have been used up.

Court Decisions

Another form of involuntary alienation occurs when title to property is conveyed by court order. The most common forms of involuntary alienation by court action are foreclosure, partition, and quiet title actions. Title to property may also change hands due to adverse possession. A claim of adverse possession is often settled by the court in a quiet title action.

Foreclosure Actions. Those holding liens against a piece of real property may force the sale of the property if the debt secured by the property is not paid. **Foreclosure** is available for any type of lien that attaches to real property, including mortgages, construction liens, tax liens, and judgment liens.

In some foreclosure actions, the court will order the sheriff to seize the debtor's property and sell it at an auction (sheriff's sale, tax sale, or execution sale). The buyer at the auction receives a certificate of sale that ripens into title if the debtor does not redeem the property within eight months (or within one year in some cases, depending on certain statutory requirements). There is no redemption period after a foreclosure action under a deed of trust. Foreclosures are discussed in greater detail in Chapter 10.

Suit for Partition. A **suit for partition** is a means of dividing property held by more than one person when the owners cannot agree among themselves how to divide it. The decision of the court is conclusive as to the parties involved. Frequently the court will order the property sold and the proceeds divided among the co-owners.

Case Example:

In 1973, Patty and Wally were planning to get married. They bought a purchaser's interest in a contract for the sale of a house. They paid $2,500 for the assignment of the purchaser's interest. The assignment was made to Wally and Patty as tenants in common. Both of them contributed to the downpayment and they intended to contribute equally in the purchase of the property. The contract called for monthly payments of $150.

In 1974, Patty and Wally were married. They lived in the house together for only seven months, until Patty moved out. She was granted a default dissolution in 1975. Wally remained in the house and continued to make the payments. Patty made no further payments after she moved out.

Patty brought a suit for partition claiming a one-half interest in the purchaser's equity on the house. Wally claimed that she had abandoned her interest and was not entitled to any interest in the house.

The court found that originally they had intended to share equally. However, after Patty moved out, Wally made all of the payments. Since they contributed unequally to the purchase price, a presumption arose that they intended to share the property proportionately to their contributions.

The court held that Patty had an equity in the property bearing the same relationship to the total equity as the ratio of her investment to the total investment of the parties. (For instance, if the amount she had paid was one-sixth of the total amount invested, she would have a one-sixth interest in the property.)

Once Wally pays Patty an amount sufficient to compensate her for her interest in the property, he may have clear title to the property. *Cummings v. Anderson*, 94 Wn. 2d 135, 614 P.2d 1283 (1980).

Quiet Title Action. A **quiet title action** is used to remove a cloud on the title when the title cannot be cleared by the more peaceable means of a quitclaim deed. The court makes a binding determination of the various parties' interests in a particular piece of real estate.

A **cloud on the title** occurs whenever doubt exists as to the validity of a seller's title. The property is unmarketable as long as the cloud exists. To clear the cloud, the seller may have to bring a quiet title action to get a judicial ruling on the title.

> **Example:** The seller has found a potential buyer for his property. A search of the recorded documents shows a gap in the title. (A gap occurs when the recorded documents don't indicate who owned the property for a certain time period.)
>
> The seller brings a quiet title action. The defendants in the action are all parties who have a potential interest in the land. (This includes the mystery person who held title during the gap, even though this person's name is unknown.)
>
> The seller asks the court to declare his title valid, thereby "quieting title" to the land. If no defendants appear to challenge the seller's title, the court will grant the seller's request. The buyer can then rely on the validity of the seller's title and purchase the property.

Adverse Possession

Adverse possession is a statutory process by which possession and use of property can mature into title to the property. The main purpose of adverse possession statutes is to encourage the fullest and most productive use of property. Adverse possession is based on the idea that it is better to give title to someone who makes good use of the property, rather than leaving title with someone who makes no attempt to use the property for a long period of time.

Owners of vacant property (for instance, owners of land held for future sale or development) should periodically inspect their property to check for any signs of adverse possession. The mere posting of "no trespassing" signs may not be sufficient to prevent a claim of adverse possession.

Public Lands. Adverse possession cannot be claimed against public lands, such as any land owned by the United States or Washington state, or land that a city, county, or other municipal district holds in a governmental capacity, such as public school lands, or public parks.

Requirements. In Washington, there are five basic requirements for adverse possession. Possession of the land must be:

1. actual,
2. open and notorious,
3. hostile,
4. exclusive, and
5. continuous and uninterrupted for a specific period of time.

Actual. Actual possession requires occupation and use of the property in a manner appropriate to the type of property. Residing on the property is not required unless residence is an appropriate use.

> **Example:** Actual possession of farmland may be achieved by fencing the land and planting crops.

Open and notorious. Possession must occur in a manner that would put a reasonable owner on notice that his or her ownership of the property was being threatened. An adverse possessor couldn't live in a hidden underground cave for ten years and then claim adverse possession, since his or her possession was not open enough to give the real owner notice.

Case Example:

The Butlers purchased property on Lake Sammamish in 1927. They believed their property line ran from a piling in the lake to the southwesterly corner of the lot. Pursuant to this belief, they planted lawn to the water line and planted a holly hedge in line with the piling. For many years they mowed the lawn, trimmed the hedge, and planted other trees, berry vines, and flowers.

In 1958, the vonMarenholtzes bought the property next to the Butlers. By this time, the Butlers' holly hedge had become overgrown and was not very well kept up, due to Mr. Butler's advanced age.

A survey by the vonMarenholtzes showed an encroachment by the holly hedge. Nothing was done about it until 1964, when they hired a contractor to erect an eight-foot cyclone fence between the properties.

In constructing the fence, the contractor bulldozed down the line to the waterfront, removing all growth on both sides of the line to a width of 15 to 20 feet. No consent was obtained from the Butlers for this bulldozing and removal of the hedge.

The Butlers brought an action to quiet title, claiming adverse possession of the narrow strip in dispute between the adjacent properties.

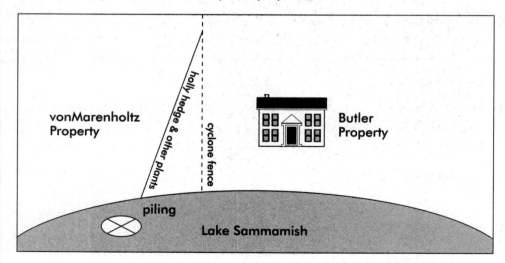

The court found that the Butlers' improvements on the strip of property were actual, open, exclusive, and continuously adverse for the statutory period, long before the vonMarenholtzes even acquired possession of the adjoining property.

The court not only gave title to the strip of property to the Butlers, but also awarded damages for the reasonable expense of restoring the destroyed hedge and plantings. *Butler v. Anderson*, 71 Wn.2d 60, 426 P.2d 467 (1967).

Many adverse possession claims involve narrow strips of land between adjoining properties. As the example shows, planting and maintaining plants and hedges can be enough to meet the requirements for adverse possession. Note, however, that just mowing the lawn on a disputed strip is probably not enough to claim actual possession.

Hostile. Hostile possession requires the occupant to treat the property as his own as against all other parties.

If the owner has given another party permission to use the property, this use can never develop into adverse possession. Use of the property must be open enough for the true owner to be aware of the use, and must be without permission.

Exclusive. Possession of the land must be exclusive, meaning that the adverse possessor may not share possession with the true owner.

> **Example:** Johnson is the true owner of beachfront property. Abbott owns the property next to Johnson and believes that his boundary extends across Johnson's lot clear to the beach.
>
> Abbott uses the beach several weekends each month. Johnson also uses the beach sometimes. He works weekends, so he typically uses the property during the week.
>
> When a dispute arises as to ownership of the beachfront property, Abbott claims the property as an adverse possessor. But his claim of adverse possession would fail because he did not have exclusive use of the property.

Continuous and uninterrupted. Under the Washington statute, the adverse possessor must be in possession of the land for ten successive years (or seven years if under color of title and taxes have been paid). Uninterrupted means that there cannot be a significant break in the period of possession. Minor breaks, such as going away on vacation for two weeks, will not end the possession period.

The requirement that possession be continuous does not mean that the adverse possessor cannot ever leave the property. Continuous use means normal continuous use that a true owner would make of the property.

> **Example:** Returning to the previous example, now suppose Johnson does not live on the property but is merely holding it as an investment. He never uses the beach; in fact he has not been out to look at the property in twelve years.
>
> During that time, Abbott has used the beach almost every weekend all summer long. Abbott seldom uses the property in winter because it is too cold and rainy.
>
> Abbott's use of the property is continuous enough to meet the requirement because it was normal use for this type of property.

The continuous and uninterrupted requirement can be met by tacking. **Tacking** is the joining together of periods of adverse possession by different parties, to make one long period.

> **Example:** Davis possessed certain property for six years before his death. In his will, he left all of his property to his son, Brent. Brent continued possession of the property for six more years. When a dispute arose, Brent claimed he had met the time period requirements for adverse possession. Brent's six years of possession may be tacked on to his father's six years for a total of twelve years.

If the possessor claims a right to the property in good faith under color of title and pays taxes on the property, the required period of continuous possession is only seven years instead of ten. A party is said to have **color of title** when he or she appears to have title, or believes he or she has valid title, but in fact his or her title is not valid. Failure of the title may be due to a defect such as a forged deed or an erroneous land description.

In order to fall under the seven-year limit, the person claiming adverse possession under color of title must not have been aware that the deed was defective. The claim to the property must be made in good faith. In other words, the possessor must actually believe that he or she has a right to the property.

Under the seven-year rule, the possessor must also have paid all taxes legally assessed on the property during the time of possession.

Condemnation

Condemnation of private property by the government is another form of involuntary alienation. Under the U.S. Constitution, the government has the power to acquire private property for public use, without the owner's consent. That power is called **eminent domain**. Exercising this power of eminent domain is referred to as **condemnation**. Based

Fig. 8.4 Requirements for adverse possession

ADVERSE POSSESSION	
10 YEARS	**7 YEARS**
1. actual, open, notorious 2. hostile 3. continuous & uninterrupted 4. exclusive	1. actual, open, notorious 2. hostile 3. continuous & uninterrupted 4. exclusive 5. good faith color of title 6. payment of taxes

Title to Real Property ■ 283

on language in the Constitution, condemnation is often referred to as a "taking" of private property. After a taking, the Constitution requires the government to pay **just compensation** to the property owner (see Chapter 1). Just compensation is ordinarily the fair market value of the property.

The power of eminent domain can be exercised by any government entity (the state, a city, a school district, and so on). Limited use of the power can be delegated to certain private entities. For example, privately owned utility companies may be authorized to condemn property for utility purposes. Whether the entity is public or private, the intended use of the property must benefit the public.

When the government (or other authorized entity) determines it needs a particular piece of property, it first offers to purchase it. If the owner rejects the offer, the government files a condemnation lawsuit. The court considers evidence concerning the fair market value of the property, and directs the government to compensate the owner. Then the court orders the property condemned.

Dedication

Another method of transferring the ownership of real property is by dedication. **Dedication** is the transfer of privately owned land to the public without compensation. Dedication may sometimes be voluntary, as when a wealthy philanthropist dedicates a portion of her estate as a public park.

More frequently, dedication is by developers or subdividers. If a developer wants government approval for a planned subdivision, he or she may be required to dedicate certain areas for public use, such as streets, sidewalks, play areas, and so forth.

Natural Changes

Sometimes the land itself changes shape, thereby changing ownership of some portions of the soil. **Accretion** is the gradual build-up of soil caused by water-borne soil deposits. These soil deposits are called **alluvion** (or alluvium). A key feature of accretion is that the build-up must be gradual and almost imperceptible. When the land is changed by accretion, the boundary line may change to include the new soil deposits.

When property is enlarged by the retreat of a body of water, the landowner acquires title to the newly exposed land. This is called **reliction** (or dereliction). As with accretion, the retreat of the waterline must be gradual and imperceptible.

Avulsion is the violent tearing away of land by flowing water or waves. The land severed by avulsion does not change title; it still legally belongs to the original owner. Avulsion must be more sudden and violent than simple erosion, which is the gradual wearing away of soil due to the action of wind or water.

Avulsion may also refer to a sudden change in a watercourse, as in the following case example.

Case Example:

The Sheldons and the Stroms owned property on opposite sides of a small stream known as "Whiskey Slough." The original deeds to both properties described the boundary as being the center or thread of the slough. In 1954, the Sheldons dredged the slough in order to widen it. The Sheldons used the enlarged slough to moor barges and trollers.

As a result of the dredging, a significant portion of the stream shifted onto the Sheldons' property, leaving the original boundary line on dry land. For many years, neither property owner was concerned about the change in the center line of the slough. Upon request from the Stroms, the Sheldons would move any craft that obstructed the Stroms' side of the slough.

In 1972, however, the Sheldons asserted a claim to the entire slough and refused to move barges from the Stroms' half. The Stroms brought an action to quiet title to the portion of land running from the original boundary to the present thread (middle of the slough).

The Sheldons argued that the sudden change in the boundary was avulsive, and that therefore the property boundary should not change. They claimed title clear up to the former boundary line, which was now on dry land on the other side of the slough.

The court found that a person may not induce an artificial change in water boundaries, and then claim for him or herself whatever advantage that change produced. Therefore, the boundary line between the property was held to be the present thread or middle of Whiskey Slough, and the Stroms' action to quiet title was granted. *Strom v. Sheldon*, 12 Wn. App. 66, 527 P.2d 1382 (1975).

Recording

The fact that someone offers to sell real property is no assurance that the seller actually owns the property. The seller simply may be lying about owning the property, or the seller's title may be defective in some way. In order to limit these potential dangers, every state has recording laws. The purpose of the **recording system** is to protect purchasers by providing a method of determining who owns what interest in a particular piece of property.

A real estate broker is not required to verify a seller's title and is certainly not required to make a title search. However, it is always helpful to know as much as possible about the property being sold. By using the recording system, a broker can find out useful information about the property, such as:

1. who is listed as the present owner of the property,
2. the legal description of the property,
3. whether there are any liens against the property, and
4. whether there are any easements or restrictive covenants that affect the property.

Recording Procedure

Many types of instruments can and should be recorded. Some of the most common are deeds, easements, covenants, certain long-term leases, mortgages and releases of mortgages, agreements relating to community or separate property, and powers of attorney to convey real estate.

To **record** a document, you simply deposit it with the recorder and pay a nominal fee. The document is then said to be filed for record. In Washington, a deed cannot be recorded until it is acknowledged.

Once a document has been given to the recorder, it is copied and placed in the public record. It may be copied by transcription, or by any photographic or photomechanical process (photocopiers, microfilm, etc.) that produces a clear, legible, and durable record. These copies are generally numbered in chronological order as they are recorded. After being recorded, the original document is returned to the person who deposited it for recording.

Usually the county auditor has the duty of recording instruments. He or she may be referred to as the **county recorder** or **county clerk.** Typically, additional people work in the recorder's office and handle the clerical and administrative work involved in maintaining the public record.

The Recording System

The recorder must keep direct and inverted general indexes. Each index is divided into seven columns that list:

1. the time of receipt,
2. the number of the volume and page where recorded,
3. the name of the grantor,
4. the name of the grantee,
5. the nature of the instrument (deed, mortgage, etc.),
6. any additional remarks, and
7. a description of the property.

The direct index (or **grantor-grantee index**) lists the names of the grantors in alphabetical order. The inverted index (or **grantee-grantor index**) lists the names of the grantees in alphabetical order.

These indexes are generally arranged according to time intervals. For instance, one set of indexes will list all instruments recorded from January 4, 2004 through June 30, 2004. When searching the records for a deed, it is usually necessary to know the names of the parties (or at least one party), and helpful to know the approximate time period when the property was transferred.

The recorder also keeps a book containing plat maps of all platted (subdivided) land within the county. An index to this **book of plats** is maintained, listing the name of each subdivision or addition.

Fig. 8.5 A grantee-grantor index, and a grantor-grantee index

WINGET							**G 07**
6.741	GENERAL INDEX · INDIRECT · COUNTY, STATE						
	01/04/88 · 06/30/88						

			RECORDED			LEGAL DESCRIPTION	
DATE & NO.	GRANTEES	GRANTORS	INSTRUMENT	REMARKS	LOT	BLOCK	ADDITION
88-01-12-0409	WINGET Charles & Agnes B	Driscoll, Frank Etux	W Deed	MF			27 26 27
88-04-26-1006	Ralph Eugene & Kathleen Mary	Shockley, Frederick Etux	W Deed	MF	03		Short Plat 107701412
88-06-21-0881	WINGROVE Philip C. & Ida D. Etal	Seattle First Natl. Bank	F Reconvy	MF			SEE 850327-0261
88-01-29-0022	WINIECKI Robert D. & Katherine L. Etal	Mason McDuffie Mtg. Corp.	F Reconvy	MF			SEE 830802-0833
88-01-19-0801	WINING Vernon K. & Glenna E. Etal	Household Finance Industrial LN CO. III	F Reconvy	MF			SEE 860519-0072
88-06-30-0964	WINKEL David J. & Sharon A.	Harrington, David Etux	W Deed	MF E100858	TRS 22. 39-43 PT		
88-04-20-1164	Mearl A. & Mary C.	Elmer, Gary Etux	W Deed	MF E995787			22 25 05
00-04-12-0365	WINKELMANN German J. & Zlato B.	Mears, Annabelle M.	W Deed	MF	03	04	Lake Hills No. 23

DOUTHIT							**B 12**
6.741	GENERAL INDEX · DIRECT · COUNTY, STATE						
	01/04/88 · 06/30/88						

			RECORDED			LEGAL DESCRIPTION	
DATE & NO.	GRANTORS	GRANTEES	INSTRUMENT	REMARKS	LOT	BLOCK	ADDITION
86-05-08-0572	DOUTHIT David T. & Norma A.	Pioneer Federal Savings Bank Etal	D of TR	MF			SEE DOCUMENT
85-05-08-0572	David V. Etal		Agreement	MF			In Sec. 10 24 05
85-11-27-0479	David V. Etal	Bankers Life Co. Etal	DT with asgn	MF			SEE DOCUMENT
85-11-27-0480	David V. Etal	Bankers Life Co.	ASM RNT & LE	MF			SEE DOCUMENT
85-12-04-0571	David V. Etal	Eastgate Sewer District	Bill of Sale	MF			SEE DOCUMENT
85-12-04-0572	David V. Etal	Eastgate Sewer District	Bill of Sale	MF			SEE DOCUMENT
85-12-04-0573	David V. Etal	Eastgate Sewer District	Easement	MF	01PT		Lincoln Executive Cntr
86-01-17-0851	David V. Etal		Easement Agr	MF	TR A		80-12R
86-04-10-0207	David V. Etal	First National Bank Menneapolis Etal	DT with Asgn	MF			SEE DOCUMENT
86-06-12-0705	Maury E. Jr. & Pamela P. Etal	Citicorp Homeowners Inc Etal	D of TR	MF			SEE DOCUMENT
85-05-29-0147	Maury & Pamela	Sanderson, C. Bevitt Etal	D of TR	MF			SEE DOCUMENT
86-06-12-0705	Maury & Pamela Etal	Citicorp Homeowners Inc Etal	D of TR	MF			SEE DOCUMENT
86-07-16-1536	DOUTHITT Robert H. & Dianne L. Etal	Hedeen, Richard Etux	F Reconvy	MT			SEE 820728-0647
85-04-09-0673	DOUTHWAITE John Etal	Washington Natural Gas Co.	UCC Filing	MF	12	09	Eastgate Add Div K
86-07-22-0538	DOUTLICK Deborah J.	Rainier Financial Services Co. Etal	D of TR	MF	09-10	17	Overland Park Add

Notice

One of the purposes of recording deeds and other documents is to provide notice of the transaction. **Notice** is knowledge of information about the property. Every purchaser or mortgagee of land is charged with notice of all prior recorded documents concerning that property.

Actual Notice. When information is acquired personally by a party, he or she is said to have actual notice. Actual notice may be gained from the seller, from other parties, or from inspection of the property.

> **Example:** Ashworth tells Simpson that he wants to sell his house. Simpson is interested. When Simpson goes to look at the property she notices that a large power transformer is located at the back of the property and power cables extend across the property. Ashworth tells Simpson that the power company has an easement across the property. Simpson has actual notice of the power company's interest in the property.

Constructive Notice. Notice may be imparted by operation of law as a result of recording. A court will not allow a party to claim ignorance of a recorded document. Even if the purchaser was not actually aware of the document, if it was in the public record the purchaser is deemed to have had constructive notice of it.

> **Example:** Smith grants an easement across his property to Jones and Jones records the easement. Smith then sells his property to King. King claims that the easement is extinguished because he could not tell that it existed simply by looking at the property and Smith never told him about it.
>
> The easement is still valid and King is deemed to have constructive notice of it. Even though he had no actual notice, a check in the recorder's office would have shown a record of the easement across the property.

Washington Recording Law

Although the rules differ somewhat, every state has **recording statutes**. Generally, these laws provide that a deed, mortgage, or other instrument is ineffective as to subsequent purchasers of the same property unless it is recorded (or unless the purchaser had actual notice of the instrument or interest). Purchasers should be able to rely on the public record and are protected against any secret, unrecorded instruments.

Document Format. The recording statute contains very specific format requirements for any document submitted for recording. Among other requirements, the document must contain an abbreviated legal description and the county assessor's tax parcel number, and each page must have margins of a certain size. Documents failing to conform to these format requirements will incur an additional fee and may be subject to a delay. If you need to record anything, check the statutory requirements and make sure your documents are in the proper format.

Washington's type of recording statute is called a **race-notice statute**, meaning that it is a race to record. Whoever records first wins, if he or she has no notice of any previous conveyances.

> **Example:** Connelly sells his property to O'Donnell and gives him a deed on June 10. O'Donnell fails to record his deed. Connelly later sells the same property to McMurphy on August 15. McMurphy has no knowledge of the sale to O'Donnell. McMurphy records her deed on August 15.

McMurphy would win an action to determine ownership of the property even though O'Donnell purchased the property first. McMurphy "won the race" by recording first, and she had no notice of the previous sale. (She had no actual notice, and could not be deemed to have constructive notice because O'Donnell's deed had not yet been recorded.)

In the example, McMurphy is what is known as a **subsequent bona fide purchaser**— someone who pays for an interest in land that has already been sold to another, without any knowledge (actual or constructive notice) of the previous sale.

A mortgagee who loans money in reliance on the public record is considered a **bona fide encumbrancer** and is likewise protected by the recording laws.

However, a subsequent purchaser who has notice of a previous conveyance can never win, even if he or she records first. Someone with notice of a previous sale is not a bona fide purchaser.

> **Example:** Majeski and Yancey are both house hunting. They have bumped into each other several times at the broker's office and have chatted about the kind of house they are looking for.
>
> Nomiama sells her property to Majeski and gives her a deed on September 6. Majeski moves onto the property on October 1. Yancey hears about Nomiama's property, and when he goes out to look at it he discovers that Majeski is living on the property. Majeski tells Yancey about the great deal she made. Yancey casually asks if Majeski has recorded her deed yet and Majeski tells him no.
>
> Yancey then purchases the property from Nomiama and records the deed on October 12. Majeski doesn't record her deed until October 20.
>
> Even though Yancey recorded first, his claim will not prevail, since Yancey had actual notice of the prior conveyance to Majeski.

An unrecorded deed or mortgage is valid between the parties, but not as to subsequent bona fide purchasers.

> **Example:** Smith sells his property to Jones and gives Jones a deed. Jones never records the deed. Even though unrecorded, the deed is valid between Smith and Jones. Smith later sells the property to White and gives White a deed. White has no knowledge of the sale to Jones. White records the deed.
>
> In a lawsuit to determine ownership of the property, White will prevail. The deed between Smith and Jones is ineffective as to the subsequent purchaser (White) because it was never recorded.
>
> Of course, Smith's action in selling the property twice was illegal and Jones could try to obtain damages from Smith, but Smith has probably skipped town by now.

The recording statutes are meant to protect purchasers. Someone who inherits property or receives it as a gift may not be protected.

> **Example:** Fritzley mortgages his property to the bank. The bank fails to record the mortgage. Fritzley later gives his son the deed to the land as a gift. The son records his

deed. The son is not protected because he is not a bona fide purchaser. The bank can still enforce the mortgage.

However, if the son sold the property to McGillicudy and McGillicudy recorded the deed, McGillicudy would get good title, free of the unrecorded mortgage, because McGillicudy is a bona fide purchaser without notice.

Problems with Recording

A county recorder may be liable for any loss or damage resulting from his or her negligence. For instance, the recorder may be liable for:

1. negligently recording or refusing to record an instrument within a reasonable time after receiving it;
2. recording any instruments untruly;
3. neglecting or refusing to keep the required indexes;
4. neglecting or refusing to make searches, or providing incomplete or defective searches or certificates; or
5. altering, changing, or obliterating any records.

The county recorder is not liable for errors not made by the recorder's office. For instance, if a name or address hand-printed or typed on the original instrument is incorrect or misspelled, the county recorder is not liable.

Torrens System

Washington has also adopted the Torrens system of registration of land. Although rarely (almost never) used, the Torrens Act provides for the registration of title to land through a procedure that establishes a title free from all rights or claims not registered.

The status of title to registered land may be discovered by examining the Torrens register, without the need to search other public records. The purchaser of property registered under the Torrens system only has to take notice of claims and rights that are registered (with the exception of construction liens, which do not have to be registered to be valid).

Title Insurance

Title insurance is a contract in which the title insurance company agrees to indemnify (reimburse) the policy holder for losses caused by defects in the title. Title insurance is typically required by a buyer or lender when a piece of real property is purchased or mortgaged. It protects the buyer or lender from losses caused by such defects in title such as tax liens, easements, or forged deeds.

The insurance policy does not normally cover every possible defect. Defects that are not covered are stated in the policy. The title insurance company usually also handles the legal defense of any claims based on defects that are covered by the policy.

Obtaining Insurance

The procedure for obtaining title insurance involves two steps. First, the title insurance company conducts a **title search**. Most title insurance companies have their own sets of records (called **title plants**) so they do not need to actually search the files in the recorder's office.

After the title search is completed, the title company issues a preliminary commitment for title insurance, setting forth the defects that will be excluded from coverage. These defects typically include recorded liens and encumbrances that, in the opinion of the insurer, currently affect title to the property. If the party requesting the insurance is satisfied with the preliminary commitment, he or she will purchase the title insurance policy by paying the required premium.

Hidden Defects. Sometimes hidden defects exist that aren't clearly shown by the recorded documents. These hidden defects include forged signatures on deeds, a deed or release of mortgage executed by a minor or mentally incompetent person, a deed or mortgage that incorrectly states marital status, and deeds that were not properly delivered. These hidden defects are usually covered by the title insurance policy.

Types of Coverage

The two most common types of title insurance policies issued in Washington are the standard coverage policy and the extended coverage policy.

The **standard coverage policy** is used to insure an owner or lender against recorded defects in title, including hidden risks such as forgery.

Standard coverage title insurance does not insure against the interests of a person in actual possession of the property, nor against other interests that would be disclosed by an inspection of the property or an accurate survey of the property.

Case Example:

W & A Development Company negotiated the sale of some of its property. Transamerica Title Insurance Company issued a preliminary title report showing W & A as the owner and also showing that the property was subject to a mortgage. Allen Bowden, an attorney and controlling owner of W & A, forged a satisfaction of the mortgage and placed it on record.

When Transamerica issued its title insurance policy, it did not include the mortgage as an exception to coverage because of the forged satisfaction.

Sometime later, a mortgage foreclosure suit was brought. The title insurance company had to pay damages because of the existence of the valid mortgage against the property. *Securities Services, Inc. v. Transamerica Title*, 20 Wn. App. 664, 583 P.2d 1217 (1978).

Fig. 8.6 Types of insurance coverage

Title Insurance Coverage	
Standard Coverage	**Extended Coverage**
Latent defects in title • forged deed • incompetent grantor Marketable title Right of access to street	Latent defects in title • forged deed • incompetent grantor Marketable title Right of access to street Defect apparent from inspection • adverse possessors • encroachments • unrecorded easements Unrecorded construction liens

In Washington, a purchase and sale agreement usually requires the seller to purchase a standard coverage title insurance policy for the buyer. This policy, referred to as an **owner's policy**, protects the buyer against title problems, including undiscovered defects such as a forged deed.

An **extended coverage policy** insures against all matters covered by the standard coverage policy, plus matters that should be revealed by an inspection of the property, such as adverse possession, an unrecorded easement, or an encroachment onto the property. It will also insure against unrecorded construction liens for work on projects that began before the closing date.

Coverage of specific items not included in the policy may be obtained by purchasing an **endorsement** to cover the particular item.

Title insurance companies will not protect a landowner from losses due to government action, such as condemnation or changes in zoning.

An extended coverage policy can be purchased by a buyer or a lender, but is typically purchased for the lender's protection. This policy, referred to as a **mortgagee's policy**, is usually paid for by the buyer.

Regulation

Washington title insurance companies are regulated by the state insurance commissioner. Each title insurance company organized in Washington must keep on deposit with the insurance commissioner a guarantee fund in an amount required by law. The required amount is determined by county population. For instance, in a county with a population of only 60,000, each insurer must have a guarantee fund of $50,000. In a county with a population of over 500,000, each insurer must have a guarantee fund of $200,000.

Title insurance companies are also subject to other regulations requiring the approval of both policy forms and the rates to be charged for specific types of insurance.

Abstract of Title

Instead of title insurance, a property owner can obtain a complete history of all the recorded interests in the property (called a **chain of title**) or a condensed history of those interests (called an **abstract of title**), and then have the history examined by an attorney who would render an opinion on the condition of the title. But the owner would still have no protection against latent or undiscovered defects in the title. Abstracts of title are no longer used in Washington; landowners prefer to protect their interests by purchasing title insurance.

Conclusion

One of the basic rights inherent in property ownership is the right to transfer the property to another party. Property can also change hands without the consent of the owner through various court procedures. When property is transferred to another party, his or her ownership can be safeguarded by recording the deed and purchasing title insurance.

An owner of real property should be certain of the property's true boundaries and should inspect it frequently to ward off the possibility of adverse possession. A broker or real estate agent should also be alert to the possibility of adverse possession.

Case Problem

The following is a hypothetical case problem. Most of the facts are taken from a real case. Based on what you have learned from this chapter, make a decision on the issues presented and then check to see if your answer matches the court's decision.

The Facts

John Mayes owned some unimproved land. Upon his death, the land was inherited by several heirs. They each received a percentage interest in the property, which they held as tenants in common. Maude Hamilton, one of the heirs, owned a ¼ interest in the property. In 1936, she executed a quitclaim deed to the property to L. E. Palm. Palm subsequently sold the property to the McGills, giving them a warranty deed that purported to convey the land in its entirety. This deed was recorded in 1936. Since 1936, the McGills have paid all of the taxes on the property.

The McGills erected fences and a goat shed on the property and used it for grazing purposes for several years. Sometime after 1940, the grazing was discontinued, and the land lay vacant and unused except as a source of firewood.

From 1936 to 1955, none of the other heirs of John Mayes made any claim to the land or attempted to occupy or use the land.

In 1955, the heirs executed quitclaim deeds to the Shugartses. When the Shugartses entered the land and cut and removed timber, the McGills brought an action to quiet title.

The Questions

When Maude Hamilton executed the quitclaim deed, what was transferred? When Palm sold to the McGills, what was transferred? Have the McGills met the requirements for adverse possession, even though they did not live on the property or even use it for many years except to cut firewood? Did the Shugartses acquire any interest in the property by the quitclaim deeds given by the heirs?

The Answer

When Maude Hamilton executed the quitclaim deed, she could only transfer the interest she possessed, which was a ¼ interest. This means that Palm only received a ¼ interest and could only transfer a ¼ interest. Since he gave the McGills a warranty deed to all of the property, he could be liable to them because he only had clear title to a ¼ interest.

However, the McGills adversely possessed the property under claim of right. They had a deed that purported to transfer all of the property to them. In addition, and probably most convincing, they paid all taxes on the property since 1936. None of the heirs had paid any taxes, made any claim to the property, or attempted to occupy or use it.

By the time the heirs attempted to convey the property to the Shugartses, they had no interest to convey. The McGills had already acquired the property by adverse possession. Since a quitclaim deed only transfers the interest the grantor possesses, the Shugartses gained no interest in the property.

Title to the property was quieted in the McGills, and the McGills were awarded damages for the Shugartses' trespass and the cutting of timber. *McGill v. Shugarts*, 58 Wn.2d 203, 361 P.2d 645 (1961).

Chapter Summary

- Transferring or alienating real property by deed is called conveyancing. Three main types of deeds are used in Washington: the general warranty deed, the special warranty deed, and the quitclaim deed.

- To be valid, a deed must have a competent grantor, be in writing, contain words of conveyance and an adequate description of the property, be transferred to an identifiable grantee, be signed by a competent grantor, and must also be acknowledged, delivered, and accepted.

- A valid will in Washington generally must be executed by a competent testator, be in writing, and be signed by the testator, and the signature must be attested to by two or more competent witnesses.

- Intestate succession is the method of distributing the property of someone who dies without a valid will. If a person dies intestate without any heirs, the property will escheat to the state.

- Property ownership may be transferred by court decisions such as foreclosure actions, suits for partition, and quiet title actions.

- Property ownership may also be acquired through adverse possession. The requirements for adverse possession are that possession be actual, open, notorious, hostile, continuous, uninterrupted, and exclusive for ten years. If the claim of adverse possession is made in good faith under color of title and the adverse possessor has paid taxes on the property, the time requirement is only seven years.

- Other methods of transferring the ownership of real property include dedication, condemnation, and natural changes such as accretion, reliction, or avulsion.

- When a document is recorded, a copy is placed in the public record and given a recording number. The county recorder's office maintains grantor/grantee and grantee/grantor indexes, listing all recorded documents.

- Every purchaser or mortgagee of land is charged with notice of all prior recorded documents. Even without actual notice, a party may be deemed to have constructive notice if the information has been recorded.

- Washington has a race-notice type of recording statute. When a dispute occurs as to ownership, the party who filed first, with no notice of previous conveyances, wins.

- Title insurance is purchased to protect the policy holder against losses caused by defects in title. A standard coverage policy insures against latent title defects; an extended coverage policy also insures against problems with the title that should be discovered in an inspection of the property.

Checklist of Problems

Real Estate Licensee's Checklist

❑ Is the seller listed as the current owner of the property? Are there any problems with title or encumbrances on the title that might block the sale?

❑ Does the listing contain an accurate and adequate description of the property?

Seller's Checklist

❑ Are you aware of the types of warranties you are offering in the deed when you transfer the property?

❑ Has standard title insurance been purchased for the buyer?

Buyer's Checklist

❑ Are there any clouds on the title?

❑ Does anyone have a possible claim to the property based on adverse possession?

❑ Has extended coverage title insurance been purchased for the lender?

❑ What type of deed are you receiving and what warranties or guarantees does this type of deed give you?

❑ Has the deed been signed by the grantor and does it indicate the grantor's marital status?

❑ Was the deed acknowledged and properly delivered?

❑ Has the deed been recorded?

Chapter Quiz

1. Johnson sells her property to Eibert. Johnson is 23 and Eibert is 17. Eibert signs the deed but Johnson does not. The deed does not specify the amount of the purchase price. Eibert never records the deed. The deed between Johnson and Eibert is invalid because:

   a. Eibert is only 17
   b. Johnson did not sign the deed
   c. the amount of the purchase price was not specified
   d. the deed was never recorded

2. A deed grants property to "Jonathan Searl Meachan and his brother Ed."

   a. The deed is invalid because it does not specify Ed's full name
   b. The deed is valid as to Jonathan but not as to Ed
   c. The deed is valid because it adequately identifies Ed even though it doesn't give his full name
   d. None of the above

3. A deed does not indicate whether the grantor is married or single. Which of the following is true?

   a. The deed is invalid because it must specify marital status
   b. Marital status is irrelevant in a deed
   c. Stating marital status is not required but is helpful and strongly recommended
   d. None of the above

4. Celia Johnson makes out a deed "to my niece upon my death" and places it in a safety deposit box. She has several nieces, although only one ever comes to visit her. Upon her death the deed is discovered. Which of the following is true?

   a. The deed is invalid because it was not adequately delivered
   b. The deed is invalid because there was no immediate intent to surrender control and pass title
   c. The deed is invalid because the grantee is not adequately identified
   d. All of the above

5. A deed promises that the grantor has good title, that the property is free from all encumbrances, and assures the grantee of quiet and peaceable possession. This type of deed is a:

   a. quitclaim deed
   b. general warranty deed
   c. special warranty deed
   d. covenant deed

6. A quitclaim deed conveys:

   a. whatever interest the grantor has
   b. only a portion of the interest held by the grantor
   c. only property acquired by adverse possession
   d. None of the above

7. A will:

   a. is a form of involuntary alienation
   b. is a form of voluntary alienation
   c. may be made out by anyone, regardless of age, if adequately witnessed
   d. must be witnessed by a notary public

8. A nuncupative will:

   a. must be entirely handwritten
   b. is invalid in Washington
   c. is an oral will
   d. can be used to convey real property

9. Which of the following is true regarding witnesses to a will?

   a. A beneficiary may never be a witness
   b. There must be at least three witnesses
   c. The witnesses must be notary publics
   d. The witnesses must be mentally competent

10. Which of these is not a requirement for adverse possession?

    a. Continuous and uninterrupted possession
    b. Possession is exclusive
    c. Constructive possession
    d. Open and notorious possession

11. Under a race-notice statute, the person who wins is:

    a. The last to purchase the property, with notice of all previous conveyances
    b. The first to record, without notice of any previous conveyances
    c. The first to purchase the property, without notice of all subsequent conveyances
    d. The first to record, with notice of all previous conveyances

12. In Washington, when someone with color of title has paid all taxes on property, the time limit required for adverse possession is:

    a. five years
    b. seven years
    c. ten years
    d. None of the above

13. A flash flood changes the course of a small river and leaves it in a new position. This type of change is known as:

    a. reliction
    b. accretion
    c. avulsion
    d. alluvion

14. Which type of title insurance policy protects against adverse possession?

    a. Only the standard coverage policy
    b. Only the extended coverage policy
    c. Both the standard policy and the extended coverage policy
    d. Neither the standard policy nor the extended coverage policy

15. A deed has been recorded but the prospective purchaser has not checked the public record. The purchaser is said to have what type of notice of this document?

    a. Actual notice
    b. Constructive notice
    c. Implied notice
    d. The purchaser has no notice until the document is discovered

9 Closing and Escrow

Outline

Key Terms

- escrow
- closing
- escrow (closing) agent
- delivery
- escrow instructions
- relation back doctrine
- RESPA
- federally related loan
- settlement statement
- credits
- debits
- proration

Chapter Overview

A seller listed property with a broker. The broker fulfilled all agency responsibilities and the property was surveyed and inspected. An interested buyer was found and a purchase and sale agreement signed. Now the process of closing begins. In most instances, escrow is opened to facilitate the closing, and settlement or closing statements are prepared. This chapter discusses the escrow and closing process and when title actually passes to the new owner.

Preparing for Closing

All of the preliminary work must be done and a clear agreement reached between the parties before a transaction is ready for closing. **Closing** is the consummation of the transaction, when the seller delivers title to the buyer in exchange for the purchase price. Typically, closing is not official until all of the documents are recorded.

When the purchase and sale agreement is signed, the broker usually helps the parties set a **closing date**. This is the legal closing date on which the documents transferring title from the seller to the buyer are delivered and recorded.

One of the most significant factors to consider when estimating a closing date is the current volume of mortgage lending. If many people are seeking financing, lenders and appraisers may be too busy to act immediately, and the closing period may be fairly lengthy (up to two or three months). However, if lenders are not particularly busy, 30 to 45 days may be enough time to close the transaction. Of course, the closing date stated in the purchase and sale agreement can be postponed if both parties agree to an extension.

Escrow

A property buyer seldom hands the seller cash in exchange for title to the property. Usually an escrow is opened to handle the details of the closing process.

Escrow is an arrangement in which money and/or documents are held by a neutral third party—an **escrow agent** (also called a **closing agent**)—on behalf of the buyer and seller. The money and documents are then transferred or distributed by the escrow agent, according to instructions from the buyer and seller.

Purpose of Escrow

Escrow is used to ensure that the concerns of the buyer, the seller, and the lender will all be met. A buyer is often reluctant to invest more than the initial earnest money deposit in the property until she is certain that the seller can convey title as agreed. And a seller doesn't want to deliver the deed until he receives the purchase price. Escrow ensures that the seller receives the purchase price, the buyer receives clear title to the property, and the lender's security interest in the property is perfected, all at the same time.

Fig. 9.1 How escrow works

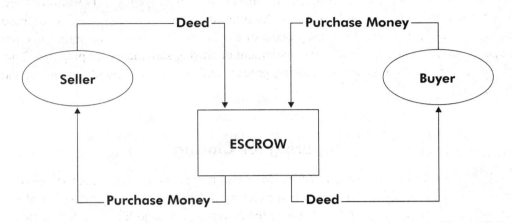

Escrow protects the parties against a one-sided change of mind. For example, after escrow has been opened, the seller cannot change his mind and refuse to deliver the deed to the buyer. Once a deed is deposited with an escrow agent, the seller no longer has any control over the deed. When the buyer meets the specified conditions (such as paying the purchase price), the escrow agent must deliver the deed.

Escrow is also a great convenience when the parties are located in different states (or even countries), travel extensively, or are occupied with other business. The use of escrow allows the closing process to continue even if both parties are not readily available to meet in person.

> **Example:** John is being transferred from Cleveland, Ohio, to the Seattle office of his corporation. He has already made several trips to Seattle and has found a house he wants to buy. He has signed the purchase and sale agreement and escrow has been opened. John agreed to and signed the escrow instructions.
>
> John has to return to Cleveland to finish up some business in that office. He cannot afford to and does not have the time to fly out to Seattle again. He does not plan to return to Seattle until he is actually transferred and ready to move. Therefore, the rest of the closing is handled by mail with the escrow company.
>
> The seller delivers into escrow a fully executed deed. Once the financing goes through and John delivers the purchase price into escrow, the escrow company delivers the deed to John. (Delivery is usually accomplished by recording the deed, with the document sent to the grantee after recording.)

Escrow Agents

An escrow agent may be a bank or other financial institution, a title insurance company, an independent escrow firm, a mortgage broker, or an attorney. In eastern Washington, attorneys frequently close real estate transactions. In the western half of the state, attorneys are not as commonly used.

State Licensing Requirements. Washington's Escrow Agent Registration Act requires companies providing escrow services to be registered and licensed as **certified escrow agents** by the Department of Financial Institutions. Before receiving certification, a company must pay a fee and have its sole proprietor, partner, or corporate officer pass a state examination and submit three affidavits of good character, proof of good credit, and a fidelity bond. A certified escrow agent may employ **escrow officers**, who must also take a state exam and be properly licensed.

Certified escrow agents must keep records of all transactions. When handling funds on behalf of a buyer or seller, an escrow agent must place the funds in a trust account maintained in a recognized Washington depository. If a certified escrow agent or escrow officer converts trust funds to personal use, or commits any other dishonest or prohibited acts, the Director of the Department of Licensing may temporarily suspend or permanently revoke the license.

Exemptions. Certain entities are exempt from the escrow registration and licensing requirements: attorneys, title companies, banks, savings and loans, credit unions, insurance companies, federally approved lenders, and those acting under the supervision of a court, such as receivers, trustees in bankruptcy, guardians, executors, and probate administrators. Real estate brokers handling escrow for their own transactions are also exempt, as long as they don't charge an additional fee for escrow services.

All escrow agents, including those exempt from the Escrow Agent Registration Act's licensing and registration requirements, are required by the law to act fairly and honestly in dealings with clients and third parties.

Limited Practice Officers. In Washington, Limited Practice Officers (LPOs) may prepare certain escrow documents and perform routine closing functions. LPOs are certified and regulated by the state Supreme Court.

The Escrow Agent's Duties. An escrow agent acts as a special agent, with authority limited to the escrow transaction. He or she is considered the agent or trustee for both parties and is essentially acting as an authorized dual agent, with duties to both parties.

An escrow agent is bound by the terms of the escrow agreement and must follow its specific instructions. If the agent acts contrary to the instructions, he or she may be liable for any resulting damages.

> **Example:** Seller delivers a deed to the closing agent. Buyer delivers the purchase price to the agent. Among other things, the escrow instructions provide that the escrow agent is to deliver the purchase price to Seller after receiving the title insurance report and pest inspection report.
>
> The escrow agent delivers the money after receiving the title insurance report, but before receipt of the pest inspection report. Seller accepts the money and moves to Rio. It turns out that the house is infested with termites. The escrow agent would be liable to Buyer for damages.

The Escrow Process

An escrow agent plays a key role in the closing process. He or she generally reviews the purchase and sale agreement and/or loan commitment to determine whether there is a valid agreement that can be closed. The escrow agent also orders title insurance and makes sure any title defects or encumbrances are cleared up.

The escrow agent prepares and explains the escrow instructions, and arranges for the execution, recording, and delivery of all necessary documents. He or she collects the funds necessary to close and prepares settlement or closing statements. A critical condition of most real estate closings in Washington is the issuance of the title insurance policy.

Choosing the Escrow Agent. Theoretically, the choice of an escrow agent is a subject for agreement between the parties. In actual practice, escrow agents are rarely specified by the parties and the decision is often made by the real estate agent handling the sale, or by the lender.

Most modern escrow agents do more than simply receive deposits. They usually create or obtain the documents required to close the transaction (for example, by ordering title insurance and preparing settlement statements).

Originally, the escrow agent was required to be a disinterested third party, independent of the seller or the buyer. Today, the closing agent must still be a third party. The seller or buyer cannot act as the escrow agent. However, it is not a specific requirement that the escrow agent be completely neutral and disinterested. (Although not a requirement, it is usually the wisest choice.) If both parties agree, the closing agent may be an attorney or real estate agent of the seller or buyer, as long as serving as the escrow agent involves no violation of his duty to the principal.

Opening Escrow. Escrow may be opened by any of the people involved in the sale transaction. It is usually opened when the real estate agent delivers a copy of the purchase and sale agreement to the closing agent specified in the agreement. It may also be opened when the lender delivers a copy of the purchase and sale agreement or a loan commitment to its escrow department or escrow subsidiary.

Enforceable contract. There must be an underlying enforceable contract between the parties before escrow can be opened. This is usually a purchase and sale agreement. Since the sale of real estate is governed by the statute of frauds, the contract must be in writing. An oral contract for the sale of real estate cannot be the basis of an escrow.

Case Example:

McLain entered into an oral agreement to exchange his land with land owned by Morgan and Pepper. Healy, an attorney, prepared the respective deeds. The deeds were executed by all of the parties except Mrs. McLain, who was out of town.

The parties agreed that Morgan and Pepper would deposit their deed with Healy. As soon as the McLain deed was executed by Mrs. McLain, it would be deposited with Healy. Healy would then deliver the deeds to the respective parties.

After depositing their deed with Healy, Morgan visited the McLain property. Dissatisfied with the land, he told Healy not to deliver their deed to McLain.

Healy received the McLain deed duly executed by Mrs. McLain. However, under the instructions from Morgan, he refused to deliver the Morgan and Pepper deed to McLain.

Fig. 9.2 A valid escrow

> ## REQUIREMENTS FOR VALID ESCROW
>
> - a valid deed,
> - an enforceable contract,
> - delivery,
> - an escrow agent,
> - instructions, and
> - conditions that must be met.

McLain brought an action to compel delivery of the deed. The court declined, holding that an enforceable escrow must rest upon an enforceable contract, and an enforceable contract for the exchange of real property must be in writing to meet the requirements of the statute of frauds. *McLain v. Healy*, 98 Wash. 489, 1168 P. 1 (1917).

The purchase and sale agreement must also contain all the required terms of the underlying transaction. For example, if the sale involves seller financing, the appropriate forms (the note and deed of trust or real estate contract) must be mentioned in and attached to the contract. Otherwise the sales agreement will be unenforceable, and therefore the escrow will be invalid. (See the discussion of purchase and sale agreements in Chapter 7.)

Where there is a binding and enforceable contract between the parties, a deposit into escrow becomes irrevocable and neither party can remove any deposits until the conditions are satisfied.

Valid deed. If the deed is invalid, it can be recalled by the seller. If an item can be recalled, it is not adequately delivered into escrow. Therefore, an invalid deed cannot be the subject of escrow.

> **Example:** Colleen McCray delivered the deed to her property into escrow. However, she never signed the deed, and to be valid, a deed must be signed by the grantor. The deposit of the deed cannot operate as a valid escrow because it lacks the required signature and it is subject to recall by Colleen. Since the deed is subject to recall, it is not adequately delivered into escrow.

Delivery. In order for escrow to be valid, there must be complete and irrevocable delivery. Delivery does not occur until the deposits are beyond the legal power of the parties to retrieve them. The depositor must part with all rights of possession or control over the deposit.

> **Example:** Maxwell deposits a deed in escrow with the instruction that it is not to be delivered to the purchaser until she notifies the escrow agent that it is okay to deliver it.
>
> Maxwell has retained control of the deed because it is to be delivered only under her direction. Since she has retained control, the deed is not validly delivered into escrow.

Neither party may withdraw documents or money unless the escrow conditions are satisfied or terminated, or both parties consent to the withdrawal.

Escrow Instructions. The obligations of the parties and the conditions that must be fulfilled are described to the escrow agent in written **escrow instructions**. Escrow instructions may differ greatly from one transaction to another, or pre-printed forms may be used. Caution should be exercised when using pre-printed forms. Sometimes a provision may be included that does not suit a particular transaction, or that is disadvantageous to one of the parties.

The buyer and seller may execute separate escrow instructions. In that case, a set of instructions from each of them would be given to the closing agent. Some buyers and sellers prefer to use joint escrow instructions. Joint instructions eliminate the risk of conflicting statements or inconsistencies in the separate instructions.

Remember, once the parties have signed the escrow instructions, they are legally bound by the provisions. If a party later attempts to cancel the sale, he or she may be subject to penalties and perhaps even legal action. The parties should take time to read and review all of the documents carefully before signing.

A problem may arise if the terms of the escrow instructions are inconsistent with the terms of the underlying purchase and sale agreement. As a general rule, if two consecutive contracts involving the same subject matter are inconsistent, the two are interpreted together to determine the whole contract. If the two contracts have material terms that are inconsistent and cannot be reconciled, the latter contract supersedes the former. So in this situation, the terms of the escrow instructions will control the outcome of the conflict.

> **Example:** The purchase and sale agreement states that Seller will pay for the pest inspection report. However, the escrow instructions provide that Buyer will pay for the pest inspection.
>
> Since the two are inconsistent, the later contract controls. The parties must follow the terms in the escrow instructions. Buyer pays for the pest inspection report.

No specific legal requirements control what must be included in escrow instructions. However, some provisions are typically included in the instructions.

Parties and property. Escrow instructions identify all of the parties by name and address. A description of the property involved is also included. There should be a statement of the nature of the transaction and the purpose of the escrow.

Obligations. A significant section of the instructions describes the obligations and duties of the parties. There should be a list of all deposits to be made by the seller. This might include the deed, bill of sale, leases, paid tax statements, service contracts, insurance policies, warranty contracts, and pest or other inspection reports. The items to be deposited by the buyer are usually the purchase price and purchase money mortgage or deed of trust, or proceeds of the mortgage or deed of trust loan. This section may also describe the duties and liabilities of the closing agent.

General instructions. A section should be included with general instructions, including when the deed is to be recorded, when deposits are to be made, and when they are to be delivered upon close of escrow. This passage should also include provisions for the return of deposits (documents and funds) if the conditions are not met.

Fees and costs. Next is a section concerning the fees and costs each party will pay. This includes directions for payment of escrow, title, and recording charges, broker's commission, and attorney's fees. Also included is a list of items to be prorated or apportioned between the parties, and the basis for such proration.

Conditions. One of the most important sections of the instructions is the portion that describes the conditions that must be met before the deposits may be delivered to the respective parties.

Even if a condition has been included in the instructions, it may be waived by the party who imposed the condition as long as it was not included for the benefit of both parties. And if escrow closes without strict compliance with the terms of the condition, a party may be held to have waived the condition by failing to make a timely objection.

> **Example:** One of the terms of the escrow instructions provides that Seller will repair or replace a broken light on the back porch. All of the other terms are met, but Seller has not yet fixed the light. Buyer is aware that the light is still broken. The parties go ahead with closing and Buyer does not raise any objection concerning the broken light. Buyer moves into the house.
>
> Buyer will probably be held to have waived the condition that Seller must repair or replace the light.

Recent case law has held escrow or closing agents to higher standards of care when it comes to making sure that all conditions and contingencies have been met or waived.

Time limits. Often an instruction is included that provides that the terms and conditions must be performed within a certain time limit. To be enforceable, the time limit must be clearly specified. Washington courts generally hold that if time has specifically been made "of the essence," the agreement becomes defunct when the time limit expires and performance has not been completed.

Case Example:

On July 26, 1965, Seller and Buyer entered into a purchase and sale agreement to purchase property. The agreement expressly made time of the essence and provided that the sale was to be closed "in any event not later than 120 days from date of this Agreement, which shall be the termination date."

Buyer delivered a promissory note in the sum of $5,000, dated July 23, 1965, payable in 60 days. This note was not paid when due and on September 25, Seller notified the escrow agent and real estate broker in writing that he did not wish to proceed with the sale. There was no response to this letter.

On November 26, 1965, Buyer tendered the full purchase price into escrow. The real estate broker and escrow agent mistakenly believed this met the specified deadline, but they had erroneously computed the time limit based upon four 30-day months. Actually, the deposit was made 123 days after the date the purchase and sale agreement was signed.

Seller refused to accept Buyer's tender on the grounds that it was over 120 days, and therefore the closing period had expired and the agreement had terminated.

Buyer brought a lawsuit requesting specific performance. The court found that time was of the essence in the agreement and a specific termination date was fixed that Buyer did not meet. Seller was not required to accept the tender and Buyer's lawsuit was dismissed. *Nadeau v. Beers*, 73 Wn.2d 608, 440 P.2d 164 (1968).

Specific time limits are a tricky area, and courts do not always adhere to such a strict rule. In some situations, a court may consider the intent of the parties, whether the parties have extended the time for performance, and surrounding circumstances (such as fluctuating property values) in order to decide if the agreement is defunct or not.

Delay may sometimes be found to be a waiver of the time limit. If one party is the cause of the delay, that party cannot hold the other party to the time limit.

Case Example:

Huffacker agreed to sell her property to Langston. On the scheduled closing date, July 25, 1980, neither party had performed. Huffacker's title had not been cleared, and Langston had not deposited the purchase price. The closing agent finally received the documents necessary to clear title on August 20. On October 9, Langston was asked to deposit a check for closing, and he immediately did so.

Huffacker refused to close the transaction because the July 25 closing date had passed.

Langston brought a lawsuit requesting specific performance of the purchase and sale agreement. The court found that Huffacker had a legal duty to clear title in a timely manner. Diligent attention to her duty to clear title would have made it possible to close the transaction on July 25. The failure to meet the time limit was the result of her lack of diligence.

Langston was ready, willing, and able to close the transaction on July 25. Langston had no duty to perform until the title was clear and Huffacker was able to perform.

Langston was entitled to specific performance of the purchase and sale agreement. *Langston v. Huffacker*, 36 Wn. App. 779, 678 P.2d 1265 (1984).

When one party has performed within the required time limit and the other has not, the performing party may cancel escrow and withdraw its deposits without any liability to

Fig. 9.3 Escrow Progress Chart

	Sch. Date	Actual Date	Escrow Operations
1.			Notice of sale to multiple listing service
2.			Buyer's deposit increased to $
3.			Escrow opened with $
4.			Preliminary title searched
5.			Clouds on title eliminated
6.			Credit report ordered from
7.			Credit report received
8.			Report of residential record ordered
9.			Report of residential record received
10.			Pest control inspection ordered
11.			Pest control report received; work—
12.			Pest control report accepted by seller
13.			Pest control work ordered
14.			Pest control work completed
15.			Other inspection ordered
16.			Report received; work—
17.			Report accepted by
18.			Special contingencies eliminated
19.			Payoff or beneficiary statement ordered
20.			Payoff or beneficiary statement received
21.			1st loan commitment ordered from
22.			Received: @ % Fee Pts.
23.			2nd loan commitment ordered from
24.			Received: @ % Fee Pts.
25.			Loan application submitted to
26.			Loan application approved
27.			Loan/assumption papers received by escrow
28.			Hazard insurance placed with
29.			Escrow closing instructions requested
30.			Client called for closing appointment
31.			Closing papers signed
32.			Closing papers to escrow holder
33.			Funds ordered
34.			Deed recorded

Received	Delivered	AFTER CLOSING OF ESCROW	Received	Delivered	AFTER CLOSING OF ESCROW
		Final adjusted closing statement			
		Check of seller's proceeds			Record deed
		Check of buyer's refund			Title insurance policy
		Commission check			

the other party. If no time limit is specified, the parties have a reasonable time period in which to perform.

Progress Chart. A real estate agent may sometimes use an escrow progress chart (see Figure 9.3) to keep track of the status of the escrow. Using such a chart will enable the agent to inform the buyer and seller of the current status of escrow. It is also a handy reminder of what steps still need to be taken in order to close the transaction.

Termination of Escrow

Escrow terminates in one of three ways: the transaction closes, the parties agree to terminate it, or one party defaults.

Upon Closing. Upon fulfillment of all conditions and transfer of all deposits, termination of escrow is automatic. Escrow is set up for a particular transaction—when that transaction concludes, the escrow terminates.

Before authorizing the escrow agent to close the sale, a buyer would be wise to inspect the property again personally. By the time escrow is ready to close, many buyers haven't seen the property for several weeks or even months. A buyer should make sure that all of the property items are in the same condition now as they were in when the sales agreement was signed.

Sometimes after closing there is money still left in escrow. This usually happens when a sum was deposited for a specific item (such as a pest inspection) and the cost of the item was less than the amount deposited. Often the parties are so concerned with all of the technicalities of closing that they forget about this leftover sum. The parties should review their closing statements to see that all amounts have been removed from escrow when escrow is closed.

Mutual Agreement. Escrow may be terminated at any time by mutual consent of the parties, even if all of the conditions have not been fulfilled and the transaction does not close. This might happen if unforeseen circumstances cause both parties to decide not to go through with the transaction.

> **Example:** The sellers were a couple that planned to retire, sell the house, and spend the next year traveling through Europe. After opening escrow, the husband died and the wife decided she would rather keep the house and not go traveling alone.
>
> At the same time, the buyers decided to get a divorce. Neither of them wants to go ahead with the purchase of the new house. The seller and the buyers discuss their situations and decide to cancel the agreement and return all deposits. (Remember that even though the parties have agreed to cancel the sale, the seller may still be liable for the broker's commission.)

If both parties agree to cancel, the escrow agent is notified of the cancellation. The agent will usually send a rescission or cancellation agreement to all of the parties involved so that everyone knows what's going on and any questions or disagreements may be resolved. This agreement should state what is to happen to the funds already in escrow and who is required to pay accumulated bills such as the cost of the pest control report. The escrow company itself may also charge a cancellation fee covering the cost of work already completed.

Default. What if both parties don't agree to cancel escrow? Often one party still wants to go through with the sale, but the other party has changed his or her mind, or has defaulted and not fulfilled the required conditions.

In many cases, the purchase and sale agreement or the escrow instructions include provisions that specifically state how the funds in escrow will be handled in the event of default by either party. For example, escrow instructions might provide that if the buyer does not deposit the remainder of the purchase price in escrow by the closing date, the escrow agent is authorized to release the earnest money deposit to the seller.

When neither the purchase agreement nor the escrow instructions specifically authorize the release of deposited funds in the event of default, the closing agent cannot simply release the funds to one party without the other's permission, even if the funds are returned to the party who deposited them, and even if that party appears to be entitled to them.

> **Example:** The buyer's $10,000 earnest money check is deposited into escrow. The closing date arrives, but the seller has not cleared her title as agreed; in fact, she hasn't even attempted to clear title.
> A week later, the buyer decides to give up and call the transaction off. He asks the escrow agent to return his $10,000. It is clear to the escrow agent that the seller has defaulted, and the buyer is legally entitled to the $10,000. The agent calls the seller and asks for authorization to return the money to the buyer. The seller refuses to authorize the release of the funds. Without the seller's written permission, the closing agent cannot release the funds.

Of course, when one of the parties in a real estate transaction defaults, the other party may decide to sue. (In the example just given, the buyer could sue the seller for specific performance or for return of the earnest money.) When that happens, the escrow agent can **interplead** the disputed funds into the court where the lawsuit was filed. In an interpleader action, the escrow agent turns the funds over to the court. The agent has no further responsibility for the money, and the court will decide which party is entitled to it. An escrow agent can also turn disputed funds over to a court without waiting for one of the parties to sue the other.

When Title Passes

In most circumstances, title to property or deposited funds usually remains with the grantor or depositor until performance of all the conditions specified in escrow. For example, the seller generally remains in possession of the property, collects any rents, and pays taxes until the day of closing.

> **Example:** Seller and Buyer agree on escrow instructions that provide that Seller will deposit the deed to the property and Buyer will deposit the purchase price with an escrow agent. Seller deposits the deed on May 15. Buyer deposits the purchase price on June 4.
>
> Although Seller has relinquished possession of the deed as of May 15, title does not pass to Buyer until June 4, when Buyer performs the required condition of paying the purchase price.

The time at which title actually passes to the buyer becomes important if some harm is suffered by the property or something happens to the deposited funds. The risk of loss as to property or funds delivered into escrow follows legal title. This means that if the escrow agent absconds with the deposited funds, the party who suffers from the loss is the one who holds title to the funds.

Case Example:

The conditions of escrow provide that Seller will deposit a deed and Buyer will deposit the purchase price. Buyer deposits the money, but Seller has not yet deposited the deed. The escrow agent absconds with the money. The loss falls on Buyer because the conditions of escrow had not yet been fulfilled. Buyer was still the legal owner of the funds. The agent was merely holding the funds until the deed was deposited. *Angell v. Ingram*, 35 Wn.2d 582, 213 P.2d 944 (1950).

Unauthorized Delivery

If the escrow agent delivers deposited funds before all the conditions are fulfilled, title does not pass unless ratified by the depositor. Delivery to one who has failed to perform the required conditions constitutes **conversion**. The injured party may recover damages from the escrow agent or from the party who has participated in the wrongful delivery.

Relation Back Doctrine

In certain circumstances, a deed may be considered delivered as of the date of deposit into escrow, instead of the date the conditions were performed. In other words, the date of delivery **relates back** to the date of deposit in escrow. This relation back doctrine is applied when:

1. the seller delivers a deed to escrow, then dies, but the conditions are fulfilled by the buyer;

2. the buyer dies after the deed has been delivered to escrow, but all of the conditions of the escrow are thereafter performed; or

3. the seller marries or becomes insane after delivery of the deed to escrow.

Case Example:

McKinnon entered into a contract to sell his property to Mallonee. In June 1950, a warranty deed, the purchase money receipt, and the escrow instructions were deposited with the Washington Escrow Company.

McKinnon died July 9, 1950. In August, Mallonee paid the balance of the purchase price to the escrow holder, who then recorded the deed to Mallonee.

Where justice requires it, a legal fiction holds that the title of the grantee (the buyer) relates back to the time of the original delivery of the deed to escrow.

If necessary, a court could find that Mallonee's title related back to the date of deposit of the deed. Thus, Mallonee may be held to have title to the property as of June, when the deed was delivered to escrow. *Washington Escrow* Co. *v. Blair*, 40 Wn.2d 432, 243 P.2d 1044 (1952).

RESPA

The Real Estate Settlement Procedures Act (RESPA) is a federal law that was passed in 1974. This law requires that disclosures be made to loan applicants concerning closing costs. It also prohibits certain practices that unnecessarily increase the cost of settlement services.

Federally Related Loans

RESPA applies to most federally related loans. A loan is **federally related** if it meets the following criteria:

1. it is secured by a first or second mortgage or deed of trust against:
   * property on which there is (or on which the loan will be used to build) a one- to four-unit dwelling;
   * a condominium unit or cooperative apartment; or
   * a lot with (or on which the loan will be used to place) a mobile home; and

2. the lender is:
   * federally regulated;
   * has federally insured accounts;
   * makes loans in connection with a federal program;
   * sells loans to FNMA, GNMA, or FHLMC; or
   * makes more than $1 million in real estate loans per year.

As you can see, RESPA applies to the majority of institutional lenders and residential loans.

Exemptions

The following loan transactions are exempt from RESPA's requirements:

- a loan used to purchase 25 acres or more;
- a loan primarily for a business, commercial, or agricultural purpose;
- a loan used to purchase vacant land (unless there will be a one- to four-unit dwelling built on it or a mobile home placed on it);
- an assumption for which the lender's approval is neither required nor obtained.

In addition, note that RESPA does not apply to seller-financed transactions, since they are not federally regulated.

Requirements

RESPA imposes a number of requirements on lenders and settlement service providers in federally related loan transactions:

1. Within three days of receiving a written loan application, the lender must give the applicant:
   - a copy of a HUD-prepared booklet on settlement procedures that explains RESPA, closing costs, and the settlement statements;
   - a good faith estimate of settlement costs with information about any settlement service provider that the lender requires the borrower to use; and
   - a mortgage servicing disclosure statement stating whether the lender intends to service the loan or transfer it to another lender.
2. The lender must itemize all loan settlement charges on a Uniform Settlement Statement form.
3. Required deposits into an impound account (to cover taxes, insurance, and other recurring costs) cannot be excessive.
4. A lender or provider of settlement services may not:
   - pay kickbacks or referral fees to anyone for referring customers;
   - accept unearned fees (for settlement services that weren't actually provided); or
   - charge a fee for preparing the Uniform Settlement Statement, an impound account statement, or the disclosure statement required by the Truth in Lending Act.
5. A settlement service provider that refers a borrower to another provider must disclose any ownership or interest in the second provider.
6. Loan servicers must provide borrowers with both an initial escrow statement and an annual escrow statement summarizing charges paid out of escrow.

Fig. 9.4 Good faith estimate form

GOOD FAITH ESTIMATE

Date: _____

Borrower: _____

Property Address: _____

This gives an **ESTIMATE** of most of the charges you will have to pay at the settlement of your loan. The figures shown **AS ESTIMATES,** are subject to change. The figures are computed on an estimated value of $_____, a loan amount of $ _____ an interest rate of _____%, a term of _____ and a LTV of _____%.
_____ owner occupied   _____ non-owner occupied   Loan Type _____
                                                                        Unless otherwise discussed rates and fees are not locked in.

ESTIMATED CLOSING COSTS

801	Loan Origination Fee _____%	_____
802	Discount _____	_____
803	Appraisal Fee	_____
804	Borrower Credit Report(s)	_____
808	Document Preparation Fee/Underwriting Fee	_____
810	Tax Registration	_____
812	Processing Fee	_____
1101	Escrow Fee	_____
1106	Flood Determination Letter/Courier/Fed. Express	_____
1108	Title Insurance Premium	_____
1201	Recording Fees	_____
	Total Closing Costs	$ _____

PREPAID ITEMS AND RESERVES

901	Interim Interest _____ Days @ $ _____	_____
902	Mortgage Insurance Premium	_____
902	Hazard Insurance Premium (12 months to be prepaid)	_____
1001	Hazard Insurance Reserve _____ mos. @ $_____	_____
1002	Mortgage Insurance Reserve _____ mos. @ $ _____	_____
1004	Property Tax Reserve for _____mos. @ $ _____	_____
	Total Prepaids and Reserves to be paid at closing	$ _____

ESTIMATED MONTHLY PAYMENT

Principal & Interest $_____

Property Tax $_____

Hazard Insurance $_____

Mortgage Insurance $_____

Total Estimated Monthly Payment $_____

ESTIMATED CASH REQUIRED AT CLOSING

Sales Price/Cost to Build/Payoff	$_____
Closing Costs	$_____
Prepaid Items & Reserves	$_____
Sub-Total	$_____
Less Earnest Money	$_____
Less Good Faith Deposit	$_____
Less Standby Takeout Fee	$_____
Less Seller Contributions	$_____
Less Loan Amount	$_____
Est. Cash Req. at Closing	$_____

The above is for information only and is not a loan commitment.

The information provided below reflects estimates of the charges which you are likely to incur at the settlement of your loan. The fees listed are estimate - the actual charges may be more or less. Your transaction may not involve a fee for every item listed. The numbers listed beside the estimates generally correspond to the numbered lines contained in the HUD-1 settlement statement which you will be receiving at settlement. The HUD-1 settlement statement will show you the actual cost for items paid at settlement.

An applicant, by signing this Good Faith Estimate, acknowledges receipt of HUD Booklet outlining settlement costs.

An applicant for an Adjustable Rate Mortgage, by signing this Good Faith Estimate, acknowledges receipt of the booklet entitled, "Consumer Handbook on Adjustable Rate Mortgages".

_____   _____
                                                                    DATE

_____   _____
                                                                    DATE

Prepared by: _____   _____
                                                                    DATE

Settlement Statements

A closing statement or settlement statement details the financial aspects of the transaction. It sets out the items to be paid by each party, the funds the buyer will have to pay into escrow, and the net cash proceeds that will go to the seller.

If the transaction is subject to RESPA, a Uniform Settlement Statement form is used. If RESPA does not apply, any one of several different forms may be used. The information for the buyer and seller may be combined into one statement. In most cases, however, a different statement is prepared for each party. The one given to the buyer presents only the buyer's closing information, and the one given to the seller presents only the seller's closing information.

Allocating Expenses

Preparing a settlement statement involves determining what charges and credits apply to a given transaction and allocating them to the proper parties. The division of expenses is usually determined by the terms of the purchase and sale agreement. The way expenses are apportioned may also be influenced by local custom, as long as the custom does not conflict with the terms of the purchase agreement.

> **Example:** A buyer usually pays the cost of the appraisal. Under local custom, the cost would be charged to the buyer at the time of settlement. However, the terms of a particular purchase and sale agreement require the seller to pay the appraisal fee. Therefore local custom will be disregarded and the expense will be a debit to the seller.

Of course, both local custom and agreements between the parties must not run contrary to local, state, or federal law.

A real estate agent should know what settlement costs are applicable to every kind of real estate transaction in order to inform the buyer and seller accordingly. The parties are entitled to know the full extent of their costs before signing a purchase and sale agreement.

Transaction Settlement Guide

A transaction settlement guide shows how the various charges and credits are usually allocated. A **debit** is an amount owed or a charge that must be paid. **Credits** are the opposite of debits. They are amounts to be received. Use of a transaction settlement guide will help the agent determine what costs will be paid by each party. For example, the purchase price is a debit to the buyer and a credit to the seller. The broker's sales commission is a debit to the seller.

Although it is virtually impossible to calculate the exact closing costs until the actual closing, a reasonably accurate estimate can be prepared in advance. (Real estate agents are often called upon to make such an estimate.)

Buyer's Costs. Obviously, the main cost for the buyer will be the **purchase price**, which is a debit to the buyer and a credit to the seller. In most transactions the purchase price will be offset by some form of **financing**, such as an institutional loan or seller financing. New loans or assumptions of existing loans are listed as credits for the buyer. The difference between the purchase price and the financing is the **downpayment**.

Earnest money deposit. An earnest money deposit (also called a **good faith deposit**) is often paid by the buyer when the purchase and sale agreement is signed. It appears as a credit to the buyer at settlement, since it has already been paid and is not owed at closing. (It constitutes part of the purchase price that has already been debited to the buyer.)

Loan fee. After the purchase price, the largest debit to the buyer at closing is typically the loan origination fee. This is a percentage of the loan amount charged by the lender to cover the administrative costs of making the loan. Lenders usually charge between 1% and 3% of the loan amount. To calculate the loan origination fee, simply multiply the loan amount (not the purchase price) by the percentage of the fee.

A loan **assumption fee** may be charged when the buyer assumes an existing loan. FHA and VA fees are minimal, but some conventional loan assumption fees are quite substantial, approximately the equivalent of a loan origination fee.

Discount points. A lender may charge discount points in connection with the loan. This fee is a percentage of the loan amount that is charged in order to increase the lender's yield on the loan. If the buyer pays points, they should be shown as a debit on the buyer's statement.

Other costs. Several other loan costs are customarily charged to the buyer in a real estate sale. These include the appraisal fee, credit report fee, amounts for impound or reserve accounts for property taxes and insurance, the lender's extended coverage title insurance premium, and prepaid interest.

The **appraisal fee** and **credit report fee** are usually set at a flat rate, which may vary depending on the location of the property and the person or firm preparing the report. Residential appraisals usually cost several hundred dollars, and credit reports are normally less than $100. The **title insurance fee** depends on the amount of the loan and may be obtained from the title company or a rate chart.

Impound or **reserve accounts** are trust accounts maintained by the lender to pay property taxes and insurance premiums. The borrower pays a portion of these expenses each month along with the principal and interest payment. When taxes or insurance premiums become due, the lender pays them out of the reserve account. When the loan is originated, the lender asks the borrower to deposit an initial amount into the reserve account. This is usually in the range of six months' to one year's worth of payments.

Prepaid (interim) **interest** is the amount of interest due on the loan during the first month of the loan term. Interest on a real estate loan is normally paid in **arrears**: the interest for a given month is paid at the end of the month. However, when a new loan is made, the interest is paid in advance for the month of closing

> **Example:** Closing occurs on June 15. Interest that will accrue between June 15 and June 30 is paid at closing. The first regular payment on the loan is then due on August 1 and covers the interest due for the month of July.

Fig. 9.5 Transaction settlement guide

	BUYER		SELLER	
	Debits	Credits	Debits	Credits
Purchase price	X			X
Earnest money deposit		X		
Sales commission			X	
Buyer's loan		X		
Loan fees	X			
Payoff of seller's loan			X	
Lender's title insurance	X			
Prepaid amounts				
◆ Interest	X			
◆ Mortgage insurance	X			
◆ Hazard insurance	X			
Reserve amounts				
◆ Mortgage insurance	X			
◆ Hazard insurance	X			
◆ Taxes	X			
Transfer tax			X	
Property tax	Varies according to what seller has already paid			
Pest inspection	Varies (usually buyer)			
Survey	Varies			
Credit report	X			
Appraisal	X			
Attorney's fees	X		X	
Recording fees	X		X	
Closing fees	X		X	

To calculate the amount of interim interest due, multiply the daily rate ($1/365$ of the annual rate) by the number of days between the closing date and the end of the month, and then multiply this figure by the amount of the loan.

Other items typically charged to the buyer include **attorney's fees, notary fees**, a share of the **escrow fee,** and **recording fees**.

If a **pest control inspection** and/or **repairs** are one of the contingencies of the sale, the buyer may be responsible for all or part of this expense.

Depending on the status of the **property taxes**, the buyer may owe an amount to the seller. If the property taxes have been paid for a period after the closing date, the buyer will have to reimburse the seller. If the taxes are in arrears, the seller owes the buyer an amount covering the period up to the closing date.

> **Example:** Assume that the closing date is June 15, and Seller has already paid taxes through the end of June. Buyer would owe Seller an amount equal to the tax for the last half of June.
> If the closing date were not until July 15, Seller would owe the amount of tax due from the end of June until July 15.

In calculating the amount of tax payable, it is necessary to know the daily rate of the tax and the number of days for which each party is responsible. The expense can then be prorated (allocated) between the parties. The process of proration is also used to allocate such items as interest on assumed loans, premiums on assumed insurance policies, and rents for income property. (See the proration discussion at the end of this section.)

Buyer's Credits. To determine the amount the buyer will actually owe at closing, certain credits must be deducted from the buyer's closing costs. For example, the buyer is credited for the amount of the **earnest money deposit** and for any deposit given to the lender to cover the **initial loan costs** such as the appraisal and credit report. The buyer may also be due a credit for any **prorated amounts** such as taxes or rents.

Seller's Costs. The seller's major cost at closing is normally the **payoff of any existing loans**. The seller may also be charged a **prepayment penalty** in connection with the payoff, and will be responsible for the **interest** due for the month of closing.

The seller is usually responsible for payment of the **broker's sales commission**, **attorney's fees**, a portion of the **escrow fee**, **notary fees**, and **recording fees**. Remember that typically, the listing broker's commission is paid by the seller and the selling broker's commission is paid through a commission split.

Depending on local custom or agreement between the parties, the seller may also be responsible for the **standard coverage title insurance** premium, the **pest control inspection** and/or **repairs**, and **discount points** for the buyer's loan. If the **property taxes** are in arrears, the seller will also owe the prorated tax due up to the date of closing.

The seller nearly always pays the **excise tax** (sometimes called a transfer tax). This is a tax levied on each sale of real property, ranging from 1.28% to 2.78% of the purchase price, depending on where the property is located.

Seller's Credits. The seller's major credit, of course, is the **purchase price**. In addition to this, the seller may be due credits for prorated taxes and insurance premiums, and the balance of any **impound accounts** in connection with existing loans. If the property is income property, there may be a credit for prorated rents.

Prorations

The term **prorate** means to divide or distribute proportionately. Often in the sale of property there are expenses that must be divided, so that each party is responsible for amounts owed during his or her ownership of the property. Some items that may need to be prorated include property taxes, fire insurance premiums, rents, and interest on loans.

Usually the seller makes the initial calculation of apportionment because the seller is more likely to have access to the necessary facts. The purchaser should check the calculations. Any disagreement must be reconciled by the closing agent before the closing.

Although prorating may seem complicated, it is really just a process of dividing an expense as of a definite date. The date most commonly used for computing prorations is the date of close of escrow, which is usually the date when the actual change of ownership occurs. Normally the buyer's responsibility begins on the date of close of escrow (the buyer pays any costs for that day).

> **Example:** Seller has paid for a one-year fire insurance policy in advance. The policy runs from January 1 through December 31. The premium was $675. The house is sold to Buyer and escrow closes on April 1. The fire insurance payment must be prorated, and Seller is entitled to a refund for the amount paid for the period from April 1 through December 31.
>
> In order to determine the amount of the proration, first determine the cost of the insurance per day. (The escrow agent is using a 365-day year and exact-day months.)
>
> $$\$675 \div 365 = \$1.85$$
>
> Seller is required to pay for the period from January 1 through March 31 (90 days). Buyer begins paying as of April 1.
>
> $$90 \times \$1.85 = \$166.50$$
>
> So Seller is responsible for $166.50. Subtract $166.50 from the total amount paid ($675).
>
> $$\$675 - \$166.50 = \$508.50$$
>
> Buyer must pay Seller $508.50 as the prorated portion of the fire insurance policy. Naturally, Buyer should be sure to get an assignment from the fire insurance company, naming the new owner as the insured party on the policy.

When figuring prorations, a 360-day year and 30-day months are sometimes used to simplify the calculations. However, now that calculators and computers are available in every office, it's common to use the exact number of days in the year or month in question.

Conclusion

Once all of the conditions have been met and settlement statements have been prepared, the parties are ready to close. Usually the actual closing occurs in the escrow agent's office.

All of the paperwork is reviewed and signed and the deed and purchase price are delivered to the respective parties.

After this formality has taken place, there are still several items to be taken care of. The deed and any release of mortgage or deed of trust must be recorded. Any service accounts such as water, gas, or electricity must be changed to the new owner's name. If the property is rental property, the tenants must be notified of the change of ownership.

The escrow agent is there to facilitate closing. Any questions or problems should be directed to the escrow agent (or to the parties' attorneys, if they are legal questions).

After escrow closes, the seller pockets the purchase price (less any debit amounts), and the buyer takes possession of the property.

Fig. 9.6 Uniform Settlement Statement form

A. Settlement Statement

U.S. Department of Housing
and Urban Development

OMB Approval No. 2502-0265
(expires 9/30/2006)

B. Type of Loan

1. ☐ FHA	2. ☐ FmHA	3. ☐ Conv. Unins.	6. File Number:
4. ☐ VA	5. ☐ Conv. Ins.		

6. File Number: 7. Loan Number: 8. Mortgage Insurance Case Number:

C. Note: This form is furnished to give you a statement of actual settlement costs. Amounts paid to and by the settlement agent are shown. Items marked "(p.o.c.)" were paid outside the closing; they are shown here for informational purposes and are not included in the totals.

D. Name & Address of Borrower:	E. Name & Address of Seller:	F. Name & Address of Lender:

G. Property Location:	H. Settlement Agent:
	Place of Settlement:
	I. Settlement Date:

J. Summary of Borrower's Transaction

100. Gross Amount Due From Borrower

101. Contract sales price	
102. Personal property	
103. Settlement charges to borrower (line 1400)	
104.	
105.	

Adjustments for items paid by seller in advance

106. City/town taxes	to	
107. County taxes	to	
108. Assessments	to	
109.		
110.		
111.		
112.		

120. Gross Amount Due From Borrower

200. Amounts Paid By Or In Behalf Of Borrower

201. Deposit or earnest money	
202. Principal amount of new loan(s)	
203. Existing loan(s) taken subject to	
204.	
205.	
206.	
207.	
208.	
209.	

Adjustments for items unpaid by seller

210. City/town taxes	to	
211. County taxes	to	
212. Assessments	to	
213.		
214.		
215.		
216.		
217.		
218.		
219.		

220. Total Paid By/For Borrower

300. Cash At Settlement From/To Borrower

301. Gross Amount due from borrower (line 120)		
302. Less amounts paid by/for borrower (line 220)	(	)

303. Cash ☐ From ☐ To Borrower

K. Summary of Seller's Transaction

400. Gross Amount Due To Seller

401. Contract sales price	
402. Personal property	
403.	
404.	
405.	

Adjustments for items paid by seller in advance

406. City/town taxes	to	
407. County taxes	to	
408. Assessments	to	
409.		
410.		
411.		
412.		

420. Gross Amount Due To Seller

500. Reductions In Amount Due To Seller

501. Excess deposit (see instructions)	
502. Settlement charges to seller (line 1400)	
503. Existing loan(s) taken subject to	
504. Payoff of first mortgage loan	
505. Payoff of second mortgage loan	
506.	
507.	
508.	
509.	

Adjustments for items unpaid by seller

510. City/town taxes	to	
511. County taxes	to	
512. Assessments	to	
513.		
514.		
515.		
516.		
517.		
518.		
519.		

520. Total Reduction Amount Due Seller

600. Cash At Settlement To/From Seller

601. Gross amount due to seller (line 420)		
602. Less reductions in amt. due seller (line 520)	(	)

603. Cash ☐ To ☐ From Seller

Section 5 of the Real Estate Settlement Procedures Act (RESPA) requires the following: • HUD must develop a Special Information Booklet to help persons borrowing money to finance the purchase of residential real estate to better understand the nature and costs of real estate settlement services; • Each lender must provide the booklet to all applicants from whom it receives or for whom it prepares a written application to borrow money to finance the purchase of residential real estate; • Lenders must prepare and distribute with the Booklet a Good Faith Estimate of the settlement costs that the borrower is likely to incur in connection with the settlement. These disclosures are manadatory.

Section 4(a) of RESPA mandates that HUD develop and prescribe this standard form to be used at the time of loan settlement to provide full disclosure of all charges imposed upon the borrower and seller. These are third party disclosures that are designed to provide the borrower with pertinent information during the settlement process in order to be a better shopper.

The Public Reporting Burden for this collection of information is estimated to average one hour per response, including the time for reviewing instructions, searching existing data sources, gathering and maintaining the data needed, and completing and reviewing the collection of information.

This agency may not collect this information, and you are not required to complete this form, unless it displays a currently valid OMB control number.

The information requested does not lend itself to confidentiality.

Previous editions are obsolete   Page 1 of 2   form HUD-1 (3/86)
ref Handbook 4305.2

L. Settlement Charges

			Paid From Borrowers Funds at Settlement	Paid From Seller's Funds at Settlement
700. Total Sales/Broker's Commission based on price $ @ % =				
Division of Commission (line 700) as follows:				
701. $	to			
702. $	to			
703. Commission paid at Settlement				
704.				
800. Items Payable In Connection With Loan				
801. Loan Origination Fee	%			
802. Loan Discount	%			
803. Appraisal Fee	to			
804. Credit Report	to			
805. Lender's Inspection Fee				
806. Mortgage Insurance Application Fee to				
807. Assumption Fee				
808.				
809.				
810.				
811.				
900. Items Required By Lender To Be Paid In Advance				
901. Interest from to	@$	/day		
902. Mortgage Insurance Premium for		months to		
903. Hazard Insurance Premium for		years to		
904.		years to		
905.				
1000. Reserves Deposited With Lender				
1001. Hazard insurance	months@$	per month		
1002. Mortgage insurance	months@$	per month		
1003. City property taxes	months@$	per month		
1004. County property taxes	months@$	per month		
1005. Annual assessments	months@$	per month		
1006.	months@$	per month		
1007.	months@$	per month		
1008.	months@$	per month		
1100. Title Charges				
1101. Settlement or closing fee	to			
1102. Abstract or title search	to			
1103. Title examination	to			
1104. Title insurance binder	to			
1105. Document preparation	to			
1106. Notary fees	to			
1107. Attorney's fees	to			
(includes above items numbers:		)		
1108. Title insurance	to			
(includes above items numbers:		)		
1109. Lender's coverage	$			
1110. Owner's coverage	$			
1111.				
1112.				
1113.				
1200. Government Recording and Transfer Charges				
1201. Recording fees: Deed $; Mortgage $; Releases $				
1202. City/county tax/stamps: Deed $; Mortgage $				
1203. State tax/stamps: Deed $; Mortgage $				
1204.				
1205.				
1300. Additional Settlement Charges				
1301. Survey to				
1302. Pest inspection to				
1303.				
1304.				
1305.				
1400. Total Settlement Charges (enter on lines 103, Section J and 502, Section K)				

Chapter Summary

- Escrow is an arrangement in which money and/or documents are held by a third party on behalf of the buyer and seller. The purpose of escrow is to ensure that the concerns of the buyer, the seller, and the lender will all be met.

- An escrow agent may be a bank, some other financial institution, a title insurance company, an independent escrow firm, a mortgage broker, or an attorney.

- The requirements for valid escrow include an enforceable contract, a valid deed, delivery, an escrow agent, instructions, and conditions.

- Escrow instructions set out the obligations of the parties and the conditions that must be met in order for the transaction to close.

- Escrow may be terminated when all of the conditions have been met and the transaction concludes, by mutual agreement of the parties, or when there is a default.

- Title does not pass to the new owner until performance of all of the conditions specified in escrow. However, the relation back doctrine provides that in certain situations, the date of delivery of the deed to the new owner relates back to the original date of its deposit in escrow.

- The Real Estate Settlement Procedures Act (RESPA) requires that disclosures be made to loan applicants concerning closing costs. When RESPA applies to a loan transaction, the lender must itemize all loan settlement charges on a Uniform Settlement Statement.

- A closing statement or settlement statement sets out the items to be paid by each party and the sums each party is to receive at closing. A transaction settlement guide shows how the various charges and credits are usually allocated.

- Upon settlement, certain items such as taxes or fire insurance premiums may need to be prorated between the parties. Proration is simply a division of expenses so that each party is responsible for amounts owed during his or her ownership of the property.

Checklist of Problem Areas

Real Estate Licensee's Checklist

❑ If the buyer or seller asked you for an estimate of closing costs, have you included all items and given an accurate estimate?

❑ Are you familiar with what costs are normally charged to the buyer or seller? Are you aware of any local customs followed in your area?

❑ Are you using an escrow progress chart to monitor the closing process? If the buyer or seller asks you what is happening, can you advise them as to what still needs to be done before escrow will close?

❑ Has a provision for the payment of your commission been included in the escrow instructions? Is there an instruction regarding payment if the transaction never closes?

Seller's Checklist

❑ Has a valid and enforceable purchase and sale agreement been signed?

❑ Have you agreed on who will be the escrow agent? Or is the buyer's lender handling escrow?

❑ Before signing final escrow documents, check to see that:

- the deed is correct,

- credit has been given for any prepaid fire insurance premiums and for your impound account,

- all of the proration calculations are correct,

- if old loans are being paid off or assumed, the payoff amount is correct,

- the sales price is correct, and

- the correct date is given for close of escrow.

Buyer's Checklist

❑ Have all of your terms been clearly expressed in the purchase and sale agreement, and is it a valid and enforceable contract?

❑ Before signing final escrow and loan documents, check to see that:

- your full name (and spouse's name) is included and spelled correctly,

- the legal description of the property is correct,

- title has been cleared,

- the prorations are calculated correctly,

- you have been credited for all loan amounts and deposits put into escrow,

- the notes are properly filled out, with the correct loan amount, interest rate, due date, and prepayment terms,

- the purchase price is correct, and

- the correct date is given for close of escrow.

Chapter Quiz

1. The time period estimated from signing the purchase and sale agreement until date of closing:

    a. is 30 days
    b. is 90 days
    c. depends on the status of the finance market and agreement of the parties
    d. None of the above

2. Escrow is opened by:

    a. the seller or buyer
    b. an attorney
    c. the real estate broker
    d. Any of the above

3. A broker may unilaterally extend the escrow period without notice for:

    a. seven days
    b. 30 days
    c. 60 days
    d. A broker may not unilaterally extend the escrow period for any number of days

4. An escrow agent is:

    a. an independent escrow agent
    b. a title company
    c. an attorney
    d. Any of the above

5. Escrow instructions are:

    a. pre-printed forms
    b. separate directions written by the seller and by the buyer
    c. joint instructions for both the seller and the buyer
    d. Any of the above

6. In Washington, courts have generally held that when the statement "time is of the essence" is specifically included in the escrow agreement:

    a. the agreement becomes defunct when the time limit expires and performance has not been carried out
    b. it is mere rhetoric and has no particular effect on the agreement
    c. the circumstances are examined, but it is very rare that the agreement will be considered defunct
    d. None of the above

7. Escrow may be terminated by:

    a. allocation
    b. mutual agreement
    c. redemption
    d. All of the above

8. Title normally passes to the new owner:

    a. as soon as the deed is deposited in escrow
    b. once title insurance has been purchased
    c. upon performance of all of the conditions specified in escrow
    d. None of the above

9. If an escrow agent wrongfully delivers a deposit before all of the specified conditions have been performed:

    a. the loss usually falls on the seller
    b. the loss usually falls on the buyer
    c. the injured party may recover damages from the escrow agent
    d. None of the above

10. The relation back doctrine provides that a deed may be considered delivered as of the date of deposit into escrow when:

    a. the seller delivers a deed to escrow and then dies
    b. the buyer dies after the deed has been delivered to escrow
    c. the seller marries or becomes insane after delivery of the deed to escrow
    d. All of the above

11. Under RESPA, a loan is considered federally related if:

    a. it will be used to finance the purchase of real property
    b. it is secured by a first or second mortgage
    c. the lender is federally regulated
    d. All of the above factors are met

12. A settlement statement:

    a. is only given to the buyer
    b. sets out the items to be paid by each party
    c. is only given to the lender
    d. None of the above

13. A buyer normally pays:

    a. the loan fee
    b. the broker's commission
    c. prepayment penalties
    d. All of the above

14. A seller normally pays:

    a. the deposit
    b. the payoff of any existing loans
    c. the loan fee
    d. All of the above

15. When an item is prorated it means that:

    a. it is deleted from the cost of the sale
    b. it is divided between the buyer and the seller
    c. it is not paid until after closing
    d. None of the above

10 Real Estate Financing

Outline

Key Terms

- promissory note
- maker
- payee
- security instrument
- default
- negotiable instrument
- holder in due course
- amortization
- straight note
- installment note
- balloon payment
- prepayment provision
- default provision
- acceleration clause
- deficiency judgment
- assumption
- due-on-sale clause
- restraint on alienation
- due-on-encumbrance clause
- subordination provision
- deed of trust

- grantor
- trustee
- beneficiary
- impound account
- power of sale
- deed of reconveyance
- mortgage
- mortgagor
- mortgagee
- satisfaction of mortgage
- nonjudicial foreclosure
- notice of default
- notice of sale
- curing a default
- reinstatement period
- redemption
- deed in lieu of foreclosure
- trustee's sale
- trustee's deed
- judicial foreclosure
- lis pendens
- decree of foreclosure

- sheriff's sale
- certificate of sale
- sheriff's deed
- equitable redemption period
- statutory redemption period
- deficiency judgment
- non-recourse provision
- real estate contract
- vendor
- vendee
- legal title
- equitable title
- Truth in Lending Act
- total finance charge
- annual percentage rate (APR)
- Mortgage Broker Practices Act
- equity skimming

Chapter Overview

It takes a lot more than pocket change to buy real estate. In fact, most real estate purchases involve a loan, and some involve more than one. Buyers, who will be borrowers, and sellers, who may act as lenders, need to understand the rights and obligations of borrowers and lenders in a real estate loan transaction. It's also important for agents to be familiar with real estate loans, since they often need to help the parties work out their financing arrangements while preparing the purchase and sale agreement.

This chapter explains promissory notes and security instruments, which are the basic financing documents. It describes the foreclosure process—what happens when a borrower defaults—and provides a brief look at real estate contracts. The chapter closes with an overview of state and federal laws designed to help protect borrowers from unscrupulous lending and business practices.

Promissory Notes

A promissory note is a written promise to repay a debt. One person loans another money, and the other signs a promissory note, promising to repay the loan (plus interest, in most cases). The borrower who signs the note is called the maker, and the lender is called the payee.

It is important to understand the relationship between a promissory note and a **security instrument**. In addition to signing a promissory note in favor of the lender, a person borrowing money to buy real estate also signs a security instrument, such as a mortgage or deed of trust. The security instrument is a contract that makes the real property collateral for the loan. It creates a lien on the property. If the borrower **defaults** on the loan (doesn't repay as agreed in the promissory note), the security instrument gives the lender the right to foreclose on the property.

A promissory note can be enforced whether or not it is accompanied by a security instrument. The payee/lender can file a lawsuit and obtain a judgment if the maker/borrower fails to repay. But without a security instrument, the judgment may turn out to be uncollectible. For example, the borrower may already have resold the property, leaving nothing for a judgment lien to attach to. By creating a lien on the property at the time of the loan, a security instrument ensures that the lender will be able to get at least some of its money back.

Because real estate loans are substantial sums, they are virtually always secured. Security instruments will be discussed in detail in the next section of the chapter. For now, let's look more closely at promissory notes.

Negotiability

A promissory note can be, but isn't necessarily, a **negotiable instrument**. (An instrument is any legal document.) The most common example of a negotiable instrument is a check. When one person writes out a check and gives it to another person, the payee has the right to demand payment at the check writer's bank. But if the payee chooses to transfer the right to payment to a third party instead, he or she can do that simply by endorsing the check and giving it to the third party. That's possible because the check is a negotiable instrument.

To be negotiable, a document must meet several requirements. It must be signed by the maker, and it must contain:

- an unconditional promise,
- to pay a sum certain in money,
- to order or to bearer,
- on demand or at a definite time.

These requirements keep a negotiable instrument simple, which makes it easy to transfer. The promise to pay should basically be the only promise in a negotiable instrument; that's why the promissory note in a real estate transaction is a separate document from the security instrument. A person accepting a negotiable instrument can be sure that he or she is getting an unconditional right to payment of a certain amount, either at any time ("on demand") or at a definite time in the future.

Fig. 10.1 Elements of a negotiable instrument

```
┌─────────────────────────────────────────┐
│        NEGOTIABLE INSTRUMENT             │
│                                          │
│   ◆ an unconditional promise             │
│   ◆ to pay a sum certain                 │
│   ◆ to order or bearer                   │
│   ◆ on demand or at a definite time      │
│   ◆ signed by the maker                  │
└─────────────────────────────────────────┘
```

A negotiable instrument can be payable to the order of a particular person, or to the bearer.

> **Example:** An ordinary check instructs the bank to pay the stated amount "to the order of" the payee named on the check. That means the payee can either ask the bank to pay him, or else direct the bank to pay someone else, by endorsing the check to that other person.
>
> Alternatively, a check can simply be made out to "the bearer." In that case, whoever is in possession of the check—whether it's the person who was originally given the check or someone who found it on the sidewalk—can demand payment at the bank.

The same rules apply to a promissory note if it meets the negotiability requirements. If it is payable to your order, you can **negotiate** it (that is, transfer the right of payment it grants) by endorsing it and giving it to another person. If it is payable to the bearer, you can negotiate it just by handing it to someone else.

Why is negotiability important? For one thing, it's easier to transfer a document just by endorsing it than by writing up an assignment. More importantly, however, a person who accepts a negotiable instrument can be a **holder in due course** and receive special legal protection.

Holder in Due Course. A holder in due course (HDC) is someone who accepts a negotiable instrument in exchange for consideration, in good faith, and without notice of any defect. An HDC is protected from certain legal defenses that the note's maker might raise against the negotiable instrument, such as fraud.

> **Example:** Using misrepresentation and other fraudulent tactics, Howard convinces Sarah to write and sign a promissory note to him for $1,000. Howard then signs the note over to Dori as payment for an old debt. Dori accepts the note in good faith, without knowing it was fraudulently obtained. Dori is a holder in due course. She can present the note for payment to Sarah and Sarah is required to pay her, even though the note was originally obtained by fraud. Sarah's recourse is limited to suing Howard to recover the $1,000 paid to Dori.

The legal protection given a holder in due course makes it much safer to accept a negotiable instrument than an assignment. As a result, negotiable instruments are very important to commerce.

The promissory notes used in real estate financing are always negotiable instruments, because these loans are routinely sold on the secondary market. Secondary market investors want the protection of being a holder in due course.

Keep in mind that a promissory note can be enforceable even if it isn't negotiable. The original payee has the right to payment and can assign that right to another party. But endorsement and delivery of the original document is not enough to transfer the payee's right to payment, and the new payee won't be a holder in due course.

Promissory Note Provisions

In its simplest form, a promissory note consists of a written promise by one person to pay a certain sum of money to another person at a specified time in the future. The note generally states:

- the loan amount (the principal),
- the amount of the payments,
- when and how the payments are to be made,
- the maturity date (when the loan is to be fully paid off), and
- the interest rate, which may be either fixed or variable.

Fig. 10.2 Basic terms of a promissory note

Promissory Note

FOR VALUE RECEIVED, Maker promises to pay to the order of

_____, or to Bearer,

THE SUM OF $_____, paid as follows:

$_____ OR MORE per month starting _____,
including interest at _____% per annum.

ACCELERATION: In the event of default, Payee or Bearer can declare all sums due and payable at once.

_____

Maker/Borrower

_____

Date

If the rate is variable, the note should include how and when the rate and payment will change, and any limitations on the change.

A promissory note used in a real estate loan transaction contains a number of additional provisions. First, the note should always state that it is secured by real property, identifying the security instrument by date or recording number. The note and the security instrument are signed on the same date, and they are linked together. If the lender negotiates or assigns the note, the security interest in the property is automatically transferred along with it. And the security instrument can't be assigned unless the right to payment under the note is transferred as well.

Straight Note vs. Installment Note. Promissory notes are classified according to whether or not the debt they secure is amortized. **Amortization** refers to the gradual repayment of a loan with installment payments that include both principal and interest.

With a **straight note**, the periodic payments are interest only, and the full amount of the principal is due in a lump sum when the loan term ends. With an **installment note**, the periodic payments include part of the principal as well as interest. If the installment note is fully amortized, the amount of the payments is enough to pay off the entire loan, both principal and interest, by the end of the term. If it is only partially amortized, the payments don't cover the full amount of principal and interest, and a balloon payment will be due at the end of the term.

A **balloon payment** is a final payment that is much larger than the earlier payments. Borrowers often find it more difficult than they anticipated to come up with the extra money at the end of the loan term. When a residential loan with a term longer than one year calls for a balloon payment, the lender is often required to send the borrower a reminder notice before the balloon payment is due.

Common Optional Loan Terms

A promissory note is a borrower's promise to repay a loan, and a security instrument gives the lender the power to have the borrower's property sold in case of default. These are the basic terms for every real estate loan. But most real estate loan agreements include additional provisions governing prepayment, default, and transfer or encumbrance of the security property. All of these provisions are recited in the promissory note.

These common additional terms generally provide extra protection for the lender. That's not surprising; when the parties work out the details of their agreement, the lender is typically in a better bargaining position than the borrower. However, there are some limits on the protective provisions a lender can impose, especially in connection with a loan secured by residential property.

Prepayment Provisions. When a contract states a specific time for performance, the law requires it to be performed at the stated time—not after that time, and also not before that time.

Example: Helen is buying Ann's house, and they've agreed that closing will take place on January 6. If Helen tenders the purchase price to Ann a week early, on December 30, Ann can refuse to accept it.

The same rule applies to a loan agreement. If the promissory note obligates the maker to pay $2,000 on the fifteenth of each month, he or she doesn't have the right to pay more or pay sooner.

However, a loan agreement may give the borrower the right to **prepay**: that is, make a larger payment than required, or pay off the entire loan before its maturity date. In fact, prepayment is permitted by the terms of most promissory notes. The note may simply state that the monthly payment is $2,000 "or more," or that the payments are due "on or before" the fifteenth of each month. Or the note may include a provision expressly stating that the borrower has the right to prepay.

On the other hand, some loan agreements specifically state that prepayment is not permitted. When a borrower is not given the option to prepay, the loan is said to be **locked in**.

Case Example:

The Georges purchased property from Fowler for $235,000, paying $50,000 cash and signing a promissory note for the balance. According to the terms of the note, the Georges were to make monthly payments of $1,657.79 over a period of 30 years. The note also specified "There shall be no prepayment."

After four years, the Georges asked Fowler for permission to pay off the entire loan balance, with interest accrued to date. When Fowler refused, the Georges sued, claiming the prepayment prohibition constituted an unreasonable restraint on alienation.

The court held that in the absence of fraud, overreaching, or inequality in the parties' bargaining power, the prepayment prohibition was valid. *George v. Fowler*, 96 Wn. App. 187 (1999).

Today, it is unusual for a loan secured by real estate to be completely locked in, but some loan agreements include a lock-in clause that prevents prepayment during a certain period, such as the first year or the first five years of the loan term.

More commonly, a loan agreement will provide that a **prepayment penalty** will be charged if the loan is prepaid. Prepayment penalties are generally enforceable if they are not unconscionable. In other words, a penalty will be upheld if the amount specified as a penalty is not outrageous or unreasonable.

Default Provisions. Many promissory notes provide for a late payment penalty. The penalty may take the form of a flat fee: for example, $35 per month is added to the debt until the overdue payment is received. Or there may be a default interest rate: for example, the interest rate on the loan balance is ordinarily 10%, but 18% is charged on any delinquent amounts.

Penalty provisions such as these generally must comply with the rules for liquidated damages (see Chapter 7). That means the amount of the late charge must have been reasonable at the time the loan agreement was made. Thus, if a promissory note provided that a $250 late fee would be added to the $500 monthly payment whenever the payment was overdue, a court would undoubtedly refuse to enforce that provision.

A default interest rate can be assessed on the delinquent amount until it is paid, but not on the entire loan balance.

> **Example:** Suppose the interest rate on my loan is 10%, but the note provides for a default rate of 12%. My payments are $500 a month, and the loan balance is currently $59,432. For one reason or another, I miss my October payment. The lender can charge 12% interest on the delinquent $500 until I pay it. However, the lender can't charge 12% on $59,432; the interest rate on the non-delinquent balance must remain at 10%.

Acceleration on default. Virtually every real estate loan agreement provides for acceleration of the loan in case of default. If the borrower defaults, the lender has the right to declare the entire balance due immediately, no matter how many years away the original maturity date might be. This is sometimes referred to as "calling the note"; the provision in the loan agreement is an **acceleration clause**.

A lender cannot accelerate the loan unless an acceleration clause was expressly included in the loan agreement. An acceleration clause in the promissory note allows the lender to accelerate if the borrower fails to make payments on time. An acceleration clause in the deed of trust gives the lender the right to accelerate if the borrower breaches any part of the security instrument—for example, by failing to pay the property taxes or keep the property insured.

Acceleration is a lender's option, not an automatic event. It's up to the lender to decide whether or not to accelerate the loan, and if so, at what point. The lender might choose to accelerate after the borrower has missed only one payment, or wait until the borrower misses five or six. But the right to accelerate ends as soon as the borrower **cures** the default by tendering payment of the delinquent amounts, renewing the insurance, or taking whatever other action is necessary.

Prepayment charges and acceleration. When a lender accelerates a loan because of default and has the property sold, the proceeds from the foreclosure sale are used to pay off the debt. This usually occurs long before the loan's original maturity date. So, in effect, acceleration and foreclosure lead to prepayment of the loan. Can the lender assess prepayment charges after a foreclosure? No—at least not in Washington.

Washington case law holds that when debtors default on a promissory note and the lender accelerates the loan, the lender cannot also demand a prepayment penalty. The court's reasoning is that acceleration, by definition, advances the maturity date of the debt, so payment thereafter is not prepayment, but instead is payment made after maturity.

Transfer Provisions. When real property is sold (or otherwise transferred), the new owner takes title subject to any existing liens. So despite the transfer, the lienholders still have the power to foreclose on the property. However, the new owner does not necessarily take on personal responsibility for the liens.

Personal responsibility becomes important if the lienholder forecloses judicially and the foreclosure sale proceeds aren't enough to pay off the full amount of the lien. In some cases, the lienholder can sue for the remainder. An award in favor of the lienholder is called a **deficiency judgment**, as it makes up for the deficiency in the sale proceeds. When a new owner takes property subject to existing liens, he or she may lose the property to foreclosure, but isn't personally liable for a deficiency judgment. The lienholder has to collect the deficiency judgment from the former owner.

Assumption. It's different if the new owner **assumes** an existing lien, instead of taking title subject to it. In an assumption, the new owner agrees to take on personal responsibility for the lien (usually a deed of trust). Then if the lender obtains a deficiency judgment, the new owner will be liable. However, the original borrower (the former owner) remains secondarily liable for a deficiency judgment. If the new owner doesn't pay, the lender can collect from the former owner. The former owner can then go after the new owner for payment, but may find it difficult to collect.

The assumption of a deed of trust can be arranged between the former owner (the original borrower) and the new owner, without the lender's consent. The assumption agreement must be in writing and signed by the new owner. There is an exception to this rule if the assumption agreement is included in the deed transferring the property; in that case, the assumption is binding even without the new owner's signature.

But lenders generally don't like it when the security property is sold or transferred without their consent, whether or not the new owner assumes the deed of trust. Although the original borrower is still liable after foreclosure, the lender's risk may be greater. The lender wants to be paid as agreed—foreclosure is a last resort. The new owner could be a much worse credit risk than the former owner, or might be more likely to allow the security property to deteriorate. Because of these concerns, nearly every real property loan agreement contains a due-on-sale clause.

Due-on-sale clauses. A lender can't include a provision in the loan agreement that prevents the borrower from selling or transferring the security property. Such a provision

Fig. 10.3 Common provisions in loans secured by real estate

- **Prepayment provision**
- **Late payment penalty**
- **Acceleration clause**
- **Due-on-sale (alienation) clause**
- **Subordination clause**

would be an **unreasonable restraint on alienation**. The law generally protects an owner's right to freely transfer property.

However, lenders can use due-on-sale clauses to protect their interests. A **due-on-sale clause** provides that if the borrower sells or transfers any interest in the property without the lender's consent, the lender has the right to accelerate the loan and demand immediate payment in full.

Because due-on-sale provisions concern the transfer or alienation of an interest in property, they are also called **alienation clauses.** While they can be considered a type of acceleration clause, don't confuse them with the provisions for acceleration on default that were discussed earlier. Here there's no default; the monthly payments, taxes, and so forth have been paid reliably. The borrower has simply exercised his or her right to sell or otherwise transfer the property.

If the lender chooses to use the due-on-sale clause to accelerate the loan, the full balance must be paid off. If it isn't, the lender can foreclose. In this case (unlike acceleration on default), the only way the former owner or new owner can stop the foreclosure is by paying off the entire loan.

As a general rule, if the new owner is a good credit risk, the lender will agree to an assumption of the loan instead of exercising its due-on-sale rights. In that case, the new owner is usually required to pay an assumption fee, or a higher interest rate on the assumed loan, or both. This kind of assumption involves a written agreement between the lender and the new owner. The former owner has no further liability for the debt.

Prepayment charges and due-on-sale clauses. In the past, if a loan agreement contained both a prepayment provision and a due-on-sale clause, when the loan was accelerated the lender could also collect prepayment charges. This is no longer allowed.

A prepayment provision and a due-on-sale clause may both be included in the agreement, but both clauses cannot operate simultaneously. If the lender elects to accelerate the debt upon the sale of the property, it may not also demand a prepayment penalty.

Case Example:

Bankers Life Insurance loaned $700,000 to the McCauslands. The note provided that no prepayment could be made during the first seven years of the loan. During the eighth through tenth years, prepayment was permitted if accompanied by a 5% fee. After the tenth year, prepayment was allowed without restriction.

The note also contained a due-on-sale clause permitting the lender to declare the entire note payable upon transfer or encumbrance of the property.

After two years, the McCauslands wanted to prepay the note. The lender refused unless they agreed to pay an additional $115,000. The McCauslands filed a lawsuit, seeking a declaration that the prepayment restrictions were invalid. The issues were:

1. Does a seven-year prepayment restriction constitute an unreasonable restraint on alienation?
2. Are due-on-sale clauses in real estate loan transactions enforceable?
3. Do both a due-on-sale clause and a prepayment restriction in the same note combine to form an unreasonable restraint on alienation?

The court held that a seven-year prepayment restriction is not an unreasonable restraint on alienation, and that due-on-sale clauses are enforceable. It further stated that the combination of a due-on-sale clause and a prepayment restriction does not unreasonably restrain alienation, so long as the two clauses do not operate simultaneously.

If the lender elects upon transfer or encumbrance to accelerate the debt, it may not also demand a prepayment penalty. *McCausland v. Bankers Life Insurance Co.*, 110 Wn.2d 716, 757 P.2d 941 (1988).

Due-on-encumbrance provision. Some due-on-sale clauses allow the lender to accelerate the loan not only if ownership is transferred, but even if the borrower encumbers the property with another lien. The borrower can't take out an additional loan using the property as security, even though the first lender's deed of trust would have higher priority than the second deed of trust.

Subordination Provisions. Lien priority is extremely important to every lender. The higher the lender's priority, the more likely that lender is to recover all (or most) of the debt if any lienholder forecloses. As you know, the priority of a deed of trust depends on the date it was recorded. A deed of trust has lower priority than any voluntary liens on the same property that were recorded earlier, and higher priority than any that were recorded later.

But a lender can agree to **subordinate** its deed of trust to another deed of trust that was (or will be) recorded later. This means the lender will accept a lower priority position than the one established by the recording date. The earlier deed of trust that takes on a lower priority is called a subordinated deed of trust. The later deed of trust that is given a higher priority is called the subordinating deed of trust.

Subordination is most common when a seller of unimproved property carries back a deed of trust for part of the purchase price. The borrower/buyer intends to improve the security property, but to do so, he or she will have to obtain a construction loan. Construction lenders generally insist on having first lien position (the highest priority). As a result, the borrower won't be able to get the construction loan unless the seller is willing to subordinate the purchase loan.

A subordination clause can be included in the earlier deed of trust, or a separate subordination agreement may be drawn up. The provision may subordinate the deed of trust to a loan that has already been arranged, or to one that the borrower intends to apply for. Because subordination can have a drastic effect on the strength of a lender's security, any subordination provision must be drafted or carefully reviewed by a lawyer.

When the other loan hasn't been arranged yet, the provision should establish strict standards for the quality and purpose of the other loan. Otherwise, the borrower could subordinate the earlier deed of trust to any kind of loan and do whatever he or she wants with the money. That could make the subordinated lender's security interest worthless.

Security Instruments

As you've seen, a loan can be secured or unsecured. An unsecured lender has a legal right to be repaid, but there's no assurance that a judgment against the borrower will be collectible. So lenders prefer to obtain a security interest in the borrower's property. Then if the borrower defaults, the lender can recover the money by having the property sold.

The oldest and simplest security arrangement is the pawnbroker's. To borrow money from a pawnbroker, you have to bring in some property as security for the loan—your grandfather's gold watch, for example. If you repay the loan within a specified period, you get the watch back. But if that period expires and you haven't paid the pawnbroker, he or she will sell the watch and keep the proceeds. The legal term for this system is **pledging**; your grandfather's watch is the pledge.

Pledging requires you to turn over possession of the security property to the lender. But the security arrangement for a real estate loan is more sophisticated. You don't have to give up possession of your house to get the loan. You only have to grant the lender the right to have the house sold in case you default. This is called **hypothecation**.

According to the original theory behind real estate security instruments, the borrower transferred title to the property to the lender (or a neutral third party) during the loan period. When the loan was paid off, title was transferred back to the borrower. The language in some security instruments still reflects this theory, stating that the borrower "conveys" the property; and after the loan is paid off, a "reconveyance" is recorded. But this is essentially a legal fiction. For all practical purposes, the security instrument merely creates a voluntary lien against the property (see Chapter 3), and no actual transfer of title is involved. The lien enables the lender to foreclose if the borrower defaults.

Two main types of real property security instruments are used today: the deed of trust and the mortgage. Both types must be in writing and must meet the formal requirements for a deed (see Chapter 8). Either creates a lien on everything that would be transferred by a deed—so it includes the fixtures and the appurtenances such as water rights, as well as the land and the improvements (see Chapter 2).

The key difference between the two types is their foreclosure procedures. A mortgage usually must be foreclosed judicially—that is, by filing a lawsuit. But a deed of trust can be foreclosed nonjudicially, without going to court. Nonjudicial foreclosure saves the lender a lot of time and trouble.

In Washington, nearly all lenders use deeds of trust instead of mortgages. Let's look at deeds of trust first.

Deeds of Trust

There are three parties to a deed of trust: the **grantor** (the borrower), the **beneficiary** (the lender), and the **trustee** (a neutral third party). The grantor makes payments to the beneficiary; the trustee steps in to conduct foreclosure proceedings in case of default.

Fig. 10.4 First page of a Deed of Trust form

After Recording Return To:

_____
_____
_____
_____

_____ **[Space Above This Line For Recording Data]** _____

DEED OF TRUST

DEFINITIONS

Words used in multiple sections of this document are defined below and other words are defined in Sections 3, 11, 13, 18, 20 and 21. Certain rules regarding the usage of words used in this document are also provided in Section 16.

(A) "Security Instrument" means this document, which is dated _____, _____, together with all Riders to this document.
(B) "Borrower" is _____. Borrower is the trustor under this Security Instrument.
(C) "Lender" is _____. Lender is a _____ organized and existing under the laws of _____.
Lender's address is _____.
Lender is the beneficiary under this Security Instrument.
(D) "Trustee" is _____.
(E) "Note" means the promissory note signed by Borrower and dated _____, _____. The Note states that Borrower owes Lender _____
Dollars (U.S. $_____) plus interest. Borrower has promised to pay this debt in regular Periodic Payments and to pay the debt in full not later than _____.
(F) "Property" means the property that is described below under the heading "Transfer of Rights in the Property."
(G) "Loan" means the debt evidenced by the Note, plus interest, any prepayment charges and late charges due under the Note, and all sums due under this Security Instrument, plus interest.
(H) "Riders" means all Riders to this Security Instrument that are executed by Borrower. The following Riders are to be executed by Borrower [check box as applicable]:

Adjustable Rate Rider	Condominium Rider	Second Home Rider
Balloon Rider	Planned Unit Development Rider	Other(s) [specify]_____
1-4 Family Rider	Biweekly Payment Rider	

WASHINGTON--Single Family--Fannie Mae/Freddie Mac UNIFORM INSTRUMENT   Form 3048   1/01 *(page 1 of 16 pages)*

Institutional lenders (banks, savings and loans, etc.) almost always use standard forms for their deeds of trust. This is necessary if the loan is going to be sold to Fannie Mae or Freddie Mac. The secondary market agencies require the use of their standard forms because they don't have time to review the terms of the security instrument used for each transaction, and also because they insist on certain protective provisions.

Basic Provisions. A deed of trust identifies the parties and includes a full legal description of the security property. Using the legal description helps prevent any confusion over about what property the lien attaches to, in case foreclosure is necessary.

The deed of trust also identifies the underlying debt and the promissory note that is evidence of that debt. Typically, the deed of trust states the total amount of the debt and the maturity date, but doesn't go into more detail about the loan. The interest rate, and the amount of the payments, late charges, and other charges are usually found only in the promissory note. However, if the loan is subject to a variable interest rate, a provision explaining the rate must be included in the deed of trust as well as the note.

Deeds of trust go into detail about the borrower's obligations regarding care of the property and the title. Generally, the borrower agrees to insure the property against fire and other hazards. The borrower also agrees not to commit waste or allow the property to deteriorate. The deed of trust grants the lender the right to inspect the property, to make sure the borrower is maintaining it properly.

The borrower agrees to keep property taxes, special assessments, and insurance premiums up to date. If the borrower allows any of these bills to become delinquent, the lender has the right (but not the obligation) to pay them. This is important to the lender, since delinquent taxes reduce the value of the security property. If the delinquencies become severe, the taxing authority can foreclose; remember, tax liens have higher priority than the deed of trust (see Chapter 3). Any amounts paid by the lender to prevent the taxes from becoming delinquent or the insurance from lapsing will be added to the borrower's debt. Usually such an advance by the lender will bear interest at a higher interest rate than the normal note rate.

Impound Accounts. Depending on the terms of the loan agreement, the borrower may be expected to pay the taxes and insurance directly, or the lender may require an **impound account**. In that case, the borrower's monthly payments to the lender are increased by an amount sufficient to cover a prorated share of the taxes and insurance. The lender puts the extra amount in a special bank account (the impound account) and pays the taxes and insurance out of that account when they fall due.

Power of Sale. The key provision in a deed of trust—the one that makes it different from a mortgage—is the **power of sale clause**. The borrower grants the trustee the power to sell the property in case of default. This provision enables the lender to foreclose nonjudicially, rather than having to file a judicial foreclosure lawsuit.

Usually, a deed of trust briefly outlines the procedures to be followed if the trustee exercises the power of sale and forecloses. For the most part, however, those procedures are prescribed by law. The foreclosure process is described later in this chapter.

Deed of Reconveyance. Once a grantor has paid off the entire amount of the debt, he or she may request a **deed of reconveyance** (also called a full reconveyance) from the trustee. This instrument is then recorded in the county where the property is situated. This makes it a matter of public record that the debt has been paid off and the deed of trust is no longer a lien on the property.

Mortgages

There are only two parties to a mortgage, the **mortgagor** (the borrower) and the **mortgagee** (the lender); there is no trustee.

Up until the point of foreclosure, the mortgagor and mortgagee have the same rights and obligations as a grantor and beneficiary. The mortgagor agrees to insure and maintain the property, and the mortgagee may require payments into an impound account for taxes and insurance.

In contrast to a deed of trust, however, a mortgage does not ordinarily contain a power of sale clause. Therefore, a mortgagee must file a lawsuit if foreclosure becomes necessary.

Satisfaction of Mortgage. As with a deed of trust, once the mortgage debt has been fully paid off, the mortgagee delivers a document to the mortgagor stating that the debt has been paid. This document, called a **satisfaction of mortgage**, releases the mortgage lien. Once the satisfaction of mortgage is recorded in the county where the property is located, the mortgage is no longer a cloud on the property's title.

Foreclosure

The purpose of a security instrument in a real estate loan transaction is to give the lender the right of **foreclosure**: if the borrower fails to repay the loan as agreed, the lender can sell the property and use the proceeds to repay the loan. The major difference between a mortgage and a deed of trust is that a mortgage doesn't ordinarily have a power of sale clause and as a result, nonjudicial foreclosure is not permitted.

It's worth noting that a power of sale clause can also be included in a mortgage (which makes the mortgage for all intents and purposes just like a deed of trust). Likewise, a deed of trust lender can foreclosure judicially. But there is usually no need for it, and rarely any advantage to it; nonjudicial foreclosure is always faster and cheaper.

Since most lenders in Washington use deeds of trust, most foreclosures are nonjudicial. We'll look at the nonjudicial foreclosure process in detail first, and then compare it to the judicial foreclosure process.

Nonjudicial Foreclosure

The nonjudicial foreclosure process involves three main steps:

1. the notice of default,
2. the notice of foreclosure and trustee's sale, and
3. the trustee's sale.

Notice of Default. When a deed of trust beneficiary (the lender) asks the trustee to start the foreclosure process, the first step is to send the grantor (the borrower) a **notice of default**. The notice identifies the deed of trust, states that the grantor has breached the terms of the deed of trust, and describes the nature of the breach. Remember, default doesn't have to be failure to make monthly payments on time. Failure to maintain the property, pay the taxes, or keep the property insured can also constitute default. So can failure to pay off the entire balance after the lender has accelerated the loan under a due-on-sale clause.

The notice of default must be given to the grantor at least 30 days before the notice of trustee's sale is recorded. This notice of default must be sent by both first-class mail and either registered or certified mail, return receipt requested, and a notice must also be posted in a conspicuous place on the premises or personally served on the grantor.

Notice of Trustee's Sale. At least 90 days before the foreclosure sale takes place, the trustee must record a **notice of sale**. A copy of the notice of sale is then sent by both first-class and either certified or registered mail, return receipt requested, to the grantor and also to:

- the grantor's successors in interest (everyone who has acquired an ownership interest in the property—heirs, for example);
- the junior deed of trust beneficiaries (the lenders with lower lien priority than the foreclosing lender);
- the vendee in a real estate contract with lower priority than the deed of trust;
- the lessee in a lease with lower priority than the deed of trust; and
- the holder of any other lien against the property that is subordinated to the deed of trust being foreclosed.

A copy of the notice of sale will also be sent to everyone who requested such notice. Anyone who wants to receive the notice of sale under a particular deed of trust can record a **request for notice**. This request must include an address so that the trustee knows where to send the notice.

A copy of the notice of sale must also be posted in a conspicuous place on the property or served upon any occupant of the property.

The notice of sale states the time and place that the trustee's sale will be held. It gives the name and address of the trustee conducting the sale; it identifies the grantor and the property to be sold. The notice states the amount of the unpaid loan balance and an estimate of the costs and expenses.

Reinstatement and Redemption. When the grantor is in default because of a failure to make the payments or to pay the taxes, assessments, or insurance, the default can be cured. (Note that if the grantor has committed waste, or if the loan has been accelerated pursuant to a due-on-sale clause, curing the default is not an option.)

Cure and reinstatement. To **cure** the default, the grantor must bring the payments current (or pay the delinquent taxes or take any other required action) and pay any accrued late charges and other costs (such as the costs of foreclosure incurred by the trustee) before a certain specified date.

The default can be cured any time until 11 days before the date of the trustee's sale. This is known as the **reinstatement period.** If the sale is postponed, the right to cure the default revives until 11 days before the new sale date.

After this date, the grantor may not reinstate the deed of trust by simply paying the back payments and other costs. At that point, the grantor may only stop the sale by paying the total principal balance, plus accrued interest and costs.

Parties other than the grantor and the grantor's successors in interest can cure the default. A junior lienholder might pay off the delinquencies, costs, and fees in order to protect its lien.

When the default is curable, the notices of default and sale must contain an explanation of the right to reinstate. The explanatory paragraphs inform the grantor that the loan may be reinstated by paying the delinquencies, costs, and fees, even though the lender has demanded full payment. They explain that the default can be cured at any time until 11 days before the sale date. The amount necessary for curing the default as of the notice date must be listed. There must also be a warning that as time passes, other expenses may be incurred and additional charges may be added, so it will be necessary to contact the trustee to learn the exact amount required.

Once a default has been cured, the loan is reinstated and the grantor may resume making the regular payments. The beneficiary can't demand higher payments or a higher interest rate because of the earlier default. The grantor can ask the beneficiary to record a **notice of discontinuance**. The notice of discontinuance provides public notice that the notice of default and notice of sale have been rescinded.

Redemption. Eleven days before the sale date, the grantor (and everyone else) loses the right to cure the default. In that 11-day period, there's still a chance to **redeem** the property—that is, to prevent the sale and retain control of the property. To redeem the property, the grantor would have to pay the lender the entire loan balance (not merely the delinquencies), plus costs and fees. If the grantor could come up with that much, he or she would own the property free and clear of the lender's interest. This doesn't happen often. Once the trustee's sale is over, the right to redeem the property is lost.

Deed in lieu of foreclosure. The only other way for the grantor to prevent a trustee's sale is by giving the beneficiary a **deed in lieu of foreclosure**. The borrower simply deeds the property to the lender, surrendering ownership. Why would a borrower do that? Often the borrower is going to lose the property anyway, since he or she can't afford to cure the default, much less pay off the entire loan. By giving the lender a deed in lieu, the borrower can avoid liability for costs and fees, and may be able to protect his or her credit rating.

A lender isn't required to accept a deed in lieu of foreclosure. The lender can decide whether accepting it will be more advantageous than foreclosing. That may not be the case, for example, if the property is encumbered with other liens. Then the lender would be acquiring ownership of the property subject to those other liens. If there are junior encumbrances against the property, most lenders will not accept a deed in lieu of foreclosure.

If the value of the property is approximately equal to the loan balance, the lender does not have to give the borrower additional consideration for the deed in lieu of foreclosure. Letting the borrower off the hook is enough. But if the property is worth more than the loan balance, the lender should make up the difference to the borrower. Otherwise (if the borrower has second thoughts and later sues) a court might consider the transaction unfair and set it aside.

Trustee's Sale. A **trustee's sale** is a public auction; the foreclosure property is sold to the highest bidder. The sale must be held during ordinary business hours, in the county where the property is located. The trustee's role is to conduct the sale in a fair and open manner, to protect all interested parties (the grantor, the foreclosing lender, and the other lienholders), and to obtain a reasonable price for the property.

The foreclosing beneficiary (the lender) is allowed to **credit bid** at the sale. With credit bidding, the amount owed is offset against the amount of the bid. No other lienholders are allowed to credit bid.

> **Example:** The amount due to the lender is $100,000 (this includes the unpaid balance on the deed of trust, plus costs and fees). The lender bids $100,000, which is the highest bid. The lender gets the property without actually paying cash for it. If the bid had been $120,000, the lender would pay only $20,000 in cash.
>
> Suppose there's a junior deed of trust on the property with a $15,000 unpaid balance. If the beneficiary on that junior deed of trust bid $100,000, he or she would have to pay the full $100,000 (not $85,000).

Postponement. The trustee can postpone the sale if necessary to protect the interests of the beneficiary or grantor. For example, the trustee might decide to postpone the sale if all the bids were unreasonably low.

Sale proceeds. After the property has been sold at the trustee's sale, the proceeds are applied in the following order:

1. first, the costs of the foreclosure are paid (including the costs of publishing, recording, and mailing notices, the cost of a title search, and the trustee's and attorney's fees);
2. next, the deed of trust that was foreclosed is paid off;
3. then any junior liens are paid off in order of priority; and finally,
4. anything left over is paid to the grantor.

If there's nothing left after the foreclosed deed of trust is paid off, the junior lienholders get nothing. Or if there's only enough left to pay the first junior lienholder, the second and

Fig. 10.5 Time frame for nonjudicial foreclosure

NONJUDICIAL FORECLOSURE	
JUDICIAL FORECLOSURE	At least 30 days before notice of sale
NOTICE OF DEFAULT	At least 90 days before sale
NOTICE OF SALE	Lasts until 11 days before sale
REINSTATEMENT PERIOD (default can be cured by paying delinquent amount, interest, and costs)	
TRUSTEE'S SALE	From 11 days before sale until date of sale, sale can be stopped by paying total balance plus interest and costs.
PURCHASER ENTITLED TO POSSESSION	20 days after sale

third get nothing (and so on). But the foreclosure **extinguishes** the junior liens regardless of whether they have been paid. That means that the junior lienholders have lost their security interest in the property; they can't foreclose later (although they can still sue the debtor for a personal judgment).

However, the foreclosure does not extinguish any liens that had higher priority than the foreclosed deed of trust (a property tax lien, for example). The purchaser at the trustee's sale takes the property subject to those senior liens. Foreclosure also does not extinguish a junior lien if the junior lienholder did not receive a notice of sale.

Trustee's deed. The purchaser at a trustee's sale receives title to the property immediately. The grantor has no further right to redeem the property. The purchaser is entitled to possession of the property on the 20th day following the sale. If the grantor refuses to surrender possession of the property, he or she can be evicted.

The purchaser is given a **trustee's deed**. Like a quitclaim deed, it conveys whatever ownership rights the grantor had, but carries no warranties of title.

Protection for Junior Lienholders. The beneficiary of a junior deed of trust (or any other junior lienholder) has the same right to foreclose as the beneficiary of the senior deed of trust. But as you've seen, if the senior lender forecloses first, the junior lender's security interest will be wiped out altogether. The junior lender may receive full payment, partial payment, or nothing at all.

The only protection for a junior lender (besides choosing the borrower carefully) is notice. If a junior lender knows that the borrower is having trouble with a senior loan, the junior lender can cure the default and reinstate the senior loan. The amount it costs to cure the default is added to what the borrower already owes the junior lender. With the senior loan reinstated, the junior lender can decide whether to foreclose on its own lien. Of course, the notice of sale alerts the junior lender that the borrower is in trouble, but in some cases the junior lender can make arrangements with the borrower to receive an earlier warning.

Judicial Foreclosure

Like nonjudicial foreclosure, judicial foreclosure involves three main steps. In this case, the steps are:

1. the foreclosure action,
2. the notice of sheriff's sale, and
3. the sheriff's sale.

Foreclosure Suit. First, the mortgagee must file a foreclosure action in the superior court of the county where the property is located. The defendants named in the foreclosure lawsuit are the borrower and any junior lienholders. The junior lienholders are brought into the suit to give them the opportunity to defend their interests.

After filing a foreclosure suit, the mortgagee will typically record a notice called a **lis pendens**. The lis pendens states that a legal action is pending that may affect title to the property. It provides constructive notice of the foreclosure, so that anyone who acquires an interest in the property takes it subject to the outcome of the foreclosure suit. For example, someone who bought a house after a lis pendens had been filed would lose the property if the foreclosure suit was successful.

When the foreclosure action is heard in court, the judge orders the property sold to satisfy the debt. This is called a **decree of foreclosure**. The decree of foreclosure establishes the amount that the defaulting mortgagor owes the mortgagee, orders the property sold to pay the debt, and also states whether or not the mortgagor is personally liable for any deficiency in the foreclosure sale proceeds. For example, if the mortgagor owes the mortgagee $210,000 and the sale of the property only raises $180,000, will the mortgagee be given a **deficiency judgment** against the mortgagor for the $30,000 deficiency? Liability for a deficiency judgment depends on the anti-deficiency rules, discussed later in this chapter.

The sale ordered by the decree of foreclosure is sometimes called a **sheriff's sale** or an **execution sale**. Up until the time of the sale, the mortgagor and junior lienholders can redeem the property by paying off the entire mortgage debt, plus any costs incurred. This is called the **equitable right of redemption**.

Notice of Sheriff's Sale. At least 30 days before the date of sale, a copy of the notice of sale must be served on the judgment debtor, or mailed to the debtor by both regular and certified mail.

For a period of not less than four weeks prior to the date of the sale, the sheriff must post a notice in two public places in the county in which the property is located. One of these notices is posted at the courthouse door, and if the property has improvements on it (such as a house or an office building), one notice must be posted at the front door of the principal building on the property.

The sheriff must also publish a notice of the sale once a week, for four consecutive weeks, in any daily or weekly legal newspaper of general circulation published in the county where the property is located.

At the sheriff's sale, the property is sold to the highest bidder, who is given a **certificate of sale.** The bidder does not get actual title to the property until he or she receives a **sheriff's deed**, which is issued at the end of the **statutory redemption period**.

Redemption. Between the filing of the lawsuit and the sheriff's sale is the **equitable redemption period**, during which the mortgagor may redeem the property by paying off the mortgage in full. After the sheriff's sale, the mortgagor has a final opportunity to redeem the property during a period known as the **statutory redemption period**. If the mortgagee has expressly waived any right to a deficiency judgment, the property may be redeemed from the purchaser at any time within eight months after the date of the sale. If the mortgagee has not waived the right to a deficiency judgment, or if it falls within the

Fig. 10.6 Time frame for judicial foreclosure

JUDICIAL FORECLOSURE	
FORECLOSURE LAWSUIT FILED	
LIS PENDENS RECORDED	
EQUITABLE RIGHT OF REDEMPTION (property may be redeemed by paying off entire debt, plus costs)	Any time until sheriff's sale
DECREE OF FORECLOSURE	
NOTICE OF SALE	At least 30 days before sale
SHERIFF'S SALE	
STATUTORY REDEMPTION PERIOD (property may be redeemed by paying amount purchaser paid at sale, plus taxes, insurance, maintenance costs, and interest)	8 months if right to deficiency waived; 1 year if not waived

agricultural exception, the property may be redeemed within one year after the date of the sale.

The right of redemption after judicial foreclosure is a substantial advantage for the mortgagor, and a substantial disadvantage for the mortgagee and the foreclosure sale purchaser.

The person who redeems the property must pay the same amount that the purchaser paid for the property at the foreclosure sale, plus whatever the purchaser has spent on taxes, insurance, and maintenance. He or she also has to pay interest on that amount, from the time of the sale until the date of redemption.

If the purchaser was a junior lienholder before the foreclosure sale, the person redeeming the property must also pay off that junior lien, plus interest. If the purchaser has used the property during the redemption period, the reasonable value of that use can be offset against the redemption price. So can any rents or profits the purchaser has received from the property.

A redemption period of one year is a long period of uncertainty for the purchaser. The purchaser won't want to improve the property during that period, because if the mortgagor decided to redeem, the value of the improvements wouldn't be included in the redemption price.

If someone redeems the property, a **certificate of redemption** is issued and recorded. If a deficiency judgment was entered after the foreclosure sale and remains unpaid, a judgment lien attaches to the redeemed property. But the junior liens that were extinguished by the foreclosure sale are not revived by the redemption. They're gone for good.

The same procedures are followed when a deed of trust beneficiary chooses to foreclose judicially instead of using the power of sale. There are real disadvantages to the judicial foreclosure process, in terms of both time and money. The long redemption period may make bids at the sheriff's sale lower than they would have been at a trustee's sale. So why would a deed of trust beneficiary choose judicial foreclosure? It's the only way to obtain a deficiency judgment. Let's take a look at the rules that govern when deficiency judgments are available.

Deficiency Judgments and Anti-Deficiency Rules. During the Great Depression in the 1930s, thousands of families lost their homes to foreclosure. Legislatures in many states passed laws to grant some relief to borrowers. For example, there was legislation that delayed foreclosure sales, extended redemption periods, and limited lenders' ability to obtain deficiency judgments. Most of these laws were temporary, emergency measures that later lapsed or were repealed. But some restrictions on the right to a deficiency judgment are still in effect.

When ordering a foreclosure sale, the court may hold a hearing to fix a minimum or **upset price** for the property. The property cannot be sold for less than the upset price. Alternatively, the court may hold a hearing after the sale to establish the fair market value of the property. If the fair market value is greater than the actual sale proceeds, the court may limit the lender's deficiency judgment to the difference between the fair market value and the amount owed. (If the fair market value is enough to completely discharge the debt, then the lender is not entitled to a deficiency judgment.)

> **Example:** The borrower owes the foreclosing lender $200,000, including foreclosure costs. At the sheriff's sale, the property was purchased for $175,000. The lender receives that $175,000, and then asks the court for a deficiency judgment.
>
> The court holds a hearing and determines that the fair market value of the property is $185,000. The court applies that amount to the $200,000 debt. The lender is granted a deficiency judgment for $15,000, the difference between the fair market value and the debt. Even if the borrower pays the deficiency judgment, the lender's total recovery will be less than the $200,000 owed: $175,000 (sale proceeds) + $15,000 (deficiency judgment) = $190,000.

This rule may seem unfair to the lender, but it prevents an abuse that was once widespread. Foreclosing lenders used to purchase the property at the foreclosure sale for much less than its fair market value, and then obtain a deficiency judgment for the difference between the sale proceeds and the debt. As a result, the lender came away from the foreclosure with far more than the borrower owed.

In Washington, a lender is never entitled to a deficiency judgment after foreclosing nonjudicially. That rule applies to all types of loans and all types of lenders. A lender who wants a deficiency judgment must go through the judicial foreclosure process. So when a deed of trust lender believes that a foreclosure sale is likely to result in a substantial deficiency, it may be worth the extra trouble to start a foreclosure lawsuit instead of exercising the power of sale.

A lender can waive the right to a deficiency judgment in the loan agreement. Sometimes a promissory note contains a **non-recourse provision**. That means the lender agrees to limit its recovery to the foreclosure sale proceeds, and will not sue the borrower if there is a deficiency.

Real Estate Contracts

You should be familiar with one other type of security instrument besides deeds of trust and mortgages. We'll refer to them as real estate contracts, although they go by a variety of similar names: land contracts, installment land contracts, installment sales contracts, real estate land contracts, or real property sales contracts.

When a **real estate contract** is used, the buyer pays the seller in installments over a long period of time. Although the buyer usually takes possession of the property immediately, the seller retains title to the property as security for payment of the contract price. The seller doesn't deliver the deed to the buyer until the full price has been paid off, which may be many years later.

The parties to a real estate contract are called the **vendor** (the seller) and the **vendee** (the buyer). The vendor has **legal title**; the vendee has **equitable title**. The vendor's interest in the property decreases as the contract is paid off, and the vendee's interest increases.

Fig. 10.7 Parties to a real estate contract

A real estate contract must comply with all of the requirements for any valid contract: capacity, mutual consent, consideration, and a legal objective. The real estate contract must be in writing and signed. A vendee may be allowed to prepay, and the vendor, like a deed of trust lender, may charge a prepayment penalty.

Most of the parties' rights and obligations are established by the terms of the contract. Because the vendor still has legal title to the property, he or she can transfer or encumber it without the vendee's consent. But the vendor is required to deliver clear, marketable title whenever the vendee pays off the contract. The vendor isn't allowed to grant any rights to third parties that would encumber the property after the vendee takes legal title (easements, for example). And if the vendor creates any liens, he or she must pay them off before delivering the deed to the vendee; if the liens are not paid off, it's a breach of contract.

The vendee also has the right to encumber the property. However, few lenders are willing to make loans with the vendee's equitable interest as the only security.

A real estate contract should be recorded, to give constructive notice of the vendee's interest in the property. If the contract is recorded, anyone who buys the property from the vendor takes it subject to the vendee's interest. When the vendee tenders full payment, the buyer will have to deliver title to the vendee, just as the vendor would have had to. But if the contract isn't recorded and someone buys the property without actual notice of the vendee's interest, the buyer can cut off the vendee's rights. (The vendor will be liable to the vendee for breach of contract, but the vendee will lose the property to the other buyer.)

The Vendor's Remedies

A real estate contract usually provides that the vendee's interest will be forfeited upon default. In other words, if the vendee stops making payments, the vendor can cancel the contract and regain possession of the property.

If the vendee stops making payments (or breaches the contract in some other manner), the vendor can file a **notice of intent to forfeit**. This notice must be in writing and signed by the vendor. It also must be recorded. Within ten days after it is recorded, a copy of the notice must be sent to the vendee and to others who have an interest in the property (such as lienholders) or who have filed a request for notice.

The notice of intent to forfeit must contain the name and address of the vendor, a description of the contract, a legal description of the property, a description of the default, and a statement that the contract will be forfeited if the default is not cured by a certain date. The date for curing the default must be at least 90 days after the notice of intent to forfeit is recorded.

If the default is not cured by the stated date, the vendor may record a **declaration of forfeiture**. The declaration must also be sent to everyone who was entitled to receive a notice of intent to forfeit, within three days after the declaration is recorded. Any right, title, or interest in the property held by the vendee will be terminated and the vendee's rights under the contract will be canceled. All sums previously paid under the contract will be retained by the vendor. All improvements made to the property (and any unharvested crops) will belong to the vendor. The vendee will be required to surrender possession of the property ten days after the declaration of forfeiture is recorded. Once the property has been forfeited, the vendee has no right to redeem the property.

The vendee may have the right to request a court to order a public sale of the property. If the court finds that the fair market value of the property substantially exceeds the unpaid portion of the vendee's obligations, it may require the property to be sold. Proceeds of the sale are then used to pay the costs of the sale and the amount owing to the vendor.

If the vendor chooses, a real estate contract may also be foreclosed in the same way as and subject to the same laws as a mortgage.

Protecting the Borrower

Real estate financing is complicated, and obtaining financing can be a confusing and difficult process for many home buyers, especially first-time buyers. Unscrupulous lenders, mortgage brokers, and other parties sometimes try to take advantage of buyers, or of homeowners who are refinancing or taking out a home equity loan. To help prevent this, there are a number of state and federal laws designed to protect buyers and homeowners from being misled or cheated in the financing or closing process.

Truth in Lending Act

The **Truth in Lending Act** (TILA) is a federal law that requires lenders to disclose the complete cost of credit to consumer loan applicants. The act also regulates advertising of consumer loans. Congress outlined these goals in the act, and delegated the responsibility for carrying them out to the Federal Reserve Board. The Federal Reserve Board's **Regulation Z** implements the Truth in Lending Act. Regulation Z sets out the detailed rules that lenders must comply with.

Loans Covered by TILA. A loan is a **consumer loan** if it is used for personal, family, or household purposes. A consumer loan is covered by the Truth in Lending Act if it is to be repaid in more than four installments, or is subject to finance charges, and is either:

- for $25,000 or less, or
- secured by real property.

Thus, any loan secured by a mortgage or deed of trust is covered by the Truth in Lending Act, as long as the proceeds are used for personal, family, or household purposes (such as buying a home, or sending the kids to college).

Exemptions. The Truth in Lending Act applies only to loans made to natural persons, so loans made to corporations or organizations are not covered. In addition, loans for business, commercial, or agricultural purposes are exempt. And a loan for more than $25,000 that is not secured by real property is not covered, regardless of how the proceeds are used.

Disclosure Requirements. The Truth in Lending Act's disclosure requirements apply not only to lenders but to **credit arrangers**: go-betweens who help would-be borrowers find willing lenders. The primary disclosures that a lender or credit arranger must make to a loan applicant are the total finance charge and the annual percentage rate.

The **total finance charge** is the sum of all fees the lender charges a borrower in exchange for granting the loan. That includes the interest on the loan, plus the origination fee, any discount points paid by the borrower, and mortgage insurance or guaranty fees. Title insurance costs, credit report charges, the appraisal fee, and points paid by the seller are not included in the total finance charge.

The **annual percentage rate** (APR) states the relationship of the total finance charge to the amount of the loan, expressed as an annual percentage. A loan's APR is higher than its annual interest rate, since it reflects all the other finance charges in addition to the interest. For example, a loan with a 9% annual interest rate might have a 9.25% APR. The APR is sometimes referred to as the effective rate of interest, as opposed to the nominal rate (the interest rate stated on the face of the promissory note).

Disclosure statement. The lender or credit arranger must give the loan applicant a clear, easily understandable disclosure statement within three days after receiving the written loan application. In addition to the total finance charge and the APR, the statement must disclose the total amount financed, the payment schedule, the total number of payments, the total amount of payments, and information regarding any balloon payments, late fees, or prepayment charges. In the case of a real estate loan, it must also state whether the loan may be assumed by someone who buys the security property from the borrower.

Adjustable-rate loans. Additional disclosures are required for adjustable-rate loans. The lender must give the applicant an informational brochure on ARM loans, *The Consumer Handbook on Adjustable-Rate Mortgages*, prepared by the Federal Reserve. The lender must also provide specific information regarding the particular ARM loan program being applied for, such as the index, the initial rate, and any rate or payment caps.

Home Equity Loans. A home equity loan is a loan secured by the borrower's existing residence, as opposed to a loan financing the purchase or construction of a residence. TILA has some special rules for home equity loans. When the security property is the borrower's principal residence, the act gives a home equity borrower a right of rescission. The borrower has the right to rescind the loan agreement up until three business days after signing the agreement, receiving the disclosure statement, or receiving notice of the right of rescission, whichever comes last. If the borrower never receives the statement or notice, the right of rescission continues for three years. (It's important to remember that this right applies only to home equity loans. There is no right of rescission for a loan to finance the purchase or construction of the borrower's principal residence.) The Truth in Lending Act also requires certain disclosures for home equity plans that involve repeated extensions of credit, as opposed to a single loan.

Advertising. The Truth in Lending Act strictly controls the advertising of credit terms. Its advertising rules apply to anyone who advertises consumer credit, not just lenders and credit arrangers. For example, a real estate broker advertising financing terms for a listed home must comply with Regulation Z.

The cash price for a property and a loan's annual percentage rate can always be advertised. But if any other particular loan terms (the downpayment or the interest rate, for example) are stated in an ad, then all the terms must also be included. For example, if an ad says, "Assume 7% VA loan," it will violate the Truth in Lending Act unless it goes on to reveal the APR and all the terms of repayment. However, general statements such as "low downpayment" or "easy terms" don't trigger the full disclosure requirement.

Washington Mortgage Broker Practices Act

Another law protecting borrowers is the state Mortgage Broker Practices Act, which regulates Washington's mortgage brokerage business. In addition to establishing licensing and practice requirements, the law specifically sets out to promote honesty and fair dealing in mortgage brokers' dealings with clients and the general public.

Prohibited Practices. The Mortgage Broker Practices Act prohibits mortgage brokers from a number of actions, including:

- defrauding or misleading borrowers, lenders, or third parties;
- engaging in unfair or deceptive practices;
- obtaining property by fraud or misrepresentation;
- contracting with a borrower to receive fees even when the borrower doesn't actually obtain a loan;
- misrepresenting available rates, points, or financing terms;
- failing to make required disclosures to loan applicants and other parties;
- bribing an appraiser;
- advertising an interest rate without disclosing the APR (or otherwise violating the Truth in Lending Act);
- failing to pay third-party service providers within 30 days of recording loan closing documents; or
- acting as a mortgage broker in his or her own transaction or a transaction handled by another licensee working for the same real estate broker.

A violation of the Mortgage Broker Practices Act is a misdemeanor.

Equity Skimming

Equity skimming refers to a type of scheme in which homeowners are defrauded out of equity in their homes. Victims of equity skimming are usually homeowners who have become financially overextended and are in default on their mortgage payments.

In one version of equity skimming, a homeowner is approached by a person offering to buy the home and assume the mortgage payments. Once the owner has sold the home, the buyer rents it out (or back to the original owner). However, the buyer never makes any of the mortgage payments, and simply pockets the money. The property goes into foreclosure and the original owner finds he is still liable for the mortgage payments.

In another equity skimming scheme, a homeowner sells her home to a buyer in a transaction that is partially or all seller-financed. The buyer takes out a second mortgage against the home with higher priority than the original mortgage. After receiving the proceeds, the buyer defaults on the second mortgage and the seller loses her equity in the home.

> **Example:** Pitts, a convicted felon with terrible credit, approached the Herberts, who held substantial equity in their home. Pitts bought the Herberts' home, financing part of the purchase with seller financing from the Herberts and part with a loan from Vega. Each loan was secured with a deed of trust. Vega's deed of trust had higher priority than the Herberts' deed of trust. Vega loaned Pitts substantially more than the amount needed and at an exorbitantly high interest rate.
>
> Pitts walked away with the loan proceeds and defaulted on the loan. Vega foreclosed on his senior priority mortgage. The foreclosure exhausted the value of the property and the Herberts were left with nothing.

In an effort to curb equity skimming schemes, the Washington legislature passed a law making equity skimming a crime. Under the law, anyone found guilty of willfully engaging in at least three acts of equity skimming within a three-year period is guilty of a felony. In addition, equity skimming is considered an unfair or deceptive act or practice punishable by civil penalty of up to $2,000 per violation.

Conclusion

Financing is an essential part of nearly every real estate transaction. Buyers can't purchase the property they want unless they can get the necessary financing. Lenders won't lend large sums of money for the purchase of real estate without a security instrument that makes the real estate collateral for the loan.

The type of promissory note and security instrument signed by the borrower can make a great deal of difference to both the borrower and the lender. In Washington, lenders generally use deeds of trust instead of mortgages. This allows them to save time and expense by foreclosing nonjudicially.

State and federal laws protect home buyers and owners from being misled or defrauded in the financing process.

Case Problem

The following is a hypothetical case problem. Most of the facts are taken from a real case. Based on what you have learned from this chapter, make a decision on the issues presented and then check to see if your answer matches the court's decision.

The Facts

The Rodgerses borrowed money to finance the purchase of some commercial property. They signed a promissory note secured by a deed of trust on the property. The note provided that it could not be prepaid during the first four years of the loan term. After the fourth year the loan could be prepaid in full only if a prepayment penalty were paid. The prepayment penalty was 5% during the fifth year and 1% thereafter.

An acceleration clause in the note also stated that if any payment was not paid when due, or in the event of any default in performance of the terms of the note, then the entire principal sum and accrued interest would at once become due and payable. The note was dated January 31, 1984.

In April 1986, the Rodgerses stopped making payments. In October 1986, the lender sent the Rodgerses notice of nonjudicial foreclosure and sale. When the Rodgerses attempted to pay off the note to prevent foreclosure, the lender demanded payment of:

1. the principal in full,
2. interest up to the date of payment,
3. costs and fees due for the foreclosure proceedings,
4. interest from the date of full payment of the principal until the end of the fourth loan year, and
5. the prepayment penalty that would have been due upon prepayment during the fifth year.

The Questions

Was the lender entitled to receive all of the above payments? If not, which are not valid demands, and why aren't they?

The Answer

The lender was entitled to receive items 1, 2, and 3 on the list; the principal in full, interest up to the date of payment, and costs and fees. It was not entitled to items 4 and 5.

The note prohibited prepayment during the first four years. However, it did not specifically provide for payment of interest for the entire four years if there was a default and acceleration during those four years. The lender chose to accelerate and make the entire principal and interest amount due and payable. Therefore it was not entitled to any interest for the period beyond the point when the note was actually paid.

The note also provided for a prepayment penalty in the fifth year. However, it did not specifically provide that the fifth year prepayment penalty would become due if there was default and acceleration before the fifth year.

A lender loses its right to a prepayment penalty by accelerating the maturity date of the debt. Acceleration advances the maturity date of the debt to the present, so that the payoff of the debt is not a prepayment but is payment made at maturity. Since the lender chose to accelerate the debt, it lost its right to a prepayment penalty. *Rodgers v. Rainier National Bank*, 111 Wn.2d 232, 757 P.2d 976 (1988).

Chapter Summary

- A promissory note is a legally binding promise to repay a debt. A security instrument is a contract that makes real property collateral for a loan. If the borrower doesn't repay as agreed in the promissory note, the security instrument gives the lender the right to foreclose on the property.

- An instrument such as a promissory note is negotiable if it can be passed freely to someone else, transferring the right to payment to the new holder. A person who accepts a negotiable instrument can be a holder in due course and thereby receive special legal protection.

- Promissory notes are classified by the way the principal and interest are to be paid off. A straight note requires payments of interest only. An installment note requires payments of principal and interest. If the payments pay off the entire loan by the end of the term, the note is fully amortized. If the payments don't cover the full amount and a balloon payment is due at the end of the term, the note is only partially amortized.

- Most loan agreements give the borrower the right to prepay the loan. However, they may forbid prepayment for a certain initial period and may require a prepayment fee.

- Almost all real estate loan agreements provide for acceleration of the loan in case of default. Upon default, the lender may declare the entire balance due immediately. If a lender accelerates a note due to default, it may not also charge a prepayment penalty.

- Many loans contain a "due-on-sale" clause that provides that if the borrower sells or transfers the property without the lender's consent, the lender has the right to accelerate the loan and demand immediate payment in full. If a lender elects to accelerate the debt, it may not also demand a prepayment penalty.

- There are three parties to a deed of trust: the grantor (borrower), the lender (beneficiary), and a neutral third party (trustee). A mortgage involves only a mortgagor (borrower) and mortgagee (lender), with no trustee.

- The most important difference between a deed of trust and a mortgage is that the deed of trust has a power of sale clause. This grants the trustee the right to sell the property in case of default. Thus the lender may foreclose nonjudicially, rather than having to file a foreclosure lawsuit.

- Nonjudicial foreclosure is usually faster and cheaper than judicial foreclosure. A judicial foreclosure may be preferable if the lender expects to get a large deficiency judgment against the borrower.

- Until the point of foreclosure, a mortgagor and mortgagee have essentially the same rights and obligations as a grantor and beneficiary.

- When property is foreclosed on in a nonjudicial sale, the trustee gives written notice of default to the debtor. The trustee must also record a notice of sale and send a copy of it to the debtor and to others with an interest in or a lien against the property.

- Until eleven days before the trustee's sale, a default can be cured and the sale prevented by bringing the payments current and paying accrued late charges and costs. This is called the reinstatement period. When it is less than eleven days until the sale, the sale may only be prevented and the property redeemed by paying the total principal balance plus accrued interest and costs.

- The sale in a judicial foreclosure is called a sheriff's sale or execution sale. Notice of the sale must be given to the debtor, posted in two public places in the county, and published in the newspaper. After a judicial foreclosure, the debtor has the right to redeem the property for eight months to one year after the sale. This is called the redemption period.

- If proceeds from a sheriff's sale do not fully satisfy the mortgagor's debt, the mortgagor may be personally liable for the deficiency. The mortgagee may ask the court for a deficiency judgment to cover the difference.

- In a real estate contract purchase, the buyer takes possession of the property immediately, but the seller retains title as security for payment of the contract price. The seller doesn't deliver the deed to the buyer until the full price has been paid.

- The Truth in Lending Act requires lenders to disclose the complete cost of credit to consumer loan applicants, and also regulates advertising of consumer loans.

- The Mortgage Broker Practices Act requires mortgage brokers to act fairly and honestly in dealing with loan applicants and other parties.

Checklist of Problem Areas

Real Estate Licensee's Checklist

❏ Do you understand the basic rights and obligations of borrowers and lenders so you can help the parties arrange financing? You should have a working knowledge of:

- promissory notes,
- mortgages,
- deeds of trust,
- real estate contracts,
- foreclosure proceedings,
- redemption rights, and
- the Truth in Lending Act.

Seller's Checklist

❏ If you are extending credit to the buyer, you need to have a firm understanding of your rights and obligations as a lender.

- Is the buyer creditworthy?
- Do you want to use a note secured by a mortgage or deed of trust, or do you want to use a real estate contract?
- What provisions or special clauses are included in the loan documents? Do they cover the possibility of transfer, assumption, or default?
- What recourse do you have if the buyer defaults?

Buyer's Checklist

❏ Are you signing a mortgage, a deed of trust, or a real estate contract?

❏ What provisions are contained in the financing documents you are signing?

- Is prepayment allowed?
- Is there a certain lock-in period before prepayment is allowed?
- Is a prepayment penalty charged? If so, how much?
- Does the security instrument contain a due-on-sale clause?
- Do the documents contain a clause providing for acceleration upon default?
- Is there a late payment penalty? If so, how much?
- Will you be charged a default interest rate on any delinquent amounts?

❏ Is the promissory note a straight note or an installment note? Is it fully or only partially amortized? Will there be a balloon payment?

Chapter Quiz

1. If a document contains an unconditional promise to pay a certain sum of money on demand or to the bearer, it is:

   a. a security instrument
   b. a negotiable instrument
   c. an HDC
   d. None of the above

2. A promissory note is usually:

   a. a mortgage
   b. in blank
   c. signed by the holder in due course
   d. a negotiable instrument

3. A security instrument:

   a. is a contract that makes real property collateral for a loan
   b. creates a lien on the property
   c. gives the lender the right to foreclose on the property if the borrower doesn't repay the loan
   d. All of the above

4. The amount of the payments on a note is enough to pay off the entire loan, both principal and interest, by the end of the term. This is called a:

   a. straight note
   b. partially amortized note
   c. fully amortized note
   d. balloon payment note

5. The provision in a deed of trust that makes it different from a mortgage is the:

   a. power of sale clause
   b. impound account clause
   c. prepayment provision
   d. acceleration clause

6. If a borrower defaults, the lender has the right to declare the entire balance due immediately. This is called a(n):

   a. prepayment provision
   b. assumption clause
   c. acceleration clause
   d. deficiency judgment

7. If the borrower sells the property without the lender's consent, the lender has the right to demand immediate payment in full. This is called a:

   a. prepayment provision
   b. due-on-sale clause
   c. deficiency judgment
   d. subordination clause

8. When the borrower has defaulted and the property is going to be foreclosed on, the trustee must record a notice of sale. This must be done:

   a. at least 30 days before the sale
   b. at least 60 days before the sale
   c. at least 90 days before the sale
   d. six months before the sale

9. Under a deed of trust, a default can be cured any time after the notice of default until a certain time period before the sale. This is called the reinstatement period. In Washington, the reinstatement period lasts until:

   a. five days before the date of sale
   b. seven days before the date of sale
   c. 11 days before the date of sale
   d. 15 days before the date of sale

10. A borrower may prevent a trustee's sale by simply deeding the property to the lender. This is called a "deed in lieu of foreclosure." A borrower may wish to do this:

    a. to avoid liability for costs and fees
    b. to protect his credit rating
    c. because he can't afford to cure the default and knows he is going to lose the property anyway
    d. All of the above

11. A deficiency judgment is available:

    a. only after a nonjudicial foreclosure
    b. only after a judicial foreclosure
    c. after either a nonjudicial or a judicial foreclosure
    d. None of the above

12. Nonjudicial foreclosure:

    a. is generally faster than judicial foreclosure
    b. is generally slower than judicial foreclosure
    c. takes about the same amount of time as judicial foreclosure but is less formal
    d. takes longer than judicial foreclosure because of the right to a deficiency judgment

13. Which are most common in Washington?

    a. Deeds of trust with nonjudicial foreclosure
    b. Deeds of trust with judicial foreclosure
    c. Mortgages with nonjudicial foreclosure
    d. Mortgages with judicial foreclosure

14. A buyer makes installment payments to the seller over a long period of time. Although the buyer takes possession, the seller retains title until the full price has been paid. This is known as:

    a. a land trust or trustee deed
    b. a real estate contract or installment sales contract
    c. an assumption sale
    d. an equitable sale contract or equity deed

15. The Truth in Lending Act:

    a. is a state law
    b. requires lenders to disclose the complete cost of credit to consumer loan applicants
    c. applies to both residential and commercial loans
    d. All of the above

11 Restrictions on Land Use

Outline

I. Public Restrictions
- A. Power to regulate land use
- B. Zoning
  1. zoning categories
  2. zoning for aesthetics
  3. exceptions to zoning regulations
     a. nonconforming uses
     b. variances
     c. conditional uses
     d. zone changes (rezones)
     e. spot zoning
  4. enforcement of zoning ordinances
- C. Building codes and permits
- D. Subdivision regulations
  1. procedural requirements
  2. Washington Land Development Act
  3. PUDs
- E. Historic preservation
- F. Land use planning and administration (Growth Management Act)
  1. comprehensive plans
  2. urban growth areas
  3. concurrency requirement
- G. Environmental legislation
  1. Comprehensive Environmental Response, Compensation and Liability Act (CERCLA)
  2. Model Toxics Control Act (MCTA)
  3. National Environmental Policy Act (NEPA)
  4. State Environmental Policy Act (SEPA)
  5. Shoreline Management Act
  6. Clean Air Act
  7. Clean Water Act
  8. other legislation
- H. Taxation
  1. general real estate taxes
  2. special assessments

II. Private Restrictions
- A. Covenants and conditions
- B. Termination of restrictions
- C. Subdivision restrictions

Key Terms

- police power
- eminent domain
- zoning ordinances
- nonconforming use
- variance
- conditional use
- rezone
- spot zone
- certificate of occupancy
- subdivision
- plat
- planned unit development (PUD)

- Growth Management Act (GMA)
- comprehensive plan
- urban growth area
- concurrency requirement
- CERCLA
- Model Toxics Control Act (MTCA)
- National Environmental Policy Act (NEPA)
- environmental impact statement (EIS)

- State Environmental Policy Act (SEPA)
- determination of non-significance
- Shoreline Management Act
- Clean Air Act
- Clean Water Act
- ad valorem
- true and fair value
- special assessment
- condition
- covenant
- CC&Rs

Chapter Overview

This chapter discusses the effects of zoning, planning, and private restrictions on the use of property. While "restrictions on land use" may seem too theoretical, or too complicated to be of much importance to the average homeowner, they can have a tremendous impact on the value of property and the ways in which that property can be used.

For example, suppose an older house is for sale in an area that has recently experienced a lot of residential growth. The owners used to run a small grocery store out of the first floor of the house. They closed the store several years ago because they were getting too old to run it by themselves.

A young couple is interested in buying the house and would like to re-open the store. Can they? Just because there was once a store here does not necessarily mean that a store can be legally operated on the property now.

A real estate agent would be negligent if she told the prospective buyers that they could open the store without first checking zoning laws, building codes, and any private restrictions that might apply to the property.

Public Restrictions

During colonial times, landowners could do whatever they liked with their property. They could build a house or raise pigs or run a blacksmith shop, or even do all three on the same piece of property. But as the population grew and cities became crowded, people began to object to pig farms right next to shopping districts. To alleviate these types of problems and to ensure that landowners did not interfere with each other's use of property, local governments began enacting zoning ordinances.

Today, zoning ordinances are the primary public restriction on land use. Building codes, state laws such as the Growth Management Act, and other regulations also serve to restrict land use in ways that benefit the public.

Power to Regulate Land Use

The power to regulate land use is rooted in the state's police power. **Police power** is a state government's constitutional power to adopt and enforce laws for the protection of the public health, safety, morals, and general welfare. (A state may delegate the police power to its local governments.) Because land use laws prevent overcrowding and its accompanying sanitation, fire protection, and law enforcement problems, they protect the public health, safety, and welfare. So as a general rule, land use laws are a legitimate use of the police power, and not an unconstitutional interference with private property rights. The U.S. Supreme Court upheld the constitutionality of zoning in a landmark case decided in 1926 (*Village of Euclid v. Ambler Realty Co.*, 272 U.S. 365).

Nevertheless, the constitutionality of a particular land use law can still be challenged if it imposes excessive restrictions on a landowner's use of his or her property. In severe cases, an **inverse condemnation** lawsuit may be filed: the landowner sues the government, claiming that the restrictions amount to a "taking" of the property. That means that the restrictions limit development of the property to such an extent that it is equivalent to the government exercising its power of eminent domain and condemning the property for public use (see Chapter 8). As a result, the landowner argues, the government is constitutionally required to pay just compensation for the property. If the court agrees, the government will be ordered either to compensate the landowner, or to repeal or modify the land use law.

To successfully challenge a land use law, the landowner must do more than simply prove that the law has lowered the value of the property. The landowner ordinarily must prove that the law makes the property virtually useless, by preventing the only kind of development it was suited for.

Zoning

The purpose of zoning is to control and regulate growth and building in a way that serves the public's best interests. **Zoning ordinances** partition a community into areas or zones and specify those uses allowed in each zone. In this way, compatible uses are located in the same area. Zoning ordinances are detailed, specific land use laws enacted by the county or city council.

Zoning Categories. Early zoning regulations used only four categories—residential, commercial, industrial, and agricultural/rural. Today's zoning regulations are much more complicated. The four basic categories may still be used, but there are numerous subcategories as well.

A residential zone may be divided into areas for single-family housing, duplexes, apartments, condominiums, or mobile homes. Industrial zones may be divided into sections for light and heavy industry. There may even be a mixture allowed (for instance, a certain percentage of multi-family housing and commercial uses in the same zone).

In addition to specifying uses, zoning ordinances may also regulate the height, size, and shape of buildings, as well as their locations on a lot.

> **Example:** A city ordinance provides that office buildings located in a commercial area may not be more than ten stories high.

Zoning ordinances are also used to control population density, and to ensure adequate open spaces and access to air and daylight. They may even provide guidelines concerning specific matters such as vehicle parking.

> **Example:** A city ordinance allows storage of recreational vehicles (RVs) and boats only on the side or back of a lot, in a front yard if the vehicle is fully screened from view, or in an extra-long driveway.

Ordinances concerning items such as the storage of vehicles are often enforced on a complaint-only basis. For example, a property owner could probably park her RV on the street in front of her house until a neighbor complained; at that point, the city would require her to move the RV.

Zoning for Aesthetics. In many areas, there is a concern that the attractiveness of the community not be marred by developments that are ugly or cheap or simply do not fit in with the general character of the other buildings in the neighborhood.

This is a difficult area to regulate, since personal tastes vary: what one person considers beautiful might be hideous to another. However, there are certain qualities that most people can agree on. For instance, a landscaped parking lot is more attractive than one that is completely asphalt with no plants or trees in sight.

When a proposal for new development is made, it must go through a plan review process to make sure that it meets all building code and zoning requirements. Many communities now also have a design review process that assesses the aesthetic quality of the buildings and landscaping.

Exceptions to Zoning Regulations. In Washington, zoning ordinances are only adopted after a public hearing has been held. This gives members of the public the opportunity to express their opinions and to state any objections.

When an area is rezoned, there are usually at least some properties that don't comply with the new zoning restrictions, or some landowners who want to make a different use of their property than the one allowed. These conflicts are resolved by seeking exceptions to the zoning rules.

Nonconforming uses. A land use that violates current zoning but was legal prior to a zoning change is called a **nonconforming use**. Typically, the owners of nonconforming use property are not required to immediately discontinue the use, because such a require-

Fig. 11.1 A zoning map

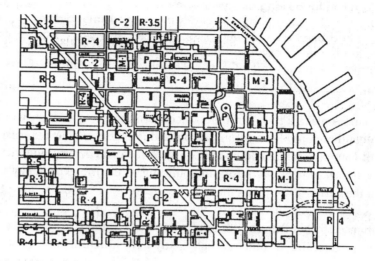

ment could be considered a "taking" of the property (and the government would then be required to compensate them). Instead, the use is permitted to continue even though it does not comply with the new or revised ordinance.

> **Example:** McGillicuddy lawfully owns and operates a bakery at the time his property is included in a rezone that changes the area to single-family residential use only. The bakery will be allowed to remain as a nonconforming use.

Although nonconforming uses are allowed to continue, they are usually subject to certain limitations or restrictions. For instance, the use may not be enlarged. (McGillicuddy can continue to run the bakery, but cannot expand or add on to the bakery.)

Also, if the use is discontinued, it cannot be resumed later on. (So if McGillicuddy closed the bakery down for a year, it could not be reopened.) However, a temporary cessation of business due to war or other causes over which the owner has no control does not constitute a discontinuance or abandonment. Most courts require proof of an intent to abandon the use.

Case Example:

The Raging River Quarry has been used as a rock quarry since about 1935. It existed prior to the adoption of the King County zoning code in 1958. The administrative department of King County determined that the quarry was a valid nonconforming use. That decision was appealed by property owners who lived near the quarry.

To qualify as a nonconforming use, the use must lawfully exist on the date specified in the zoning code. If a nonconforming use is abandoned or discontinued, the right to continue as a nonconforming use comes to an end.

It is the nature of rock quarries to operate only when there is a need for material sufficient to justify quantity production. When the need is not present, quarry operations may cease for as long as a year or more.

Just because the quarry was not actively in use at all times did not necessarily mean the quarry had been discontinued or abandoned. Instead, it was necessary to find an intent to abandon or an overt act or failure to act that carried the implication of abandonment. *Andrew v. King County*, 21 Wn. App. 566, 586 P.2d 509 (1978).

Some ordinances place a time limit on nonconforming uses. In other words, they will be allowed to continue only for a certain amount of time. So long as the time limit is reasonable, it will generally be upheld by the courts. A factor in determining reasonableness is the life expectancy of the nonconforming building. If the life expectancy of the bakery building from the earlier example is thirty years, the ordinance may require that the nonconforming use be discontinued in thirty years.

Some ordinances forbid the rebuilding of a nonconforming structure that has been destroyed by earthquake, fire, or other casualty. Any new structure built must comply with the current zoning regulations. In our example, if McGillicuddy's building burned down, a house could be built on the property, but the bakery could not be rebuilt.

Nonconforming uses usually run with the land. This means that if the property is sold, the new owner can continue the nonconforming use. However, all of the same restrictions that applied to the previous owner would also apply to the new owner. A potential purchaser of property that is a nonconforming use should check whether there is a time limit or other restrictions on enlarging or rebuilding the structures.

Variances. A **variance** permits an owner to build a structure or conduct a use not otherwise allowed. Even well-planned zoning ordinances may cause unintentional hardship to certain property owners. A variance is a built-in safety valve that gives community officials flexibility when the injury to the property owner would outweigh the benefit of strict zoning enforcement.

Where peculiarities of a specific property make it difficult or impossible to meet the zoning guidelines, a variance can be granted. Generally, a variance allows only a minor deviation from the requirements of the zoning ordinance.

> **Example:** Judith's property is located in a single-family residential zone that requires all structures to be set back at least 20 feet from the road. Judith's lot is an odd-shaped end lot. No matter how the plans are oriented, Judith finds it impossible to build her house 20 feet from the road. Judith applies for and obtains a variance to build her house only 18 feet from the road.

When a variance is sought, the proposed use must not change the essential character of the area, or reduce the value of the surrounding properties.

Case Example:

The Stromgrens owned a large, woodsy lot (36,840 square feet) in an area zoned RE (residential estate), which required a minimum lot size of 20,000 square feet.

Their home was located in one corner of the lot. They wanted to short plat the land and create a second lot. However, the zoning ordinance prohibited any change that would establish a new lot smaller than the permitted 20,000 square feet.

The Stromgrens applied for a variance, but several neighbors opposed it. The board of adjustment held two full hearings concerning the issue.

Evidence showed that the Stromgren lot was one of only four oversized corner lots in the zone. It was bounded on two sides by land zoned with a minimum lot size of only 7,300 square feet. In addition, 25 of the lots in the zone were smaller than 20,000 square feet because they were platted before the zoning ordinance. Therefore a smaller lot would not substantially change the character of the neighborhood. The Stromgrens' variance was granted. *Martel v. City of Vancouver Board of Adjustment*, 35 Wn. App. 250, 666 P.2d 916 (1983).

To obtain a variance, a property owner applies to the local zoning authority. As in the case example above, there may be an administrative hearing, which is similar to a court proceeding but less formal. Notice of the hearing is given to neighboring property owners. If the requested variance is minor and there are no objections, the hearing is perfunctory and the variance is easily granted. If the variance is a large deviation from the zoning requirements and there are objections, the hearing may be quite lengthy. Expert witnesses or neighbors may be called to testify.

In some communities, routine variances are handled by a board of adjustment, and a hearing is held only if there are objections to the requested variance.

In any case, certain factors must be present before a variance is granted. The owner must show that the zoning causes undue hardship. The hardship suffered must be that reasonable use cannot be made of the land, not simply that more money could be made by devoting the land to another use.

Personal hardship such as the owner's age or physical condition cannot justify a variance. And the hardship claimed cannot be self-created or the result of the owner's own action.

Fig. 11.2 Types of zoning exceptions

EXCEPTIONS TO ZONING REGULATIONS

- ◆ Nonconforming Use
- ◆ Variance
- ◆ Conditional Use
- ◆ Rezone

370 ■ Chapter 11

Fig. 11.3 Basic requirements for a variance

VARIANCE

- ◆ Owner must show undue hardship
- ◆ Must not change character of area
- ◆ Must not reduce value of surrounding property

Example: Johnson departs from the plans and specifications attached to his building permit and intentionally builds his house five feet closer to the road than the zoning ordinance allows. The building inspector spots the deviation. Johnson then seeks a variance.

Johnson will not be granted the variance, because it's clear that his hardship was self-created. He intentionally departed from the permitted plans. An owner cannot knowingly build a structure that does not comply with the zoning ordinance and then seek a variance.

Conditional uses. A common provision in zoning ordinances allows the zoning board to issue special permits for certain uses that are inconsistent with the designated zone, but are necessary or beneficial to the community. Such **conditional uses** (also called **special exceptions**) include schools, hospitals, churches, cemeteries, public utility structures, and parks. These uses must be located somewhere, but they are controlled to ensure proper placement in the community and limit possible adverse effects on neighboring property. Most people would be dismayed to learn that the vacant lot next door is going to be developed as a cemetery.

In contrast to the requirements for variances, evidence of hardship in developing the property is not required for a conditional use permit. However, the use must meet a specific need of the community. As long as the proposed location meets the requirements detailed in the zoning code, the owner will generally be granted a permit to construct the special use.

Case Example:

The state Department of Corrections applied for a conditional use permit for a prison work release facility in downtown Kennewick. The location was chosen in part due to its proximity to businesses that would provide employment opportunities for inmates.

Under the city's zoning laws, a conditional use permit could be issued only if the use would not be materially detrimental to the public welfare or injurious to local property or improvements. In addition, a conditional use permit for a penal institution located near facilities serving children or the elderly could be granted only if the city planning director made specific findings justifying the location, and found that the location was not detrimental to those uses.

Kennewick's city planning director found that the site conformed to the requirements of the code, and issued the permit. Neighboring property owners appealed to the city planning commission, which reversed the director's decision. The Kennewick City Council upheld the commission's reversal, stating that the fear of increased crime constituted a material detriment to the value of local businesses and properties. The Department of Corrections sought judicial review.

The court ordered the City of Kennewick to issue the conditional use permit, holding that unsubstantiated, generalized community fear was an irrelevant consideration when deciding where to build essential public facilities, and an improper basis for denying a land use permit. *DOC v. Kennewick*, 86 Wn. App. 521 (1997).

Zone changes (rezones). If a property owner believes a zoning classification is improper, a petition may be made for a **rezone**. Generally the party seeking the change is a landowner or developer who wants to make a different use of the land than is permitted under its current zoning classification. Rezones may also be initiated by the local government based on recommendations from citizens' advisory committees or planning officials.

Notice must be given to surrounding property owners and a hearing must be held before any rezone or zoning change can occur. The change must be justified by the current needs of the community; it can be made only if it makes more sense than the current zoning category and will not damage the rights of those relying on the current zoning. The community should look to its overall plan to determine what use would best serve future as well as present owners.

Case Example:

In 1964, the city of Redmond zoned an area in the Sammamish River Valley for light industrial use. Valley View Industrial Park was a general partnership formed to develop a specific parcel of land located in this zone.

During the 1970s, the farmlands preservation movement began applying pressure for agricultural zoning of the parcel. In 1977, a citizens' advisory committee was formed to make recommendations on the land use plan. The committee conducted numerous public hearings and meetings.

In September 1978, Valley View submitted a preliminary site plan for its proposed development.

In June 1979, based on the citizens' advisory committee's findings, the Redmond City Council enacted a revised zoning code that downzoned the Valley View property from light industrial to agricultural use.

Valley View filed a lawsuit claiming that the zoning change was unconstitutional or, in the alternative, that it was an uncompensated taking requiring the payment of damages.

The court found that the zoning change was unconstitutional. A property owner has a right to use property under the terms of the current zoning ordinance. This right vests or accrues at the time the building permit is applied for.

In other words, Valley View applied for approval for industrial development while the land was zoned for industrial use. If the permit application is complete and complies with the existing zoning ordinance and building codes, the developer has the right to rely on the current zoning.

Once a proper building permit is filed, the zoning classification it carries at the moment of the filing is fixed on the property. The city could no longer simply change the category. *Valley View Industrial Park v. City of Redmond*, 107 Wn.2d 621, 733 P.2d 182 (1987).

Spot zoning. Some forms of zoning changes are illegal. For instance, **spot zoning**—when one piece of property is singled out and rezoned without any clear justification for the change—is illegal.

> **Example:** A rich developer owns property in an area classified as residential. He does favors for several members of the local zoning authority, and his property alone is rezoned light industrial. (Industrial property can be much more profitable than residential property.) This type of spot zoning is illegal.

Some legitimate zone changes may appear to be spot zoning. If the zone change is based on sound planning policy and is clearly justified, the change is not illegal.

> **Example:** A new area on the outskirts of the city is zoned residential. Because residents complain about having to travel all the way into the city to find a gas station or convenience store, four corner lots in the developing neighborhood are rezoned for commercial use. This would probably be considered a justifiable reclassification.

In deciding whether or not a particular rezone is spot zoning, a court considers several factors:

- the size of the area rezoned,
- the character of the surrounding areas,
- whether the new use meets community needs or fits within the comprehensive plan, and
- whether the rezone benefits the individual owner without any corresponding benefit to the community.

Case Example:

In July 1979, Snohomish County adopted a comprehensive plan that designated the Soper Hill area as a suburban residential zone. In August 1979, the Hewlett-Packard Company proposed development of an electronic facility on the Soper Hill site. Hewlett-Packard suggested amending the comprehensive plan to provide for a business park zone.

In 1980, the county council formally enacted the plan amendment. Save Our Rural Environment (SORE), a nonprofit corporation organized to oppose the rezone, filed a lawsuit charging that the Soper Hill rezone constituted a spot zone.

In deciding to uphold the rezone, the court noted that environmental impact statements were prepared and the county planning commission conducted public hearings on the proposal. The county took traffic counts and arranged for road improvements to the area. The county also imposed certain conditions to mitigate the environmental impact on the area.

The rezone was found to bear a substantial relationship to the general welfare of the community. The court found the rezone valid and not an illegal spot zone. *Save Our Rural Environment v. Snohomish County*, 99 Wn.2d 326, 662 P.2d 816 (1983).

Enforcement of Zoning Ordinances. In Washington, zoning ordinances may be enforced by either city or county officials, depending on where the property is located. Fines or other penalties may be imposed on parties who violate zoning regulations. In addition, neighbors or the local government may bring court actions seeking to enjoin a particular use of the property.

One of the best methods for enforcing zoning regulations is the system of building codes and permits, which we'll discuss next. If a proposed use is in violation of the zoning ordinance, a building permit simply will not be granted. If construction begins without a permit, the owner and the builder may be penalized.

Building Codes and Permits

Building code regulations are intended to protect the public health and safety. Building codes are generally divided into specialized areas, such as the fire code or the plumbing code. These codes specify construction standards as well as requirements for the materials used. Building codes are usually enforced by requiring a building permit to be obtained before a building can be built, repaired, or altered.

A structure built before a new, stricter building code standard is implemented may still be required to meet the new standard.

> **Example:** A new building code regulation provides that all apartment buildings containing more than four units must have smoke detectors in each unit. The Commodore Apartments were built in 1960, long before the smoke detector requirement was initiated. Nevertheless, because the Commodore has more than four units, it must now install smoke detectors in each unit to meet the new requirement.

The building permit system allows officials to inspect building plans to verify that building codes and zoning ordinances will be complied with during construction. With luck, if there are any problems, they will be recognized at the planning stage and corrected before any of the actual construction begins.

Once construction begins, a building inspector will come and examine various phases of the construction. If there are problems noted, these problems must be resolved before construction may continue. Once the building is completed, it is inspected again. If it is found to be satisfactory, a **certificate of occupancy** is issued.

It's a good idea for real estate agents or prospective buyers to check with the building department to verify that the structures on a property have been inspected and approved, and that a certificate of occupancy has been issued. Most building departments also have records showing any improvements made to a building (such as a new roof, decks, or room additions). Some building departments have records showing where the sewer and utility lines run.

Subdivision Regulations

There are two types of subdivision regulations in Washington. The first type is concerned with the physical aspects of subdivisions, such as provisions for streets and utilities, the size of lots, and locations of schools, parks, and other community services, and these determine the procedures for subdividing and developing land. The second type of subdivision regulation is concerned with protecting the interests of consumers in real estate transactions.

Procedural Requirements. Regulations that set forth the procedures for subdividing land are adopted and administered by each county. Before subdividing, a landowner generally must notify the officials of the county where the property is located. If the property is within one mile of a city or within city limits, notice must also be given to city officials (usually the planning commission).

Notice is usually given by filing a map called a **plat**. A plat is a type of map that shows the location and boundaries of the proposed lots within the subdivision and the location of streets and public areas, and provides information about public services such as utilities, schools, and parks.

Most city and county regulations provide that a developer may not divide and sell or make improvements to the land until the proposed design of the subdivision has been approved by the planning authority. This often means that the developer must submit a preliminary plat for consideration. After any required changes or improvements have been made, the subdivider files a final plat for approval.

Subdivision regulations may control the size of the individual lots, the location of streets and sidewalks, the placing of sewer and water lines, and the presence of open spaces and recreation areas.

Washington Land Development Act. The Washington Land Development Act is a consumer protection law that applies to sales of land subdivided into 26 or more lots and sold or advertised to the general public.

Requirements. Developers are required to provide purchasers with a **public offering statement** at least two days prior to the closing of a sale of a lot. The public offering statement must include a variety of information about the developer and the development, including (but not limited to):

- the name and address of the developer and the development;
- a brief description of the permitted uses and use restrictions pertaining to the development and the purchaser's individual lot;
- the number of existing lots in the development and the maximum number of lots that may be added to the development; and
- a list of the principal common amenities in the development.

Furthermore, the public offering statement must include copies of pertinent CC&Rs, surveys, plat maps, articles of incorporation, bylaws, current or proposed budgets for any owners' association, and other important documents.

The Land Development Act also makes it unlawful to sell a lot that is subject to a blanket encumbrance unless the purchaser of the lot will obtain legal title, free and clear of the blanket encumbrance. This means that if the developer has financed the development by using all of the parcels as security for the loan, the lender must be obligated to release each individual lot from the lien when it is purchased by the individual buyer. This way, the purchasers will be able to obtain title to the individual lots free and clear of the developer's debt.

A developer's failure to comply with any of these requirements may lead to:

1. liability for actual damages,
2. an injunctive order prohibiting future sales, and
3. cancellation of any sales agreements made with purchasers who did not receive a copy of the public offering statement.

Exemptions. The Land Development Act does not apply if all of the lots in the development are at least five acres. A subdivision is also exempt if all of the lots have buildings on them or if buildings are to be constructed by the developer within two years. Finally, a subdivision that is entirely within the limits of a city is not subject to the act.

Planned Unit Developments. Some communities use **planned unit developments (PUDs)** to provide flexibility in zoning requirements. PUDs differ greatly from each other, but usually have certain characteristics in common. Generally, PUDs are larger than traditional subdivisions, and houses are clustered close together on slightly undersized lots in order to provide more open space to all of the residents.

A developer may also be able to mix residential and retail uses, single- and multi-family uses, or some other combination of uses that would not normally be permitted in one area. In return, the developer must usually provide more open space, dedicate more land to the public, or take other actions beneficial to the public welfare.

Some communities designate specific areas as PUD zones. More commonly, a floating zone system is used, which means that a PUD could be put in any area if an adequate proposal is made and approved by the community and the local zoning authority.

To get approval for a PUD, a developer must submit detailed plans of the proposed development to the planning authority. The planning authority may require additional concessions to the community before approval for the PUD is granted.

Historic Preservation

In some areas of the country, particularly older urban areas, certain buildings or districts have been designated as historical sites. This affects land use because the historical designation protects the buildings from destruction. In addition, a permit must be obtained before any significant changes can be made to the buildings.

Land Use Planning and Administration

In Washington, land use planning and administration changed dramatically with the passage of the Growth Management Act (GMA) in 1990, and its subsequent amendments. The GMA has four major goals:

1. to change Washington's previous patterns of "sprawling settlement" by concentrating new development in already existing urban growth areas;
2. to ensure adequate public facilities are available to serve all new development by requiring thorough infrastructure planning;
3. to protect critical areas from environmentally harmful activities, and to protect natural resource lands from incompatible development; and
4. to encourage regional responsibility by coordinating the plans and regulations of neighboring communities.

The GMA created a framework for land use planning, outlining the steps local governments must take to achieve the goals of the act. The GMA also contains deadlines for compliance, and it established three regional hearing boards to adjudicate disputes under the act. However, the act leaves the bulk of land use planning to the local governments themselves.

Comprehensive Plans. All states—not just Washington—have adopted legislation authorizing local governments to develop comprehensive plans. A **comprehensive plan** (sometimes referred to as a comp plan) sets forth general guidelines for development in a community, to prevent the problems caused by haphazard and unplanned growth. A comp plan addresses many issues, including building intensity, housing, sewers, roads, utilities, and transportation. Comp plans are usually developed by **planning commissions** appointed by local legislative bodies (the county council or city council).

In Washington, the land use planning objectives of the GMA are achieved using comprehensive plans. The GMA requires most counties in Washington, as well as the cities within those counties, to prepare comp plans. Other local governments may choose whether or not to prepare a plan.

Requirements. The Growth Management Act requires comprehensive plans to be:

1. internally consistent;
2. coordinated and consistent with the plans of adjacent counties and cities within a region; and
3. implemented by development regulations (such as zoning ordinances) that are consistent with those plans.

Furthermore, comprehensive plans must address a number of land use planning issues. Among other things, a comp plan must:

- include comprehensive information on required land uses, especially housing;
- address the housing needs of all economic segments of society, by providing for low-income housing, government-subsidized housing, manufactured housing, group homes, and foster care facilities;
- explore the relationship between land use and transportation, inventory current transportation facilities, forecast future transportation needs, and plan the financing of future transportation facilities;
- determine the location and distribution of various land uses, set forth the appropriate population densities and building intensities in relation to the various land uses, and project future population growth; and
- provide for the protection of ground water quality and quantity, and the management of drainage, flooding, and storm water run-off.

Generally, comprehensive plans are implemented by zoning ordinances. Local zoning ordinances can never conflict with the goals set forth in a community's comp plan. Amendments to the plan can only be considered once a year.

In a large city, in addition to a planning commission, there are often several agencies that administer the zoning ordinances and other land use laws. There may be a board of adjustment that grants variances and conditional use permits, a hearing examiner who decides quasi-judicial disputes, a board for subdivision approval, a department that issues building permits, and an enforcement division. In a small town, the town council may handle all of those matters and also serve as the planning commission.

Urban Growth Areas. The Growth Management Act requires new development to be concentrated in compact **urban growth areas** that are contiguous with presently urbanized areas. Counties and cities planning under the GMA must designate the areas to which new urban growth will be limited. Urban growth areas must consist of areas that are or will be adequately served by public facilities and services, and must contain greenbelt and open space areas. Each county's urban growth area must contain enough space to accommodate the county's projected 20-year population growth.

The resulting high density in urban growth areas minimizes the number of areas that will be developed and helps protect natural resource areas and critical areas. Using urban growth areas also helps ensure that public facilities are provided more efficiently and with less environmental damage.

Concurrency Requirement. Another important element of the Growth Management Act is its **concurrency** requirement. Under this requirement, public facilities that are adequate to serve new development must be made available when the impact of development occurs and without decreasing current service levels below certain minimum standards. This means that development cannot take place unless it is accompanied by sufficient public facilities and services.

Case Example:

In 1996, Mason County adopted a comprehensive plan and accompanying development regulations. Members of local community group filed a petition with the local Growth Management Hearings Board, challenging the plan. The board determined that the comp plan and regulations failed to comply with several GMA requirements.

First, the board found that the county had used the wrong population growth projections and had therefore allocated too much land for urban growth areas. The comp plan also provided for density levels in rural areas that were high enough to be essentially "urban in nature." These density levels would allow excessive population growth and prevent growth from concentrating in urban growth areas.

In addition, the comp plan did not meet the GMA's concurrency requirement: the comp plan used inaccurate growth projections, contained no rural transportation plan, and failed to discuss the future levels of service that would be required from major public facilities.

The board also found that the comp plan did not make adequate provisions for affordable housing and failed to identify open space areas and greenbelts.

The board ordered Mason County to re-evaluate the comp plan and regulations and bring them into compliance with the GMA. When the county appealed, the court upheld the board's order. *Diehl v. Mason County*, 94 Wn. App. 645 (1999).

Environmental Legislation

The federal and state governments have enacted environmental legislation to preserve and protect the natural environment and the health and welfare of their citizens. These laws affect land use in a number of ways.

Compensation and Liability Act (CERCLA)

The Comprehensive Environmental Response, Compensation and Liability Act is a federal law that concerns liability for environmental cleanup costs. This act is responsible for dramatically changing the way property owners view potential environmental liability.

CERCLA is well known for its creation of **Superfund**, a multibillion dollar fund used to clean up hazardous waste dumps and respond to spills of hazardous materials. CERCLA also created a process that is used to identify liable parties and make them responsible for cleanup costs.

The Environmental Protection Agency (EPA) is responsible for enforcing CERCLA. Once the EPA determines that a release of hazardous materials has occurred, it can begin remedial action. First, the EPA determines who is responsible for the release of hazardous materials. These parties, which may include present and previous landowners as well as industrial generators of waste, are referred to as "potentially responsible parties." If the potentially responsible parties fail to cooperate voluntarily in the cleanup, the EPA can begin the cleanup work itself. The EPA will then charge the cleanup costs to the responsible parties. Cleanup costs may include both the cost of cleaning up that particular property and the cost of cleaning up any neighboring property that may have been contaminated by the hazardous substances.

Liability under CERCLA is **joint and several**: any one property owner can be held responsible for the entire cost of the cleanup, regardless of the liability of any other owners. If only one owner can afford the cleanup, he or she must pay for it, and can then try to get reimbursed by the other owners.

In some cases, the current owners of contaminated property may be required to pay for the cleanup even if they did not cause the contamination. This kind of liability is referred to as **retroactive liability**, and does not depend on any findings of fault.

Model Toxics Control Act

Washington's Model Toxics Control Act (MTCA) is a state law analogous to CERCLA. Like CERCLA, MTCA imposes joint and several liability for hazardous waste cleanup on "potentially liable parties" that include past and present landowners and waste generators. Cleanup under MTCA is coordinated by the state Department of Ecology and is funded in part through taxation of hazardous materials.

Potentially liable parties may conduct cleanup without the assistance and oversight of the state, but the cleanup results must still be reported to the Department of Ecology. If the potentially liable parties do not begin cleanup voluntarily, the department may handle the cleanup and then recover up to three times the amount spent from the responsible party.

National Environmental Policy Act

The National Environmental Policy Act (NEPA) requires federal agencies to provide an **environmental impact statement** (EIS) for any action that would have a significant effect on the environment.

NEPA applies to all types of federal development, such as construction projects, the building of highways, and waste control. NEPA also applies to private actions when the use or development requires the approval of a federal agency in the form of licenses, permits, or even federal loans. In these cases, federal agencies may require submission of an EIS before approving the use or development.

An EIS should disclose the impact of the development on energy consumption, sewage systems, school population, drainage, water facilities, and other environmental, economic, and social factors.

State Environmental Policy Act

Many states have developed specific state versions of NEPA—sometimes known as "little NEPAs." Washington's "little NEPA" is the State Environmental Policy Act (SEPA). It is similar to the federal legislation in that it requires the issuance of an environmental impact statement for all acts of local and state agencies that may have a significant effect on the quality of the environment.

SEPA applies to all state and local developments and also to private developments that require the approval of state, city, or county government agencies. For instance, SEPA requirements must be met before a city or county can give approval for rezones, variances, conditional use permits, or building permits.

SEPA Procedures. When a government agency is considering its own project or whether to issue a permit for a private project, the agency must review the environmental considerations. This review is based on information found in an **environmental checklist**, which is provided by the project applicant. After reviewing the checklist, the agency decides if the project may have significant environmental effects that would require the preparation of an environmental impact statement.

If the proposal will have only a moderate or minor effect on the environment, the agency may issue a **determination of nonsignificance**. When a determination of nonsignificance is issued, additional SEPA procedures do not have to be met, and an environmental impact statement does not have to be prepared.

When the effect is deemed significant, an EIS is required. The state or local agency may prepare the statement itself. But commonly, the developer provides the necessary environmental information to the agency, or may even be involved in the actual preparation of the EIS. The agency makes its decision to approve or deny the proposed project after considering the findings in the EIS.

If a buyer is purchasing property with plans to improve it, the buyer needs to consider what impact the improvements will have on the surrounding environment. Even if the proposed development meets all zoning and building code requirements, a building permit may still be refused based on adverse information in an environmental impact statement.

Case Example:

Polygon Corporation applied for a permit to build a 13-story condominium in an area of Seattle zoned "Multiple Residence High Density." The city's building department determined that the proposed project was a major action with significant environmental impacts. An environmental impact statement was prepared.

The EIS disclosed a number of adverse impacts, including "view obstruction, excessive bulk and excessive relative scale, increases in traffic and noise, and shadow effect." The EIS also contained comments of numerous local residents who opposed the project.

The Superintendent of Buildings denied Polygon's permit application, stating that the project was inconsistent with SEPA's goals. Polygon appealed the denial, arguing that its project complied with existing zoning regulations.

The court held that since SEPA "overlays" existing local ordinances, the city could deny the permit even though the project conformed to local zoning laws. SEPA gives a municipality the discretion to deny a building permit application on the basis of adverse environmental impacts disclosed by an EIS. *Polygon Corp. v. Seattle*, 90 Wn.2d 59 (1978).

Shoreline Management Act

Washington's Shoreline Management Act protects shorelines by regulating development within 200 feet of high water marks. The act applies to coastal shorelines, to the shores of lakes larger than 20 acres, and to streams that flow at a rate in excess of 20 cubic feet per second.

Since there is so much water in the state, the Shoreline Management Act affects quite a large amount of property. Anyone purchasing shoreline property needs to consider what impact this law may have on the use they hope to make of the property.

The Shoreline Management Act requires cities and counties to adopt **shoreline master programs**. These programs regulate development in shoreline areas. The programs preempt other zoning laws that may apply to shoreline regions.

Developers of shoreline property are required to obtain a **substantial development permit** from the local city or county government before beginning any work. A development is considered "substantial" if its value exceeds $2,500, or if it would materially interfere with the normal public use of the water or shoreline.

Case Example:

Clam Shacks of America, Inc., leases approximately 1,500 acres of mud-flat tidelands in Skagit Bay, where it harvests clams. In 1983, Clam Shacks planned to begin harvesting clams with a newly developed hydraulic clam rake. The rake injects salt water into the sand, which causes the clams to break free and float to the surface.

The Skagit County Planning Department placed certain conditions on Clam Shacks concerning the use of the clam rake. Clam Shacks filed a petition seeking a determination that it was not subject to the regulatory requirements of the Shoreline Management Act or the Skagit County Shoreline Master Program because its use of the clam rake was not a "development."

The court determined that the Shoreline Management Act should be construed to provide the greatest protection to the shoreline environment and concluded that a permit may be required for an activity affecting the shoreline even though it is not a "development." *Clam Shacks of America v. Skagit County,* 45 Wn. App. 346, 725 P.2d 459 (1986).

Violation of the Shoreline Management Act may result in fines and damages. A court may also order that the shoreline be restored to its original condition—even if this means the complete removal of any buildings or improvements.

Clean Air Act

The federal Clean Air Act requires the Environmental Protection Agency (EPA) to control the emission of air pollutants that are harmful to the public health and welfare. National standards have been issued for certain pollutants. Each state is required to prepare a **state implementation plan** (SIP) for meeting the national standards.

The air quality of an area can have a significant effect on land use and development. A state must be concerned with how any new development or use of the property will affect the air quality. Refusal to grant a building permit may be based on how the proposed use would adversely affect air quality.

Developers of projects that will cause direct emissions of pollutants into the air must obtain permits from the State Department of Ecology or from regional air pollution control authorities.

Clean Water Act

The federal Clean Water Act is meant to safeguard water and prevent water pollution. Required water quality standards may affect land use by prohibiting the construction of certain industrial uses that would discharge an unacceptable level of water pollutants. Permits are required for the discharge of pollutants into a lake, stream, or other waterway.

The Clean Water Act also regulates wastewater treatment systems. It encourages local governments to investigate new technology and alternatives to the traditional sewage treatment plants. The wastewater facilities available may have a significant effect on the type and amount of new construction permitted. New construction will not be permitted in an area that does not have adequate sewage treatment facilities.

Fig. 11.4 Federal and state environmental laws

ENVIRONMENTAL REGULATIONS
CERCLA
NEPA
SEPA
Shoreline Management Act
Clean Air Act
Clean Water Act

Other Legislation

The Coastal Zone Management Act, Resource Conservation and Recovery Act, and Noise Control Act may also affect land use.

In addition, other federal and state regulations that don't immediately seem to apply to real estate may also have an effect on land use.

> **Example:** Due to a declining population in the district, an old grade school building has been closed and unused for several years. The school district is anxious to sell the building. A broker has a client who is interested in purchasing the building and turning it into offices.
>
> Unfortunately, many of the construction materials used in the building contain asbestos. The Occupational Safety and Health Act (OSHA) provides health and safety standards to protect employees in the workplace. It has set specific asbestos standards that must be met. The building cannot be approved for use as offices until the asbestos has been removed.

A real estate agent should advise his or her clients that there may be significant expenses above and beyond the price of the property. In the example above, substantial renovations may have to be made before the school can be approved and used as office space. (In addition to this concern, the broker would need to know the zoning regulations in this area. Is it zoned for office space? Most schools are located in residential areas.)

Taxation

Although taxes are not levied primarily to control land use, the tax liability that attaches to certain properties can affect their use. For instance, high taxes on farmland in an urban area may encourage or even force the owner to convert the land to nonagricultural use.

Conversely, an agricultural or forestland tax exemption may encourage a property owner to keep the land undeveloped.

There are two types of taxes on real property: general real estate taxes and special assessments.

General Real Estate Taxes

General real estate taxes are levied annually and used to support the government's general operations and services. For example, police and fire protection are usually paid for out of general tax revenues.

General real estate taxes are sometimes referred to as **ad valorem taxes** because the amount of the tax is calculated based on the value of the property. (*Ad valorem* means "according to value" in Latin.) The taxable value is periodically determined by a county assessor.

Assessing Value. In Washington, real property is valued at its "true and fair value" unless otherwise specifically provided by law. **True and fair value** means market value. In other words, how much would the property sell for if it were currently on the market? For assessment purposes, land is valued as if vacant and available for development to its highest and best use. **Highest and best use** means the use of the property that would produce the highest net return.

> **Example:** Property located in the middle of the downtown business district is used as a parking lot. The highest and best use of the lot is as a site for an office building.
>
> The property taxes are based on the lot's value to someone who wants to purchase a site for an office building—not the lot's value to someone who wants to continue operating the parking lot.

Thus, a property owner generally pays taxes based on the highest and best use of the land rather than the use to which it is actually devoted. However, the projected use must be legal and in compliance with zoning regulations and any city or county ordinances.

> **Example:** A parcel of property would be worth a great deal of money if its owner could use it as a site for an office building. However, the lot is in an area that is zoned for single-family residences.
>
> The value of the lot will be assessed according to its value as a building site for single-family homes. This is the highest and best use of the lot because it is the only use permitted under current zoning regulations.

The value of improvements to property (such as office buildings, houses, etc.) is assessed separately from the value of the land.

> **Example:** A residential property is assessed for tax purposes. The lot is valued at $80,000; the house itself is valued at $100,000. Thus, the total assessed value of the property is $180,000.

Exceptions. Some specific types of property are not taxed at their highest and best use. For example, the Washington legislature has decided that it is in the best interest of the state to maintain and preserve open space for the production of food, fiber, and forest crops, and to assure the use and enjoyment of natural resources and scenic beauty for the well-being of its citizens.

To help preserve these open spaces, the state has provided that open space will be taxed on the basis of its current use rather than its highest and best use. For instance, if agricultural property is used for farming but is located in an area that is experiencing suburban growth, the land will be taxed on its value as agricultural property, not its value as if subdivided for residential use.

The legislature has also declared that it is in the public interest to encourage the preservation of historic landmarks. Therefore it has provided a special tax valuation for improvements to historic property.

Exemptions. Certain types of property are exempt from general real estate taxes. Some of the most important exemptions include publicly owned property, church property, cemeteries, property owned by nonprofit organizations and veterans' organizations, libraries, heath care facilities, schools, and museums.

Tax Amounts. In Washington, the total amount of all general taxes on real and personal property in any year cannot exceed 1% of the true and fair value of the property. (This limit does not apply to port district or public utility district levies, or to special levies voted for by the people.)

In most taxing districts the rate is set at a certain number of dollars per thousand dollars of value. That rate is then applied to the assessed value of each taxpayer's property.

Collection of Taxes. Tax bills are usually mailed in the middle of February. Payment of one-half of the tax is due on April 30 and the balance is due on October 31.

Special Assessments

Special assessments (also called **improvement taxes**) are levied to pay for public improvements that benefit specific pieces of property. These taxes are usually a one-time expense to pay for particular improvements, such as installing street lights or sewers.

Only those pieces of property that benefit from the improvement are taxed. The theory behind this rule is that the value of these properties will increase because of the improvements, so the property owners should bear the cost of the improvements.

Case Example:

Samis owned over 200 platted, undeveloped lots in Soap Lake. The city imposed an annual $60 "standby" charge on any vacant, unimproved land that abuts but is not connected to a water or sewer line. Samis challenged the fee as an unconstitutional property tax. The city argued the charge was a regulatory fee assessed in exchange for benefits conferred.

Based on the following considerations, the court held that the charge was an illegal property tax. First, the primary purpose of the charge was to raise revenue and not to regulate the fee payers. Second, the collected funds were not segregated and used to benefit the parties being assessed, but rather were used to pay the cost of general utility improvements. And last, there was no relationship between the fee charged and any service received by the lots.

The $60 charge therefore constituted a property tax. Because the tax was imposed selectively and without regard to property value, it was unconstitutional. *Samis Land Co. v. Soap Lake*, 143 Wn.2d 798 (2001).

Private Restrictions

So far this chapter has discussed only governmental or public restrictions on land use. However, there may also be private restrictions on a property. Private restrictions are agreements between a seller and a buyer or between neighbors. Private restrictions are usually found in the deed to the property, and they generally run with the land. If the land is transferred or sold, the new owner is also bound by the restrictions.

Covenants and Conditions

Private restrictions may be either covenants or conditions. A **covenant** is a promise to do or not do something. A **condition** in a deed places a restriction on the owner's title. A condition is much more serious than a covenant: a breach of a condition can result in forfeiture of the owner's title through a reversion clause (see Chapter 3).

Since forfeiture is an extremely harsh punishment, if there is any ambiguity in the wording of the clause, a court will usually construe a restriction as a covenant rather than a condition. Almost all private restrictions (especially those found in subdivision restrictions) are covenants.

The violation of a covenant can lead to a court order requiring compliance with the covenant, or a judgment for money damages. Failure to abide by the court order can result in punishment for contempt of court, which is usually time spent in jail.

Example: Leonard purchased a home with a view overlooking Lake Sammamish. All building lots in this subdivision were bound by a restrictive covenant stating that no structure should exceed one story in height, except that the architectural control committee could grant a special variance if the proposed building or addition would not restrict the view for others within the area.

Leonard built a one-story house. Several years later he added a second story addition that blocked his neighbor Winston's view of the lake. Winston brought a lawsuit requesting that his view be restored.

Leonard argued that Winston was only entitled to money damages. The court determined that a view is a unique asset for which a monetary value is very difficult to determine. Winston testified that one of the main reasons he bought this particular house was because of the view.

Leonard was required to remodel or remove the addition in its entirety so as to restore Winston's view.

Termination of Restrictions

Most restrictive covenants have no time limit and may be enforced indefinitely. However, some restrictive covenants include a time limit. If a covenant contains a time limit, the covenant simply terminates at the end of the specified time period.

A few states impose time limits on restrictive covenants even if no time limit is specified in the covenant itself. For example, in New York private restrictions terminate automatically after thirty years, unless formally renewed. However, Washington and most other states impose no time limitations.

A restrictive covenant may also terminate by abandonment.

Example: A developer planned to create a residential subdivision and placed a restrictive covenant in some of the deeds. Then the developer's plans changed and the remaining portions of the subdivision were used for commercial buildings. The restrictive covenant for residential use was abandoned.

Similarly, a restrictive covenant may no longer be enforceable if the nature of the restricted neighborhood has changed.

Example: All of the deeds in a particular neighborhood contained a restrictive covenant restricting the properties to residential use. Over the years, however, several other uses crept in.

Now the neighborhood includes a gas station, a convenience store, and several restaurants. A property owner would have difficulty enforcing the restrictive covenant because the neighborhood has changed so much. The covenant may be deemed inoperative because it is no longer appropriate or suited to the neighborhood.

Subdivision Restrictions

Probably the most common example of private land use regulation is the list of restrictions placed by a subdivider on lots within a subdivision. The restrictions may be referred to as a **declaration of restrictions** or as **CC&Rs** (covenants, conditions, and restrictions).

Subdivision restrictions usually cover matters such as the permitted uses of the property (e.g., single-family detached dwellings for residential use only), and may specify items such as minimum square footage, maximum height, setback requirements, and permitted exterior materials. They may also address aesthetic concerns, such as limiting overnight parking on the streets, and may even limit the types of pets or other animals the property owners may keep.

> **Example:** Although all the lots in a particular subdivision are at least one acre, the CC&Rs prohibit property owners from keeping horses on their property, because the neighborhood is essentially residential rather than rural in character.

> **Example:** A particular subdivision in the Snoqualmie Valley consists of two- to four-acre lots, and many families keep horses and small farm animals on their properties for their own enjoyment. However, the CC&Rs prohibit property owners from keeping animals for commercial purposes. One property owner decided to operate an ostrich farm on the property, keeping ten to twenty ostriches on the land and selling their eggs and offspring.
>
> Several other property owners sued the ostrich farmers, claiming that the nine-foot birds were nuisances (because of the resulting odor and noise) and a violation of the CC&Rs.
>
> Even though ostrich farming in this area does not violate any zoning ordinance, health laws, or other public regulations, the property owners will probably have to give up their ostriches to comply with the CC&Rs in effect in the neighborhood.

General Plans. Often subdividers or other land developers devise a general plan for uniformity among all of the lots in the development. The most common way of setting up restrictions in this type of development is with a recorded plat or map of the area that lists all of the uniform restrictions that will apply to every lot. The individual deed to each lot then states that the lot is subject to the restrictions in the recorded plat. The recorded restrictions are incorporated by reference in each individual deed, and the title conveyed is subject to those restrictions.

Enforcement. If there is a general plan, any lot owner may enforce the restrictions in the plan against any other owner. Some developers create a homeowners association made up of the lot owners. The association has the right to enforce the restrictions or bring a lawsuit if the restrictions are violated.

> **Example:** The CC&Rs of a subdivision imposed strict aesthetic requirements on the property owners. The owners of one home repainted it mauve and eggplant. The subdivision homeowners association insisted that they repaint the house in more traditional colors. The owners refused, claiming the mauve and eggplant color scheme was contemporary, yet tasteful. The homeowners association sued the owners and won, forcing them to repaint their house.

Restrictions that violate public policy will not be enforced. For example, a restriction prohibiting the sale of the property to members of a particular race or religion is unenforceable.

Any doubts about the meaning or application of a restriction are usually resolved in favor of the free use of the land, rather than a more restrictive use.

Conclusion

Private property is subject to a considerable variety of public restrictions. Before developing or building on their property, landowners may have to comply with subdivision regulations or environmental laws. Owners also cannot use their property or build on it in a way that violates zoning or building codes, and they have to pay property taxes.

In addition to the government regulations that affect a property, there may be private restrictions. Prospective property buyers should always make sure that there are no restrictions prohibiting the use they plan to make of the property.

Case Problem

The following is a hypothetical case problem. Most of the facts are taken from a real case. Based on what you have learned from this chapter, make a decision on the issues presented, and then check to see if your answer matches the court's decision.

The Facts

The Wilhelms owned a lot in a residential subdivision that was partially surrounded by adjoining lots. In 1980, the Wilhelms began construction of an enclosure for their swimming pool so that it could be used year-round. The back portion of the enclosure was less than 15 feet from the rear property line.

The enclosure was sided with cedar drop siding the same color as the siding on the house, with windows, doors, and trim similar to the house. It was entered through a recreation room in the house, with no separation between the house and the pool enclosure.

The Wilhelms filed an application and received a building permit for an addition to their home.

The Dixons and the Whites (neighbors of the Wilhelms) objected to the construction of the pool enclosure and claimed that it violated the subdivision covenants.

When the subdivision was developed in 1962, the developers filed an instrument containing residential area covenants. They also formed an architectural control committee to approve building plans prior to construction, but by 1980 the committee had not functioned for several years.

The neighbors claimed that building the swimming pool enclosure violated the following three covenants:

1. No building shall be erected other than one detached single-family dwelling and a private garage.
2. No building shall be erected until the construction plans and specifications have been approved by the architectural control committee.
3. No dwelling shall be located on any interior lot closer than 15 feet to the rear lot line.

The Questions

Was the construction of the pool enclosure a violation of the restrictive covenants? Should the structure be allowed to remain?

The Answer

The pool enclosure did not violate restriction number one, because it was not a separate building. An addition to a home does not violate a restrictive covenant against building more than one building on the lot.

The pool enclosure was technically a violation of restriction number two, which required approval by the architectural control committee before building. However, the committee had not been operating for several years. If a covenant is habitually and substantially violated so as to create the impression that it has been abandoned, it will not be enforced.

In this particular case, it was pointed out that the Whites and the Dixons had also violated this covenant. The Dixons' house was actually built without approval of the committee, and the Whites had altered a deck and added a storage shed without approval of the committee. Someone who has violated a building restriction cannot enforce the same restriction against others.

The court decided that restriction number three was ambiguous because it did not define an "interior lot." The Wilhelms' lot was only partially surrounded by adjoining lots. Any doubts about restrictions should be resolved in favor of the free use of land.

In this case, the Wilhelms' pool enclosure was allowed to remain. *White v. Wilhelm*, 34 Wn. App. 763, 665 P.2d 407 (1983).

Chapter Summary

- Police power is the power a state has to adopt and enforce laws and regulations necessary to protect the public. This includes planning, zoning, and taxation.

- The purpose of zoning ordinances is to implement a community's comprehensive plan, control and regulate growth, and promote the health, safety, morals, and general welfare of the inhabitants of the community.

- A nonconforming use is a use that was already legally in place when a new zoning ordinance came into effect, and which does not comply with the requirements of the new ordinance. Nonconforming uses are generally allowed to remain but may be subject to certain restrictions.

- A variance is a permit to build a structure or conduct a use that would not otherwise be allowed. In order to receive a variance, a property owner must show undue hardship.

- Conditional use or special exception permits are generally granted for schools, hospitals, churches, cemeteries, public utility structures, and parks.

- If a property owner believes a zoning classification is incorrect, a rezone or zone change may be requested. However, spot zoning—a change in zone category for a single piece of property without clear justification—is illegal.

- The purpose of building codes is to protect the public health and safety. A building permit must be granted before construction can begin. Once a building is completed, it must be inspected and a certificate of occupancy issued.

- The purpose of the Growth Management Act is to concentrate development into already existing urban growth areas, help protect environmentally critical areas and natural resource areas, and increase the efficiency of community transportation, services, and utilities. The GMA requires most counties and cities in Washington to conduct land use planning and administration using comprehensive plans.

- Taxation of real property can have an effect on land use by promoting or discouraging certain uses of property based on the tax levied on different uses. Most real estate is taxed based on the assessed value of its highest and best use. However, there are some exceptions and exemptions.

- Significant environmental legislation that affects land use includes the National Environmental Policy Act, State Environmental Policy Act, Shoreline Management Act, Clean Air Act, Clean Water Act, Model Toxics Control Act, and CERCLA.

- Most private restrictions are covenants rather than conditions. Subdividers commonly impose restrictions (CC&Rs) on the entire subdivision. Violation of private restrictions may result in a court order to comply or a judgment for money damages.

Checklist of Problem Areas

Real Estate Licensee's Checklist

❑ Agents should check the zoning of all listed property. Some brokerage offices have copies of local zoning maps and regulations available.

❑ A potential buyer tells you what he or she wants to do with the property. Is this use compatible with the zone the property is located in?

❑ Has the property been designated as a historical site? If so, it could be protected from destruction and a permit would have to be obtained before any significant changes could be made to the building. Is your potential purchaser aware of this?

❑ If there were subdivision restrictions when the subdivision was first created, are they still in force?

Buyer's Checklist

❑ What type of zone is the property you're considering buying located in? Is the character of the neighborhood consistent with the zoning ordinance?

❑ Are there any private restrictions on the property, such as deed restrictions or CC&Rs?

❑ If you are planning to develop the property, will your proposed development be allowed in this area? Not only do you need to check the zoning guidelines, but you must also consider whether the development will have any adverse impact on the environment. Will it affect air and water quality, traffic patterns, noise levels, etc.?

❑ Will the property be regulated by the Shoreline Management Act? If you decide to build on or otherwise develop the property, will you be able to obtain a shoreline substantial development permit, or could your proposed development be refused?

Chapter Quiz

1. Which of the following has the power to regulate and restrict the use of private property?

    a. The federal government
    b. State governments
    c. Local (city or county) governments
    d. All of the above

2. An area of the city has recently been rezoned residential. John McAllister has been operating a retail upholstery shop in this zone. He will be allowed to continue using his property for commercial purposes. This is known as a:

    a. variance
    b. nonconforming use
    c. spot zone
    d. conditional use

3. In order to be granted a variance, you must show:

    a. that the proposed use will result in a financial benefit
    b. that the proposed use will change the character of the area
    c. that a hardship will be suffered if the variance is not granted
    d. All of the above

4. A wealthy, philanthropic landowner owns property in a residential area. He is a member of the First Presbyterian Church and wants to build a new church building on the lot as a charitable gift to the church. Will he be allowed to build the church on this lot?

    a. No, because it is zoned residential
    b. Yes, if he is granted a conditional use permit
    c. No, he will not be granted a variance, since he has suffered no true hardship
    d. Yes, because it is a nonconforming use

5. Johnson owns property in a large commercial zone. His property alone is rezoned for industrial use, and he builds a lucrative industrial plant on the property. This is an example of:

    a. a spot zone
    b. a variance
    c. justified zone modification
    d. comprehensive planning

6. Subdivision regulations may control:

    a. lot size
    b. location of streets and sidewalks
    c. provisions for public services such as utilities
    d. All of the above

7. Generally, comprehensive plans are implemented by:

    a. inverse condemnation
    b. variances
    c. building codes
    d. zoning ordinances

8. A planned unit development (PUD):

    a. is generally smaller than most subdivisions
    b. usually places houses on larger than average lots
    c. generally clusters houses close together on undersized lots
    d. may only be located in a commercial zone

9. One of the main methods of enforcing zoning ordinances is:

    a. through the use of building permits
    b. by bringing criminal charges for violations
    c. neighborhood watch programs
    d. None of the above

10. A new addition to the plumbing code requires the use of non-lead pipes in daycare facilities because of the harmful effects of lead on children. The Kiddie Care Center has been located in the Hansen Building for 15 years. The Hansen Building has lead pipes. The Kiddie Care Center:

    a. doesn't have to comply with this requirement because the plumbing code only applies to new buildings
    b. may be required to meet the new standard
    c. is not the only tenant in the Hansen Building, so the plumbing code requirement does not apply
    d. must have non-lead pipes to meet the new standard within 90 days

11. Once a building is completed, if a building inspector finds it satisfactory:

    a. a building permit will be issued
    b. a certificate of occupancy will be issued
    c. an environmental impact statement will be prepared
    d. None of the above

12. General real estate taxes:

    a. are also called ad valorem taxes
    b. are assessed annually
    c. often pay for police and fire protection
    d. All of the above

13. In Washington, the value of agricultural property is assessed for tax purposes:

    a. based on its current use
    b. every six months
    c. based on its highest and best use
    d. None of the above

14. Under the State Environmental Policy Act (SEPA):

    a. every building project must submit an environmental impact statement
    b. environmental impact statements are only required for state or federal projects
    c. no environmental impact statement is required if there has been a determination of nonsignificance
    d. None of the above

15. If there is ambiguity in the wording of a private restriction, a court will usually construe the restriction as a:

    a. covenant rather than a condition because a condition can result in forfeiture
    b. covenant rather than a condition because a covenant can result in forfeiture
    c. condition rather than a covenant because a condition can result in forfeiture
    d. condition rather than a covenant because a covenant can result in forfeiture

12 Civil Rights and Fair Housing

Outline

Key Terms

- Civil Rights Act of 1866
- Federal Fair Housing Act
- Mrs. Murphy exemption
- blockbusting
- steering
- redlining
- reasonable accommodations and modifications
- Dept. of Housing and Urban Development (HUD)

- Equal Credit Opportunity Act
- Home Mortgage Disclosure Act
- Americans with Disabilities Act
- public accommodation
- readily achievable modification

- Washington Law Against Discrimination
- Washington Fairness in Lending Act
- disparate impact
- compensatory damages
- punitive damages
- testers

Chapter Overview

Many federal and state civil rights and fair housing laws prohibit discrimination, and these laws apply to sellers and buyers, landlords and tenants, and real estate agents. Real estate agents charged with violating antidiscrimination laws could have their licenses suspended or revoked, and could also be subject to a lawsuit.

This chapter discusses the most important federal and Washington state antidiscrimination laws that apply to real estate transactions, including the fair housing laws that govern the day-to-day relationships of residential real estate agents and their clients and customers.

State Action vs. Private Action

The first federal civil rights laws in the U.S. were passed more than 125 years ago. These laws were originally interpreted to forbid discrimination only if it involved "state action"—action by federal, state, or local government entities or officials. For instance, if a city law prohibited loitering, but only African-Americans were arrested for loitering (even though white people were doing exactly the same thing), the police could be accused of discrimination. Examples of discriminatory state action include discriminatory laws and regulations, discriminatory enforcement of the law by police or courts, and court orders to enforce discriminatory private covenants or restrictions.

Case Example:

A party brought suit to enforce private covenants that restricted ownership of property based on race and/or religion. The Supreme Court held that it was unconstitutional to enforce such restrictive covenants. The covenants themselves were not unlawful, but the government could not enforce them (by issuing orders prohibiting their violation or by hearing lawsuits for damages based on their violation). That would be discriminatory state action. *Shelley v. Kraemer,* 334 U.S. 1 (1948).

In the last few decades, the courts and legislatures have extended antidiscrimination laws to purely private acts, as well as state action. The right to buy or lease property can be impaired just as effectively by sellers or landlords as by the state or local government. It is now unlawful to include discriminatory covenants in deeds or other documents, to honor or attempt to honor similar provisions in existing documents, or for county recorders to even record documents containing such covenants.

As you read the following discussion of federal discrimination laws, keep in mind that Washington state laws are often stricter than federal laws, prohibiting more types of discrimination in more transactions and with fewer exceptions. It is always the stricter law that must be followed, so you should treat the material covering exemptions from the Federal Fair Housing Act as general background information, recognizing that for the most part, those exemptions do not exist under Washington law.

Federal Laws

The eradication of discrimination began on the federal level with the Thirteenth and Fourteenth Amendments to the Constitution. These amendments, passed after the Civil War, abolished slavery and guaranteed equal protection under the law.

Federal laws prohibiting discrimination include the Civil Rights Act of 1866, Title VIII of the Civil Rights Act of 1968 (usually referred to as the Federal Fair Housing Act), the Equal Credit Opportunity Act, and the Home Mortgage Disclosure Act. For the most part, these laws are based on the Thirteenth and Fourteenth Amendments.

Civil Rights Act of 1866

Suppose Mr. and Mrs. Jones try to buy a home in a subdivision. Their offer is refused because they are African-American. What can Mr. and Mrs. Jones do? What can the agent who is representing the Joneses do? What kind of liability, if any, would the sellers have? The agent of the sellers?

The Civil Rights Act of 1866 prohibits discrimination based on race or ancestry in any property transaction in the United States. The act states, ". . . all citizens of the United States shall have the same right, in every state and territory as is enjoyed by white citizens thereof to inherit, purchase, lease, sell, hold and convey real and personal property."

Application. The 1866 Civil Rights Act contains no exceptions and applies to all property, whether real or personal, residential or commercial, improved or unimproved. However, this act applies only to discrimination based on race or ancestry.

The constitutionality of the 1866 Act was challenged in a landmark case decided by the U.S. Supreme Court just a few weeks after Congress passed the 1968 Civil Rights Act.

Landmark Case:

Mr. and Mrs. Joseph Jones tried to buy a home, or to have one built for them, in a subdivision being developed by the Mayer Company near St. Louis. When their offer was refused, they brought suit against the Mayer Company based on the 1866 Civil Rights Act, claiming the refusal was evidence of racial discrimination. The court ruled in favor of the Joneses and held that the 1866 Act was constitutional. *Jones v. Alfred H. Mayer Co.*, 392 U.S. 409 (1968).

This court decision established three important precepts:

1. The 1866 Act prohibits all racial discrimination in the sale and rental of property, whether through private or state action, because the right to buy or lease property can be impaired as effectively by those who place property on the market as by state or local governments.
2. The act is constitutional under the Thirteenth Amendment to the U.S. Constitution. This amendment abolished slavery and also gave Congress the power to enforce the amendment through appropriate legislation.

   The 1866 Civil Rights Act is "appropriate legislation." The Thirteenth Amendment was intended to eliminate not only slavery but also the various conditions and aspects associated with slavery, often referred to as "badges of slavery." One of these "badges" was the inability to own or exchange property. Therefore, it was proper for Congress to eliminate this badge of slavery through legislation authorized by the Thirteenth Amendment.
3. The provisions of the 1866 Act are independent of and not superseded by the 1968 Civil Rights Act. The Court noted that the 1866 Act is not a comprehensive fair housing law. It does not address discrimination on grounds other than race or ancestry; it does not deal with discrimination in services or facilities connected with housing, financing, advertising, or brokerage services; and it does not provide for any federal agency to assist aggrieved parties or for intervention by the attorney general. The 1866 Act is a general statute, enforceable only by private parties bringing their own private lawsuits.

In contrast, the Fair Housing Act of 1968 is a detailed housing law covering a great variety of discriminatory practices and enforceable by the complete range of federal authorities.

Enforcement. You are a real estate agent representing a party whose offer is rejected because of her race. What remedies does she have?

The injured party can bring a lawsuit against the seller. Anyone who is unlawfully discriminated against under the 1866 Act may bring a lawsuit in federal district court. The federal law does not specify a time limit for filing an action, so the lawsuit must be filed within the time limit specified by state law for similar claims.

Fig. 12.1 Civil Rights Act of 1866

CIVIL RIGHTS ACT OF 1866
In property transactions, prohibits discrimination based on: **Race or Ancestry**
Exceptions: **None**

If the plaintiff wins the discrimination suit, the following remedies are available:

- injunctive relief,
- actual damages, and
- punitive damages.

Injunctive relief is a court order requiring the defendant to do or refrain from doing a particular act. For example, the court might order the owner to sell the house to the plaintiff.

Actual (compensatory) damages is a money award that will compensate the plaintiff for the damages caused by the discrimination. This may include out-of-pocket expenses (such as rent or transportation payments) or compensation for emotional distress. In some cases, awards for actual damages can total thousands of dollars, and in exceptional cases even hundreds of thousands of dollars.

Punitive damages are intended to punish the wrongdoer and discourage others from engaging in similar behavior. There is no limit to the amount of punitive damages that may be awarded for claims brought under the 1866 Act. In some cases, punitive damage awards have exceeded $100,000.

The Federal Fair Housing Act

Another federal act prohibiting discrimination is Title VIII of the Civil Rights Act of 1968 (referred to as the Federal Fair Housing Act), which states: "It is the policy of the United States to provide, within constitutional limitations, for fair housing throughout the United States."

The act prohibits discrimination based on **race**, **color**, **national origin**, **religion**, **sex**, **handicap, or familial status** (families with children) in the sale or lease of residential property or vacant land intended to be used for residential purposes. The law also prohibits discrimination in advertising, lending, real estate brokerage, and certain other services in connection with residential transactions.

Application. Most sales, rentals, and exchanges of residential property are covered by the act. Unless specifically exempt, the law covers transactions involving:

1. any building or structure, or portion of a building or structure that is occupied as, or designed or intended to be occupied as, a residence; and,
2. vacant land offered for sale or lease for the construction of any building(s) or portion(s) of building(s) to be used for residential purposes.

Exemptions. Although the act covers the majority of residential transactions, it does contain several specific exemptions. The provisions regarding discrimination based on familial status generally don't apply to retirement communities. And there are strictly limited exemptions for persons owning up to three homes, owner-occupants of small rental properties, private clubs, and religious, educational, and charitable organizations. Here are the details of those exemptions:

1. The law doesn't apply to a single-family home sold or rented by a private individual owner, provided that:
   - the owner owns no more than three such homes,
   - no discriminatory advertising is used, and
   - no real estate broker (or anyone else in the business of selling or renting homes) is employed.

   If the owner is not the occupant or most recent occupant, he or she may use this exemption only once every 24 months.

2. The law doesn't apply to the rental of a room or unit in a dwelling with up to four units, provided that:
   - the owner occupies one unit as his or her residence,
   - no discriminatory advertising is used, and
   - no real estate broker is employed.

   This is sometimes referred to as the **Mrs. Murphy exemption.**

3. In dealing with their own property in noncommercial transactions, religious organizations or societies or affiliated nonprofit organizations may limit occupancy to or give preference to their own members, provided that membership isn't restricted on the basis of race, color, or national origin.

4. Private clubs with lodgings that aren't open to the public and that aren't operated for a commercial purpose may limit occupancy to or give preference to their own members.

These limited exemptions apply very rarely. Remember, the 1866 Civil Rights Act prohibits discrimination based on race or ancestry in any property transaction, regardless of any exemptions available under the Fair Housing Act. Also, there is no exemption for any transaction involving a real estate licensee. Finally, and most importantly for Washington residents, these exemptions do not exist at all under Washington law. The Washington Law Against Discrimination has no exemptions.

Fig. 12.2 Fair Housing poster

U.S. Department of Housing and Urban Development

**EQUAL HOUSING
OPPORTUNITY**

We Do Business in Accordance With the Federal Fair Housing Law

(The Fair Housing Amendments Act of 1988)

> # It is Illegal to Discriminate Against Any Person Because of Race, Color, Religion, Sex, Handicap, Familial Status, or National Origin

- In the sale or rental of housing or residential lots
- In advertising the sale or rental of housing
- In the financing of housing

- In the provision of real estate brokerage services
- In the appraisal of housing
- Blockbusting is also illegal

Anyone who feels he or she has been discriminated against may file a complaint of housing discrimination:
 1-800-669-9777 (Toll Free)
 1-800-927-9275 (TDD)

U.S. Department of Housing and Urban Development
Assistant Secretary for Fair Housing and Equal Opportunity
Washington, D.C. 20410

Previous editions are obsolete

form HUD-928.1A(8-93)

Prohibited Acts. Under the Federal Fair Housing Act, the following acts are unlawful if based upon race, color, religion, sex, national origin, handicap, or familial status:

1. refusing to rent or sell residential property after receiving a bona fide offer;
2. refusing to negotiate for the sale or rental of residential property;

3. any action that would make residential property unavailable or deny it to any person (under this general clause, actions such as **steering** and **redlining** are prohibited, as well as many other discriminatory practices and marketing methods);

4. discriminating in the terms or conditions of any sale or rental of residential property or in providing any services or facilities in connection with such property;

5. discriminatory advertising or any other notice that indicates a limitation or preference or intent to make any limitation, preference, or discrimination;

6. making any representation that property is not available for inspection, sale, or rent when it is in fact available;

7. inducing or attempting to induce, for profit, any person to sell or rent property based on representations regarding entry into the neighborhood of persons of a particular race, color, religion, sex, or national origin (**blockbusting**);

8. discrimination by a commercial lender in making a loan for buying, building, repairing, improving, or maintaining a dwelling, or in the terms of such financing;

9. denying access to a multiple listing service or any similar real estate broker's organization or discriminating in the terms or conditions for access to the organization;

10. coercing, intimidating, threatening, or interfering with anyone on account of his or her enjoyment, attempt to enjoy, or encouragement or assistance to others in enjoying the rights granted by the Fair Housing Act.

Three terms that frequently arise in discussions of fair housing and fair lending laws are:

*   steering,
*   blockbusting, and
*   redlining.

Steering. The term **steering** refers to the channeling of prospective buyers or renters to specific neighborhoods, based on race or other protected classes. For instance, white customers might be shown homes only in white neighborhoods and black customers shown homes only in black neighborhoods.

> **Example:** In some areas, it used to be a widespread practice to code listing agreements with an "X" or some other mark to indicate that the home could be shown to African-American prospects.

Case Example:

One real estate brokerage used a separate phone number when advertising properties located in African-American neighborhoods. The person answering the phone could tell if the call was coming in on the special line, and could direct the caller to one of the African-American agents working in the office. *U.S. v. Real Estate One*, 433 F. Supp. 1140 (E.D. Mich. 1977).

In most states, a real estate agent's good faith answer to a buyer's question about the neighborhood's composition (racial, ethnic, religious, etc.) would not violate antidiscrimination laws if there was no intent to discriminate. However, an agent cannot direct or advise a buyer to buy or not buy based on the neighborhoods' racial or ethnic composition.

Example: The following statements could be construed as steering:

"You probably wouldn't be interested in looking at that house; it's in a Latino neighborhood."

"You wouldn't want to buy in this area, since it's a changing neighborhood."

Since it's difficult to prove or deny discriminatory intent, an agent should avoid all statements regarding the racial or ethnic composition of a neighborhood.

Blockbusting. The act of blockbusting, or panic selling, occurs when someone (such as a real estate agent) predicts the entry of minorities into a neighborhood and forecasts lower property values, higher crime rates, a decline in schools, or some other undesirable consequence. As a result of these statements, panicked property owners list and sell their property in a hurry, often at reduced prices. This allows the person making the statements to make a quick profit on the transactions.

Many blockbusting "techniques" commonly practiced have been cited in various court cases, including:

- passing out literature stating that a member of a minority group has purchased a home nearby;
- "wrong number" phone calls where the callers indicate that they thought they were calling "the black family that just moved in";
- obtaining numerous listings in the area and placing "For Sale" signs on the properties, in an effort to frighten local residents into selling;
- purchasing a home in the area and then selling it on contract to a minority buyer in order to frighten local residents into selling;
- telling owners that the influx of minorities will adversely affect the schools; and
- implying that homes in the neighborhood are being sold to minorities and that the police will no longer be able to patrol the area effectively.

These are particularly egregious examples of blockbusting. Of course, more subtle blockbusting methods must not be practiced or condoned either.

Redlining. A lender's refusal to make loans on property located in a particular neighborhood will be considered **redlining** if the refusal is for discriminatory reasons. Many lenders used to assume that property values in any predominantly African-American or integrated neighborhood were automatically declining. They would then refuse to make loans in those neighborhoods. Frequently, this was a self-fulfilling prophecy. The inability to obtain purchase or renovation loans made it difficult to sell, maintain, or improve homes in the neighborhood, which caused property values to decline.

Lenders may still refuse to lend money for a property in a neighborhood where values are declining. However, the refusal must be based on objective, economic criteria concerning the condition and value of the property and surrounding neighborhood, without regard to the racial composition of the neighborhood. A lender may not simply equate a minority or integrated neighborhood with declining values.

Reasonable accommodations and modifications. An important element of the Fair Housing Act is its inclusion of handicapped persons as a protected class. The act requires landlords to permit reasonable accommodations or modifications necessary for a handicapped person to fully use and enjoy a housing unit.

Under the act's **reasonable accommodations** requirement, it is unlawful to refuse to make reasonable accommodations in rules, policies, practices, or services if such accommodations are necessary for a handicapped person to have an equal opportunity to use and enjoy a housing unit. This requirement applies to public and common use areas as well as individual living areas.

> **Example:** Bonnie is blind and uses a seeing eye dog. She applies to live in an apartment building that does not allow pets. The landlord must allow Bonnie to keep her seeing eye dog because the dog is necessary for Bonnie to have an equal opportunity to use and enjoy the apartment.

Under the Fair Housing Act's **reasonable modifications** requirement, a landlord must permit a handicapped person to make reasonable modifications to existing housing if such modifications are necessary for the handicapped person's full enjoyment. The tenant may be required to pay for the modifications. The landlord may also require the tenant to return the premises to its original condition, as long as it is reasonable to do so.

> **Example:** A family moves into an apartment and finds that the bathroom doorway is too narrow for their daughter's wheelchair. They ask the landlord for permission to widen the doorways, at their expense. This is a reasonable modification and landlord must allow it. The landlord cannot require the family to change the doorway back when they move out, unless the wider doorway somehow interferes with the landlord's or future tenant's use and enjoyment of the apartment.

Enforcement. An individual unlawfully discriminated against under the Fair Housing Act may file a complaint with the Office of Equal Opportunity (OEO) of the Department of Housing and Urban Development (HUD), or may file a lawsuit in federal or state court. HUD may also file a complaint on its own initiative. A complaint must be filed with HUD within one year of the discriminatory conduct; a lawsuit must be brought within two years.

If a complaint is filed with HUD, agency employees will negotiate for "voluntary" compliance. If that is unsuccessful, the case will be decided by HUD or by a federal district

Fig. 12.3 Fair Housing Act

FEDERAL FAIR HOUSING ACT
Prohibits discrimination based on race, color, religion, sex, handicap, or national origin, or against families with children

Exemptions:
 1. Single-family home sold/rented by owner if:
    a. owner owns no more than three homes
    b. no discriminatory advertising
    c. no real estate agent
    If owner is not the most recent occupant, only one transaction every 24 months.
 2. Mrs. Murphy Exemption
 3. Religious groups preferring their own members
 4. Private clubs preferring their own members
 5. Retirement communities excluding children

court. Compensatory damages, injunctions, and civil penalties ranging from a maximum of $11,000 for a first offense to $55,000 for a third offense may be awarded.

In states such as Washington where there are state or local fair housing laws similar to the federal law, HUD may refer complaints to the equivalent state or local agency. (In Washington, this agency is the Human Rights Commission.)

A suit may be filed in federal district court or in the state trial court having general jurisdiction (in Washington, this would be superior court). The court may grant an injured party:

- a temporary restraining order,
- a permanent injunction,
- actual damages,
- punitive damages, and
- attorney's fees.

The defendant may also be ordered to take certain steps to prevent future discrimination.

The U.S. Attorney General may bring a civil suit in federal district court if there is evidence of a pattern of discriminatory activities, or if there is a group of people who have been denied their rights in such a way as to raise an issue of public importance. The Attorney General may request temporary or permanent injunctions or other orders necessary to insure that everyone receives the rights granted under the act. The court may also impose civil penalties of up to $100,000.

Fair Lending

In addition to real estate agents and sellers, lenders must also avoid discriminatory activities. The following federal laws and regulations are designed to eliminate discrimination in lending:

- the Federal Fair Housing Act (discussed above),
- the Equal Credit Opportunity Act,
- the Home Mortgage Disclosure Act, and
- regulations that implement and explain these statutes.

The Fair Housing Act prohibits discrimination in home loans and other aspects of residential financing. It does not apply to any other credit transactions.

The **Equal Credit Opportunity Act (ECOA)** applies to all consumer credit, including residential real estate loans. Consumer credit is credit that is extended to an individual (not a corporation or business) for personal, family, or household purposes. The act prohibits lenders from discriminating based on race, color, religion, national origin, sex, marital status, age (as long as the applicant is of legal age), or because the applicant's income is derived partly or wholly from public assistance.

The **Home Mortgage Disclosure Act** addresses whether lenders are fulfilling their obligation to serve the housing needs of the communities where they are located. The act facilitates the enforcement of federal laws against redlining.

Under the Home Mortgage Disclosure Act, institutional lenders in metropolitan areas with assets of over $10 million must make annual reports on residential mortgage loans (both purchase and improvement loans) that were originated or purchased during the fiscal year. The information is categorized as to number and dollar amount, type of loan (FHA, VA, or other), and geographic location by census tract or county (for small counties with no established census tracts). The reports disclose areas where few or no home loans have been made and alert investigators to potential redlining.

Equal Access to Facilities

The **Americans with Disabilities Act (ADA)**, which became effective in January 1992, is a federal law that was passed to ensure that disabled persons have equal access to public facilities. The ADA requires any business or other facility open to the public to be accessible to the disabled.

Under the ADA, no one can be discriminated against on the basis of disability in any place of public accommodation. A **disability** is defined as any physical or mental impairment that substantially limits one or more of the individual's major life activities. A **public accommodation** is defined as any private entity that owns, operates, leases, or leases to, a place open to the public, as long as the operation of the facility affects commerce.

Real estate offices are considered to be public accommodations, along with hotels, restaurants, retail stores, shopping centers, banks, convention centers, museums, parks, schools, and the offices of attorneys, accountants and doctors.

The ADA requires each of the following to be accomplished, as long as they are readily achievable:

- Reasonable modifications must be made in policies, practices, and procedures in order to make goods or services accessible to individuals with disabilities.
- Architectural barriers, structural communication barriers, and transportation barriers must be removed so that goods and services are accessible to the disabled.
- Auxiliary aids and services must be provided so that no disabled person is excluded, denied services, segregated, or otherwise treated differently than other individuals.
- All new commercial construction must be accessible to the disabled, unless structurally impractical.

Readily achievable is defined by the ADA as action that can be easily accomplished, without much difficulty or expense. Some examples of readily achievable modifications would be:

- The owner of a commercial building with no elevator installs automatic entry doors and a buzzer at street level so that customers of a second-floor business can ask for assistance.
- A commercial building owner alters the height of a pay phone to make it accessible to someone in a wheelchair, adds grab bars to restroom stalls, and takes a variety of other steps to make the building's facilities accessible.
- A department store rearranges its racks and adjusts the layout of its shelves to permit access to wheelchair users.

Exemptions. Private clubs and religious organizations are exempt from the public accommodations requirements of the ADA.

Enforcement. An individual who is being discriminated against, or who reasonably believes he or she is about to be discriminated against, may bring a civil action and obtain a temporary or permanent injunction or restraining order from the court. An individual may also file a complaint with the U.S. Attorney General, who will investigate the alleged violation.

If the Attorney General finds that a case of general public importance exists, or that a person is engaging in a pattern or practice of discrimination under the ADA, the Attorney General may file a lawsuit seeking injunctive relief, monetary damages for the victim(s), and civil penalties payable to the government.

State and Local Laws

Agents, sellers, and landlords must also comply with state laws prohibiting discrimination. The Washington Law Against Discrimination, the Fairness in Lending Act, and the Washington Real Estate License Law all include provisions designed to promote fair housing within the state. In addition, many local jurisdictions have their own regulations barring discrimination in housing.

Washington Law Against Discrimination

The Washington Law Against Discrimination declares that discrimination is a matter of state concern because it threatens the rights and privileges of state inhabitants and the very foundations of a free democratic society. In fact, the Washington Law Against Discrimination is stricter than any of the federal laws discussed above, both as to the types of activities covered and the classes of persons protected from discrimination.

This law prohibits discrimination based on **race**, **creed**, **color**, **national origin**, **sex**, **age**, **marital status**, **familial status**, or **sensory**, **physical**, **or mental disability**, or the **use of a trained guide dog or service dog**. Note that those infected or perceived to be infected with HIV are protected from discrimination in the same manner as those suffering from any other sensory, physical, or mental disability.

To further the purposes of the Washington Law Against Discrimination, the Human Rights Commission was created and given the mission of eliminating and preventing discrimination in this state.

Unlawful Discriminatory Practices. The Washington Law Against Discrimination is not just a fair housing law. It prohibits a wide range of discriminatory practices in employment, insurance and credit transactions, places of public accommodation and amusement (such as restaurants, movie theaters, hotels, beauty shops, and most other commercial enterprises), and in regard to all types of real property.

The law prohibits unfair practices with respect to real estate transactions. This means discrimination is prohibited in any real estate transaction, including the sale, appraisal, brokering, exchange, purchase, rental, or lease of real property; transacting or applying for a real estate loan; and the provision of brokerage services.

If based on discrimination against a protected class, it is an unlawful unfair practice to:

1. refuse to engage in a real estate transaction;
2. discriminate in the terms or conditions of a transaction;
3. discriminate in providing services or facilities in connection with a real estate transaction;
4. refuse to receive or fail to transmit a bona fide offer;
5. refuse to negotiate;
6. represent that property is not available for inspection, sale, rental, or lease when it is in fact available;
7. fail to advise a prospect about a property listing or refuse to allow him or her to inspect the property;
8. discriminate in the sale or rental of, or otherwise make unavailable, a dwelling to any person;

9. publish any advertisement, notice or sign which indicates, directly or indirectly, an intent to discriminate;

10. use any application form or make any record or inquiry which indicates, directly or indirectly, an intent to discriminate;

11. offer, solicit, accept, or retain a listing with the understanding that a person may be discriminated against;

12. expel a person from occupancy;

13. discriminate in negotiating, executing, or financing a real estate transaction;

14. discriminate in negotiating or executing any service or item in connection with a real estate transaction (such as title insurance or mortgage insurance);

15. induce or attempt to induce, for profit, anyone to sell or rent by making representations regarding entry into the neighborhood of a person of a particular race, creed, color, or national origin, or with a sensory, mental, or physical handicap (blockbusting);

16. insert into a written instrument relating to real property, or honor or attempt to honor, any condition, restriction, or prohibition based on race, creed, color, national origin, or sensory, mental, or physical handicap; or

17. discriminate in any credit transaction (whether or not real estate related) in denying credit, increasing fees, requiring collateral, or in any other terms or conditions.

In short, just about every form of discrimination in real estate transactions or any services associated with real estate transactions is unlawful if it is because the person is a member of any of the protected classes.

It is important for real estate agents, property sellers, and landlords to remember that, unlike the Federal Fair Housing Act, the Washington law has no exemptions for individual owners. A person who owns only one home is still prohibited from discriminating in selling or renting that home. People are also prohibited from discriminating when renting rooms in their own homes.

Note that based on the right of privacy, including the right to choose the sex of persons with whom one lives, the Human Rights Commission has ruled that it will not hear cases involving discrimination based on sex in the rental of rooms where the parties are to share living space. This ruling was prompted by an inquiry from a woman who wanted to let a room in her home only if she could rent it to another woman. However, this exemption is very limited, as the following case illustrates.

Case Example:

A property owner lived on the first floor of her home and rented several rooms on the second floor. She refused to rent one of the rooms to a prospective tenant because he was African-American. The tenant brought an action for discrimination and the Human Rights Commission ruled in his favor. On appeal, the owner argued that:

1. the Commission ruling relating to room rentals with shared facilities should apply to her;
2. applicable city and county ordinances exempted rentals in owner-occupied, single-family residences; and
3. her right of privacy in choosing persons to share her home outweighed the state's interest in preventing discrimination.

The court rejected all three arguments. It stated that even if the Commission's previous ruling not to hear cases in certain circumstances was constitutional (and the court expressed some doubt about this), her situation did not fall within that voluntary, self-imposed limitation.

The court also stated that the right to privacy was not absolute. When the state has a compelling interest, such as eliminating racial discrimination, reasonable regulations may be imposed on the right to privacy. When a person opens his or her home to the public by renting rooms for monetary gain, rights of privacy are deemed subordinate to compelling state interests. *Voris v. The Human Rights Commission*, 41 Wn. App. 283, 704 P.2d 632 (1985).

Exemptions. The Washington law has very few exemptions. Educational institutions may discriminate based on sex or marital status in student housing, and private clubs and certain cemeteries and mausoleums operated by religious or sectarian institutions are also exempt as to religious preference. There are no exemptions for the typical seller or lessor of real property, and certainly none for a real estate broker or salesperson engaged in professional activity.

Enforcement. A party injured by an unfair real estate practice may file a complaint with the Human Rights Commission within one year after the alleged discrimination took place. The Commission will then conduct an investigation. If the investigation reveals a reasonable basis for a belief that discrimination occurred, the Commission will act on the complaint. First, the Commission will try to eliminate the unlawful discrimination by conference, conciliation, and persuasion.

If that is unsuccessful, the Commission may schedule a hearing before an administrative law judge. If the judge finds unlawful discrimination, a cease and desist order will be issued. The judge may require affirmative relief, such as requiring an apartment owner to give the next available apartment to the victim or to solicit minority tenants for future vacancies. The judge may also award damages to the victim. In addition, a civil penalty payable to the state may be imposed. For a first offense, the penalty is limited to $10,000. For a second offense in the previous five years, the penalty may be up to $25,000. If two or more other unfair practices have been committed in the previous seven years, or if the offender has previously been found guilty for the same act, the penalty may be as much as $50,000.

The outcome of the administrative hearing may be appealed to the superior court by filing an appeal within 30 days after being served with the final order.

As an alternative to an administrative hearing, the injured party may choose to have the state Attorney General bring a civil action against the alleged discriminator.

Washington Fairness in Lending Act

The Washington Fairness in Lending Act prohibits redlining. Under this act, financial institutions may not deny single-family home loan applications because the home is located in a particular geographic area. In addition, they may not vary the terms of the loan (such as by requiring a higher downpayment, higher interest rate, or shorter amortization term, or by deliberately under-appraising the value of the property).

The act does not prevent a lending institution from using sound underwriting practices (including considering the borrower's creditworthiness and the market value of the property), but it outlaws the use of lending standards that have no financial basis.

Washington Real Estate License Law

In addition to complying with the federal and state laws already discussed, real estate licensees must also adhere to the provisions of the license laws and regulations.

According to the license law, violating any fair housing or civil rights laws or regulations is grounds for disciplinary action. If a broker or salesperson discriminates in sales or hiring activity on the basis of a protected class, his or her license could be suspended or revoked. Furthermore, the licensee could face a fine of up to $1,000 for each offense, and/or be required to complete an educational course in civil rights laws and nondiscriminatory real estate practices. Violations of the license law are also punishable as gross misdemeanors.

Effects of Antidiscrimination Legislation

In all property transactions, discrimination based on race or ancestry is prohibited, with no exceptions. Generally, discrimination based wholly or even partly on any of the other specified classes (creed, color, national origin, sex, familial status, or sensory, physical, or mental handicap) is also prohibited in Washington.

In most cases, discrimination by an owner, agent, real estate broker, or salesperson violates one or more of the laws we have discussed. Some examples of violations are briefly discussed below to give you an idea of the types of practices that have violated civil rights laws in renting and selling real property, MLS membership and practices, brokers' employment and business practices, advertising, lending, municipal zoning, and other regulatory actions.

Selling and Renting

Refusing to sell or rent after receiving a bona fide offer is prohibited if it can be shown that race (or some other class such as religion, national origin, or disability) is a factor, even if it is not the only reason for refusing to sell or rent. In one case, a landlord claimed that a sublessee was an unacceptable tenant. Despite the fact that there were a number of legitimate reasons for rejecting the tenant, a federal court held that the tenant could not be turned down if race was one of the factors for the denial.

Refusal to negotiate for a sale or rental may be a straightforward refusal to talk to or deal with a potential purchaser or renter. Or the lessor or seller simply may refuse to answer the door or to act on an application.

Case Example:

The manager's apartment was located so that she could observe the front door of the building from her own apartment door. When the buzzer rang, she looked down the hall and if the person standing at the door was African-American, she simply went back inside and refused to answer the door. Since she was visible by persons ringing the buzzer, this practice was easily discovered and a complaint was filed with the Human Rights Commission.

After the complaint was filed, the owners installed a peephole in the manager's door. Although the owner maintained this was for the manager's safety, at least one member of the hearing tribunal thought that it could also be for the purpose of allowing the manager to continue her practice without being seen by persons ringing the buzzer. *Skold v. Johnson*, 29 Wn. App. 541, 630 P.2d 456 (1981).

Another method of discrimination involves ignoring rental applications. A property manager takes the rental application and tells the minority applicant that he or she will be contacted later, or when a vacancy arises. Instead, the manager throws away the application, or never contacts the minority applicant.

In one case, it was the owner's practice not to process rental applications that were not accompanied by a deposit. White applicants were told of this procedure and, accordingly, made a deposit with their applications. African-American applicants were not informed; therefore, few made deposits with their applications, and so their applications were never processed.

The methods used to discriminate can be simple or complex. For example, the salespeople in a model home might dash out the back door when an "undesirable" potential purchaser drives up or approaches the front door. Or a developer might discriminate in the terms or conditions of a sale by making minority purchasers pay higher closing costs. Discrimination can also entail an elaborate scheme, as illustrated by the following case example.

Case Example:

A house was for sale in an exclusive residential district near Chicago. The asking price was $850,000, but after some negotiation, the seller and a African-American couple signed an agreement with a sales price of $675,000. The buyers made an earnest money deposit of $75,000.

News spread that a African-American couple had bought the home, upsetting a number of the community residents. Covenants in the community required all sales to be reported to the homeowners association. The association had a 30-day assignable option to buy the property. In an unprecedented action, the president of the association called a special meeting to discuss the situation. In 16 or 17 previous sales, the option right had been routinely waived without discussion.

At the meeting, talk centered on the buyers' race and occupation (they operated a number of car washes) and ways to prevent the sale. Although the seller was a member of the board of governors and vice president of the association, he was not told of the meeting.

The association's attorney suggested that it might not be advisable for the association itself to buy the property to frustrate the sale, but that perhaps they could form a separate syndicate or find another buyer. Shortly before the 30-day period expired, another buyer (a white person) who had viewed the home earlier was contacted and agreed to buy the association's option.

The African-American purchasers brought suit against the homeowners association and against the white buyer alleging a conspiracy to deny them housing based on their race. The court found in favor of the African-American purchasers.

While the white buyer claimed ignorance as to the race of the first purchasers, the court did not believe her. It also did not believe that the failure to notify the seller of the meeting was an oversight, or that the association's main concern was that the low sales price would lessen the value of other properties in the community. The court noted that price had not been discussed at all at the meeting and that the association had entered into an agreement to have another buyer purchase the property at exactly the same price.

The court noted that the only difference between the second deal and the first was that the second buyer was a white professional businesswoman and the first buyer was an African-American car wash owner.

The court entered judgments in favor of both husband and wife against both the association and the white buyer for out-of-pocket expenses, emotional distress, and punitive damages. The total judgment was $288,691. *Phillips v. Hunter Trails*, 785 F.2d 184 (7th Cir. 1982).

MLS Membership and Practices

Discrimination has also been found in the denial of access to a multiple listing service and in the practices of MLS members.

Case Example:

A case from Indiana concerned the efforts of a number of brokers in a large city to gain access to multiple listings. The chain of events began in early 1973 and eventually led to several interrelated lawsuits.

In 1973, there was a multiple listing service called Northwest MLS operating in the city, serving the local Board of Realtors. The board was made up of 40 white brokers and four African-American brokers. The MLS had 26 broker members, all of whom were white. The four African-American members of the board repeatedly applied for membership in the MLS but were denied. Towards the end of the year, Northwest MLS ceased operations but was soon replaced by another multiple listing service. This MLS was made up of 18 white brokers and three African-American brokers. At the same time, eight white brokers in the city MLS joined an MLS and local board in a neighboring suburb.

All of the members of the suburban MLS and board were white. The eight white brokers who belonged to both the metropolitan and the suburban multiple listing services began directing all listings they obtained to the suburban MLS, even though they continued doing most of their business in the city.

Since the African-American brokers were not members of the suburban MLS, they were unable to obtain access to those listings. Sometime in the middle of 1977, the white brokers withdrew from the metropolitan MLS altogether and operated solely out of the suburban MLS, although most of their business continued to be with properties located in the city.

The drastic reduction in the number of brokers and listings in the city MLS caused it to cease operations almost immediately. Seven African-American brokers then attempted to join the suburban MLS but were unable to do so. To qualify for membership, it was necessary to belong to the local board, and to qualify for membership in the board, a broker was required to maintain an office in the suburban area.

The African-American brokers alleged that although they attempted to do so, they were unable to rent office space in that suburb because of discriminatory racial attitudes prevalent in the area. They were therefore unable to gain admission to the only operating MLS in the area and were denied access to a majority of the real estate listings in the area.

They sued the multiple listing service, the local board, and eight individual white brokers. They were able to obtain a consent order in federal district court in which the board waived the requirement that members maintain an office within the suburban area. *U.S. v. South Suburban MLS,* and *Wilkes Realty, Inc. v. South Suburban MLS,* No. H77-417 and No. 80-307 (N.D. Ind. 1984).

Employment by Brokers

It is a violation of antidiscrimination laws and the Washington real estate license law for a broker to discriminate based on race or any other protected class in hiring sales associates or in determining compensation, work assignments, or other terms and conditions of employment.

Case Example:

A large metropolitan brokerage corporation with over 20 offices and over 300 sales-people had a policy of nondiscrimination in hiring and, in fact, took affirmative steps to recruit, train, and keep licensed African-American salespersons. Several of its officers were recognized leaders throughout the city and state in educating real estate sales-people regarding fair housing laws and the necessity of complying with those laws.

When the lawsuit began, the company was the only real estate firm in the state that operated on a large scale both in predominantly white suburban neighborhoods and in predominantly African-American urban neighborhoods with a biracial sales force.

The problem arose because almost all of the African-American salespeople were assigned to offices located in predominantly African-American urban neighborhoods and almost all of the white salespeople were assigned to offices located in predominantly white suburbs. The judge felt that this practice had the effect of racial steering because:

1. an all-African-American office has a tendency to attract African-American buyers and discourage white buyers;
2. an all-white office has a tendency to attract white buyers and discourage African-American buyers; and
3. agents tend to sell homes in the area near their offices.

The judge believed that an integrated sales staff would foster racially integrated neighborhoods. The brokerage was ordered to give all salespeople information about all offices and neighborhoods served by the firm. Sales associates were to be allowed to visit other offices and typical homes listed by each office, and African-American salespeople were to be encouraged to work out of suburban offices on a full- or part-time basis, without losing the right to be reassigned to the offices in the city if they desired. *U.S. v. Real Estate One, Inc.*, 433 F. Supp. 1140 (E.D. Mich. 1977).

Advertising

Both federal and Washington state law prohibit any advertising that indicates a restriction, preference, or intent to discriminate based on race or other protected class. Discriminatory advertising or solicitations may be very subtle, and apparently innocent statements may sometimes be intended or interpreted as discriminatory.

Example: In some areas of the country, an advertisement that states "Near schools and churches" may be taken to mean that it is a gentile neighborhood and that Jewish people (who attend temple or synagogue, not church) are not welcome.

Many brokers send advertisements to the neighbors of listed homes in search of potential buyers. While such solicitations are not necessarily discriminatory, they can have a discriminatory effect when:

1. the solicitations are used only in neighborhoods where the residents are predominantly of the same race and/or religious or ethnic background;

2. persons in the neighborhood of a particular race or ethnic background are not sent copies of the solicitation; or

3. the solicitation suggests that the recipient can control the type or character of the person who will buy the property. For example, if the solicitation suggests that a neighbor can, by referring potential buyers, "uphold the standards of the community" (when the "standards" are unspecified), the neighbor is likely to infer that he or she can control the race or ethnic background of the buyer.

Solicitations used under those circumstances are considered an unfair practice and a violation of licensing regulations, as are solicitations that invite or provoke discriminatory feelings or actions.

Newspaper advertising is perhaps the most common form of advertising used by real estate licensees. In certain circumstances, even the choice of newspapers used for advertising purposes may be deemed to have the effect of racial steering.

Case Example:

A real estate brokerage in a large metropolitan area advertised listed properties in two newspapers that were distributed over the entire area, a number of smaller newspapers that were circulated primarily in certain communities or neighborhoods, and in a weekly newspaper circulated primarily in African-American neighborhoods and sold primarily to African-American readers.

The practice that attracted the attention of the attorney general was the company's standard policy of advertising listings in the so-called "changing" areas of the city in the African-American newspaper and not regularly advertising those homes in the newspapers of general distribution.

The court believed this had an impermissible steering effect because, for the most part, only persons who read the African-American newspaper (mostly African-Americans) were made aware of available homes in the "changing" neighborhoods. The judge believed this would have the effect of accelerating the change from a mixed neighborhood to an all or predominantly African-American neighborhood. This would create a segregated neighborhood in violation of the government's policy of fostering integrated neighborhoods.

The company was ordered to maintain the same level of advertising in the newspaper circulated primarily to African-Americans and at the same time advertise the same homes in the two newspapers of general distribution, with some advertising in the smaller community papers nearby. *U.S. v. Real Estate One, Inc.*, 433 F. Supp. 1140 (E.D. Mich. 1977).

The type of models used in advertising can also lead to charges of discrimination.

Example: A broker is the listing agent for a large, exclusive housing development. He advertises homes in the development by putting display ads in the local paper. (Display ads are larger than the average classified ad and typically include illustrations or photos.)

In every ad placed by the broker, the buyers and sellers depicted are white, even though 30% of the city's population is non-white. The use of only white models could be the grounds for a discrimination suit.

Lending

Aside from redlining, which is the most common discrimination charge in real estate lending, discrimination in financing includes different treatment in foreclosure practices, in granting loans, and in setting application fees and other financing charges.

A lender who has been charged with redlining may be ordered (or may voluntarily agree) to undertake affirmative lending activities to increase lending in neighborhoods where few loans have been made.

Action to correct the situation may include:

* appointing a bank officer to institute and oversee the affirmative lending program;
* setting goals for the number of mortgage loans to be made in particular areas;
* consulting with minority advertising and marketing experts to implement advertising programs in the target areas; and
* conducting regular fair lending and training seminars for personnel.

In one case, a lender hired two additional loan agents to serve the targeted areas; paid them a guaranteed minimum salary (which was not paid to agents outside the target areas); and paid them a higher rate of commission on the loans they made (because the average amount of those loans was lower than the average amount of loans made in other areas, since property values tended to be lower). [Settlement agreement, *United Neighbors in Action v. American Savings*, No. C-78-1799 (N.D. Calif. 1979).]

Zoning and Other Municipal Regulations

Antidiscrimination laws prohibit zoning practices that have the effect of denying housing to minorities. Since it is unlikely that any state or municipality would currently enact a blatantly racist ordinance, these cases normally involve arguments based on the concept of **disparate impact**. This means that even though the ordinance or regulation may be neutral on its face, its effect is discriminatory because the impact of the law falls more heavily on a particular class than it does on others.

For example, in the field of employment discrimination there have been a number of cases alleging that height restrictions for police or fire departments discriminated against women and certain minorities because they tended to be shorter than white males and because there was no evidence to indicate that the height restriction was related to job requirements.

Discriminatory or **exclusionary** zoning cases usually arise out of zoning practices that prohibit or unreasonably restrict zones or permits for multi-family or low-income housing. The argument is that since far more minorities are low-income, any ordinance that limits or restricts lower-cost housing has the effect of excluding minorities or severely restricting their ability to live in the community.

Case Example:

In one of the leading discriminatory zoning cases, a municipality refused to rezone so as to permit construction of multi-family dwellings within the city. In that case, the general metropolitan area (Chicago) had a population that was approximately 18% African-American, but the municipality in question had only 27 African-American residents out of a population of approximately 65,000 (.04%).

Since a greater percentage of the occupants of multi-family dwellings were African-American than were white, the court felt that this zoning practice had the effect of denying housing to African-Americans within the municipality. *Metropolitan Housing Development Corp. v. Arlington Heights*, 517 F.2d 409 (7th Cir. 1975).

Case Example:

Under similar reasoning, a city was found guilty of discrimination based on its practice of approving low-income housing in only one (predominantly African-American) section of the city.

The court found this had the discriminatory effect of preventing African-Americans from moving into predominantly white sections of the city, since there was little or no housing available in those areas for low- or middle-income residents. *U.S. v. Yonkers Board of Education*, 624 F. Supp. 1276 (S.D.N.Y. 1985).

The Right to Sue

As the case examples show, the scope of civil rights laws and the potential consequences of a violation are greater than is immediately obvious from the language of the statutes. Successful plaintiffs are entitled to:

- actual damages,
- punitive damages (in certain cases),
- attorneys' fees, and
- costs.

As we discussed earlier, **actual damages** (also called **compensatory damages**) are intended to reimburse the plaintiff for expenses caused by the discrimination—such as additional rent, or transportation, storage, or moving costs. They also provide compensation for mental distress resulting from the humiliation or embarrassment of discrimination. **Punitive damages** are intended both to punish the wrongdoer and to serve as a deterrent to others.

Awards for both compensatory damages and punitive damages have been growing much larger in recent years. One possible reason for larger judgments is that fair housing and civil rights laws have now existed for more than several decades—which is plenty of time to assimilate and implement all the legal requirements. Whatever the reason, as the following case indicates, the awards can be substantial.

Case Example:

This case arose out of what is probably the most common violation of fair housing laws: telling a minority applicant that no apartment is available for rent when in fact there is an available apartment.

The plaintiffs were African-American women employed as air traffic controllers by the FAA. They attempted to rent apartments at a complex near their jobs at MacArthur Airport on Long Island after reading advertisements for the complex. Both were repeatedly told over a period of several months that no apartments were available for rent. However, the complex continued to run newspaper advertisements for available apartments, and white "testers" who visited the apartments were shown vacant apartments and told space was available. The plaintiffs themselves were told apartments were available when they called on the phone and did not identify themselves.

The jury had no trouble finding the defendant, a realty company, guilty of discriminatory conduct. The jury entered a verdict for the following damages: compensatory damages of $40,000 for one plaintiff and $25,000 for the other, and punitive damages of $250,000 for each plaintiff, for a total damages award of $565,000. *Grayson v. Rotundi & Sons Realty Co.*, CV 83-0844 (E.D.N.Y. 1984).

Note that in Washington, punitive damages are generally not available unless expressly authorized by statute. The Washington Law Against Discrimination does not authorize punitive damages. However, the punitive damages are available under the Federal Fair Housing Act.

It is important to understand that a housing discrimination case may involve many more people as plaintiffs than just the one denied housing, and more defendants than just the one who actually denied the housing. For example, **testers** may also become plaintiffs in a discrimination case.

One of the most common methods of proving violations of fair housing laws is through the use of testers. When a person feels that he or she has been lied to about the availability of housing, that person complains to a government agency, an attorney, or a community fair housing organization. This entity then sends out testers. These testers may be volunteers, although they are more often paid expenses and a nominal fee.

The most frequent type of test is the so-called **sandwich test** in which a white tester (or couple) asks to see available apartments and is shown available space. Immediately on this tester's departure, a minority tester (or minority or mixed-race couple) appears and asks to see available apartments. The minority tester is told that there are no vacancies. Immediately on his or her departure, a second white tester (or couple) appears, asks to see available apartments, and is shown space. This sort of test is generally successful in proving that the property owner or agent is discriminating based on race or some other prohibited grounds.

Obviously, the original applicant (the one who made the complaint) is entitled to damages upon proving that he or she was discriminated against. What might not be so obvious is that the African-American and white testers and the fair housing organization may also be entitled to sue and recover damages from the agent and/or property owner.

Case Example:

An African-American man inquired about available apartments at a complex near Richmond, Virginia. He was told there were no vacancies. He complained to a local nonprofit organization whose purpose was to promote equal housing opportunities. The organization sent out an African-American tester and a white tester. On four different occasions, the African-American tester was told that no apartments were available yet. The white tester was shown vacant apartments.

The realty corporation was then sued by the renter applicant, the African-American tester, the white tester, and the fair housing organization. The court allowed them all to proceed with their lawsuits for damages. The African-American renter's claim was based on straightforward allegations of denial of housing and racial steering.

The African-American tester's claim was based on a provision of the Fair Housing Act that makes it unlawful for anyone to misrepresent that housing is not available when it is in fact available. To recover under that provision, it is not necessary to be actually seeking housing. Even testers who expect to be lied to have a right to sue.

The white tester was truthfully told that apartments were available. His claim was based on a right to enjoy the benefits of an integrated society. The prohibited activities of the defendants interfered with that right.

The fair housing organization's claim was based on the theory that the discriminatory activities of the defendant interfered with the organization's efforts to provide housing counseling and referral services, with a resulting drain on its financial resources. *Havens Realty v. Coleman*, 455 U.S. 363 (1982).

In short, there are often many people connected with an act or practice of unlawful discrimination who can sue those connected with the violation. Those sued often include a property manager or real estate salesperson, a broker, and an owner, based on their own acts or on the basis of agency liability.

If a seller refuses to go through with a transaction because the buyer is a minority, the broker may sue the seller for the commission.

Fig. 12.4 Overview of civil rights laws

	Civil Rights Act of 1866	Federal Fair Housing Act	Washington Law Against Discrimination
Race	X	X	X
Color		X	X
Religion (creed)		X	X
Sex		X	X
National origin		X	X
Ancestry	X		*
Handicap		X	X
Use of guide dog			X
Familial status		X	X
Marital status			X
Age			X
All property	X		X
Housing only		X	

* The law doesn't specifically mention this type of discrimination, but it has been interpreted to prohibit all arbitrary discrimination in housing.

A minority broker who sues an MLS and member brokers for denying him or her membership could even sue brokers who refuse to co-broker with him or her after the lawsuit.

Case Example:

After several African-American brokers brought suit against the MLS and its members for denying them membership, a number of the white brokers refused to split commissions or co-broker any transactions with the plaintiff African-American brokers.

The African-American brokers then sued the white brokers in a separate lawsuit alleging that the refusal to cooperate was in retaliation for their lawsuit under the Fair Housing Act. The white brokers freely admitted that they refused to cooperate because of the lawsuit. They did not choose to work with or share commissions with anyone who was suing them.

Their position may seem reasonable. After all, who wants to do business with or share commissions with someone who is suing you? In this case, though, it was a violation of the law. The Fair Housing Act has a provision which makes it unlawful to "interfere" with the rights guaranteed under the act.

The lawsuit was based on the African-American brokers' rights under the law. The court held the refusal by the white brokers to cooperate was in retaliation for the lawsuit to enforce rights guaranteed under the Fair Housing Act, and was therefore "interference" with the exercise of their rights under the law. *U.S. v. South Suburban MLS*, No. H 80-307 (N.D. Ind. 1984).

Conclusion

As illustrated by some of the preceding cases, damages awards can run into hundreds of thousands of dollars and licensees may be subject to license suspension or revocation for violating fair housing laws. It is extremely important for all real estate licensees to understand the application, effect, and consequences of state and federal antidiscrimination laws, both for their own protection and to provide more professional service to their clients and customer.

Case Problem

The following is a hypothetical case problem. Most of the facts are taken from a real case. Based on what you have learned from this chapter, make a decision on the issues presented and then check to see if your answer matches the court's decision.

The Facts

Starrett City is the largest housing development in the nation, consisting of 46 high-rise buildings containing over 5,000 apartments in Brooklyn, New York. The project was originally conceived by the United Housing Foundation, which planned to build cooperative apartments. However, this project was abandoned.

Starrett City Associates then proposed to construct rental units on the condition that the city real estate tax abatement granted to the original project be transferred to Starrett. This transfer created a great deal of community opposition because of the fear that rental apartments (rather than co-ops) would make Starrett City an overwhelmingly minority development. The community was concerned about "white flight." The transfer was approved only upon assurances that Starrett City was intended to be a racially integrated community.

Starrett City began renting apartments in 1973. Starrett sought to maintain a racial distribution that was approximately 64% white, 22% African-American, and 8% Hispanic. All eligible applicants were told that no apartments were available, but their application would be placed in the active file and they would be notified when a unit became available. When an apartment became available, applicants of a race or national origin similar to that of the departing tenants were selected from the active file and offered the apartment.

Starrett maintained that these procedures were adopted solely to achieve and maintain integration and were not motivated by any racial animus.

Experts at trial testified concerning "white flight" and the "tipping" phenomenon, in which white residents leave a community as the minority population increases, resulting in a predominantly minority community. (The experts disagreed about what the tipping point would be for a particular development.) Starrett claimed that its use of quotas kept the number of minorities in Starrett City low enough to avoid setting off a wave of "white flight." However, Starrett City's quota system also meant that minority applicants waited up to ten times longer than the average white applicant before they were offered an apartment.

The Question

Was Starrett City's quota system a violation of Title VIII of the Civil Rights Act of 1968 (the Fair Housing Act)?

The Answer

Yes. Housing practices that are unlawful under Title VIII include not only those motivated by a racially discriminatory purpose, but also those that disproportionately affect minorities.

In the real case of *U.S. v. Starrett City Associates*, 840 F.2d 1096 (2nd Cir. 1988), the court said that although quotas promote Title VIII's integration policy, they contravene its antidiscrimination policy.

In efforts to promote integrated housing, race may sometimes be an appropriate consideration. A race-conscious affirmative action plan does not necessarily violate the Fair Housing Act. However, a race-conscious plan should not use rigid racial quotas of indefinite duration to maintain a fixed level of integration.

In other words, it may have been all right for Starrett to attempt to achieve a certain level of racial integration when the apartments were first rented. It is also legitimate to continue to promote an integrated community. However, strict racial quotas that seriously disadvantage minorities are not an acceptable method for attempting to maintain integration.

Chapter Summary

- Real estate licensees must be aware of both state and federal antidiscrimination laws and regulations. The earliest of these is the federal Civil Rights Act of 1866. This law, the constitutionality of which is based on the Thirteenth Amendment, prohibits discrimination based on race or ancestry in all property transactions. There are no exceptions to the act.

- The Federal Fair Housing Act of 1968 prohibits discrimination based on race, color, religion, sex, national origin, handicap, or familial status in the sale or lease of residential property. Several exemptions exist, including the Mrs. Murphy exemption, an exemption for certain religious or secular groups who may prefer their own members over outsiders, and one for a person selling a single-family residence under certain conditions.

- Three specifically prohibited actions under the Fair Housing Act are steering, redlining, and blockbusting. Steering is the channeling of buyers or renters to specific neighborhoods based on race or other protected characteristics. Redlining is the refusal to make loans on property located in particular areas for discriminatory reasons. Blockbusting is attempting to obtain listings or arrange sales in a neighborhood by predicting the entry of a minority into the neighborhood and representing that this will cause a decline in the neighborhood.

- Several federal laws and regulations prohibit discrimination in credit transactions: the Federal Fair Housing Act, the Equal Credit Opportunity Act, and the Home Mortgage Disclosure Act.

- The Americans with Disabilities Act prohibits discrimination against disabled people in any place of public accommodation. Under the ADA, a property owner may be required to modify the property to make its facilities accessible to the disabled.

- Washington state law prohibits discrimination not just in housing, but also in employment, insurance, and credit transactions, places of public accommodation and most other commercial enterprises, and all types of real property transactions. There are very few exemptions.

Checklist of Problem Areas

Real Estate Licensee's Checklist

❑ Has there been any discrimination in hiring salespeople or working with co-brokers? Is there any discriminatory practice in your office, such as minority salespeople working only with minority clients or only in minority neighborhoods?

❑ Is your advertising free of any discriminatory language? Do you advertise all properties in the various available newspapers, not selecting certain properties to be advertised only in certain newspapers?

❑ If you have sent out letters of solicitation, is there anything in the wording that could have a discriminatory effect? Were the letters sent out to everyone in the neighborhood, regardless of race, religion, etc.?

❑ Remember that even though there are some exemptions under the federal laws, these exemptions are generally not available under Washington law and are never available to real estate licensees.

Seller or Landlord's Checklist

❑ Remember that Washington law is much stricter than federal antidiscrimination laws. Under Washington law, there are generally no exemptions, not even for sellers of single-family residences who do not use a real estate agent.

❑ If you refuse to go through with a sale or lease and the potential buyer or tenant is someone who fits into one of the protected categories (minority, handicapped, etc.), what is your reason for refusal? You may be liable under federal or state law if the refusal is in any way based on discriminatory reasons.

Buyer or Tenant's Checklist

❑ If you are told that an apartment is not available or that a house has already sold, is there any reason to suspect otherwise?

❑ Have you been shown houses primarily in one area of town? When you ask about houses in a different area, has the agent tried to steer you away from that area?

❑ If you suspect you have been discriminated against, you can contact local nonprofit housing organizations, the Washington Human Rights Commission, the Department of Licensing (Real Estate Division), the Attorney General's Office, or the Office of Equal Opportunity at HUD.

Chapter Quiz

1. Under the Washington law relating to discrimination in housing, complaints are taken to the:

    a. Department of Fair Employment and Housing
    b. state Human Rights Commission
    c. state Housing Council
    d. Washington Association of Realtors

2. Title VIII of the Civil Rights Act of 1968 is also called the:

    a. Voting Rights Act
    b. Federal Fair Housing Act
    c. Equal Opportunity in Housing Act
    d. Washington Law Against Discrimination

3. The Federal Fair Housing Act declares a U.S. policy of:

    a. building housing for minority groups throughout the U.S.
    b. guaranteeing separate but equal housing in all states
    c. providing fair housing throughout the U.S.
    d. eliminating prejudice throughout the U.S.

4. Title VIII of the Civil Rights Act of 1968 prohibits:

    a. discrimination in housing
    b. discrimination in residential lending
    c. Both a) and b)
    d. Neither a) nor b)

5. The Federal Fair Housing Act has a direct impact on:

    a. federally subsidized housing
    b. federally insured loans
    c. nonfederal housing
    d. All of the above

6. Which of the following is exempt from the Federal Fair Housing Act of 1968?

    a. A broker selling vacant lots in a subdivision
    b. A salesperson helping to sell a single-family home
    c. An owner selling his six-unit apartment house
    d. None of the above

7. Under the Federal Fair Housing Act, a person who feels he or she has been unlawfully discriminated against can:

    a. seek injunctive relief and sue for damages in state or federal court
    b. file criminal charges in a federal court
    c. file criminal charges in the state supreme court
    d. only sue for damages in federal court

8. The Home Mortgage Disclosure Act helps to enforce the prohibition against:

    a. redlining
    b. steering
    c. blockbusting
    d. None of the above

9. Under Washington law, it would be permissible for a landlord to refuse to rent to a prospective tenant because the tenant:

    a. has a child
    b. was born in Ireland
    c. has a low income
    d. None of the above

10. A developer who intended to rent housing in a particular development only to persons 55 years of age or over would be in violation of:

    a. the Civil Rights Act of 1866
    b. the Civil Rights Act of 1968
    c. the Washington Law Against Discrimination
    d. None of the above

11. Generally speaking, the Washington Law Against Discrimination:

    a. is broader in application, with fewer exemptions, than the federal laws
    b. is narrower in scope than federal legislation
    c. provides exactly the same coverage as federal legislation because of the principle of federal supremacy
    d. is enforceable only in so far as it provides the same protection against discrimination as is provided by federal laws

12. Blockbusting is an acceptable practice:

    a. only under the supervision of licensed real estate brokers
    b. only when approved by HUD or the Department of State
    c. only if the buyer and seller are notified and agree
    d. under no circumstances

13. The term "racial steering" refers to:

    a. directing brokers to minority prospects
    b. directing prospects toward housing choices based on the racial composition of the neighborhoods
    c. directing minority prospects toward affordable property, based on their income and assets
    d. None of the above

14. All of the following would be considered public accommodations under the ADA except:

    a. the office of the local credit union
    b. a lab in the home of a self-employed scientific researcher who uses it to complete tests for a well-known company
    c. a real estate office
    d. a property management office that only has one employee

15. An investor owns a five-story office building. She ramped the curb and the steps leading to the office building, altered the height of a pay phone in the lobby, widened restroom doors throughout the building, and added grab bars in certain restroom stalls. The investor did this in an effort to comply with the:

    a. 1988 Handicap Amendment to the Fair Housing Act
    b. Americans with Disabilities Act
    c. Civil Rights Act of 1866
    d. Civil Rights Act of 1964

13 Landlord/Tenant Law

Outline

I. Leases
   A. Requirements
      1. terms in a lease
   B. Types of leases
      1. gross lease
      2. graduated lease
      3. net lease
      4. percentage lease
      5. ground lease
   C. Transferring a leasehold
      1. sale
      2. assignment
      3. sublease
      4. novation

II. Residential Landlord-Tenant Act
   A. Application and exemptions
   B. Rights, duties, and liabilities of landlord and tenant
      1. duties of the landlord prior to possession
      2. possession
      3. covenant of quiet enjoyment
      4. privacy
      5. rent
      6. damage and security deposits
      7. nonrefundable fees
      8. locks
      9. criminal acts
      10. codes and rules
      11. pests
      12. maintenance
      13. habitability
      14. utilities and appliances
      15. structural components
      16. repairs
      17. access to landlord

III. Termination of a Lease
   A. Mutual agreement
      1. exceptions
      2. renewal
   B. Abandonment

        C. Eviction
            1. retaliation
            2. unlawful detainer
            3. self-help eviction
            4. constructive eviction
            5. personal property
        D. Destruction of the premises
    IV. Rent Control

Key Terms

- leasehold estate
- lease
- gross (fixed or flat) lease
- graduated lease
- net lease
- percentage lease
- ground lease
- assignment
- sublease

- novation
- Residential Landlord-Tenant Act (RLTA)
- consequential damages
- covenant of quiet enjoyment
- common areas
- implied warranty of habitability

- surrender
- abandonment
- eviction
- retaliatory eviction
- unlawful detainer
- self-help eviction
- constructive eviction
- rent control

Chapter Overview

One of the most common of all real estate transactions is the rental or lease of a place to live or work. Although people who rent or lease an apartment, home, office, or business property do not own the premises, they have certain rights or interests in that property. These interests are called **leasehold estates**. (Leasehold estates are discussed in detail in Chapter 3.) The parties to a leasehold estate have certain obligations and privileges based on the law and the terms of the lease agreement.

A real estate agent should have a basic knowledge of landlord/tenant law. Many people own rental properties for investment purposes. Sometimes when property is for sale but no immediate buyer can be found, the seller decides to rent the property with an option to buy, or until a buyer can be found. Real estate licensees often act as rental agents for these parties. In addition, many licensees are involved in property management for rental properties.

This chapter explains the different types of leases and the rights, duties, and liabilities of the landlord and tenant. Both commercial and residential landlord/tenant law is covered, although particular attention is paid to the state Residential Landlord-Tenant Act. Note that local jurisdictions may have additional landlord/tenant rules that are not covered in this book.

Leases

A **lease** is an agreement that transfers the right of possession and use of real property from the owner or landlord to the tenant. A lease is both a conveyance and a contract. As a conveyance, it transfers the right of possession or occupancy. As a contract, a lease provides for the payment of rent and sets forth the other rights and duties of the landlord and tenant. The parties are free to bargain or negotiate the terms of the contract.

Requirements

Since a lease is a contract, the basic requirements of a contract must be met. First, a valid lease is an agreement between parties who are legally capable of entering into a contract: the parties must not be mentally incompetent or under age.

The lease must also be supported by consideration. The normal consideration is a set dollar amount that is paid as rent. Usually the lease specifies that rent is to be paid at the beginning of the rental period. However, if the lease does not specify when rent is to be paid, it is not due until the end of the rental period.

The purpose of the lease must be legal. For instance, in Washington prostitution is illegal. Therefore, it would be illegal to lease a house for that purpose, and the lease would be invalid.

Under Washington law, a lease for over one year must be in writing and acknowledged. A lease for a specific term of one year or less must also be in writing, but does not need to be acknowledged. Other leases, such as periodic tenancies or tenancies at will (see Chapter 3), do not have to be in writing to be enforceable.

If a lease has been put into writing, it must be signed by the landlord. A tenant usually signs the lease as well, but the tenant's signature is not required. If the tenant takes possession of the leased property and pays rent, those actions are considered to constitute acceptance of the lease, even without a signature.

Terms in a Lease. Certain basic information, such as identification of the parties, a description of the premises, the duration of the lease, and the rental amount should be included in all leases.

Most leases also contain clauses concerning acceptable uses of the property, the right to assign or sublet, required security and damage deposits, and the responsibility for repairs and maintenance. Other information concerning the landlord's access to the premises, and the consequences of alterations, damage or destruction of the premises, or default by the tenant may also be included.

Types of Leases

Gross Lease. Most residential leases are gross leases. Under a **gross lease** (which may also be called a fixed, flat, or straight lease), the tenant pays a set rent amount, and the landlord pays all additional expenses such as maintenance and repairs, taxes, special assessments, and insurance. Most tenants under a gross lease still pay for their utilities, such as electricity and water.

Graduated Lease. A **graduated lease** is similar to a gross lease except that it includes periodic increases in the rental amount. These increases are usually set at specific future dates and are often based on the cost-of-living index.

Net Lease. Many commercial leases are net leases. In a **net lease**, a tenant pays rent plus maintenance and operating expenses, such as utilities, taxes, insurance, and repairs.

There are different gradations of net leases. The terms of a particular lease will vary, but generally under each type of lease a tenant pays a base rent plus the following:

- **net lease**: some maintenance and operating expenses;
- **net-net lease** (also called a double net lease or an NN lease): property taxes, insurance premiums and some other maintenance and operating expenses; and
- **net-net-net lease** (also called a triple net lease or an NNN lease): property taxes, insurance premiums, and all other maintenance and operating expenses.

Percentage Lease. Some commercial leases are percentage leases. In a **percentage lease**, the rental amount is usually based on a percentage of the tenant's monthly or annual gross sales. Percentage leases are common for retail stores, especially in large shopping centers.

There are many types of percentage leases. For instance, under a pure percentage lease, the entire rental amount is a percentage of the tenant's gross sales. Under the most common type of percentage lease, a fixed minimum rental amount is required along with a percentage of gross sales (or a percentage of gross sales above a certain specified amount).

> **Example:** Dapper Dan, a men's clothing outlet, rents a retail location in a large mall. The lease agreement provides for a minimum rent of $1,500 per month, plus an additional rental amount of 4% of all gross sales above an annual amount of $200,000.

The percentage varies based on the business involved. For instance, parking lots make a much higher percentage of profit on every dollar earned than other businesses. A parking lot might pay a percentage rental of 50% or 60%, while a grocery store would probably pay only 1% or 2%.

A problem with percentage leases is that disagreement often arises concerning what is meant by the term "gross sales." Does it include mail orders, sales and excise tax, credit sales, inter-store transactions, or income from vending machines? The lease should clearly define what is included under the term "gross sales," so that there is no question about the amount the percentage is based on.

Ground Lease. In a **ground lease**, the landowner leases vacant land to a tenant who wants to erect a building on the property. This type of lease is popular in large metropolitan areas and is usually long-term in order to make the construction of a building desirable and profitable.

For example, a tenant might lease a parcel of land and build a 20-story office building on it. Then the tenant would lease office space to different tenants. This creates a **sandwich lease**. The original tenant who constructed the building is both a tenant (as to the land) and a landlord (as to the building).

Transferring a Leasehold

Sale. A landlord is free to sell the leased property at any time. The buyer takes the property subject to existing leases. The new owner must honor the terms of the current lease agreements.

Once the current tenants have been notified of the sale, the new owner has the right to collect all rents. A problem sometimes arises when a tenant has prepaid rent and then the property is sold. The new owner assumes that he or she is entitled to certain rent, but the tenant has already paid the former owner and does not want to pay again.

Courts disagree on how to handle this situation. Sometimes the new owner is simply out of luck and the prepaid rent remains with the former owner. Sometimes the former owner is required to turn over prepaid rent to the new owner. And sometimes, if there is no record of the prepaid rent and the former owner is unavailable, the unfortunate tenant may be required to pay the rent again, this time to the new owner.

If a tenant prepays rent, he or she should be sure to get a receipt for the amount paid. A purchaser acquiring property with a pre-existing lease should find out what rent has already been paid, and how much is currently owing.

Assignment. Unless the lease provides otherwise, a tenant may assign the lease to someone else. An **assignment** transfers the entire remaining portion of the lease to a new party.

> **Example:** Kirk leases an apartment from October 1, 2004, through September 30, 2005. In March, Kirk changes jobs and wants to move to a new area of the city. He assigns the remainder of the lease to Mary Alice. Mary Alice agrees to pay the rent to the landlord from April 1 through September 30.

In an assignment situation, the original tenant becomes secondarily liable for the rent. In the above example, this means that Mary Alice has the primary responsibility for paying the rent. If Mary Alice does not pay, Kirk is still liable to the landlord for payment of the rent.

Sublease. A **sublease** is similar to an assignment except that it is for a shorter period than the entire remainder of the lease. In a sublease, the subtenant pays the rent to the original tenant rather than to the landlord.

> **Example:** Kirk leases an apartment from October 1, 2004, through September 30, 2005. In March, Kirk accepts a special three-month job in Taiwan. He subleases his

apartment for the three months he will be gone. Mary Alice agrees to pay rent to Kirk from April 1 through June 30. Kirk continues to pay rent to the landlord.

A sublease does not alter the original landlord-tenant agreement. The original tenant is still primarily liable for payment of rent to the landlord.

Most commercial leases prohibit both assignments and subleases without the landlord's consent. The tenant must get the landlord's approval before assigning or subleasing. In most cases, denial of approval must not be unreasonable or without just cause.

Case Example:

Ernst Home Center leased commercial space in a mall. The lease stated that the tenants could not assign or sublet the premises without the written consent of the lessors, "whose consent shall not be unreasonably withheld."

Ernst decided to close its store and requested permission to assign the lease to Value Village, a retailer selling used clothing that had been donated to charities. The landlord did not consent and Ernst sued for breach of the lease.

At trial, the court found that the landlord withheld consent because it objected to the type of merchandise sold by Value Village and the "tone" the store presented. No consideration had been given to the financial stability of Value Village.

The lease contained no restrictions as to the nature of the business to be operated on the leased premises. The court held that consent to the assignment was unreasonably withheld. The landlord was ordered to allow assignment of the lease to Value Village. *Ernst Home Center Inc. v. Sato*, 80 Wn .App. 473, 910 P.2d 486 (1996).

In general, courts do not favor restrictions on the right to transfer real property. A landlord must be careful in drafting a limitation on assignment or subleasing. If there is any question or ambiguity, a court will generally favor the right to assign or sublease.

Novation. In a **novation**, a new contract is created and the old contract is extinguished. The purpose of a novation is to terminate the liability of the tenant under the terms of the original lease. A novation may occur when the tenant and landlord negotiate and replace the original lease with a new one, or when the landlord agrees to release the tenant from the lease and create a new lease with a third party.

Example: Kirk leases an apartment from October 1, 2004, through September 30, 2005. In March, Kirk is transferred by his firm to their Taiwan office. His friend Mary Alice likes Kirk's apartment and wants to rent it when he leaves.

Kirk explains his situation to the landlord. The landlord agrees to terminate the lease with Kirk and create a new lease with Mary Alice. Kirk's lease and liability terminate on March 31, 2005, and Mary Alice signs a new lease from April 1, 2005, through March 31, 2006.

Kirk no longer has any responsibility to the landlord. Even if Mary Alice doesn't pay the rent, Kirk is not liable because his contract has terminated and a new contract was created with Mary Alice.

Fig. 13.1 Ways to transfer a leasehold

TRANSFERRING A LEASEHOLD	
SALE	New owner takes subject to existing leases
ASSIGNMENT	Original tenant becomes secondarily liable
SUBLEASE	Original tenant remains primarily liable
NOVATION	Liability of original tenant is completely terminated

Residential Landlord-Tenant Act

In 1973, Washington adopted the Residential Landlord-Tenant Act (RLTA). The act's basic purpose is to protect residential tenants from unfair practices and poor living conditions. It imposes a number of duties on residential landlords that other landlords aren't required to fulfill. Nonresidential (commercial or industrial) tenants are presumed to be more sophisticated than residential tenants, and better able to protect their interests during lease negotiations.

The remainder of this chapter focuses on residential tenancies and the rights and duties of landlords and tenants under the RLTA.

Application and Exemptions

Although the RLTA applies to the rental of almost any form of housing, a number of exceptions exist:

1. residents of public or private medical, religious, educational, recreational, or correctional institutions, including correctional facilities, nursing homes, monasteries and convents, and hospitals (but not college dormitories);
2. tenants under a purchase and sale agreement to buy the dwelling;
3. residents of a hotel, motel, or other transient lodging;
4. temporary tenants of property condemned for public use, where the tenant is the owner;
5. residents of land rented incidental to land leased for agricultural purposes;
6. residents of housing for seasonal agricultural employees;
7. tenants leasing public lands from the state of Washington;
8. tenants employed by the landlord, where the right to occupy is conditioned on employment on the property; and
9. tenants in a single-family dwelling with a lease for one year or more, or with an option to purchase, as long as their attorney has approved the lease.

In addition, relationships between landlords and tenants of mobile or floating homes may be subject to different or additional rules.

Mobile Homes. Washington also has a Mobile Home Landlord-Tenant Act (MHLTA). In a mobile home park, tenants usually own their mobile homes and rent a space from the park owners. It's often difficult for a mobile home owner to move. In many communities, there are few mobile home parks and few vacancies in those parks.

To address this problem, some provisions in the MHLTA differ from the RLTA. For instance, a landlord may not offer a mobile home lot for rent for less than one year. If a tenant wishes to rent a lot for less than a year, or on a month-to-month basis, the tenant must waive the right to a one-year lease in writing.

When a tenant is renting the mobile home itself (rather than just the lot), the RLTA applies instead of the MHLTA.

Floating Homes. In Washington, especially around the Seattle area, many people own floating homes. Specific city ordinances have been passed concerning floating homes. For instance, six months' notice is required for termination of a floating home moorage in Seattle. These specific ordinances override any differing provisions in the RLTA involving floating homes.

Agricultural Leases. Sometimes a residential lease is incidental to an agricultural lease. For instance, a farm is rented and a farmhouse goes along with the farm. The tenant moves into the farmhouse and farms the property. Even though the farmhouse is a residence, if its rental is part of the agricultural lease, it may be excluded from the RLTA.

Rights, Duties, and Liabilities

Whenever two parties enter into a contractual agreement, they agree to certain terms and obligations. Since a lease is a contract, the parties to a lease are bound by the terms agreed to in the lease. Under the RLTA, the parties are also required to fulfill certain other duties and obligations, even if these duties are not specifically mentioned in the lease.

Duties of the Landlord Prior to Possession. There are certain restrictions on what a landlord can require of a prospective tenant prior to occupancy. For example, a landlord cannot require a prospective tenant to pay a fee for the privilege of being placed on a waiting list to be considered as a tenant for a dwelling unit.

A landlord who has offered a prospective tenant a unit may charge a fee to ensure that the prospective tenant will actually move into that unit. However, the landlord must provide the prospective tenant with a receipt for the deposit along with a statement describing the conditions under which the fee is refundable. If the tenant does move in, the landlord must credit the fee against the first month's rent or the required security deposit. If the tenant does not move in, the landlord may keep the full amount of the fee if so agreed. This fee cannot include any amount used to pay for a screening service or background check.

If the landlord uses a tenant **screening** service, the landlord may charge the tenant only the actual costs incurred; if the landlord conducts his or her own screening, the landlord may charge the tenant for the actual costs of the screening, as long as those costs do not exceed the customary fee charged by a screening service. Before charging a tenant a screening fee, the landlord must notify the tenant in writing: 1) about what a tenant screen entails, 2) the tenant's rights to dispute the accuracy of the information provided, and 3) the name and address of the tenant screening service to be used.

Possession. A tenant has the right to possession of the rented premises on the agreed date. Implied in every lease is a covenant to deliver possession to the tenant. If the tenant is prevented from gaining possession, this implied covenant has been breached and the tenant may be excused from paying some or all of the rent.

The general rule is that if the covenant to deliver possession is breached, the tenant may rescind or cancel the agreement. But if the tenant elects not to rescind and merely waits for the landlord to clear the premises, the tenant may request only consequential damages.

Consequential damages are an award of money made by a court to compensate a party for the consequences or results of some act. For instance, suppose a lease calls for the new tenant to take possession on April 1, but the old tenant does not leave until April 5. The new tenant moves in on April 6. Since the new tenant did not rescind the lease, but merely waited for the premises to be vacated, the new tenant must still pay rent, but may request consequential damages. In this case, the rent would probably be prorated to subtract the amount for April 1 through April 5. In addition, the new tenant might also claim damages for storage fees or additional rent in another location for the extra five days.

Case Example:

Hagbert agreed to rent a piece of property from Draper from July 1, 1980, through June 30, 1983. Hagbert paid a security deposit and the first one-half month's rent.

At the time the lease began, trucks owned by the prior tenant were still using part of the property. There was some disagreement about how long the trucks remained (possibly several weeks). Although Hagbert moved onto the premises, he did not pay any additional rent.

Draper sent Hagbert a notice to pay rent. When Hagbert did not pay, Draper filed a lawsuit. Hagbert claimed that he did not have to pay rent because Draper had breached the implied covenant to deliver possession.

Draper did breach the implied covenant to deliver full possession (because of the presence of the former tenant's trucks). However, Hagbert did not exercise his option to rescind the lease but continued in possession of the property until at least October. Therefore, he only had a claim for consequential damages.

In other words, Hagbert could not completely avoid paying rent, because he took possession of the property. However, he could request damages for the time period between when he was supposed to be able to take complete possession and when the former tenant's trucks were removed. *Draper Mach. Works, Inc. v. Hagbert*, 34 Wn. App. 483, 663 P.2d 141 (1983).

Covenant of Quiet Enjoyment. The landlord's covenant of quiet enjoyment promises that the tenant shall enjoy possession of the premises in peace and without disturbance. This doesn't refer to a noisy neighborhood, but to the right to undisturbed possession.

Under the covenant of quiet enjoyment, a tenant is protected from intrusion by the landlord or anyone else claiming a right to the property. This covenant is breached upon **eviction** of the tenant (either **actual** or **constructive eviction**).

> **Example:** Mother Goose Day Care Center rented a portion of the Talmage Building. A chemical company rented another section of the building. An accident in the chemical company caused a harmful chemical spill. Environmental guidelines required the whole building to be shut down while the extent of the danger was investigated. Mother Goose was forced to vacate the building and had to rent a new location. The covenant of quiet enjoyment was violated.
>
> Mother Goose has effectively been evicted from the building. Even if it is only a temporary situation, Mother Goose may have a claim against the landlord for breach of the covenant of quiet enjoyment and constructive eviction. (Note that depending on the specific facts of the case, both Mother Goose and the landlord may also have claims against the chemical company.)

Privacy. Once a tenant has taken possession of the property, he or she has a right of privacy. The landlord may not enter the property without the tenant's consent, except in an emergency. An emergency is any sudden and unexpected threatened or actual injury to property or people.

> **Example:** A water pipe bursts and begins flooding a tenant's apartment. The tenant is not at home. This is an emergency in which the landlord would be authorized to immediately enter the apartment to attempt to stop the flood.

> **Example:** Several apartments have had trouble with bathroom ceiling fans that turn off-center, causing a loud noise when the fan is used. The landlord decides to have a repairman inspect all of the fans in the building. This is not an emergency. The landlord must give the tenants notice and request consent for this inspection.

When requesting entry to inspect the unit, make non-emergency repairs, or provide other services, the landlord must give the tenant two days' notice. The landlord may enter the unit to show it to a prospective buyer or new tenant at a specified time, after giving the current tenant one day's notice. The landlord has a right of access only at times that are reasonable for the tenant. (For instance, the landlord could not request access at two o'clock in the morning.) If the landlord has complied with these requirements, the tenant may not unreasonably withhold permission to enter.

Rent. Not surprisingly, the tenant's most important duty is to pay the agreed rental amount on time. Most rental agreements specify when rent is due (usually the first day of the month). If there is no agreement as to when rent is due, the common law provides that rent is due at the end of the rental term.

A landlord has the right to terminate a lease or evict a tenant for nonpayment of rent. Many landlords impose a late charge if the rent is not paid by a certain date. A late charge is enforceable only if it is reasonable and was called to the tenant's attention at the beginning of the tenancy.

Damage and Security Deposits. A tenant should leave the property in essentially the same condition that it was in at the beginning of the tenancy. The tenant must not intentionally or negligently damage the rental unit. A tenant is liable for any alterations made to the property without the landlord's approval, and for any damage beyond normal wear and tear. A tenant cannot be charged for reasonable wear and tear caused by normal use of the premises.

A **security deposit** or **damage deposit** is money paid by the tenant over and above rent, for the security of the landlord. An average security deposit is about one month's rent, although there is no specific dollar requirement, so the amount may vary. This deposit secures the landlord against the cost of repairing damage caused by the tenant, or against a tenant who abandons the property before the term of the lease is up or without paying the current month's rent.

No security deposit may be collected by a landlord unless the rental agreement is in writing and a written checklist is provided that specifically describes the current condition and cleanliness of the premises and furnishings. This checklist must be signed and dated by both the landlord and the tenant, and a copy must be given to the tenant.

Under the RLTA, a landlord must return a security deposit to the tenant within 14 days after termination of the rental agreement. (Mailing the deposit within the 14-day period is sufficient, even if the tenant doesn't receive it until a few days later.) The landlord may retain no more of the deposit than is needed to pay for damage or overdue rent. If any portion of the deposit is retained, the landlord must give the tenant a written statement explaining why it was retained (also within 14 days). A court may award the tenant up to two times the amount of the deposit if the landlord intentionally refuses to give the required written statement or pay the refund due.

Nonrefundable Fees. Any nonrefundable amounts required by the landlord (such as a carpet cleaning fee) must be designated in writing as nonrefundable. These amounts may not be taken out of a deposit or designated as a deposit.

If a tenant has caused severe damage and the cost to repair is greater than the amount of the security deposit, the landlord may bring an action against the former tenant for the amount exceeding the deposit. The fact that a security deposit was paid does not protect the tenant from liability for additional damages.

Case Example:

Charron rented a luxury apartment for more than a year. Upon renting the apartment, he paid a security deposit of $225. When he vacated the apartment, the manager discovered that the living room carpet was damaged by rust or mildew stains from plant containers, and the area in front of the wet bar was described as "mutilated." There were also cigarette burns in the carpet in the den. Carpeting in the bedroom and hallway was undamaged.

The manager made inquiries about cleaning or repairing the carpeting but was told that it could not be restored. This particular pattern of carpet had been discontinued, so the damaged areas could not be replaced.

The owners ended up replacing all of the carpeting throughout the entire apartment. The total cost of replacement was $2,723.19. The owners requested additional damages from Charron, over and above the security deposit. Charron argued that he could not be required to pay more than the security deposit.

At trial, the court determined that (especially in light of the fact that this was a luxury apartment) it was reasonable to replace all of the carpeting. The court also found that payment of a security deposit does not protect a tenant from additional liability. The court ordered Charron to pay damages of $1,200. *James S. Black & Co. v. Charron*, 22 Wn. App. 11, 587 P.2d 196 (1978).

Locks. A landlord must provide tenants with reasonably adequate locks and furnish keys for the locks. Some local housing codes may contain more specific requirements for locks.

> **Example:** In Seattle, landlords are required to provide dead-bolt locks on all buildings other than detached single-family houses.

Criminal Acts. In the past, landlords have had no duty to protect tenants against criminal acts of third parties. However, some courts are moving toward imposing liability on landlords for "failure to protect" if the act was foreseeable. This is especially true if the landlord has advertised security protection or if the building is in a high-crime area where criminal activity is likely and foreseeable.

Case Example:

A tenant was assaulted inside her apartment by a neighboring tenant, who entered the victim's apartment through a hole in the wall separating the attic space of the two apartments. The assailant had previously entered the victim's apartment in the same manner. The victim had complained to the landlord, who had merely nailed a piece of lumber over the hole.

The victim sued her landlord for negligence. The court held the landlord liable, holding that a residential landlord has a duty to protect its tenants against foreseeable criminal acts of third parties. *Griffin v. West RS, Inc.* 97 Wn. App. 557 (1999).

Under certain circumstances, threatening behavior can be grounds for terminating a lease. If a tenant is threatened by another tenant with a deadly weapon, that other tenant is arrested as a result of the threatening behavior, and the landlord fails to file an unlawful detainer action against that tenant, then the threatened tenant may immediately terminate the rental agreement without any further liability for rent.

If a tenant is threatened by a landlord with a deadly weapon, and the threat leads to the arrest of the landlord, the tenant may immediately terminate the rental agreement without further obligations.

If a tenant has a valid protection order (which is available for the landlord's inspection), the order is violated while the tenant is occupying the rental unit, and the tenant notifies the proper authorities of the violation, then the tenant may terminate the rental agreement and leave the premises without any further obligations under the lease.

Codes and Rules. A landlord must maintain the premises in compliance with all state and local statutes and ordinances that substantially affect the tenant's health and safety. This includes ensuring that the building meets all building code requirements.

In order to enforce a code or regulation, a tenant must show that the violation poses a threat to health or safety. Violations based on faulty wiring or plumbing will be much easier to enforce than something that is not life-threatening like a door that is inches narrower than the code requirement.

Along with the landlord, the tenant must also comply with obligations imposed by municipal, county, and state codes, statutes, ordinances, and regulations. For example, a tenant is required to keep all smoke alarms in proper working order and refrain from dangerous and threatening behavior. In addition, a tenant has a duty to obey any reasonable rules or obligations imposed by the landlord that are noted upon moving in or later adopted with proper written notice from the landlord. All rules brought to the tenant's attention at the beginning of the tenancy automatically become part of the rental agreement. The landlord has the right to terminate the lease or evict the tenant for violating those rules or the terms of the lease.

Pests. A landlord must provide a reasonable program for the control of insects, rodents, and other pests. However, there is no obligation to control infestation in a single-family residence if the problem did not arise until after the tenancy began. The landlord also has no duty when the infestation is caused by the tenant.

> **Example:** Tenant consistently leaves food uncovered on counters and in cabinets. This attracts ants. It will be Tenant's responsibility to get rid of the ants.

Maintenance. The landlord has a duty to maintain any shared or common areas in a reasonably clean, sanitary, and safe condition. This includes keeping them free from anything that would increase the hazard of fire or accident, such as old rags at the bottom of a stairwell, or snow and ice on an entryway. Common areas are those areas of a building that are used by all of the tenants or by the public. Typical common areas include entries, elevators, hallways, stairways, and lobbies.

Case Example:

Lulu Geise, a tenant in a mobile home park, injured herself by slipping on snow and ice that had accumulated in a common area of the park. She brought a lawsuit against the Lees, owners of the Lazy Wheels Mobile Home Park.

The Lees had actual notice of the dangerous icy condition because they had been informed by several tenants and because other residents of the park had already fallen, one even having to go to the hospital.

The court stated that a landlord has an obligation to keep common areas in a reasonably safe condition for the tenants' use. This doesn't mean that the landlord guarantees the tenants' safety. It simply means that the landlord must exercise reasonable care in keeping all common areas reasonably safe from hazards likely to cause injury, if the landlord has actual or constructive notice of the danger. *Geise v. Lee*, 84 Wn.2d 866, 529 P.2d 1054 (1975).

While a landlord must keep the common areas clean and safe, the tenant must keep his or her private portion of the premises clean and safe. This rule requires the tenant to maintain cleanliness standards that will not cause health problems, attract pests, or interfere with other tenants' use or enjoyment of the property. A tenant must properly dispose of all waste and eliminate pest infestations caused by the tenant.

Case Example:

Richard Taylor resided in the Gill Street Apartments. He was served with a notice of termination. The notice stated that he had breached the rental agreement because he did not keep his apartment in a clean and safe condition, he did not properly dispose of garbage, and he unreasonably disturbed his neighbors' peaceful enjoyment of the premises.

Taylor did not move by the stated deadline, and filed a complaint against the apartment owners protesting the eviction notice. In the court proceeding, there was testimony that Taylor's apartment badly needed cleaning and exuded a very bad odor. Taylor essentially admitted that he left his drapes open when he walked around his apartment in the nude (this apartment was near the children's play area). Taylor had refused to move his car to permit snow removal when requested to do so. He would sit in the parking lot blowing his horn for an extended period of time if his parking place was occupied. Several witnesses testified to seeing Taylor frequently intoxicated and driving while intoxicated, and one tenant testified that he had seen Taylor hit a parked car while intoxicated.

Based on this evidence, the court agreed that Taylor had breached the rental agreement. The court entered a writ of eviction ordering Taylor to leave the premises. *Taylor v. Gill Street Investments*, 743 P.2d 345 (Alaska 1987).

Habitability. In all residential rental agreements, there is an **implied warranty of habitability**. This warranty places a duty on the landlord to keep the premises fit for human habitation at all times during the tenancy. Any clause in a lease in which the tenant waives this right is against public policy and will not be enforced. A breach of this warranty may relieve the tenant from the obligation to pay rent.

Case Example:

Ronald Foisy rented a house from Richard Wyman. Foisy signed a six-month lease that required payment of $300 ($50 per month). During the term of the lease, Foisy only paid $95, leaving $205 still owing.

Wyman brought a lawsuit seeking unpaid rent and damages. In his defense, Foisy argued that Wyman had breached the implied warranty of habitability.

The house contained a number of severe defects, including: no heat, no hot water tank, broken windows, a broken door, water running through the bedroom, an improperly seated and leaking toilet, a leaking sink, broken water pipes, and termites in the basement.

Foisy knew about most of these problems when he signed the lease. In fact, because of these defects, the rent was reduced from $87 per month to $50 per month. (As a side note, the court stated that this type of bargaining is contrary to public policy and the purpose of the doctrine of the implied warranty of habitability. A disadvantaged tenant should not be placed in a position of agreeing to live in an uninhabitable dwelling.)

The court stated that if the premises were found to be totally uninhabitable because of these defects, Foisy's obligation to pay rent could be relieved by the landlord's breach of the implied warranty of habitability. However, if the premises were found to be partially habitable, Foisy would be liable for the reasonable rental value of the house in its substandard condition. *Foisy v. Wyman*, 83 Wn.2d 22, 515 P.2d 160 (1973).

Utilities and Appliances. Facilities adequate to supply heat and hot and cold water as reasonably required by the tenant must be provided. This does not mean that the landlord must pay for these services, but merely that the facilities must be available.

It is unlawful for a landlord to intentionally cause the termination of utility services, except for a reasonable time in order to make repairs. A landlord who unlawfully terminates utilities may be liable to the tenant for any actual damages sustained, plus up to $100 for each day the tenant was deprived of service.

The landlord must maintain all electrical, plumbing, heating, and other facilities and appliances supplied by the landlord. The landlord has no responsibility to maintain any appliances supplied by the tenant. For instance, if the tenant owns and installs his or her own washer and dryer, the landlord is not responsible if the washer malfunctions and overflows. The tenant is responsible for all of his or her own appliances. Fixtures and appliances supplied by the landlord must be properly used and maintained by the tenant. A tenant may be responsible if an appliance has problems caused by the tenant's ill-considered use of it.

Example: Tenant does not own a washer and dryer, but hates going to the laundromat. Tenant has been washing the dishrags in the dishwasher along with the dishes. One of the dishrags gets caught in the dishwasher motor. Tenant will be responsible for the cost of repairs to the dishwasher, because her improper use of the dishwasher was the cause of the problem.

Except in the case of a single-family residence, the landlord must provide garbage cans and arrange for regular trash removal.

Structural Components. A building must be kept in a reasonably weathertight condition, and all structural components of the building (the chimney, roof, floors, etc.) must be maintained by the landlord. It is not required that these be in perfect condition, but merely that they be in reasonably good repair to safely perform the function for which they were intended.

Repairs. Formerly, under common law, a landlord had no duty to repair rental property. Tenants simply took the property as they found it. If they noticed defects in the property, they had two options: not to rent the property, or to arrange for repairs themselves. If defects arose during the rental period, it was up to the tenant to repair them. In modern times, this rule has swung completely around, and now the duty to repair rests mainly on the landlord's shoulders.

Under the RLTA, the landlord has a duty to make repairs to keep the premises habitable. If the premises were substandard to begin with, it is not enough simply to maintain the status quo. Repairs must be made to bring the residence up to a habitable standard.

When a repair needs to be made, the tenant must give the landlord written notice and allow a reasonable time for the repair. In general, a landlord has 24 hours to begin to restore heat, hot or cold water, or electricity, or to repair a hazardous condition. If the tenant is deprived of the use of the refrigerator, range, oven, or a major plumbing fixture supplied by the landlord, repairs must be started within 48 hours. In all other cases, the landlord must begin repairs within 10 days after receiving notice of the problem.

A landlord has no duty to repair a defective condition caused by the conduct of the tenant. This includes the conduct of the tenant's family or guests. A landlord is also not responsible for repairs when the tenant refuses to allow the landlord access for repairs.

If a landlord has a duty to repair but does not begin repairs within the applicable statutory time limit, the tenant has several possible remedies:

- The tenant may notify the landlord of intent to vacate and then move out, without further obligation and without forfeiting any prepaid rent or deposit.
- The tenant may arrange to have the repairs performed by a competent third party, after providing the landlord with an estimate of the cost. The tenant may then pay the third party and deduct the cost from the rent. The deduction cannot exceed one month's rent, and if the tenant uses this remedy more than once, the deductions in any 12-month period cannot exceed two months' rent. The landlord must be given an opportunity to inspect the repair work.
- When repairs will cost no more than half of one month's rent, the tenant may choose to perform them (as long as no license is required for the type of work involved).

Fig. 13.2 Deadlines for making repairs

REPAIR DEADLINES	
24 HOURS	Heat, hot or cold water, electricity, or hazardous condition
72 HOURS	Refrigerator, range, oven, or major plumbing fixture
10 DAYS	All other non-urgent repairs

The tenant must make the repairs in a workmanlike manner and allow the landlord to inspect the repairs. The tenant may then deduct the cost of materials and labor from the next month's rent. A tenant may not deduct more than half of one month's rent per repair, or more than one month's rent in any 12-month period.

- A tenant may ask a court or arbitrator to determine that the rent should be reduced until the defect is corrected or repaired.
- When a dangerous problem exists, and the repair and deduct remedy is not adequate to correct it, the tenant can establish a rent escrow. The tenant must first arrange with the local government to have the property inspected. If the inspector certifies that the problem threatens the tenant's health or safety, the tenant may deposit rent into an escrow account when it is due, instead of paying it to the landlord. The tenant must send the landlord written notice of the deposit and disclose the location of the account.

To get the funds released from the escrow account, the landlord must provide a certification from the local government that the defective condition has been repaired. Or the landlord may file a court action for release of the funds, or to have the property's mortgage, insurance, utilities, and the necessary repairs paid out of the escrow account.

Access to Landlord. A landlord must provide a tenant with the name and address of the landlord. A tenant must also be immediately notified of any change of landlord. Many of the tenant's remedies or obligations require giving notice to the landlord. Therefore, the landlord must be available to receive notice, or must appoint someone to receive it on his or her behalf.

Termination of a Lease

A lease may be terminated in a variety of ways. The rights of the parties will vary depending on the reason for termination.

Mutual Agreement

A landlord and tenant may mutually agree to terminate a lease at any time. This mutual agreement is called a **surrender**. However, many leases simply terminate on the date specified in the lease agreement. If a lease is a periodic (month-to-month) lease, it may be terminated by either party upon proper **notice of termination**. The written notice of termination must be given to the other party at least 30 days before the end of the rental period. If the tenancy is covered by the Residential Landlord-Tenant Act, the written notice of termination must be given to the other party at least 20 days before the end of the rental period.

Exceptions. In certain situations, a tenant may terminate a residential lease with less than 20 days' notice. If a tenant is in the armed forces and receives reassignment or deployment orders that do not allow for 20 days' notice, the tenant and his or her spouse and dependents may terminate a lease without 20 days' notice.

A tenant that has been the victim of domestic violence, sexual assault, or stalking may also terminate a lease without the required 20 days' notice. In this situation, the tenant must provide the landlord with a report of the incident that has been signed by a qualified third party such as a law enforcement officer, mental health professional, or member of the clergy.

Renewal. Sometimes when a lease expires, or is near expiration, the parties decide to renew the lease. Upon renewal, the terms of the lease may be renegotiated and the rent amount may be increased or decreased. Thirty days' notice is required for a rental increase or other change in the lease terms.

Abandonment

Abandonment is defined as an absolute relinquishment of the premises by the tenant before the end of the lease. When a tenant abandons the leased property, the landlord usually wants to retake possession of the property without waiting until the end of the lease term. Most leases contain a clause permitting reentry by the landlord after abandonment, but reserving the right to collect rent from the absent tenant.

When the tenancy is month-to-month, the tenant is liable for rent for the 30 days following the date the landlord learns of the abandonment, or the date the next regular rental payment would have become due, whichever occurs first.

When the tenancy is for a term greater than one month, the tenant is liable for either the entire rent for the remainder of the term, or the rent accrued during the period reasonably necessary to rent the premises again, plus additional costs.

The landlord has a duty to try to mitigate the damages by renting the property to a new tenant as soon as possible. However, if a new tenant cannot be found after reasonable attempts by the landlord, the original tenant remains liable for damages caused by the abandonment.

Example: Landlord leases an apartment to Tenant from June 1, 2004, through May 31, 2005. Tenant abandons the apartment in October. Landlord retakes possession and attempts to rent the apartment. However, with Christmas coming up, most people don't want to move until after the first of the year. Although Landlord advertises extensively, he is unable to find a new tenant until January 15.

The original tenant is liable for the rent owed for October, November, December, and half of January. Since the landlord found a new tenant, the original tenant is not required to pay rent from mid-January through May, even though this was the original lease agreement. However, the original tenant may also be liable for expenses incurred in finding a new tenant. He could be required to pay for the cost of advertising and any additional work necessary to rent the apartment.

Case Example:

The Meyers owned and leased business premises to Western Farmers Association. The lease was then assigned to Higgins. Without any notification, Higgins abandoned the premises. The Meyers attempted, without success, to find another tenant for the building. The Meyers brought a lawsuit against Western Farmers for the unpaid rent and for reimbursement for repairs.

Western Farmers brought a cross-complaint charging that the Meyers failed to mitigate their damages by leasing to a new tenant. The court found that the Meyers had tried to mitigate but no new tenant was found. An honest and reasonable effort is all that is required.

Western Farmers was therefore liable for unpaid rent and for repairs. *Meyers v. Western Farmers Association*, 75 Wn.2d 133, 449 P.2d 104 (1969).

Eviction

Almost all leases provide that the lease may be forfeited and the tenant evicted for non-payment of rent or for violation of the terms of the lease. However, if the tenant fails to pay the rent, the lease is not automatically terminated. The landlord must first give notice to the tenant of the nonpayment. If the tenant still fails to pay, the landlord may begin legal proceedings to recover rent payments or evict the tenant.

If the tenant breaches the terms of the lease or uses the premises in a manner not authorized by the lease, the landlord may terminate the lease and evict the tenant. Also, if the tenant uses the premises for illegal activity, the landlord may demand that the tenant cease the illegal activity or vacate the premises.

Washington's Residential Landlord-Tenant Act specifically allows a landlord to evict a tenant based upon a reasonable belief that illegal drug activity is taking place in the unit.

Example: Landlord discovers that Tenant is using his apartment to manufacture and sell drugs. Landlord may begin eviction proceedings to remove the tenant from the premises, and notify law enforcement agencies that illegal drug activity is taking place.

Retaliation. When a landlord evicts a tenant in response to complaints made by the tenant, it is considered **retaliatory eviction**. Under the RLTA, a landlord cannot retaliate against a tenant simply because that tenant has requested necessary repairs or has complained in good faith to the proper authorities concerning violations of health or building code regulations.

Retaliatory action includes eviction, increasing the rent, reduction of services, or increasing the obligations of the tenant.

Presumptions. If a landlord initiates any of the actions listed above within 90 days after the tenant's complaint or after inspection by an agency resulting from the tenant's complaint, it creates a presumption that the landlord's action was retaliatory. This presumption may be rebutted by evidence from the landlord showing that the action was not retaliatory.

It is sometimes difficult to judge whether an action is retaliatory or not. For instance, raising a particular tenant's rent as a punishment for the tenant's complaints is unlawful. However, raising all tenants' rents in order to pay for necessary repairs complained about by a tenant is acceptable.

A landlord may not single out and evict one tenant who has made complaints. However, if code violations or necessary repairs are so extensive that the landlord cannot afford to bring the building up to the required standards, the landlord may take the entire building off the rental market.

Results. In any lawsuit or eviction proceeding where the tenant prevails on a claim of retaliatory action, the tenant is entitled to recover costs and attorney's fees. If the landlord prevails by showing that the action was not retaliatory, the landlord may recover costs and attorney's fees.

Unlawful Detainer. An action in unlawful detainer is the most common procedure used by a landlord to recover possession of property from a **defaulting** tenant (a tenant who has failed to pay rent when due). The landlord must give the tenant proper notice of default and allow an opportunity to cure the default. If the tenant fails to **cure** (pay all rent owed), the landlord may file an unlawful detainer action. If the court finds the tenant in default, it issues a **writ of possession**, which requires the tenant to leave the premises or be forcibly removed by the sheriff.

Self-help Eviction. The process of legal eviction is often slow. However, a landlord should be warned against any attempt at self-help eviction. A landlord may not remove or exclude a tenant without a court order. Sometimes a landlord attempts to force a tenant to leave by cutting off utilities. This is illegal, and the landlord may be fined $100 for each day the tenant is without utility service, plus damages and reasonable attorney's fees.

Lockouts. A **lockout** is another method of self-help eviction: the landlord locks the tenant out of the rental unit by changing the locks while the tenant is out. Lockouts are generally prohibited. If a lockout is prohibited by a local ordinance, the police may assist a tenant who has been locked out.

Example: In Seattle, police enforce the section of the housing code prohibiting lock-outs. The police may arrest or issue a citation to a landlord who has unlawfully locked out a tenant.

Constructive Eviction. Eviction can occur when the landlord causes or permits a substantial interference with the tenant's possession of the property. **Constructive eviction** happens when an act materially disturbs the tenant's use or enjoyment of the premises so that the tenant is forced to move out.

Example: Tenant rents a small studio apartment from Landlord in August. Landlord tells Tenant that the apartment is heated by radiant heat. Tenant notices an old-fashioned radiator along one wall. When winter arrives, Tenant discovers that the radiator is broken and produces no heat. Landlord fails to repair the radiator or supply any heat.

Tenant has been constructively evicted because of lack of heat. Tenant can terminate the lease without liability for any further rent.

In the past, a tenant was required to actually move out before being entitled to claim constructive eviction. However, this rule has been somewhat relaxed. In these days of tight housing markets, high rent, and high deposit requirements, it is often hard or even impossible for a tenant to immediately find a new apartment to move into. Therefore even though a tenant has not actually moved from the premises, the tenant may sometimes claim constructive eviction and sue for damages or an abatement of rent.

Personal Property. A landlord may not take or detain a tenant's personal property unless the tenant has been evicted by a court order or the premises have been abandoned. If a landlord takes personal property in any other circumstances, or refuses to return property after a written demand by the tenant, the landlord may be liable for the value of the property, actual damages, and up to $100 per day for each day that the tenant is deprived of his or her property, up to $1,000.

If a tenant abandons the premises or is evicted and leaves personal property behind, it must be stored by the landlord and can be sold only if written notice is given to the former tenant or mailed to the tenant's last known address. If the property is sold, proceeds that are in excess of the landlord's claim must be kept by the landlord for at least one year. After one year, if no claim is made by the tenant for the balance of the proceeds, they become the property of the landlord.

Destruction of the Premises

If a lease is for a part of a building, such as an office, apartment, or commercial space, the destruction of the building will frustrate the entire purpose of the lease and the tenant will be released from the duty to pay rent.

If the lease is for the land and any buildings thereon, or for the use of an entire building, the destruction of the building or part of the building does not necessarily terminate the lease. The tenant may still be required to pay rent to the end of the rental period. This situation usually occurs only in a commercial or agricultural lease.

A lease should contain provisions concerning how the parties will handle destruction of the premises. Normally, a lease specifies who will maintain insurance on the property, and who is liable for rebuilding if a structure is destroyed by fire or other casualty. If there is no express stipulation, and the building is destroyed without fault, the loss generally falls on the landlord.

Case Example:

Frank Payne leased two hydroponic greenhouses from Washington Hydroculture, Inc. The lease contained a general maintenance and delivery clause that stated that Payne would maintain the greenhouses and, upon expiration of the term, would surrender them in as good a condition as they were in when possession was taken.

Both greenhouses burned down in a fire. Washington Hydroculture alleged that because of the maintenance and delivery clause, Payne was required to rebuild the greenhouses.

In construing covenants in a lease, a court looks to the plain meaning of the language used and the intention of the parties. In this lease, there was no express stipulation to restore buildings destroyed by fire or other casualty. The clause merely talked about maintenance. The general meaning of the word "maintain" is not "rebuild." If there is no express stipulation requiring the tenant to rebuild, then the loss will fall on the landlord. Payne was not required to rebuild the greenhouses. *Washington Hydroculture, Inc. v. Payne*, 96 Wn.2d 322, 635 P.2d 138 (1981).

Rent Control

Ordinances called **rent controls** set maximum limits on the amount of rent that a landlord may charge. Rent controls are intended to make property available at reasonable rates when there is a housing shortage.

Many economists believe that rent controls are not effective in accomplishing their primary goal of providing affordable housing. They argue that rents become high because demand for housing exceeds supply. In order for rents to come down, demand and supply must be brought into balance, either by reducing demand or by increasing supply. Rent controls usually have little positive effect toward either of these aims. Artificially low rents may in fact increase demand. In addition, the resulting low yields to property owners may discourage the construction of new housing.

Rent control laws are common in California and some other states. No rent control laws currently exist in Washington. Should any rent control laws be enacted in the future, they would have to be state laws, because rent control laws cannot be enacted by local ordinance in Washington.

Conclusion

Renting property can be a good situation for everyone involved. A broker who acts as a rental agent will earn a commission on the rental unit. A landlord can make money on the property while still retaining ownership. A tenant can gain possession and use of the property for a fraction of what it would cost to buy it. In the ideal rental situation, all those involved get what they want. But problems do sometimes arise.

The best way to avoid problems is to make sure that the rental agreement covers all of the situations in which problems commonly arise. The agreement should be a signed, valid contract. It should specify the duties and responsibilities of both parties and the consequences if either party breaches the agreement. In addition, each party has rights and duties established by law, regardless of the terms of their agreement.

Case Problem

The following is a hypothetical case problem. Most of the facts are taken from a real case. Based on what you have learned from this chapter, make a decision on the issues presented and then check to see if your answer matches the real decision by the court.

The Facts

Safeway Stores leased a commercial building for a term of 40 years, starting in 1941 and extending to 1981. The lease provided that Safeway "shall have the right to assign or transfer this lease or to underlease or sublet the whole or any part of said leased premises."

In the lease, Safeway agreed to pay a base rental of $120.83 per month. Safeway also paid all utility charges and taxes. In addition, the lease provided that if sales exceeded $207,000 in any one year, Safeway would pay additional rent of ¾ of 1% on all sales in excess of $207,000.

Safeway operated a grocery store out of the leased premises from 1941 to 1959. During this period, Safeway paid approximately $27,550 in base rent, and over $52,000 in additional rent based on gross sales in excess of $207,000.

In 1960, Safeway subleased the property to Hill Bros. Distributors, who operated the premises as a shoe store. Under the sublease, Hill Bros. paid Safeway $500 per month. Safeway continued to pay all utilities and taxes and paid the monthly base rental of $120.83 to the owners.

The sublease to Hill Bros. also contained a provision for rental based on a percentage of sales similar to the clause in the original lease. This percentage amount was to be paid directly to the owners (instead of through Safeway). While Hill Bros. operated the shoe store, no rental based upon percentage of gross sales was earned. (In other words, the shoe store did not have gross sales in excess of $207,000.)

The owners sought cancellation of the lease, claiming an implied restriction against any assignment or sublease for a use that would not yield a percentage rental comparable to that paid by Safeway.

The Questions

Was Safeway within its rights in subleasing the property? Was it required to sublease only to another grocery store or to a business with comparable sales amounts? Can the owners cancel the lease simply because the subtenant does not have gross sales as high as Safeway's?

The Answer

The court found that the lease did not place any restriction on use, so the building did not have to remain a grocery store. Safeway was completely within its rights in making the sublease, and could sublease to any type of business, since no restrictions were stated.

Restrictions against assignment are not favored by the courts. Any restrictions will be strictly construed against the owner and will not be extended by implication. The owners may have assumed that the property would remain a grocery store, but there were no such restrictions in the lease, and such a restriction will not be implied.

Requiring a subtenant with comparable sales to Safeway, so that the percentage portion of the rent would remain stable, would have the effect of changing the percentage rental to a fixed rental. The purpose of a percentage lease is to allow for increases or decreases in the tenant's sales. Safeway was not required to sublease to a business with comparable sales. If the shoe store's sales were to increase, the building owners might collect an additional percentage rental in the future.

The court found the terms of the lease clear and unambiguous, and the owners were not allowed to cancel the sublease. *Williams v. Safeway Stores, Inc.*, 198 Kan. 331, 424 P.2d 541 (1967).

Chapter Summary

- A lease must meet basic contract requirements in order to be valid. Certain information, such as identification of the parties, a description of the premises, the duration of the tenancy, and the rental amount, should always be included in a lease.

- There are many different types of leases, including fixed leases, graduated leases, net leases, percentage leases, and ground leases.

- The owner of property that is being leased is free to sell or transfer the property, but the new owner takes title subject to the lease. Unless otherwise agreed, a tenant has the right to assign his or her interest or sublet the property.

- The Residential Landlord-Tenant Act sets forth the rights and duties of residential landlords and tenants. Some of these rights and duties are different than those for parties to a commercial lease.

- A tenant has the rights of possession, quiet enjoyment, and privacy.

- A tenant also has a duty to pay rent and follow the terms of the lease. If a tenant defaults, a landlord may begin eviction proceedings.

- A tenant may be liable for damage to the premises beyond normal wear and tear. If the damage is greater than the amount of the security deposit, the landlord can seek additional damages. Money from a security deposit cannot be used for normal wear and tear.

- A landlord must provide locks and keys and, in certain circumstances, may be liable for the criminal actions of third parties against a tenant.

- Both landlord and tenant must follow local codes and regulations and maintain the premises in a clean and safe condition.

- The implied warranty of habitability in every residential lease requires the landlord to keep the premises fit for human habitation.

- A residential landlord also has the duty to make repairs. A tenant has certain specific remedies if the landlord refuses to make repairs.

- A lease may be terminated on the date specified in the lease agreement, upon proper notice, or by mutual surrender.

- If a tenant abandons the premises, the landlord has a duty to try to mitigate the damages by renting again as soon as possible. The tenant who abandoned may be liable for damages.

- A landlord has the right to evict a tenant for certain specified reasons. The landlord should follow the legal procedures instead of attempting self-help eviction.

- If leased premises are destroyed, the lease may indicate which party is responsible for rebuilding them. Without such a provision, the loss normally falls on the landlord.

Checklist of Problem Areas

Real Estate Licensee's Checklist

❑ If you are helping to sell property that is currently being leased, is the buyer aware of the existing lease? Does the buyer understand that he or she will purchase the property subject to the existing lease?

❑ If you are acting as a rental agent, do you understand the terms of the rental agreement, and are you familiar with the duties imposed on the landlord (your client) by law?

Landlord/Owner's Checklist

❑ Have you signed the lease and have all other requirements been met to make the lease valid?

❑ In a commercial percentage lease, has the exact percentage been specified and has the term "gross sales" been defined so there is no question as to what is included?

❑ If this is a residential lease, is the property fit for human habitation? Have all building code and statutory requirements been met? Are there any problems that need to be corrected or at least pointed out to the tenant?

❑ Will the property be vacant and ready for possession and occupancy by the new tenant on the specified date?

❑ Does the lease specify who is responsible for utility payments and insurance coverage?

❑ When terminating a lease, has proper notice been given to the tenant? Remember that retaliatory eviction is unlawful. Also remember that a lease cannot be arbitrarily terminated by the landlord before its specified ending date except for just cause. If a tenant is wrongfully evicted, the landlord will be liable for damages.

Tenant's Checklist

❑ What type of lease are you signing?

❑ What is the duration of the lease? Does it allow assignment or subleasing? Is an assignment or sublease subject to the landlord's approval?

❑ Have you paid the required security deposit and any required nonrefundable fees?

❑ If repairs are required, have you given proper notice to the landlord and allowed enough time for repairs to begin?

❑ When terminating a lease, have you given proper notice? Have you left the premises in as good a condition (except for normal wear and tear) as they were in at the beginning of the tenancy?

Chapter Quiz

1. Johnson signs a lease that provides for periodic increases in the rental amount based on the cost-of-living index. This type of lease is called a:

   a. fixed lease
   b. net lease
   c. graduated lease
   d. percentage lease

2. Thomas Nomiama signs an apartment lease for September 1, 2004, through August 31, 2005. In February, his brother buys a house and asks Tom to move in with him. Tom finds another person, Elizabeth Jenkins, to rent his apartment from February 15 through August 31. This is called:

   a. a sale
   b. an assignment
   c. a sublease
   d. a novation

3. Dave Albert signs a commercial lease that contains a clause stating that Dave may not assign or sublease without Landlord's consent. Dave wants to sublease to Leon Jones, who is African-American. Landlord refuses to give his consent. Which of the following is correct?

   a. Landlord is within his rights in refusing
   b. In most cases, a refusal to consent to an assignment or sublease must be reasonable—if Landlord's refusal is unreasonable, a court could order Landlord to allow the sublease
   c. Even if Landlord would otherwise be within his rights in arbitrarily refusing to give consent, Landlord's refusal could be considered discriminatory, which is a violation of state and federal laws
   d. Both b) and c)

4. A new tenant signs a lease that begins on March 1. On March 1, the old tenant is still living in the apartment. This means that:

   a. the new tenant must begin eviction proceedings against the old tenant
   b. the landlord has the duty to remove the old tenant so that the new tenant can take possession
   c. the new tenant's lease is automatically canceled, since the apartment is not available for possession
   d. None of the above

5. Tenant pays a security deposit of $200. Tenant has not caused any damage to the apartment beyond normal wear and tear. Under the Residential Landlord-Tenant Act, after Tenant moves out, how long does Landlord have to return the deposit?

   a. 7 days
   b. 14 days
   c. 30 days
   d. 45 days

6. A plumber is fixing the plumbing in apartment 4C. He discovers that the pipes have been leaking inside the walls for quite some time. He tells Landlord that the leaking pipes are probably causing damage behind the walls of all four apartments in building C. Landlord wants the leaking pipes repaired, but the repair work must be done from inside each apartment.

   a. Since this is an emergency, Landlord can enter all of the apartments without the tenants' permission
   b. This is not an emergency, as the pipes have been leaking for some time and a little longer won't matter—Landlord must give tenants one day's notice
   c. This is not an emergency, ast he pipes have been leaking for some time and a little longer won't matter—Landlord must give tenants two days' notice
   d. This is not an emergency—Landlord must give tenants one week's notice

7. Providing for garbage removal is a residential landlord's responsibility:

    a. only if the lease expressly assigns that duty to the landlord
    b. unless the rental property is a single-family home
    c. unless the lease makes it the tenant's duty
    d. except in the case of a fixed lease

8. Tenant rents office space in a high-rise office building downtown. After a heavy snowstorm, ice builds up on the entryway into the lobby. If Tenant slips and falls, breaking her leg:

    a. Landlord may be liable for failing to maintain the premises in a reasonably safe condition
    b. Landlord is not liable, because a snowstorm is an act of nature that cannot be foreseen
    c. other tenants in the building may be liable for failing to keep the common areas in a safe condition
    d. None of the above

9. Tenant lives in a high-crime area. He rents an apartment that is rundown, but it is all that he can afford. There is a lock on the outer building door, but the lock on Tenant's apartment door is broken. Tenant's apartment is vandalized and everything he owns is broken or stolen. Which is correct?

    a. Landlord cannot be liable because it was Tenant's duty to replace the door lock himself
    b. Even though Landlord did not provide a lock as required, he cannot be held liable for the criminal actions of third parties
    c. Landlord may be liable because of his failure to provide an adequate lock
    d. Landlord will be liable because all rental units must be supplied with dead-bolt locks

10. Tenant has a wild party in his apartment. One of his guests attempts to swing from the chandelier and pulls it out of the ceiling. Which of the following is correct?

    a. Landlord has the duty to repair any damage to the premises
    b. Landlord has no duty to repair a condition caused by Tenant; however, since this was a guest, Landlord is still obligated to repair
    c. Landlord has no duty to repair a condition caused by Tenant, or by family members or guests of Tenant
    d. None of the above

11. It is mid-January in Spokane. The temperature is about 20°. Suddenly the furnace quits working. Tenant immediately notifies Landlord. How long does Landlord have to begin repairs?

    a. 24 hours
    b. 48 hours
    c. 72 hours
    d. 10 days

12. Tenant has notified Landlord that her garbage disposal has stopped working. Landlord failed to repair it within a reasonable time. Tenant decides to take matters into her own hands. She buys a book on garbage disposal repairs and makes the repairs herself. Tenant figures her materials and labor cost approximately $65; her monthly rent is $400. Which of the following statements is true?

    a. Tenant is out $65 and Landlord has no obligation to repay her, since Tenant chose to make the repairs herself
    b. If the repairs were done in a workmanlike manner, and Tenant allows Landlord to inspect them, Tenant may deduct the $65 from the next month's rent
    c. Tenant may only deduct $50 from the next month's rent, since this is the statutory limit on self-help repairs
    d. None of the above

13. Landlord lives in a ground-floor apartment and Tenant lives upstairs. Landlord and Tenant have had several disagreements. Landlord knows that Tenant hates the smell of cooked cabbage. Several times a week Landlord makes cooked cabbage for dinner. The smell travels up the heat vent into Tenant's apartment. This is an example of:

    a. retaliatory eviction
    b. constructive eviction
    c. self-help eviction
    d. None of the above—normal cooking smells are not enough to establish any form of eviction

14. Tenant signs a one-year lease. After three months, he abandons the premises. Which of the following statements is correct?

    a. Tenant is liable for the remaining rent owed under the lease
    b. Landlord has a duty to mitigate by attempting to rent the premises to a new tenant as soon as possible
    c. Even if Landlord rents the premises to a new tenant, the first tenant may still be liable for damages, such as the cost of finding a new tenant
    d. All of the above

15. Tenant abandons the property but leaves behind some expensive stereo equipment. Landlord sends written notice to Tenant's last known address that the personal property will be sold. After a proper time period, the property is sold. If the proceeds are in excess of the amount owed to Landlord:

    a. Landlord immediately gets all of the money, no matter what the amount
    b. Landlord must hold onto the excess money for at least one year, in case Tenant attempts to reclaim it
    c. Landlord must mail the excess money to Tenant's last known address
    d. The money must be turned over to the city or the municipal organization in charge of landlord-tenant actions

14 Condominiums, Cooperatives, and Securities

Outline

Key Terms

- condominium
- Condominium Act
- common areas
- declaration
- declarant
- conversion
- unit owners association
- right of first refusal
- public offering statement

- right of rescission
- implied warranties of quality
- resale certificate
- CCARA
- townhouse
- timeshare
- interval ownership

- vacation license
- right to use
- cooperative
- proprietary lease
- cooperative association
- blanket mortgage
- real estate securities
- REIT

Chapter Overview

As cities have grown more crowded, single-family homes have become harder to find and more expensive to buy and maintain. In many communities, condominiums have become a popular ownership alternative. This chapter describes the laws that govern development and ownership of condominiums in Washington. It also looks at timesharing arrangements, cooperatives, and real estate securities.

Condominiums

Most condominiums look like apartment buildings, but a condominium isn't owned by a landlord who rents apartment units to tenants. Instead, it is owned by its residents.

The buyer of a condominium unit acquires separate title to the unit itself. The other parts of the condominium property—the grounds, the parking lot, the recreational facilities, the building's lobby, elevators, and hallways—are called the **common areas** or **common elements**. These areas are owned by all of the residents as tenants in common. Each unit owner has an undivided interest in the common areas.

> **Example:** Sheila buys a unit in a 24-unit condominium. The deed describes her property as "Unit 11 in Hemlock Ridge, a condominium, together with an undivided $1/24$ interest in the common areas of said condominium."

Although the majority of condominiums are residential, office buildings and retail centers have also been developed as condominiums. Some condominiums include a mixture of commercial and residential units. For instance, the street level might contain shops and a restaurant, with living units on the floors above.

History

The basic concept of condominium ownership has existed for centuries. In modern times, individual ownership of separate floors or "flats" in a building became common in

Fig. 14.1 Two ways condominiums are created

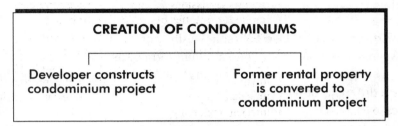

Paris and other French cities in the 1920s. Legislation governing this form of ownership began appearing in many parts of Europe in the 1930s and 1940s, and in South America in the late 1940s and the 1950s.

In the United States, condominium ownership was rare until the 1960s. Condominium development got a boost from the passage of the National Housing Act of 1961, which provided federal mortgage insurance for condominium units. By 1968, all 50 states had adopted some form of condominium law.

In 1989, the Washington State Legislature passed a new Condominium Act. (It is a version of the Uniform Condominium Act, which has also been adopted by several other states.) This law applies to all condominiums created in Washington after July 1, 1990. Many of its provisions also apply to condominiums established before that date, but those condominiums are still governed to some extent by the previous 1963 state condominium law (the Horizontal Property Regimes Act). This discussion will focus on the rules and procedures established in the 1989 law.

Creation of Condominiums

A condominium can be created in two ways. The property can be initially developed as a condominium, or an existing building (usually an apartment building) can be converted into a condominium. In either case, condominium status is established by recording a **condominium declaration**.

The declaration must contain the name of the condominium and a legal description of the property. The entire development must be described—both the land and the buildings. Specific information about each unit must be included, such as the square footage and the number of bathrooms, bedrooms, and fireplaces. Any restrictions on the use, occupancy, or alienation of the units must be listed. The declaration will also contain provisions concerning the ownership and use of the common areas. If the developer (called the declarant in the Condominium Act) is reserving any special rights in regard to the property, those rights must be described in the declaration.

At the same time that the declaration is recorded, the declarant also must record a survey map of the property and building plans for the project. The plans must show the vertical and horizontal boundaries of each unit in sufficient detail to establish the position of the unit in relation to the land. (See Chapter 2 for a discussion of property descriptions that involve air lots.)

Condominiums and Land Use Laws. In Washington, local zoning ordinances and other land use laws may not prohibit the condominium form of ownership. Land use laws may not impose any requirements on condominiums that do not also apply to identical developments under a different form of ownership (such as an ordinary apartment complex).

In some cases, large condominiums are considered subdivisions and are subject to local subdivision regulations. Condominium developments also must comply with environmental laws.

Case Example:

The decision to grant preliminary approval for a condominium project on Cooper Point near Olympia was "a major action significantly affecting the quality of the environment." An environmental impact statement was therefore necessary to comply with SEPA. *Loveless v. Yantis*, 82 Wn.2d 754, 513 P.2d 1023 (1973).

Conversion. In some cases, the owner of a rental property decides to **convert** the existing building to condominium status in response to a steep rise in operating expenses or taxes. Or the owner may decide to convert the building because selling it piecemeal, one unit at a time, will be more profitable than selling the whole property to a single investor.

The Condominium Act has some special rules that apply when residential rental property (such as an apartment building) is converted into a condominium. If there are tenants living in the building when the decision is made, the owner is required to take certain steps to protect the tenants' interests.

The owner must give each tenant at least 90 days' notice that the building is going to be converted into a condominium. The tenancies cannot be terminated before that 90-day period expires, unless a tenant stops paying rent or does something else that would be grounds for eviction under the Residential Landlord-Tenant Act.

If the conversion condominium will be residential, the owner is required to give each tenant a public offering statement (explained later in this chapter). Each tenant must also be given a 60-day **first right of refusal** on his or her unit. That means the tenant may choose to buy the unit, on specified terms, once the building has become a condominium. If the tenant doesn't decide to buy the unit during that 60-day period, in the following 180 days the building owner may not offer the unit to anyone else on more favorable terms than the terms offered to the tenant.

Common Areas

A condominium's common areas include every part of the property except the individual units. As explained earlier, ownership of the common areas is shared by all of the unit owners, as tenants in common. All of the unit owners have the right to use the common areas—to ride in the elevator, swim in the pool, and so on.

The declaration must assign a specific fraction or percentage of interest in the common areas to each unit. In some cases, each unit has an equal interest in the common areas; for instance, in a 30-unit condominium, each unit might have a $1/30$ undivided interest in the common areas. In many condominiums, however, the percentage is based on the value of the individual unit in relation to the total value of the property. The larger, more expensive units have a larger percentage of interest in the common areas.

> **Example:** Pete bought Unit 403 for $250,000, which is 3% of the total value of the entire condominium complex ($8,333,300). Pete's deed gives him full fee simple ownership of his unit, plus a 3% undivided interest in the common areas.
>
> In the same condominium, Marsha bought Unit 801, which is much larger than Unit 403 and has a better view. Marsha paid $416,665, 5% of the condominium's total value. She owns her unit in fee simple and has a 5% undivided interest in the common areas.

When a condominium unit is conveyed, its undivided interest in the common areas is automatically conveyed, too. An interest in the common areas cannot be transferred separately from a unit.

> **Example:** The Cochrans live down the street from a condominium, and they would like to be able to use its pool and other recreational facilities. Gregor owns Unit 6 in the condominium, together with an undivided $1/15$ interest in the common areas. He never uses the recreational facilities, so he would be willing to sell his interest in the common areas to the Cochrans. It won't work; a deed granting Gregor's undivided interest in the common areas to the Cochrans would be void.

In many condominiums, certain common areas are designated **limited common areas**. These are parts of the property that may be used only by the owners of specific units, rather than by all the residents. For example, a particular patio might be a limited common area shared by the owners of units in Building C; the unit owners in Building D would not be entitled to use that patio. The declaration must list the limited common areas and specify which units may use each of the areas.

Unit Owners Association

A condominium is required to have a **unit owners association** (sometimes called a **condominium association**). The association must be organized as either a profit or nonprofit corporation under the Condominium Act. Every unit owner is automatically a member of the association, and only unit owners may be members. The association controls the affairs of the condominium as a whole; its primary concern is the regulation and maintenance of the common areas.

Most decisions are made by the association's board of directors. The board is elected by the association's members, and a majority of the directors must be members (unit owners) themselves. The directors are required to exercise ordinary and reasonable care in performing their duties.

Like any other corporation, a unit owners association has bylaws that govern its management. The bylaws provide for the election of the board of directors, specify the powers and duties of the directors, and outline the schedule and procedures for association meetings. Under the Condominium Act, meetings must be held at least once a year and all unit owners must be notified.

The association has the power to collect assessments from each unit owner to pay for the common expenses, such as common area maintenance, repair, and insurance costs. Some assessments are routine, and are paid every month; others are for special expenses (for example, a new fence in the pool area, or emergency repairs to the roof). An unpaid assessment creates a lien against the unit owner's title. The lien attaches automatically, as soon as the assessment is due; it is not necessary for the association to record a claim of lien.

Some owners associations retain a first right of refusal on the sale of any unit. So if an individual unit owner decides to sell his or her unit, the association has the option to purchase it. If the association declines, the owner can sell to a third party, but only at the same (or higher) price.

The association's lien can be foreclosed judicially or (if certain procedures are followed and the declaration includes a power of sale) nonjudicially. If the lien is foreclosed judicially, it has priority over all other liens except for property tax and special assessment liens, certain mortgages and deeds of trust, and liens recorded before the condominium declaration was filed.

An owner's share of the common expenses is usually based on the owner's percentage of interest in the common areas, as is an owner's voting power in the unit owners association. For instance, if a unit owner has a 3% interest in the common areas, she is responsible for 3% of the common expenses, and her vote would be counted as 3% of all the association's votes.

Sale of Condominium Units

The Condominium Act establishes rules that a **declarant** (condominium developer) must follow when selling a unit to its first unit owner. The act also has rules that a unit owner must follow when reselling his or her unit.

These rules apply to any type of condominium, except that the purchaser of a unit in a nonresidential condominium can agree in writing to waive them. A residential purchaser cannot waive these requirements.

Sale by Declarant. The declarant is required to prepare a **public offering statement** that discloses certain information about the declarant, the condominium, and the unit being purchased. For example, if the declarant has completed other condominium projects in the past five years, the names of the five most recent projects must be listed in the public offering statement. Building code violations and physical hazards affecting the condominium have to be listed; so do liens against the property, and pending lawsuits that might result in a judgment lien.

Some of the many other required disclosures include an estimate of the unit owner's share of the common expenses, and any additional fees for the use of the common areas. In addition, the public offering statement must contain copies of the declaration, survey map, and plans, along with copies of the articles of incorporation and bylaws for the unit owners association, any rules and regulations adopted by the association, and the association's current budget and balance sheet.

For any sale requiring a public offering statement, the declarant cannot convey the unit until after the declaration, survey map, and plans have been recorded. In addition, the unit must be substantially completed and available for occupancy at the time of conveyance, unless the buyer and the declarant have agreed in writing that the unit will not be ready for occupancy. However, the declarant is allowed to execute a purchase and sale agreement before the declaration and other documents are recorded, or before the unit is completed.

Right of rescission. When someone decides to buy a unit from the declarant, the declarant should give the prospective buyer the public offering statement more than seven days before the purchase and sale agreement is executed. If the buyer isn't given the statement seven days in advance, he or she has a seven-day **right of rescission** that runs from the time the statement is received.

> **Example:** Mike wants to buy Unit 6B in the Harbor Heights condominium. Unit 6B has never been purchased before, so the seller is the declarant.
> The declarant's agent gives Mike a copy of the condominium's public offering statement on October 2. Mike reads the statement that evening and decides to go ahead with the purchase. The next day, October 3, he and the declarant sign a purchase and sale agreement, and he gives the declarant an earnest money deposit. They agree on November 1 as the closing date.
> Mike has a right of rescission until October 9, seven days after he received the public offering statement. If he changes his mind about Unit 6B before October 9, he can withdraw from the purchase agreement without penalty.

A declarant is required to keep all earnest money deposits in an escrow account until closing. If Mike chose to rescind the contract, the declarant would have to refund his earnest money deposit.

The buyer can also move the closing date if necessary to allow seven days between receipt of the public offering statement and closing.

> **Example:** As in the example above, Mike receives the public offering statement on October 2, and signs the contract on October 3. But now suppose that Mike is in a

hurry and doesn't need to arrange financing, so that he agrees to make October 6 the closing date.

The day after signing the contract, Mike decides he may be acting a little too hastily. He has the right to call the declarant and delay the closing until October 9 (seven days after he received the offering statement). The declarant can't insist on an October 6 closing.

In some cases, the declarant may fail to give the buyer a public offering statement. If so, the buyer can sue the declarant either for actual damages or for a refund of a portion of the purchase price. If the declarant's failure to provide the statement was willful, the buyer is entitled to a refund of 10% of the price paid. If the declarant's failure to provide the statement was unintentional, the refund would be 3% of the price.

Release of liens. When the declarant begins selling units, there may be some liens against the entire condominium property (a deed of trust for the construction financing, for example, or construction liens from the construction itself). When a unit is sold, the declarant is required to do one of three things: pay off any liens affecting that unit; provide title insurance for that unit which will protect the new owner from the liens; or record a partial release for that unit. A **partial release** removes the liens from the new unit owner's title, although the liens remain attached to the rest of the condominium property.

Warranties. The purchaser of a condominium unit is not entitled to rely on any express warranties of quality or representations concerning the property unless they are included in the public offering statement, or made in writing and signed by the declarant (or the declarant's agent).

However, the Condominium Act creates several **implied warranties of quality** that automatically apply to the sale of a unit by the declarant. For example, the declarant warrants that the unit and the common areas are suitable for ordinary uses, and that the improvements are free from defective materials and constructed in a workmanlike manner.

These implied warranties can be modified or waived in a written agreement between the declarant and the buyer. But in the sale of a residential unit, the declarant cannot make a general disclaimer of implied warranties, although he or she may disclaim liability for a particular defect (in writing).

Resale by Unit Owner. A unit owner who resells his or her unit must provide the buyer with a **resale certificate**.

The resale certificate is prepared by the association or an agent of the association. It contains information pertaining to the unit being resold, such as the unit's monthly common expense assessment and fees, and any other assessments that are currently due or have been levied. It contains a copy of the declarations, bylaws, and rules and regulations of the association. It also contains detailed financial information about the association, including an annual financial statement and the current operating budget. In addition, the resale certificate gives information about other units that could affect the unit being resold. For example, if there is an assessment against another unit that's more than 30 days overdue, it must be listed in the certificate. And if the unit owners association has a right of first refusal, this must be disclosed as well.

The unit owner is supposed to give the resale certificate and other documents to a prospective buyer before the purchase and sale agreement is signed. The agreement is voidable by the buyer until five days after he or she receives the certificate, or until the unit is actually conveyed, whichever happens first. For assessments due or levied as of the date of the certificate, the buyer cannot be required to pay more than the amounts stated in the certificate (unless the buyer had actual notice of additional assessments or greater amounts).

The declarant's implied warranties of quality, and any express warranties made by the declarant or any other previous seller, are passed along to the buyer when a unit is resold.

After closing, the buyer (the new unit owner) must notify the association of his or her name and address and the date of conveyance.

Deeds. When a unit is sold, the deed does not have to give a full legal description of the entire condominium property. It simply has to state the unit number, the name of the condominium, the declaration's recording number, and the county where the property is located. It's standard practice for the deed to mention what percentage of interest in the common areas goes along with the unit, but that is not required by the Condominium Act. That information (and the full legal description of the property) can always be found in the declaration.

Like any other deed, the deed to a condominium unit should be recorded to protect the new owner's interest.

Consumer Protection

As condominiums became common, certain problems also became common. Many of them were caused by unscrupulous or incompetent developers.

One frequent source of problems was the developer's failure to disclose all the costs involved in condominium ownership. Some unsophisticated buyers committed themselves to purchasing a unit without understanding that they would have to pay monthly assessments and fees on top of their mortgage payments.

The public offering statement or resale certificate required by Washington's Condominium Act alleviates this type of problem, since they must disclose all the financial consequences of unit ownership. However, some buyers who receive a public offering statement or resale certificate never read it. A real estate agent involved in a condominium sale should explain the importance of the information in the statement or certificate and encourage the buyers to go over it carefully.

Developer self-dealing was another source of problems. Some developers would make arrangements for the condominium to benefit themselves, rather than the unit owners. They would set up long-term property management contracts for themselves or affiliated companies, or lease recreational facilities to the condominium at high rates, and make ratification of these agreements a condition of purchasing a unit. Now, under the Condominium Act, any management contract, lease of facilities, or other contract arranged by the developer may be terminated by the board of directors of the unit owners association. The board must give 90 days' notice of termination.

Another common hazard for prospective condominium buyers was losing an earnest money deposit. Buyers would give the developer deposits for units in a condominium that was still under construction—or hadn't even been started yet. The developer would accept the deposits and spend them, but construction would never be completed. Although the buyers had the right to sue for return of their deposits, as often as not construction had stopped because the developer had gone bankrupt. In many cases, the buyers couldn't recover their deposits. This problem is addressed by the Condominium Act's requirement that developers keep all earnest money deposits in an escrow account until closing.

CCARA. The Federal Housing and Community Development Act was signed into law in 1980. Title VI of this act is the Condominium and Cooperative Abuse Relief Act (CCARA). CCARA applies to all condo and co-op projects with five or more residential units in each structure. It does not apply when all of the units in a project are restricted to commercial use.

The stated purposes of the CCARA are to minimize the adverse impact of condominium conversions (especially for low-income, elderly, and handicapped tenants); to ensure that fair and equitable principles are followed in establishing condominiums and cooperatives; and to provide relief where long-term leases of facilities are determined to be unconscionable.

Unfortunately, the CCARA is a very limited enactment that does little in a practical sense to meet its stated goals. Washington's Condominium Act is a much more useful law. In Washington, when a condominium developer has acted unscrupulously, a lawsuit will nearly always be filed under the Condominium Act instead of the CCARA. However, note that the CCARA (unlike the Condominium Act) applies to cooperatives as well as condominiums. Cooperatives are discussed later in this chapter.

Condominiums vs. Townhouses

A type of home ownership that mixes attributes of condominiums and single-family homes is the townhouse. A **townhouse** is typically a multi-story home on a small lot that may or may not share walls with neighboring units. Townhouse ownership is similar to condominium ownership in that a townhouse owner has both a separate interest in his individual unit and an undivided interest in the common areas of the townhouse development. However, a townhouse owner also has title to the parcel of land on which the townhouse is situated.

Although the statutory restrictions of the Condominium Act do not apply to townhouses, townhouse developments may have homeowners associations similar to condominium unit owners associations. Homeowners association membership and fees may be mandatory. In addition, homeowners associations may restrict changes to the exterior appearances of the individual townhouses.

Timeshare Condominiums

Another nontraditional form of ownership is the timeshare arrangement. Rather than purchasing all rights to an individual unit, a timeshare arrangement allows a buyer to purchase a time slot of ownership. In Washington, a **timeshare** is defined as a right to occupy a unit during three or more separate time periods over a period of at least three years.

The concept of real estate timesharing was first conceived in Europe in the early 1960s. Timesharing began to appear in the United States in about the mid-1970s. By 1985, the number of timeshare owners was estimated at approximately 500,000, and it has continued to rise.

Most timeshare condominiums are found in vacation areas where ownership of the unit for the entire year is expensive and unnecessary or unwanted.

> **Example:** The Slaters like to vacation in Hawaii, but do not want to live there full time. They do not want to purchase a house or condominium, since they would use it only a small portion of the year. The Slaters purchase a two-week share in a timeshare condominium unit for the first two weeks in March.
>
> The Slaters have the right to possess and occupy the property only during the first two weeks in March. Other buyers have the right to use the unit at other times of the year.

Types of Timeshare Ownership

The ownership interest in a timeshare unit may be held in one of three different ways. The first is a **tenancy in common,** in which all of the buyers are deeded an undivided interest in a particular unit as tenants in common. The buyers then agree to limit their use of the unit to a specific time period.

A timeshare may also be an **interval ownership**, in which the buyers are granted an estate for years for a specific time period each year.

Under tenancy in common or interval ownership, the owner has all of the responsibilities of property ownership, such as property taxes and potential liability if someone is injured on the property.

The third type of timeshare arrangement is called a **vacation license** or **right to use**. In this arrangement, the developer retains ownership of the timeshare unit and agrees to

Fig. 14.2 Types of timeshares

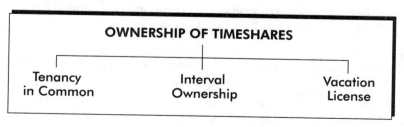

OWNERSHIP OF TIMESHARES

| Tenancy in Common | Interval Ownership | Vacation License |

allow the buyers to use the premises for a specific time period each year. The timeshare purchasers do not have actual ownership of the property and are not liable for property taxes or injuries that might occur on the property. The purchaser does not build any equity in the property or have any voice in its operation.

In 1983, Washington adopted the Washington Timeshare Act, which was enacted mainly as a protection for the consumer. It requires registration of any timeshare property and disclosure of pertinent information to potential purchasers, and provides for remedial measures in the event that the act is violated.

Disclosure Statement

Washington law requires that any person who offers or sells a timeshare must provide the prospective purchaser with a written disclosure document before the purchase and sale agreement is signed. The disclosure document must contain the official name and address of the promoter, the location and description of the timeshare property, and a list of all units offered.

It must also include the types, prices, and number of units, location of units, types and durations of timeshares, and the maximum number of timeshares that may be created. Certain financial information must also be included, along with copies of any agreements or leases to be signed at the time of purchase.

Under the Washington Timeshare Act, a purchaser may cancel any agreement for the purchase of a timeshare within **seven days** after receipt of the disclosure document or the signing of the timeshare purchase agreement, whichever is later. This cancellation must be in writing and delivered or mailed to the promoter to be effective.

Cooperatives

Stock and non-stock **cooperatives** are another type of nontraditional ownership of real property. Like condominiums, cooperatives are usually residential buildings, although they may also be established for commercial uses.

Title to a cooperative building (and the surrounding property) is generally held by a nonprofit corporation formed for that purpose. A person who wants to live in the building buys shares of stock in the corporation, instead of renting or buying a unit. The building's residents are the corporation's shareholders. The corporation owns the building, but the residents own the corporation. (Instead of a corporation, ownership of the land and building could be in the form of a trust or partnership, but this is not as common as corporate ownership.)

A less common form of cooperative ownership is the **membership cooperative**. A person who wants to live in the building buys a membership in the cooperative; instead of buying stock, the owner pays a membership fee. Usually all members have the same voting power when they vote on items of concern to the membership. The cooperative owns the building, the individual has a membership interest.

History

After World War II and up until 1961, many cooperative housing corporations came into existence. Before 1970, most rental units that were converted to resident ownership were converted to cooperatives. But starting in about 1970, most conversions outside of New York have been made into condominiums rather than cooperatives. New York is still the center for most of the co-ops in this country.

The cooperative has never been a major portion of the real estate market in Washington state. However, there are some cooperatives in existence, both residential and commercial. In the early 1980s there was renewed interest in the cooperative, but this interest did not last very long.

Creation of Cooperatives

As with condominiums, a project may be developed initially as a cooperative, or an existing building may be converted into a co-op.

Individual unit residents own stock in the corporation and have a proprietary lease for their unit. In order to acquire the lease on a specific unit, a person must purchase a certain number of shares of stock. Shares are allocated to each unit based on the value of the unit compared to the total value of the entire building or complex.

> **Example:** A cooperative has a total of 33 units. There are one-, two-, and three-bedroom units. The units on the west side of the building have a view overlooking the lake, and are therefore valued higher than the units with no view. The units are assigned individual values running from 20 to 40 shares. The total value of the complex is 1,000 shares.
>
> Johnson wants to acquire an interest in a one-bedroom unit with no view. Her unit is valued at 20 shares. She must purchase 20 shares of stock in the cooperative corporation.
>
> Davis wants to purchase a two-bedroom unit with a view of the lake. His unit is valued at 35 shares. He must purchase 35 shares of stock in the corporation.

Each unit owner in a cooperative is not really an owner, but rather a shareholder in the corporation that owns the complex in which the unit is located. Johnson owns 20 shares or 2% of the total value of the complex. Davis owns 35 shares or 3½% of the total value of the complex.

Each of the shareholders has a proprietary lease for their particular unit. A **proprietary lease** has a longer term than most ordinary leases and gives the shareholder considerably more rights than an ordinary tenant would have. The cooperative tenants participate in the running of the cooperative through their stock interest in the corporation.

The lease does not state a fixed rental amount for the term of the lease. Instead, each year the amount that will be needed to pay the building's mortgage, insurance, and operating expenses is determined. Each leaseholder is then assessed an amount based on his or her percentage of ownership. For instance, Johnson's assessment would be 2% of the total, while Davis's assessment would be 3½%.

Co-op Associations and Bylaws. Cooperatives are generally run by a **cooperative association**. The association is managed by a board of directors. In Washington, the board must consist of at least three directors. The directors are shareholders (unit owners) and members of the association and are elected by the members of the association.

The association usually passes bylaws for the governing of the cooperative. The association and the board of directors manage the cooperative according to the guidelines set out in the bylaws. They generally have the right to level charges required for maintenance, repairs, and the general cost of effectively running the cooperative.

Comparison of Condos and Co-ops

There are some similarities between condos and co-ops. In both instances, the individual owner has a right to possess a certain unit and has an interest in the common areas. However, there are also many differences between ownership of a condo and ownership of a co-op.

Ownership. One of the major differences is the fact that a condominium owner actually owns his or her individual unit and receives a deed for that unit. A cooperative owner merely has a lease for a specific unit. However, the co-op owner acquires equity in the shares of the cooperative's stock. If the market value of the property increases, the market value of the stock increases, and the owner would reap the profits at the time of sale, as with any other type of property.

Mortgages. In a co-op, the corporation may take out a single mortgage on the entire building. In a condominium, there is no blanket mortgage on the entire building, but there may be separate mortgages on some or all of the individual units. Thus financing is often easier for a condominium unit than for a co-op.

One of the major disadvantages of the co-op is the financial interdependence of all of the shareholders. Because a blanket mortgage is used, one shareholder's financial instability could jeopardize the whole cooperative. There is a possibility that the entire building could be foreclosed and your lease could be extinguished, even if you were never delinquent in your own payments.

> **Example:** Ten percent of the tenants in a co-op building were unable to pay their rent. Ninety percent was not enough money to make the mortgage payment. The other tenants would have to pay the remaining amount themselves, or else the mortgage on the entire building could be foreclosed and all leases extinguished. This type of situation could easily occur during a severe economic recession.

In some cases, a lender may make a loan against the shares or the membership in the co-op owned by an individual.

Fig. 14.3 Condominiums vs. cooperatives

	CONDOMINIUMS	COOPERATIVES
Ownership	Buyer owns individual unit and receives deed	Buyer owns shares in corporation or membership interest and has proprietary lease of unit
Mortgage	Individual mortgages on separate units	Blanket mortgage on entire building
Restrictions	Condo association may have right of first refusal	Tighter restrictions—may need approval of board to sell
Transfer upon owner's death	Fee simple estate can be freely passed to any successor	No automatic right; person who inherits must be approved by board
Eviction	Difficult	Easier than with condo
Taxes	Individual taxes on each unit	Taxes assessed on entire building
Liens	Attach only to individual unit	May attach to entire building

Restrictions. Another difference between condos and co-ops is in the type of restrictions on the ability to sell. A co-op tenant generally needs the approval of the board of directors in order to sell to a new tenant.

These tight restrictions are necessary because of the financial interdependence of the co-op tenants. Since they may be personally affected by a tenant with financial problems, they have the right to evaluate and approve any potential new tenants.

Upon the death of a co-op tenant, the person who inherits the co-op unit must be approved by the board of directors or a membership committee. There is no automatic right to continue the co-op lease. By contrast, a condominium owner has a fee simple estate in the unit. It can be freely passed on to any successor.

Eviction. It is easier to get rid of an incompatible resident in a co-op than in a condominium. Other tenants may view this as an advantage of the co-op. A tenant who refuses to comply with the co-op rules can be evicted. It is much harder to get rid of a condo unit owner. If a condo owner is delinquent in paying assessments, a lien foreclosure action can be brought against the owner. However, the procedure is likely to be time-consuming and expensive.

Taxes. In a condominium, each unit owner receives an individual property tax assessment and is responsible only for that amount. In a cooperative, a tax assessment is made on the entire building. Each owner is assessed an amount in proportion to the amount of stock owned. (In other words, in proportion to the value of the unit.) If an individual owner in a co-op defaults on tax payments, the other shareholders must see that these taxes are paid or risk that the entire building could be sold at a tax sale.

Liens. An individual owner may have work done or services performed on a particular unit. In a condominium, a construction lien attaches only to the unit where the work was done. In a cooperative, work done or materials ordered by one tenant could result in a construction lien attaching to the entire building.

Real Estate Securities

Real estate is usually considered to be a good investment. However, many people don't have the money, time, or experience necessary to locate good investment property on their own. Sometimes a group of friends or business associates get together and pool their money to invest in real estate. Or a promoter may offer an interest in a real estate investment opportunity to the public.

These kinds of arrangements typically involve the sale of real estate securities. A **real estate security** is any kind of arrangement in which someone invests money in an enterprise involving real estate, with the expectation of earning profits from the efforts of a promoter or some other third party.

Securities Regulation and Registration

If a transaction meets the definition of a security, the promoter must comply with federal and state **securities regulations.** The purpose of securities regulations is to protect the consumer by requiring registration of securities and disclosure of certain information.

Before offering to sell any property that meets the definition of a security, the promoter must register with the Securities and Exchange Commission (SEC). Once the promoter has registered, the property can be advertised and offers can be made. However, purchasers cannot enter into binding contracts and sales cannot be concluded until the SEC declares the registration statement effective.

Condominiums as Securities

Normally, the sale of a condominium unit is not considered to be the sale of a security. But if a condominium unit is purchased as an investment (rather than for personal use) it may be considered a security.

Usually a condominium project will not be deemed a security simply because some of the owners intend to rent out their units rather than live there themselves, as long as each owner is free either to rent or not rent. However, if owners are required to rent out their units and the plan is to have the developer or some other person manage this rental operation, the arrangement will be treated as a security.

Case Example:

Ford Hill Investment Company built a six-unit condominium near a snow skiing recreation area. The Lowerys signed an installment sales contract with Ford Hill for one of the units.

The contract provided that Ford Hill was the exclusive management and rental agent for each unit owner. Each owner was assessed a monthly rental promotion and management fee. Rental rates were to be determined and fixed solely by the manager. Owners were required to maintain their units in a rentable condition. If the owners wanted to reserve the right to occupy their unit for personal use, they were required to give six months' advance written notice.

The court found that the sale of condominium property, when accompanied by agreements of this type, constitutes the sale of a security. *Lowery v. Ford Hill Investment Co.*, 556 P.2d 1201 (Colorado 1976).

If condominium advertisements or other documents make reference to providing rental services for buyers, the purchase may be treated as an investment contract and securities regulations will apply. Some timeshare arrangements have also been subject to securities regulation on the basis of the investment contract theory.

Whether or not a condominium (or other type of investment) is considered a security is a fairly complicated question that should be answered only by an attorney who deals in this area.

Real Estate Investment Trusts (REITs)

A **real estate investment trust (REIT)** is a real estate investment transaction that is considered a security. When an REIT is established, a group of investors form a trust and purchase certificates of ownership in the trust. The trust invests in real estate and real estate mortgages and distributes any profits to the investors. An REIT must have a minimum of 100 investors.

A trust is unincorporated; it is not taxed like a corporation, but is only taxed on its retained earnings. As long as most of its income is distributed to the investors, any significant taxation of the trust is avoided. The profits distributed to the investors are taxed as ordinary income to the individual investors.

With an REIT, small investors can take advantage of big investment opportunities by pooling their resources.

Conclusion

Condominiums, cooperatives, and timeshare arrangements offer alternatives to traditional property ownership. In a condominium, a buyer owns a particular unit in fee simple and an undivided interest in the common areas. In a co-op, a buyer holds shares in the cooperative corporation and has a proprietary lease for an individual unit. Timeshare owners have the right to occupy a particular unit only during a specified time period.

In certain cases, condominium or timeshare sales are deemed to be securities transactions, so the promoter is required to comply with federal and state securities regulations. A real estate investment trust is another form of real estate investment that is subject to securities regulations.

Case Problem

The following is a hypothetical case problem. Most of the facts are taken from a real case. Based on what you have learned from this chapter, make a decision on the issues presented and then check to see if your answer matches the real decision by the court.

The Facts

The Riva Ridge North Chalet is a building composed of approximately ten condominiums in Vail, Colorado. The complex is managed by the Broadmoor Management Company. The individual owners of the condo units and the condominium corporation signed a management agreement. This agreement provided that in return for management and rental agent responsibilities, Broadmoor was to receive $30 per month for each unit, 40% of all rental commissions, an amount equal to one day's rental during the prime season, and three days' use of each unit for promotional purposes.

In addition to the above amounts provided for in the management agreement, Broadmoor also charged the condominium association for all common expenses, including resort association dues, housekeeping and security services, and advertising.

Several individual owners and the condo association brought a lawsuit against Broadmoor, claiming that the common expenses should have been paid out of the monthly fees provided for in the management agreement, and not charged as an additional amount.

The Questions

Can a condominium association file a lawsuit, or does it have to be brought by each individual owner? Should the management company be allowed to charge additional fees for common expenses? If the condo association wins the lawsuit, how will damages be apportioned?

The Answer

Where a condominium association has signed a contract (such as the management agreement), it is a proper party to file a lawsuit for damages. The bylaws of this condo association granted it the power to collect and disburse all funds necessary to manage the building. Each individual owner was required to be a member of the association. Thus, the association was in an ideal position to represent all of the owners.

The management company was found to have overcharged the condo association. (This decision was basically a matter of interpreting the contract. A management company might be allowed to charge additional monthly common expenses if the management agreement so provides.)

The court awarded damages for the amount overcharged, plus interest, to the association. The association was ordered to distribute the award among the individual unit owners in proportion to their percentage of ownership in the building. *Andrikopoulos v. Broadmoor Management Co.*, 670 P.2d 435 (Colo. App. 1983).

Chapter Summary

- The owner of a condominium unit receives fee simple ownership of the individual unit, plus an undivided interest in the common areas. The percentage of interest in the common areas assigned to each unit is usually based on the value of the unit in relation to the total value of the property.

- A unit owners association and its board of directors regulates and maintains the common areas of a condominium. It has the power to collect assessments from each unit owner to pay for the common expenses.

- The Washington Condominium Act requires a condominium developer to record a declaration, survey map, and plans, and to give a public offering statement to prospective buyers. A unit owner reselling a unit must give the buyer a resale certificate and other documents.

- A timeshare arrangement allows a buyer to purchase a time slot of ownership. A timeshare may involve tenancy in common, interval ownership, or a vacation license.

- For a cooperative, a nonprofit corporation owns the land and building, and the residents each own stock in the corporation or a membership interest and have a long-term lease in a specific unit. A blanket mortgage covers the entire cooperative property. If several of the tenants do not pay their rent, the entire building could be foreclosed on. This financial interdependence is one of the major disadvantages of cooperatives.

- A real estate security is an arrangement in which someone invests money in an enterprise involving real estate, with the expectation of earning profits from the efforts of a promoter or some other third party.

- If a condominium is purchased for investment purposes, it may be considered a security, and the parties must comply with state and federal securities regulations.

- When a group of over 100 investors forms a trust to invest in real estate, it is called a real estate investment trust (REIT). An REIT will also have to be registered as a security.

Checklist of Problem Areas

Real Estate Licensee's Checklist

❑ Does the unit owners association have a right of first refusal before a unit can be sold?

❑ How many of the units in the building or complex are owner-occupied, and how many are rented out?

❑ Are there specific restrictions on the unit or the common areas (such as no pets, or no drinking within the pool area)?

❑ Is the sale of the unit considered a real estate security, and if so, has it been registered in compliance with both state and federal law?

Seller's Checklist

❑ Does the unit owners association have a right of first refusal?

❑ Have you given the buyer a resale certificate?

❑ If you're selling a timeshare unit, has full disclosure been made to the potential purchaser?

Buyer's Checklist

❑ If you're purchasing a condominium unit from the declarant, have you received (and studied) a copy of the public offering statement?

❑ If you're purchasing a unit from the previous unit owner, have you been given a resale certificate?

❑ Does the unit owners association have a right of first refusal? In other words, even if your offer is acceptable to the seller, could the association block the sale to you?

❑ What undivided interest in the common areas is assigned to this particular unit?

❑ What monthly assessments and fees must be paid to the association?

❑ What is the current condition of all of the common areas? Will there be big expenses coming up in the future when major items have to be repaired?

❑ Does the association's insurance cover the interior of your unit?

❑ If you're purchasing a timeshare unit, exactly what type of ownership interest will you acquire?

Chapter Quiz

1. Condominiums are used:

   a. in resort communities
   b. in large metropolitan areas
   c. for residential and commercial purposes
   d. All of the above

2. A condominium declaration and survey map must be recorded:

   a. only for residential condominiums
   b. only for property initially developed as a condominium, not for a conversion
   c. to establish any type of condominium
   d. only if the condominium must be registered with the Securities and Exchange Commission

3. Hannah just bought Unit 10 in a 50-unit condominium. Which of the following is true?

   a. Hannah does not have a direct ownership interest in the common areas, since they are owned by the association
   b. Hannah did not acquire an interest in the common areas unless that interest was stated in her deed
   c. Hannah must have acquired an undivided interest in the common areas, but her percentage of interest is not necessarily the same as her neighbor's percentage
   d. Hannah must have acquired a 2% interest in the common areas

4. A condominium association is made up of:

   a. only those unit owners who choose to join
   b. all the unit owners
   c. directors and officers appointed by the declarant
   d. the declarant, the board of directors, and selected unit owners

5. For condominiums:

   a. an individual unit deed should be recorded for each unit
   b. a master deed is recorded for the entire complex, so that individual deeds for each unit are unnecessary
   c. an individual unit deed is given to each owner, but does not need to be recorded
   d. None of the above

6. When a residential apartment building is converted from rental units into condominium units, the existing tenants must be given how many days' notice?

   a. 30 days
   b. 60 days
   c. 90 days
   d. 120 days

7. Carlton buys into a timeshare condominium. All of the buyers are deeded an undivided interest in a unit, and then agree to limit their use to a specific time period. This type of timeshare is called:

   a. interval ownership
   b. a vacation license
   c. a right to use
   d. a tenancy in common

8. The Washington timeshare statute requires that a prospective purchaser be given a written disclosure statement. After being given this disclosure, the purchaser:

   a. must close the deal within seven days
   b. may cancel the agreement within seven days
   c. must record a copy of the disclosure
   d. None of the above

9. The financing of a cooperative involves:

   a. a blanket mortgage on the entire building
   b. individual mortgages on the individual units
   c. both a blanket mortgage and individual mortgages
   d. None of the above

10. A cooperative owner has some remodeling work done on his individual unit. He does not pay the bill, and a construction lien is filed for the work. Which of the following statements is correct?

   a. The lien attaches only to the unit where the work was done
   b. The lien may attach to the entire building
   c. A construction lien cannot attach to a co-op, since the shareholder does not actually own the unit
   d. None of the above

11. A tax lien is filed against a condominium owner. Which of the following statements is true?

   a. The lien attaches only to her individual unit
   b. The lien attaches to the entire building and could result in a tax sale of the whole building
   c. The lien attaches to the whole building, but the other individual owners would be protected in a tax sale
   d. None of the above

12. Real estate securities must be registered with the Securities and Exchange Commission. Which of the following statements is true?

   a. Condominiums are always securities that must be registered
   b. Not all condominiums are securities, but timeshares are always securities and must be registered
   c. Some, but not all, condominiums and timeshares are securities that must be registered
   d. All condominiums and timeshares are securities and must be registered

13. A real estate investment trust (REIT) must have:

   a. at least 50 investors
   b. at least 75 investors
   c. at least 100 investors
   d. There is no minimum requirement, but an REIT cannot have more than 100 investors

14. A group of people decide to purchase all the condominium units in a building, rent them out, and turn the management of the units over to a particular property management firm. This kind of arrangement:

   a. is illegal under the Washington Condominium Act
   b. would be considered a real property security
   c. would constitute a timeshare ownership interest
   d. would require the services of a real estate broker

15. Harrison is a condominium developer. Before he sells any condo units in a particular project, he enters into a management agreement (in the name of the condominium association) with Condos, Inc. Under the terms of the agreement, Condos, Inc. will handle the repairs and maintenance of the project for a healthy fee. If Harrison is the sole stockholder of Condos, Inc.:

    a. there is nothing wrong with this agreement, and Harrison should make a tidy profit
    b. this agreement is unfair, but the board of directors of the unit owners association can do nothing about it
    c. while Washington law does not prevent this type of agreement, it is a federal crime
    d. the board of directors of the unit owners association can terminate the agreement with 90 days' notice

Chapter Quiz Answer Key

Chapter 1

1. d
2. a
3. b
4. c
5. a
6. d
7. a
8. c
9. d
10. b
11. c
12. a
13. c
14. b
15. a
16. d
17. c
18. d
19. b
20. d
21. b
22. a
23. b
24. c
25. d

Chapter 2

1. b
2. c
3. a
4. b
5. b
6. c
7. b
8. c
9. c
10. c
11. b
12. c
13. b
14. a
15. b

Chapter 3

1. b
2. b
3. c
4. c
5. b
6. b
7. a
8. c
9. b
10. a
11. c
12. d
13. c
14. d
15. c

Chapter 4

1. a
2. c
3. b
4. d
5. b
6. c
7. a
8. d
9. a
10. b
11. c
12. a
13. a
14. d
15. b

Chapter 5

1. c
2. b
3. d
4. b
5. d
6. d
7. b
8. b
9. b
10. c
11. a
12. b
13. d
14. c
15. c

Chapter 6

1. c
2. b
3. a
4. b
5. d
6. a
7. b
8. b
9. b
10. d
11. a
12. b
13. c
14. d
15. b

Chapter 7

1. b
2. c
3. d
4. a
5. d
6. b
7. c
8. b
9. c
10. c
11. a
12. b
13. b
14. d
15. a

Chapter 8

1. b
2. c
3. c
4. d
5. b
6. a
7. b
8. c
9. d
10. c
11. b
12. b
13. c
14. b
15. b

Chapter 9

1. c
2. d
3. d
4. d
5. d
6. a
7. b
8. c
9. c
10. d
11. d
12. b
13. a
14. b
15. b

Chapter 10

1. b
2. d
3. d
4. c
5. a
6. c
7. b
8. c
9. c
10. d
11. b
12. a
13. a
14. b
15. b

Chapter 11

1. d
2. b
3. c
4. b
5. a
6. d
7. d
8. c
9. a
10. b
11. b
12. d
13. a
14. c
15. a

Chapter 12

1. b
2. b
3. c
4. c
5. d
6. d
7. a
8. a
9. c
10. d
11. a
12. d
13. b
14. b
15. b

Chapter 13

1. c
2. b
3. d
4. b
5. b
6. c
7. b
8. a
9. c
10. c
11. a
12. b
13. d
14. d
15. b

Chapter 14

1. d
2. c
3. c
4. b
5. a
6. c
7. d
8. b
9. a
10. b
11. a
12. c
13. c
14. b
15. d

Glossary

Abandonment—Failure to occupy and use property, which may result in loss of rights.

Absolute Fee—*See:* Fee Simple.

Abstract of Judgment—A summary of the provisions of a court judgment which, when recorded, creates a lien on all of the real property of the debtor within the county where recorded.

Abstract of Title—A brief, chronological summary of the recorded documents affecting the title to a particular piece of property.

Abut—To touch, border on, be adjacent to, or share a common boundary with.

Acceleration Clause—A provision in a promissory note or a security instrument allowing the lender to declare the entire debt due immediately if the borrower breaches one or more provisions of the loan agreement. Also referred to as a call provision.

Acceptance—1. Agreeing to the terms of an offer to enter into a contract, thereby creating a binding contract. 2. Taking delivery of a deed from the grantor.

Accord and Satisfaction—An agreement to accept something different than, and usually less than, what was called for in the original agreement.

Accretion—A gradual addition to dry land by the forces of nature, as when waterborne sediment is deposited on waterfront property.

Acknowledgment—When a person who has signed a document formally declares to an authorized official, such as a notary public or county clerk, that he or she signed willingly. The official can then attest that the signature is voluntary and genuine.

Acre—An area of land equal to 43,560 square feet; or 4,840 square yards. There are 640 acres in a section of land in the government survey system.

Actual Notice—Actual knowledge of a fact, as opposed to knowledge imputed by law.

ADA—*See:* Americans with Disabilities Act.

Adjacent—Nearby, next to, bordering, or neighboring; may or may not be in actual contact.

Adjustable-Rate Mortgage—A mortgage loan with an interest rate that is periodically increased or decreased during the loan term.

Administrator—A person appointed by the probate court to manage and distribute the estate of a deceased person when no executor is named in the will, or there is no will.

Ad Valorem—A Latin phrase meaning "according to value," used to refer to taxes assessed on the value of property. Ad valorem taxes are also known as general real estate taxes.

Adverse Possession—Acquiring title to real property owned by someone else, by means of open, notorious, exclusive, continuous and uninterrupted possession of the property, in a manner hostile to the title of the owner, for ten years. If the adverse possessor is claiming under color of title and has paid all taxes assessed on the property, the time period is only seven years.

Affirm—1. To confirm or ratify. 2. To make a solemn declaration that is not under oath.

After-Acquired Title—Title acquired by a grantor after he or she attempted to convey an interest in property that he or she did not own.

Agency—A relationship of trust created when one person, the principal, delegates to another, the agent, authority to represent the principal in dealings with third parties.

Agency, Apparent—When third parties are given the impression that someone who has not been authorized to represent another is that person's agent, or else given the impression that an agent has been authorized to perform acts which are in fact beyond the scope of his or her authority. Also called ostensible agency.

Agency, Dual—When an agent represents both parties to a transaction, as when a broker represents both the buyer and the seller.

Agency, Exclusive—*See:* Listing, Exclusive Agency.

Agency, Ostensible—*See:* Agency, Apparent.

Agency Coupled With an Interest—When an agent has a claim against the property that is the subject of the agency, so that the principal cannot revoke the agent's authority.

Agent—A person authorized to represent another (the principal) in dealings with third parties.

Agent, Dual—*See:* Agency, Dual.

Agent, General—An agent authorized to handle all of the principal's affairs in one area or in specified areas.

Agent, Special—An agent with limited authority to do a specific thing or conduct a specific transaction.

Agent, Universal—An agent authorized to do everything that can be lawfully delegated to a representative.

Agreement—*See:* Contract.

Air Lot—A parcel of property above the surface of the earth, not containing any land; for example, a condominium unit on the third floor.

Air Rights—The right to undisturbed use and control of the airspace over a given parcel of land; may be transferred separately from the land.

Alienation—The transfer of title, ownership, or an interest in property from one person to another, by any means.

Alienation, Involuntary—Transfer of an interest in property against the will of the owner, or without action by the owner, occurring by operation of law, through natural processes, or by adverse possession.

Alienation, Voluntary—Voluntary transfer of real property from one person to another.

Alienation Clause—A provision in a security instrument that gives the lender the right to declare the entire loan balance due immediately if the borrower sells or otherwise transfers the security property. Also called a due-on-sale clause.

Alluvion—The solid material deposited along a river bank or shore by accretion. Also called alluvium.

Amenities—Features of a property that contribute to the pleasure or convenience of owning it, such as proximity to public transportation, schools, or shopping, as well as panoramic views, architectural excellence, or the prestige that goes with living in a given community.

Americans with Disabilities Act—A federal law that prohibits employment discrimination based on disability, and mandates equal access to public accommodations for the disabled.

Amortize—To gradually pay off a debt with installment payments that include both principal and interest.

Annexation, Actual—When personal property is physically attached to real property, so that it becomes part of the real property.

Annexation, Constructive—When personal property becomes associated with real property in such a way that the law treats it as a fixture, even though it is not physically attached; for example, a house key is constructively annexed to the house.

Annual Percentage Rate (APR)—All of the charges the borrower will pay for the loan (including the interest rate, origination fee, discount points, and mortgage insurance fees), expressed as an annual percentage of the loan amount.

Anticipatory Repudiation—When one party to a contract informs the other before the time set for performance that he or she does not intend to fulfill the terms of the contract.

Anti-Deficiency Rules—Laws that prohibit a secured lender from suing the borrower for a deficiency judgment in certain circumstances (for example, after nonjudicial foreclosure of a deed of trust).

Appeal—When one of the parties to a lawsuit asks a higher court to review the judgment or verdict reached in a lower court.

Appellant—The party appealing a decision or ruling. Also called the petitioner.

Appellee—In an appeal, the party who did not file the appeal. Also called the respondent.

Apportionment—A division of property (as among tenants in common when the property is sold or partitioned) or liability (as when responsibility for closing costs is allocated between the buyer and the seller) into proportionate, but not necessarily equal, parts.

Appraisal—An estimate or opinion of the value of a piece of property as of a certain date. Also called a valuation.

Appraiser—One who estimates the value of real or personal property, especially an expert qualified to do so by training and experience.

Appreciation—An increase in value; the opposite of depreciation.

Appropriation—Taking property or reducing it to personal possession, to the exclusion of others.

Appropriation, Prior—A system of allocating water rights, under which a person who wants to use water from a certain lake or river in a way that will diminish the quantity or flow is required to apply for a permit. The permit will have priority over other permits that are issued later. *Compare:* Riparian Rights.

Appropriative Rights—The water rights of a person who holds an appropriation permit.

Appurtenances—Rights that go along with ownership of a particular piece of property, such as air rights or mineral rights; they are ordinarily transferred with the property, but may, in some cases, be sold separately.

Appurtenances, Intangible—Rights that go with ownership of real property which do not involve physical objects or substances; for example, an access easement (as opposed to mineral rights).

Arbitration—Submitting a disputed matter to a private party (rather than to the judicial system) for resolution.

Area—1. Locale or region. 2. The size of a surface, usually stated in square units of measure, such as square feet or square miles.

Artificial Person—A person created by law, with legal rights and responsibilities, such as a corporation, as distinguished from a natural person (a human being). Compare: Nautral person.

Assessment—1. The valuation of property for taxation. 2. A non-recurring specific charge against property for a definite purpose, such as curbs or sewers. Usually called a special assessment.

Assessor—An official who determines the value of property for purposes of taxation.

Asset—Anything of value that a person owns.

Assets, Liquid—Cash, and other assets that can readily be turned into cash (liquidated). Real estate holdings are not considered to be liquid assets.

Assign—To transfer rights or interests to another.

Assignee—One to whom rights or interests have been assigned.

Assignment—1. A transfer of contract rights from one person to another. 2. In the case of a lease, when the original tenant transfers his or her entire leasehold estate to another. *Compare:* Sublease.

Assignment of Contract and Deed—The instrument used to substitute a new vendor for the original vendor in a land contract.

Assignor—One who has assigned his or her rights or interests to another.

Assumption—When a buyer takes on personal liability for paying off the seller's existing mortgage or deed of trust.

Assumption Fee—A fee paid to the lender, usually by the buyer, when a mortgage is assumed.

Attachment—Court-ordered seizure of property belonging to a defendant in a lawsuit, so that it will be available to satisfy a judgment if the plaintiff wins. In the case of real property, attachment creates a lien.

Attachments, Man-Made—*See:* Fixture.

Attachments, Natural—Plants growing on a piece of land, such as trees, shrubs, or crops.

Attestation—The act of witnessing the execution of an instrument (such as a deed or will).

Attorney in Fact—Any person authorized to represent another by a power of attorney; not necessarily a lawyer (an attorney at law).

Authority, Actual—Authority actually given to an agent by the principal, either expressly or by implication.

Authority, Apparent—Authority to represent another that someone appears to have, although no actual authority has been granted.

Authority, Express—Authority that is specifically communicated from the principal to the agent, either orally or in writing.

Authority, Implied—An agent's authority to do everything reasonably necessary to carry out the principal's express orders.

Avulsion—1. When land is suddenly (not gradually) torn away by the action of water. 2. A sudden shift in a watercourse.

Balance Sheet—A summary of facts showing the financial condition of an individual or business, including a detailed list of assets and liabilities. Also called a financial statement.

Balloon Payment—A payment on a loan (usually the final payment) that is significantly larger than the regular installment payments.

Bankruptcy—1. When the liabilities of a person, firm, or corporation exceed its assets. 2. When a court declares a person, firm, or corporation to be insolvent, so that the assets and debts will be administered under the bankruptcy laws.

Bargain and Sale Deed—A deed that conveys title but does not make the same promises as a full warranty deed.

Base Line—In the government survey system, a main east-west line from which township lines are established. Each principal meridian has one base line associated with it.

Bench Mark—A surveyor's mark on a stationary object at a known point of elevation, used as a reference point in calculating other elevations in a surveyed area; often a metal disk set into cement or rock.

Beneficiary—1. One for whom a trust is created and on whose behalf the trustee administers the trust. 2. One entitled to receive real or personal property under a will; a devisee or legatee. 3. The lender in a deed of trust transaction.

Bequeath—To transfer personal property to another by will.

Bequest—Personal property (including money) that is transferred by a will.

Bilateral Contract—*See:* Contract, Bilateral.

Bill of Sale—A document used to transfer title to personal property from one person to another.

Binder—1. An instrument providing immediate insurance coverage to an insured person until the regular policy is issued. 2. Any payment or preliminary written statement intended to make an agreement legally binding until a formal contract has been drawn up.

Blanket Mortgage—*See:* Mortgage, Blanket.

Block—In a subdivision, a group of lots surrounded by streets or unimproved land.

Blockbusting—Attempting to induce owners to list or sell their homes by predicting that members of another race or ethnic group, or people suffering from some disability, will be moving into the neighborhood, with the suggestion that this will lower property values. Also called panic selling.

Bona Fide—In good faith; not fraudulent.

Boundary—The perimeter or border of a parcel of land; the dividing line between one piece of property and another.

Bounds—Boundaries. *See:* Metes and Bounds Description.

Branch Manager—An associate broker designated by a firm's primary broker to manage the operations of a branch office.

Breach—Violation of an obligation, duty, or law.

Breach, Material—A breach of contract serious enough that the other party is excused from performing his or her side of the bargain.

Breach of Contract—The unexcused failure to perform according to the terms of a contract.

Broker—A natural or artificial person that is licensed to represent members of the public in real estate transactions for compensation.

Broker, Associate—A person who has qualified as a real estate broker, but is affiliated with another broker.

Broker, Designated—A corporate officer or general partner, licensed as a broker, who is responsible for the brokerage activities of a corporation or partnership.

Brokerage—A real estate broker's business.

Brokerage Fee—The commission or other compensation charged for a real estate broker's services.

Building Codes—Rules set up by local governments regarding minimum construction standards.

Building Restrictions—Rules concerning building size, placement, or type; they may be public restrictions (in a zoning ordinance, for example) or private restrictions (CC&Rs, for example).

Bump Clause—A provision in a purchase and sale agreement that allows the seller to keep the property on the market while waiting for a contingency clause to be fulfilled; if the seller receives another good offer in the meantime, he or she can require the buyer to either waive the contingency clause or terminate the contract.

Bundle of Rights—The rights inherent in ownership of real property, including the right to use, lease, enjoy, encumber, will, sell, or do nothing with the property.

Business Opportunity—A business that is for sale.

Call—In a metes and bounds description, a specification that describes a segment of the boundary; for example, "south 15° west 120 feet" is a call.

Cancellation—Termination of a contract without undoing acts that have already been performed under the contract.

Capacity—The legal ability or competency to perform some act, such as entering into a contract or executing a deed or will. *See:* Competent.

Capture, Rule of—A legal rule that grants a landowner the right to all oil or gas produced from wells on his or her land, even if the oil or gas migrated from underneath land belonging to someone else.

CC&Rs—A declaration of covenants, conditions, and restrictions; usually recorded by a developer to place restrictions on all lots within a new subdivision.

CCARA—The Condominium and Co-operative Abuse Relief Act, a federal law enacted to minimize the adverse impact of condominium and cooperative conversions.

Cease and Desist Order—An order issued by the Director of the Department of Licensing in a disciplinary action, to stop a violation of the license law.

CERCLA—The Comprehensive Environmental Response, Compensation and Liability Act; a federal law that established a fund to clean up hazardous substances, and a process for determining liability for the cleanup costs.

Certificate of Occupancy—A statement issued by a local government verifying that a newly constructed building is in compliance with all building codes and may be occupied.

Certificate of Title—A statement of opinion by an attorney that describes the status of title to the property.

Chain of Title—*See:* Title, Chain of.

Civil Law—The body of law concerned with the rights and liabilities of one private party in relation to another, as distinguished from criminal law. Contract law is an example of civil law.

Civil Rights—Fundamental rights guaranteed to a person by the law. The term is most often used in reference to constitutional and statutory protections against discrimination or government interference.

Civil Rights Act of 1866—A federal law guaranteeing all citizens the right to purchase, lease, sell, convey, and inherit property, regardless of race or ancestry.

Civil Wrong—*See:* Tort.

Clean Air Act—A federal law passed to maintain and enhance air quality.

Clean Water Act—A federal law passed to maintain and enhance the quality of the nation's water resources.

Client—One who employs a broker, a lawyer, or an appraiser. A real estate broker's client can be the seller, the buyer, or both, but is usually the seller.

Closing—The final stage in a real estate transaction, when the seller delivers the deed and the buyer pays the purchase price. Also called settlement.

Closing Costs—The expenses incurred in the transfer of real estate in addition to the purchase price. A typical list might include the appraisal fee, title insurance premium, real estate commission, excise tax, etc.

Closing Date—The date by which the terms of a contract must be met, or else the contract is terminated.

Closing Statement—*See:* Settlement Statement.

Cloud on Title—Any claim, encumbrance, or apparent defect that makes title to real property unmarketable. *See:* Title, Marketable.

Codicil—An addition to or revision of a will. It must be executed with the same formalities as a will.

Codification—The collection and organization of piecemeal laws into a systematic, comprehensive statute called a code.

Collateral—Anything of value used as security for a debt or obligation.

Collusion—An agreement between two or more persons to defraud another.

Color of Title—Title that appears to be good title, but which in fact is not; commonly based on a defective instrument, such as an invalid deed.

Commercial Bank—A type of financial institution that has traditionally emphasized commercial lending (loans to businesses), but which also makes many residential mortgage loans.

Commercial Property—Property zoned and used for business purposes, such as restaurants, hotels, retail stores, and office buildings; distinguished from residential, industrial, or agricultural property.

Commingling—Illegally mixing trust funds held on behalf of a client with personal or general business funds.

Commission—1. The compensation or fee paid to a broker for services rendered in a real estate transaction. 2. A group of people organized for a particular purpose or function.

Common Areas—1. In a condominium, planned unit development, or cooperative housing project, the land and improvements that are owned and used collectively by all the residents. Common areas usually include driveways, recreational facilities, and stairwells. Also called common elements. 2. In a building with leased units or space, the areas that are available for use by all of the tenants.

Common Elements, Limited—In a condominium, areas outside of the units (such as balconies or assigned parking spaces) that are designated for the use of particular unit owners, rather than all of the residents.

Common Law—The body of law based on the decisions of judges, developed in England and incorporated into the American system of justice. It is the basis of the laws of every state but Louisiana, which based its laws on French civil law.

Community Property—Property owned jointly by a married couple in Washington and other community property states, as distinguished from each spouse's separate property; generally, any property acquired during marriage through the labor or skill of either spouse (but not through gift or inheritance) belongs to both spouses equally.

Competent—1. Of sound mind. 2. Legally qualified to enter into a contract, by virtue of being of sound mind and having reached the age of majority.

Complaint—Legal papers that outline a dispute, which must be filed to start a lawsuit.

Compliance Inspection—An inspection of a building to determine, for the benefit of a real estate lender, whether building codes, specifications, or conditions established by a prior inspection have been met before a loan is made.

Comprehensive Environmental Response, Compensation and Liability Act—*See:* CERCLA.

Comprehensive Plan—An overall plan for the development of a city or county, which is used as a guide for the development of zoning regulations. Also called a master plan.

Concurrent Ownership—A form of ownership in which two or more people share title to one property at the same time. Also called a co-tenancy.

Condemnation—1. The taking of private property for public use (for streets, sewers, airports, railroads, etc.) through the government's power of eminent domain. 2. A declaration that a structure is unsafe and must be closed or destroyed.

Condition—A provision in an agreement or contract, limiting the rights and obligations of the parties or making them contingent on the occurrence or nonoccurrence of a specified event.

Conditional Fee—An ownership estate that may be terminated by the previous owner if specified conditions are not met. Also called a fee simple subject to condition subsequent. *See:* Fee Simple Defeasible.

Conditional Use Permit—A permit that allows a special use, such as a school or hospital, to operate in a neighborhood where it would otherwise be prohibited by the zoning. Also called a special exception permit.

Condominium—Property developed for concurrent ownership, where each co-owner has a separate interest in an individual dwelling unit, combined with an undivided interest in the property's common areas.

Condominium Act—A state law passed in Washington in 1989 which governs all condominiums created after July 1, 1990.

Condominium Association—*See:* Unit Owners Association.

Condominium Bylaws—The rules governing the operation of a condominium development.

Condominium Declaration—A document recorded to establish a condominium, which contains detailed information about the project.

Confidential Information—Information from or concerning a principal that was acquired during the course of an agency relationship, that the principal expects to be kept confidential, that the principal reasonably expects to be confidential, that the principal has not disclosed to third parties, that would operate to the detriment of the principal, and that the principal would not be legally obligated to disclose to the other party.

Confirmation of Sale—Court approval of a sale by an executor, administrator, or guardian.

Consent—To agree, to give permission or assent.

Conservation—1. Regarding real estate, preservation of structures or neighborhoods in a sound and favorable condition. 2. Regarding natural resources, preserving or using them in a way that provides the most long-term benefit.

Consideration—Anything of value given to induce another person to enter into a contract, such as money, services, goods, or a promise. Sometimes called valuable consideration.

Conspiracy—An agreement or plan between two or more persons to perform an unlawful act.

Construction Lien—*See:* Lien, Construction.

Constructive Annexation—A doctrine holding that some moveable items are so strongly connected with real property that they are considered fixtures.

Constructive Eviction—When a landlord's actions interfere with a tenant's rights seriously enough to force the tenant to vacate the premises.

Contiguous—Physically adjoining, abutting, or in close proximity.

Contingency—An event or condition that must occur before a contract becomes binding.

Contour—The surface shape or configuration of land. A contour map depicts the topography by means of lines, called contour lines, which connect points of equal elevation.

Contract—An agreement, for consideration and between competent parties, to do or not do a certain thing. It is an agreement enforceable at law.

Contract, Bilateral—A contract in which each party promises to perform something in exchange for the other's promise to perform.

Contract, Executory—A contract in which one or both parties have not yet completed performance. (An executed contract, on the other hand, is one in which both parties have completely performed their obligations under the contract.)

Contract, Express—A clear and definite contract set forth in words.

Contract, Implied—One implied by the actions of the principals; in contrast to an express contract, in which the words forming the agreement are stated, orally or in writing.

Contract, Oral—A spoken agreement.

Contract, Real Estate—1. A contract for the sale of real property in which the buyer (the vendee) pays in installments; the buyer takes possession of the property immediately, but the seller (the vendor) retains legal title until the full price has been paid. Also called a land contract, installment sales contract, or contract for deed. 2. An earnest money agreement. 3. Any contract having to do with real property.

Contract, Unenforceable—One that will not be enforced through the courts because its contents can't be proven (usually an oral contract); or because it is of a type required to be in writing (such as a real estate contract), but is not.

Contract, Unilateral—A contract that is accepted by performance. The offeror is not required to perform his or her part of the contract until the offeree has performed.

Contract, Valid—A binding, legally enforceable contract.

Contract, Void—A "contract" that is really not a contract because it lacks one of the key elements, such as consideration or a lawful objective.

Contract, Voidable—A valid contract that may be terminated without liability by one or both of the parties (because of fraud, undue influence, duress, or mistake, or because the party seeking to terminate the agreement is a minor).

Contract of Sale—An agreement in which a buyer agrees to buy a parcel of land for a certain price and the seller agrees to convey title; also called an earnest money agreement, purchase and sale agreement, or deposit receipt.

Contractor—One who contracts to provide labor or materials, or construct a building, or do other work for a certain price.

Conversion—1. Misappropriating property or funds belonging to another; for example, converting trust funds to one's own use. 2. The process by which an existing building is turned into a condominium. The Washington Condominium Act has special rules for residential conversions.

Conveyance—The transfer of title to real property from one person to another by means of a written document, such as a deed.

Cooperating Agent—A member of a multiple listing association who helps find a buyer for property listed by another brokerage company within the same multiple listing association.

Cooperative—A building or project owned by a nonprofit corporation. In a cooperative, the residents purchase shares in the corporation that owns the building. A resident receives a proprietary lease on a living unit and the right to use the common areas.

Corporation—An association organized according to certain laws, in which individuals may purchase ownership shares; regarded by the law as an artificial person, separate from the individual shareholders.

Corporation, Domestic—A corporation doing business in the state where it was created (incorporated).

Corporation, Foreign—A corporation doing business in one state, but created (incorporated) in another state.

Corporation, Nonprofit—A corporation formed for the purpose of serving a purpose of public or mutual benefit other than the pursuit or accumulation of profits.

Correction Lines—Adjustment lines used in the government survey system to compensate for curvature of the earth. They occur at 24-mile intervals, every fourth township line, where the distance between north and south range lines is corrected to six miles.

Co-Tenancy—*See:* Concurrent Ownership.

Counteroffer—A new offer made by the offeree in reply to an offer to enter into a contract. It constitutes a rejection of the first offer, and the roles of the two parties are now reversed. The original offeror is the offeree and can accept or reject the counteroffer. This situation commonly arises when the original offeree wants to make some change in the offer he or she has received. Any change, however slight, constitutes a rejection of the original offer.

County—An administrative subdivision of the State, created by the State and deriving all of its powers from the State.

Course—In a metes and bounds description, a direction, stated in terms of a compass bearing.

Covenant—1. A written agreement or promise to do or not do something. 2. A stipulation that a property will be used or will not be used for a particular purpose or purposes. 3. A guarantee that some state of facts exists (such as the fact that a grantor has good title to real property).

Covenant, Restrictive—A promise to do or refrain from doing an act relating to real property, especially such a promise that runs with the land; usually imposed by a grantor on all subsequent owners of the property. Also called deed restrictions.

Covenant Against Encumbrances—In a warranty deed, a promise that the property is not burdened by any encumbrances other than those that are disclosed in the deed.

Covenant of Quiet Enjoyment—A promise that a buyer or tenant's possession of the property will not be disturbed by the previous owner, the landlord, or anyone else making a lawful claim against the property.

Covenant of Right to Convey—In a warranty deed, a promise that the grantor has the legal ability to make a valid conveyance.

Covenant of Seisin—In a warranty deed, a promise that the grantor actually owns the interest he or she is conveying to the grantee.

Covenant of Warranty—In a warranty deed, a promise that the grantor will defend the grantee's title if it is challenged in court.

Credit—A payment that is receivable (as opposed to a debit, which is a payment due).

Creditor, Secured—A creditor who has a lien on specific property, such as a mortgagee.

Customer—In real estate, usually a prospective purchaser.

Damage Deposit—*See:* Security Deposit.

Damages—The amount of money one can recover as compensation for an injury to his or her person or property resulting from an act or failure to act.

Damages, Compensatory—The amount of money awarded for an injury, or a loss incurred.

Damages, Liquidated—A sum that the parties to a contract agree in advance (at the time the contract is made) will serve as full compensation in the event of a breach.

Datum—A reference point used by surveyors to determine elevation.

Debit—A charge listed on a settlement statement, showing a debt or payment owed by one of the parties.

Debtor—One who owes something (usually money) to another.

Decedent—A person who has died.

Decisional Law—Law that evolves from published opinions of the courts. Also called case law.

Declarant—The term used to refer to the developer of a condominium in the Washington Condominium Act.

Declaration of Abandonment—A recorded document voluntarily releasing a property from homestead protection.

Declaration of Homestead—A document claiming homestead protection for a property.

Declaration of Restrictions—*See:* CC&Rs.

Dedication—An appropriation or granting of private property for public use; may be a grant of the entire fee simple interest or just an easement (such as an easement for sidewalks or streets).

Dedication, Common Law—Transfer of land from private to public ownership or use by virtue of the private owner's acquiescence in public use of the land for an extended period of time.

Dedication, Statutory—Transfer of land from private to public ownership as required by law, as a prerequisite to subdivision approval, for example.

Deed—A written instrument that, when properly executed and delivered, conveys title to real property from the grantor to the grantee.

Deed, Bargain and Sale—A deed that conveys title but does not make the same promises as a full warranty deed.

Deed, Correction—A deed used to correct minor mistakes in an earlier deed, such as misspellings of names or errors in description of the parcel.

Deed, General Warranty—A deed in which the grantor warrants the title against defects that might have arisen before or during his or her period of ownership.

Deed, Gift—A deed freely given in which the consideration is love and affection (rather than valuable consideration such as money, goods, or services).

Deed, Partial Reconveyance—The document used to release a portion of the secured property from the lien of a blanket deed of trust.

Deed, Quitclaim—A deed that operates to convey and release any interest in a piece of real property that the grantor may have. It contains no warranties of any kind, but does transfer any right, title, or interest the grantor has at the time the deed is executed.

Deed, Sheriff's—A deed delivered by the sheriff, on court order, to the holder of the Certificate of Sale following the period of redemption after a mortgage foreclosure.

Deed, Special Warranty—A deed in which the grantor warrants title only against defects that may have arisen during his or her period of ownership.

Deed, Tax—A deed given to the successful bidder when property is sold to satisfy unpaid property taxes.

Deed, Trustee's—A deed given to the successful bidder at a trustee's sale in the nonjudicial foreclosure of a deed of trust.

Deed, Warranty—A deed containing warranties or guarantees of clear title and the right to convey, as well as the grantor's willingness to defend against claims that the title conveyed is not good.

Deed, Wild—A deed that cannot be located under the grantor-grantee system of indexing.

Deed Executed Under Court Order—A deed, such as a sheriff's deed or tax deed, that is the result of a court action, such as foreclosure.

Deed in Lieu of Foreclosure—A deed given by a borrower to a lender to satisfy the debt and to avoid a foreclosure suit.

Deed of Partition—A deed used by co-owners, such as joint tenants or tenants in common, to divide up the co-owned property so that each can own a separate portion.

Deed of Release—A deed used to release property (or part of it) from a lien created by a land contract. Most often used when the contract covers more than one parcel of land.

Deed of Reconveyance—The instrument used to release the security property from the lien created by a deed of trust when the debt has been repaid.

Deed of Trust—One of the two main types of security instruments used to finance the purchase of real estate, the other being a mortgage. Under the deed of trust, the power to sell the secured property in the event of default by the trustor (the borrower) is given to an independent third party (the trustee) to protect the interests of the beneficiary (the lender) and the trustor. A deed of trust can be foreclosed at a trustee's sale. Unlike foreclosure of a mortgage, judicial intervention is not required, and there is no period of redemption following the trustee's sale. A trustee's deed is issued after the sale.

Deed Restrictions—Limitations in a deed restricting the use of the property, such as "Residential use only" or "No building over 35 feet in height." Also called restrictive covenants.

Default—Failure to fulfill an obligation, duty, or promise, as when a borrower fails to make loan payments or a tenant fails to pay rent.

Default Judgment—*See:* Judgment, Default.

Defeasance Clause—A clause in a mortgage, deed of trust, or lease that cancels or defeats a certain right upon the occurrence of a certain event.

Defeasible Fee—*See:* Fee Simple Defeasible.

Deficiency Judgment—*See:* Judgment, Deficiency.

Degree—In surveying, a unit of circular measurement equal to $1/360\text{th}$ of one complete rotation around a point in a plane.

Delivery—The legal transfer of an instrument evidencing title or ownership. A valid deed does not convey title unless it has been delivered (actually or constructively) to the grantee.

Density—The number of buildings or the number of occupants per unit of land (square mile, acre, etc.).

Department of Licensing—The state agency in charge of administering the real estate license law in Washington.

Deposit—1. Money offered as an indication of good faith in regard to the future performance of a contract to purchase real property. Also called earnest money. 2. A security deposit given to a landlord by a tenant.

Deposit Receipt—A written instrument used as a receipt for the earnest money deposit and as an offer to purchase real property, which becomes a binding contract if accepted by the seller. Also called an earnest money agreement or a purchase and sale agreement.

Deposition—Formal out-of-court testimony of a witness taken before trial, for possible use later in the trial. Testimony taken either for discovery, to determine the facts of the case, or when a witness will be unable to attend the trial, or both.

Depreciation—A loss in value. For appraisal purposes, depreciation results from physical deterioration (such as cracks in the foundation), functional obsolescence (such as old fashioned plumbing or lighting fixtures), or economic obsolescence (such as deterioration in the neighborhood).

Detached Residence—A home physically separated from other houses; not connected to another house by a common wall.

Detrimental Reliance—*See:* Promissory Estoppel.

Developed Land—Land that has been improved by man-made additions, such as buildings, roads, or sidewalks.

Developer—Someone who makes changes to bring land to its most profitable use by subdividing and/or improving it.

Devise—1. A gift of real property transferred by will. The donor is the testator and the recipient is the devisee. 2. To transfer real property by will. *Compare:* Bequest; Legacy.

Devisee—A recipient of real property under a will. *Compare:* Beneficiary; Legatee.

Disability—According to the Americans with Disabilities Act and the Fair Housing Act, a physical or mental impairment that substantially limits a person in one or more major life activities.

Disaffirm—To ask a court to terminate a voidable contract.

Discount—1. An amount paid to the lender or withheld from the loan amount at the time a loan is made, to increase the lender's yield on the loan. 2. To sell a note at a reduced value or less than face value.

Discrimination—Unequal treatment, either favorable or unfavorable, based on the class, race, or other group to which a person or persons belong.

Diversity Jurisdiction—The federal courts' power to hear cases in which a citizen of one state sues a citizen of another state (or country).

Domestic Corporation—*See:* Corporation, Domestic.

Dominant Tenement—Property that receives the benefit of an appurtenant easement.

Downzoning—Rezoning land for a more restricted use.

Dual Agent—An agent who represents both the buyer and the seller in the same transaction.

Due-on-Sale Clause—A clause in a loan agreement giving the lender the right to declare the entire loan balance due immediately if the security property is sold or otherwise transferred without the lender's consent. Also called an alienation clause.

Due Process—A fair hearing by an impartial judge. Under the U.S. Constitution, no one may be deprived of life, liberty, or property without due process of law.

Duress—Unlawful force, constraint, threats, or other actions used to compel someone to do something (such as sign a contract) against his or her will.

Dwelling—A building or part of a building used or intended to be used as living quarters.

Earnest Money—A deposit made by a prospective purchaser of real estate as evidence of a good faith intention to complete the purchase. Also called a good faith deposit.

Earnest Money Agreement—A contract in which a property owner agrees to sell the property to a buyer for a specified price. Also called a purchase and sale agreement or deposit receipt.

Easement—A right to use some part of another person's property for a particular purpose; for example, as a driveway, or for installing and maintaining a water line.

Easement, Implied—*See:* Easement by Implication.

Easement, Negative—An easement that prevents the landowner from using the land in a certain way; essentially the same thing as a restrictive covenant.

Easement, Positive—An easement that allows a landowner to use another's land for a specific purpose.

Easement Appurtenant—An easement for the benefit of a particular piece of property (the dominant tenement). *Compare:* Easement in Gross.

Easement by Express Grant—An easement granted to another by means of a deed or other document.

Easement by Express Reservation—An easement created by deed in favor of the grantor, who transfers the property (or part of the property) but reserves an easement for his or her own use.

Easement by Implication—An easement created by law (not by express grant) when a property is divided into more than one parcel, when there was apparent prior use of the easement and it is reasonably necessary for the enjoyment of the dominant tenement. Also called an implied easement.

Easement by Necessity—An easement implied by law when a property is divided into more than one parcel if the dominant tenement would be completely useless without an easement, even though it was not a long-standing, apparent use.

Easement in Gross—An easement for the benefit of a person instead of a piece of land. *Compare:* Easement Appurtenant.

Egress—A passageway leading from property; a means of exiting. It is the opposite of ingress (entry). The terms ingress and egress usually refer to easements.

Emancipated Minor—A person under 18 who is or has been married, is on active duty in the military, or has a declaration of emancipation from a court.

Emblements—Crops, such as wheat or corn, that are produced annually through the labor of the cultivator.

Emblements, Doctrine of—The right of an agricultural tenant to enter land after termination of the lease for the purpose of harvesting crops.

Eminent Domain—The power of the government to take (condemn) private property for public use, upon payment of just compensation to the owner.

Employee—Someone who works under the direction and control of another. *Compare:* Independent Contractor.

Encroachment—Unlawful physical intrusion onto the property of another, usually as the result of mistake.

Encumber—To place a lien or other encumbrance against the title to a property.

Encumbrance—A nonpossessory interest in property; a lien, easement, or restrictive covenant burdening the property owner's title.

Enjoin—To prohibit an act, or command performance of an act, by court order; to issue an injunction.

Environmental Impact Statement (EIS)—A statement evaluating the impact of a development on the surrounding community and the environment.

Equal Credit Opportunity Act—A federal law prohibiting providers of consumer credit from discriminating based on race, color, religion, national origin, sex, marital status, age, or because the applicant receives public assistance.

Equal Protection—Under the U.S. Constitution, all citizens are entitled to the equal protection of the laws; no law may arbitrarily discriminate between different groups, or be applied to different groups in a discriminatory manner.

Equitable Redemption Period—The period between the initial complaint and the sale of a foreclosed property, during which time a borrower may redeem the property by paying the amount of the debt plus costs.

Equitable Remedy—A remedy granted to a plaintiff that is something other than an award of money (damages), when money alone cannot adequately correct the problem, such as an injunction or an order of specific performance.

Equity—1. The difference between the value of a piece of property and the liens against it; an owner's unencumbered interest in his or her property. 2. In law, a judge's power to soften or set aside strict legal rules, to bring about a fair and just result in a particular case.

Equity Skimming—An illegal scheme in which homeowners are defrauded out of equity in their homes.

Erosion—Gradual loss of soil due to the action of water or wind.

Escheat—The reversion of property to the State when a person dies without leaving a will and no heirs entitled to the property can be located.

Escrow—An arrangement in which something of value (such as money or a deed) is held by a disinterested third party, called an escrow agent, until certain conditions specified in the escrow instructions have been fulfilled.

Escrow Agent—1. A neutral third party who holds money and documents in trust and carries out the closing process. 2. A company (not a natural person) that is licensed to engage in the escrow business.

Escrow Instructions—A written document that tells the escrow agent how to proceed and states the conditions each party must fulfill before the transaction can close.

Escrow Officer—A person licensed to work for an escrow agent.

Estate—1. A possessory interest in real property; either a freehold or a leasehold. 2. The property left by someone who has died.

Estate at Will—A leasehold estate for an indefinite period of time, which can be terminated at any time by either landlord or tenant without notice. Also called a tenancy at will.

Estate for Life—*See:* Life Estate.

Estate for Years—A leasehold estate set to last for a definite period of time (one week, six months, three years, etc.), after which it terminates automatically.

Estate, Fee Simple—*See:* Fee Simple.

Estate in Remainder—*See:* Remainder.

Estate in Reversion—*See:* Reversion.

Estate of Inheritance—An estate that can be inherited by the owner's heirs, such as a fee simple estate.

Estoppel—A legal doctrine that prevents a person from asserting rights or facts that are inconsistent with his or her earlier actions or statements.

Eviction—Dispossession, expulsion, or ejection of a person from real property.

Eviction, Actual—Physically forcing someone off of property (or preventing them from re-entering), or using the legal process to make someone leave.

Eviction, Constructive—When a landlord's act (or failure to act) interferes with the tenant's quiet enjoyment of the property, or makes the property unfit for its intended use, to such an extent that the tenant is forced to move out.

Eviction, Retaliatory—When a landlord evicts a tenant in retaliation for requesting repairs, filing a complaint against the landlord, or organizing or participating in a tenants' rights group.

Eviction, Self-Help—When a landlord uses physical force, a lock-out, or a utility shut-off to get rid of a tenant, instead of using the legal process. (This is generally illegal.)

Excise Tax—*See:* Tax, Excise.

Exclusive Right to Sell—*See:* Listing, Exclusive Right to Sell.

Execute—1. To perform or complete. 2. To sign a document and take any other formal steps that may be necessary for its validity (such as acknowledgment).

Execution—A legal process in which the court orders the sheriff or another official to seize and sell the property of a debtor to satisfy a judgment lien or other lien.

Executor—A person named in a will to carry out the provisions of the will. (If it is a woman, she may be referred to as the executrix, although that term is passing out of use.)

Exemption—A provision holding that a law or regulation does not apply to a particular person or group. For example, a person entitled to a property tax exemption is not required to pay property taxes. An exemption can be full or partial.

Express—Stated in words, spoken or written (rather than merely implied by actions). *Compare:* Implied.

Extender Clause—A clause in a listing agreement providing that the broker will still receive the commission if the property is sold during a specified period of time after the listing expires to someone who was a prospect during the listing term. Also called a carryover clause or safety clause.

Failure of Purpose—An excuse for rescinding a contract; if the contract cannot achieve its intended purpose, the parties are released from their obligations.

Fair Housing Act—A law enacted in 1968 that makes it illegal to discriminate in the sale or rental of residential property or vacant land that will be used for residential construction.

Fairness in Lending Act—A state law prohibiting financial institutions from redlining.

Fannie Mae—A popular name for the Federal National Mortgage Association (FNMA).

Fed—The Federal Reserve.

Federal Deposit Insurance Corporation (FDIC)—A federal agency that insures deposits in state and federally chartered banks (through the Bank Insurance Fund) and savings and loan associations (through the Savings Association Fund).

Federal Home Loan Mortgage Corporation (FHLMC)—A private corporation supervised by HUD; one of the three major secondary market agencies. Also called Freddie Mac.

Federal Housing Administration (FHA)—An agency within the Department of Housing and Urban Development that provides mortgage insurance to encourage lenders to make more affordable home loans.

Federal National Mortgage Association (FNMA)—A private corporation supervised by HUD; one of the three major secondary market agencies. Commonly called Fannie Mae.

Federal Question—A legal question involving the U.S. Constitution, a treaty, or a federal statute. Federal question cases may be heard in federal court.

Federal Reserve System—The government body that regulates commercial banks and implements monetary policy in an attempt to control the national economy.

Federal Trade Commission (FTC)—A federal agency responsible for investigating and eliminating unfair and deceptive business practices. It is also the agency charged with enforcing the Truth in Lending Law.

Fee—*See:* Fee Simple.

Fee Simple—The greatest estate one can have in real property; of indefinite duration; with no conditions on the title; freely transferable or inheritable. Also known as a fee or a fee simple absolute.

Fee Simple Defeasible—A fee estate in real property that is subject to being defeated or undone if a certain event occurs or a certain condition is not met.

Fee Simple Determinable—A defeasible fee that is terminated automatically if certain events occur.

Fee Simple Subject to Condition Subsequent—A defeasible fee that may be terminated by the grantor after breach of a condition specified in the grant. The grantor has a power of termination.

FHA—Federal Housing Administration.

Fiduciary Relationship—A relationship of trust and confidence, in which one party owes the other (or both parties owe each other) loyalty and a higher standard of good faith than they owe to third parties. For example, an agent is a fiduciary in relation to the principal; husband and wife are fiduciaries in relation to one another.

Finance Charge—Any charge a borrower is assessed, directly or indirectly, in connection with a loan.

Financing Statement—A brief document that, when recorded, gives notice of a creditor's security interest in an item of personal property.

Finder's Fee—A referral fee paid to someone for directing a buyer or seller to a real estate agent.

First Lien Position—The position held by a mortgage or deed of trust that has higher lien priority than any other mortgage or deed of trust against the property.

First Refusal, Right of—*See:* Right of First Refusal.

Fiscal Year—Any 12-month period used as a business year for accounting, tax, and other financial purposes, as opposed to the calendar year.

Fixed Term—A period of time which has a definite beginning date and ending date.

Fixture—An item that was personal property, but which has become affixed to or associated with real property in such a way that it has legally become part of the real property.

Fixture, Trade—Article of personal property annexed to real property by a tenant for use in his or her trade or business, which the tenant is allowed to remove at the end of the lease.

Foreclosure—When a lienholder causes property to be sold, so that the unpaid lien can be satisfied from the sale proceeds.

Foreclosure, Judicial—A lawsuit filed by a mortgagee or deed of trust beneficiary to foreclose on the security property when the borrower has defaulted.

Foreclosure, Nonjudicial—Foreclosure by a trustee under the power of sale clause in a deed of trust.

Foreign Corporation—*See:* Corporation, Foreign.

Forfeiture—Loss of a right or something else of value as a result of failure to perform an obligation or condition.

Fraud—An intentional or negligent misrepresentation or concealment of a material fact, which is relied upon by another, who is induced to enter a transaction and harmed as a result.

Fraud, Actual—Intentional deceit or misrepresentation.

Fraud, Constructive—Negligent misrepresentation, or a breach of duty that misleads the person the duty was owed to, without an intention to deceive.

Freddie Mac—A popular name for the Federal Home Loan Mortgage Corporation (FHLMC).

Free and Clear—Title to real property that is completely free of encumbrances such as mortgages, liens, and so forth.

Freehold—An ownership estate in real property; either a fee simple or a life estate. The holder of a freehold estate has title, whereas the holder of a less-than-freehold estate (leasehold estate) is merely a tenant, having a temporary right to possession, but no title.

Future Estate—An interest in property that will or may become possessory at some point in the future, such as an estate in remainder or an estate in reversion.

Garnishment—A legal process by which a creditor may gain access to a debtor's personal property or funds that are in the hands of a third party. Items that may be garnished include wages, debts owed, security interests, and goods or personal effects concealed in the possession of third parties.

General Agent—*See:* Agent, General.

General Lien—*See:* Lien, General.

General Warranty Deed—*See:* Deed, General Warranty.

Ginnie Mae—A popular name for the Government National Mortgage Association (GNMA).

Goodwill—An intangible asset of a business resulting from a good reputation with the public, serving as an indication of future return business.

Government Lot—In the government survey system, a parcel of land that is not a regular section (one mile square), because of the convergence of range lines, or because of a body of water or some other obstacle; assigned a government lot number.

Government National Mortgage Association (GNMA)—A government agency within HUD, popularly known as Ginnie Mae; one of the major secondary market agencies, along with Fannie Mae and Freddie Mac.

Government Survey System—A system of land description in which the land is divided into squares called townships, each approximately six miles square (containing 36 square miles), which are divided into 36 sections, each approximately one mile square and containing approximately 640 acres. Also called the rectangular survey system or section, township, and range system.

Grant—To transfer or convey an interest in real property by means of a written instrument.

Grantee—One who receives a grant of real property.

Granting Clause—Words in a deed that indicate an intent to transfer an interest in land.

Grantor—One who grants an interest in real property to another.

Grantor/Grantee Indexes—Indexes of recorded documents maintained by the recorder, with each document listed in alphabetical order according to the last name of the grantor (in the grantor index) or the grantee (in the grantee index); the indexes list the recording number of each document, so that it can be located in the public record.

Growth Management Act—A Washington state law aimed at limiting sprawl and concentrating growth in existing urban areas.

Guardian—A person appointed by a court to administer the affairs of a minor or a mentally incompetent person.

Guide Meridian—*See:* Meridian, Guide.

Habitability—*See:* Implied Warranty of Habitability.

Heir—Someone entitled to inherit another's property under the laws of intestate succession.

Highest and Best Use—The use that is most likely to produce the greatest net return from the property over a given period of time.

Historic Preservation—The protection of historic buildings from destruction or unauthorized modifications.

Holder in Due Course—A person who obtains a negotiable instrument for value, in good faith, and without notice of any defenses against it.

Holdover Tenant—A tenant who fails to surrender possession of the premises at the end of the tenancy.

Home Mortgage Disclosure Act—A federal law requiring institutional lenders to make annual disclosures of all mortgage loans made, as a means of enforcing prohibitions against redlining.

Homeowners Association—A nonprofit association made up of homeowners in a subdivision, responsible for enforcing the CC&Rs and managing other community affairs.

Homestead—An owner-occupied dwelling, together with any appurtenant outbuildings and land.

Homestead Law—A state law that provides limited protection against creditors' claims for homestead property.

Housing Codes—Local regulations setting minimum standards for aspects of housing that affect health and safety.

HUD—The Department of Housing and Urban Development.

Hypothecate—To give real or personal property as security for an obligation without giving up possession of it. *Compare:* Pledge.

Implied—Not expressed in words, but understood from actions or circumstances. *Compare:* Express.

Implied Warranty of Habitability—A warranty implied by law in every residential lease, that the property is fit for habitation.

Implied Warranties of Quality—Under the Condominium Act, certain guarantees that automatically apply to the sale of a unit by the declarant.

Impound Account—A bank account maintained by a lender for payment of property taxes and insurance premiums on the security property; the lender requires the borrower to make regular deposits, and pays the expenses out of the account. Also called a reserve account.

Improvements—Man-made additions to real property.

Imputed Knowledge—A legal doctrine stating that a principal is considered to have notice of information that the agent has, even if the agent never passed that information on to the principal.

Incompetent—1. Not legally qualified to enter into contracts, as in the case of a minor or a mentally ill person. 2. Not of sound mind.

Independent Contractor—A person who contracts to do certain work for another person, agreeing to achieve a certain result but retaining control over how he or she will carry out the task, rather than submitting to the control of the other person. Real estate brokers are usually independent contractors. *Compare:* Employee.

Indexing—A means of cataloging deeds and other documents in the recording office; deeds are indexed according to grantor and grantee, and sometimes according to the location of the land.

Ingress—A means of entering a piece of property, such as a driveway. The opposite of egress.

In-House Transaction—A sale in which the buyer and the seller are brought together by salespeople working for the same broker.

Injunction—A court order prohibiting someone from performing an act or commanding performance of an act.

Instrument—A legal document, usually one that transfers title (such as a deed), creates a lien (such as a mortgage), or establishes a right to payment (such as a promissory note or contract).

Insurance, Hazard—Insurance against losses on property caused by fire, flood, theft, or other disaster. Also called casualty insurance.

Insurance, Homeowner's—Casualty insurance that covers the homeowner's personal property as well as the real property.

Insurance, Title—Insurance that protects against losses resulting from undiscovered title defects. An owner's policy protects the buyer, while a mortgagee's policy protects the lien position of the buyer's lender.

Insurance, Title, Extended Coverage—A policy of title insurance that covers problems which should be discovered in an inspection of the property, such as adverse possession or encroachments.

Insurance, Title, Standard Coverage—Title insurance that protects against latent title defects (such as forged deeds) and undiscovered recorded encumbrances, but does not protect against problems that would only be discovered by an inspection of the property, such as adverse possessors or unrecorded easements.

Integration Clause—A clause in a contract which states that the document is the entire agreement between the parties.

Interest—1. A charge a borrower pays to a lender for the use of the lender's money. 2. A right or share in something (such as a piece of real estate).

Interest, Future—An interest in property that will or may become possessory at some point in the future, such as an estate in remainder or an estate in reversion.

Interest, Prepaid—Interest on a new loan that must be paid at the time of closing; covers the interest due for the first month of the loan term. Sometimes called interim interest.

Interest, Simple—Interest that is computed on the principal amount of the loan only. (This is the type of interest charged in connection with real estate loans.)

Interest, Undivided—A co-owner's interest, giving him or her the right to shared possession of the whole property, rather than exclusive possession of a particular section of it.

Interpleader—A court action filed by someone who is holding funds that two or more people are claiming. The holder turns the funds over to the court; the court resolves the dispute and delivers the money to the party who is entitled to it.

Interrogatories—A discovery tool similar to a deposition but conducted by mail instead of in person. One party sends a series of questions to the other and the other party must send back answers.

Interval Ownership—A form of time-share ownership in which buyers are granted an estate for years for a specific time period.

Intestate—Without a valid will.

Intestate Succession—Distribution of the property of a person who died intestate to his or her heirs.

Inverse Condemnation Action—A court action by a private landowner against the government, seeking compensation for damage to property caused by government action.

Inverted Pyramid—A way of visualizing ownership of real property; in theory, a property owner owns all the earth, water, and air enclosed by an inverted pyramid with its tip at the center of the earth and its base corresponding to the boundaries of the property and then continuing into the airspace.

Investment Property—Unimproved property that produces no income, but is held in the expectation that it will appreciate in value.

Involuntary Lien—*See:* Lien, Involuntary.

Joint and Several Liability—*See:* Liability, Joint and Several.

Joint Tenancy—*See:* Tenancy, Joint.

Joint Venture—Two or more individuals joining together for one specific project as partners. A joint venture is of limited duration; if the members of the venture undertake another project together, the association may become a partnership.

Judgment—1. A court's binding determination of the rights and duties of the parties to a lawsuit. 2. A court order requiring one party to pay damages to the other.

Judgment, Default—A court judgment in favor of the plaintiff due to the defendant's failure to answer the complaint or appear at a hearing.

Judgment, Deficiency—A personal judgment entered against a borrower in favor of the lender if the proceeds from a foreclosure sale of the security property are not enough to pay off the debt.

Judgment Creditor—A person to whom money is owed by virtue of a judgment in a lawsuit.

Judgment Debtor—A person who owes money by virtue of a judgment in a lawsuit.

Judgment Lien—*See:* Lien, Judgment.

Judicial Foreclosure—*See:* Foreclosure, Judicial.

Just Compensation—The compensation that the Constitution requires the government to pay a property owner when the property is taken under the power of eminent domain.

Land—In a legal sense, the solid part of the surface of the earth (as distinguished from water), everything affixed to it, by nature or by human beings, or anything on it or in it, such as minerals and water.

Landlocked—A parcel of land without access to any type of road or highway. The owner of landlocked land may be able to obtain an easement by necessity from the court.

Landlord—A landowner who has leased his or her property. Also called a lessor.

Landmark—A monument, natural or artificial, set up on the boundary line of two adjacent estates in order to mark the boundary.

Latent Defects—Defects in property that are not visible or apparent.

Lateral Support—*See:* Support, Lateral.

Lawful Purpose—An objective of a contract that is not against the law.

Lease—A contract in which a landlord (lessor) grants a tenant (lessee) the possession of real estate in exchange for rent.

Lease, Fixed—A lease in which the tenant pays the landlord a fixed sum as rent each month, and the landlord pays all of the property's operating expenses. Also called a flat lease, gross lease, or straight lease.

Lease, Graduated—A lease in which the rent is increased at agreed intervals during the term of the lease.

Lease, Gross—*See:* Lease, Fixed.

Lease, Ground—A lease of the land only, usually for a long term, and sometimes secured by improvements placed on the land by the tenant.

Lease, Net—A lease requiring the tenant to pay some or all of the property's operating expenses (such as taxes, utilities, and insurance), in addition to the rent paid to the landlord.

Lease, Percentage—A lease in which the rent includes a percentage of the tenant's monthly or annual gross sales.

Leasehold Estate—The possessory interest that a tenant has in the leased property during the term of the lease.

Legal Description—A method of describing a parcel of real estate that is recognized by law, including the lot and block (recorded plat) method, the government survey method (also called the township and range or rectangular survey method), or the metes and bounds method.

Legal Person—*See:* Artificial Person.

Legatee—A recipient of personal property under a will.

Lender, Institutional—A bank, savings and loan association, life insurance company, or similar organization that invests others' funds in mortgages and other loans; as distinguished from individual or private lenders who invest their own money.

Lessee—One who possesses or occupies property owned by another under the terms of a lease. Also called a tenant.

Lessor—One who has leased property to another. Also called a landlord.

Leverage—The effective use of borrowed money to finance an investment such as real estate.

Liability, Joint and Several—A form of liability in which several persons are responsible for a debt both individually and as a group. Any one of the individuals can be required to pay the entire debt if the others fail to pay their shares.

Liability, Vicarious—A legal doctrine stating that a principal can be held liable for harm to third parties resulting from an agent's actions.

Liable—Legally responsible.

License—1. Official permission to perform certain acts that the law does not allow everyone to do. 2. Revocable, non-assignable permission to enter land owned by someone else for a particular purpose. *Compare:* Easement.

License, Inactive—Any real estate license that has been turned over to the Director temporarily. The holder of an inactive license is not permitted to engage in activities requiring a license.

Lien—A nonpossessory interest in property, giving the lienholder the right to foreclose if the owner does not pay a debt owed to the lienholder; a financial encumbrance on the owner's title.

Lien, Attachment—A lien on property intended to prevent transfer of the property pending the outcome of litigation.

Lien, Construction—A specific lien claimed by someone who performed work on the property (construction, repairs, or improvements) and has not been paid. Also called a mechanic's lien.

Lien, Equitable—A lien arising as a matter of fairness, rather than by agreement or by operation of law.

Lien, General—A lien against all of the property of a debtor.

Lien, Involuntary—A lien that arises by operation of law, without consent of the property owner.

Lien, Judgment—A general lien against all of the property of a judgment debtor, making it possible for the judgment creditor to have the property sold to satisfy the debt.

Lien, Materialman's—Similar to a construction lien, but it refers specifically to sums owed suppliers, as opposed to laborers, for materials provided in connection with a construction project.

Lien, Mechanic's—*See:* Construction Lien.

Lien, Property Tax—A specific lien on property to secure payment of the property taxes.

Lien, Specific—A lien that attaches only to a particular piece of property, as opposed to a general lien, which attaches to all of the debtor's property.

Lien, Statutory—A lien created by operation of law, rather than by contract, such as a tax lien.

Lien, Tax—A lien on property to secure the payment of taxes.

Lien, Voluntary—A lien placed against property with the consent of the owner.

Lienholder, Junior—A secured creditor whose lien has lower priority than another lien against the same property.

Lien Priority—The order in which liens are paid off out of proceeds of the foreclosure sale.

Lien Theory—A legal theory holding that upon giving a mortgage or deed of trust as security for a debt, the borrower does not transfer title to the lender. The lender has a security interest during the period of indebtedness, but not title. *Compare:* Title Theory.

Life Estate—A freehold estate that lasts only as long as a specified person lives. That person is referred to as the measuring life.

Life Tenant—Someone who owns a life estate; the person entitled to possession of the property during the measuring life.

Limited Liability Company—A business entity that combines the management and tax advantages of a partnership with the limited liability of a corporation.

Limited Partnership—A partnership in which the liability of some of the partners (the limited partners) is limited to the amount they invested.

Liquidated Damages—*See:* Damages, Liquidated.

Lis Pendens—A recorded notice stating that there is a lawsuit pending that may affect title to the defendant's real estate.

Listing—A written contract between a principal and an agent stipulating that the agent will be paid a commission for finding or attempting to find a ready, willing, and able buyer to purchase the seller's property on terms acceptable to the seller. Also called a listing agreement.

Listing, Exclusive—Either an exclusive agency listing or an exclusive right to sell listing.

Listing, Exclusive Agency—A listing agreement that entitles the broker to a commission if anyone other than the seller finds a buyer for the property during the listing term.

Listing, Exclusive Right to Sell—A listing agreement that entitles the broker to a commission if anyone—including the seller—finds a buyer for the property during the listing term.

Listing, Open—A nonexclusive listing, given by an owner to as many different brokers as he or she chooses. If the property is sold, a broker is only entitled to a commission if he or she is the procuring cause of the sale.

Loan, Conventional—A loan that is not insured or guaranteed by any government agency (such as the FHA or VA).

Loan Assumption Fee—A fee charged to the buyer by the existing lender in return for permission to assume an existing loan.

Loan Origination Fee—A fee charged by a lender to cover the administrative costs of making a loan. Also called a loan fee.

Loan-to-Value Ratio—The relationship between the loan amount and either the sales price or the appraised value of the property (whichever is less), expressed as a percentage.

Lock-In Clause—A clause in a promissory note or an installment sales contract prohibiting full payment of the debt before a date specified in the contract.

Lot—A parcel of land in a subdivision.

Lot and Block Description—A type of legal description; a piece of land is described by reference to a lot and block appearing on the subdivision plat map recorded by the county auditor or county recorder. Sometimes called a maps and plats description.

LTV—*See:* Loan-to-Value Ratio.

Majority, Age of—Age at which a person becomes legally competent to enter into contracts and transactions; usually 18 years old.

Marketable Title—*See:* Title, Marketable

Market Price—The price actually paid for property. *Compare:* Value, Market.

Material Breach—*See:* Breach, Material.

Material Fact—Information that has a substantial negative impact on the value of the property, on a party's ability to perform, or on the purpose of the transaction.

Measuring Life—*See:* Life Estate.

Meeting of the Minds—*See:* Mutual Consent.

Meretricious Relationship—A stable, marital-like relationship between cohabitating, unmarried parties.

Merger—Uniting two or more separate properties by transferring ownership of all of them to one person.

Meridian—An imaginary line running north and south, passing through the earth's poles. Also called a longitude line.

Meridian, Guide—In the government survey system, one of the north-south lines, spaced 24 miles apart.

Meridian, Principal—In the government survey system, the main north-south line in a particular grid, used as the starting point in numbering the ranges.

Metes—Measurements. *See:* Metes and Bounds Description.

Metes and Bounds Description—A method of legal description that starts at an easily identifiable point of beginning, then describes the property's boundaries in terms of courses (compass directions) and distances, ultimately returning to the point of beginning.

Mill—One-tenth of one cent; the measure used to state the property tax rate. A tax rate of one mill on the dollar is the same as a rate of one-tenth of 1% of the assessed value of property.

Mineral Rights—Rights to the minerals located beneath the surface of a piece of property.

Minor—A person who has not reached the age at which the law recognizes a general contractual capacity (usually 18 years old).

Misrepresentation—An incorrect or false statement. *See:* Fraud.

Mitigation—When the nonbreaching party takes action to minimize the losses resulting from a breach of contract.

MLS—Multiple Listing Service.

Model Toxics Control Act (MCTA)—A Washington state law analogous to CERCLA that imposes joint and several liability for hazardous waste cleanup on potentially liable parties.

Monetary Policy—The Federal Reserve Board's effort to control the supply and cost of money in the United States.

Monument—A visible marker, natural or artificial, used in a survey or a metes and bounds description to establish the boundaries of a piece of property.

Mortgage—1. An instrument that creates a voluntary lien on real property to secure repayment of a debt. The parties to a mortgage are the mortgagor (borrower) and mortgagee (lender). 2. The term is often used more generally, to refer to either a mortgage or a deed of trust.

Mortgage, Assumption of—Taking over the primary liability on an existing mortgage from the original borrower, usually in connection with the purchase of the security property.

Mortgage, Balloon—A mortgage that provides for payments that do not fully amortize the loan by the loan's maturity date. The balance of the mortgage is then due in one lump sum (called a balloon payment) at the end of the term.

Mortgage, Blanket—A mortgage or deed of trust that covers more than one piece of real estate.

Mortgage, First—The mortgage or deed of trust that has higher lien priority than any other on a property. Without a subordination agreement, this will be the one that is recorded first. Also called a senior mortgage.

Mortgage, Junior—A mortgage or deed of trust that has lower lien priority than another mortgage or deed of trust against the same property. Sometimes called a second mortgage.

Mortgage, Satisfaction of—The document a mortgagee gives the mortgagor when the mortgage debt has been paid in full, acknowledging that the debt has been paid and the mortgage is no longer a lien against the property.

Mortgage, Senior—*See:* Mortgage, First.

Mortgage Broker—An intermediary who brings real estate lenders and borrowers together and negotiates loan agreements between them.

Mortgage Broker Practices Act—A Washington state law regulating the mortgage broker business.

Mortgage Company—A type of real estate lender that originates and services loans on behalf of large investors or for immediate resale on the secondary market.

Mortgagee—The one who receives a mortgage; the lender.

Mortgaging Clause—A clause in a mortgage that describes the security interest given to the mortgagee.

Multiple Listing Service—An organization of real estate brokers who share their exclusive listings.

Mortgagor—A property owner (usually a borrower) who gives a mortgage against the property to another (usually a lender) as security for payment of an obligation.

Mutual Consent—When all parties freely agree to the terms of a contract, without fraud, undue influence, duress, menace, or mistake. Mutual consent is achieved through offer and acceptance. Sometimes called mutuality or "a meeting of the minds."

Mutuality—*See:* Mutual Consent.

N.A.R.—National Association of Realtors.

National Environmental Policy Act—*See:* NEPA.

Natural Person—A human being, an individual (as distinguished from an artificial person, such as a corporation).

Navigable Waters—A body of water that is capable of being used practically for the carriage of commerce.

Negligence—Conduct that falls below the standard of care that a reasonable person would exercise under the circumstances; carelessness or recklessness.

Negotiable Instrument—An instrument containing an unconditional promise to pay a certain sum of money, to order or to bearer, on demand or at a particular time. It may be a check, a promissory note, a bond, a draft, or stock.

NEPA—The National Environmental Policy Act; federal legislation requiring the preparation of an environmental impact statement (EIS) before any government action that would have a significant effect on the environment.

Nominal Interest Rate—The interest rate stated in a promissory note.

Nonconforming Use—A property use that does not conform to current zoning requirements, but is allowed because the property was being used in that way before the present zoning ordinance was enacted.

Nonpossessory Interest—An interest in property that does not include the right to possess and occupy the property; an encumbrance, such as a lien or an easement.

Nonprofit Corporation—*See:* Corporation, Nonprofit.

Non-Recourse Provision—A promissory note provision in which a lender agrees to limit its recovery on a loan default to proceeds from a foreclosure sale.

Notary Public—An official whose primary function is to witness and certify the acknowledgment made by someone signing a legal document.

Note—*See:* Note, Promissory.

Note, Demand—A promissory note that is due whenever the holder of the note demands payment.

Note, Installment—A promissory note that calls for periodic payments of principal and interest until the debt is fully paid.

Note, Joint—A note signed by two or more persons with joint and several liability for payment; that is, each can be required to pay the full amount, not merely his or her share.

Note, Promissory—A written promise to repay a debt.

Note, Straight—A promissory note that calls for regular payments of interest only, so that the entire principal amount is due in one lump sum at the end of the loan term.

Notice, Actual—Actual knowledge of a fact, as opposed to knowledge imputed by law.

Notice, Constructive—Knowledge of a fact imputed to a person by law. A person is held to have constructive notice of something when he or she should have known it, even if he or she did not actually know it.

Notice of Cessation—A notice recorded by a property owner when construction on the property has ceased, although the project has not been completed; it limits the period during which construction liens can be filed.

Notice of Completion—A recorded notice that announces the completion of a construction project and limits the period in which construction liens may be filed.

Notice of Default—A notice sent by a secured creditor to a debtor, informing the debtor of a breach of the loan agreement.

Notice of Non-Responsibility—A notice which, if recorded and posted on the property in a timely manner, will protect a property owner from construction liens filed for work that was requested by someone other than the owner (a tenant, for example).

Notice of Sale—A notice sent to a defaulting borrower, to junior lienholders, and to other interested parties, setting the date for a foreclosure sale.

Notice to Quit—A notice given to a tenant by a landlord, demanding that the tenant cure a default (e.g., by paying overdue rent) or else vacate the leased property.

Novation—1. When one party to a contract withdraws and a new party is substituted, relieving the withdrawing party of liability. 2. The substitution of a new obligation for an old one.

Obligatory Advances—Disbursements of construction loan funds that the lender is obligated to make (by prior agreement with the borrower) when certain phases of construction have been completed.

Offer—When one person (the offeror) proposes a contract to another (the offeree); if the offeree accepts the offer, a binding contract is formed.

Offer, Illusory—An offer that is not a valid contract offer, because it requires something more than simple acceptance in order to create a contract.

Offer, Tender—An unconditional offer by one of the parties to a contract to perform his or her part of the agreement; made when the offeror believes the other party is breaching the contract, it establishes the offeror's right to sue if the other party doesn't accept it.

Offeree—One to whom an offer is made.

Offeror—One who makes an offer.

Officer—In a corporation, an executive authorized by the board of directors to manage the business of the corporation.

Off-Site Improvements—Improvements that add to the usefulness of a site but are not located directly on it, such as curbs, street lights, and sidewalks.

Open Listing—*See:* Listing, Open.

Option—A contract giving one party the right to do something, without obligating him or her to do it.

Optionee—The person to whom an option is given.

Optionor—The person who gives an option.

Option to Purchase—An option giving the optionee the right to buy property owned by the optionor at an agreed price during a specified period.

Origination Fee—*See:* Loan Origination Fee.

"Or More"—A provision in a promissory note that allows the borrower to prepay the debt (i.e., pay it off before payment is required).

Ownership—Title to property, dominion over property; the rights of possession and control.

Ownership, Concurrent—Any form of ownership in which two or more people share title to a piece of property, holding undivided interests; includes joint tenancy, tenancy in common, and community property.

Ownership in Severalty—Ownership by one person alone.

Panic Selling—*See:* Blockbusting.

Parcel—A lot or piece of real estate, especially a specified part of a larger tract.

Parol Evidence—Evidence concerning negotiations or oral agreements that were not included in a written contract, often altering or contradicting the terms of the written contract.

Partial Release Clause—A clause in a blanket mortgage or deed of trust which allows the borrower to get part of the security property released from the lien when a certain portion of the debt has been paid or other conditions are fulfilled.

Partial Satisfaction—The instrument given to the borrower when part of the security property is released from a blanket mortgage under a partial release clause.

Partition—The division of property among its co-owners, so that each owns part of it in severalty; this may occur by agreement of all the co-owners (voluntary partition) or by court order (judicial partition). In many cases, the property is sold and the sale proceeds are divided among the former co-owners.

Partner, General—A partner who has the authority to manage and contract for a general or limited partnership, and who is personally liable for the partnership's debts.

Partner, Limited—A partner in a limited partnership who is primarily an investor and does not participate in the management of the business, and who is not personally liable for the partnership's debts.

Partnership—According to the Uniform Partnership Act, "an association of two or more persons to carry on, as co-owners, a business for profit." The law regards a partnership as a collection of individuals, not as an entity separate from its owners.

Partnership, General—A partnership in which each member has an equal right to manage the business and share in the profits, as well as equal responsibility for the debts of the business.

Partnership, Limited—A partnership made up of one or more general partners and one or more limited partners.

Partnership Property—All property that partners bring into their business at the outset or later acquire for their business; property owned as tenants in partnership.

Patent—The instrument used to convey government land to a private individual.

Patent Defect—A problem that is readily observable in an ordinary inspection of the property (as opposed to a latent defect, which is not readily observable).

Personal Property—Any property that is not real property; movable property not affixed to land. Also called chattels or personalty.

Personalty—Personal property.

Physical Life—An estimate of the time a building will remain structurally sound and capable of being used.

Plaintiff—The party who starts a civil lawsuit; the one who sues.

Planned Unit Development (PUD)—A development (usually residential) with small, clustered lots, designed to leave more open space than traditional subdivisions have.

Planning Commission—A local government agency responsible for preparing the community's master plan or comprehensive plan for development.

Plat—A detailed survey map of a subdivision, recorded in the county where the land is located. Subdivided property is often called platted property.

Plat Book—A book containing the subdivision plat maps of all the subdivided property in the county, maintained at the county recorder's office.

Pledge—When a debtor transfers possession of property to the creditor as security for the repayment of a debt. *Compare:* Hypothecate.

Plottage—The consolidation of several parcels of land into one, resulting in greater utility and consequently higher value. The additional value that results is called the plottage increment.

Point of Beginning—The starting point in a metes and bounds description; a monument or a point described by reference to a monument.

Points—One point is 1% of the principal amount of a loan, paid to the lender at the time the loan is made to give the lender an additional yield above the interest rate. Because of the points paid at the outset, the lender is willing to make the loan at a lower interest rate.

Police Power—The constitutional power of state and local governments to enact and enforce laws to protect or promote the public's health, safety, morals, and general welfare.

Possession—1. The holding and enjoyment of property. 2. Actual physical occupation of real property.

Possessory Interest—An interest in property that includes the right to possess and occupy the property. The term includes all estates (leasehold as well as freehold), but does not include encumbrances.

Possibility of Reverter—The possibility that a defeasible fee estate may revert to the grantor (or the grantor's heirs or assigns) if a condition is not met or if a particular event occurs.

Power of Attorney—An instrument authorizing one person (the attorney in fact) to act as another's agent, to the extent stated in the instrument.

Power of Sale Clause—A clause in a deed of trust that gives the trustee the right to foreclose nonjudicially (sell the debtor's property without a court action) if the borrower defaults.

Power of Termination—The right to terminate a fee simple subject to condition subsequent if the estate holder fails to meet required conditions. Also called the right of reentry.

Precedent—A published judicial opinion that serves as authority for deciding a similar issue in a later case. A binding precedent is a precedent that a particular court is required to follow.

Prepayment—Paying off all or part of a loan before payment is due.

Prepayment Penalty—A penalty charged to a borrower who prepays.

Prepayment Provision—A provision in a promissory note that gives the borrower the right to pay off the loan before it is due.

Prescription—A method of acquiring an interest in real property (usually an easement) by using it openly and without the owner's permission for the period of time required by statute (in Washington, ten years). *Compare:* Adverse Possession.

Primary Mortgage Market—The market in which loans are originated, where lenders make loans to borrowers. *Compare:* Secondary Mortgage Market.

Principal—1. One of the parties to a transaction (such as the buyer or seller of a home), as opposed to those who are involved as agents or employees (such as a broker or escrow agent). 2. One who grants another person (an agent) authority to represent him or her in dealings with third parties. 3. In regard to a loan, the amount originally borrowed, as opposed to the interest.

Principal Meridian—*See:* Meridian, Principal.

Prior Appropriation—*See:* Appropriation, Prior.

Private Restrictions—*See:* Restrictions, Private.

Privity—The relationship between two people who have simultaneous or successive interests in a contract or a property. For example, in an easement agreement, the dominant and servient tenants are in privity to one another; so are the seller and buyer of a property.

Probate—A judicial proceeding in which the validity of a will is established and the executor is authorized to distribute the estate property; or, when there is no valid will, in which an administrator is appointed to distribute the estate to the heirs.

Probate Court—A court that oversees the distribution of property under a will or by intestate succession.

Procedural Law—A law that establishes the legal procedure for enforcing a substantive right. *Compare:* Substantive Law.

Procuring Cause—The real estate agent who is primarily responsible for bringing about a sale; for example, by negotiating the agreement between the buyer and the seller.

Promisee—Someone who has been promised something; someone who is supposed to receive the benefit of a contractual promise.

Promisor—Someone who has made a contractual promise.

Promissory Estoppel—A doctrine applied when someone has made a technically unenforceable promise to another, and the other person has acted in reasonable reliance on the promise. If the person who relied on the promise will suffer harm unless it is enforced, a court may enforce it. Also called the doctrine of detrimental reliance.

Promissory Note—*See:* Note, Promissory.

Property—1. The rights of ownership in a thing, such as the right to use, possess, transfer, or encumber it. 2. Something that is owned.

Property Held for Production of Income—Property that generates rent or other income for the owner, such as an apartment building.

Property Manager—A person hired by a property owner to administer, merchandise, and maintain property, especially rental property.

Property Tax—*See:* Tax, Property.

Property Used in a Trade or Business—Under the federal income tax code, property such as business sites and factories used in a taxpayer's trade or business.

Proprietary Lease—A lease of a unit in a cooperative building, held by a tenant who has purchased stock in the cooperative corporation.

Proprietorship, Individual or Sole—A business owned and operated by one person.

Proration—The process of dividing or allocating something (especially a sum of money or an expense) proportionately, according to time, interest, or benefit.

Public Offering Statement—A special document that the Washington Condominium Act requires a condominium developer to prepare, which discloses certain information to buyers about the unit being offered, the condominium project, and the developer.

Public Record—The official collection of legal documents that individuals have filed with the county recorder in order to provide constructive notice to the public of the information contained in them.

Public Restrictions—*See:* Restrictions, Public.

Public Use—A use that benefits the public. For a condemnation action to be constitutional, it must be for a public use.

Puffing—Superlative statements about the quality of a property that should not be considered assertions of fact.

Punitive Damages—Damages awarded to a plaintiff in a civil suit as a punishment to the wrongdoer (the defendant) and as a deterrent to others.

Pur Autre Vie—For another's life. A life estate based on the life of someone other than the holder of the life estate is called a life estate pur autre vie.

Purchase and Sale Agreement—A contract in which a seller promises to convey title to real property to a buyer in exchange for the purchase price. Also called an earnest money agreement, deposit receipt, sales contract, purchase contract, or contract of sale.

Qualified Acceptance—*See:* Counteroffer.

Qualifying Standards—The standards a lender requires a loan applicant to meet before a loan will be approved. Also called underwriting standards.

Quiet Enjoyment—Use and possession of real property without interference from the previous owner, the lessor, or anyone else claiming title.

Quiet Title Action—A lawsuit to determine who has title to a piece of property, or to remove a cloud from the title.

Quitclaim Deed—*See:* Deed, Quitclaim.

Range—In the government survey system of land description, a strip of land six miles wide, running north and south.

Range Lines—In the government survey system of land description, the north-south lines (meridians) located six miles apart.

Ratification—The later confirmation or affirmation of an act that was not authorized when it was performed.

Ready, Willing and Able—A buyer is ready, willing and able if he makes an offer that meets the seller's stated terms, and has the contractual capacity and financial resources to complete the transaction.

Real Estate—*See:* Real Property.

Real Estate Brokerage—A real estate broker's business; the business of bringing a buyer and seller together and negotiating a sales contract between the two parties.

Real Estate Brokerage Relationships Act—A Washington state law that significantly changes traditional agency law in regards to real estate transactions. It governs when and how real estate agency relationships are created and terminated, the duties owed by real estate licensees to the parties in a real estate transaction, and when and how agency disclosures are to be made.

Real Estate Commission—A state commission appointed by the Governor, consisting of the Director of the Departing of Licensing and six commissioners; responsible for preparing and conducting the real estate licensing examinations.

Real Estate Contract—1. A contract for the sale of real property in which the buyer (the vendee) pays in installments; the buyer takes possession of the property immediately, but the seller (the vendor) retains legal title until the full price has been paid. Also called a land contract, installment sales contract, or contract for deed. 2. An earnest money agreement. 3. Any contract having to do with real property.

Real Estate Investment Trust (REIT)—An unincorporated real estate investment business, with a minimum of 100 investors, organized as a trust.

Real Estate Salesperson—A person who is licensed to work for and represent a broker in real estate transactions.

Real Estate Security—An arrangement in which someone invests money in an enterprise involving real estate with the expectation of earning profits from the efforts of another party.

Real Estate Settlement Procedures Act—*See:* RESPA.

Real Property—Land and everything attached or appurtenant to the land. Also called realty or real estate. *Compare:* Personal Property.

Realtor—A real estate agent who is an active member of a state and local real estate board that is affiliated with the National Association of Realtors.

Realty—*See:* Real Property.

Reasonable Use Doctrine—A limitation of riparian water rights, holding that there is no right to waste water.

Reconveyance—Releasing the security property from the lien created by a deed of trust, by recording a deed of reconveyance.

Recording—Filing a document at the county auditor's or county recorder's office so that it will be placed in the public record, providing constructive notice to the public of the contents of the document.

Rectangular Survey—*See:* Government Survey System.

Redemption—1. When a defaulting borrower prevents foreclosure by paying the full amount of the debt, plus costs. 2. When a mortgagor regains the property after foreclosure by paying whatever the foreclosure sale purchaser paid for it, plus interest and expenses.

Redemption, Equitable Right of—The right of a mortgagor to redeem property prior to the foreclosure sale, by paying off the debt, plus costs.

Redemption, Statutory Right of—The right of a mortgagor to get the property back during a specified period after a foreclosure sale, by paying whatever the foreclosure sale purchaser paid for it, plus interest and expenses.

Redemption Period, Statutory—The period of time (set by statute) after a judicial foreclosure sale during which the debtor can reclaim foreclosed property by paying the full amount of the debt plus costs.

Redlining—When a lender refuses to make loans secured by properties in a certain neighborhood because of the racial or ethnic composition of the neighborhood.

Reformation—A legal action to correct a mistake, such as a typographical error, in a deed or other document. The instrument used is known as a reformation deed or correction deed.

Regulation Z—The Federal Reserve's regulation that implements the Truth in Lending Act.

Reinstatement—When foreclosure proceedings are stopped and the loan agreement is restored after the borrower cures the default (for example, by paying the delinquent payments, plus costs).

Relation Back—A legal doctrine holding that, under certain circumstances, title acquired by deed relates back to the point at which the deed was delivered to the escrow agent.

Release—1. To give up a legal right. 2. A document in which a legal right is given up.

Release Clause—1. A clause in a blanket mortgage or deed of trust that allows the borrower to have certain parcels of land released from the lien when a certain portion of the debt has been paid off. 2. A clause in a real estate contract providing for a deed to a portion of the land to be delivered when a certain portion of the contract price has been paid. Also known as a deed release provision.

Reliction—When a body of water gradually recedes, exposing land that was previously under water. Also called dereliction.

Remainder—A future interest that becomes possessory when a life estate terminates, and that is held by someone other than the grantor of the life estate (as opposed to an estate in reversion, which is a future interest held by the grantor or the grantor's successors in interest).

Remainderman—The person who has an estate in remainder.

Remand—To send back. When an appellate court remands a case, it is sent back to the lower court for additional proceedings or a new trial.

Remise—To give up; a term used in quitclaim deeds.

Rent—Compensation paid by a tenant to the landlord in exchange for the use and possession of the leased property.

Rent Control—Governmental restrictions on the amount of rent a landlord can charge.

Renunciation—When someone who has been granted something or has accepted something later gives it up or rejects it; as when an agent withdraws from the agency relationship. *Compare:* Revocation.

Resale Certificate—A written document prepared by an owners' association when a condominium unit is resold, providing prospective buyers with information about assessments on the unit being sold, other units, and the association's finances.

Rescission—When a contract is terminated and each party gives anything acquired under the contract back to the other party, restoring the parties, as nearly as possible, to the positions they were in before entering into the contract.

Reservation—A right retained by a grantor when conveying property; for example, mineral rights, an easement, or a life estate can be reserved in the deed.

Reserve Account—*See:* Impound Account.

Resident Manager—A salaried manager of an apartment building or complex, who resides on the property.

Residential Landlord-Tenant Act (RLTA)—A Washington law that sets forth the rights and duties of residential landlords and tenants.

Res Judicata—The legal doctrine holding that once a lawsuit between two parties has been tried and a final judgment has been issued, neither one can sue the other over the same dispute again.

RESPA—The Real Estate Settlement Procedures Act, a law that requires lenders making loans secured by residential property to provide the borrower with a good faith estimate of closing costs and use the Uniform Settlement Statement form.

Restitution—Restoring something to a person that he or she was unjustly deprived of.

Restrictions—Limitations on the use of real property. Restrictions may be private (such as restrictive covenants) or public (such as zoning ordinances).

Restrictions, Private—Restrictions on the use of land that have been imposed by private parties in deeds or contracts (as opposed to public restrictions, which are imposed by law).

Restrictions, Public—Law or governmental regulations limiting or restricting the use of real property.

Restrictive Covenant—*See:* Covenant, Restrictive.

Retainer—A fee paid up front to a licensee when entering into a real estate agency (usually a buyer agency) relationship.

Reversion—A future estate that becomes possessory when a life estate terminates, and that is held by the grantor (or his or her successors in interest). *Compare:* Remainder.

Revocation—When someone who granted or offered something withdraws the grant or offer; as when a principal withdraws the authority granted to the agent. *Compare:* Renunciation.

Rezone—*See:* Zoning Amendment.

Right of First Refusal—A right that gives the holder the first opportunity to purchase or lease a particular piece of property, should the owner decide to sell or lease it.

Right of Survivorship—A characteristic of joint tenancy; surviving co-tenants acquire a deceased joint tenant's interest in the property.

Right of Way—An easement that gives the holder the right to cross another person's land.

Right to Use—*See:* Vacation License.

Riparian Rights—The water rights of a landowner whose property is adjacent to or crossed by a body of water. *Compare:* Appropriation, Prior.

Rule of Capture—*See:* Capture, Rule of.

Running with the Land—Binding or benefiting the successive owners of a piece of property, rather than terminating when a particular owner transfers his or her interest. Usually used in reference to an easement appurtenant or a restrictive covenant.

Safety Clause—*See:* Extender Clause.

Satisfaction of Mortgage—*See*: Mortgage, Satisfaction of.

Savings and Loan Association—A type of financial institution that emphasizes consumer loans and home mortgages.

Secondary Financing—Money borrowed to pay part of the required downpayment or closing costs for a first loan, when the second loan is secured by the same property that secures the first loan.

Secondary Mortgage Market—The market in which investors (including Fannie Mae, Freddie Mac, and Ginnie Mae) purchase real estate loans from lenders; also called the national market.

Secret Profit—A financial benefit that an agent takes from a transaction without informing the principal.

Section—In the government survey system of land description, a section is one mile square and contains 640 acres. There are 36 sections in a township.

Security—A real estate security is an arrangement in which people invest money in an enterprise involving real estate, with the expectation of earning profits from the efforts of a promoter or some other third party.

Security Agreement—Under the Uniform Commercial Code, a document that creates a lien on personal property being used to secure a loan.

Security Deposit—Money a tenant gives a landlord at the beginning of the tenancy to protect the landlord in case the tenant defaults; the landlord may retain all or part of the deposit to cover unpaid rent or repair costs at the end of the tenancy. Also called a damage deposit.

Security Instrument—A document that creates a voluntary lien on real property to secure repayment of a loan; either a deed of trust or a mortgage.

Security Interest—The interest a creditor may acquire in the debtor's property to ensure that the debt will be paid; if the debt is not paid as agreed, the creditor may foreclose (force the sale of the property) and collect the amount owed from the sale proceeds.

Security Property—The collateral for a loan; the property that a borrower gives a lender a voluntary lien against, so that the lender can foreclose if the borrower defaults.

Seisin—The possession of a freehold estate; ownership.

Seller Disclosure Statement—A statement containing information about the property that a seller of residential property is required to give to the buyer. Formerly called a transfer disclosure statement.

Selling Broker—The broker responsible for procuring a buyer for real estate; may represent either the seller or the buyer.

SEPA—The State Environmental Policy Act; a Washington state law analogous to NEPA that requires environmental impact statements before government actions that would have a significant effect on the environment.

Separate Property—Property owned by a married person that is not community property; includes property acquired before marriage, or by gift, devise, or inheritance after marriage.

Setback Requirements—Provisions in a zoning ordinance that do not allow structures to be built within a certain distance of the property line.

Settlement—1. An agreement between the parties to a civil lawsuit, in which the plaintiff agrees to drop the suit in exchange for money or the defendant's promise to do or refrain from doing something. 2. Closing.

Settlement Statement—A document that presents a final, detailed accounting for a real estate transaction, listing each party's debits and credits and the amount each will receive or be required to pay at closing. Also called a closing statement.

Severalty Ownership—Ownership by one person alone. *Compare:* Concurrent Ownership.

Severance—1. Termination of a joint tenancy. 2. The permanent removal of a natural attachment, fixture, or appurtenance from real property, which transforms the item into personal property.

Shareholder—Individual who purchases shares in a company as an investment and has limited liability in regard to the corporation's debts. Also called stockholder.

Sheriff's Deed—*See:* Deed, Sheriff's.

Sheriff's Sale—A foreclosure sale held pursuant to a court order in a judicial foreclosure. Also called an execution sale.

Shoreline Management Act—A Washington law enacted to protect shorelines by regulating development within 200 feet of the high water mark.

Short Platting—Subdivision of a parcel of land into four or fewer lots.

Special Assessment—A tax levied only against the properties that have benefited from a public improvement (such as a sewer or street light), to cover the cost of the improvement; creates a special assessment lien.

Special Exception Permit—*See:* Conditional Use Permit.

Special Warranty Deed—*See:* Deed, Special Warranty.

Specific Lien—*See:* Lien, Specific.

Specific Performance—A legal remedy for breach of contract in which a court orders the breaching party to actually perform the contract as agreed, rather than simply paying monetary damages.

Spot Zoning—*See:* Zoning, Spot.

Stare Decisis—The legal doctrine holding that in resolving a lawsuit, a court should try to follow precedents decided in the same jurisdiction, to make the law evenhanded and predictable.

State Environmental Policy Act—*See:* SEPA.

Statute—A law enacted by a state legislature or the U.S. Congress.

Statute of Frauds—A law that requires certain types of contracts to be in writing and signed by the party to be bound in order to be enforceable.

Statute of Limitations—A law requiring a particular type of lawsuit to be filed within a specified time after the event giving rise to the suit occurred.

Statutory Redemption Period—*See:* Redemption Period, Statutory.

Steering—Channeling prospective buyers or tenants to particular neighborhoods based on their race, religion, national origin, or ancestry.

Stockholder—*See:* Shareholder.

Subagent—A person that an agent has delegated authority to, so that the subagent can assist in carrying out the principal's orders; sometimes described as the agent of an agent.

Subcontractor—A contractor who, at the request of the general contractor, performs a specific job, such as plumbing or drywalling, in connection with the overall construction project.

Subdivision—A piece of land divided into two or more parcels.

Subdivision Plat—*See:* Plat.

Subdivision Regulations—Local laws and regulations that must be complied with before land can be subdivided.

Subjacent Support—*See:* Support, Subjacent.

Subject To—When a purchaser takes property subject to a deed of trust or mortgage, he or she is not personally liable for paying off the loan; in case of default, however, the property can still be foreclosed on. *Compare:* Assumption.

Sublease—When a tenant grants someone else the right to possession of the leased property for part of the remainder of the lease term; as opposed to an assignment, in which the tenant gives up possession for the entire remainder of the lease term.

Subordination Clause—A provision in a mortgage or deed of trust that permits a subsequent mortgage or deed of trust to have higher lien priority than the one containing the clause.

Subpoena—A document ordering a person to appear at a deposition or court proceeding to testify or to produce documentary or physical evidence.

Substantial Performance—Performance that is sufficient to discharge a party to a contract from further obligation under the contract, even though there has not been full performance.

Substantive Law—A law that establishes and defines rights and duties. *Compare:* Procedural Law.

Substitution of Liability—A buyer wishing to assume an existing loan may apply for lender approval to do so. Once approved, the buyer assumes liability for repayment of the loan, and the original borrower is released from liability.

Succession—Acquiring property through descent, by will or inheritance.

Successor in Interest—A person who has acquired property previously held by someone else; for example, a buyer or an heir.

Summons—A notice telling the defendant in a lawsuit that a complaint has been filed.

Support, Lateral—The right to have the soil of a piece of property supported by the land adjoining it. An owner is protected by law from excavation on neighboring property that would deny this support.

Support, Subjacent—The support that the surface of land receives from the subsurface soil.

Support Rights—The right to the support of land that is provided by adjacent (lateral) or underlying (subjacent) land.

Surrender—Yielding or giving up an estate (such as a life estate or a leasehold) before it has expired.

Survey—The process of precisely measuring the boundaries and determining the area of a parcel of land.

Survivorship, Right of—A characteristic of a joint tenancy; the surviving joint tenants automatically acquire a deceased joint tenant's interest in the property.

Syndicate—An association formed to operate an investment business. A syndicate is not a recognized legal entity; it can be a corporation, real estate investment trust, or partnership.

Tacking—When successive periods of use or possession by more than one person are added together to make up the period required for prescription or adverse possession.

Taking—When the government acquires private property for public use by condemnation, it's called "a taking." The term is also used in inverse condemnation lawsuits, when a government action has severely reduced the usefulness of a piece of private property.

Tax, Ad Valorem—A tax assessed on the value of property. Also called general real estate tax.

Tax, Excise—A tax on the transfer of real property; revenue stamps or some other evidence of payment of the tax may have to be attached to a deed before it can be recorded. Also called a documentary transfer tax.

Tax, General Real Estate—An annual ad valorem tax levied on real property.

Tax, Improvement—*See:* Special Assessment.

Tax, Property—1. The general real estate tax. 2. Any ad valorem tax levied on real or personal property.

Tax Deed—The deed given to the person who purchases property at a tax sale.

Tax Foreclosure—Foreclosure by a government agency to obtain payment of delinquent taxes.

Tax Lien—A lien against property to secure payment of taxes, such as the general real estate taxes.

Tax Sale—Sale of property after foreclosure of a tax lien.

Tenancy—Lawful possession of real property; an estate.

Tenancy, Joint—A form of concurrent ownership of property in which the co-owners have unity of time, title, interest, and possession and the right of survivorship. *Compare:* Tenancy in Common.

Tenancy, Periodic—A leasehold estate that continues for successive periods of equal length (for example, from week to week or month to month), until terminated by proper notice from either party.

Tenancy, Term—*See:* Estate for Years.

Tenancy at Sufferance—When a tenant (who entered into possession of the property lawfully) stays on after the lease ends without the landlord's permission.

Tenancy at Will—When a tenant is in possession with the owner's permission, but there is no definite lease term; as when a landlord allows a holdover tenant to remain on the premises until another tenant is found.

Tenancy by the Entirety—A form of joint ownership of property by husband and wife recognized in most states that don't use a community property system; not recognized in Washington.

Tenancy in Common—A form of concurrent ownership of real property in which two or more persons each have an undivided interest in the entire property, but no right of survivorship. *Compare:* Tenancy, Joint.

Tenancy in Partnership—The form of concurrent ownership in which general partners own partnership property, whether or not title to the property is in the partnership's name. Each partner has an equal undivided interest, but no right to transfer the interest to someone outside the partnership.

Tenant—Someone in lawful possession of real property; especially, someone who has leased property from the owner.

Tenant, Dominant—A person who has easement rights on another's property; either the owner of a dominant tenement, or someone who has an easement in gross.

Tenant, Holdover—A lessee who remains in possession of the property after the lease term has expired.

Tenant, Life—Someone who has a life estate, with the right to possess the property until the death of the person whose life is the measuring life. (In many cases, the life tenant's own life is the measuring life.)

Tenant, Servient—A property owner whose property is encumbered by an easement.

Tender Offer—*See:* Offer, Tender.

Tenements—Everything of a permanent nature associated with a piece of land that is ordinarily transferred with the land. Tenements are both tangible (buildings, for example) and intangible (air rights, for example).

Tenement, Dominant—Property that receives the benefit of an easement appurtenant.

Tenement, Servient—Property burdened by an easement, so that the owner is required to allow someone else to use the property for a specified purpose.

Term—A prescribed period of time; especially, the length of time a borrower has to pay off a loan, or the duration of a lease.

Testament—A will.

Testate—Refers to someone who has executed a will. *Compare:* Intestate.

Testator—A person who makes a will. (If it is a woman, she may be referred to as a testatrix, although that term is passing out of use.)

Third Party—1. A person seeking to deal with a principal through an agent. 2. In a transaction, someone who is not one of the principals.

Tier—A row of townships running east-west.

Tight Money Market—When loan funds are scarce, leading lenders to charge high interest rates and discount points.

TILA—Truth in Lending Act.

Time is of the Essence—A clause in a contract that means performance on the exact dates specified is an essential element of the contract; failure to perform on time is a material breach.

Timeshare—An ownership interest or license that gives the holder a right to possession of the property only for a specific, limited period each year.

Title—Lawful ownership of real property. Also, the deed or other document that is evidence of that ownership.

Title, Abstract of—A brief chronological summary of the recorded documents affecting title to a particular piece of property.

Title, After-Acquired—Title acquired by a grantor after he or she attempted to convey an interest in property that he or she did not own.

Title, Chain of—The chain of deeds (and other documents) transferring title to a piece of property from one owner to the next, as disclosed in the public record.

Title, Clear—Title that is free of encumbrances or defects; marketable title.

Title, Color of—*See:* Color of Title.

Title, Equitable—The vendee's interest in property under a real estate contract. Also called an equitable interest. *Compare:* Title, Legal.

Title, Legal—The vendor's interest in property under a real estate contract. *Compare:* Title, Equitable.

Title, Marketable—Title free and clear of objectionable liens, encumbrances, or defects, so that a reasonably prudent person with full knowledge of the facts would not hesitate to purchase the property. Also called merchantable title.

Title Company—A title insurance company.

Title Insurance—*See:* Insurance, Title.

Title Plant—A duplicate (usually micro-filmed) of the county's public record, maintained by a title company at its offices for use in title searches.

Title Report—A report issued by a title company, disclosing the condition of the title to a specific piece of property. A preliminary title report is one issued early on in a transaction, before the actual title insurance policy is issued.

Title Search—An inspection of the public record to determine all rights and encumbrances affecting title to a piece of property.

Title Theory—A legal theory holding that a mortgage or deed of trust gives the lender legal title to the security property while the debt is being repaid. *Compare:* Lien Theory.

Torrens System—A system of land registration used in some states, which allows title to be verified without the necessity of a title search; title to registered land is free of all encumbrances or claims not registered with the title registrar. (Almost never used in Washington.)

Tort—A breach of a duty imposed by law (as opposed to a duty voluntarily taken on in a contract) that causes harm to another person, giving the injured person the right to sue the one who breached the duty. Also called a civil wrong (in contrast to a criminal wrong, a crime).

Township—In the government survey system of land description, a parcel of land six miles square, containing 36 sections; the intersection of a range and a township tier.

Township Lines—Lines running east-west, spaced six miles apart, in the government survey system.

Township Tier—In the government survey system, a strip of land running east-west, six miles wide and bounded on the north and south by township lines.

Tract—1. A piece of land of undefined size. 2. In the government survey system of land description, an area made up of 16 townships; 24 miles on each side.

Trade Fixture—*See:* Fixture, Trade.

Transferability—If an object is transferable, then ownership and possession of that object can be conveyed from one person to another.

Trespass—An unlawful physical invasion of property owned by another.

Trust—An arrangement in which title to property (or funds) is vested in one or more trustees, who manage the property on behalf of the trust's beneficiaries, in accordance with instructions set forth in the document establishing the trust.

Trust Account—A bank account, separate from a real estate broker's personal and general business accounts, used to segregate trust funds from the broker's own funds.

Trust Deed—*See* Deed of Trust.

Trustee—1. A person appointed to manage a trust on behalf of the beneficiaries. 2. A neutral third party appointed in a deed of trust to handle the nonjudicial foreclosure process in case of default.

Trustee in Bankruptcy—An individual appointed by the court to handle the assets of a person in bankruptcy.

Trustee's Sale—A nonjudicial foreclosure sale under a deed of trust.

Trust Funds—Money or things of value received by an agent, not belonging to the agent but being held for the benefit of others.

Trustor—The borrower in a deed of trust. Also called the grantor.

Truth in Lending Act (TILA)—A federal law, implemented by the Federal Reserve Board's Regulation Z, which requires disclosure of certain information to applicants for consumer loans (including residential mortgage loans). The required disclosures include the annual percentage rate and the total finance charge.

Unauthorized Practice of Law—Offering legal advice or otherwise practicing law without the required license.

Underwriting—In real estate lending, the process of evaluating a loan application to determine the probability that the applicant would repay the loan, and matching the risk to an appropriate rate of return. Sometimes called risk analysis.

Undivided Interest—A co-owner's interest, giving him or her the right to possession of the whole property, rather than to a particular section of it.

Undue Influence—Exerting excessive pressure on someone so as to overpower the person's free will and prevent him or her from making a rational or prudent decision; often involves abusing a relationship of trust.

Unenforceable—*See:* Contract, Unenforceable.

Uniform Commercial Code—A body of law adopted in slightly varying versions in most states (including Washington), which attempts to standardize commercial law dealing with such matters as negotiable instruments and sales of personal property. Its main applications to real estate law concern security interests in fixtures and bulk transfers.

Uniform Settlement Statement—A settlement statement required for any transaction involving a loan that is subject to the Real Estate Settlement Procedures Act (RESPA).

Unit Owners Association—The organization (made up of unit owners) that handles the operation of the condominium; its managerial duties include making assessments needed for the upkeep of the common areas and arranging for repairs or special improvements. Also known as a condominium association.

Unity of Interest—In reference to concurrent ownership, when each co-owner has an equal interest (equal share of ownership) in the property. A requirement for joint tenancy.

Unity of Possession—When property is owned concurrently by two or more individuals, each co-owner is equally entitled to possession of the entire property, because their interests are undivided. This is a requirement for joint tenancy, but it is also a characteristic of all concurrent ownership.

Unity of Time—In reference to concurrent ownership, when each co-owner acquired title at the same time. A requirement for joint tenancy.

Unity of Title—In reference to concurrent ownership, when each co-owner acquired title through the same instrument (deed, will, or court order). A requirement for joint tenancy.

Unjust Enrichment—An undeserved benefit; a court generally will not allow a remedy (such as forfeiture of a real estate contract) if that remedy would result in the unjust enrichment of one of the parties.

Unlawful Detainer—A summary legal action to regain possession of real property; especially, a suit filed by a landlord to evict a defaulting tenant.

Urban Growth Area—Under the Growth Management Act, areas in which new development must be concentrated.

Usury—Charging an interest rate that exceeds legal limits.

VA—Department of Veterans Affairs.

Vacation License—A timeshare arrangement in which the developer retains ownership and sells only the right to use the premises for a specific time each year.

Valid—Binding and enforceable in a court of law.

Valuable Consideration—*See:* Consideration.

Valuation—*See*: Appraisal.

Value—The amount of goods or services offered in the marketplace in exchange for a given product; the present worth of future benefits.

Value, Assessed—The value placed on property by the taxing authority (the county assessor, for example) for the purposes of taxation.

Value, Market—The most probable price that a property should bring in a competitive and open market under all conditions requisite to a fair sale, the buyer and seller each acting prudently and knowledgeably, and assuming the price is not affected by undue stimulus. (This is the definition from the Uniform Standards of Appraisal Practice.) Also called fair market value, value in exchange, or objective value.

Variable Interest Rate—An interest rate charged on a loan that is periodically increased or decreased during the loan term.

Variance—Permission obtained from proper authorities to use property or build a structure in a way that violates the strict terms of the zoning ordinance.

Vendee—A buyer or purchaser; especially, someone buying property under a real estate contract.

Vendor—A seller; especially, someone selling property under a real estate contract.

Vested—A person who has a present, fixed right or interest in property has a vested right or interest, even though he or she may not have the right to possession until sometime in the future. For example, a remainderman's interest in the property vests when it is granted (not when the life estate ends).

Vicarious Liability—*See:* Liability, Vicarious.

Void—Having no legal force or effect.

Voidable—*See:* Contract, Voidable.

Voluntary Lien—*See:* Lien, Voluntary.

Waiver—The voluntary relinquishment or surrender of a right.

Warranty, Implied—In the sale of property, a warranty created by operation of law for the protection of the buyer, whether or not the seller intended to offer it.

Warranty Deed—*See:* Deed, Warranty.

Washington Human Rights Commission—The state agency that enforces the Law Against Discrimination.

Washington Law Against Discrimination—A state law that is stricter than the Fair Housing Act in its prohibition against discrimination in housing and other transactions on the basis of race, creed, color, national origin, sex, marital status, familial status, disability, or use of a service animal.

Waste—The destruction, damage, or material alteration of property by someone in possession of the property who holds less than a fee estate (such as a life tenant or lessee), or by a co-tenant.

Water Rights—*See:* Riparian Rights, Appropriative Rights.

Will—A person's formal stipulation regarding how his or her estate will be disposed of after death. Also called a testament.

Will, Formal—A will that meets the statutory requirements for a valid will; it must be signed by two witnesses.

Will, Holographic—A will written and dated entirely in the testator's handwriting, which may be valid even if it was not witnessed. Not recognized in Washington.

Will, Nuncupative—An oral will made on the testator's deathbed; valid only as to bequests of personal property worth under $1,000.

Writ of Execution—A court order directing a public officer (usually the sheriff) to seize and sell property to satisfy a debt.

Yield—The return of profit to an investor on an investment, stated as a percentage of the amount invested.

Zone—An area of land set off for a particular use or uses in a zoning law.

Zoning—Government regulation of the uses of property within specified areas.

Zoning, Spot—An illegal rezone that favors (or restricts) a particular property owner (or a small group of owners) without justification.

Zoning Amendment—A revision of a zoning ordinance, usually changing the uses allowed in a particular zone. Also called a rezone.

Index